Informing Business:
Research and Education on
a Rugged Landscape

Informing Business:
Research and Education on a Rugged Landscape

T. Grandon Gill

Informing Science Press

Informing Business: Research and Education on a Rugged Landscape

ISBN: 1-932886-29-X
       978-1-932886-29-0

Published by

Informing Science Press
publishing arm of the Informing Science Institute:

131 Brookhill Court
Santa Rosa
California
95409
USA
Phone: +1 707 531 4925
Fax: +1 480 247 5724
ISPress.org
InformingScience.org

Printed in the US

This book is dedicated to Clare.

T. Grandon Gill
Informing Business
Santa Rosa, California: Informing Science Press.

Acknowledgements

Given the controversial nature of many of the ideas presented in this book, I fear that acknowledging any participation in its creation might be viewed as more curse than blessing. Let me therefore begin by asserting that any sensible idea that emerges from the book is the doubtless the product of many researchers, reviewers and individuals kind enough to comment on earlier drafts. Those individuals who sacrificed their time trying to help me see the error of my ways must not be held accountable for my inability to see the light.

Because the *Informing Science Institute* operates entirely on a volunteer basis, there was no budget to pay reviewers. Early drafts of the manuscript were therefore reviewed by my parents, Richard T. Gill and Elizabeth Gill, Professor Marion Becker, Eli Cohen and Betty Boyd, and Zbigniew Gackowski, all of whom provided comments that were both extensive and highly useful.

As the manuscript reached its later stages, I sent email messages to at least one author of each "Foundational Reference" (those references listed at the end of each chapter). What I asked these individuals to do was to check to see if I had used their work correctly. I heard back from many of these individuals, including Daniel Ariely, Jason Colquitt (whose comments were particularly extensive), Ray Goldberg, Chip Heath, Raymond Hubbard, Deirdre McCloskey, Nassim Nicholas Taleb and Daniel Willingham. I was honored that so many eminent scholars took the time to do a spot check of what I had written.

During this period, I also received comments from Bob Travica, Mary Shelman and Bill Murphy, who is presently a doctoral student at the University of South Florida.

At the very end of the review process, I made the manuscript available to some of my MBA sectionmates from *Harvard Business School*, hoping to gain some practitioner perspective. I am particularly grateful to Julian Bene and Jeff Kohler for taking the time not only to read the manuscript, but to send me useful comments to think about.

Finally, although I mentioned them earlier, I want to re-emphasize the pivotal role played by Eli Cohen and Betty Boyd of the *Informing Science*

Institute. Had it not been for them, the book might never have been conceived, it probably would never have been written and it certainly would never have been published. The selfless generosity exhibited by these two in managing virtually every aspect of the institute and in building an atmosphere of true collegiality and mentorship is unprecedented in my experience.

T. Grandon Gill
Informing Business
Santa Rosa, California: Informing Science Press.

Informing Business:
Research and Education on a Rugged Landscape

Contents

Acknowledgements...vii

Contents ix

Preface xi

Chapter 1: The Crisis of Informing 1

Chapter 2: Academic Informing Systems 27

Chapter 3: Complexity, Fitness, and Theory 47

Chapter 4: The Complexity of Business...87

Chapter 5: Mental Models and Heuristics...117

Chapter 6: Learning and Expertise 159

Chapter 7: Complexity and Individual Resonance 193

Chapter 8: Non-Routine Informing and Networks 227

Chapter 9: Complexity and Time Horizons 249

Chapter 10: The Question of Rigor 283

Chapter 11: A Research Case Study..337

Chapter 12: Complex Informing: A Synthesis 359

Chapter 13: Informing Ourselves..373

Chapter 14: Informing the Student Client..415

Chapter 15: Informing Practice 471

Chapter 16: Progress and the Future..509

Chapter 17: Reflections 557

References 567

About the Author... 593

Index 595

Preface

As a professor employed by a business school within a research university, my ultimate goal should be to inform business. I try to achieve this goal through a variety of activities. Before I can presume to inform anyone, I must first inform myself. We call this activity *research*. Once I have acquired knowledge that I believe to be useful, I engage in a series of activities intended to communicate it both to my colleagues and directly to practice. Publications, presentations, and consulting represent just a small fraction of the channels that are available for this task. Finally, and most importantly, I must inform business through my students, who will then take what they have learned and apply it in their future professional positions, as well as communicating some of these ideas to their future colleagues. We call the role I play in this process *educating*.

Knowing that the value of what I accomplish in my professional life ultimately depends on my effectiveness in informing business, I am naturally motivated to assess my success in these efforts. My hope is that other business faculty members—who are the targeted audience for this book—might feel the same. Unfortunately, assessing the impact of our research and educational activities is far from straightforward. Even an exploratory attempt to do justice to that task requires a considerable amount of thought relating to the business landscapes that we study and to the mechanisms by which we examine problems and communicate our findings. That understanding these informing processes requires us to venture beyond the boundaries of what is strictly "business" should come as little surprise. There are few business problems today that can be addressed without considering a broad array of more general issues that may include technology, psychology, cultural history, environmental systems, and communications—as well as many other disciplines.

It will become quickly obvious—a few paragraphs into the first chapter, if not before—that I harbor deep suspicions regarding how well today's business schools are informing business. The source of these suspicions can be framed in terms of three questions that relate to both our research and teaching priorities, later referred to as Priorities 1, 2 and 3:

1. Is our emphasis on understanding the general principles of business behavior or on building a tool bag of techniques for dealing with individual problems?

2. Are we utilizing one way channels to communicate our knowledge or are we interactively constructing knowledge with our practitioner and student clients?

3. Is our focus on exploring the routine activities of business or on creatively responding to the unexpected?

Naturally, any sensible informing approach will require a mixture in each of the three areas. But as I look at most business schools today, particularly in the U.S., what I see is a gradual drift towards emphasizing general principles (a.k.a. theory-building), towards relying on one-way channels (e.g., scholarly publications and lectures) and towards curricula and research agenda that focus on surveying the routine.

I find this drift troubling. Many business scholars would disagree with me on this matter, however. They can point to domains of inquiry—particularly in the physical sciences—where huge advances in our understanding have resulted from precisely such a movement towards general principles and explaining replicable behaviors, all communicated through channels dominated by peer-reviewed journals and lectures. In this book I will argue, on the other hand, that the domains studied by the hard sciences are fundamentally different in their underlying behavior than social environments such as business. My case builds upon my assessment of the underlying complexity of the two distinct domains of study. Certainly, physical domains can be made arbitrarily complicated—any engineer can tell you that. Nevertheless, for a variety of reasons (e.g., the principle of superposition, immutable nature of physical laws) they rarely achieve the level of complexity inherent in most social systems. What I mean by complexity and *why it plays such a critical role in the character of the knowledge we can expect to extract from a domain* is at the core of this book.

For readers familiar with *informing science*, the transdisciplinary research area that strives to further our understanding of general informing processes, it will come as no surprise that my arguments draw from many disciplines. Effective informing requires a basic understanding of how we communicate, problem solve, and learn. Most advances in these areas have been made outside the sphere of business research, in disciplines such as psychology, education, sociology, and even computer science. Exploring the features that make a domain of study complex benefits from consideration of models developed in fields such as evolutionary biology and cognitive science. Conjectures regarding the suitability of our research methods for the areas we study cannot be made without some discussion of the underlying assumptions of the statistical and mathematical models that we routinely employ.

As a consequence of the transdisciplinary approach, the book necessarily moves back and forth between topics that are directly relevant to informing business and topics that—on the surface—seem to have little or nothing to do with business. As an aid to the reader, I offer a short "Objectives" block at the beginning of each chapter that identifies the one or two key points I am hoping to make in the chapter. If such summaries seem more at home in a textbook than in a monograph, I once again offer up the transdisciplinary nature of informing science as my excuse. Because so many disciplines contribute to our understanding of informing, we cannot assume that each reader will have sufficient background to understand what is being presented and why. In endeavoring to provide the necessary explanations, a bit of the textbook flavor necessarily surfaces.

The roadmap to the book that follows may also prove useful to the reader:

Chapters 1 & 2: The purpose of these chapters is to present the case that informing business has become a serious and widespread concern (Chapter 1) and that if we fail to address this concern it could have serious unpleasant consequences for those of us plying our trade as business researchers and educators (Chapter 2).

Chapters 3 & 4: These chapters explore the complexity of the business landscape, the core theme that drives all the subsequent chapters. Chapter 3 specifically establishes what I mean by complexity and how we identify its presence. It draws upon domains almost entirely outside of business research—evolutionary biology in particular. The closest it comes to business is an example of how business school rankings might differ in a complex landscape vs. a decomposable (less complex) landscape. Chapter 4, in contrast, focuses specifically on making the case that business landscapes are generally complex and draws heavily on findings from many areas of business research. The presence of such complexity necessarily means that the principles describing the business landscape will be dominated by "exceptional cases". Naturally, this reduces the feasibility of identifying a small set of general principles (see Priority 1).

Chapters 5 & 6: These chapters explore the cognitive nature of problem solving and learning, with relatively little effort to tie the findings directly to business—although a number of the findings presented were first observed in a business context. Chapter 5 considers how we solve problems in general, particularly emphasizing the types of errors we frequently make in unfamiliar settings. This starts to build an argument for why we might be better off focusing on unexpected, rather than routine, situations (see Priority 3). In Chapter 6, we consider the process of learning. A key point here is that we tend to retain very little of that knowledge that we do not repeatedly apply. Thus, if business activities tend to be governed by a large set of situation-specific rules (as would be implied by a complex landscape), it is unlikely that students will remember much from comprehensive survey courses that describe these rules but do not offer the chance to repeatedly apply them, an important observation in considering balancing principles vs. problem solving (see Priority 1).

Chapters 7 & 8: These chapters consider the processes of informing at the individual (Chapter 7) and collective (Chapter 8) levels. Like the previous two chapters, they are presented in general, rather than business-specific, terms. In Chapter 7, the obstacles in the way of achieving effective informing are identified; these obstacles grow with the complexity of the content being conveyed. The key to effective informing in these situations is developing a clear picture of the client's initial knowledge. Developing such a picture virtually demands a process of back-and-forth interaction with the client (see Priority 2). In Chapter 8, research relating to the diffusion of ideas into a group is summarized. Here, the evidence is clear that one-way channels, such as publications and lectures, are likely to become far less effective as complexity grows (again, see Priority 2).

Chapter 9: Addresses the important issue of time horizons, mixing general and business-specific observations. The key conclusion of this chapter is that as the complexity of the business environment grows, the degree to which non-routine situations are encountered and their role in shaping overall system behavior will grow correspondingly (Priority 3).

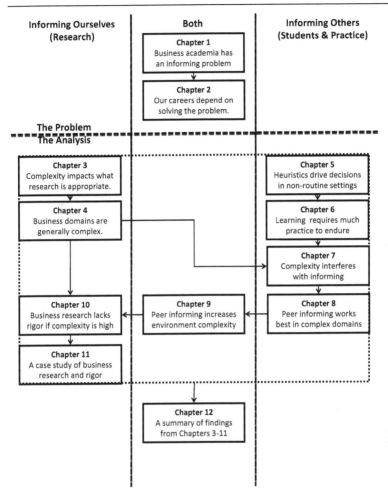

Figure P.1: Conceptual map of problem and analysis portion of the book, Chapters 1 through 12

Chapters 10 & 11: These chapters narrowly address the rigor of business research, since the widespread existence of business theories and models would seem to be inconsistent with the conclusion that business landscapes are truly complex. In recent decades, many of the criticisms of business schools have revolved around their emphasis on rigor as opposed to relevance. In Chapter 10, I make the argument that the underlying complexity of the business landscape can create the appearance of rigor where true rigor does not actually exist. As a consequence, many of the general principles supported by our empirical research may prove far more brittle than we imagine (see Priority 1). Chapter 11 is a case study that revisits an empirical research project that I conducted in the early 1990s. Throughout the chapter, I identify threats to rigor and dissect flaws that I have only lately recognized.

Chapter 12: This chapter summarizes the key ideas developed in Chapters 3 through 11, ending the conceptual portion of the book. The general flow of these chapters is illustrated in Figure P.1.

Chapters 13, 14 & 15: These chapters examine how a business school might be redesigned if effective informing were the sole criterion for fitness being employed. Chapter 13 deals with how we might inform ourselves more effectively in our research activities. It particularly emphasizes the need to consider the diffusion of ideas as an integral part of the research process, and why we should stress communicating through relationships rather than through publications (see Priority 2). Chapter 14 focuses on how we inform our students. It argues that the typical program design, built around many lecture-oriented survey courses with only limited opportunities to apply the knowledge being presented, will lead to very low levels of retention. As an alternative, it proposes that greater attention should be paid to core problem solving skills (see Priority 1) and providing opportunities to apply these skills to specific business problems. Chapter 15 examines how we might inform businesses directly. It makes the case that publications, even in practitioner-oriented journals, are likely to exert minimal impact on practice. Instead, we should be focusing on working side-by-side with practitioners in problem solving situations, such as case-writing and consulting (see Priority 2).

Chapter 16: This chapter looks towards the future, arguing that if business schools are to serve as more than trade schools, we need to embrace the process of progress and act to balance the many forces—particularly within academia—that would seek to constrain that process. It concludes that our most valuable role could be in helping individuals prepare for the unexpected (see Priority 3), since the continuation of progress guarantees that the unexpected will exert an ever-growing influence on business landscapes.

Chapter 17: Reflections intended to tie together the disparate threads that run throughout the book and to address directly the three questions presented in this Preface. I also hope it will serve to help the casual reader quickly ascertain "the point" of this book.

The solutions and synthesis portion of the book is illustrated in Figure P.2.

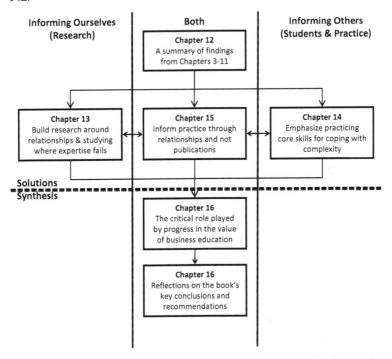

Figure P.2: Conceptual map of the solutions and synthesis portions of the book, Chapters 13 through 17

*   *   *

Before concluding, I will make a few quick comments about some quirks in the structure of the book. To begin, I have chosen to place notes at the conclusion of each chapter, rather than at the end of the book. When I am a reader, I find that particular organization to be the more convenient. In these notes, I generally include supporting remarks that cannot easily be summarized or identified with a single reference. Some of these notes are quite lengthy. Occasionally, however, I cannot resist using them to make the odd whimsical or sardonic comment. The reader's degree of amusement (or annoyance) with these comments is likely to be a matter of taste.

A complete reference list is included at the end of the book, just before the index. At the end of each chapter, however, I also include a list of no more than five citations under the heading "Foundational References". What I am doing here is identifying those writings that exerted an unmistakable imprint on the shape of the chapter. Whether or not I actually agreed with their substance, the chapter would not have been the same without them. Why I believe this to be a good idea is discussed in Chapter 13.

With respect to the usage of the collective "we" throughout the book, I am referring to the worldwide fellowship of business faculty. While I very much hope that some practicing managers will read this book and derive value from it, I believe that we, as business academics, bear particular responsibility for the sad state of many of today's business schools. Thus, it is to my colleagues, as well as to me, that I address most of the recommendations presented here.

I have no doubt that much of analysis I present and many of the suggestions that I have made in this book will be controversial. My hope, however, is that I can convince the open-minded reader that most—if not all—of my conclusions flow fairly naturally from the assumptions that I make regarding the complexity of a continuously adapting business domain. Naturally, if a reader does not believe business practice is as complex as I make it out to be, it will be relatively easy to dismiss this book. If, however, my assumptions seem to make sense, I hope that the reader will finish this book with an appreciation of the fundamental changes that may be necessary if we are to become effective in informing business.

The primary intended audience of this book is, quite obviously, business educators: the faculty members and administrators responsible for directing and conducting the research and teaching activities of today's business schools. I further believe the lessons presented in this book could be of value to two other audiences. The first secondary audience is business practitioners, who depend heavily on business schools for many of their future employees and who frequently make large investments in these schools. Through their hiring and financial support decisions, practice has the power to exert great influence over the future direction of business schools. Today, that power is largely unused. This book offers many examples of activities that practitioners can and should actively encourage if they wish to see greater value from these institutions. The second secondary audience is educators from other disciplines, particularly in the social sciences. Arguably, the conceptual scheme that I present is readily applicable to many areas—such as education, public administration, and social work—where the indicators of landscape ruggedness suggest a qualitatively similar environment. Obviously, the business-specific recommendations presented here would need to be tailored to the goals of the field. Nevertheless, the underlying principles guiding the research and education challenges facing these disciplines may prove to be quite similar.

Professor T. Grandon Gill
Information Systems and Decision Sciences Department
University of South Florida

April 2010

T. Grandon Gill
Informing Business
Santa Rosa, California: Informing Science Press.

Chapter 1

The Crisis of Informing

Roadmap & Objectives: Before jumping into the topic of how to inform business more effectively, we need to ask the question: How good a job are we doing right now? This chapter presents evidence that business schools today face an informing problem and offers some details regarding the nature of that problem.

During the last half of 2008, the world was rocked by a series of crises that eroded our confidence in U.S. business to a degree that was nothing less than cataclysmic. Financial institutions, including many of the world's major banks, came dangerously close to closing their doors after having made bets on a rising real estate market that, in retrospect, seem incomprehensible. America's top three automakers all appeared to be on the brink of failure; two actually entering bankruptcy. The largest Ponzi scheme in human history was detected; it was operated by the former head of the NASDAQ exchange and remained undetected despite repeated demands to the U.S. Securities and Exchange Commission (SEC) that it be investigated. It looked as if the world economic system was about to collapse. Indeed it might have if the U.S. and many other governments had not intervened with massive infusions of funds and guarantees. Not the best of years for capitalism.

Hidden by the headlines of that tumultuous year, another business crisis continued to brew. It is a crisis of informing, and its epicenter is the business schools of the U.S. The heart of the problem is the failure of these schools to improve the conduct of management in any visible way. The public's trust in business executives has reached its lowest level since we began to measure it. How can the institutions that pride themselves on being the source of so many of these executives escape being tarred with the same brush?

In this chapter, we consider if U.S. business schools are truly failing to inform business. Such informing can take place in many ways. We can inform business through the discoveries we make in our research. Are our findings having an impact on the way we manage? Is that impact positive? We can also inform business through the knowledge we impart to the students that we graduate. Are they learning what we want them to learn? Is what we are teaching them helping, or are our lessons making the problem worse?

Before considering these specific questions, we review how public trust has been impacted by recent economic events. The particular importance of that topic becomes apparent when we consider the track record of business schools in producing trustworthy students.

The Trust Catastrophe

Under the capitalist system, a vibrant and evolving economy depends upon trust. On an individual level, without trust consumers are reluctant to commit to a purchase. Without trust, suppliers will not extend the credit that companies need to grow and adapt. Without trust, banks will not lend. Without trust, our focus turns to defending what we have rather than on building what we have not. Collectively, the continued existence of the free enterprise system depends on our willingness to trust where the system is taking us. A central theme that runs throughout this book is that complex systems nearly always exhibit certain perverse tendencies; they are prone to unpredictable shocks and they tend to lead to distributions of "things", such as wealth and power, that seem wildly inequitable. If we cannot trust that the system is fair, then we will surely choose to replace it.

Trust and Evolution of U.S. Business Schools

The lack of trust in business at the turn of the 20th century was one of the principal forces leading to the establishment of U.S. business schools. As Rakesh Khurana (2007) explains in his history of U.S. business schools, it was during this period that the traditional owner-managed business gave way to corporate ownership and the professional manager emerged. During this same period, government often took an adversarial view of these new entities—with trust-busting activities peaking around 1912. The social status accorded to individuals pursuing these new managerial careers was also vastly inferior to their economic status. Memories of the age of "robber barons" were still fresh and heated disputes with labor often led to bloodshed. It was to counter forces such as these that institutions such as Harvard's Graduate School of Business Administration and Dartmouth's Tuck School were founded.

During the late 1950s, another crisis of trust transformed U.S. business schools. In this case, it was a lack of trust in the institutions themselves. Strong criticisms were leveled in reports funded by the Carnegie Foundation (Pierson, 1959) and the Ford Foundation (Gordon & Howell, 1959). The latter report, for example, asserted the following:

> [There is] strong and widespread dissatisfaction with the quality of business education in American colleges and universities today. What passes as the going standard of acceptability is embarrassingly low, and many schools of business do not even meet these low standards. While the schools are bedeviled by uncertainty, there is growing recognition that the present situation is intolerable. The gap between what society needs and what the business schools are offering has grown wide enough for all to see (Gordon & Howell, 1959, p. 6).

Stung by criticisms such as these, and funded with foundation dollars, top business schools began to remake themselves according to the model of the sciences in the 1960s and 1970s. The direction of research became more focused; its quantity magnified many times. By the 1980s, business research had come to be viewed in a new light. It had gained a considerable amount of respectability in the eyes of other disciplines.

Trust in Business

As the research of business schools gained credibility in the academic sphere, the level of trust enjoyed by business seemed improve at the same time, particularly in the U.S. In recent years, the trend was quite pronounced. According to the Edelman Trust Barometer (StrategyOne, 2009a, p. 5), when asked about their trust in business, European opinion leader responses were positive between 32% and 41% of the time between 2001 and 2008, with no particular trend. Asked the same question, U.S. leaders responded positively 44% of the time in 2001 (right in the midst of the Enron scandal and the dot-com bust). For the next six years, that number improved almost continuously, reaching 58% in the 2008 survey (taken at the beginning of the year). By the 2009 survey, the trust level had plummeted to 38%—just slightly ahead of Europe's 36% for the same year. This contrasts with trust levels in emerging economies, most notably China and Brazil, where trust in business remained high (71% in China, 69% in Brazil) and actually rose between 2008 and 2009 (StrategyOne, 2009a, p. 7).

With the decline of trust in business in both the U.S. and Europe came a strong sentiment that business needs to be reined in. When asked to agree or disagree with the statement "your government should in the future impose stricter regulations and greater control over business across all industry sectors", agreement levels were high, ranging from 84% in France to 61% in the U.S. (where trust in government also fell, from 39% to 30%; StrategyOne, 2009a, pp. 7 & 15). Such public support certainly impacted the U.S. government's willingness to become heavily involved in the financial, automobile, housing, and health sectors.

Trust in the Students We Graduate

As of the time of this writing, relatively little attention has been directed towards the role, if any, that business schools played in the recent crisis. In the long run, however, we are unlikely to escape so easily. Many of the events that transpired had a strong ethical element; some—such as Madoff's Ponzi scheme—were indisputably criminal. How long can it be before the ethics, as well as the competence, of the students we graduate are called into question?

Unfortunately, when it comes to the ethics of our students, we stand on particularly weak ground. A well known study in this area was conducted by Donald McCabe, Kenneth Butterfield and Linda Trevino (2006). These researchers collected data on the subject of academic dishonesty from over 5000 business and non-business graduate students[1]. That study found that 56% of graduate business students admitted to having cheated one or more times in the previous year, compared with 47% of non-business graduate students. These results could, of course, be interpreted in two ways—business schools attract students with lower-than-average ethical values or business schools are not doing a good job in helping their students acquire good ethical values. The best research available seems to suggest that the truth probably lies somewhere in the middle. One study, for example found that while entering business students score significantly lower on an ethics questionnaire than other undergraduate students when entering school, no improvement in scores was found by the end of their fourth year (Milner, Mahaffey, MacCaulay & Hynes, 1999). In fact, their scores dropped slightly, but the difference was not large enough to be significant. For my own part, I would not be eager to sit before a state legislative committee justifying our programs on the grounds that we do not do so much damage as to be measureable.

It is, in fact, unfair to judge business schools on a single dimension. The U.S. business school is today expected to perform many missions, particularly at a research university. In addition to teaching our students (the education mission), we are expected to create knowledge (the pure research mission) and to disseminate that knowledge to practice (the applied research mission). In pursuit of our pure research mission, we are mainly informing ourselves; later in the book our effectiveness in this regard is considered. For the remainder of this chapter, we focus on the degree to which we have been judged effective in informing our students and informing practice.

How Are We Educating Our Students?

In considering how well business schools are doing, both with respect to students and practice, the two fundamental questions we need to be asking are the following:

1. Are our informing efforts having an impact?

2. Is the net impact we are having a positive one?

We turn to these questions first in the context of our students.

Do Managers Need a Business Education?

In most professions, some form of licensing is a prerequisite to practice. As a prerequisite to the licensing process, individuals may also need a professional degree. In medicine it is the M.D., in law it might be an LLB or JD, and so forth. Management has no such licensing and no such degree requirements, leading some to argue that it is not a true profession (e.g., Khurana, 2007).

Despite this fact, business degrees—both at the undergraduate and master's degree levels—are widespread, particularly in the U.S. For example, between 1965 and 1985, the number of MBAs awarded in the

U.S. grew from 7% of all master's degrees to 23% (Cheit, 1985, p. 49). By the same year, 1985, business degrees had risen to about 24% of all undergraduate degrees awarded, according to the U.S. Department of Education. Since that time, however, the rapid increase in business degrees stopped, as illustrated in Figure 1.1, and the percentage flattened out—although the total number of degrees rose considerably since total undergraduate degrees (all subjects) awarded nearly doubled during the period and total and master's degrees rose by a factor of nearly two and a half .

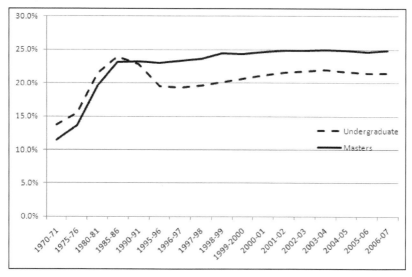

Figure 1.1: Business degrees conferred in the U.S. from 1970-2007 as a percent of all undergraduate and master's degrees. Source: *U.S. Department of Education, National Center for Educational Statistics,* **Tables 271 and 272.**

With such a large pool of graduates educated in business, were business education to be a true prerequisite to business success, we would expect that an overwhelming percentage of the most successful business executives would have such degrees. It is probably too early to make a final judgment on that score, since the largest cluster of business graduates are just starting to reach the age at which they would normally become executives. In one area—the world's most successful entrepreneurs—the initial indications do not suggest that business education is an overwhelming advantage, however. If you look at the names on the list of the richest people in the U.S., it becomes clear that a small number of companies have been responsible for creating a huge amount of wealth. These include Walmart (numerous Walton family members), Microsoft (Bill Gates, Paul Allen, Steve Ballmer), Berkshire Hathaway (Warren Buffet), Oracle (Larry Ellison), Koch Industries (Charles Koch, David Koch), Bloomberg L.P. (Michael Bloomberg), Google (Sergey Brin, Larry Page), and Dell (Michael Dell). In fact, these 8 companies are responsible for the top 13 places on the list. If we look at the founders of the eight companies, only two (Michael Bloomberg and Warren Buffet) had formal education in business, both acquired before the business education boom. Four, on the other hand, did not complete an undergraduate degree: Sam Walton, Bill Gates, Larry Ellison, and Michael Dell[2], the last three being of an age where business education was commonplace. In other words, it would probably be an overstatement to claim that business education provides any "needed" skills that cannot be acquired elsewhere.

Another source of evidence that a full degree is not a prerequisite to success in business comes from *business boot camps*, discussed further in Chapter 14. These are short programs, typically 6-8 weeks, offered by a number of top business schools—such as Dartmouth's Tuck School and the University of California at Berkeley—that prepare undergraduate students with engineering and liberal arts degrees for careers in business. What these programs focus on is conveying the facts and vocabulary that students *need* to know, rather than on developing a general knowledge of business functions and analytical methods. Consider the following quote from the flyer for *2008 Global Summit on Business Education in the 21ˢᵗ Century* conducted by Harvard Business School:

> In the financial services sector, long the biggest employer of graduating MBAs, having an MBA does not increase the odds of promotion. McKinsey now hires in a 50/50 split, with half of new employees coming from MBA programs and the other half consisting of Ph.D.s, MDs, law school graduates, or graduates with other degrees. Their non-MBA employees go through a six-week training period and are deemed ready to perform—without needing an MBA. (HBS, 2008)

Questions have also been raised with respect to the level at which business graduates have mastered their subject matter. Jeffrey Pfeffer and Christina Fong (2002, p. 82) report the following:

Recently, an investment bank was horrified to find that an MBA graduate it hired from a leading business school, an individual who had apparently taken a number of courses in finance, could not calculate the net present value of a future stream of payments.

I have noticed the same problem in my own master's degree program, where I teach the capstone course. Even basic analytical skills, such as performing a simple break-even analysis, are often lacking despite the full complement of prerequisite core courses in each business function that the students have previously taken and passed.

Concern regarding what students are actually learning in our business programs has been sufficiently great that in 2003 *AACSB International*, the principal accrediting body for research-oriented business schools in the U.S. and, increasingly, the world, changed its accreditation standards so that *assurance of learning* became a major goal.

With respect to organizational performance, there is also a question as to whether or not a business degree—most particularly, the MBA—actually impacts performance very much. For example, in a study of mutual fund performance, Judith Chevalier and Glenn Ellison (1999) found that while the average SAT score reported by the manager's undergraduate institution did seem to have a small impact on overall fund performance, the coefficient for having an MBA was not significant[3]. Similar findings were reported by Aron Gottesman and Matthew Morey (2006a, 2006b) for a broader cross-section of CEOs. In a complementary vein, a number of elite consulting firms, including McKinsey and the Boston Consulting Group, experimented with hiring non-MBA graduates. Their initial evaluation of the effectiveness of these hires was highly positive, and they indicated that they planned to hire more (Mintzberg, 2004, p. 88-89). As noted previously, the split of MBA/non-MBA hires has now risen to 50/50 at McKinsey.

The fact that these findings and observations are coming out of financial services and consulting should be of particular concern to the most elite MBA programs, whose graduates disproportionately favor these occupations[4]. The perception that the MBA lacks value has also alarmed Harvard Business School, where professor David Garvin (HBS, 2008) reports the following in the materials for their *Global Summit*:

> A top recruiter at Harvard Business School said, 'If given a choice between the admit list and the graduation list, the admit list is what you want.'

There is also evidence that the return on investment of an MBA degree has started to decline, causing its perceived value in the marketplace to be reduced. Ariel Nelson (2008), in a CNBC "By the Numbers" column, used numbers compiled in *Business Week* to estimate how quickly the graduate of a top 10 MBA program recouped tuition and lost income through higher salary. In 1998, the payback period was only 2.9 years; by 2008 that period had more than doubled, to 6.3 years, as a result of rising tuition (from $52,000 in 1998 to $95,000 in 2008) and reduced pre- and post-MBA salary differentials[5].

Trends and observations such as these aside, what is perhaps most disturbing here is the strong attachment to the status quo that we exhibit in our role as business educators. The burden of proof clearly falls on those trying to argue that business education is having a negligible impact on student performance once they graduate. Paradoxically, demanding such proof for the "no impact" case is diametrically opposed to how we conduct most of our disciplinary research. In our "real" research, it would be more natural to accept the null hypothesis (i.e., we have no impact on our students) until such impact has been demonstrated to exist[6]. Fortunately, for the sake of our egos, we have become very adept at rationalizing why the very principles that we would have business practitioners learn from us, those of research rigor, should not apply to those activities where we are, in effect, acting as practitioners—such as our instructional duties.

But perhaps I am being unfair here. After all, there are some very distinguished researchers who argue that the education we provide does have an important impact on our students. Regrettably, their argument is that our impact is almost entirely negative.

Are Managers Being Hurt by Their Education?

In considering if management education is actually damaging our students, criticisms tend to fall into one (or more) of three categories:

1. Business education is encouraging students to focus on the wrong things.

2. Business education is cultivating the wrong attitudes among our students.

3. Business education is conveying invalid theories to students that they are then acting upon.

Because the last of these represents a criticism relating to business research in general, to be taken up in Chapter 10, we focus on the first two in this section.

The wrong focus

After the earlier-mentioned criticisms leveled by the Ford and Carnegie Foundations in the late 1950s, nearly two decades passed before the next wave of criticism of business education arrived. Many scholars (e.g., Cheit, 1985) place particular importance on an article titled "Managing Our Way to Economic Decline" published in the *Harvard Business Review* by Robert Hayes and William Abernathy (1980, p. 5). In the article's most quoted paragraph, the authors stated:

> ...during the past two decades American managers have increasingly relied on principles that prize analytical detachment and methodological elegance over insight, based on experience, into the subtleties and complexities of strategic decisions. As a result, maximum short-term financial returns have become the overriding criteria for many companies.

The assertions made in the article set off a firestorm of debate within business schools, since the change in research philosophy that had taken place in the mid-1960s led universities to incorporate more and more quantitative and analytical content into their curriculum. It has been echoed in numerous commentaries since then. For example, in Lyman Porter and Lawrence McKibbin's (1988, p. 65) influential *Management Education and Development*:

> If there is one area that many critics seem to agree receives *too much* emphasis in the modern business school, it is quantitatively based analytical techniques.

Or, to quote Henry Mintzberg (2004, p. 101):

> An obsession with "facts" blinds the calculating manager to everything but the present.

What I find rather interesting about the Hayes and Abernathy criticisms is the degree to which the outcomes they predicted *were not* realized[7]. For example, the authors idolized European and, to a lesser extent, Japanese management; by their reckoning both regions should have—by now—far outpaced us. In reality, of course, starting in the late 1980s, the U.S. grew at a substantially faster rate. They also criticized the U.S. for its lack of innovative spirit. Ironically, this criticism was leveled right at the start of the IT boom, a period then followed by the Internet boom, during which the U.S. appeared to lead the world in technological innovation. Thus, whatever the validity of their criticisms[8], their predictive accuracy was not particularly great. As we shall see throughout the book, this type of problem is universally experienced when experts attempt to predict the behavior of complex environments.

Cultivating the wrong attitudes

Upon reading Henry Mintzberg's (2004) *Managers Not MBAs*, you definitely get the sense that he has a special purgatory in his heart for MBAs in general and graduates of Harvard Business School in particular. He even expresses his opinions in the form of an equation:

$$\text{CONFIDENCE} - \text{COMPETENCE} = \text{ARROGANCE}$$

To this, he adds:

> Humility is not a word often pegged on MBAs. Arrogance is. That the label has been used so often is not an indication that all MBAs are arrogant, only that a noticeable number of them are (Mintzberg, 2004, p. 74)

In fact, in a series of four chapters he accuses the type of calculating and inexperienced manager produced by MBA programs of: 1) corrupting the educational process, 2) corrupting managerial practice, 3) corrupting existing organizations, and 4) corrupting society.

In addition to promoting arrogance and corruption, some individuals such as Robert Giacalone (2004, p. 415), an ethics professor at Temple University, accuses business schools of removing the very hearts of their students:

> We promulgate a worldview that facilitates questionable decisions. We create brilliant tacticians who know how to play the

end game of wealth creation, where financial success is defined without transcendent responsibilities. We teach a path without a heart where tacticians can cheat themselves and others of good lives. We are proud, excellent drill sergeants teaching tactical reductionism: The worthiness of a tactic depends on whether it results in profits for oneself or for one's company. But in search of a personal or corporate gain, proponents of this instruction aid and abet physical, psychological, and spiritual toxins for our students, the organizations they work for, and society at large.

While opinions such as these make for entertaining reading, as well as marvelous opportunities for block quoting, I have two key reservations. First, they carry with them the implicit assumption that a particular treatment—a business degree "applied" to a student—will exert a reasonably consistent effect across students. In Chapter 3, we will see the theoretical justification as to why such uniformity of effect is *very unlikely* in complex informing situations. Responding directly to Mintzberg's fascination with Harvard, my alma mater, I certainly recognize—in *some* of my MBA classmates—the often disagreeable characteristics he describes. Having gone through the process, however, I would also comment that I personally observed a number of individuals who became *less arrogant* as a result of their MBA experience[9]. This is not surprising since nearly all my classmates had been at or near the top of their respective undergraduate and high school classes, yet half of this group found themselves in the bottom half of their HBS class, whether or not they cared to acknowledge it.

My second reservation deals with the inconsistency of accepting criticisms that business education has little or no effect while, at the same time, being willing to ascribe a strong negative influence to that same process. As for me, I count myself lucky when I can get my students to read the syllabus carefully. That I could make them markedly more arrogant or could affect the theft of their very souls while they appear to be attending to barely anything that I say strikes me as improbable. Thus, I tend fall on the "failing to inform" side of the debate.

Is Our Research Helping Practice?

At a typical U.S. research university, research productivity is often the principal criterion by which tenure earning faculty members are judged.

Does that research actually help practitioners? Once again, we can break this into two questions: 1) Are we impacting practice? and 2) Is what impact we exert positive?

Does Our Research Have Impact?

That we, as academic researchers in business, wish that our research had greater impact on practice is not in dispute[10]. A more interesting question is as follows: Does our research have *any* impact on practice?

Thomas Davenport and Laurence Prusak published a study of the flow of ideas into management (Davenport, Prusak & Wilson, 2003, p. 81). With respect to the contribution of business academics, they concluded the following:

> We believe that most business schools—and the academics that inhabit them—have not been very effective in the creation of *useful* business ideas. Sure, a lot of business ideas are explored in business school research, but for the most part, they are created elsewhere and are seldom even discussed in an accessible fashion by academics.

The authors were much more enthusiastic about the roles played by consultants, practicing managers, and journalists. Indeed, many of the academics involved in idea creation they prefer to describe as "academic refugees", since their contributions evolved and were disseminated outside of the academic mainstream.

Warren Bennis and James O'Toole (2005, p. 1) argue that lack of relevance to managers is a serious problem and one that is growing worse because of our focus on scientific research. They state:

> During the past several decades, many leading B schools have quietly adopted an inappropriate—and ultimately self-defeating—model of academic excellence. Instead of measuring themselves in terms of the competence of their graduates, or by how well their faculties understand important drivers of business performance, they measure themselves almost solely by the rigor of their scientific research. They have adopted a model of science that uses abstract financial and economic analysis, statistical multiple regressions, and laboratory psychology. Some of the research produced is excellent, but because so little of it is grounded in actual business practices, the

focus of graduate business education has become increasingly circumscribed—and less and less relevant to practitioners.

Jeffrey Pfeffer (2007), a distinguished professor at Stanford University has been a particularly vocal critic of the impact of research on management. He comments that in a recent book that reviewed major contributions to the practice of management (Mol & Birkinshaw, 2008), not one the 50 innovations they listed appeared to be the result of academic research. With his co-author Christina Fong (Pfeffer & Fong, 2002), he also points out the relatively small percentage of business books that are actually written by business academics.

Concerns about research impact are sufficiently great that *AACSB International* assembled a task force on the subject, just as it did for learning impact. The study and the subsequent rounds of revisions involved many people:

> Nearly 1,000 business deans, directors, and professors have participated in formal discussions about the report or offered comments and suggestions. (AACSB, 2008, p. 4)

Its preface begins with the words: "It is not easy to fix something when people cannot agree it is broken." To this comment might be added: "It is not easy to tell if something is broken if the people you ask are the ones who broke it."

One intriguing aspect of the study was its effort to identify instances of academic research that have impacted practice. These examples are summarized by discipline in Table 1.1. What is particularly interesting about the list they presented is the disparity across disciplines. In the case of finance, the evidence of impact is clear—I have observed every single item applied in practice and have even used a few myself while consulting (and finance is most definitely *not* my research area). With respect to the remaining areas, they seem to be very narrow, have their origins in practice (e.g., Hofstede's work, which is well known, benefited heavily from his time employed at IBM), or are of questionable practical impact (e.g., did accountants really learn that the stock market reacts to announcements from academics?).

Moreover, the evidence supporting actual impact is quite weak. AACSB's (2008) sole empirical support comes from a study that found a *small* correlation between 120 articles that practitioners felt could be relevant to them and the number of times they were cited by other researchers (Baldridge, Floyd & Markoczy, 2004). This is like saying that because we like the same flavors of ice cream as practitioners, our preference impacts theirs. In fact, to the extent that ideas do flow between academia and practice, it is probably in the direction of practice to academia. At least that was the conclusion of management researchers Barley, Meyer and Gash (1988, p. 52), who attempted to track the flow of concepts and concluded "the data suggest that symbolic and conceptual influence flowed in only one direction: from practitioners to academics."

Table 1.1: Examples of areas where business research has impacted practice (quoted from AACSB, 2008, p. 18-19)

Area	Impactful Research Examples
Finance	Theories of portfolio selection, irrelevance of capital structure, capital asset pricing, efficient markets, option pricing, and agency theory.
Accounting	Building on efficient market theory, the foundational research of William Beaver demonstrated that the stock market reacts strongly to corporate earnings announcements. Applying agency theory, the work of Watts and Zimmerman has been influential in creating a research stream that addresses how managers choose among accounting methods.
Marketing	Keller is well known for his contributions to understanding the construction, measurement, and management of brands. Green and Rao are credited with developing conjoint analysis approaches to consumer research based on seminal work by Luce and Tukey in mathematical psychology. Today, conjoint analysis is widely used to test new product designs and assess the appeal of advertisements.
MIS	The research of Malhotra has helped companies to understand why knowledge management systems fail and Bass's Diffusion Model has had practical applications for forecasting demand of new technologies.
Management	Hofstede has conducted the most comprehensive study of how values in the workplace are influenced by culture, and Vroom made seminal contributions to understanding employee motivation.

Perhaps not coincidentally, finance is quite different from the other disciplines in two respects. First, as already noted, it clearly does exert an influence on practice. Indeed, individuals with finance and economics PhD's are prized by Wall Street and government and are frequently found in positions where they influence decision-making and policy; I know of no other business discipline that can make the same boast. Second, finance is the area where we find most debate regarding whether or not the impact of research has been positive. It is to that question that we now turn.

Is Our Theory Hurting Business?

The discipline of finance and its reference discipline, economics, have produced a great many theories that exert some practical influence. The question therefore becomes "Has that influence been beneficial or negative?" Many of the users of such theories, as well as its creators, view the impact as being beneficial. Suffice it to say that there are many such supporters—almost as many are there are users and creators of the theory. There are, however, some strong detractors as well. Some question the theories as a consequence of their underlying qualitative assumptions; some are concerned about their more quantitative impacts. Two of the most influential detractors, one from each camp, are now profiled.

Ghoshal's critiques of assumptions regarding behavior

Some of the strongest criticisms of business research were leveled by the late Sumantra Ghoshal (2005). He was particularly critical of agency theory and transaction cost economics. The first of these is an area where AACSB specifically asserted that our research has had impact; the second is closely related to the first. It is worth looking at the substance of Ghoshal's arguments as to why these theories can promote unethical behaviors. In preparation for doing so, it is useful to review these theories.

We begin with agency theory. The gist of the theory presented by Jensen & Meckling (1976) is as follows. It begins by arguing that the entire notion of a collective "firm" is misplaced; that it is better to view the firm as a nexus of contractual relationships between agents (e.g., employees) and principals (e.g., owners). In a sole proprietorship, the chief executive is also the principal. As a consequence, he or she fully bears the entire cost of increasing his or her utility. Such costs include those for pecuniary benefits—which is to say benefits defined in monetary terms, such as salary—and non-pecuniary benefits—such as the psychic satisfaction of having a corporate jet at one's beck and call. As ownership share declines, however, the personal cost to the chief executive of acquiring these benefits similarly declines. For example, a CEO who owns 80% of a firm pays for only 80% of the cost of his or her salary and other benefits. In the worst case, a CEO who has no ownership stake effectively experiences zero costs from engaging in activities that maximize personal utility as opposed to maximizing the fitness of the firm. Because shareholders are aware of this problem, as management's ownership declines, they become increasingly willing to expend resources on monitoring and bonding activities intended to ensure the cost of these personal benefits are controlled. They must also accept the reality that some residual costs will be experienced owing to their inability to fully control agent behavior. All these factors can be placed into a mathematical form that can be optimized, with implications for capital structure and many other rational management behaviors.

Transaction cost economics theory is similar in spirit. Oliver Williamson (1975), who happened to receive the 2009 Nobel Prize in economics as I was writing this chapter, makes the argument that the natural mechanism for exchange is a market in which participants exchange goods and services. Unfortunately, markets are not very effective at certain types of activities—such as those involving a lot of coordination or where asset specificity is high—because participants will behave opportunistically if allowed to do so unchecked. As a consequence, hierarchical organizations are established to control undesired behaviors. In the words of Ghoshal and Moran (1996, p. 14):

> According to this theory, organizations exist because of their superior ability to attenuate human opportunism through the exercise of hierarchical controls that are not accessible to markets.

Ghoshal (2005) asserts that these theories are not well supported by empirical data. Many experiments, for example, demonstrate that humans actually place a high weight on perceived fairness. They also engage in altruistic behaviors provided they are in an environment that encourages them to do. They are far from being the rational utility maximizers assumed by the models of economic theory. Thus, these theories are based on flimsy foundations.

What is worse, he argues, is that social theories tend to be self-fulfilling. In other words, if we tell a manager (or a student wishing to become a manager) that he or she should be strictly guided by rational self-interest, he or she will tend to behave that way. Ghoshal (2005, p. 85) asserts:

> Combine agency theory with transaction cost economics, add in standard versions of game theory and negotiations analysis, and the picture of the manager that emerges is one that is now very familiar in practice: the ruthlessly hard-driving, strictly top-down, command-and-control focused, shareholder-value-obsessed, win-at-any-cost business leader of which Scott Paper's "Chainsaw" Al Dunlap and Tyco's Dennis Koslowski are only the most extreme examples. This is what Isaiah Berlin implied when he wrote about absurdities of theory leading to de-humanization of practice.

His words, written five years before this book, seem prescient. To his list, a brand new cast of rascals has been added—some considerably worse than the last batch.

Taleb's critique of assumptions relating to risk

As a complement Ghoshal's criticism of the qualitative behavioral assumptions employed in business research, Nassim Nicholas Taleb (2007) takes on the quantitative assumptions employed in finance theory with considerable gusto. In his book *The Black Swan*, he argues that academic theory—and those elements of practice that are guided by that theory—fundamentally misunderstand the nature of *uncertainty*, which cannot be quantified, and *risk*, which can be. He refers to this packaging of uncertainty as quantifiable risk as the *ludic fallacy*. The metaphor used to title his book is that of the swan. Based upon observations made in Europe—where all swans *are* white—it was assumed that the probability of finding a swan of some other color was zero. That all changed, however, when a black swan was discovered in Australia. In other words, it is very imprudent to assume that you understand risk based upon past observations.

Much of the conceptual scheme presented in this book is devoted to exploring how the nature of complexity and complex systems supports Taleb's perspective, so we will not discuss it further here. If you accept his thesis, however, it undermines the basis of portfolio theory, the mathematically derived irrelevance of capital structure, the capital asset pricing model and options pricing. In other words, his ideas combined with Ghoshal's lead us to question nearly all the areas of the finance discipline's impact listed by the AACSB.

Taleb is very emphatic about the practical implications of his concerns. In fact, he argues that we are living in a fool's paradise when we allow our decision-making to be guided by existing financial theory. He admits to having felt very lonely in his concerns, working as a trader in his "day job", until October 1987. At that point, the stock market fell around 25% in a single day—an event that simply could not have happened given the academic consensus regarding the distribution of risk. Since the market seemed to go pretty much back to normal after that event, his warnings regarding the inadequacy of existing theories once again became easier to discount. After all, these theories had been developed by researchers who, one after another, were being awarded the Nobel Prize[11] during the same period[12]. Then, many of these researchers got together to form a firm called *Long Term Capital Management*. Taleb (207, p. 281-282) describes his vindication as follows:

> Robert Merton, Jr. and Myron Scholes were founding partners in the large speculative trading firm called Long-Term Capital Management, or LTCM… It was a collection of people with top-notch resumes, from the highest ranks of academia. They were considered geniuses. The ideas of portfolio theory inspired their risk management of possible outcomes—thanks to their sophisticated "calculations". They managed to enlarge the ludic fallacy to industrial proportions.

> Then, during the summer of 1998, a combination of large events, triggered by a Russian financial crisis, took place outside their models. It was a Black Swan. LTCM went bust and almost took down the entire financial system with it, as its exposures were massive. Since their models ruled out the possibility of large deviations, they allowed themselves to take a monstrous amount of risk. The ideas of Merton and Scholes, as well as those of Modern Portfolio Theory, were starting to bust. The magnitude of the losses was spectacular, too spectacular to allow us to ignore the intellectual comedy. Many friends and I thought that the portfolio theorists would suffer the same fate as the tobacco companies: they were endangering

people's savings and would soon be brought to account for the consequences...

None of that happened.

Instead, MBAs in business schools went on learning portfolio theory...

Of course, immediately after the LTCM event we experienced the peak of the Internet bubble, followed by its painful puncturing. Perhaps there was something to Taleb's reasoning after all.

Unfortunately, it is relatively easy to shape past events so as to create a compelling case for your particular position[13]. Taleb himself mentions this and refers to it as the *narrative fallacy*. Thus, a more rigorous test requires predicting something will happen. Part of what therefore impressed me about his book was certain observations he made no later than 2007, when the book was published. For example (Taleb, 2007, p. 225), he asserted the following about the globalization of world finance:

> ...creates interlocking fragility, while reducing volatility and giving the appearance of stability. In other words, it creates devastating Black Swans. We never lived before under the threat of global collapse...Almost all banks are now interrelated...when one falls, they all fall.

On the same page, in a footnote, he also mentioned:

> ...the government sponsored institution Fannie Mae, when I look at their risks, seems to be sitting on a barrel of dynamite, vulnerable to the slightest hiccup. But not to worry: their large staff of scientists deemed these events unlikely.

Of course, he might be faulted for not predicting that it would be the collapse of Fanny Mae and the housing market that would help to trigger the global financial meltdown that actually occurred. But Taleb is quick to acknowledge that experts, including himself, cannot be counted upon to accurately predict the future; indeed they are unlikely to do much better than random guessing—a proposition explored at length later in this book. So, I suppose he will have to content himself merely with being a better judge of the situation than nearly anyone else in the world.

Seven Fundamental Questions

In presenting these perspectives on ethics, education, and research, it has not been my intention to offer a balanced survey. The casual reader can quickly find *plenty* of editorials and articles in which we, as business faculty, congratulate ourselves for our research and educational accomplishments. Even the fiercest critics of business schools admit to the possibility that we may occasionally come up with ideas that are not entirely misplaced. Here are some examples:

- "We have much to be proud about and little to be ashamed of relative to most other countries." (Hayes & Abernathy, 1980, p. 12-13).

- "To be fair, some of what is published in A-list journals is excellent, imaginative, and valuable." (Bennis & O'Toole, 2005, p. 3).

- "The fact is that many of today's most influential management writers—serious thinkers widely read—have made their careers in academia" (Mintzberg, 2004, p. 395).

- "Adoption of scientific methods has yielded some significant benefits for both our research and our pedagogy" (Ghoshal, 2005, p. 77).

Taleb (2007) himself concedes that the Nobel committee may not have been too far off the mark in awarding the Nobel Memorial Prize in Economics to Friedrich von Hayek (a philosopher) and later Daniel Kahneman (a psychologist).

My goal in emphasizing the negative view of business school performance is not to suggest that there is nothing good about these schools. If I truly believed that to be the case, I would not permit myself to be employed by one. Rather it is to motivate a series of fundamental questions that I will be addressing throughout the book. The most important of these include the following:

1. *Can business schools continue doing "business as usual"?* Chapter 2, in particular, addresses the issue of the availability of resources, using the ongoing evolution—perhaps better described as the imminent extinction—of the MIS discipline as an example of

how a research discipline that does not pay attention to informing can pay a heavy price.

2. *Why do some disciplines seem to have so much more impact than others?* Ways in which finance and economics differ from other business research disciplines are considered, along with their implications for diffusion.

3. *Is the type of research we are conducting consistent with the domains we are researching?* Using a model drawn from complexity research, the likelihood that attractive theory—the goal of most of our research—will *ever* be found is considered.

4. *Is our research rigorous?* Using the same complexity model, the rigor of our theory-building and empirical research is questioned.

5. *Can the knowledge creation and dissemination processes really be separated?* Arguments for the inseparability of diffusion and research activities are examined.

6. *Are our curricula effective in informing our students?* Using the complexity and informing lenses, the adequacy of existing models of business education is considered.

7. *Are we teaching our students what they need to learn?* Given the nature of the business environment, the set of skills likely to be most valuable to students is proposed.

In addition to trying to answer these questions, the book—in Chapters 13 through 15—offers a number of concrete suggestions as to how our institutions might be transformed to accomplish greater informing. Chapter 16 then speculates upon what might happen to progress itself if we fail in that transformation.

Conclusions

Momentous events have shined a spotlight on the weaknesses of our economic system. It seems inconceivable that business schools will escape its glare. Business schools, particularly in the U.S., should be very concerned about this eventuality. By our own reckoning, there is room for much improvement in the ethics we impart, in the effectiveness of our teaching and in the impact of our research.

Those leveling these criticisms are not malcontents unable to succeed under the current system; most concerns have been raised by researchers from the very highest echelons of academia. Nor have they been offered out of malice; all have expressed a genuine desire to see business schools improve and have provided concrete suggestions towards that end.

There is a certain paradoxical quality to the criticisms. The two almost universal themes are suspicion of overly quantitative research and regret that we have become so disconnected from practice. At the same time, we must acknowledge that our quantitative research—developed by economists and finance researchers—is precisely where we have had our greatest tangible influence on practice. Critics argue that our educational efforts have had little effect and yet, in almost the same breath, bemoan the negative impact that our theories are having on the human side of management. Some, such as Mintzberg, go so far as to suggest that we would do well to consider abandoning our efforts to teach undergraduates and MBAs, focusing instead on more experienced students who have the wisdom to appreciate the knowledge we are exchanging with them. What they have failed to clarify is how—having eliminated virtually our entire existing source of students as we continue to pursue a generally impact-free research agenda—we can expect our activities to be funded.

Understanding how we might better inform business is the central goal of this book. For us to make progress in informing business, we first need to understand what complexity means and how it can impact the types of research we should be doing and how we educate our students. For too long we have acknowledged that business is complex without fully understanding the profound implications the statement carries. Thus, before we can assess possible techniques for improving the impact of our research and education, we begin by examining the nature of our dependence upon informing (Chapter 2), the meaning of complexity (Chapter 3) and the many ways in which the two interact (Chapters 4 through 12).

Chapter 1 Foundational References

Ghoshal, S. (2005). Bad management theories are destroying good management practices. *Academy of Management Learning & Education,* 4(1), 75-91.

Khurana, R. (2007). *From higher aims to hired hands.* Princeton, NJ: Princeton University Press.

Mintzberg, H. (2004). *Managers not MBAs.* San Francisco, CA: Berrett-Koehler.

Pfeffer, J. (2007). A modest proposal: How we might change the process and product of managerial research. *Academy of Management Journal, 50*(6), 1334-1345.

Taleb, N. N. (2007). *The Black Swan.* New York, NY: Random House.

Chapter 1 Notes

[1] These results were consistent with those of an earlier study in which business undergraduates were found to be more prone to cheating than other undergraduates (McCabe & Trevino, 1995).

[2] I relied on the Wikipedia biographies of the respective individuals to determine their educational background. I also used the Forbes list included on Wikipedia to identify the wealthiest individuals.

[3] These results probably undermine the value of business education even more than might first appear. Much of the mutual fund industry in the U.S. is headquartered in the northeast and, for that reason, recruits heavily from Ivy League schools—meaning that the high end of "average SAT" will be heavily composed of Ivy League graduates. These top schools, including Harvard, Princeton and Yale, do not offer undergraduate business concentrations, meaning that the high SAT group that performed well in the sample is likely to be singularly lacking in undergraduate business majors (a variable not included in the study).

[4] Consider, for example, the 2006 placement patterns at three of these schools. At Harvard Business School, 63% of the class of 2006 accepted jobs in finance and consulting (Finance: 42%, Consulting: 21%; Datar, Garvin & Knoop, 2008a). At Stanford, the total was 65% (Finance: 41%, Consulting: 24%; Datar, Garvin & Knoop, 2008b). Not to be outdone, at Yale the percentage was 73% (Finance: 49%, Consulting: 24%; Datar, Garvin & Weber, 2008b). The undisputed champion in the competition, however, was the University of Chicago, coming in at 81% (Finance: 59%, Consulting: 22%; Datar, Garvin & Weber, 2008a).

[5] There is some evidence that an MBA may be of value in signaling a shift in career priorities. For example, one study of IT workforce salaries between 1999 and 2002 found that an MBA yielded a 24% increase over the period, as opposed to less that 1% for non-MBA degree employees (Garvey, 2004). We need to be careful how heavily we weigh this observation, however. The period examined was a very unusual one in IT history since it involved both the most extreme years in the run-up of the Internet bubble *and* Y2K along with the subsequent disillusionment in IT that followed.

[6] In Chapter 10 there is considerable discussion of how we choose to set up our research analyses in such a way that reducing Type I error (assuming an effect exists when it does not) is given a much higher priority than reducing Type II error (missing an effect that is present).

[7] In the *Harvard Business Review* reprint of the Hayes & Abernathy (1980, p. 3) article, Hayes provides an explanation as to why they were really correct. To accept their explanation, however, you need to believe two unsupported assertions he made. First, that U.S. management became much less focused on "the numbers" during the 1980s—the decade during which both PCs and spreadsheets were invented and then proliferated to the desktop of virtually ever manager in the U.S. Second, that the "get rich quick" mentality of the Internet bubble was the principal cause of our decline in competitiveness over the past decade (as opposed to alternative explanations, such as anything that the Chinese might happen to be doing).

[8] As it happens, I believe that the relationship Hayes & Abernathy (1980) proposed between quantitative focus and shortened time horizons is extraordinarily insightful and largely valid—a subject considered at length in Chapter 9. I would also suggest, however, that the relationship is far more complicated than they originally supposed.

[9] Regrettably, I would be forced to place myself in Mintzberg's "became more arrogant as a result of the HBS MBA experience" camp, so observing that not everyone was so affected is not a backhanded attempt to compliment myself on my personal humility.

[10] We see calls for greater impact, for example, in management (e.g., Pfeffer, 2007), MIS (e.g., Gill & Bhattacherjee, 2009), marketing (e.g., Tapp, 2004), accounting (Maher, 1995), and operations re-

search/management science (e.g., Barman, Buckley & DeVaughn, 1997). Notably absent from these fields—where calls for relevance abound (the examples above are just a tiny fraction)—is finance. Why this may be expected is briefly mentioned later in this chapter and discussed more fully throughout the book.

[11] Taleb (20, p. 277-278) specifically mentions Nobel Laureates Sharpe, Markowitz, Merton and Scholes.

[12] When economists Sharpe and Markowitz, who helped develop portfolio theory, were awarded the prize, Taleb (2007, p. 277) commented "In a world where these two get the Nobel, anything can happen. Anyone can become president." Amusingly, two years later in the U.S. we have a president who was once widely regarded as extremely unlikely to be elected who just won an equally improbable Nobel Prize.

[13] Later in the book, we will find that ability to shape events into a supporting narrative is particularly enabled by systems that are complex. In such systems, there will nearly always be regions that behave according to a particular pattern—you just need to look for them hard enough.

T. Grandon Gill
Informing Business
Santa Rosa, California: Informing Science Press.

Chapter 2

Academic Informing Systems

Roadmap & Objectives: A frequent refrain of academics is that an educational institution cannot be run as if it were a business. The implication is clear: as business academics, any failure on our parts to inform will not necessarily impact our livelihoods. Since we are not like a business, why should we be *required* to provide a service that clients would willingly pay for? This chapter presents the opposing argument: if we ignore our informing problem we may well find ourselves without resources in the future.

The theme of this chapter is understanding academic informing systems. Such systems consist of two interrelated sub-systems. *Disciplinary informing systems* are built around disciplines and serve as the primary engines responsible for informing student and practitioner clients. *Institutional informing systems*, on the other hand, serve principally to acquire the resources necessary to support the activities of the disciplinary informing systems at a typical research university. The interaction between these two systems will determine, to a great extent, the long term prospects of both disciplines and institutions. Most significantly, a discipline or set of disciplines that do not meet the informing needs of the institution may well become starved for resources. This should be a frightening prospect for many of today's business schools.

To illustrate the challenges of acquiring resources in an academic environment, I profile my own discipline: management information systems (MIS). It represents a good example of an area that has had considerable success in pursuing its own research agenda while, at the same time, placing little emphasis on its practitioner stakeholders. What is happening to the discipline should, therefore, be of interest to business researchers in general. Nearly all business research seems to be heading in the direction chosen by MIS. We just reached the destination a little bit earlier.

Before looking at this practical example, however, we need to introduce the core building block of informing science—the informing system. Informing systems will then be used as the unit for much of the analysis performed throughout this book.

Informing Science and Informing Systems

Informing science[1] is a transdiscipline that has emerged mainly over the past decade. It was established as a result of the observation that many disciplines, including MIS, education, library science, computer science, and others, were studying the movement of information between senders and receivers in ways that were far more similar than they were different. In the seminal article that launched informing science, Eli Cohen (1999) defined the transdiscipline as follows:

> The fields that comprise the discipline of Informing Science *provide* their *clientele* with *information* in a *form, format,* and *schedule* that maximizes its effectiveness.

Cohen further identifies three underlying precepts of informing science:

1. A framework for characterizing such systems that involves a sender, a communications pathway, and a receiver. These are respectively referred to as the *informing environment*, the *delivery system* and the *task completion environment*.

2. The ability to characterize such systems at many levels. Three such levels include the level at which actual informing occurs, the level at which new informing system instances are created, and the level at which overall designs for such systems are specified.

3. The inherent inter-relatedness of the components of such systems: task, technology, structure, and people.

Each of these precepts is now explored briefly.

Informing Framework

Cohen (1999) uses Shannon's (Shannon and Weaver, 1949) communications model (sender, encoder, medium, decoder, and receiver) as the principal lens through which informing systems are viewed. A simplified version of that model is presented in Figure 2.1.

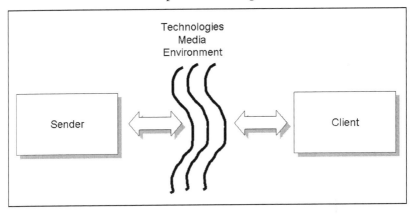

Figure 2.1: Basic Informing System Model

In practical situations, such a simple model rarely suffices. Many factors make "real world" informing systems much more complex. Examples of these include:

1. Sender and client components are rarely homogeneous. Rather, senders consist of complex *informing environments* that involve sub-systems that may, themselves, be informing systems. The same can be said of clients, described by Cohen (1999) as participants in *task completion systems*.

2. Senders may be members of multiple informing systems that inform different clients. Drucker (1989), for example, refers to the inherent tension that knowledge workers experience as they divide their loyalties between profession (e.g., accounting, law, medicine) and the organization that employs them.

3. Multiple senders may compete to inform the same client. For example different departments (disciplines) may compete for the same set of students; doctors from different specialties may compete to diagnose the same patients, etc.

4. Multiple communications pathways may be utilized within the same informing system. For example, an advertising campaign may involve the use of print, broadcast, and web-based media in order to reach its entire client base.

5. Multiple clients may be informed by the same sender and may have to compete for that sender's attention. For example, a patient may find his or her case is neglected as a consequence of the attention a doctor pays to the needs of other patients.

6. Clients may, themselves, serve as part of an extended informing system. For example, a company may depend heavily on "word of mouth" advertising to gain new clients.

The types of complexities these factors can add to a system are illustrated in Figure 2.2.

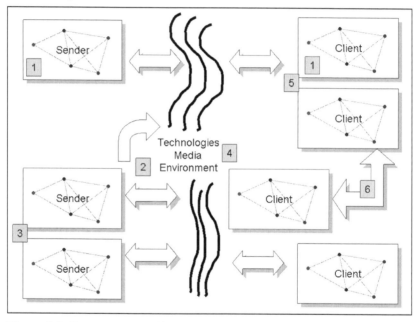

Figure 2.2: Complexities in "real world" informing systems

Levels of Abstraction

A second precept of informing science is that systems can be examined at multiple levels of abstraction. Cohen (1999) lists three specifically: the informing instance itself, the system responsible for constructing new informing system instances, and, finally, the system that designs new types of informing systems. He presents two examples. The academic example: teaching a course designed by others (instance), creating a new course (constructing), and formulating a new curriculum (design). The business example: using an existing transaction processing system (TPS; instance), building a new TPS from existing rules (constructing), and creating a new type of TPS (design). From these examples, we see that different levels of abstraction may also correspond to different levels or areas of the organization where the informing system is housed. We may also conclude that the boundaries of informing system levels are somewhat permeable. For example, redesigning an existing course and designing a new course obviously represent part of a continuum between instance construction and design.

Interrelatedness

A final precept of informing science is that the elements of an informing system (e.g., task, technology, structure, and people) interact in a manner that is so strongly interrelated that changing the characteristics of one component (e.g., technology) can have a significant impact on the behavior of other components (Cohen, 1999). Systems with such characteristics tend to resist decomposition (Simon, 1981), meaning that behavior is best examined at the system level, since understanding individual component behaviors does not necessarily lead to a valid picture of how the system as a whole will behave—indeed, such is essentially how Herbert Simon (1981) defines system complexity and is central to the concept of complexity used throughout this book.

An important implication of this interrelatedness is that technology must play a particularly crucial role in informing science research, since it tends to be the element within such systems that is changing most rapidly and is, therefore, the engine that drives much of the change in system behavior. A further implication of interrelatedness and technology's role is that informing science research must, of necessity, proceed at a rapid pace, since technology-induced changes to system behavior will tend to occur continuously. Should the time between observation and dissemination of such research be too great, the behaviors being observed will likely cease to be relevant.

Academic Informing Systems

Academic informing systems, such as business schools, are best viewed as a pair of interdependent systems. On the one hand, we have the *disciplinary informing system*. This is the principal system through which research and advanced instruction is conducted. Conceptually, these systems span across many institutions; through conferences, publications, collaborations, and service activities, researchers in many locations all contribute to disciplinary informing activities.

The other key component of the academic informing system is the *institutional informing system*. Its principal functions are to supply resources to the disciplinary informing systems, coordinate the activities of the many disciplinary systems within the university, and to engage in those informing activities that acquire the resources necessary for institutional survival.

Multiple clients exist for both disciplinary and institutional systems, and these clients overlap to some degree. For example, both systems have student clients. In the case of the disciplinary system, these students are the ultimate source of the next generation of disciplinary participants. Thus, advanced graduate students and, particularly, doctoral students tend to be especially high-priority clients. On the institutional side, students are a source of resources, both while they are enrolled—through tuition and through government subsidies—and subsequently, through giving when they become alumni.

For disciplinary systems, the content of informing tends to be built on research. Clients may be *internal clients*, which is to say other researchers within the discipline, or *external clients*—such as students, practitioners, and researchers in other disciplines. These clients are served by four types of research, illustrated in Figure 2.3:

- *Pure research:* Research that is principally aimed at *internal clients*. Such research is an essential part of a discipline's ability to advance.

- *Applied research:* Research that is directed towards other clients. Among these are included practitioners, interested members of the public, or other disciplines (e.g., applied mathematics describes the use of mathematical techniques in physics, chemistry, economics, etc.)

- *Scholarship of teaching (SOT) and ancillary research:* Research that is specifically directed towards improving the effectiveness of teaching (i.e., informing student clients) or other aspects of the discipline outside of its traditional research focus. It makes sense to distinguish SOT/ancillary research from other forms of applied research because it can easily draw upon an entirely different set of reference disciplines (e.g., psychology, education) than those of the discipline itself (e.g., engineering, science, fine arts).

- *Unrelated research:* Research that is outside of disciplinary paradigms and is not necessarily directed towards disciplinary clients. Interdisciplinary collaborations frequently fall into this category.

	Discipline Paradigms	Other Paradigms
Internal Client	Pure Research	Scholarship of Teaching and Ancillary Research
External Client	Applied Research	Unrelated Research

Figure 2.3: Categories of research

Institutional systems, on the other hand, are much more varied in their informing activities and tend to involve a broad range of client constituencies (Trieschmann, Dennis, Northcraft & Niemi, 2000). These could include students, regulators, employers, benefactors, community leaders, accreditation organizations, ranking organizations, and others. These relationships for the two systems are illustrated in Figure 2.4. As suggested by the dotted line down the middle of the diagram, many participants are shared between the disciplinary and institutional systems (e.g., colleges, departments, faculty members). These participants necessarily face choices regarding how to allocate their activities between systems. All other things being equal, it is reasonable to suppose that priorities will, to a great extent, be shaped according to how the activities impact each participant's access to resources. For the individual faculty member with an active research program, this pull is likely to be in the direction of maximizing disciplinary participation—since research productivity translates directly to compensation (Gill, 2001). For department/college organizational units, on the other hand, the greatest return is likely to come from activities that impact position in the institution's resource queue. These units are therefore likely to gravitate towards increased institutional participation.

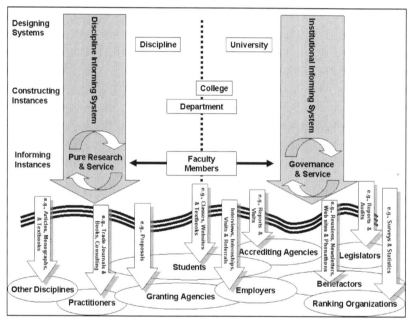

Figure 2.4: Disciplinary and Institutional Informing Systems

As part of its role of coordinating the disciplinary activities, the institutional system must necessarily decide on how resources are allocated between disciplines. The degree of overlap between a discipline's clients and the clients of a specific institution is likely to have a profound impact on its share. Disciplines that attract a large number of students will be given high priority. Similarly, institutions may be willing to invest heavily in building up disciplines that can attract their own resources through grants, such as medicine and engineering. Some resources will also be available for activities with enviable intra-disciplinary informing track records. For example, a strong research reputation in a particular department might lead to a higher overall ranking of the university in *U.S. News & World Report*; reducing funding to a particular department below a certain threshold might impact an institution's accreditation status. Nonetheless, a discipline that focuses exclusively on internal clients, thereby ignoring the informing needs of its potential external clients, runs a high risk. Just how serious this risk can be is illustrated by the case study of the MIS discipline that follows.

MIS Disciplinary Informing System

An interesting case study of the interaction between disciplinary and institutional informing systems can be found in the case of the management information systems (MIS) discipline. This discipline emerged in the 1970s, as it became clear that the challenges presented by rapidly changing information technologies had important managerial consequences. By the early 1980s, the discipline had established significant outlets for published research, such as the journal *MIS Quarterly* (MISQ). Moreover, there is some evidence that the discipline was actively engaged with its practitioner clients. For example:

1. The field's leading journal, MISQ, was established as a joint publication of academia and the *Society for Information Management* (SIM), a practitioner organization.

2. In 1980, over 40% of the articles in MISQ had at least one practitioner co-author.

3. When a symposium on the MIS research challenge was convened at Harvard in 1985, practitioners were invited and actively participated (McFarlan, 1985).

In the decades that followed, the MIS research discipline changed dramatically. Part of this change can be attributed to wildly fluctuating enrollment patterns. For example, in the mid-1990s, student interest in MIS began to skyrocket. Undergraduate MIS major enrollment increasing by a factor of three between 1994 and 2001—as happened at my university—was the rule rather than the exception. For example, when I joined the University of South Florida in 2001, MIS had just become the largest business department, with around 1100 majors. By acting as a magnet for students, MIS was serving the informing needs of the institution's single most important client. As a consequence, resources—in the form of new faculty lines, salary increases, and reduced teaching loads—were lavished upon MIS departments around the world.

Shortly after the Internet bubble burst in the 2000-2001 time period, the enrollment situation reversed itself. Students left the MIS major in droves. At USF, for example, we saw an 80% decline in major enrollments during the period from 2001 to 2007. We went from being the largest department in our college, based upon the number of majors, to the smallest. MIS faculty salaries lagged behind those of almost every other area and hiring dried up.

Table 2.1: Rankings by business discipline from Dennis, et al (2002)

Rank 1997-2001	Rank 1986-1998	University	Accounting	Finance	Ins, IB	Management	MIS	Mgt. Science	Marketing	POM
1	1	Pennsylvania	1	2	1	4	37	2	1	63
2	2	Michigan	7	14	10	1	14	7	13	8
3	9	Harvard	9	3	12	11	18	11	8	49
4	3	Stanford	4	9	69	7	45	5	15	7
5	5	Chicago	3	1	35	37		24	14	7

There are other pieces of evidence that show how far the MIS discipline has plummeted. For example, of the top 5 business schools in the U.S. (ranked by research output), not one has an MIS department ranked in the top 10, as shown in Table 2.1. This is highly significant since four of the five are private institutions which boast both the resources and the reputation to achieve excellence in whatever research areas they choose to pursue aggressively. No other discipline fares as badly. Evidence from the education side is equally telling. Among *Business Week's* top 20 schools, not a single school now requires an MIS course as part of its MBA program (Gill & Bhattacherjee, 2009).

It would be easy to claim that the rise and fall of MIS as being purely a matter of the fickleness of student tastes. This explanation does not seem sufficient, however. Why did student preferences change so quickly—and why haven't enrollments bounced back more, now that MIS employment has returned to and exceeded its 2000-2001 peaks?

What I propose is that the low priority placed upon informing external clients by the MIS discipline is an important part of the explanation for its demise. We now consider how MIS research has served three of these clients: MIS practitioners, its students, and researchers in other disciplines.

Practitioner Clients

The MIS discipline's failure to inform its practitioner clients is highlighted in the AACSB's (2008) attempt to list areas where MIS has exerted an impact on practice (see Table 1.1 in Chapter 1). The report's authors, a group of business school deans, were able to identify only two areas. The first involved applying a model actually developed by a marketing professor and the second involved a researcher whose principal impact has been through consulting, rather than published research. Talk about being damned with faint praise![2]

Table 2.2: Industry and academic author contributions to MISQ at 5 year intervals

Year	Count of Articles	Academic Authors	Industry Authors	Total Authors	Percent of Authors from Industry
1980	18	16	11	27	41%
1985	23	32	8	40	20%
1990	23	45	11	56	20%
1995	24	60	3	63	5%
2000	23	55	3	58	5%
2005	28	66	0	66	0%

Even within the MIS research discipline, there is recognition that our informing of practitioner clients leaves much to be desired. Opinions range from "the business community would question the relevance of IS research as published in the leading journals of our field" (Benbasat & Zmud, 1999) to "the extent to which IS research is relevant to IS practice is, objectively speaking, unknown" (Lee, 1999). Some have also proposed that we are informing practice through our students (Davenport & Markus, 1999), with textbooks playing an important role (Lyytinen, 1999). If so, then the amount of informing we are doing has declined significantly as a result of our plummeting enrollments.

What we can say objectively on the subject is that the evidence of academic-practitioner collaboration that was so striking in the early 1980s has largely reversed itself. In the 1990s, the *Society for Information Management* essentially divorced itself from MISQ by eliminating the free subscription that had previously come with membership—at which point most members dropped their subscription (Benbasat & Zmud, 1999). Practitioners are almost entirely absent from the discipline's most prestigious conferences. Perhaps most striking is the pattern of academic-practitioner contributions to MISQ. Over the past quarter century, it has fallen from 41% (in 1980) to 0% (in 2005), as shown in Table 2.2.

Student Clients

The second natural client for the MIS discipline is its students. It turns out to be very difficult to make a rigorous assessment of the degree to which student clients are being served, since both faculty and students are, potentially, participants in both the disciplinary and institutional informing systems presented earlier in Figure 2.4.

One indicator of how we prioritize our student clients involves examining the overlap between what we research and what we teach. Where the overlap is high, it is reasonable to conclude that our research activities make a strong contribution to informing our students. Where the overlap is low, disciplinary informing activities would seem to be peripheral to informing student clients. Some care needs to be taken in applying this measure, however. Since research doctoral students have demonstrated their intent to join the disciplinary system, doctoral courses and research seminars would fall under the heading of internal informing[3]. Similarly, it would be unreasonable to expect ongoing faculty research activities to make a major contribution to introductory survey courses. Such courses are frequently referred to as "service courses" precisely because they serve institutional needs, rather than those of the discipline.

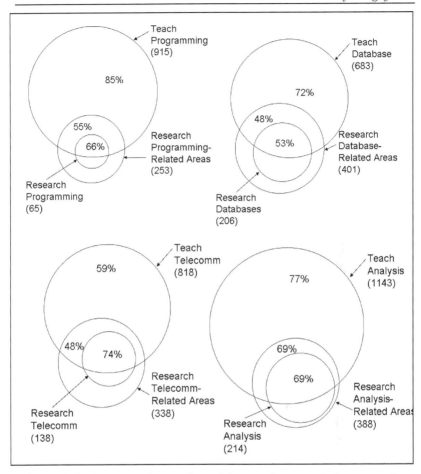

Figure 2.5: A comparison of teaching and research interests for AIS members. Numbers in the non-overlapping portion of the large circle represent percentage of faculty members who teach in a particular area but do not research in that area. Numbers in the smaller overlapping circles represent the percentage of faculty who perform research in the specified area (or related area) and also teach in it. (Adapted from Gill and Bhattacherjee, 2009)

An assessment of overlap between teaching and research interests, compiled from the AIS database, is presented in Figure 2.5[4]. It takes four core course topics that are widely taught at both the undergraduate and graduate levels and compares them with faculty research interests. The figure presents a paradoxical picture. On the one hand, those faculty members who research a given area are very likely to teach it. For example, 74% of AIS members who research telecommunications also teach that subject. On the other hand, most of the AIS members who teach a particular subject are not doing research in that subject. For example, 85% of the individuals teaching programming are not doing research directly or indirectly related to programming.

The explanation for this situation derives from the nature of the research conducted within the disciplinary informing system. Specifically, MIS has always engaged in research in two areas: the behavioral and the technical. Over time, however, that research has increasingly favored the behavioral. MIS educational programs, however, have retained a large technical component. Thus, a mismatch has developed between what MIS teaches and what it researches. If a researcher happens to engage in technically-focused research, opportunities to teach the same content are readily available. On the hand, if the researcher studies behavioral topics, he or she is likely to have to teach some technical courses since there just are not sufficient technical researchers available to support the teaching demand.

Another issue relating to informing student clients is the low level of status accorded to scholarship of teaching research (SOT) within the MIS discipline. For example, the top ranked MIS journal focused on teaching, the *Journal of IS Education*, ranks 80th on the AIS composite list. While education-related research is denigrated in many fields (outside of education), a healthy respect for SOT within a discipline suggests a high priority being placed on informing student clients. Not surprisingly, education-oriented research has much higher status in computer science—where education-related conferences are highly competitive *and*, more importantly from the resource acquisition perspective, substantial funding is available for teaching-related research from agencies such as the National Science Foundation (NSF).

Researcher Clients from Other Disciplines

One remaining set of possible external clients that warrants consideration is researchers in other disciplines outside of MIS. Given the increasingly universal impact of IT on all business functions, a reasonable case can be made that MIS *should* serve as a reference discipline for other fields (Baskerville & Meyers, 2002). Unfortunately, citation analysis fails to support the view that MIS research is actively informing other business disciplines. In a study of out-of-field citations among top journals (Wade, Biehl & Kim 2006), MIS scored near the bottom (just ahead of ethics) with 0.19 out-of-field citations per article (for comparison purposes, General Management averaged 5.03, Organizational Behavior scored 1.96 and Finance scored 1.30; p. 254). Furthermore, the same research found that non-MIS citations to MIS articles have been dropping over time (since their peak in 1997), with external citations as a percentage of citable articles dropping even faster, since 1992 (p. 259). The situation appears even worse when MIS is contrasted with International Business—another relatively young discipline—where outside citations have risen materially during the same period (p. 260).

Question: Is Pure Research Enough?

To summarize: MIS appears to be doing very little to inform its practitioner clients, has a research agenda that is misaligned with the bulk of its teaching activities, and does not appear to be producing much research that is of interest to other fields. The question then becomes, is doing research for your own consumption enough to sustain a discipline?

Based upon the evidence of the past few years, the answer would seem to be no. For example, two of the top ten performing MIS research departments (according to the same publication metrics used in Table 2.1) have been disbanded and merged into other departments.

Even more disheartening for the field is the case of the MIS department of the University of Central Florida[5] (UCF), a large state university located in Orlando. During the late 1990s, that university decided to make its MIS department a high priority. Towards that end, it hired some of the most respected and productive researchers in the field—including the soon-to-be Editor-in-Chief of *MISQ*—raised its promotion and tenure standards and expanded its doctoral program. Doing so required substantial institutional resources but resulted in a department whose research faculty's reputation was international in scope and far beyond what was typical for that particular institution.

Not long after the new departmental focus was established, the rapid drop in MIS enrollments experienced by virtually all business schools began. Despite the department's stellar research reputation, administrative concerns regarding the high cost per student were expressed. Even relatively strong assistant professors were denied tenure. By 2008, the department's doctoral program was discontinued. In the summer of 2009, the university announced that it was disbanding the department as of spring 2010 and terminating the employment of departmental faculty, irrespective of their tenure status.

The conclusion we can draw from this example is that while research that seeks mainly to inform our disciplinary colleagues may be a necessary condition for disciplinary success, it is not sufficient. Disciplines that do not identify and inform institutional clients are at risk in the long term.

Implications for Business Schools

The disciplinary model and MIS example I have just presented can be generalized to business schools as a whole. In terms of resources, the collective profile of business at most institutions is one of high enrollment combined with a high reliance on the institution for resources. This profile can be contrasted with that of other disciplines, as illustrated in Figure 2.6. It is, for example, the opposite of computer science, which suffers from enrollment problems, particularly among women[6], but remains very good at attracting grant funding. It is similar to medicine in terms of popularity with students (e.g., pre-med programs) but differs greatly in its ability to attract external funding; on that score, business is more similar to classic language programs[7].

A number of disturbing parallels can be drawn between business in general and the recent experiences of MIS. To begin, the cost of business faculty is among the highest at a university[8]. As business faculty, we justify this disparity by pointing out that we are paid far less than our practitioner colleagues. That argument is likely to hold water only as long as student demand for business courses is high. Should business become less of a student draw, the opposing argument—why should we be paid twice as much as an education professor when our work activities are nearly identical?—will gain credence. Moreover, participants in other more highly paid disciplines are frequently required to pay part of their own way. My colleagues in medicine and engineering, for example, are shocked when I tell them that grants play a relatively unimportant role in most business schools. Acquiring such grants is absolutely central to the career prospects of faculty in most other highly paid fields.

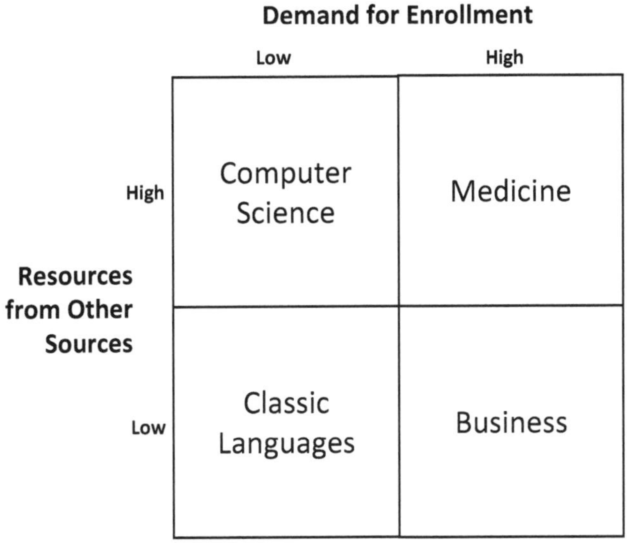

Demand for Enrollment

	Low	High
High	Computer Science	Medicine
Low	Classic Languages	Business

Resources from Other Sources

Figure 2.6: Comparison of business and other selected disciplines

In Chapter 1, I pointed out that business research in general—not just MIS research—has exerted relatively modest impact on practice. Concerns on this score led the AACSB to write an entire report on the impact of research, concluding that it needed to be improved. Unfortunately, the events of the past year have suggested they may have been too charitable in their assessment. In terms of research impact, the bright spot has always been the economics and finance disciplines. As we saw in Chapter 1, there is ample evidence of ideas (and people) moving from academia to practice in these areas. What has happened over the past year, however, has been that nearly all of the risk and economic models used to forecast outcomes and guide policy have produced results little better than random guessing and considerably worse than might have been achieved through the application of common sense. The fact that the research we generate offers guidance that doesn't work terribly well is not a great endorsement.

Our effectiveness at informing students was also called into question in Chapter 1. The theme of this argument is that many of our most prized theories, such as transaction cost economics and agency theory, tend to encourage a certain moral laxity on the part of our students. While I am not personally convinced by these arguments—I want proof whenever the assumption is made that our student's are actually impacted by what we teach—they certainly will resonate with those who are inclined to see corruption at all levels of business. Nor does it help when respected firms like McKinsey believe that a seven week boot camp for undergraduates is roughly equivalent to an MBA from a prestigious graduate business school.

What this all means is that the very existence of business schools is predicated on continuing high enrollments. Should we see a significant drop in enrollments, as happened to MIS, we are vulnerable to denial of institutional resources. On this subject I hasten to add that I have yet to meet a colleague outside of business who would shed a tear should our funding be cut back. Such vulnerability will remain for as long as our resource flow depends solely on our stream of student clients.

Conclusions

The purpose of this chapter has been to reframe the challenges faced by business schools in informing terms. Many of the concerns expressed in Chapter 1 can be characterized as a failure to inform our external clients: practitioners and students, in particular. What I have argued here is that failing to inform has practical long term consequences. If business schools are to thrive, a critical reassessment of our informing practices is needed.

What has not been explored in this chapter is the question of why we have so much trouble informing these clients. You would be hard pressed to find a business researcher who sees informing practice as undesirable or irrelevant. It would be even harder to find one who feels that way about informing students. Yet the problem persists, despite our desire to solve it.

The informing problem we face could arise from two sources. First, it could be a consequence of our research being invalid. Practice, in particular, would have little incentive to pay attention to *findings* that are inconsistent with their observed reality. Second, it could be a consequence of our failure to *communicate* what we know in an effective manner.

As we enter the analysis portion of the book, I take the position that both of these sources, findings *and* communications, contribute to our informing problem. I also argue that the problems experienced in both areas derive from a common source: the complexity of the underlying business environment. Because of this common source, it makes little sense to treat our research and education activities separately.

Over the next ten chapters, we consider the nature of complexity and the challenges presented by complex informing. What I will argue is that effective informing of our external clients will require fundamental changes on our part. These changes will involve both how we inform these clients and the methods we employ in conducting our research. Later in the book, in Chapters 13 through 15, examples of the types of changes we might consider are presented.

Chapter 2 Foundational References

Cohen, E. (1999). Reconceptualizing information systems as a field of the transdiscipline informing science: From ugly duckling to swan. *Journal of Computing and Information Technology, 7*(3), 213-219.

Gill, T. G., & Bhattacherjee, A. (2007). The informing sciences at a crossroads: The role of the client. *Informing Science: The International Journal of an Emerging Transdiscipline, 10,* 17-39. Retrieved from http://www.inform.nu/Articles/Vol10/ISJv10p017-039Gill317.pdf

Chapter 2 Notes

[1] The description of informing science, as well as all but the last section of the chapter, was adapted from Chapter 3 of Gill & Cohen, (2009) *Foundations of Informing Science.*

[2] I am unwilling to reject the possibility that alcohol was involved in AACSB's identification of areas of MIS research impact. The very fact that a bunch of deans had to stretch so far to come up with anything useful that MIS has done is, in itself, significant to my mind.

[3] Professional doctorates clearly represent a different case but, at the present time, do not play a major role in U.S. programs.

[4] After eliminating doctoral and service courses from the mix, what remains are MIS-specific courses that are taught at the undergraduate and graduate level to students whose principal goal is NOT to become MIS researchers. Because of the highly dynamic character of IT in gen-

eral, we would expect that cutting edge findings from MIS research should rapidly make their way into the classroom to the extent that what we research overlaps what we teach.

5 The mini-case describing the elimination of the MIS department at the University of Central Florida was developed through personal sources. I first became aware of their newly developed research focus when I considered applying for a faculty position there in late 2000. The subsequent elimination of their doctoral program followed by the laying off of their tenured faculty was widely reported in the media throughout Florida. This was confirmed by one of their faculty members, a personal friend, who learned of her termination, effective 2010, in a brief email from the university.

6 The decline in women enrolled in computer science programs has been extraordinary over the past decade. To quote an article on computer science from the Boston Globe, "In the early 1980s, it had one of the highest proportions of female undergraduates in science and engineering. And yet with remarkable speed, it has become one of the least gender-balanced fields in American society." (Bombardieri, 2005). The process appears to be continuing. According to NSF statistics, U.S. undergraduate degrees granted to women in computer science dropped from 27% of the all degrees to 20% between 1997 and 2006.

7 Carol Saunders, at the University of Central Florida, suggested this particular presentation of positioning to me.

8 In a recent presentation to the business faculty, for example, our provost remarked that he could acquire two or three physics faculty members for the price of every new business faculty member. From the context of the comment, we gathered that his preference was for the former.

T. Grandon Gill
Informing Business
Santa Rosa, California: Informing Science Press.

Chapter 3

Complexity, Fitness, and Theory

Roadmap & Objectives: There would seem to be two possible explanations as to why we have an informing problem: 1) Our findings are not valid, or 2) We are not communicating them properly. In fact, this book takes the position that we are failing in both areas and that both failures stem from a common source: complexity. This chapter explores the general nature of the complexity that arises when many elements interact in the presence of dynamic goals and identifies the behaviors we can expect when such complexity is present.

A business school exists at the intersection of the business and education domains. The unifying theme of this book is that both of these domains are *complex;* understanding the implications of this assertion is central to addressing the informing challenge.

In this chapter, we consider precisely what is meant by complexity. In doing so, we need to disambiguate the many related and not so related meanings that have been assigned to the term. I will also introduce the concept of a *fitness landscape*, a conceptual tool most widely used in evolutionary biology, as a means of exploring decision-making under conditions of complexity. We shall see, for example, that assessment schemes—such as college ranking systems—behave very differently in the presence or absence of complexity. We conclude by considering how the nature of informing changes as what we need to communicate becomes more complex.

This chapter is the first of several (e.g., Chapters 5, 6, 7, & 8) that serve to define problem solving and informing processes in terms that are general as opposed to being business-specific. In fact, one of the principal conceptual schemes developed in the chapter is that of a complexity-based continuum of science to art that could be used to characterize many different disciplines. In Chapter 4, we return to a discussion that specifically addresses the complexity of business.

What is Complexity?

If I were to make the casual statement that "business and education are complex," I doubt the typical listener would raise any serious objection. Nonetheless, a great deal of this book is devoted to exploring that statement and understanding its implications.

The main problem with using the term complexity[1] stems from its ambiguity. When Richard Hicks and I analyzed several hundred articles that either defined or applied the term "task complexity", we found thirteen distinct definitions (Gill & Hicks, 2006). These definitions, in turn, fell into five different classes, summarized in Table 3.1.

Table 3.1: Task Complexity Classes

Name	Form of Definition	Example
Experienced	Task Complexity → Psychological state	*Example*: If an individual perceives a task to be difficult, then the task is complex
Information Processing	Task Complexity → IP Activity	*Example:* If a task a task produces high information processing (IP) levels, then the task is complex
Problem Space	Problem Space Attributes → Task Complexity	*Example*: A task's complexity is defined by the minimum size of the computer program required to perform the task.
Structure	Lack of Structure → Task Complexity	*Example:* The more routine a task, the less complex it is
Objective	Task Characteristics → Task Complexity	*Example:* A task's complexity is determined by the number of task elements, the degree of interrelationship between the elements and the degree to which task objectives are changing (Wood, 1986).

Of the five classes, the first two define task complexity in terms of its consequences. They differ most notably in how these consequences change with repetitive practice. Specifically, *experienced complexity* tends to decline with practice while our *information processing* rate and capacity tends to grow.

The next pair of definitions deal with how we represent the knowledge associated with a task. A problem space is analogous to a computer program; it is the collection of factual knowledge, procedures, and goals that we employ to perform a task. *Problem space complexity* measures characteristics of our internal "program". As a consequence, these measures tend to *grow* as we become more expert. *Lack of structure complexity*, on the other hand, describes the degree to which we are lacking in the task-specific knowledge that would allow us to perform a task efficiently. Absent such knowledge, we are forced to rely on inefficient general reasoning techniques, such as logic and analogy. Thus, lack of structure complexity tends to *decline* with expertise. We return to these concepts in Chapter 5.

It is possible to draw some linkages between the first four of these task complexity definitions. While lacking the force of a theory, the following relationships tend to hold more often than not:

Lack of structure	→	Task complexity I	→	Perceived difficulty
Problem space attributes	→	Task Complexity II	→	Amount of information processed

What these relationships state, in essence, is as follows: *the less we know about a task, the more difficult we perceive it to be.* This can be characterized as complexity arising from uncertainty. Similarly, *the greater our store of task knowledge, the more efficiently we can process task-related information.* This may be characterized as the complexity associated with expertise; in the broadest terms, it provides insights into how much we need to learn in order to perform a task effectively. Understanding the distinction between the two general patterns of complexity becomes useful in the coming chapters; they tend to be accompanied by different obstacles to informing.

The remaining definition, *objective complexity*, asserts task complexity to be a strict function of task characteristics. The most widely used version of objective complexity was proposed by Wood (1986), who described it as a function of three attributes:

1. The number of elements in the task (*component complexity*)

2. The level of interrelationship between these elements (*coordinative complexity*)

3. The degree to which the goals and relationships associated with the task change as the task is being performed (*dynamic complexity*)

Because the construct is independent of task performer knowledge, it offers few insights into either perceived difficulty or amount of information processed. This statement is particularly true where the task performer has discretion regarding how to perform a task. A business owner facing an "objectively complex" decision task may choose to spend hours deliberating on it (high IP, high difficulty) or may decide to make the selection by flipping a coin (low IP, low difficulty). In either case, the job gets done. In fact:

> *The more objectively complex the task to be performed, the greater the incentive to employ a simplifying strategy.*

There is ample experimental evidence to support this proposition[2]. Because many simplifying strategies are accompanied by undesirable side-effects, dealing with the consequences of this proposition is fundamental to the informing recommendations presented later in this book.

Compared with other task-related management constructs, such as goal setting and intrinsic motivation, objective complexity has exerted a relatively minor impact on research. I attribute this lack of use to two factors: 1) it is hard to measure, and 2) it is not immediately clear what the construct is good for. Interestingly, the same cannot be said of other disciplines. In fact, in the study of evolutionary biology, a nearly identical construct has become central to a particular school of thought. We now turn to examining how the objective complexity construct can be applied to the study of *fitness*.

Fitness Functions and Landscapes

A fitness function[3] serves to map a set of attributes into a single value that is indicative of the desirability of the particular combination. Conceptually, this function can be represented as:

$$F = f(x_1, x_2, \ldots, x_N)$$

In this notation, F is the fitness associated with a particular combination of specific values for the attributes x_1 through x_N. The term fitness landscape is used to refer to the behavior of the fitness function across the set of all possible values of its attributes. Conceptually, this corresponds to the "shape" of the function.

The desirability aspect of a fitness function typically manifests itself in one or both of two ways:

1. *It may signify the survivability of a particular attribute combination.* In biology and in genetic algorithms, for example, entities with higher fitness values are more likely to survive from one generation to the next than those with much lower values.

2. *It may serve to guide choice.* In economics, for example, an underlying axiom of individual behavior involves choosing that basket of goods and services that maximizes utility, which is to say the perceived fitness of the combination.

The differences between the two forms of fitness may be less significant than might first appear. Evolutionary economists, for example, argue that our utility preferences are, in fact, simply the evolved manifestation of characteristics that have—at least in the past—contributed to individual survival (Gandolfi, Gandolfi, & Barash, 2002). Similarly, the survivability of a particular product is likely to depend heavily on the utility it inspires in its prospective customers.

The simplicity of our conceptual representation of a fitness function should not be taken as suggesting that such functions are simple. On the contrary, beyond the question of how the function behaves—which, as we shall find, can be quite complex—just finding a suitable representation for the attributes being considered is far from a trivial matter. Suppose, for example, we wanted to construct the fitness function for a particular recipe that predicts—based upon the arguments supplied—how tasty the resulting dish would be. Among the elements we would need to represent are included:

- The nature and quantity of the ingredients

- The timing of insertion of the ingredients

- The specific actions that we would need to perform upon those ingredients

- The timing of those actions, and

- The tools and equipment required.

Furthermore, among those attributes that are quantitative in character, such as ingredient amounts in our example, the relationship between fitness (taste) and quantity is unlikely to be linear. For example, as shown in Figure 3.1, it is likely that some optimal amount of each ingredient, such as a sugar, will be present. Either more or less than that amount will lead to lower fitness—meaning the resulting dish will be less tasty.

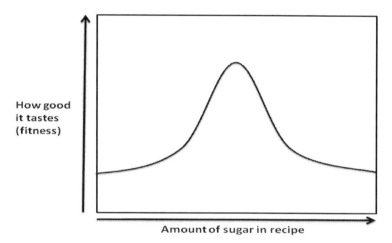

Figure 3.1: Mapping between taste and amount of sugar in a hypothetical recipe

The shape of the curve presented in Figure 3.1 is an example of a fitness peak. In our cooking example, we might anticipate that every ingredient (i.e., argument to the fitness function) would exert a qualitatively similar influence on fitness, as would other continuous measures such as oven temperature. If we had only two ingredients, the resulting fitness space would look like a mountain with the peak representing the optimal combination of the two ingredients. With more ingredients, the precise shape of the function is harder to visualize but, conceptually, can still be thought of as a peak.

Rugged Fitness Landscapes

The *decomposability* of a fitness function defines the degree to which the impact of each individual attribute upon fitness is independent of the values of the other attributes. For example, suppose a particular fitness function can be represented as:

$$F = f(x_1, x_2, \ldots, x_N)$$

That function is fully decomposable if we can also represent it as:

$$F = y_1(x_1) + y_2(x_2) + \ldots + y_N(x_N)$$

where y_1 through y_N are functions that transform the raw x values into their marginal contribution to fitness. For example, the y_{SUGAR} in the recipe example would take into account the peaked shape of sugar's impact on taste. At the other extreme, a fitness function may be completely non-decomposable—leading to a *maximally rugged fitness landscape,* later referred to as a *chaotic landscape.* What this means is that the contribution of a particular attribute to fitness cannot be determined without knowing the value of the other attributes.

The distinction between decomposable and interacting variables is illustrated in Figure 3.2. In the decomposable version, on the left, fitness can be represented as a stacked bar, with each value of X_i contributing a specific amount to fitness. In the interacting case, on the other hand, the influence of individual variables cannot be separated out. Thus, for one set of values $X_1 \ldots X_N$, a change of X_i to X_i^* could exert a large impact on fitness (as shown on the right). For another set of values, X_1' to X_N', the same change might have no impact on fitness at all, or might even change fitness in the opposite direction.

To return to our cooking example, suppose you were attempting to create a function that predicted the "fitness" of a recipe based upon its list of ingredients. If cooking could be described by a decomposable fitness function, then each ingredient would make the same predictable contribution to every recipe. If, for example, adding garlic improves the taste of one recipe, then it would have the same positive impact on taste for every recipe. The same would be true of ingredients that had no impact. If adding some baking powder had an undetectable influence on the taste of a chicken curry recipe, then we would anticipate that omitting it from a cake recipe would have no particular impact. Another consequence of decomposability would be the existence of a single "optimal" recipe in which each ingredient is either included or excluded depending upon whether or not it impacts fitness positively. Indeed, we would not expect cookbooks to exist for such a landscape. Why would any chef prepare anything but the recipe with the peak fitness value?

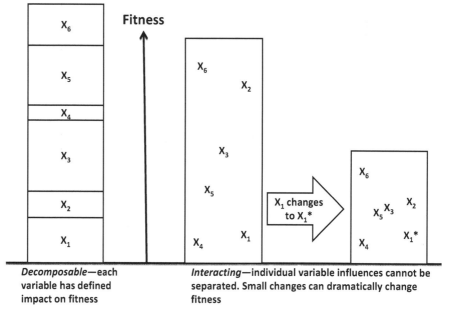

Decomposable—each variable has defined impact on fitness

Interacting—individual variable influences cannot be separated. Small changes can dramatically change fitness

Figure 3.2: Decomposable versus interacting contributions to fitness

Kauffman's NK Model

Kauffman's (1993) NK landscape model provides a tool for characterizing the decomposability of fitness functions. Originally developed to simulate the fitness of a chromosome, the N refers to the number of genes. The K, in turn, refers to the average number of other genes whose values must be ascertained before the contribution of a particular gene to fitness can be determined. It is, therefore, a measure of interdependence between arguments. The model has two extreme points:

- **N, 0**: At this point each gene contributes to fitness independently, leading to a *fully decomposable landscape*.

- **N, N-1**: At this point the impact of a given characteristic on fitness can only be determined by considering the value of every other characteristic. As a consequence of this complete interdependency, no meaningful estimate of fitness can be made without knowing the values of all N characteristics. We'll refer to this landscape as the *chaotic landscape*.

For a decomposable (N,0) fitness landscape, there will be a single fitness peak at which point the fitness values y_1 through y_N are individually maximized. Somewhat less immediately obvious, and at the other extreme, the chaotic (N, N-1) fitness landscape can, for all intents and purposes, be simulated using a set of 2^N random numbers (Kauffman, 1993), thereby ensuring that no fully separable relationships between a subset of elements and fitness are likely to occur.

A third aspect of the Kauffman model is the impact of co-evolution. A fundamental precept of the model is that the shape of the fitness function for a particular entity will, necessarily, depend upon the characteristics of its environment. For example, the ability to digest grass will contribute substantially to the fitness of a species that exists on a prairie while contributing much less to the fitness of a species living in the forest. The environment may, in turn, be impacted by the presence of other species. Continuing the previous example, if multiple species graze the same prairie, then other characteristics—such as the ability to shift food sources in the event of overgrazing—may contribute more strongly to fitness.

In addition to co-evolution, the positioning of entities within a landscape can also change its shape. Cooperative and competitive effects can dramatically alter the fitness of (or cost to attain) a particular state. On the competitive side, once a Walmart has established itself as a low cost competitor, it becomes much harder for another organization to succeed by employing the same strategy. At the other extreme, some landscapes may exhibit network effects that grow with adoption. An example from the 1980s that is commonly used involves VCR standards. Two competing types of cassettes—VHS and Betamax—

competed for dominance of the marketplace. As VHS sales began to pull ahead of Betamax, rental companies and retailers increasingly emphasized the former. Seeing this, consumers chose to purchase VHS equipment in preference to Betamax and the domination grew even greater. Eventually, what started as a slight edge became a cascade, as everyone recognized that Betamax was dying and moved to VHS. Ultimately, Sony abandoned Betamax. A similar phenomenon played out in the high definition DVD market. In this case, however, Sony's Blue Ray standard came to dominate its HD-DVD competition[4].

Another type of occupancy function involves tradeoff between cooperation and competition. In this situation, there are cooperative benefits of grouping together until the point where entities find themselves having to compete for resources. Herds of wild horses and flocks of birds fall into this category. In both cases, there are defensive benefits of travelling in groups that need to be weighed against the availability of food sources for high concentrations of entities. A similar set of conflicting considerations influences retail location decisions, where the presence of "foot traffic" depends upon having a concentration of retailers that is ultimately limited by the firm's willingness to be located in close proximity to competitors.

Listing the three components of the rugged fitness landscape model together—number of elements (N), degree of interrelationship between them (K) and dynamic changes to fitness—we find that we have returned to objective complexity. Because objective complexity is a task measure while NK complexity describes a landscape, how the two concepts relate may not be immediately obvious. Where the two become aligned is when the "task" at hand is research—the task of achieving better understanding or predicting the shape of the landscape or the behavior of entities on that landscape. As it turns out, many—and perhaps most—business research activities fall into that category. Any model intended to improve a company's profitability involves understanding a fitness landscape faced by organizations. Any model of motivation involves understanding how individuals perceive their fitness landscape. Decision-making models nearly all assume maximization of some fitness-related value, such as utility. Human resource models commonly attempt to explain employee performance. The study of competitive dynamics involves understanding how firms explore and interact with their environment. Leadership models examine how different styles impact individual success. What Kauffman's formulation provides is a tool for better understanding how the presence of objective complexity in any of these domains is likely to impact the findings of our research.

The most obvious way to assess the impact of objective complexity is to contrast the no-coordinative-complexity case (K=0) with the maximal coordinative complexity case (K=N-1). As we have already noted, the K=0 case leads to a single fitness peak, with all N attributes set to their highest fitness value. The maximally complex case, on the other hand, can be simulated by choosing a random number to each possible combination of attributes. Under this scenario, the estimated number of these peaks will be given by a formula (Kauffman, 1993, p. 47)[5]:

$$2^N / (N+1)$$

As Kauffman points out, as K approaches N, the height of the typical peak tends to get lower, as there will be a higher percentage of possible combinations that are peaks. This, he argues, would tend to make "chaotic" fitness functions relatively inefficient in terms of survival because an entity trying to maximize fitness is likely to get hung up on relatively low fitness local peaks. On the other hand, fully decomposable fitness functions will necessarily lead to entities highly tuned to a particular peak. Such tuning will tend to lead to brittleness; in the event of significant changes to the fitness function, survival will be low. For example, the koala's singular dependence on eucalyptus leaves as a food source has made it highly susceptible to habitat loss.

What Kauffman proposes, therefore, is that successful organisms tend to exist on fitness environments where some interdependence (K>0) exists—leading to entities existing on multiple peaks (reducing the threat produced by changing fitness relationships)—but that are also far from chaotic (meaning that for large N, K<<N), implying that local migration to high fitness is possible. We would also expect that higher K values (favoring diversity and adaptability) would be beneficial in environments that are heavily affected by co-evolution, whereas lower K values (favoring fewer, higher peaks) would be beneficial where landscapes are more static. It also turns out high interactivity tends to produce certain patterns of adaptive behavior that are almost universally observed across landscapes. We consider these patterns next.

Adaptive Behavior on Complex Landscapes

As we have seen in the Kauffman model, complex landscapes are normally presented as being part of a continuum or discrete range, existing between "ordered" and "chaotic". Entities on each of these landscapes constitute *systems*. Extensive study in the field of complex adaptive systems[6] has led to a wealth of findings that seem to hold across nearly all observed systems. The most relevant of these is that systems tend to exhibit characteristic patterns of behavior that vary according to the underlying landscape.

In an ordered system, there tends to be a single peak so individual entities tend to move towards a steady state. As a consequence, it is often possible to model the behavior of pieces of the system without needing to know the state of every component in the system. In a chaotic system, on the other hand, interdependency typically leads to an extreme sensitivity to initial conditions. While such systems may exhibit discernible patterns of behavior, these patterns are not typically very useful for long term prediction for two reasons. First, the state of every system component needs to be known in order to predict long term system behavior—a task that is essentially impossible for large systems (such as the weather). Second, the slightest error in assessing initial conditions totally confounds long term prediction, meaning that the only systems whose long-term behavior can be predicted with any accuracy are digital systems, such as cellular automata[7].

Complex systems are seen as existing on the boundary between order and chaos. Their most interesting characteristic behavior is that of punctuated equilibrium (Bak, 1996). As a matter of empirical observation, such systems routinely exhibit ordered behavior for sustained periods then suddenly, and without warning, experience sharp changes in behavior. After these sudden changes—such as the occasional avalanches that occur when grains of sand are dropped on a sand pile—the system may revert to its previous behavior or, particularly in adaptive systems, may enter into an entirely new pattern of behavior. What makes such punctuated equilibrium behavior particularly intriguing is that, although the sudden transitions often fall into predictable patterns of frequency and size (Bak, 1996), the actual timing of specific transitions invariably defies prediction by any means. In Chapter 9, we examine these behaviors in greater detail.

The observation that complex systems tend to exhibit discontinuous change is very consistent with the structure of the NK landscape model. As I have previously emphasized, complex landscapes provide many fitness peaks. As these landscapes are transformed by co-evolution or other forces, some peaks are likely to become more desirable and some will become less desirable. Once the desirability of a particular peak falls beneath a certain threshold, there will be a tendency for entities to migrate. The process of changing from one peak to another will necessarily be rapid, since the intervening states will be in lower fitness troughs (valleys). Migration will be further accelerated in cases where entities (e.g., organizations) are reasonably cognizant of the landscape and, therefore, can establish a clear destination for their migration and in cases where entities can observe the behavior of other entities. The latter sets the stage for an information cascade (Gill, 2008c), a process whereby individuals choose their state based upon their observations of what others are doing. Such cascades are frequently cited as the cause for rapid changes in taste, such as those observed in fashion.

The phenomenon of discontinuous vs. gradual shifts is not necessarily limited to multiple entity systems. If we look at other phenomena that are the result of complex interactions between system components—such as attention, which is a phenomenon that emerges from the complex connected architecture of the brain—we see similar patterns. When shifting our thoughts from one topic to another, we do not consciously experience a midpoint during which each topic is receiving equal partial attention.

Assessing Landscape Complexity

Unfortunately, fitness functions do not advertise their N-K values. As a consequence, assessing landscape complexity is by no means trivial. There are, however, some reasonable indicators that we can use. I will now propose both a "big picture" approach and a series of specific indicators.

Problems of Fit

It is probably no coincidence that the root of the word "fitness" is "fit". In every day usage, it is relatively unusual for our concept of fitness to be independent of context. Even physical fitness becomes specialized by sport—what constitutes good fitness for a gymnast would seem highly out of place in a U.S. football tackle or a sumo wrestler. Certainly there would be some common traits (e.g., strength, endurance) but even these would be weighted differently.

If we look at an activity and it seems likely that achieving fit will be important, it is very likely that the fitness landscape will be rugged. In decomposable landscapes, attributes tend to contribute to fitness like rectangular tiles or the building blocks of Figure 3.2. There are many ways they can be assembled to produce a desired effect. Complex landscapes are more like a collection of puzzle pieces. To get a coherent whole, you need to match the pieces up correctly.

A lot of times, the first concrete indicator that a landscape is likely to involve problems of fit comes when we discover that different participants have very different profiles. For example, in research that is familiar to anyone who has studied international business, Geert Hofstede (2001) proposed a series of cultural dimensions that vary widely across nations and regions. These include power distance, individualism vs. collectivism, masculinity vs. femininity, uncertainty avoidance, and time horizons. Many of these dimensions seem as if they could exert quite a significant impact on behavior. On the other hand, it is hard to assess whether a particular orientation is necessarily more fit than another.

The assessment of fitness becomes quite different when a specific task is performed, however. In *Outliers*, Malcolm Gladwell (2008) relates the story of commercial airliner crashes. By way of background, although flying under routine conditions is quite straightforward[8], when unusual events occur it becomes vital for the pilot and co-pilot to communicate. In some cases, the co-pilot even has the authority to take control away from the pilot in order to maintain the safety of the aircraft.

Because it was the birthplace of aviation, the task of flying commercial airliners was largely designed in the U.S. Mapped to Hofstede's dimensions, the U.S. is quite low with respect to power distance. In practical terms, what this means is that workers in the U.S. are much more willing to contradict or override a supervisor than they would be in high power distance countries. Thus, designing a task that included the possibility of a co-pilot correcting the pilot made perfect sense. The problem with the fitness of this arrangement arises in cultures with much higher power distances.

As it turns out, if you map power distance to airline crashes, you find that high power distance countries tend to have unusually high rates of crashes. The specific case Gladwell focuses on is Korean Air (South Korea second only to Brazil in terms of power distance) which had a crash rate 17 times higher than that of U.S. airlines. Not only was the statistical evidence of lack of fitness strong, it was confirmed by flight recorder transcripts that, in many cases, clearly showed co-pilots identifying problems to the pilot but refusing to be assertive about them. For example, the pilots of one airliner making an approach to Guam airport in poor visibility got confused with respect to its position. When the first officer realized the problem (shortly after radar indicated that the ground was much closer than it was supposed to be), he gently suggested:

"Let's make a missed approach." (Gladwell, 2008, p. 179)

This was about seven seconds prior to crashing into the side of a mountain three miles away from the airport. A comparable U.S. pilot would likely have reacted more along the lines of:

"Sh*t!!![9] Pull up! Pull up!"

At the same time, he (or she) would probably be pulling up on the controls, overriding whatever the pilot was doing. But doing so would have been a huge breach of protocol in the South Korean culture, with its tradition of deference to authority (i.e., high power distance).

Given the extraordinary economic growth of South Korea over the past decades, it is self-evident that high power distance is not necessarily detrimental to fitness across the entire range economic activities. It just happens to be *a poor fit* with a particular task specifically designed with low power distance participants in mind.

The existence of individuals or entities with different profiles will not necessarily lead to outcomes as spectacular as the Korean Air example. A good example of this is learning styles, a subject not directly relevant to business but certainly relevant to the overall theme of this book. A wide number of different dimensions have been profiled (Hawk & Shah, 2007), many of which—such as whether you prefer visual or auditory learning—seem to be self-evidently important. The problem is, when you attempt to test the statistical significance of their impact, results are inconsistent at best (Hawk & Shah, 2007; Willingham, 2009). This has led to two divergent conclusions: 1) they are not that important compared to other factors (Willingham, 2009), and 2) their importance is likely to become better understood through future research (Christensen, Horn, & Johnson, 2008; Hawk & Shah, 2007).

Having done a small (unpublished) study in which learning style appeared to have no discernable impact, I am acutely aware of the problem of working with classifications that seemed *obviously* relevant to me, yet fail to produce statistically significant results[10]. In later chapters of this book, however, I make the case that *the statistical tools we routinely employ in business research are spectacularly bad when employed to analyze observations sampled from a rugged landscape.* Not only do they fail to detect important interactions that are present, they are also prone to "detecting" high significances for effects that are not present. Thus, our inability to develop a clear understanding may be as much a consequence of flawed methodology as one of lack of underlying effect[11].

Specific Indicators of Ruggedness

If concluding that a landscape looks like a "fit problem" seems too subjective, evidence of ruggedness can also be found in the observed behaviors of entities on the landscape. In fact, we would expect to see very different patterns where a landscape is highly decomposable versus where it is not. The indicators of ruggedness include:

1. *Different approaches to fitness succeed.* Where highly dissimilar examples of high fitness can be identified, the presence of multiple local fitness peaks distributed throughout the landscape is suggested. Dissimilarity is particularly important in this context, since similar examples of high fitness could simply be entities close to the same peak.

2. *Inconsistent changes to fitness result when variables are changed in different contexts.* Incremental changes to fitness—resulting from manipulating the same variable in the same manner—mean that a variable's effect cannot be established independent of the values of other variables that determine fitness. Using a previous example, omitting the baking powder from a cake recipe may drastically reduce the fitness of the resulting cake, even though the quantity of the ingredient is small and its impact upon taste negligible. This differs from decomposable landscapes, where the impact of a particular variable is always the same, and if

many variables participate in determining fitness, the average incremental impact of each will be relatively small.

3. *Inconsistent research findings.* Fitness behavior in a particular setting that varies significantly from findings well supported by previous research; like the second, this suggests a situation-dependence that implies interactions between variables. It could also indicate the presence of a dynamic component to fitness. On theoretical grounds, entities existing on a dynamic landscape will be more likely to survive if a diverse set of high fitness peaks are always occupied. Obviously, replication research will not tend to be very supportive on such a landscape.

4. *Little changes sometimes make a big difference to fitness.* When a landscape is decomposable, changes in most variables exert a predictable (and usually small) impact on fitness. Where the underlying landscape is complex, variable changes can act through interaction and a small change can dramatically change fitness. For example, what would have happened to the fitness of the Mona Lisa if da Vinci had employed a few extra milligrams of paint to make the smile just a bit more obvious?

5. *Stickiness of entities.* Ruggedness implies local peaks and entities on established peaks naturally resist incremental change; when change does occur, it tends to be discontinuous in nature. When you are on a fitness peak, incremental change always leads to a decline in fitness; this assertion is purely a consequence of how we define "peak". When attempting to migrate to another peak, changing many attributes tends to entail either high risk or extended periods transitioning through valleys of low fitness. Thus, entities that have already reached fitness peaks are likely to try to remain on those peaks for as long as possible. Only entities who know that they are not on a peak (e.g., new entrants to an industry) or whose particular peak has been disrupted (e.g., manufacturers of photographic film in an age rapidly transitioning to digital photography) will tend to be motivated towards significant change. When such change does occur, it will be rapid.

6. *Turbulent dynamics.* Punctuated equilibrium behavior has previously been noted to be a characteristic of nearly all complex landscapes.

Even knowing these rules, our natural tendency to try to view the world as orderly can influence us towards taking decomposable fitness constructs too seriously. College rankings provide an interesting example.

College Rankings: An Example

College rankings have long been taken as a measure of institutional fitness. For this reason, it is not unusual for institutions to undertake changes specifically to increase ratings. For example, it was recently suggested that Clemson University had made a significant number of decisions—impacting tuition, class size, and faculty salaries—with the specific goal of improving its national ranking (Van Der Werf, 2009), as opposed to basing the decisions strictly on educational merit. There were also accusations that its administrators gave very low peer assessments to other schools (25% of the fitness estimate for some rating systems) while rating itself very highly so as to increase its relative position (McGurn, 2009). It is therefore interesting to consider the underlying behavior of this particular fitness function.

As it happens, back in the late 1980s, I spent 9 months developing a commercial program, the College Expert™, that could be used to generate undergraduate academic rankings. While doing so, I learned quite a bit about how such programs are constructed. Most typically, the rankings are constructed by taking a set of attributes (x_1 through x_N), each weighted by some undisclosed proprietary factor (a_i) and then summed, to compute a score (S) for every university, e.g.,

$$S = a_1x_1 + a_2x_2 + ... + a_Nx_N$$

This formula would obviously meet the criteria of a fully decomposable fitness function since the contribution of a particular attribute—e.g., whether or not the institution has a football team—would be the same no matter what other attributes the institution has or doesn't have.

For an institution seeking to maximize "fitness" according to such a formula, it would be relatively easy to come up with approximate estimates for the publication's proprietary coefficients (e.g., $a_1 ... a_N$). For example, to determine the impact of the football team attribute, an institution could add a football team and see what happened to its ranking. If fielding a team seemed too expensive for the sake of information gathering, the researcher might attempt to find two institutions whose characteristics differed mainly through the presence/absence of a football team and observe how their rankings differed on the list. If such a comparison were not available, the researcher might gather the characteristics of a sample of universities and then use a statistical tool—such as multiple regression analysis—to estimate the coefficient weights for each characteristic including the presence/absence of a football team. Any of these techniques would work because each attribute's impact is entirely independent of the impact of any other attribute.

Even where a fitness function is fully decomposable, the process of achieving optimal fitness may prove far from trivial. There may, for example, be constraints—such as the availability of budgetary resources—that prevent an entity from optimizing all attributes simultaneously. The fitness benefits of a football team may need to be weighed against the construction of a new science building, since sufficient funds are not available for both. Where decomposability is present, however, algorithmic approaches to optimizing fitness—such as linear or integer programming—are often available that dramatically reduce the amount of searching that must be done in order to achieve maximum fitness given a particular set of constraints.

Rankings Using the College Expert™

Analysis of the type just described makes sense only if college rankings actually are a reasonable measure of an institution's fitness. To address this question, it is useful to look at the *College Expert* in a bit more depth. The program had two different data sources. The first was a database of about 500 characteristics related to an individual U.S. college. These included location details, special characteristics, sports offered, majors offered, difficulty of admission, student body characteristics, extracurricular activities, and social opportunities. Data for this list was acquired from a commercial source, the same source supplying the *Arco College Guide* series. The second data source was entered by the user and included academic performance details (e.g., grades, test scores), athletic accomplishments, extracurricular activities, and a wide range of preferences and priorities. The program's output was an ordered list of schools—optionally filtered by admissions likelihood—based upon the student's preferences and the weights given these preferences.

Earlier I mentioned that the program could be used to generate ranking lists. To create a list comparable to those published in the media, all you would need to do is to enter a student with the following character-istics:

- SAT scores in the 99th percentile

- Straight A grades in both humanities and sciences

- At least one outstanding extracurricular activity

- No location preference—geographic region and campus set-ting don't matter

- No religious preference and no objections to any particular re-ligion

- Indifferent to public or private education

- Indifferent to post graduate requirements for military service

- No financial constraints, but interested in a school with good financial aid

- Of undetermined gender (since single sex schools still exist)

- Very interested in sports, but not in any particular sport

- Very interested in academics, but not in any particular field

- Interested in social activities and extracurricular activities, but none in particular

For such an individual, magazine rankings might well serve as an excel-lent basis for making a college choice. As a publisher, however, I'd probably be concerned about the size of my market if individuals with these characteristics were my only target audience.

A Rugged College Fitness Landscape

As the *College Expert* example suggests, the problem with magazine rankings is that they are attempting to characterize fitness without knowing at least half the equation that determines "fit": the nature of the specific student. Suppose, then, an institution were to define fitness in an entirely different manner? Inspired by a quote from Yash Gupta[12], suppose we assert the fitness of a school to be as follows:

Being the best choice of college for as many students as possible...

Immediately, we see that many attributes that would independently contribute to fitness in traditional ranking systems, such as scores on standardized college entry tests, would impact the "best choice" metric quite differently. For example, elite universities often boast S.A.T. scores in the top 1% of all students; under the "best choice" system such a criterion would eliminate 99% of the population of potential students from consideration, vastly reducing the applicable population. Similarly, some attributes that would not impact rankings under normal systems, such as whether an institution was liberal or conservative in its political leanings, might exert a great impact on determining whether or not it was a good fit for a particular student—for one group of students a left-wing outlook might increase fit, while for others it would reduce it. Another aspect of the best choice ranking system would be a strong motivation for institutions to migrate towards customized missions that target particular clusters of students. In the traditional ranking system, universities would tend to maximize fitness in the same way, since fitness for each is determined using the same set of attributes. Under best choice fitness, institutions would benefit from continuously searching for large subsets of the potential student universe whose needs were not being well met by other universities. Making incremental changes to attract these students would be an excellent way to increase fitness.

It should be evident that the principal challenge presented by best choice fitness stems from the lack of decomposability in the relationship between institutional attributes and student characteristics. For example, universities targeting students who want to leave home for college might do best by investing money in dormitories and emphasizing classes that meet during the day so as to match the desires of full-time students; universities targeting the local population, particularly the local working population, might emphasize night classes and part time programs. In regions serving the economically disadvantaged, low cost community colleges might exhibit far greater fitness than more traditional, higher-priced schools that focus on a national pool of affluent students by providing luxurious surroundings at a high price tag. On the other hand, because we assume the landscape is not chaotic, and that K is probably much closer to 0 than to N, we may also reasonably expect than some attributes may contribute to fitness relatively independently of other attributes. The ephemeral "quality of teaching" might be an example of such an attribute—although a counter-argument could also be made that teaching quality could have less of an impact on fitness in institutions whose target clientele is high achieving self-motivated students than for institutions targeting first-in-family college students.

Increasing fitness in a rugged landscape is vastly more difficult than it is for decomposable landscapes. This difficulty stems from two sources. First, it is much harder to assess if fitness changes that are observed in one entity are going to generalize to another. For example, the observed positive fitness impact of adding a football program to a small full time college may be quite different than it would be for a large urban university whose student base consists mainly of part time commuters. Second, although experimenting with individual characteristics one at a time can lead to incremental fitness increases, eventually the entity will reach a point at which every change leads to declines in fitness. Some missions, no matter how perfectly they are carried out, may never be the best fit for a significant number of students. Thus, if acceptable fitness levels are to be achieved, an entity may, from time to time, need to consciously jump from one place in the landscape to another in the quest for alternative (higher) fitness peaks.

If we look at the landscape of actual colleges in the U.S. and internationally, the pattern seems far more consistent with that of a rugged landscape than a decomposable landscape. The most obvious indicator is the diversity of missions, locations, sizes, and configurations of different colleges. In a decomposable landscape, all would be trying to achieve success according to the same criterion. We also can see evidence of activities producing—or being judged to produce—impacts on fitness in different directions. For example, just as Western Washington University was abandoning its football program owing to the deficit it produced, other colleges, such as Georgia State University, were launching football programs in the hope of building community.

Why are Rankings Popular?

Before leaving the subject of college rankings, we would do well to ask ourselves a question: If published rankings are such a poor indicator of fitness for the typical student, why do they have such demonstrated impact on college choice?

The answer, I believe, lies in one of the heuristic rules of informing that I have proposed in my past research (Gill, 2008d, p. 267): the *Law of Limited Visibility*. What this law basically states is that if our criteria for determining fitness are fuzzy or our knowledge of the fitness landscape is very limited, we will naturally seek out and place a heavy reliance on any clear indicators of fitness that are available. These indicators may consist of observed high fitness—if you see long lines waiting to buy coffee down the street, you wonder if you should be opening a coffee shop—or techniques for estimating fitness, such as college rankings.

The potential importance of the law of limited visibility cannot be overstated for two reasons. First, unlike the relationships between attributes and actual fitness—which can vary dramatically from region to region—any fitness estimator we accept must apply over a clearly defined region of the fitness space, otherwise it is unusable. For example, if we believe that stock price serves to estimate the underlying value of a public company, then we must believe it is applicable to all companies that trade in good faith[13]. If we do not believe this to be true, then we lose confidence in share price as an estimator. We are not necessarily required to believe our estimators perfectly reflect fitness; the efficient market hypothesis, for example, allows for the possibility that share price fails to reflect underlying fitness (Siegel, 2009). We only require that the domain over which our estimator is applicable be well defined and, preferably, as large as possible.

The second reason that limited visibility is important is that the validation of fitness estimators generally takes a long time. In biological settings, for example, a simple snapshot of an ecology is rarely enough to determine how successful the different participating organisms will be many generations later. To assess that type of fitness, you need a long term perspective as well as many observations over time. You also need to beware of projecting short term trends, since many biological populations exhibit natural cyclical fluctuations.

The development of a reliable estimate-of-fitness has important consequences because, as we saw in the college example, once a fitness estimator has been established in a limited visibility environment, entities in that environment are likely to start acting to impact the indicator, as a proxy for underlying fitness. If you tell companies that consistent and rising quarterly profits signify an organization's health, then they will naturally attempt to employ accounting techniques that produce the appearance of rising quarterly profits. Stated another way, an estimate-of-fitness easily becomes confused with actual fitness. We return to this topic frequently as the book progresses.

Complexity and Theory-of-Fitness

The creation and testing of theory has become a central objective of business research. In some business disciplines, particularly management, theory building and testing has become the discipline's paramount goal, as later discussed in Chapter 10. Understanding a landscape's complexity, however, can tell us a great deal about what types of theories we are most likely to produce. We now turn to that topic.

Attractive vs. Ugly Theory

Any theory must serve to explain or predict some phenomenon or set of phenomena. An *attractive theory*, however, possesses three additional characteristics: it is *compact*, it is *generalizable* and it is *stable*. Compactness has a number of virtues. First, it is easy to communicate. Second, it lacks the extraneous constructions that are so often exposed as being unnecessary once a proper theory has been established. For example, when Copernicus proposed the heliocentric solar system, the prediction of planetary positions—once requiring special charts or complex mechanisms such as an antikythera—became much less involved. The heuristic we use is that less is more when it comes to theory, also referred to as Occam's Razor or the law of parsimony[14].

Generalizability refers to the ability of our theory to be useful in circumstances to which it has not been applied before. A theory that is not generalizable offers value only for those situations where it has been extensively tested.

Stability refers to the degree to which the theory is stable over time. Theories that continuously change, such as those depending on very specific tastes or technologies, have a short shelf life. This can be particularly problematic from an academic perspective, since long publication cycles may exceed the useful life of the theory being proposed.

A particularly important subset of theory can be described as *theory-of-fitness*. Theory within this subset seeks to understand the relationship between a particular type of fitness and the factors that determine it. Stated another way, it is a theory that pertains to a fitness landscape. Naturally, not all theory meets these criteria. The theory of evolution, for example, does not attempt to predict the fitness of a particular landscape. Instead, it seeks to understand the process by which increases to biological fitness are achieved, later referred to as *theory-of-process*. On the other hand, a great many theories in business fall into the theory-of-fitness category. Shareholder wealth, employee performance, information systems success, and market share all are measures related to fitness. Any theory that attempts to map specific states or actions to these types of values, therefore, qualifies as being within the theory-of-fitness category.

Theory-of-fitness differs from our earlier estimate-of-fitness (e.g., college rankings) in a number of important ways. These differences become particularly apparent when the underlying fitness space is complex:

1. Theory-of-fitness is based on a model that involves causality. Estimates-of-fitness can be constructed purely based upon correlation. For example, one predictor of stock market behavior that gained a lot of attention was based on whether a team from the National Football League (NFL) or American Football League (AFL) won the annual Super Bowl, an approach that worked for 18 of 19 years (Mlodinow, 2008).

2. Estimates-of-fitness generally apply over a large, well defined portion of the fitness landscape. Where that landscape is decomposable, of course, the same can be said of theory-of-fitness; where the landscapes are rugged, however, theory-of-fitness may only be applicable locally.

3. Theory-of-fitness is particularly interested in the question of whether or not a particular attribute contributes to fitness[15] and may therefore focus on partially explaining fitness by examining the effects of one or several characteristics. For example, in a typical psychology experiment, some variables are controlled so that the impact of others can be examined in isolation. Estimates-of-fitness, on the other hand, need to predict the entire value of fitness in order to be useful.

Where the two types of fitness construct exhibit a strong similarity is in the perceived desirability of compactness. A good fitness estimator should be easy to acquire or compute; the attractiveness of a theory-of-fitness is inversely related to its size.

Unfortunately, the presence of underlying complexity dramatically impacts our ability to build an attractive theory-of-fitness. To understand this, let us consider the extreme cases: a completely decomposable landscape and maximally rugged landscape of N variables. In the decomposable case, our theory of fitness can be expressed as a single expression:

$$F = y_1(x_1) + y_2(x_2) + \ldots + y_N(x_N)$$

In the maximally rugged (i.e., chaotic) landscape, on the other hand, each possible combination maps to a separate random number. Thus, N variables $(x_1, \ldots, x_N)$ require 2^N expressions, one for each combination, when our X values are binary. When we are dealing with more complicated independent variables, the number of possible combinations effectively becomes infinite. Stated another way, *as complexity grows, our theory becomes less compact*[16].

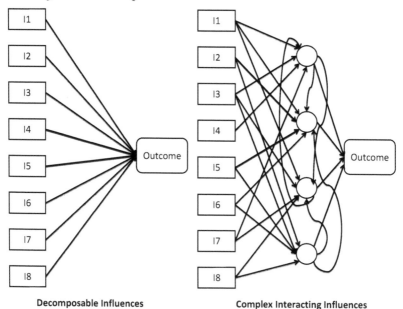

Decomposable Influences   **Complex Interacting Influences**

Figure 3.3: Diagrams of a hypothetical decomposable versus complex system with eight factors influencing fitness.

Presented graphically, the difference between attractive and ugly theory-of-fitness might look something like Figure 3.3. On the left, a series of factors (I1 through I8) each contribute either positively or negatively to the fitness outcome. On the right, these same eight factors interact to form four clusters of interaction—clusters that may themselves interact. Only then can the outcome be determined.

Complexity also impacts generalizability. In a decomposable landscape (with binary variables), once you have a pair of observations for each variable, you can start to develop your theory. If there is no measurement error, you can then quickly develop an expression for fitness that generalizes to any combination. In a chaotic landscape, on the other hand, each combination maps to a different random value. As a result, unless a particular combination has been observed, your theory tells you nothing about it.

The stability of theory is also impacted by complexity, as one of the sources of objective complexity is dynamic complexity. Thus the co-evolving forces that tend to encourage an NK landscape with a high interaction (K) value also tend to undermine a theory's stability.

Development and Products of Research

Ultimately, underlying complexity can dramatically impact the type of research we are able to conduct, assuming that we are interested in seeing that research applied to practice. To explore what I mean by this, it is useful to consider a framework proposed by Fritz Roethlisberger, whose long career as a business researcher at Harvard Business School spanned from the late 1920s to the 1970s and whose investigations included the famous studies at Western Electric's Hawthorne plant[17]. He argued that knowledge is *developed* through a series of stages (moving up in Figure 3.4) towards theory, while its *application* tends to proceed from theory towards more the more specific and practical.

If we consider how complexity impacts this process of creation and application, what should be evident is the degree to which it limits our ability to reach the top levels. As our example of NK landscapes demonstrates, truly complex phenomena cannot be described using a compact deductive system. Indeed, even statements of the form "$\underline{x}$ varies directly or indirectly with $\underline{y}$ under [a] given condition" become so numerous in a highly rugged landscape that a complete collection can probably never be assembled. Complexity also dramatically reduces our ability to create solid estimates-of-fitness of the form "$\underline{x}$ varies with $\underline{y}$", meaning that we can expect such estimators to misbehave frequently.

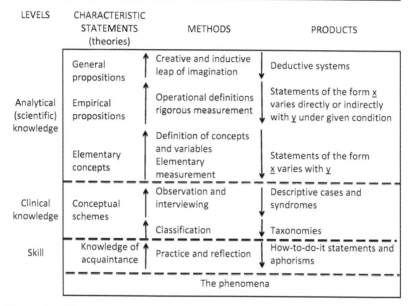

Figure 3.4: The knowledge enterprise (Roethlisberger, 1977, p. 393). For development of knowledge, read from the bottom up; for the practice of knowledge, read from the top down.

Thus, if we are researchers whose goal is to develop attractive theory, our best hope is that the landscape we are studying is not actually rugged and that, some day, a "creative and inductive leap of imagination" will occur that reorganizes our thinking into an attractive theory. Until that time, we may need to content ourselves with the products at the lower levels.

Roethlisberger also emphasized the distinction between conceptual schemes and theory. Conceptual schemes allow us to identify and classify what we have observed; good ones may also organize what we know in a manner that makes that knowledge relatively easy to recall. As such, they may prove to be quite useful in improving our skills as observers and practitioners. They will not necessarily offer deep and unifying explanations, however. I will refer to knowledge of this form as *ugly theory* since it is unlikely to be compact, generalizable, or even stable. Nonetheless, if the underlying landscape we are studying is truly complex, it may be the best we can do.

The Science vs. Art Continuum

As was discussed in Chapter 2, it has only been 50 years since we began viewing the study of business as a science, rather than as an art. The same can be said about education, although its scientific treatment predates that of business by several decades. Economics has been given a scientific treatment for much longer—perhaps as far back as 1776, the year Adam Smith's *The Wealth of Nations* was published. Nonetheless, none of these fields can boast a long history of scientific study, especially when compared with other disciplines such as physics or chemistry.

Complexity and Science vs. Art

As it turns out, the question of what is science vs. what is art has more to do with complexity than may first be apparent. To understand this, it is useful to consider Table 3.2, where characteristics from a range of disciplines are presented.

Table 3.2: Examples of Different Disciplines

Characteristic	Newtonian Mechanics	Internal Medicine	Painting
Nature of elements	Particles or bodies	Organs and systems	Gobs of paint
Number of elements	Small	Medium	Huge
Interactions between elements	Decomposable	Near decomposability	High Interaction
Reliability of fitness measure	High	Medium	Low
Dynamics of fitness measure	None	Low	High
Adaptation to fitness	None	Some	High
Characterization of discipline	Physical Sciences	Life Science	Art

We begin with the Newtonian mechanics column. This is the domain of every introductory physics course. In the systems studied, we typically are dealing with a few bodies (e.g., planets, balls, particles) since systems involving larger numbers cannot be mathematically solved in closed form. Fortunately, the behavior of systems with many bodies can be computed as a result of the principle of *superposition*. What this principle states is that the net force acting on one body is the sum of the individual forces. This is precisely consistent with how decomposability was previously defined. While it means that physics problems may be made arbitrarily complicated (by adding bodies), they are not necessarily complex as we have defined it here.

Physics does not, for the most part, study behavior on fitness landscapes. On the other hand, it is possible to assign a fitness value to the theories themselves: how well they predict observed behavior. It is axiomatic that this form of fitness will not change for a given theory; such a change would imply that the physical laws that govern our universe are changing. Where adaptation is relevant is, therefore, in respect to our theories themselves; the adaptive processes through which these theories change are sometimes referred to as normal science and paradigm shifts (Kuhn, 1970).

At the other extreme we have painting, the quintessential art form. Conceptually, we may view a typical painting as a set of "gobs" of paint[18] distributed over a two dimensional canvas. The number of gobs is clearly huge, since they need to be smaller than the eye can distinguish—analogous to pixels on a computer screen but with depth and other properties. These gobs necessarily interact, since the fitness of a particular dot of color in the painting cannot be determined independent of its neighboring gobs, both near and far. What would have happened to the overall fitness of the Mona Lisa, for example, if her two eyes had each been painted a different color? Our measure of painting fitness also happens to be quite unreliable since it will vary by observer[19]. Furthermore, even a given observer may react differently to it at different times, meaning fitness is highly dynamic. Indeed, perceived fitness in many of the arts is driven by what is in fashion—with individual artists adapting their work to what is selling or to what critics assert to be in vogue. In this respect, fitness in the arts could not be more different from fitness in the physical sciences.

Between the physical sciences and the arts, we find the life sciences. Here, what we frequently have is the assumption of near decomposability, the term coined by Nobel Laureate Herbert Simon (1981). In internal medicine, for example, the entire fitness landscape of just one body includes a substantial number of systems, organs, and component parts of the elements, all the way down to the cellular level. Specialization, however, will reduce the number of interactions that a particular doctor or researcher needs to consider. For example, an ophthalmologist specializes in the eye.

While specialization allows for some assumed decomposability, there are distinct limits to that assumption. For example, in examining the eyes a doctor may find evidence of conditions, such as diabetes, whose origins have nothing to do with sight-related systems (although they may later affect sight).

With respect to reliability, a variety of objective measures that are correlated with fitness—such as body temperature—are available but none of these tests are guaranteed to be perfect indicators of fitness[20]. Moreover, our understanding of what constitutes fitness may change as a patient ages. What an individual patient considers acceptable fitness may also vary considerably across individuals. For example, modest nearsightedness is generally considered a trivial affliction. To a U.S. Navy midshipman hoping to qualify as a pilot—which happens to require perfect uncorrected vision—it could be heartbreaking. A substantial amount of adaptation to achieve higher fitness is also present in medicine. The nearsighted midshipman's acquisition of eyeglasses would represent an example of this.

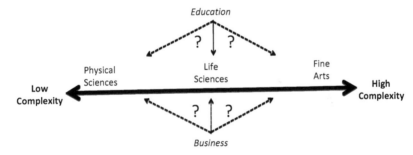

Figure 3.5: **Continuum of disciplines in terms of complexity**

This analysis suggests a continuum of disciplines rated in terms of their complexity, along the lines of that presented in Figure 3.5. We need to be very specific, however, in interpreting such a figure. What the figure presents has to do with underlying theory that governs the discipline—such as physical laws and the principle of superposition—and not necessarily the characteristics of the problems being studied. The science of meteorology, for example, is dedicated to understanding and predicting the weather. While we expect water and gas molecules to obey physical laws, when you have a huge number of them banging into each other, excited by energy sources such as the sun in the presence of a heterogeneous environment that includes oceans, mountains, forests, deserts, and urban areas, the fundamental character of the problem changes. Indeed, it was in modeling the weather that the phenomenon of *chaos* was first encountered[21]. Where chaos is present, long term predictions of system behavior are generally impossible, much the same as they would be in high complexity systems.

Clarifying where the domain of business falls on the Figure 3.5 science-to-art continuum is perhaps the most critical single factor impacting the ultimate design of an informing business school. As suggested by the dotted lines (with question marks) from business, there are three categories of possibilities. First, towards the left of the continuum, it may prove that business is less complex than medicine. If that is the case, then we can expect our research efforts will ultimately produce attractive theory-of-fitness that can be applied in practice. That same theory should be relatively easy to communicate to students.

If business falls to the right of the life sciences, towards the "art" side of the continuum, our efforts to develop attractive theory-of-fitness that is actually applicable to practice will be thwarted. Instead, it will be as if our research is like a giant game of "whack-a-mole"—each time we adjust our theory to nail down one exception, another contradictory case will raise its ugly head. This is not a criticism of research in the arts. What I am criticizing here is only the attempt to apply attractive theory-of-fitness to an underlying domain that is inconsistent with such theory[22].

The alternative I have placed in the middle is the life sciences, as exemplified by medicine. If our domain of particular interest, business, exhibits this complexity level, then how we train doctors could give us important insights into how we should be educating managers. It could also offer some insights into the likelihood that our research efforts will yield success.

To explain the last conjecture, let us consider an example of medical research. Specifically, we ask how medical research has addressed the seemingly straightforward question: "Is coffee good for you?"

The first comment I would make on this subject is that every time I suggest this to be a "simple" question *to anyone who actually does medical research*, they look at me in horror[23]. Knowing the impact of interactions as they do, they immediately recognize that such a theory-of-fitness question will invariably prove unanswerable in any general way.

In fact, if you consult WebMD, you'll find that the coffee question has been addressed quite a few times According that article (Kirchheimer, 2004), "In recent decades, some 19,000 studies have been done examining coffee's impact on health." To put this number in perspective, that single question has been addressed in a number of studies comparable to the estimated number of articles published globally in business and management over the course of an entire year (AACSB, 2008, p. 10). Does this imply the findings are so equivocal that the subject must be continually revisited? Consider the following: one survey conducted over the course of 18 years involving 126,000 people found that men who had six cups per day or more experienced a reduced risk for type II diabetes of 54% (there was an interaction with sex, however, since the reduction was only 30% for women). Despite the presence of incredibly strong statistical significance, *the overriding conclusion was that more research was necessary*.

Should we conclude that the business domain is *merely* as complex as medicine, this example suggests is that we are going to need vastly more resources to conduct our research if we want to make progress comparable to that made by medical sciences. Should our complexity prove to be to the right of medicine on the continuum (more complex), however, then we probably need to completely rethink our current approach to business research and educating managers.

Explanation and Science vs. Art

Interestingly, a continuum very similar to that of Figure 3.5 was proposed by Elster (1983) and adapted by Ghoshal (2005). Rather than being based upon the fitness function, however, it was based upon the type of explanation typically employed in describing phenomena. There were three categories of explanation:

1. *Causal:* Explanations presented in the form X causes Y based upon axiomatic principles, such as the inverse square law defining the strength of gravitational and electrostatic fields.

2. *Functional:* Explanations in which phenomena are described as interactions between systems, each of which has a specific function.

3. *Intentional:* Explanations in which behaviors are characterized in terms of actions that are consciously controlled by participants, driven by forces such as motivation and preference.

The argument they present is that if you examine the physical sciences, causal explanations dominate to the exclusion of all others. In biological sciences, on the other hand, functional explanations play the dominant role—evolution provides the basis for assuming that functional specialization of systems can arise without the need for conscious control. In the social sciences, including management, Ghoshal (2005) asserts that intention-guided explanations are most likely. While there is still room for causal and functional explanations, they will generally be less directly relevant and useful. In the arts, the utility of explanations of any kind are diminished. This is illustrated in Figure 3.6, suggesting that social sciences need to be placed *to the right* of life sciences. In Chapter 4, we consider more carefully the justification for such a placement.

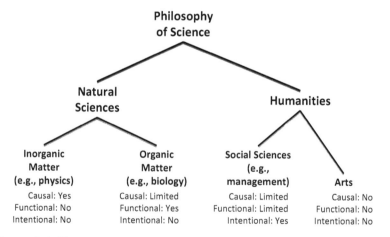

Figure 3.6: Explanation-based taxonomy of disciplines, adapted from Ghoshal (2005, p. 78) that was, in turn, adapted from Elster (1983).

Conclusions

Decision-making is fundamental to virtually everything we teach in a business school. In this chapter, I have considered how complexity might impact the outcomes we face. Although complexity is often equated to difficulty, I use the term differently here. Objective complexity, where present, tends to provide us with many outcomes that are local maxima, but which may be far from the best available. In a complex landscape, it is far easier to find yourself on top a foothill than the highest peak.

True complexity, where it is present, has significant implications for the type of theory-of-fitness we can expect to develop for the purpose of explaining our environment. Environments that are decomposable can, with patience and commitment, be rigorously described using attractive theory. Properly refined and tested, that theory will be compact, generalizable, and stable. Where a landscape is truly complex, however, the best we can hope for is ugly theory—filled with numerous qualifications, not particularly generalizable, and continuously changing as a consequence of external forces. Notice that I never said useless; towards the end of the book I will argue that the pursuit of ugly theory has many virtues to recommend it. Nonetheless, it will never be pretty.

What I have not asserted in this chapter is that the domain of business is necessarily complex. The next chapter, in its entirety, is devoted to exploring whether or not the assumption of landscape complexity in business is reasonable to make. This question is pivotal to the remainder of the book. If you accept that the complexity exists, it influences every aspect of our research and informing activities.

Chapter 3 Foundational References

Gill, T. G., & Hicks, R. (2006). Task complexity and informing science: A synthesis. *Informing Science: The International Journal of an Emerging Transdiscipline, 9*, 1-30. Retrieved from http://inform.nu/Articles/Vol9/v9p001-030Gill46.pdf

Kauffman, S. A. (1993). *The origins of order*. Oxford, UK: Oxford University Press.

Roethlisberger, F. (1977). *The elusive phenomena*, Boston, MA: HBS Press.

Simon, H. A. (1981). *The sciences of the artificial* (2nd ed.). Cambridge: MIT Press.

Wood, R. (1986). Task complexity: Definition of the construct. *Organizational Behavior and Human Decision Processes, 37*, 60-82.

Chapter 3 Notes

[1] The section on task complexity draws heavily upon Chapter 7 of Gill, T.G. & Cohen, E. (Eds.) (2009) *Foundations of Informing Science*, Santa Rosa, CA: Informing Science Press. That chapter was adapted from a previously published article (Gill & Hicks, 2006).

[2] A good place to find examples of how increasing complexity leads to simplification strategies is the research of Payne (1976; Payne, Bettman, & Johnson, 1983). In his early experiment's, for example, he found that students given a pair of hypothetical apartments to choose between would employ a cognitively intensive strategy where every attribute was compared. As they were given a much larger set of apartment options, they employed mechanical strategies—such as throwing out all choices lacking in a particular attribute—so as to simplify the decision-making process.

[3] The section on fitness landscapes draws heavily upon Chapter 16 of Gill, T.G. & Cohen, E. (Eds.) (2009) *Foundations of Informing Science*, Santa Rosa, CA: Informing Science Press. That chapter was adapted from a previously published article (Gill, 2008b). Some of the summarizing material was adapted from a study Joni Jones and I wrote on the complexity of teaching situations (Gill & Jones, 2010).

[4] W. Brian Arthur (1988, 1989) used the VHS/Betamax example to demonstrate self-reinforcing mechanisms.

[5] The curious reader can easily derive this formula. A peak exists where a particular value is higher than that of all N of its local neighbors (i.e., neighbors differing by only one attribute value). Given we are simulating fitness by using random numbers, the likelihood of a particular combination meeting this criterion is $1/(N+1)$. Since there are 2^N possible combinations of attributes, the number of peaks can be estimated by taking the number of combinations times the likelihood that each one is a peak, leading to the formula $2^N/(N+1)$.

[6] Mitchell Waldrop's *Complexity: The Emerging Science at the Edge of Order and Chaos* (1992; New York: Simon & Schuster) provides an excellent

summary of the origins of the field and its early findings, including those of Stuart Kauffman and Per Bak.

[7] Cellular automata are simulations, normally computer-based, of cells that can exist in two or more states. The state of one cell typically impacts the state of neighboring cells, leading to complex patterns. The nature of these patterns can be dramatically impacted by changing the nature of the states and the rules for interaction.

[8] With respect to the simplicity of routine flying, the computerized autopilot is so sophisticated that in an episode of the U.S. TV show *Mythbusters*, the hosts were able to successfully land a large commercial jet in a simulator with just a few hours of instruction and no prior flying experience.

[9] I'm speculating here that a bit of profanity might help getting the message past the pilot's attention filter (see Chapter 6).

[10] The fact that my study went unpublished *and* that the results showed no significance was, of course, not coincidental. Indeed, after my preliminary analysis of the data I abandoned all thoughts of writing up the project—which was an attempt to measure how different forms of assessment related to each other.

[11] The problem then becomes that what appears to be *"obviously relevant"* tends to have a large subjective component, meaning that the experience and judgment of the observer tends to be very important in assessing the credibility of a conclusion involving landscapes where statistical tests are prone to failure. In Chapter 10, we return to this issue in considering the drawbacks of anonymous peer review for research that investigates complex landscapes.

[12] When taking over as the first dean of the new Carey School of Business at Johns Hopkins University, Gupta stated: "Our goal is not to become the best business school *in* the world, it is to become the best business school *for* the world".

[13] Even where stock prices are concerned, it is probably wise to leave open the possibility that some public companies will engage in activities—often criminal in nature—that may intentionally distort stock price. Recognizing this, we would then concede that stock price is not a

perfect estimate of underlying public company fitness, just one of the best ones available.

[14] As is so often the case, I find Wikipedia to be invaluable in dredging up information that I probably first encountered either in school or on the Discovery Channel. The entries on Occam's Razor and antikythera mechanisms were particularly helpful in this instance.

[15] Because whether-or-not a variable contributes is more important than how much it contributes, academics interested in developing theory tend to focus on statistical significance rather than the practical impact of findings. This is a central complaint of Ziliak and McCloskey (2007) that we consider in detail in Chapter 10 of this book.

[16] If the functional form I have used does not make it clear why complex landscapes produce less compact theory than decomposable landscapes, imagine two cities—one laid out on a grid, like many modern U.S. cities and one laid out mainly on the basis of ancient cow paths, such as Boston, Massachusetts. If someone asked you how to get to a particular address in each city, how long would the directions be? The grid directions would tend to be very compact, decomposed along the lines of East-West and North-South travel. The Boston directions would need to be much more elaborate, contenting with curved streets, lots of one-way traffic, five-way intersections, rotaries (known as traffic circles in much of the world) and many unsigned streets. Moreover, the price of making a turning error is much greater in Boston, as getting back to where you were is often far more complicated than simply going around a 4-sided block or turning the same way at the next opportunity. That is perhaps the reason that tourists often comment on the unwillingness of natives to give directions in Boston—they would be too long for the tourist to follow. (And more than likely wrong, if I am to judge by personal experience).

[17] These studies, directed by Elton Mayo, were particularly famous for having identified the "Hawthorne Effect", in which the mere act of observing workers enhanced their productivity.

In an unanticipated example of the frequent emergence of complex interactions, Professor Zbigniew Gackowski, while reviewing an early draft of this book, made the following comment:

I am pleased to inform you that this "famous effect" based on Polish and [my own] time and motion studies, yielded just the opposite result: Polish workers immediately slow down, act meticulously concerned with details to log more time and lower the expected performance standards. In the rugged landscape of human behaviors, the US results hit a peak and a valley in Poland.

[18] I seriously doubt that "gob" is the preferred term of the art world. I use the term, as opposed to some term such as pixel or point, to suggest a small element having properties that could include color, shininess, and depth.

[19] In cases where fitness is very hard to determine, we tend to bring in experts to help. Hence the arts are full of experts and critics who provide estimates-of-fitness that we can use to tune our own judgments.

[20] While there is no universal indicator of health, the onset of rigor mortis is a pretty good indicator of extremely low fitness.

[21] An excellent history of the study of chaos is James Gleick's (1988) book *Chaos* (New York, NY: Penguin Books USA). Chaos differs from randomness in two important ways. First, it tends to exhibit sensitive dependence on initial conditions. This means that tiny changes in the initial state of a system, often below the threshold of measurability, can ultimately lead to huge changes in the system state later on. Often, this is referred to as the "butterfly effect". The description is intended to suggest that a butterfly's single flap of its wing in one part of the world could, ultimately, precipitate a major weather event, such as a hurricane, in some other part of the world. Such a chain of events would be far less plausible in a system driven by entirely randomness, since many sources of randomness acting together tend to average out in their effect.

The other key phenomenon associated with chaos is that of strange attractors. While chaotic systems never repeat a state (if they did, they would become cyclical, not chaotic), they will tend to favor certain patterns of behavior over other patterns. Thus, when the state of a chaotic system is plotted over time, the resulting diagram often looks distinctly non-random.

[22] Malcolm Gladwell (2005) begins *Blink* with a wonderful story in which an art expert detects a forgery at the Getty Museum in California by virtue of the fact that some indiscernible aspect of the sculpture didn't feel right. Such insights could only be the product of years of experience in the field; they are genuine expertise. What is important to understand here is that expertise in the arts tends to be acquired using approaches far different from those used to gain expertise in the physical sciences. The point, therefore, is that it makes sense to tailor how we education experts to the shape of the underlying domain.

[23] When trying to illustrate the impact of complexity on research, I often pose the question to individuals: "Which is a more complex question: 1) Is coffee good for you? or 2) What are the factors that determine if an information system will be successful?" When I ask this of MIS or business researchers, I generally get a look of disbelief followed by an assertion that the latter is obviously more complex. I ask the same question of someone involved in medical research and get the same look of disbelief, followed by the assertion that it is obviously the former. Through hard experience, medical researchers know that type of question that is bound to be unanswerable in any general way as a consequence of the interactions involved.

Chapter 4

The Complexity of Business

Roadmap & Objectives: The previous chapter describes the differences between decomposable (simple) and rugged (complex) landscapes. The next logical step is to look specifically at business landscapes. This chapter makes the case that the general indicators of complexity are present in a typical business landscape and explores why some areas of business research seem to be more impactful than others. Later in the book, in Chapters 10 and 11, we specifically consider whether our prevailing research approaches fit a complex environment.

The previous chapter presented a model of complex landscapes and theory. It did not attempt to justify why such a model might be applicable to business schools. This omission is significant. Many, and probably most, researchers in business-related disciplines start from an assumption that the domain they study will ultimately be describable as a series of relatively independent cause-and-effect influences; in other words, that business processes can be modeled using attractive theory. To justify this assumption, researchers can cite numerous examples from the natural sciences where such a pattern of discovery has, in fact, unfolded. The implications of these historical precedents are obvious: we just need to give our researchers more time to explore, a position that sits well with our personal preferences to continue doing just as we have been.

In this chapter, we explore both sides of the question "Are business landscapes generally complex?" We begin with the argument that the business domain is not truly complex and that, given sufficient time, we will develop a body of attractive theory-of-fitness that will do a good job describing it. This case depends principally upon historical examples drawn from other sciences. We then consider the opposing case:

that business involves processes that are not likely to be decomposable. Here the argument is primarily based upon observed differences between business and the natural sciences. In particular, evidence is presented that the prerequisites for complexity are commonly met for most business landscapes and that patterns of behavior consistent with complexity are routinely observed. Given such complexity, it is reasonable to argue that our understanding of the business domain will not be much improved as a result of continuing efforts to apply the techniques for research and teaching that we have employed in the past. Instead, a paradigm shift will be needed if we are to better understand business landscapes. The status quo will not take us where we need to go.

The Case for Decomposability

The belief that we will ultimately develop broadly applicable theories that explain a wide range of behaviors in the business domain is deeply held by many researchers in the field. The strongest arguments for this assumed decomposability appear to come from two directions: 1) historical precedents, and 2) existing findings. We now consider both of these arguments.

Historical Precedent

The historical precedent argument is based on the irrefutable observation that much of what was once deemed beyond our understanding has ultimately proven to be explainable through science. Clayton Christensen does an excellent job of presenting this argument in the context of education, an argument that generalizes well to business (brackets are mine):

> ... the contention that ... phenomena are unfathomably complex, with unpredictable outcomes, is not unique to education [or business]. For example, prior to 1700, people said similar things about understanding the natural world. Some things seemed so inexplicable that the only plausible explanation was the wrath of the gods. But the development of the scientific method changed all that, and now we understand and can predict with reasonable certainty many things in the world around us. For example, understanding gravity allowed humans to predict that if someone walks off a cliff, he or she will fall— and therefore we do not need to collect experimental data on

that particular question. We can predict the level of stress at which a given material will fracture, the conditions under which certain elements will bond chemically with others, and so on. (Christensen, Horn, & Johnson, 2008, p. 161-162)

In the late 1950s, the Ford Foundation report—the influence of which was discussed in Chapter 1 of this book—expressed a similar optimism that deeper understanding would arise from our continued research efforts and from the development of theory. For example:

> Whether the aim is to improve our understanding of business behavior (i.e., to search for significant generalizations) or to develop better techniques and rules for decision-making, it is clear that business research needs to become more analytical, to develop more solid theoretical underpinning, and to utilize a more sophisticated methodology. This means not only more applied research of the sort that makes the best possible use of the methods of analysis that we now have, but also the development of new and more useful theories and concepts. This in turn requires that the business schools turn for help to the underlying disciplines such as the behavior sciences and mathematics and statistics, as well as to economics…
>
> None of the preceding discussion is intended to minimize the importance of field investigations, detailed case studies, and, in general, the systematic collection of more and better information about business behavior. This is the essential raw material for the study of business—but it is only the raw material. Similarly, case collection is an important activity for the business school, both because of its contribution to teaching and because of its value as training for the faculty member. But case collection by itself is not research in the usual sense of that term. It can, however, become the raw material for research since, through careful and discriminating analysis, significant generalizations can sometimes be drawn from the study of a large number of cases. (Gordon & Howell, 1959, p. 384-385)

Implicit in these assertions, particularly those of the second paragraph, is the belief that continued research of the proper type will lead to *generalizations* (clear evidence of presumed decomposability) that will ultimately prove useful to managers. These beliefs remain widely held today. Their strength is evidenced by the high esteem in which attractive theory—including many examples of theory-of-fitness—is held by the various business disciplines (e.g., Hambrick, 2007)[1].

Results of Existing Research

The other line of argument that would seem to support broad decomposability of the business domain is the large body of research that: a) makes the assumption of decomposability (either in the models proposed or the models tested), and b) the degree to which such research has demonstrated statistically significant results when tested empirically.

Obviously, it is beyond the scope of this chapter (or this book, or this author's knowledge, or anyone's knowledge) to review the entire body of business research. Without even attempting to make estimates of the amount of such research, a casual survey of the literature in any business domain should convince the reader that:

1. A substantial fraction of business research either proposes or tests theory-of-fitness models. To review what this means, a model falls into this category if it attempts to predict or understand what factors contributes to some variable that is generally considered desirable to achieve (e.g., profit, employee performance, technology usage, and so forth).

2. Statistical approaches that assume decomposability of contributions to fitness (e.g., analysis of variance, multiple regression, factor analysis, structural equation modeling) are frequently employed to test such models.

3. The findings of these tests almost invariably show one or more variables that contribute to fitness at a level of statistical significance that is unlikely to be coincidental (e.g., less that a 1 in 20 chance of being observed randomly).

Given this pattern of research and results, it seems reasonable to conclude that the assumption of decomposability in theory-of-fitness is generally warranted. Even researchers who have been critical of business research—such as Pfeffer (2007), Hambrick (2007), and Mintzberg (2004)—have established stellar reputations through a body of personal research that incorporates some decomposability as an implicit assumption. The consensus for the assumption is so strong that it is hard to imagine building a business research career without it.

Paradoxically, the paradigmatic nature of the decomposability assumption proves to be a major obstacle in building a case to support the assumption. It is ingrained so deeply in the research we read, in our training as doctoral students, and in the feedback we receive on our own research that an explicit justification assuming decomposability is rarely required or offered. Few reviewers will object if we simply propose inherently decomposable models—without explaining why we do not expect interactions to play a major role—and conduct our tests using tools that assume it. As a result, my arguments in support of the assumption prove to be much less comprehensive than I would have preferred. There just doesn't seem to be much of a literature in place that attempts to defend the status quo assumption. I believe that is because it so rarely comes under serious attack[2].

The Case for Ruggedness

Whereas the status quo, assuming that a particular business landscape is largely decomposable, will generally be accepted by colleagues, editors, and reviewers with minimal justification, making the case that these landscapes are inherently quite rugged is an entirely different matter. There are some strong arguments, however, that assuming substantial landscape complexity is a far more appropriate starting point for business research. We now consider several of these, including:

- Direct responses to the two justifications for decomposability presented previously

- Observed behaviors consistent with those expected from a rugged landscape

- Existence of widely used business models more consistent with ruggedness than decomposability

- Evidence that theory-of-fitness models are inconsistent and are not mapping well to the reality of the landscape

Taken collectively, these support the conclusion that the landscapes of business are generally far more rugged than is generally assumed.

Response to Historical Precedent Argument

As previously summarized, the arguments for decomposability tend to fall into two categories: historical precedent and body of supporting research. According to the historical precedent argument, we are merely being short-sighted if we assume, based upon today's limited knowledge, that the domain we study will always seem complex. It is hard to deny that the physical sciences and medicine seemed "unfathomably complex" (to use Clayton Christensen's term) several hundred years ago but that much of that apparent mystery has been removed as a result of systematic research. Moreover, even where considerable doubt remains—for example, with respect to behaviors at the subatomic level—we remain optimistic that new ideas and new tools (such as giant particle accelerators) will eventually clarify what is actually going on.

Lacking a crystal ball that allows us to see into the future, we do not have the tools to refute—with complete certainty—this optimistic view of future discovery. There are, however, some important differences between the systems that we have succeeded in understanding and those that remain unclear. This is particularly true for social systems, the domain of most business research. Consider, for example, the following:

1. *Social systems tend to have many interacting elements.* Even among physical systems, such interactions frequently lead to chaotic behavior—such as that exhibited by the weather—that limit our ability to make meaningful long term predictions.

2. *There is no definitive evidence of an analog to the principle of superposition for social interactions.* We can model many-planet solar systems and predict the behavior of many colliding gas molecules because, in physics, net force on a body can be computed as the sum of all forces. If this were true of humans, then every time we were presented with two competing, and equally compelling arguments, we would end up in a state of "no opinion"[3].

3. *Individual entities within a social system are continuously adapting—often within the time frame being modeled.* The concept of adaptation is largely irrelevant when applied to physical systems; our *theories* of how they behave may change to accommodate new evidence, the *physical rules* governing these systems do not. When we deal with the life sciences, such as medicine, adaptation does occur in the systems being studied. The time scale of that adaptation, however, tends to be evolutionary[4] in most cases. Thus, the underlying principles expected to govern behavior typically do not change during the period in which it is being

studied. In social systems—particularly those systems where learning is occurring—we can reasonably expect the entities in the system being studied to behave differently at the end of study than they did at the beginning. Indeed, if the system is an educational system, we have arguably failed in our mission if such behavioral change is not observed.

It is important to recognize that it is perfectly possible to develop theories that help explain the behavior of systems such as these. Indeed, one of the most spectacularly successful theories in human history—the theory of evolution—was developed precisely to explain how living systems behave over long periods of time. Evolution, however, is not a theory-of-fitness. It does not, for example, generally attempt to use its axioms[5] to predict the factors that lead to the "optimal" human being[5]. Instead, it is a theory-of-process that attempts to understand the mechanisms through which increasing fitness is achieved.

All these observations do not provide enough evidence to make the assertion that business and other social domains are fundamentally different from the sciences that have advanced in the past. They do, however, provide a basis for arguing that business research may well follow a very different trajectory.

Response to Body of Existing Research Argument

The case that existing research appears to support the assumption of decomposability cannot easily be dismissed. This is particularly true for empirical research that employs the scientific method in its attempts to validate decomposable theory[6].

Let us begin by accepting as fact that a large body of research exists in which multivariate techniques that assume the underlying decomposability of the landscape—such as multiple regression—show statistically significant influences for individual variables. Is it possible that a complex landscape could produce patterns similar to what we see in empirical findings of business research?

The least involved answer to this question is yes. Even in a highly rugged landscape, there is no reason to assume that the average effect of a given variable will be 0. Depending upon the nature of the sample that is taken, we can therefore reasonably expect these average effects—referred to as main effects—will be detected for some variables. Interaction effects can easily hide themselves *unless you are explicitly looking for them.*

To explore this proposition, let us take a simple example of a situation where we know interaction will be present. Imagine that you are given a choice of a main dish (roast beef or ice cream) and a topping (gravy or fudge sauce). If your tastes are anything like mine, the resulting fitness plot would look something like Figure 4.1.

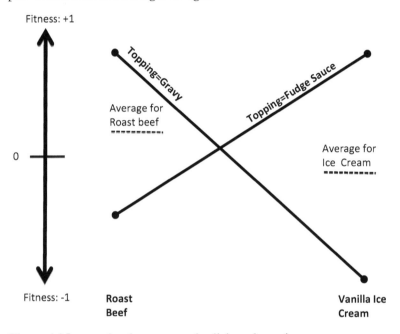

Figure 4.1 Interaction between main dish and toppings

This plot—of a type you can find in a large percentage of experimental psychology papers—can be interpreted as follows. On the left, we see the fitness of roast beef with gravy (high) and fudge sauce (low). On the right, we see the fitness of ice cream with gravy (low) and fudge sauce (high). (The lines connecting the dots are to help us visualize what happens when the sauce is held constant). The plot also shows the average fitness of roast beef (low, but > 0) and of ice cream (somewhat less than 0). What these averages suggest is that if we had a large number of observations and performed regression using main dish and topping as explanatory variables—with no interaction terms—we would find a small but statistically significant positive coefficient for roast beef[7]. The other implication of this example relationship is that the size and significance of the coefficient will be highly dependent upon the actual make up of the observations. If, for example, we have a lot more observations with gravy than fudge sauce, while the number of roast beef and ice cream observations are roughly balanced, we will find that the magnitude and significance of the positive roast beef coefficient will rise accordingly. Thus, if a lot of researchers are performing research on the relative fitness of roast beef and ice cream—without recognizing the inherent interaction with topping—we would expect to see a common pattern of significance but a lot of variation in the magnitude of the coefficients.

In what I believe to be more than coincidental, these observations about the results of regressing interacting variables map very nicely to the research of Ziliak and McCloskey (2008). In their book, *The Cult of Statistical Significance*, they discuss their extensive studies of the application of multivariate statistics in economics and other disciplines. The most central of their conclusions is that we are paying much too much attention to statistical significance and far too little to economic significance. The problem results from using large samples that can detect significance at a level that is too small to be of practical impact. It is compounded by research that reports significance without making clear the units of the variables being measured. What is interesting is that although the authors did not mention interaction effects as being central to the issue, the presence of complexity would produce precisely the same pattern that they observed. In fact, reporting coefficient values and attempting to characterize their impact would likely cause considerable dissonance in the research community if the underlying landscape is complex, since we would expect to see substantial variations in values owing to the previously mentioned sampling effects. Reporting significances only, being unclear with respect to units, or making no attempt to clarify the practical implications of the findings would increase the consistency of reported results, thereby reducing that dissonance.

The obvious rejoinder to this argument is that it is perfectly possible to incorporate specific interactions into regression models. While this is true in principle, in the presence of a complex landscape the number of combinations grows so rapidly that it outstrips our ability to model them. We would need 3 variables and a base case to model the interaction in Figure 4.1. Suppose, however, we add another interacting variable—whether the dish is served hot or cold, as shown in Figure 4.2. This brings the number up to 7 interaction variables plus a base case. We could then allow for the case where the "no topping" case was allowed—this would add another 4 interactions (Roast beef-no topping-hot, roast beef-no topping-cold, ice cream-no topping-hot, ice cream-no topping-cold). Then, suppose we add another variable—extremely thirsty or not extremely thirsty. This might lower the fitness of all solid choices (roast beef more so than ice cream) and might actually raise the fitness of the hot ice cream choices (since it would be liquid). Indeed, if you were thirsty enough, the dreaded vanilla ice cream/gravy/served hot combination might move into the positive fitness category[8].

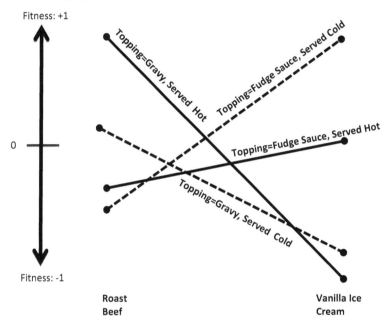

Figure 4.2: Interaction effects of dish and topping, adding whether or not it is served hot or cold.

What we see in the preceding example is the early stages of ugly theory development. As I mentioned in the previous chapter, such theory is the natural result of trying to model a complex environment.

I earlier referred to this interaction model as the "least involved" answer to our question as to whether or not a complex environment could produce statistically significant research results. In Chapter 10, we return to this subject in the context of examining research rigor. At that time, I identify a number of additional mechanisms through which even stronger—and much more misleading—statistically significant results could be produced.

Complexity Indicators in Business Environments

In the preceding section, we have seen the arguments that historical precedents and consensus of existing research may not be sufficient to justify the decomposability assumed for so many business research domains. An entirely different set of arguments can be presented to support the position that ruggedness is likely to characterize such environments. The first of these arguments involves the widespread presence of characteristics consistent with a rugged landscape. To make this argument, we employ the list of complexity indicators presented in Chapter 3. For each of these indicators, we consider an example of the phenomenon and point out a body of existing theory consistent with the observed indicator.

Multiple peaks exhibiting high fitness

To review: where a fitness function is decomposable, maximal fitness for all entities will exist at a single peak. There may, of course, be some variation from entity to entity, since some contributors to fitness may not be entirely under an entity's control. A technology firm started in the Silicon Valley might have inherently greater fitness than one started in rural Kansas. Similarly, there can only be one sales leader in an industry. Nonetheless, for all variables contributing to fitness that can be controlled, entities would ultimately migrate towards the same set of values. If universities are all making adjustments based solely upon improving their magazine rankings, they will all start to look the same.

In a rugged environment, on the other hand, we would expect adapting entities to be distributed across a wide range of local peaks. Even though some peaks will be lower and some higher, once a peak is reached an entity would find that incremental adaptation always reduces fitness. That is how a peak is defined.

If we look at the U.S. and world economies, I believe the wide variety of business firms that exists—breathtakingly diverse, even within a typical industry—is much more consistent with the rugged landscape than the decomposable one. If you disagree that such diversity actually exists, of course, then this argument is not very compelling. And, perhaps, you ought to get out more…

A plausible counterargument would be to concede the diversity, but to point out that we do not really know if these diverse entities exist on, or close to, peaks. This argument leads to an intriguing paradox. I will refer to it as the "baby and bath paradox". The core of nearly all economic theory—at least in a free enterprise environment—is that individual business entities selfishly maximize individual fitness. In qualitative theory, the result is "the invisible hand" that guides the growth of the economy as a whole. In mathematical economics, the result is general equilibrium. If we were to argue against ruggedness by saying that entities do not adapt towards increased fitness, we would then need to toss out nearly all existing theory in economics, finance, and most other business disciplines—throwing out the baby with the bath water.

To provide an example of the existence of distinct peaks, consider the airline industry in the early 1980s. During that period, competition was intense as the effects of deregulation became very apparent. One of the most important contributors to an airlines success was ownership of a reservation system. Such as system facilitated the hub-and-spoke route design that deregulation encouraged, it helped lock in travel agents, it allowed its owners to design and roll out new pricing strategies quickly, and it provided owners with immediate access to competitor's pricing and promotions[9]. The two airline competitors operating major reservation systems—American Airlines and United—continue to operate today. Mere survival for 25 years would not seem like high fitness in most industries, but in the airline industry, where most major carriers have gone out of business, it is a prodigious achievement.

What is interesting about the airline fitness landscape is that there was another peak. One major carrier, Southwest Airlines, refused to adopt the hub-and-spoke system and instead concentrated on point-to-point short hops. It did not participate in any reservation system. It maintained a simple pricing structure. It viewed its major competitors to be rental car and bus companies, not other airlines. And it consistently thrived throughout the entire period—unlike its hub-and-spoke competitors. Thus, we see two very distinct peaks—employing inherently incompatible strategies—in the same industry.

As it turns out, there is also widely held business theory specifically asserting landscape ruggedness. A good example of this is the business strategy research of Porter (1980, 1985). He proposes that three generic competitive strategies exist—cost leadership, differentiation, and segmentation—and asserts that the rules for effective competition (i.e., fitness) are fundamentally different depending upon which of these is chosen. He also warns of the danger of being "stuck in the middle" (Porter, 1985, p. 16), rather than pursuing one of the strategies. This is clear evidence that distinct peaks are presumed to exist.

Inconsistent results from incremental change

To review: in a decomposable landscape, the same change in fitness should always result from changing a particular variable. This is a simple consequence of the generalizability we expect to see in such landscapes. In complex landscapes, on the other hand, we expect to see rules that work in one context to have either no effect or the opposite effect in other contexts. Indeed, if a rule behaves reasonably consistently across an entire environment, then the particular cluster of variables involved can be treated as nearly decomposable.

An example of a behavior that behaves differently in different contexts can be found in a 2003 "all-you-can-eat" crab legs promotion run by the Red Lobster restaurant chain. This was one of a series of all-you-can-eat promotions run by the restaurant (e.g., all-you-can-eat shrimp) that had previously been very successful in building traffic. This particular promotion, however, proved so costly—as diners paying $20 returned for numerous refills—that the company's profits were seriously impacted and the CEO was dismissed. The counterargument: the economics of crab legs are so different from other entrees that the effect was not comparable to prior offerings. Even today, however, local Chinese buffets offer all-you-can-eat crab legs (along with unlimited servings of all the other dishes they serve) for as little as $13.98. This suggests another interaction: if the only all-you-can eat item on the menu is your most expensive item, you may be in trouble. If, however, everything is all-you-can-eat, diners will tend to fill up with less expensive items as well so as to experience more variety[10].

Observed inconsistency has become central to the tenets of behavioral economics, particularly as it relates to individual preference. As mentioned in the previous chapter, preference is guided by the individual's utility function (Gill, 2008a). The utility function, in turn, is the result of thousands of generations of evolution and is therefore presumed to guide the user in the direction of higher fitness. If it did not, the species could not have survived.

As we will see in Chapters 5 and 9, however, experimental evidence, is unequivocal in its findings that preferences can be manipulated relatively easily (e.g., Kahneman & Tversky, 1982; Ariely, 2008; Thaler & Sunstein, 2008). For example, identical lotteries produce inconsistent preferences depending upon how they are framed as a sequence of gains and losses. Our preference for buying a particular product is influenced by the presence of other products that we would not even consider buying. We can even be primed by irrelevant numbers in a way that affects our perceived value for a product or service. In a decomposable world, such inconsistency in our perception of fitness would not exist.

Behaviors at odds with research findings

To review: in a complex environment, we would expect to find many significant exceptions to any decomposable theory-of-fitness that is proposed or that is a finding derived from decomposable analytical techniques. The example we now consider combines both experimental evidence and theory-building.

Recently, the *Academy of Management Journal* (AMJ) ran a special issue (Volume 50, No. 5) on evidence-based management in the human resources field. Of particular concern to researchers was the degree to which practitioners were unaware of, or chose to ignore, some of the most significant findings of academic research. At the head of the AMJ list was the finding that "Intelligence predicts job performance better than conscientiousness (Schmidt & Hunter, 1998)," which elicited a particularly high level of disagreement from practitioners (Rynes, Giluk, & Brown, 2007, p. 988).

Two general comments can be made about the specific finding. First, the dependent variable—job performance—is clearly a fitness measure. Indeed, in the military, annual employee evaluations are referred to as "fitness reports". Second, we can readily identify examples where the opposite of the rule—choosing conscientiousness over intelligence— would have been a better contributor to fitness when viewed in retrospect. Consider the following three cases:

1. Barings ("Barings debacle," 2008). A trader who failed to follow established trading guidelines took a firm that had survived the Napoleonic Wars and put it out of business.

2. Societe Generale ("French bank blames," 2007). An employee who failed to follow established trading guidelines lost $7 billion of the firm's money, crippling it.

3. Chernobyl (INSAG-7, 1992). Although the principal cause of the worst nuclear accident in history was an appallingly unstable reactor design, a lackadaisical attitude towards testing procedures on the part of operators was a significant contributor to the actual disaster.

In these cases, with the benefit of hindsight, conscientiousness outweighed intelligence[11]. Thus—bearing in mind that a large body of research found intelligence correlated with job performance (e.g., Schmidt & Hunter, 1998)—we may conclude that neither intelligence nor conscientiousness prevails across the entire landscape. Their relative contribution to fitness will vary according to the values of other characteristics related to the job and, possibly, upon each other—with the highly intelligent/highly non-conscientious interaction perhaps posing a particularly serious threat.

The example just presented also illustrates another characteristic of fitness. True fitness can almost never be known for entities existing on a rugged landscape. As a result, we need to rely on estimates-of-fitness. In these cases, the existing theory-of-fitness predicted intelligence would be the most critical contributor to job fitness. Thus, researchers used performance ratings, an estimate-of-fitness, to test their theory. But the individuals involved in the incidents described may well have had high performance ratings. Thus, the danger of over-reliance on a single estimate-of-fitness, mentioned in the previous chapter, is once again illustrated.

One might, of course, argue that the counter-examples I presented are simply a case of "the exception that proves the rule," the old adage that allows us to dismiss any evidence that makes us uncomfortable. But, the arguments of this book suggest that a better restatement of adage might be: "the exception that proves ruggedness."

Sensitivity to small changes

To review: because interacting variables impact fitness through the force of the interaction, as opposed to individually, there is the potential that even small changes can be magnified. This is similar to the sensitivity to initial conditions effect exhibited by chaotic systems.

As an example, consider the early days of Bill Gates. After dropping out of Harvard, he founded Microsoft, a small software company whose principal product was a BASIC interpreter for the newly created microcomputer market. IBM was creating its own product for that category, to be known as the IBM Personal Computer, but did not want to invest a great deal of time and effort into the product. As a consequence they approached Gates about licensing his version of BASIC. They also needed an operating system, so they attempted to meet with the founder of Digital Research, Inc.—developer of the popular CP/M operating system used on other microcomputers—but they could not get together to ensure the proper paperwork was signed. While meeting with Gates, IBM mentioned that they needed an operating system. He replied that he knew of one that might be available (the DOS operating system) and asked them if they wanted to acquire it or if he should get it himself. They indicated that he should go ahead and acquire it[12], which he did, retaining the rights to sell it to other microcomputer producers.

What is interesting about this story is the huge impact that retaining the rights to DOS had over the long term. Although not considered to be critical decision by either party at the time (according to the previous account), nearly all of Microsoft's current market position can be traced back to that decision. By being allowed to resell DOS, Microsoft enabled the PC clone industry. By controlling the operating system, the company also acquired an advantage in creating and enhancing newly acquired productivity software (e.g., MS-Word) and development tools. IBM began to recognize its mistake in the mid-1980s and decided to co-develop, with Microsoft, its OS/2 operating system that was intended to complement its new, largely proprietary next generation of PC hardware, the PS/2. Microsoft, however, decided to split with IBM and continue evolving its own commercially unsuccessful graphic operating system, MS-Windows, which ran as a layer on top of DOS. Ultimately, Windows evolved to the point where it was largely independent of DOS and became the launching pad for most of Microsoft's subsequent product initiatives. Meanwhile, OS/2—perceived to be the clear technological winner in its early days—withered and died.

Malcolm Gladwell presents a very interesting perspective on the issue of the impact of small changes. In his book *The Tipping Point* (Gladwell, 2000)—subtitled: "How little things can make a big difference"—he places considerable emphasis on threshold effects. These effects drive behaviors such as mobs and information cascades (Gill, 2008c), where behaviors die out very quickly unless a threshold is attained, in which case they grow rapidly. The same phenomenon can be observed in highly interactive physical systems such as a nuclear reactor; a few millimeters in control rod position can make the difference between low power output sub-criticality and super-criticality, where power output grows exponentially. On the other hand, his book *Outliers* (Gladwell, 2008) appears to emphasize the opposite—that much of the individual success that we attribute to luck (such as the story of Bill Gates) is actually much better characterized as the result of a confluence of factors that actually prepared the individual, and those like him or her, to follow a similar trajectory[13].

What unites these two seemingly inconsistent perspectives is the underlying complexity of the landscape. While small changes in attributes *can* lead to big changes in fitness, this is true only in unusual situations. In fact, fitness behavior on a complex landscape is likely to depend much less on assumed randomness than on landscapes assumed to be decomposable. To explain large fitness changes resulting from small attribute changes in a decomposable landscape, you more or less need to assume that a giant random error term has been encountered[14]. In a complex landscape, on the other hand, such giant leaps in fitness will occasionally occur *but they will be accessible mainly to entities that have a set of attributes already in place that allows them to make the step required to enter the new state of high fitness.*

Stickiness and discontinuous change

To review: A complex fitness landscape is characterized by many local peaks. In consequence, incremental changes to attributes tend to reduce fitness. This will tend to inhibit an entity's willingness to change (stickiness) and when an entity does change, discontinuous jumps from one peak to another are more likely to occur.

An example of stickiness that I found in my own research was the case of Batterymarch Financial Management (Gill, 1995a). This firm, which managed stock portfolios, was the early leader in automated trading and in algorithmic analysis of portfolios. The model it used for stock picking was distinctly contrarian in its outlook and, during the period from 1974 to 1983, the firm outperformed the S&P 500 9 out of 10 years— beating it by over 20 points in two of those years. In 1982, however, the behavior of the stock market changed; the weak market of the 1970s was replaced by the longest bull market in history. Batterymarch continued to apply the same models that had brought it success in the past, incrementally tuning them as new data came in. The outcome was that during the period from 1983 to 1993 it achieved the amazing feat of underperforming the market every year and by 1991 it had made the "major losers" category in the Pension Olympics for five years in a row.

As a consequence of stickiness, we would expect examples of discontinuous change to be infrequent. Where they do occur, however, changes are likely to be quite sweeping—as transitioning from one peak to another would require. One good example can be found in IBM's transformation in the 1990s (Applegate, Austin, & Collins, 2005). By the early 1990s, it had become clear that IBM's existing business model, built around selling and leasing mainframe hardware, had been made obsolete by advances in computing hardware. Indeed, the value of the pieces of the firm was perceived to be greater than that of the firm as a whole. As a consequence, when Lou Gerstner—former CEO of American Express—was hired to take over, the intention was that he would oversee the dismantling and sale of the company's pieces. Based on his interviews with customers, however, he perceived that the type of integration that IBM could provide though its various divisions was actually of great value. That value, however, would not come from being a hardware vendor. Instead, he took the bold step of reconfiguring the company as a systems integration services supplier. This change, taking place over just a few years, produced one of the biggest rebounds in the history of business.

An example of a theory-of-process that embodies the notion of stickiness is Clayton Christensen's theory of disruptive innovation (Christensen, Horn, & Johnson, 2008). The essence of the theory is that once a firm establishes a market position, it is possible for technologies to come along that will ultimately displace it. Often, these technologies emerge in a different market (e.g., early microcomputers originally targeted an entirely different market segment, consumers and individuals, than other computer types), making them largely invisible or uninteresting to established participants in the marketplace. While the established competitors continue to innovate along their existing path (i.e., stick to their current fitness peak, in landscape parlance), however, advances in the disruptive technology ultimately make it possible for the new entrants to compete with the original participants; by this time, the disruptive version of the technology is often much cheaper or more capable.

Punctuated equilibrium

To review: systems that involve interactions between many elements, whether adaptive or not, frequently exhibit a pattern which is orderly most of the time but occasionally experiences rapid transitions. Because many interacting elements are also a source of objective complexity, we would expect to see punctuated equilibrium behaviors on such landscapes.

We have already mentioned a number of examples of landscapes changing rapidly after having behaved in a much more orderly fashion. The sudden cascade in the video cassette format preference—towards VHS and away from Betamax—is one example. The sudden transition from an indifferent stock market to a bull market in 1982 is another, as was the sudden market crash in October 1987.

On the theory side, the phenomenon has been widely recognized in business environments. Aside from punctuated equilibrium (Gersick, 1991), the phenomenon has been referred to by many names, including discontinuous change (Handy, 1990), turbulence, (Edwards & Harris, 1977), jolts (Meyer, 1982), high velocity (Bourgeois & Eisenhardt, 1988; Virany, Tushman, and Romanelli, 1992), divergent change (Moss Kanter, Schlesinger, & Richardson, 1989) and Black/Grey Swans (Taleb, 2007).

The Research-Practice Gap

As noted in the previous section, attempts to apply theory-of-fitness to practice when the underlying landscape is complex would result in a great many anomalies. These anomalies, in turn, would render the theory less valuable to practitioners. As a consequence, if researchers continue to focus on developing attractive theory, we would expect a research-practice gap to develop. The evidence that such a gap does exist was presented in the first chapter. Thus, what we observe is consistent with what we would expect given a complex underlying landscape.

There is a problem with this broad assessment, however. Although the consensus that academic research has very low impact is well supported for many disciplines—such as management, MIS, and marketing—the case is much less strong for other business-related disciplines, most notably finance and its reference discipline, economics. For one thing, a number of widely known theories in these disciplines have their origins in academia (AACSB, 2008). Perhaps even more impressive, we often see commercial and government entities competing with academia to hire economics and finance doctoral students. Indeed, even faculty members may be recruited by practice and government from time to time[15].

At first glance, this evidence of academic theory diffusing to practice would seem to call into question the entire notion that business theory does not map to the underlying fitness landscape. That, in turn, would seem to suggest that the landscape is not as complex as I have proposed.

I believe the contradiction presented by economics and finance is not as great as it initially appears to be. Let us begin by considering economics. Even a casual inspection of the field will quickly reveal that "economic theory" is really a misnomer. "Economic theories" would be a much better description. Indeed, for virtually any intended economic action, a school of economic thought that supports it (and argues against it) can be found. This became particularly obvious to me during the recent debates regarding the U.S. economic stimulus. Drawing parallels to the actions taken in the Great Depression, on any day one could find economists arguing that the actions taken by Roosevelt were too timid (thereby prolonging the depression) or too aggressive (thereby prolonging the depression) or were just about right. Given that we have had 75 years to study the historical period, this lack of consensus could lead one to suspect that the hiring of an economist might be best justified on ideological grounds, as opposed to scientific ones. Economist Russ Roberts (2010, p. A13) voiced his concerns in a recent Wall Street Journal opinion piece as follows:

> I once thought econometrics—the application of statistics to economic questions—would settle these disputes and the truth would out. Econometrics is often used to measure the inde-

pendent impact of one variable holding the rest of the relevant factors constant. But I've come to believe there are too many factors we don't have data on, too many connections between the variables we don't understand and can't model or identify.

I've started asking economists if they can name a study that applied sophisticated econometrics to a controversial policy issue where the study was so well done that one side's proponents had to admit they were wrong. I don't know of any. One economist told me that in general my point was well taken, but that his own work (of course!) had been decisive in settling a particular dispute.

Perhaps what we're really doing is confirming our biases. Ed Leamer, a professor of economics at UCLA, calls it "faith-based" econometrics. When the debate is over $2 trillion in additional government spending vs. zero, we've stopped being scientists and become philosophers. Do we want to be more like France with a bigger role for government, or less like France?

The sense that economic theory is heavily influenced by the predisposition of the economist, as opposed to being the best attempt to systematically account for all that is known, derives further support from the field of behavioral economics, which has spent the last few decades questioning the underlying assumptions upon which economics is based. To quote Duke University's Dan Ariely:

> Though practitioners of traditional economics reluctantly admitted that people may behave irrationally from time to time, they have tended to stick to their theoretical guns. They have argued that experiments conducted by behavioral economists and psychologists, albeit interesting, do not undercut rational models because they are carried out under controlled conditions and without the most important regulator of rational behavior: the large, competitive environment of the market. (Ariely, 2009, p. 3)

Stated another way, much of economic theory appears to be based upon mathematical derivations from simple behavioral axioms that do not conform to actual behavior.

So why on earth would anyone need an economist? The answer, I believe, stems from the fact that while economists develop some theory-of-fitness and theory-of-process, they are particularly attuned to developing estimates-of-fitness. As was introduced in the previous chapter, in the context of college rankings, the underlying fitness of an entity or particular position on a fitness landscape is not always readily evident. In biological settings, for example, it may take thousands of generations before a species can be characterized as "successful". The same can be said of an economy. One of the most important roles that economists play is to supervise the gathering and interpretation of data that helps policy makers to judge the fitness of the economy or some subset of the economy. Numbers like unemployment rates, inflation rates, gross national product (GNP), national income, per capita income, income distribution, and so forth all contribute to our assessment of past and current fitness. Economic forecasts help us to estimate expected future fitness. Understanding what these numbers mean—and none of them are straightforward—and how they are gathered is critical to the assessment of national or regional fitness. To do so properly requires a considerable amount of advanced training in econometrics.

As we noted in the case of college rankings, easy to acquire estimates-of-fitness are likely to be welcomed by individuals participating on a rugged landscape. While mindful of the inherent weaknesses of such estimates, any estimate is better than none at all (a topic we shall return to in Chapter 5). It is also beneficial that estimators be easy to explain, making simple estimators (in line with attractive theory) much preferable to complicated ones[16]. Even where policy-makers proceed from entirely different theories-of-fitness and, therefore, vehemently disagree on what actions should be taken in a particular economic situation, they may nonetheless employ the same estimates-of-fitness in their decision-making processes and in making their forecasts.

The case of finance resembles that of economics. Rather than focusing on the fitness of an entire economy or industry, however, the most common unit of analysis is the company. The core problem addressed by finance is, therefore, estimating the underlying fitness of a company. For a public company, the estimate translates directly to the company's market value. When a company's stock price is volatile—except in direct response to a specific event—the implication is not that the underlying fitness of the company is continuously changing by large amounts. Rather, it is the market's estimates of that value that are changing.

Once we recognize that market value is, in fact, an estimate of fitness, it becomes clear that finance—much like economics—is heavily invested in fitness estimation. A value investor, for example, is simply someone who believes he or she has a better estimate of underlying fitness than market value. A technical investor is someone who believes that he or she can beat the market by detecting common patterns in the behavior of the market's fitness estimates. A mergers and acquisitions specialist attempts to assess how the market value of a combined entity will compare with the sum of the market values of the original entities. A divestiture specialist does the reverse.

As was the case with economics, there are a wide range of financial schools of theory. Some believe markets are efficient, others do not. Some believe that capital structure is irrelevant, others disagree. There is little guarantee that you will make a killing in the market by following the advice of a finance professor. As mentioned in Chapter 1, when Robert Merton, Myron Scholes, and other leading research experts in the field of finance founded a company based upon principles derived from finance research—Long-Term Capital Management (LTCM)—the performance was less that exemplary. Indeed, the firm's collapse in 1999 almost took the entire financial systems down with it; a harbinger of things to come. Nassim Talep (2007) argues that this failure resulted from a huge and completely predictable misunderstanding of the nature of uncertainty. By estimating uncertainty as if it were the result of normally distributed error, the researchers could dismiss the likelihood of the high impact, low frequency events that Taleb calls "Black Swans". Thus, as was the case for economics, the underlying assumptions upon which financial models are based are definitely subject to question.

Despite the disagreements between schools of financial thought, however, a common set of analytical and research skills are required to make and interpret estimates of organizational fitness. Lots of data must also be acquired and analyzed. Thus, we would expect some research findings (and researchers) to migrate to practice.

In conclusion, some business disciplines—such as management, marketing, and MIS—are heavily invested in developing theory to explain the underlying fitness of the organization. If the body of theory does not conform to the shape of the fitness landscape, then we would expect practice to show little interest in the theory. On a rugged landscape, the factors impacting fitness tend to be very situation specific; general theories do not necessarily apply. Other disciplines, such as economics, finance, and—to a lesser extent—accounting are more concerned with developing estimates of fitness. On landscapes where fitness is hard to assess, whether they are complex or decomposable, techniques for estimating fitness consistently will always be welcome— even where controversy remains regarding how fitness can be enhanced. As a consequence, we would expect such techniques to diffuse to practice much more easily.

Conclusions

If business landscapes are complex, as complexity is defined in this book, it has important implications for how we research them and how we teach students to thrive in them. This chapter has made the argument for complexity two different ways:

1. *Pointing out that existing arguments for the decomposability of the business landscape are far from watertight.* Those natural science domains that have been greatly clarified though continued scientific investigation have lacked the adaptive character of business; the statistical significance observed when decomposable models are tested can be explained in other ways.

2. *Identifying observed characteristics of business domains that are consistent with underlying ruggedness.* These include evidence of multiple fitness peaks, inconsistent behaviors resulting from the same changes made to an attribute, noteworthy exceptions to general findings of research, large changes in fitness resulting from small changes in attributes, a tendency of business entities to stick to established peaks even when forces suggest they should move, and the patterns of punctuated equilibrium frequently observed in business systems.

In addition, the very existence of a research-practice gap suggests that many of the theory-driven findings of researchers are not considered applicable to practice. There are two exceptions to this rule: economics and finance. In these fields, there is considerable evidence of research being applied to practice. Here, I advance the proposition—to be justified later in the book—that research focused on developing estimates-of-fitness is likely to get a more positive reception from practice than theory-of-fitness. Because a great deal of economics research deals with estimating key aggregate fitness indicators (e.g., GNP, income distribution, growth rate) and finance is heavily focused on estimates of business fitness (e.g., market value of the firm), these fields should naturally tend to develop a closer relationships to practice than disciplines that do not. We would also anticipate that government entities and financial services firms would seek to employ individuals with academic training in these disciplines, consistent with what we actually see happening.

Having presented the case that business is complex we can now turn to how a rugged fitness domain impacts informing. That is the subject of the next series of chapters.

Chapter 4 Foundational References

Ariely, D. (2008). *Predictably irrational.* New York: Harper Collins.

Gill, T. G. (2008b). Reflections on researching the rugged fitness landscape. *Informing Science: The International Journal of an Emerging Transdiscipline, 11*, 165-196. Retrieved from http://inform.nu/Articles/Vol11/ISJv11p165-196Gill219.pdf

Handy, C. (1990). *The age of unreason.* Boston, MA: Harvard Business School Press.

Taleb, N. N. (2007). *The Black Swan.* New York, NY: Random House.

Ziliak, S. T., & McCloskey, D. N. (2008). *The cult of statistical significance.* Ann Arbor, MI: University of Michigan Press.

Chapter 4 Notes

[1] The relationship of generalizable theory to decomposability only applies to theory-of-fitness. Theories that describe a process through which fitness is achieved, such as the theory of evolution or experiential learning theory (Kolb & Kolb, 2009) do not necessarily make any assumptions about the underlying decomposability of the fitness landscape.

[2] Consider how differently business researchers treat potential interactions in contrast to medical researchers. As illustrated by the "Is coffee good for you?" example of Chapter 3, even highly material effects accompanied by astronomical statistical significances are routinely discounted in epidemiological studies precisely because interaction effects have so often proved problematic in the past.

[3] I would actually conjecture that the state of "no opinion" is a highly unstable one for many people—particularly amongst the academics that

I have spend much of my life observing. Lacking an opinion, it would be nearly impossible for us to engage in our favorite pastime: hearing ourselves talk.

[4] Medicine is continually developing new ways to improve overall fitness—in terms of life-span or quality-adjusted-lifespan—without attempting to change the underlying biological principles governing how the human bodies operate. The rules of fitness governing the human bodies may change, but only very slowly. I would, for example, be rather uncomfortable if my doctor, upon observing my weight, were to respond: don't worry about it, in a few hundred thousand years natural selection and adaptation will have changed our bodies to the point where obesity will not matter. More likely, he would suggest a course of diet and exercise designed to increase fitness under the existing set of rules by which my body is constrained to live.

[5] On the subject of evolution and human design, the field of eugenics (popularized by Nazi Germany but having strong roots in Britain and the U.S.) was based on the premise that we could achieve an "optimal" human through selective breeding and culling sub-optimal specimens—using evolutionary theory as its justification. Implicit in that discipline was the assumption that the overall fitness of a human could be achieved through individually optimizing selected traits—in other words, it assumed that the human fitness function was largely decomposable. What is particularly interesting about this is that many of the individuals who were leaders in the study of eugenics were the very same individuals who pioneered the multivariate statistical techniques that we use today—techniques that, as I have already noted, assume decomposability. For example, Egon Pearson, well known for his correlation coefficient and other advances to statistical theory, occupied a joint chair in statistics and eugenics at University College. When he retired in 1933, that department was split into two departments. Appointed to chair the newly formed eugenics department was Ronald Fisher, the individual most directly responsible for popularizing the use of statistical significance testing in conjunction with multiple regression analysis. Thus, we find that the origins of many of the statistical techniques overlap with a now discredited field that assumed the decomposability of traits contributing to human fitness. I learned these facts from Ziliak and McCloskey's (2009) fascinating account of the decid-

edly unscientific origins of the statistics field that now guides so many of our scientific investigations in business research.

6 The existence of theory that has been proposed but not tested, on the other hand, presents a much weaker argument for decomposability. It is quite possible for widely held theories to evolve independently of reality. The pre-scientific days of human history were rife with such theories; magic and the acts of troublesome gods were used to explain many unforeseen events.

7 Since we are constrained to either roast beef OR ice cream in the example, I assume here that ice cream is the base case. Thus, only roast beef would have a computed coefficient value.

8 That warm vanilla ice cream served with gravy might ever prove attractive is pure speculation on my part. I have been told, however, that people in the desert may become thirsty enough to drink their own urine. Given the forced choice between urine and warm ice cream with gravy, I would definitely choose the latter in my current state of thirst. Since I have never been thirsty enough to be willing to drink either, however, I cannot state with certainty which option I would prefer if I were dying of thirst. This illustrates why researching a complex landscape is so different from researching a decomposable one and, as will be discussed later, why in-depth observations play such an important role in understanding complex landscapes.

9 For decades, I have opened my MIS graduate courses with the *Frontier Airlines* case (HBS Case 9-189-074) to illustrate the power that can be exerted by an information system.

10 The desire to seek variety when dining is well established in research. It can even lead to choices for dining in the future that are inconsistent with the diner's actual taste preferences (e.g., Gilbert, 2007, p. 133).

11 From a statistical standpoint, non-survival also presents a serious empirical sampling issue. In our example, it would have been impossible to include either Barings or Chernobyl in any post-event study of the intelligence vs. conscientiousness tradeoff since one organization was disbanded and the referenced employees in the other all died. Thus, if conscientiousness-related failures occur at a rate higher than that of intelligence-related failures—and I make no assertions or conjectures on this point—the relative contribution of conscientiousness to

survival could be severely under-sampled. Were this to be the case, employers with a sensible level of risk-aversion might be quite rational in preferring conscientiousness to intelligence in spite of the substantial body of empirical evidence that seems to support the benefits of intelligence.

[12] Accounts vary as to what actually happened, since what transpired at these meetings subsequently became hacker folklore. My description is based on Mlodinow's (2009) account, which in turn was largely based on what IBM's representative reported.

[13] As an example of how external factors contribute to success, Gladwell (2008) tells the story of Bill Gates emphasizing how key aspects of his background—the availability of a timeshare linkup at his private school in 1968, personal connections that allowed him to begin programming commercially early in life, and the fact that he was born at just the right time (1955)—all contributed to his success. In fact, Gladwell offered a list of 9 individuals sharing many of these factors (all born between 1953 and 1956) and all of whom went on to achieve great wealth and success in the computer industry. Quite honestly, as an individual born in 1955, who attended a private school that installed a timeshare system in 1968, who had family connections (an uncle) that allowed him to begin programming early, and who went to Harvard as an undergraduate (as 3 of the 9 did, a fact that Gladwell was kind enough not to mention), I found the whole story to be quite depressing. It showed me to be the slacker that I always suspected I was.

[14] The assumption that giant variations from expected behavior in a system is caused by randomness provides the justification for omitting those observations that fail to conform to a model from a sample and calling them "outliers". We return to this subject frequently in later chapters.

[15] While I was teaching at Florida Atlantic University, for example, a assistant professor in finance took my intermediate undergraduate programming course prior to departing for Wall Street, where he had been hired as a technical analyst. With respect to government, all one has to do is look at the number of economics faculty members joining a typical U.S. administration after an election has been held.

[16] The insight that simple estimates-of-fitness are much preferred to complex ones in economics (and other fields) came to me as a result of an e-mail exchange I had with Dr. Paul Frijters, a leading economist in the area of utility theory. After I had written a paper on the relationship of goals to utility, I thought I had better get a reality check on what I had written. Since Dr. Frijters had recently published an important article on the subject (Clark, Frijters, & Shields, 2008), I sent him a draft and asked if he would kindly look it over and tell me if "I was crazy". His kind response (with a few names omitted), came within a few hours and was as follows [emphasis is mine]:

> I can give you a very quick reaction:
>
> a) you are not mad. Nearly all of the authors in this field have put up diagrams of the type you propose (Figures 3 and 4: your goal oriented diagram). I myself had one similar to this (though with different labels) when I was a PhD student. My PhD supervisor…had a huge diagram in his thesis, my own PhD student …just last month gave me a diagram of similar proportions. Lots of boxes and arrows between them.
>
> b) ***it's a dead horse in terms of publishing. The power of economics is the power of good simplifications.*** We didn't have the data for my diagrams and we don't have the data for yours.
>
> c) it's a good horse in terms of reminding yourself that we are making grandiose abstractions.
>
> Happy to provide more feedback if you need it, but the above is pretty much my gut reaction,
>
> Paul Frijters

According to evolutionary economics, utility is our evolved estimator for fitness. Even the estimator of an estimator needs to be attractive in its characteristics in order to be acceptable, or so it appears.

T. Grandon Gill
Informing Business
Santa Rosa, California: Informing Science Press.

Chapter 5

Mental Models and Heuristics

Objectives: Before we can draw any conclusions about how best to inform our students and practice, we need to develop a conceptual scheme for what we mean by informing. To develop such a scheme we need to consider a number of areas: how we store and process knowledge (this chapter), how knowledge accumulates through learning and practice (Chapter 6), and what occurs when we transfer knowledge through informing (Chapter 7). This chapter examines the basic mechanisms of human information processing and explores why problem solving in unfamiliar settings is so prone to error.

At first glance, it might seem that examining human information processing, as we do in this chapter, is a bit far afield from our central goal of understanding how to better inform business. In fact, the topic of mental models is at the heart of informing. For informing to occur, the client's view of the world must be altered in some way. If it is not, then whatever communication has taken place has had no effect and the process cannot be characterized as informing[1]. In this book, that loosely defined "view of the world" is characterized as a set of *mental models*. For our purposes, of particular interest are those models that relate to specific tasks or problem solving activities on the part of the client. These are referred to as *problem spaces*.

The problem spaces contained within the mind of the client are not limited to well understood activities. Over hundreds of thousands of years of evolution, we have developed mental shortcuts—known as *heuristics*—that allow us to deal with unfamiliar situations. For most of the history of the human species, these shortcuts have served us fairly well, largely because we did not encounter completely unfamiliar situa333333tions very often and because we lived in a world where predictable patterns of behavior were enforced by economic and social realities. Over the past three centuries, however, the diversity of situations that we encounter has increased dramatically, as has the underlying complexity of the world that produced them. Heuristics that once enhanced fitness now often detract from it. As a result, understanding what heuristics are failing us and why can be an important source of insights with respect to what the practitioner and the graduating student needs to know.

In order to view the informing process in its entirety, we need to examine three elements of the process: 1) what we mean by a mental model, 2) how these models change, and 3) how the messages we send influence that change. This chapter begins a three chapter examination of informing processes. Our focus here is on what we mean by mental models. In Chapter 6, we examine how these models change. Finally, in Chapter 7, we consider how the form of the information we receive influences these changes.

Throughout the chapter, I will employ a conceptual scheme advanced by Alan Newell and Herbert Simon (1972; Newell, 1990) in their landmark book *Human Problem Solving*. The field of cognitive science has advanced considerably since that scheme was proposed—particularly in its understanding of non-symbolic processes and neuroscience—but the basic model still provides a useful framework for organizing and understanding the higher level processes of information processing and learning.

The Problem Space

A mental model is the representation, maintained within our minds, that holds our understanding of how a particular piece of the world works. If you believe, for example, that basketball players develop a "hot hand" that causes them to sink baskets at a higher rate than normal, then that is part of your mental model of the game of basketball. The model does not have to be correct[2]; it is simply what you believe. Effective informing occurs when an informer changes a client's mental model in some intended way; ineffective informing occurs when the client's model changes in an unintended manner (known as *misinforming*[3]) and *no informing* occurs when a client's mental models are unaffected by the process.

The mental model associated with a particular task or other goal-directed activity is often referred to as a *problem space*. Since nearly all business education involves decision situations, we will henceforth assume that the client mental models that we are interested in changing through our informing efforts are also problem spaces.

A problem space can be defined as follows:

> *Definition:* A *problem space* is a representation of the cognitive system that will be used to perform a task "described in terms of (1) a set of *states of knowledge*, (2) *operators* for changing one state into another, (3) constraints on applying operators, and (4) *control knowledge* for deciding what knowledge to apply next." (Card, Moran, & Newell, 1983, p. 87)

To organize our problem space, we will describe the set of knowledge states as the *state space* and the set of operators, constraints, and control knowledge as the *operator space*. We will also assume the existence of a *goal space*, containing specialized operators (i.e., estimates-of-fitness) that allow the task performer to assess the fitness of a particular state space with respect to task goals and to determine relative progress towards these goals.

The simplified cognitive architecture that we will be using in this book is presented in Figure 5.1. It begins with the almost universally accepted premise that we have two forms of memory: *long term memory*, which holds knowledge for a very long time, and *working memory*, which represents that portion of our knowledge that we are actively attending. Working memory performs a dual purpose. It processes incoming information and, some of the time, it may then enable that information to be stored in long term memory where it can later be recalled and used. Working memory also holds information recalled from long term memory in order that it can be further processed. This is the activity we would commonly refer to as *thinking* or *deliberating*. It is important to note that in the model presented, all conscious activity takes place in working memory. Long term memory is simply an associative storage unit, meaning that retrieval is accomplished through past associations with the contents of working memory. Long term memory does not, on its own, process any information nor is retrieval as reliable as it would be in more structured storage systems, such as a computer database.

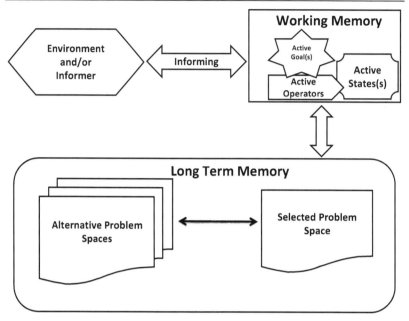

Figure 5.1: Simplistic task performance architecture. Adapted from Willingham (2009, p. 11).

Ignoring informing processes for the time being, one of the greatest challenges presented by the human cognitive system is the fact that working memory has a very limited capacity. What this means is that it may not be possible to fit an entire problem space into working memory at any given time—although we have evolved some mechanisms (discussed in Chapter 6) to reduce the impact of this limitation. Thus, problem solving and other forms of task performance may involve continuously retrieving and storing pieces of the problem space. Generally, this is done by moving information to and from long term memory. Sometimes, however, we reduce that cognitive load by offloading the information to the environment. Why try to do long division entirely in your head when you can write down intermediate results on paper so you can easily retrieve them later?[4]

An important aspect of Figure 5.1 is the notion that a particular task might have more than one problem space that may be applicable. This is particularly true for tasks that are unfamiliar. In mathematics, for example, students may be able to solve an equation presented to them yet fail to perform precisely the same exercise presented as a word problem. Identifying the problem space appropriate to a particular task case can therefore be an important aspect of task performance.

To clarify the overall problem space concept, let us now examine several sample tasks and consider how they can be described in problem space terms.

A Chess Game

Although chess is a challenging game to play well, it is relatively easy to describe in problem space terms. Indeed, many of the early experiments in human information processing involved chess[5].

The *state space* in chess involves representing the position of the various pieces on the board. In this context, there are two observations to be made. First, the actual mental representation used to store board positions does not appear to be anything like a snapshot of the actual board. Expert chess players, for example, demonstrate an extraordinary ability to recall actual game board positions after a brief inspection; that ability disappears when the pieces are simply placed randomly on the board (Charness, 1991). Second, the state space not only represents the current board position, it is also used to visualize possible future board positions. In order to play chess competently, you need to look several moves ahead, anticipating possible opponent responses to each move you are considering.

The *operator space* in chess is the simplest part of the problem space. It holds the rules for changing the state space, which is to say the knowledge of how each piece moves. As expertise grows, it also holds memorized sequences of moves. For example, your typical chess master knows by name many classic opening sequences.

The *goal space* contains heuristic rules for evaluating board positions. Using the terminology employed in the previous chapters, these are estimates-of-fitness. Soon after novices start learning to play chess, they are given rules for valuing pieces: 1 point for pawns, 3 points for bishops and knights, 5 points for rooks and 10 points for the queen. These allow the player to make a crude evaluation of the fitness of different board positions. They may also be given other rules, such as control the center of the board, don't expose your queen too early in the game, and so forth. Using these rules, they can make comparisons of alternative board outcomes as they look ahead in the game.

Experts and intermediate players appear to apply a similar process as they play the game. Once players reach an intermediate level, the number of moves they look ahead appears to flatten out. Where grand masters appear to excel, however, is in their enhanced ability to overlook moves that are unsuitable without conscious thought (Charness, 1991). Stated another way, they develop vastly improved board position estimates-of-fitness, making expertise closely tied to increasing sophistication of the goal space for this particular task.

Medical Diagnosis

A very different problem space can be constructed in the domain of medical diagnosis. Like chess, this domain has been studied extensively, particularly in the expert systems subfield of artificial intelligence.

The state space in diagnosis includes, but is not limited to, four distinct types of knowledge. The first is specific knowledge that maps symptoms to various underlying causes, including information on the relative likelihood of the causes. The second is general knowledge of body systems and medical systems that can be used to generate conclusions and hypotheses in situations where mappings from symptoms are inconclusive. The third is cost-related information, reflecting how much money, time, risk, and patient discomfort/inconvenience is associated with different actions. The fourth type of state space knowledge involves the acquired ability to translate what is observed into knowledge that can be employed in the diagnosis process. For example, listening to a patient's heart would be a fruitless exercise if you do not have training with respect to what a normal and abnormal beat sounds like.

The operator space consists of the set of tests, observations, questions, or other actions (such as a referral) that the physician can use to acquire information during the diagnosis process. As was the case for possible moves on the chess board, the impact of any of these operators on the state space cannot be fully determined, since the results of applying a diagnostic operator cannot be known prior to actually invoking the operator. Otherwise, it would not qualify as a diagnostic operator.

The goal space for diagnosis consists of the set of possible conditions that the physician may look for. It may also include other goals; the "avoid getting sued" goal, for example, might cause the physician to practice defensive medicine and order a full battery of tests even where they do not appear to be fully justified by the initial set of symptoms.

The diagnosis task is likely to begin with a general information gathering goal, where the patient fills out a checklist that provides background information. Where an unusual pattern is detected[6], a particular diagnosis that would explain the pattern may be triggered immediately, in which case the goal of verifying or rejecting that specific conclusion would be moved into working memory and subsequent operators would be chosen based on their ability to confirm or disconfirm the diagnosis. This would continue until sufficient evidence supporting the diagnosis was obtained or until the likelihood that the diagnosis would be confirmed becomes sufficiently low so that pursuing other possible diagnoses are activated as alternative goals. For example, when a patient comes in showing obvious symptoms of the flu, a doctor's first line of questioning and tests are likely to revolve around confirming or rejecting a flu diagnosis.

Where no diagnosis immediately suggests itself, the process proceeds with the gathering of additional information. In this case, the operators to be applied are likely to be selected based upon balancing the likelihood that they will detect useful information with the cost of applying them. Ideally, low cost tests with a high likelihood of obtaining useful information would be performed first. After such tests are exhausted, the physician might proceed to low cost options that detect something unusual or to higher cost options that detect more common underlying causes. Physicians are given considerable training in this process, since the interpretation of test results is not necessarily straightforward[7].

Unlike a game of chess, the diagnosis process does not necessarily have a definitive end point. The condition causing a patient's symptoms, for example, may be outside the physician's personal set of problem spaces. It might, for example, prove to be a rare or unknown disease. Like the game of chess, on the other hand, low cost estimates-of-fitness that reflect the match between the accumulated evidence and possible diagnoses for a particular patient would be very valuable in deciding when to end the task.

Writing a Business Plan

Our final example differs from the previous two in that it is less well defined; it can be described as a *low structure problem*. Let us assume that you are an engineer who has just developed a new product and you want to create a business plan for a startup company based around the product. Let us also assume that this is your first business plan.

As is the case for virtually all low structure tasks, neither the state space, the operator space, nor the goal space starts out very well defined. This, however, does not prevent the task from being performed. It simply means that instead of task-specific knowledge we need to apply general purpose operators. Examples of such operators might include:

1. Identify and buy a book on < specific topic> and read it

2. Search the internet for <specific topic>

3. Identify and acquire software designed to assist in <specific topic>

4. Identify and ask an expert on <specific topic>

In this case, we just substitute "writing a business plan" for <specific topic> and the operators can be used to get us started.

Having these operators available is not sufficient to begin performing the task. We also need a means of choosing which to apply and in what sequence. Whenever economists are confronted with a choice situation, they postulate the existence of a utility function[8]. What such a function does is to capture the preferences of the decision-maker. The highest utility option wins.

Stated another way, a utility function acts as the estimate-of-fitness used to make choices. There are many factors that could come into play here; in low structure tasks there is virtually never a "correct" choice. You may enjoy browsing bookstores, in which case the first option may be preferred. Because Option 2 is so easy, you may decide to apply that operator first before making any additional decisions. You may not have the money to hire a consultant, in which case Option 4 would seem unattractive. On the other hand, you may personally know someone, such as a neighbor or former instructor, who has done a lot of business planning and who might give you some quick advice at no charge.

After applying the initial operators, the task-specific state space should begin to take shape. Conceptually, the state space mirrors the actual document being prepared, in organization and content. Thus, if a book gives you a particular business plan outline that you like (again, the utility function serving to estimate state space fitness comes into play), that may become the basis of your state space.

As the task progresses, the state space becomes increasingly well developed. In some cases, new subtasks may emerge. If you are not familiar with creating financial projections, for example, acquiring such familiarity may become an entirely new low structure subtask. The operators you apply now revolve around writing the plan content; these draw upon the generalized writing skills you acquired throughout your education as well as that product-specific knowledge that you have. Meanwhile, as the task progresses you continually estimate the fitness of what you have created, with additional problem solving efforts being directed at portions where you assess fitness to be unsatisfactory.

Having drafted a complete plan (or complete plan section) that you view to be of acceptable fitness, you will probably—if you are wise—try to find some friends or other outsiders who are willing to read your plan and offer you their own estimates of its fitness. Based upon their comments, you will likely revisit your own estimates and do some rewriting. Finally, you will send the plan out to one or more potential funding sources who, based upon their own estimate-of-fitness for the plan, will decide whether to fund it.

What this example shows, as did the previous two examples, is the critical role that good estimates-of-fitness can play in task performance. In the two preceding chapters, we saw how fitness estimates (i.e., college rankings, market value of firms) seem to make their way into practice more readily than theory-of-fitness. The examples just presented help explain why.

Heuristics for Low Structure Tasks

Why take on a low structure task? From a species survival standpoint, the benefits are obvious. By our willingness to confront the unknown, we may stumble on to an unexplored region of high fitness. When many of us do this, we end up distributing ourselves over the fitness landscape. What such a distribution accomplishes, in turn, is resilience in the face of landscape changes. As a consequence, individuals receptive to low structure tasks should survive at a higher rate than the general population when the landscape is dynamic. This means the trait should eventually become imprinted into the utility functions of a substantial fraction of the population. The more dynamic the fitness landscape, the faster this will happen.

The eagerness to explore is an example of an *evolutionarily stable strategy*, meaning that it can reach a steady state even when imprinted on some—but not all—of a population. The reason for this is that the strategy of avoiding low structure activities and, instead, focusing on efficiency can also produce high survival rates (so long as the environment does not change too rapidly). As a result, we could expect to see a population become increasingly dominated by "efficiency" specialists while the environment remains relatively static. From time to time, however, the "adapter" proportion surviving will spike when environmental change disrupts existing patterns of fitness. This tradeoff between focused efficiency vs. adaptability will be revisited many times as the book proceeds.

Fundamental Drives

In order to perform low structure tasks, we need to begin somewhere. One starting point is to postulate a set of built-in sources of utility. Paul Lawrence and Nitin Noria (2002), for example, propose that there are four fundamental drives that have become imprinted into the human cognitive system in such a manner. These are:

1. The drive to acquire
2. The drive to bond
3. The drive to learn
4. The drive to defend

In evolutionary economics, these drives principally act through the individual's utility function. Unlike many economic axioms, the utility maximization assumption is inherently reasonable (and largely definitional); if an individual makes a choice that seems irrational, we can simply blame it on a badly constructed utility function.

Each of the four drives can manifest itself in a number of specific ways, both individually and in interaction with the other drives. For example, the drive to acquire includes a component *drive to win or dominate*—that is, to achieve a high relative position in the outcome of activities. From an evolutionary perspective, this makes great sense. As Nobel Laureate Amartya Sen points out, even in a famine there is always some food;

that food is likely to be accessible only to those with the highest relative status (Lawrence & Noria, 2002, p. 67). It can also be used to explain the Easterlin paradox (Clark, Frijters, & Shields, 2008), where absolute income seems to have little impact on average happiness across nations, yet relative income within a nation does impact the individual's happiness.

When drives interact, new component drives can emerge. For example, the drive to acquire and the drive to bond lead to a *drive for fairness*. Much acquisition can be accomplished only in cooperation with others. Try to build a house entirely your own! Yet bonding comes with a price. Individuals become increasingly unwilling to cooperate with someone who only looks out for his or her own acquisitive interests. At the same time they recognize that a need to acquire is a necessary force if any progress is to be made. As a consequence, each of us develops a personal concept of what constitutes a fair exchange. Within that range, we tolerate satisfying another individual's desire to acquire part of what is ours (e.g., a salesperson trying to negotiate a higher price) without triggering our drive to defend—which could lead us to walk away (a.k.a. flight) or strike out (a.k.a. fight).

It is relatively easy to construct situations where the interaction between drives leads to behaviors that are counterproductive to all involved. Perhaps the most famous of these is the Prisoner's Dilemma (Axelrod, 1984). A typical scenario might be described as follows. Two miscreants are picked up by the police. The police know that they participated jointly in a crime and have enough evidence to convict them. The police do not, however, have enough evidence to convict the two on the most severe of the charges. The police separate the two and provide each one independently the same set of choices:

1. If neither of you confesses, you will both likely get 2 years in prison.

2. If both of you confess, you will both get 5 years in prison.

3. If you confess and your partner does not, your partner will get 15 years in prison, you will get parole.

4. If your partner confesses and you do not, you will get 15 years in prison and your partner will get parole.

The problem this presents is that the "best" outcome, in terms of total years in prison, is the first—no one confesses (4 years total). From the individual's perspective, however, you always do much better by confessing than not confessing (e.g., 0 years versus 2 years if your partner does not confess, 5 years versus 15 years if your partner confesses). Thus, unless you trust your partner very much, you end up in option 2.

As discussed at greater length in the next chapter, low structure situations are far more likely to produce drive-directed behavior than routine tasks. An excellent illustration of this principle was offered by Ori and Rom Brofman (2008) in *Sway*. They describe an exercise used by a Harvard Business School professor in a negotiations class that I will now summarize. The protocol for the exercise is as follows:

- The professor holds out a $20 bill. He tells the students that he will hold an auction where the students will have the opportunity to bid for it.

- The rules of the bidding are that the winner gets the $20 bill, less whatever he or she bids. The second highest bidder, however, must pay the professor the full amount of the losing bid (actually, the money goes to charity when the exercise ends, unbeknownst to the students).

- He starts the bidding.

While the bidding is low, students do not realize that this "opportunity" is actually a trap. Once it reaches the $12-$16 range, however, the true nature of the game becomes clear. At this point everyone but the two highest bidders drops out because this is a game that you do not want to play. Quickly, the desire to acquire—that initiated the process—is replaced by the desire to defend, which translates to not being the second highest bidder. Much like the prisoner's dilemma, a participant always does better ($19 better, to be precise) by bidding $1 over the bid of his or her competitor. The result is that bidding tends to go well over $20. In fact, the highest bid recorded was $204.

The key point of this exercise is that once you understand it, you will never again participate[9]. That is why it is so important to distinguish our reactions to situations that we do not understand from those for routine situations where we have developed specific and presumably more "rational" rules.

Drives Supporting Low Structure Problem Solving

Of the four basic drives, the third, the drive to learn, would naturally tend to encourage an individual to seek activities—such as low structure tasks—that are likely to lead to learning. Using the problem space conceptual scheme, we can look at the learning drive as consisting of at least three interrelated component drives:

- *Curiosity.* Humans are naturally curious (Willingham, 2009). It has been posited to be the result of an information gap (Loewenstein, 1994), where curiosity is maximized when the gap is neither too small nor too large. This idea of curiosity being maximized within bounds is consistent with earlier research describing what is *interesting* (Davis, 1971). In our conceptual scheme, curiosity can be characterized as an intrinsic desire to add knowledge to the state space.

- *Control.* Humans appear to have a strong drive towards control (Gilbert, 2007). In the problem space model, control is exerted by applying operators, so the desire for new forms of control would encourage the expansion of that space.

- *Feedback.* Feedback has long been recognized as an important source of intrinsic motivation (e.g., Hackman & Oldham, 1980). In our model, such feedback could either be used to refine the contents of the state and operator space or it could serve as a source of fitness estimates, allowing for increasing refinement of the goal space.

The utility offered by undertaking these activities motivates acceptance of low structure tasks, well before specific goals and task-specific knowledge have been acquired. General purpose heuristics are also available to aid in low structure tasks. Some of these are now discussed.

State Space Heuristics

The space-state challenges presented by low structure tasks are mapping observations to existing knowledge, weighing the validity of what we have seen, and drawing conclusions rapidly, often with a small amount of information. We appear to have a number of built in shortcuts—referred to as *heuristics*—that have been widely observed in experimental settings. We now consider some of these.

Judgment by Representativeness (e.g., Teigen, 2004; Tversky & Kahneman, 1982c). Representativeness is a mental shortcut that we use to avoid the need for extensive data gathering. It involves acquiring a small amount of information that is then mapped to some pre-existing schemata—a representative case—after which our actions and conclusions are based upon the representative case. Consider the following example:

> You observe a person on the pavement who appears to be talking to himself. He is alone but smiling and gesturing. You decide that he is probably crazy. (Teigen, 2004, p. 165)

This example also illustrates the limitations inherent in representativeness. If an additional piece of information is provided or observed—that the individual was wearing a cellular phone ear piece—we might reach a radically different conclusion. Indeed, viewed in the context of a later time period (e.g., 2008 vs. 2004), many of us might have jumped to the cellular phone conclusion initially—since most of us have probably already observed such behavior.

Availability (e.g., Reber, 2004). Availability is characterized as making decisions based upon that information that is readily available to the task performer. Since availability, in turn, can be influenced by salience (i.e., how vivid the information is) and recency (Tversky & Kahneman, 1982a), judgments that are based on availability can be significantly influenced by factors that are outside of the domain of the task. The availability effect can work in two ways. First, it can occur in conjunction with representativeness; readily available examples become the most likely to be accessed as being representative. Second, it can lead to a pronounced *recency effect*—also known as the serial position effect (Frensch, 1994)—in which the client recall for information acquired at the beginning and end of the informing process is amplified in comparison with that information transferred in the middle of the process.

Confirmation Heuristic (e.g., Oswald & Grosjean, 2004). We tend to search for and interpret information that confirms to our existing schemata. As a consequence, where information is encountered that supports our existing mental models, we are likely to interpret it as being entirely consistent with those models and give it substantial weight.

Recognition Heuristic (Gigerenzer, 2004). New information may include a mixture of familiar and unfamiliar content. The recognition heuristic posits that when the two forms of information are comingled, the recognized information will be given much greater weight in subsequent decision-making. An interesting demonstration of this heuristic occurred when separate groups of U.S. and German students were asked the question "Which city has more inhabitants: San Diego or San Antonio." Most U.S. students got the answer correct. What was more remarkable was the performance of the German students:

> ...most Germans know little about San Diego, and many have not even heard of San Antonio... Despite a considerable lack of knowledge, 100 percent of the Germans answered the question correctly. How can people who know less about a subject nevertheless make more correct inferences? The answer is that the Germans used a fast and frugal heuristic: the recognition heuristic: If you recognize the name of one city but not the other, then infer that the recognized city has the larger population. The Americans could not use that heuristic because they had heard of both cities... (Gigerenzer, 2004, p. 68)

Pattern detection heuristics (Mlodinow, 2008; Tversky & Kahneman, 1982b): When observing phenomena, we tend to detect patterns very quickly. Viewed in a not-so-positive light, this leads to biases such as the *gambler's fallacy* and *the "law" of small numbers*.

Operator Space Heuristics

There are two categories of operators that seem to be particularly well-suited to low structure tasks. The first is operators that take existing knowledge to form new knowledge. The second is operators that winnow down a large set of alternatives.

Creating new knowledge from existing knowledge

A very important set of knowledge schemata in the state space is assertions of truth. These serve as the raw material upon which many operators act. There are a number of types of operators that we can use to obtain new truths from old truths. We now consider three categories of these: mathematical/deductive, inductive, and abductive.

Mathematical/Deductive Operators: These operators take one or more assumed truths and, through symbolic manipulation, come up with new truths. For example, if you are assumed to have $1000 in period 1 that you want to save for a year and are being given 10% interest, compounded annually with no taxes, then we can derive the new assumption that you will have $1100 a year after period 1. Similarly, if we assume that A implies B and that B implies C, we can then derive the new relationship that A implies C by applying the deduction operator.

Unlike induction and abduction, the mathematical operators—properly applied—are not heuristics in the sense that they guarantee correctness. Thus, what is heuristic about them tends to be the assumptions necessary to put knowledge into a form that is tractable. We have noted, for example, that actual human behavior differs from the behaviors assumed by mathematical economists. It is, however, necessary to assume the behaviors of the economic man, referred to by Richard Thaler (2000) as *homo economicus*, in order to build the elegant theories that the field is famous for.

The other difference between mathematical/deductive techniques and the other heuristic techniques is that humans do not appear to have any innate capacity for this type of reasoning. Thus, to apply these operators effectively, the individual will need some formal training in mathematics and logic.

Induction. Induction is the process of generalizing knowledge from a set of observations. A variety of techniques may be employed in this process. Categorization and taxonomies are often used initially. Statistical methods, such as multiple regression, and even computational approaches[10] can be applied as the set of observations grows larger.

The title of *The Black Swan* (Taleb, 2007) signifies the problem inherent with generalizing from a known set of data. As mentioned in Chapter 1, in Europe, all the swans that anyone had ever seen were white. That seemed to provide a good basis for asserting, as fact, that swans were necessarily white. The weakness in this approach is that it did not even recognize the possibility that swans of a different color might be found elsewhere. As it turns out, black swans were then found in Australia.

Abduction. The most heuristic of the techniques, abduction asserts causality based on as little as one observation. Take a simple example. Suppose you were a Native American in what is today New England and your happened to be growing corn as your major food source. One day, late summer, you walk into your field and you notice that the corn in one area of the field is much higher, and more robust, than in the rest of the field. You go over to that portion of the field and, on the ground, you notice some fish bones. That reminds you of a gathering you had in late May where some of the participants had tossed the remains of the fish that they were eating onto that portion of the field that you were tending. At the time, you were quite annoyed. Now, however, you conclude that scattering fish bones on a field increases the yield of corn. Thus, you have assumed causality based on a relationship you observed.

Abduction provides a very robust tool for generating new relationships. Its principle weakness is that a huge proportion of the relationships generated through abduction are later likely to prove false. Causality is a tricky thing to prove. Correlations can be coincidental, a result of shared relationships (e.g., B appears to cause C based upon observed relationships where, in fact, A causes B and A causes C, causing both B and C to occur at the same time) and causality may act in the reverse direction (e.g., users who work with an information system every day may report it is easy to use; does that mean: a) perceived-ease-of-use causes daily usage, or b) daily usage causes perceived-ease-of-use? Or does it mean neither of the above?).

One well established consequence of applying abduction is that individuals frequently perceive their actions have caused a particular outcome even when logic suggests there was no causal link. The phenomenon is referred to as *illusions of control* (e.g., Thompson, 2004, p. 119). For example, in a laboratory study subjects were asked to assess whether pressing a computer's space bar influenced whether an X appeared on the screen as (opposed to an O). They had 40 trials and could choose, in each case, whether or not to press the bar. Unbeknownst to the subjects, the space bar had no influence on what characters appeared. Despite this fact, subject perceptions of the degree of control they were exerting were much higher when 75% Xs appeared (meaning that many of the space bar presses coincided with an X) than when 25% Xs appeared (meaning that most presses did not coincide with an X).

Visceral influences also appear to exert an influence over this particular illusion: depressed people have a reduced sense of control, whereas individuals in a positive mood are more likely to experience this illusion. Similarly, individuals having a high level of desire for a particular task outcome tend to perceive that they have control (Thompson, 2004).

Given the inherent weaknesses of abduction, you would expect that serious scientists would never apply it. This does not seem to be the reality. In the last chapter, I pointed out the peculiar case of mathematical economics—a field whose underlying assumptions are being increasingly called into question by experimental research. The field remains viable based upon reasoning such as the following:

(1)   Assumptions of "rational" behavior lead to a series of predictions, such as general equilibrium

(2)   We have observed some behaviors consistent with these behaviors in actual economies

(3)   Therefore, the assumptions we have made are justified in a practical sense, and the "anomalies" observed in experiments are just that—behaviors so atypical in real world settings that they can be safely ignored.

This is a classic abductive argument since it ignores the possibility that some other explanation—other than homo economicus—may actually produce the resulting observed behaviors. We should also be careful not to single out economists in this regard. According to Thomas Kuhn (1971), the natural sciences have never seen a case where an existing paradigm was abandoned before a competing paradigm was available to displace it. In other words, simply discovering that our abduction does not work is insufficient to cause us to discard it. In Chapter 6, we refer to this extreme reluctance to renounce existing beliefs as the *Law of Abandoned Expertise*.

Choosing between many alternatives

Many generic strategies specifically designed to reduce the cognitive load of choice problems have been observed or proposed (e.g., Payne, Bettman, & Johnson, 1993). In such problems, individuals are presented with a set of alternatives, each of which has attributes that impact an alternative's attractiveness. Some of the most important choice heuristics (adapted from the list provided by Payne et al., 1993, p. 25-29) include:

- *Equal weight heuristic* (Einhorn & Hogarth, 1975): Alternatives are compared across all relevant attributes, with each attribute being given an equal weight.

- *Satisficing* (Simon, 1955): Alternatives are considered until a predetermined or adaptively determined cut point for fitness is reached.

- *Lexicographic heuristic* (Tversky, 1969): Alternatives are compared across the most important attribute and only those at the top are retained. Then the second most important attribute is considered and the process continues until only one alternative remains.

- *Elimination by aspects* (Tversky, 1972): Similar to lexicographic comparison, alternatives are compared across the most important attribute and only those meeting a desired cut point are retained. Then the second most important attribute is considered and the process continues until only one alternative remains.

- *Majority of confirming dimensions* (Russo & Dosher, 1983): Alternatives are pair-wise compared attribute by attribute and the choice with the greatest number of winners is retained for comparison with the next alternative.

- *Frequency of good and bad features* (Alba & Marmorstein, 1987): The positive and negative attributes of each alternative are counted. Choice can then be made based on the fewest number of bad features or the largest number of good features.

These options generally assume that no overall estimate-of-fitness is available but that some estimates of the desirability of individual attributes can be made. As a consequence, these would tend to be generally bad approaches to choice-making unless the fitness landscape is decomposable. The one exception to this is Simon's (1955) satisficing, which assumes an overall fitness estimate or value is available. Not surprisingly, that particular heuristic seems to be the only one that has its origins outside of a laboratory setting.

Goal Space Heuristics

In the three previous examples, we saw how the contents of the goal space—particularly our ability to estimate fitness of solutions as the task was being performed—was crucial in determining the effectiveness of our task performance. The problem with very low structure tasks, however, is that we often have few insights into fitness when we begin.

How, for example, do you gauge the attractiveness of a new product that is dissimilar to all previous products, such as the Ipod when it was first introduced?

In examining the goal space, we need to move away from an implicit assumption included in the descriptions of the state and operator spaces, that of *symbolic processing*. Assuming the use of symbols, such as words and images, is a convenient abstraction when considering the representation and processing of information. It also fits nicely with our conscious perceptions of how we think; we reason things out using language (a symbolic form of expression), we manipulate these symbols using symbolic rule systems such as algebra and logic, and we visualize and transform images in our head when we design things. Unfortunately, symbols do not serve as nearly as well when it comes to how we make choices and judgment. For these types of goal-based activities, absolutely critical in the performance of low structure tasks, strength of feelings or intuitions often prove to be a better description of what guides us.

At the outset, it is important to recognize that although a great deal of research has been conducted on the nature and source of human preferences, what we do not yet know is far greater than what we do know. Chances are that fields such as cognitive neuroscience will eventually help us figure out how the brain's architecture handles utility. For the time being, the best we can do is to construct a conceptual scheme that organizes what we know as well as possible. That scheme is based upon connectionism.

Connectionist Models

Connectionism takes a very different—although not incompatible—view of cognition from symbolic models. It is based upon the presumed architecture of the brain. That architecture involves processing units, known as neurons, that transmit signals to many other *neurons* through structures called *axons* and receive transmissions through structures called *dendrites*. The signals transmitted are both electrical and chemical in nature. There are hundreds of billions of these neurons, each of which is typically connected to thousands of other neurons. Sensation, cognition, and consciousness are all emergent properties of this architecture; we do not yet know precisely why these capabilities emerge. The human brain is truly the ultimate complex system.

Since the late 1950s, attempts have been made to build computing systems based around the way the brain appears to be organized. Some of the earliest cognitive models, such as Oliver Selfridge's (1958) *Pandemonium*, focused on word identification and employed a detector-accumulator model[11]. This type of model consists of connected elements (nodes) that can be excited or inhibited by signals from other elements. These nodes, which are intended to mimic the neurons in the brain[12], may adapt to serve a number of different roles, including:

- *Feature detection*, where connections to sensory and other cognitive systems cause the node to become excited when a particular pattern is detected[13].

- *Accumulation*, where a node accumulates signals from other nodes.

- *Comparison*, where signals from other nodes are detected and a signal in some way related to the difference is generated.

In addition, the linkages between nodes can either excite or inhibit the activation of the nodes to which they are connected. The strengths of the signals that pass through the links are also weighted. Excitation of one node will have a strong effect on a node to which it is connected when the linkage has a high weight, yet will exert a very low impact on a similarly connected node where the connection weight is low. Learning in such a computational architecture is presumed to occur mainly through a continuous process of changing the weights on the linkages.

A simple, and as it turns out inadequate, model for utility would be to assume that various detectors (such as those for the four drives and other learned sources of utility, such as money) exist in the brain and that they are connected to an accumulator node that sums their signals and represents utility. This architecture is presented in Figure 5.2, which is similar to a computational device known as a *perceptron*.

Unfortunately, the perceptron architecture had a flaw. In a landmark book, Marvin Minsky and Seymour Papert (1969) demonstrated mathematically that there were a great many types of patterns, such as the exclusive OR (one and only one unit is sending a signal above a certain threshold), that a perceptron simply could not learn. With this book, the two scientists nearly destroyed the emerging science of connectionism. In fact, what they were demonstrating is basically the same problem that occurs when you try to fit a decomposable fitness function to a rugged landscape.

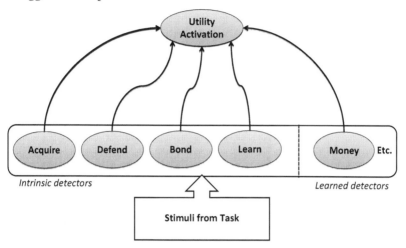

Figure 5.2 Perceptron-style connectionist model of utility

As it turns out, however, the accumulator-detector architecture is perfectly capable of learning to recognize very complex patterns[14]. You simply need to add layers of intermediate nodes that, in effect, store information relating to interactions. When this fact became widely recognized in the early 1980s, the field of connectionism—also known as neural networks—experienced a rebirth and is, today, widely used in pattern detection problems. The multi-layer architecture is conceptualized in Figure 5.3.

Since we will address learning in the next chapter, for now let us look at the case where we are attempting to evaluate the utility of an unfamiliar choice. In this case, we would expect that detectors would exist for characteristics satisfying the basic drives (i.e., acquire, defend, learn, bond) as well as other more specialized detectors that have been acquired as we grew up. For example, there is considerable evidence that we detect and react differently to choices where money (in the form of cash) is involved (Ariely, 2008). These detectors, in turn, feed through as series of layers to an overall valence node, summing all the detected sources of utility and disutility (i.e., features we want to avoid). Because we also frequently find ourselves needing to make choices, we may also expect that comparator nodes—specifically aimed at distinguishing preferences between alternatives—are available.

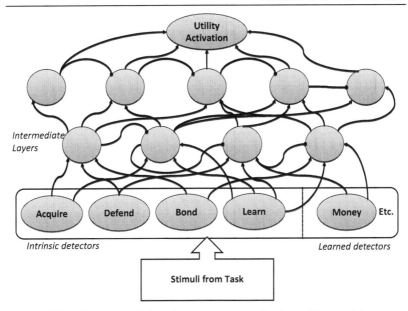

Figure 5.3: Conceptual drawing for connectionist utility architecture. Detectors at the bottom layer identify potential sources of utility, both intrinsic and learned. These are passed through multiple layers of node that allow non-linear responses to detected stimuli to be learned. The top node is activated according to the utility of an alternative.

There are two key things we need to recognize about an architecture of this type. First, it is not a *reasoning* architecture. Being transmitted between nodes are not text messages, they are just signals (e.g., electro-chemical impulses in the brain). In other words, this part of the cognitive architecture simply creates signals—feelings, if you will—based upon genetic pre-wiring and patterns that have been learned in the past. Second, the very structure of a connectionist network—lots of participating computational units, high levels of interactions between units, changes brought about by learning—guarantees that the system will acquire multiple combinations of inputs that lead to utility peaks. As a consequence, it is relatively easy to produce inconsistencies in our choices when the setting is unfamiliar. This is easily demonstrated through a series of examples.

Example 1: Framing. Consider the following two choice problems presented to experimental subjects (taken directly from Tversky & Kahneman, 1988, p. 173-174):

First choice problem:

> Assume yourself richer by $300 than you are today. You have to choose between:
>
> A.   A sure gain of $100
>
> B.   50% chance to gain $200 and 50% to gain nothing

Second choice problem:

> Assume yourself richer by $500 than you are today. You have to choose between:
>
> A.   A sure loss of $100
>
> B.   50% chance to lose nothing, 50% to lose $200

The actual results of this experiment were that most (72%) chose A in the first problem, while most (64%) chose B in the second. This distinct preference is inconsistent since options A and B across both choice problems lead to precisely the same outcomes: a $400 gain for option A, a 50-50 distribution between $300 and $500 for option B.

This is an example of a framing problem, which exploits the gain-loss asymmetry that most people exhibit. What this means is that the signal from a gain detector (associated with the "acquire" basic need) is weaker than the signal from the loss detector (associated with the "defend" basic need). As a consequence, if you frame a problem such that it appears to have a loss involved, we will try harder to avoid the loss than to achieve a gain. Similarly, we have a poorly developed sense of randomness. Thus, certainty produces a disproportionately strong signal when compared to some probability (even near certainty). A similar problem occurs at the low end of the scale—intuitively, we do not do well distinguishing a one in a thousand chance from a one in a million chance, which is why lotteries thrive.

Example 2: Anchoring. Anchoring effects (e.g., Mussweiler, Englich, & Strack, 2004) are similar to framing effects; they occur when some initial value or alternative encountered in the task—often relatively arbitrary in nature—impacts subsequent decision making. These effects can influence decisions in two ways: 1) they may present the sender a means of manipulating client preferences and decision making or 2) they may lead the sender to influence client preferences and decision-making inadvertently.

Anchoring frequently occurs as a consequence of detecting favorable comparisons and similar options among choices. Common effects involving three or more options include (Usher & McClelland, 2004):

- *Attraction:* Where three options are presented to a decision-maker and two are similar, with one clearly dominating the other, decision-maker preference tends to skew towards the dominant option in the pair, regardless of the characteristics of the third.

- *Similarity:* Where three options are presented and two are similar (with neither dominating), decision-maker preference skews towards the third, non-similar option.

- *Compromise:* Where three options are presented and one option could be viewed as a compromise between the other two, that option is disproportionately selected.

Illustrative examples of these types of effects abound in consumer marketing. For example, the "decoy effect," a variation of attraction, involves using one product model to anchor perceptions of another model. Consider the following example:

> When Williams-Sonoma first introduced a home "bread bakery" machine (for $275), most consumers were not interested. What was a home bread-making machine anyway? ... Flustered by poor sales, the manufacturer of the bread machine brought in a marketing research firm, which suggested a fix: introduce an additional model of the bread maker, one that was not only larger but priced about 50 percent higher than the initial machine.
>
> Now sales began to rise... [Consumers] could say, "Well, I don't know much about bread makers, but I do know that if I were to buy one, I'd rather have the smaller one for less money." And that's when bread makers began to fly off the shelves. (Ariely, 2008, p. 14-15)

Anchors can be even stranger, however. In a number of experiments, when students were asked to write down the last two digits of their social security numbers prior to being asked how much they would be willing to pay for selected items, it was clear that the social security number digits were influencing the prices they settled on (Ariely, 2008, p. 28).

Example 3: Priming. A particularly remarkable demonstration of the power of visceral influences influencing our fitness assessments can found in a phenomenon called *priming* (e.g., Gladwell, 2005). Priming occurs when mere exposure to certain words and behaviors prior to an activity exerts a strong impact on subsequent performance of that activity. Experimental psychologists use priming frequently; it proves to be a very useful tool in laboratory studies where the impact of emotional state on cognition or learning is being tested. Numerous examples exist of the phenomenon, which can be astonishingly powerful in its impact. For example:

> Two Dutch researchers did a study in which they had groups of students answer forty-two demanding questions from the board game Trivial Pursuit. Half were asked to take five minutes beforehand to think about what it means to be a professor and write down everything that came to mind. Those students got 55.6 percent of the questions right. The other half of the students were asked to first sit and think about soccer hooligans. They ended up getting 42.6 percent of the Trivial Pursuit questions right. The "professor" group didn't know any more than the "soccer hooligan" group. They were simply in a "smart" frame of mind... (Dijksterhuis & van Knippenberg, 1998, as cited in Gladwell, 2005, p. 56)

Priming can also impact how we experience and disambiguate stimuli—a critical element in informing processes. For example:

> ...volunteers in one study were told that they would be eating a delicious but unhealthy ice cream sundae (ice cream eaters), and others were told that they would be eating a bitter but healthful plate of fresh kale (kale eaters). Before actually eating these foods, the researchers asked volunteers to rate the similarity of a number of foods, including ice cream sundaes, kale, and Spam (which everyone considered both unpalatable and unhealthful). The results showed that ice cream eaters thought Spam was more like kale than it was like ice cream. Why? Because for some odd reason, ice cream eaters were thinking

about food in terms of its *taste*... On the other hand, kale eaters thought that Spam was more like ice cream than it was like kale. Why? Because for some odd reason, kale eaters were thinking about food in terms of its *healthfulness*... (Gilbert, 2007, pp. 159-160)

Example 4: Social influence. When attempting to estimate the value of a particular choice, a very plausible approach is to observe the preferences of others. We see evidence that individuals value such information in a number of contexts: in weekly box office scores for movies reported by many newspapers and newscasters, on web sites such as Amazon.com and Youtube.com where purchase ranks and number of views are reported, in the previously mentioned popularity of magazine issues ranking different educational institutions. Such a heuristic, in fact, seems to make perfect sense.

Knowledge of what other people are doing can have a significant impact on our behavior. For example, in one experiment (Cialidini, 2005), guests in a hotel were encouraged to recycle towels with one of three different messages:

I. HELP SAVE THE ENVIRONMENT.

You can show your respect for nature and help save the environment by reusing your towels during your stay.

II. PARTNER WITH US TO HELP SAVE THE ENVIRONMENT

In exchange for your participation in this program, we at the hotel will donate a percentage of the energy savings to a non-profit environmental protection organization. The environment deserves our combined efforts. You can join us by reusing your towels during your stay.

III. JOIN YOUR FELLOW GUESTS IN HELPING TO SAVE THE ENVIRONMENT

Almost 75% of guests who are asked to participate in our new resource savings program do help by using their towels more than once. You can join your fellow guests to help save the environment by reusing your towels during your stay.

The response clearly favored the third message, which was based on the social influence approach. (The rate of actual recycling for each message was 38%, 36% and 48% respectively). A similar result was found in a study of Minnesota tax compliance (Thaler & Sunstein, 2008; Coleman, 1996). A large number of Minnesotans were each sent letters encouraging them to comply with their taxes. The first letter justified complying on moral and ethical grounds. The second included the following text:

> According to a recent public opinion survey, many Minnesotans believe other people routinely cheat on their taxes. This is not true, however. Audits by the Internal Revenue Service show that people who file tax returns report correctly and pay voluntarily 93 percent of the income taxes they owe.

The second proved more effective, as measured by the smaller average size of their refunds, with the second letter averaging $45 less in refunds than the first (p<0.05).

One consequence of establishing personal preference in response to the preference of others is that it tends to enable phenomena referred to as *information cascades*. Described in greater detail in Chapter 8, what can happen when observed preferences are used to determine individual choice is that a small positive blip in preference in the early stages of a particular decision, such as going to a new restaurant or a movie, can influence more people to make that choice. These observed decisions, in turn, make the choice irresistible for even more people until the choice ends up disproportionately popular relative to its actual merits.

Example 5: Projection heuristic. The complement to using other people's preferences is making the assumption that other people's preferences mirror our own. This becomes important in decision-making situations where the potential behavior of others must be considered as part of the task. Absent strong evidence to the contrary, we frequently assume that others share our perspective. For example, many studies have found that a physician's own views regarding end-of-life treatments strongly influence his or her perceptions of what the patient wants; much more so than the patient's actual preferences (Chapman, 2004).

Example 6: Endowment effect. The asymmetry between our drive to acquire and drive to defend is illustrated particularly well by the fact that we seem to value what is in our possession much more highly than what is not. For example, Dan Ariely (2008, p. 130) conducted a survey of Duke students who had won tickets to a Final Four basketball game in a lottery and compared their asking price with the offering price of students in the lottery who had not won tickets. Those who had the tickets wanted about $2400 to sell; those without tickets were willing to pay only about $170.

Example 7: Money and price heuristics. Dan Ariely (2008) has documented a wide range of choice heuristics that specifically deal with money and price. Obviously, when our principle goal is to better understand informing business this domain is of considerable interest. As it turns out, many of these can reasonably be explained—or at least rationalized[15]—in terms of the fundamental drives operating within the goal space.

The effect of cold, hard cash: One particularly unusual set of effects Ariely demonstrated deals with the effects of cash as opposed to other forms of money (such as checks or credit cards). Specifically, we seem to be much more reluctant to part with it. This fact has long been recognized by the retail and credit industries; we tend to spend more when using credit cards than we would when using cash (Prelec & Simester, 2001) even when we pay our balances off each month. But it turns out that the effects are even more profound. For example, the presence of cash seems to make us more honest. Ariely (2008, p. 220-221) and his colleagues demonstrated this in an experiment in which students were asked to complete a simple 20 question math test and were offered payment for each question. The test was designed so that it would be nearly impossible to complete in the available 5 minutes and students were paid $0.50 per correct answer. Students graded their own work. There were three groups:

1. A control group that turned in their answer sheets for direct payment from the investigator.

2. A group that was told to tear up their answer sheet, to put it in their backpack, then to approach the investigator and report the score, after which they received direct payment.

3. A group that was instructed to tear up their answer sheets (following the instructions for group 2) after which they reported their score to one of the investigators, receiving tokens worth $0.50 each. They then had to walk about 12 feet to another investigator who took the tokens and exchanged them for cash.

Based on earlier versions of the experiments, the investigators knew that some cheating would take place in group 2. Consistent with this expectation, the second group reported an average of 6.2 questions right as opposed to 3.5 in the control group. What surprised them, however, was that the third group, differing from the second only in the use of tokens, reported an average of 9.4 questions right—a highly significant difference from the second group. Thus, the mere act of substituting tokens for cash appears to have increased dishonesty.

Using the fundamental drive conceptual scheme, it is relatively easy to produce a plausible explanation for these peculiar effects. Cash has the property of being difficult to come by yet easy to lose (either accidentally, as a result of theft or through impulsive behavior). We learn this quickly as children (or at least I did[16]). As a consequence, it would be entirely natural for the possession of cash to stimulate our defensive drive. That would make us loath to part with cash; far more so than would be the case for cash equivalents that could be replaced if lost. In addition, and here I admit to speculating, cheating seems to be an activity inconsistent with high defensive activation. From an evolutionary standpoint, the principal benefit we each accrue from laws and ethical codes is that they prevent others from taking advantage of us. Thus, when our defensive center is stimulated we may well prove less disposed to take advantage of others.

The effect of prices and "free": Ariely (2008, p. 182-183) and his colleagues conducted a number of other experiments that demonstrated some remarkable effects. With respect to prices, one experiment involved the effectiveness of pharmaceuticals, run on 100 Boston-area subjects. All the subjects were subjected to discomfort in the form of electric shocks. There were however two treatment groups. Both were initially given shocks with no treatment for pain. Then the groups were:

1. Given a placebo treatment for pain (actually a vitamin C pill) which, they were told, cost $2.50 a pill.

2. Given a placebo treatment for pain (actually a vitamin C pill) which, they were told, cost $0.10 a pill.

Both groups 1 and 2 reported less discomfort; this is the long recognized placebo effect. What was surprising, however, is that while nearly all the individuals in Group 1 reported relief, only half the individuals in Group 2 did. Thus, the stated price altered their perception of efficacy.

The second effect convincingly demonstrated by Ariely (2008, p. 52) is the power of "free" goods. In one experiment, he and his colleagues set up a candy table at which customers could purchase a single Lindy truffle (a high end chocolate) for $0.15 or a Hershey's Kiss (a less elite chocolate) for $0.01. Among those who purchased, 73% chose the truffle, 27% the Kiss. The experiment was then repeated, with the prices lowered by $0.01, making the truffle $0.14 and the Kiss free. The preferences were reversed—69% chose the Kiss, 31% the truffle. From a purely rational standpoint, such a reversal does not seem to make sense. After all, the difference in prices remained the same.

The explanations that I would propose for the seemingly contradictory effects of higher price producing higher efficacy while, at the same time, the lure of "free" seeming to be irresistible both involve the same underlying force: *price is inherently an estimate-of-fitness.*

Consider the following. Where you have absolutely no idea about the underlying fitness of the object being priced, then price becomes your only estimate of fitness. This was clearly the case for the non-existent drug. If a placebo effect exists, it is therefore reasonable to expect that it would be enhanced by price. By the same token, we would expect someone with little knowledge of jewelry but lots of money to be attracted to high priced items; people who know very little about underlying companies should be impressed by high flying companies. Indeed, when price is the only estimate-of-fitness that is available, we can expect high levels of volatility in situations where the market determines the price. We will consider the phenomenon further in Chapter 8, when information cascades are explored.

Another situation occurs where we have some underlying idea of the fitness of the object and a price estimate as well. Since Ariely's experiment did not interview students as to why they chose a particular chocolate, we do not know how familiar they were with respect to the two choices. Given that the experiment took place in the U.S., however, most were probably familiar with the ubiquitous Kiss while a much smaller number were familiar with the truffle. Unless they were quite familiar with both, however, the price likely contributed to their assessment of relative fitness. In this case, the $0.01 works against the Kiss, since it implies much lower estimate-of-fitness than the $0.15 truffle. Given the fact that the amounts involved were relatively trivial in any case, it is not surprising that the higher fitness estimate was more popular.

By making the Kiss free, on the other hand, price was eliminated as a plausible fitness estimator. As a consequence, participants needed to estimate the fitness of that choice using other means, such as past experience eating Kisses. In other words, moving from a low price to free removes a negative estimate-of-fitness from the equation.

All this changes, of course, when we are dealing with individuals who are highly knowledgeable about the item being priced. These individuals—such as the experienced commercial real estate investor buying a rental property—have their own independent techniques for estimating fitness. For them, choice is likely to be heavily dependent on the difference between the final price, which represents the prevailing (or seller's) estimate-of-fitness, and their own personal estimate. Where their own estimate is the higher of the two, the likelihood of a good value is great. The lure of "free" is also likely to be much reduced[17].

Are Our Heuristics Irrational?

With relatively few exceptions (e.g., Gigerenzer, 2004; Lo, 2005), the heuristics for handling low structure problems that I have just described are viewed very negatively, characterized as "biases" or "fallacies." In fact, it has been argued that that they collectively constitute such a systematic attack on the assumption of individual rationality that underlies most economic theory that we need to reconsider whether such theory is warranted (e.g., Ariely, 2009). While I am certainly in agreement with that last concern, I am hesitant about concluding that these "irrationalities" are necessarily "bad."

The problem here is one of context. If we assert that these behaviors are entirely negative in their effect, we are effectively arguing that traits that undermine fitness have become widely distributed across the population. This is inconsistent with any evolutionary explanation of how our utility preferences developed. Not only would this play havoc with the field of evolutionary economics, it would also leave us with some very quirky unexplained behaviors.

A better way of looking at the question involves complexity. If you consider the history of civilization, there have occasionally been local episodes of exceptional progress: the Greeks, the Romans, the Mayans, the Chinese all experienced such bursts, as have many other civilizations. The sustained progress of the past 500 or so years—a brief instant in evolutionary terms—has been without parallel, however. Starting in the west with the Renaissance and the printing press, then moving east more recently, advances in transportation, communication, computing, agriculture, medicine, and other areas have transformed the world. These advances have fundamentally altered the structure of our activities. Globalization and mass communication have us interacting with many more people than a 14th century farmer—who probably lived in a community of around 150 people[18]. Computing and rapid transportation also increase the pace at which these interactions occur.

In other words, over the past 500 years or so, we have seen dramatic changes in:

1. The number of people in the system

2. The degree of interconnectivity between them

3. The rate at which they can react to each other

All of this occurs, of course, in a dynamic technological and social environment. Thus, all the prerequisites for increasing complexity have been met.

The question then becomes, would today's heuristics have seemed so bad in a world of lesser complexity? To begin with, a great many of the preference anomalies that have been identified relate to randomness—failure to make the right choice under known odds. But, as Taleb (2007) points out many times in his book, situations where you actually know the odds you are encountering are rare. Moreover, much of the "randomness" we encounter today—particularly in financial systems such as the stock market—isn't really randomness at all. We simply treat the system behavior that way because we cannot predict it and so, from the observer's standpoint, it might as well be random. I'll refer to such systems as pseudo-random.

Many of the pseudo-random systems we encounter today, however, are quite recent in origin. Go back 1000 years—still a few ticks on an evolutionary scale—and far fewer of these systems existed. In fact, it wasn't until the mid-1500s that a formal understanding of randomness started to emerge (Mlodinow, 2008). I suggest that this was because, for the typical individual of the time, there was little need for one. Using Kauffman's (1993) model, when the complexity of a fitness landscape declines (e.g., fewer attributes, fewer interactions) what we see is a decline in both the number of peaks and a corresponding rise in their relative fitness. Thus, what we might anticipate is that the clustering of entities would be more pronounced.

Put in practical terms, while there might be considerable diversity across communities, we could expect to see stable patterns of uniformity develop within communities and clans—of dress, of religious beliefs, of behaviors; far more than we would likely see in communities of comparable size today. A similar pattern would likely exist for occupations, where a particular approach to fitness would be passed down through apprenticeships and observations.

Where these clusters of similarity existed, heuristics such as representativeness and availability would be much more effective. Learn where a person came from and you could tell a great deal about that person, particularly if you had met someone from there before. Knowing an individual's clan and occupation would similarly be more valuable during that period than they are today. Perhaps that is why location, clan, and occupation figure so prominently into our last names.

Even today, a person's specific occupation may tell you much more about him or her than you might initially suspect. Malcolm Gladwell's (2008) *Outliers*, for example, documents the progression of a cohort of Jewish lawyers—all of whose parents had worked in New York's garment district—that came to dominate a particular category of law firm on Wall Street. A similar phenomenon occurred in the high tech world, where an early exposure to computers combined with a birth date near 1955 is common to nearly all the individuals who achieved success as a result of the PC revolution. Even birth month can matter in sports contexts—being born in the first part of the year proves to be a *huge* advantage in Canadian hockey[19], where junior leagues are based upon age cohorts divided by age as of 31 December, so players born earlier in the year are older than their counterparts born at the end of the year[20]. To summarize, the mapping between individuals and occupations is certainly complex but may not be all that random.

An evolved asymmetry in preference for gains vs. losses would also be an understandable trait for much of human history. Up until very recently, the last century or two, the vast majority of humans were at or very close to subsistence. Under those circumstances, whatever the magnitude of a gain presented by an opportunity, it needed to be weighed against the non-survival that could result from a loss.

There is also another point to be considered. If we look back over the course of human history, I feel confident in asserting that the typical number of low structure decisions an individual would encounter over his or her lifetime would be quite low. For most people, geographic mobility was low, occupation was heavily influenced by birth, alternative prospects for a spouse were very limited (and often specified by parents), and even choice of belief system was not available—the punishments for heresy were not pleasant and an individual's failure to abide by social norms looked like witchcraft to a lot of people. Thus, since the heuristics described here are most useful in low structure decision-making, individuals would not have needed to resort to them very often.

Fast forwarding to today, the situation has totally changed. Low structure decision-making situations occur all the time. Our need for rapid decision-making has also increased, as a consequence of the pace of modern life. Under these circumstances, it makes a lot of sense to be on guard against decision-making rules that probably served a hunter-gatherer quite well but that present problems when applied to the typical fitness landscapes that we now face.

Conclusions

The particular emphasis of this chapter has been on low structure task performance. The conclusions are as follows:

1. Humans have many general purpose mental tools for addressing low structure tasks. As long as we have a reasonable estimator of how well we are doing—in other words, an estimate-of-fitness—we can perform even unfamiliar tasks.

2. The tools we use to perform low structure tasks provide many shortcuts, referred to as heuristics, that reduce the load we place on working memory—the scarcest resource in the human information processing system. A particularly pronounced theme of these heuristics is that they encourage us to view new knowledge as being consistent with what we already know. Unfortunately, as the world becomes increasingly complex, the adequacy of these heuristics has declined.

3. Low structure task performance is hard. It is hard because it requires thinking, which is also hard.

The first of these points—the value of having an estimate of how well we are doing while performing an unfamiliar task—needs to be re-emphasized. Many of the heuristics described in the chapter are expressed as preferences. Preferences, by their very nature, are intended to guide us towards higher fitness. As mentioned in Chapter 4, the benefits of having fitness estimates makes research based on developing them much more palatable to practice. Even an unreliable estimator may be better than none at all. Inaction is the paralysis that generally accompanies no direction; it is often less desirable than a series of wrong actions and subsequent adjustments. This is particularly true on a complex and dynamic fitness landscape.

The material presented in this chapter is critically important to the rest of the book because, in an increasingly complex environment, we can expect that low structure tasks will be encountered frequently. It is also important because, as becomes clear in Chapters 6 and 7, learning and informing processes are critically impacted by a client's existing mental models. While it may be convenient to treat our students (and even, from time-to-time, practitioners) as blank slates, such an assumption is almost never valid. The widely observed human heuristics for low structure task performance will always be present. We must be aware of these heuristics because they can seriously interfere with the knowledge we intend to convey.

Chapter 5 Foundational References

Ariely, D. (2008). *Predictably irrational*. New York: Harper Collins.

Gill, T. G. (2008a). A psychologically plausible goal-based utility function. *Informing Science: The International Journal of an Emerging Transdiscipline, 11*, 227-252. Retrieved from http://inform.nu/Articles/Vol11/ISJv11p227-252Gill220.pdf

Kahneman, D., Slovic, P., & Tversky, A. (Eds.). (1982). *Judgement under uncertainty: Heuristics and biases* (pp. 493-508). Cambridge, UK: Cambridge University Press.

Newell, A., & Simon, H. A. (1972). *Human problem solving*. Englewood Cliffs, NJ: Prentice-Hall.

Willingham, D.T. (2009). *Why don't students like school?* San Francisco, CA: Jossey Bass.

Chapter 5 Notes

[1] A number of researchers in informing science, such as Zbigniew Gackowski, take a more general view of informing, one that does not involve mental models. I see advantages to this perspective in understanding the physical layer of informing processes. In this book, however, I refer these more general processes of information transfer as *communications*, of which *informing* represents that subset applicable to processes involving the intentional transfer of information to human clients. I do not assert that this is the "correct" definition of informing, only that it is the one that I use.

[2] I chose the "hot hand" example specifically because there is statistical evidence that the phenomenon could be explained as the result of random chance—in other words, that it may be a myth (see Thaler and Sunstein, p. 30). Unfortunately, that leads many researchers to assert that it *is* a myth. I feel that ruling out some hot hand effect—on the basis that it could just be random—is just as sloppy science as assuming that "hot hands" exist because spectators and players feel they do. Asserting randomness effectively forces us to accept one of two propositions: 1) that achieving a streak does not impact a player's psychological state, or 2) that a player's psychological state has no impact on his or her ability to continue performing. For streaks involving games of chance, such as roulette, I find (2) to be a perfectly acceptable assumption. For games of skill, I find it much harder to swallow (I could, however, accept the possibility that two forces—confidence boosting the likelihood of continuing and anxiety that the streak will end increasingly undermining that same likelihood—may interact in a complex way to produce a pattern not so different from random). Then, of course, there is Joe Dimaggio's hitting 56 game hitting streak in 1941. Even those favoring the pure chance explanation of sports performance find that one hard to fit into the model. You can, however, with enough tweaking come to the conclusion that there is a reasonable possibility that *some* baseball player would have experienced such a streak during the 100+ years that the game has been played. But even this explanation runs into problems: given those assumptions, it is hard to understand why no streaks comparable in length have yet to be achieved (the next longest was 45 games), and how it could be that the same Joe Dimaggio also happens to hold the record for the second longest streak

in the history of the minor leagues (61 games in 1933), a fact that showed up in Wikipedia's entry on hitting streaks when I was researching this topic.

3 Another type of informing, *disinforming*, occurs when a sender intentionally provides information to the client for the purpose of creating a misleading mental model.

4 Of course an equally relevant question might be: Why do long division at all when you have calculators readily available? This is an illustration of how problem spaces can be altered by the availability of technology.

5 In fact, chess has been described as the drosophila (fruit fly) of the cognitive sciences owing to its frequent use in the study of problem solving (Charness, 1991, p. 39).

6 Chip and Dan Heath (2007) provide a compelling example of this in their book *Made to Stick*. In a premature birth intensive care ward, a baby was in obvious and severe distress. Because the heart monitor was normal, the physicians and other nurses were focused on other possible causes for the problem. One of the nurses, however, had previously seen the same unusual combination of symptoms in an episode where the child had died; in that case the problem was that the heart muscle had ceased to beat despite the fact that the nervous system was still sending electrical signals (which is what a heart monitor actually detects). Based on what she recognized, she concluded her diagnosis was correct and forcefully intervened to save the child's life.

7 Leonard Mlodinow (2008, p. 114), in *The Drunkard's Walk*, relates how his doctor had told him that there was a 999 out of 1000 chance that he'd be dead within a decade. The reason for this gloomy prognosis was that the HIV test that he had been given only had a 1 in 1000 rate of false positives. What the doctor had failed to take into account was that among married, monogamous heterosexual men the rate of HIV was extremely low (Mlodinow used 1 in 10,000 in his example). Taking this into account, there would likely be 10 false positives in this population for each valid detection—making the odds less than 10% that the diagnosis was valid as, indeed, it was not.

8 My own thoughts on utility functions and learning can be found in a recent paper that I wrote on the subject (Gill, 2008a).

[9] Actually, asserting that you would never participate in the negotiation exercise once you understand how it plays out might be overstating the case a bit. For my part, if I happened to be in that classroom and in the (very unlikely) event that I already understood the dynamic, I would probably try very hard to be the first bidder. I would then bid $21. When asked what I could possibly be thinking—as I surely would be—I would then say: "It is easily worth $1 to me not to see this soul-destroying exercise played out, and it is worth far more than $21 for me to discover who my enemies are."

While I would certainly be out a buck, and more than likely would be out $21 (given my experience with HBS classmates), the macho reputation that such a move would inspire would be well worth its cost—particularly in a negotiations course such as the one described.

Of course, if I did not get the first bid I would simply shut up and hoot when the hapless participants discovered their folly.

[10] For example, one of the distinguishing features of the successful PC-based expert system package, VP-Expert, was the ability to place facts or observations in a spreadsheet-like form. These were then transformed into logical rules by the program's induction engine.

[11] The original detector-accumulator architecture proposed was Pandemonium (Selfridge, 1958), which treated cognitive architecture as a series of layers. At the bottom layer, feature detectors (referred to as daemons) identified letter features—e.g., slanted lines, vertical lines, horizontal lines, and arcs—that sent signals to a second layer containing accumulators associated with each letter that, in turn, sent signals to word accumulators that identified words. This original model was then extended in HEARSAY and then in the interactive activation model (McClelland & Rumelhart, 1981; Rumelhart & McClelland, 1982). More recently, the leaky accumulator model (Usher & McClelland, 2001, 2004) has been specifically applied to explaining many of the rational inconsistencies that seem to routine appear in studies of human preference. In common, all the models assume:

- Parallel processing of inputs.

- The existence of feature detectors and the ability to develop new feature detectors.

- The existence of layers of elements (e.g., detectors, accumulators) at different levels of abstraction.

Common to the later models, heavily influenced by findings in neural networks, are the following additional similarities:

- A substantial amount of "knowledge" is contained in the strength of linkages between system elements.

- Linkages can both excite and inhibit accumulators and detectors

- Learning occurs through changes in the strength of connections between elements.

Where models tend to diverge is in relation to the process by which links change, the degree to which symbolic versus connectionist processes dominate, and the nature of activation signals (e.g., linear versus non-linear). For the present purposes, however, we need not dwell on these differences; ultimately these will most likely be settled in the domain of neuroscience.

[12] Since early cognitive models of the brain were first developed, our appreciation for the complexity of individual neuron behavior has grown significantly. This does not necessarily prevent connectionist architectures—whose nodes tend to be quite simple—from being valid. It does, however, suggest that any one-to-one correspondence between neurons and model nodes may be misleading. The neuron's behavior itself may need to be modeled as a network of nodes.

[13] Recent discoveries by neuroscientists strongly support the extraordinary feature detection capabilities of neurons. In brain studies, for example, scientists detected three individual neurons in a patient that were activated *only* by the presence of Ronald Reagan, Halle Barre, and Mother Teresa, respectively (Hotz, 2009).

[14] Early versions of the detector-accumulator architecture, such as the perceptron, were not able to handle interacting inputs, such as the exclusive OR (one input must be on while the other must be off). This limitation stunted the development of the field until it was recognized that multilayer architectures did not suffer from this limitation and could, in fact, learn very complex patterns.

15 The difference between explaining versus rationalizing is frequently razor thin in a complex environment. This is a key reason why I prefer to use the term conceptual scheme to theory, or even model, in describing what I am presenting. Explaining implies some proof of causality; such proof is hard to come by. Rationalizing speculates that causality may exist, but does not get pushy in pressing the point. In a theory, we demand explanation. In a conceptual scheme, we can allow for a bit of either; the purpose of the scheme is to help us organize materials in a manner that allows us to better recall, apply, and communicate them. If some of our linkages are rationalizations that later prove to be less than completely accurate, that fact does not prevent the scheme from being useful. For example, the strict notion that lower level drives must be satisfied before we can pursue higher level drives, as portrayed in Maslow's Hierarchy of Needs, has been largely discredited. Nonetheless, I would not hesitate to apply it during my initial pass at understanding a complex motivational situation. The spectrum of needs it describes would discourage me from taking a narrow perspective; its notion that "base" needs, such as hunger, must be taken care of before we turn our full attention to higher needs, such as self-actualization, is still likely to hold a lot more often then it fails. The key is that we must not take these schemes, or ourselves, too seriously.

16 I can still easily recall episodes from my youth where I lost money or had it stolen from me by bullies and where I spent it imprudently and later regretted the fact. Since my intention in writing this book was to inform the reader, not provide therapeutic release for its author, I will not relate these traumatic episodes here.

17 For example, popular U.S. electronics chains such as Best Buy and the now defunct Circuit City frequently include free printers as part of a complete computer/monitor/printer package. Often, the combined package is priced cheaper than the computer alone. Experienced computer buyers recognize, however, that a "free" printer normally runs slowly, holds very little paper and comes with exorbitant long-term ink costs. In many cases, for such individuals taking the printer is more of an inconvenience than an incentive. We currently have three such printers at my house, all of which are out of ink. Experience considerably dims the allure of free.

[18] I use an estimate of 150 because that seems to be an "optimal" size for communities, according to Gladwell (2000).

[19] For example, in the team Gladwell (2008) profiled, the 2007 Medicine Hat Tigers, only 4 out of the 25 players were born in the second half of the year. A psychologist first noticed the widespread nature of this discrepancy in the 1980s and it has been found to hold in other sports as well.

[20] One should not become too jealous of the hockey-playing advantages of January babies, however. A recent *Wall Street Journal* article reported that, "Study after study has shown that they test poorly, don't get as far in school, earn less, are less healthy, and don't live as long as children born at other times of year" (Lahart, 2009, p. A14). Research suggests that part of the effect may be a consequence of their home environment. For example, compared with May (the "optimal" month), January babies were less likely to be born to an two-parent family (about 67.5% versus 70%) and more likely to be born to a teenager (13.2% vs. 12%), with an additional small (but statistically significant) tendency towards less educated mothers. Competing effects, such as sports advantages vs. upbringing disadvantages, highlight the essential ruggedness of the fitness environments we face. Indeed, it is even plausible that there could be interaction between the two forms of fitness, as time spent on sports or on scholarship necessarily reduces the time available for the alternative pursuit.

Chapter 6

Learning and Expertise

Roadmap & Objectives: In Chapter 5 we considered what is meant by mental models and the types of knowledge we employ when encountering a task that is unfamiliar. Effective informing, on the other hand, depends on our ability to alter these models within the client's mind in some predictable way. What next needs to be considered, therefore, is how mental models change as additional knowledge is acquired—regardless of where it comes from. Subsequently, we can consider knowledge acquired specifically as a result of informing processes (Chapter 7). This chapter examines the general mechanisms through which expertise is acquired with a particular emphasis on the critical role played by repetition and practice. Of particular interest is the role that existing knowledge can play in that process.

The goal of this book is to show how business schools can become more effective at informing their external clients, particular students and practitioners. In other words, we want them to learn more from us. As it turns out, this process will necessarily turn out to be a two way street: if they are to learn more from us, we will need to learn more from them. But, if we are to make progress in either direction, we need achieve a clearer understanding of what *learning* actually means.

We are most interested in learning that changes a client's mental models in a manner suitable for subsequent use. Although an individual can "learn" that it is currently raining outside, that learned fact is not likely to be retained for very long, nor should it be. Rather, our focus is the type of learning that changes the way we think about or do things in the future: the type of learning that research and education is supposed to foster.

For conceptual purposes, the learning process can be broken down into two components: *stimulus* and *response*. The stimulus is the information the client receives that initiates the learning process. That will be the subject of Chapter 7, where we look at how a message makes its way through the client's mental systems. The response refers to how the mental models used by the client change as a result of the stimulus. What is meant by mental models was discussed in Chapter 5. How learning occurs, the actual response, is the subject of this chapter.

Because effective management is a skill that is generally acquired over a substantial period of time, the particular form of learning that will be emphasized is the acquisition of expertise. This process can be further broken down into two components: practice and concept acquisition. Both components of learning exert a strong influence on task performance and problem solving.

The conceptual scheme employed will continue to be the problem space model introduced in the last chapter. At the very end of the chapter, however, we compare that scheme with another model, one widely employed in education: Bloom's Taxonomy. What we find is that the two approaches describe the learning phenomenon in ways that are quite similar.

Acquisition of Expertise

The acquisition of expertise is the obvious remedy to the problems associated with low structure problem solving. Conceptually, we can divide this process into two basic activities[1]:

1. *Practice*: Repeatedly performing the same or similar tasks.

2. *Concept Acquisition*: Changing the contents of the problem space by incorporating new knowledge.

Expertise generally cannot be acquired without both activities.

Expertise and Practice

It is easy to dismiss practice and drilling as being inconsequential to expertise, particularly if you work at an educational institution where the emphasis is more likely to be on concept acquisition, as narrowly defined above. What cognitive scientists have found, however, is that there is probably nothing more central to expertise than the effects of practice. This finding was recently popularized in Gladwell's (2008) *Outliers*, with its chapter titled "The 10,000 Hour Rule"—the minimum number of hours of exposure to a task required to achieve true expertise[2].

To understand the role played by practice, it is useful to return to the simplistic task performance model presented in Figure 5.1. As was mentioned at the time, the portion of the model where actual thinking and attention are concentrated is working memory. Working memory, however, has very limited capacity. In fact, early psychological estimates of a 5 to 7 item limit (e.g., Miller, 1967) have proven to be remarkably resilient. This limit creates a significant stumbling block to thinking.

Fortunately, our brain has found a way around the working memory limitation. While the number of items in working memory is limited, the size of the items is not. Thus, as we work with the same conceptual structures (schemata) on a routine basis, all the necessary information assembles itself into a single cohesive unit known as a *chunk*. In terms of our connectionist model of the last chapter, this means that all the nodes and links holding information relevant to the task become activated, making them simultaneously available for use in processing. The more we practice, the larger and more comprehensive the chunks become. This allows us to perform much more involved tasks without going back and forth to long term memory.

If we conceive *chunking* to be a phenomenon of the state space, then a similar phenomenon—*automatization* (Shiffrin & Dumais, 1981)—takes place that allows operators and goals to be applied more efficiently and with less conscious attention. The basic evolution occurs as follows. Initially, when we perform a task we mainly rely on what are called *control processes*. These processes involve a conscious selection of operators one by one, normally directed by their perceived fitness as detected by the goal space. This process places extreme demands on working memory and, therefore, requires all our concentration. Over time, however, common sequences of operators become associated in memory. In a phenomenon closely analogous to chunking, these sequences become automatic—we invoke one operator after another with no conscious thought or attention.

Anyone who has ever learned to drive can probably recognize the automatization process. When you first slide into the driver's seat, every action requires conscious thought[3]. Even simple activities, like adjusting the steering to stay in your lane on an empty road, require attention. Because so many driving activities are repetitive, however, they rapidly become automatized. Thus, it becomes possible for us to drive in routine conditions paying virtually no attention whatsoever. Consequently, many drivers therefore perceive that they can safely drive while engaging in other activities, such as talking on a cell phone or eating (or both) while driving. Unfortunately, this perception is inconsistent with automatic behaviors; while they lead to superior performance as long as conditions remain unchanged, they are not designed to handle unexpected contingencies, as so often occur in traffic situations. Automatic behaviors halt as soon as decisions need to be made.

There are many types of expert behavior that simply could not exist in the absence of chunking and automatization. The chess master who plays ten or more opponents in a chess demonstration relies on chunking to help recall similar board positions and sequences of moves. There are many musical pieces that require performance speeds beyond the capability of conscious human processing. You cannot play them until they become automatized. The chunking and automatization phenomena collectively are referred to as *knowledge compilation*.

The law of practice

As expertise is acquired through practice, performance tends to improve according to a remarkably consistent pattern, sometimes referred to as the *law of practice* or the *learning curve* (Newell & Rosenbloom, 1981). The learning curve is one of our first examples of behaviors that follow a power law (which will prove to be particularly important when we look at time horizons, in Chapter 9). A power law relationship occurs where a given percentage increase in one variable leads to a consistent percentage change in another. In a learning curve setting, the two variables would typically be *number of repetitions* and *fitness of performance* (which could be measured in terms of time or some other quality we are trying to improve). For example, we might find by doubling the time spent on a task, we drop our performance time by 0.8. Suppose, then, after 10 repetitions our time for a single performance was 100 seconds. Then after 20 repetitions, it would drop to 80 seconds. After 40 repetitions, it would drop to 64 seconds, and so forth. Power law plots appear as straight lines when plotted on log-log scales, as shown in Figure 6.1.

Interestingly, learning curve improvements often accompany task performance in general, not just practice situations. It has also been observed in many business settings. For example, the airplane manufacturing industry counts on it in estimating future costs for a particular model of jet airliner.

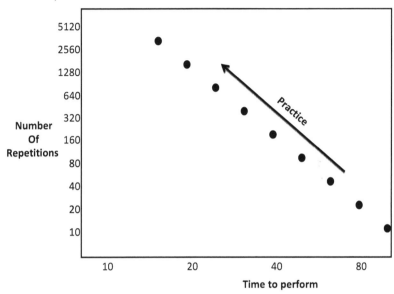

Figure 6.1: Hypothetical learning curve where performance time decreases by 0.8 with each doubling in the number of repetitions

Practice and retention

Practice also plays an important role in memory retention. Human long term storage is associative, which means it is generally stored and retrieved though the use of related concepts. Knowledge with many strong associations is therefore easy to retrieve. Most of us will not forget out first job (or driving lesson). Memories with weak associations, such as what we had for dinner a month ago, can quickly become irretrievable[4].

Through the formation of chunks and automatized procedures, we build and strengthen links between the knowledge elements employed. As a result, knowledge that we have practiced using tends to be much better retained than knowledge we have merely acquired and rarely used. The strength of the relationship between practice and retention can be quite staggering.

A particularly good example of the effect was presented by Willingham (2009, p. 89). The domain was mathematics, which happens to be a good domain for this type of study since computations in higher mathematics (e.g., calculus) frequently require us to apply concepts learned in lower level mathematics (e.g., algebra). The particular study involved giving individuals a simple algebra multiple choice test at different intervals after they had completed school. The thrust of the results were as follows:

- Individuals who had advanced beyond calculus had nearly perfect scores from 5 to 55 years out.

- Individuals who had taken calculus had scores that declined slightly between 5 and 55 years but which generally remained in the 90% range.

- Individuals who had taken more than one algebra course started at about 80% right after school, but declined to about 50% at the 55 year point.

- Individuals who had taken a single algebra course scored about 60% right after school but their scores effectively converged with the group that had never taken algebra by the 55 year point.

These findings also illustrate two other recommendations for effective practice (see Willingham, 2009, p. 94). First, practice is best if it is spaced out over time, rather than being highly concentrated, referred to as spacing vs. massing (Rohrer & Pashler, 2007). Second, practice on basic skills can be folded into the process of learning more advanced skills.

These findings and recommendations tend to confirm a rule of thumb that I have heard in the past[5]: you will remember quite a bit of the material covered in the second-to-last course in a sequence of related courses that you take. It further suggests two other principles:

1. If you *really* want a student to remember a concept forever, design your curriculum so that it is covered in the first course of a three course sequence, making sure that it is practiced in the remaining courses.

2. If you do not care if a student remembers a concept over the long term, introduce it near the end of a sequence or teach it in a course by itself.

We return to these observations when we look at curriculum design for the informing business school in Chapter 14 of this book.

Expertise and Concept Acquisition

Building upon our information processing conceptual scheme, we can organize concept acquisition into three component processes:

1. *Storing knowledge*: Concepts, relationships, procedures, fitness criteria, and other forms of knowledge must be placed in long term memory, so they are available for later application.

2. *Retrieving knowledge*: In order apply knowledge we must be able to access relevant concepts and operators and bring them into working memory.

3. *Directing processing*: Where required knowledge is not in a form where it can be directly retrieved from storage, we must have a mechanism for choosing how to transform the knowledge. For example, an individual will have many different problem spaces. Choosing the one most applicable to a particular task is often the key to success. Sometimes knowledge about problem solving techniques, rather than knowledge about how to solve a specific problem, is referred to as *meta-knowledge*.

We will consider each of these areas in turn. But first, we need to look briefly at what we mean by knowledge.

Levels of knowledge structure

When we have referred to complexity thus far, we have typically meant objective complexity—number of elements, interactions between elements, and changing fitness. As was mentioned in Chapter 3 (Table 3.1), however, there are a number of other common uses of the term. One of these is structural complexity, although it might better be called "lack of structure" complexity, since the less structured the task, the more complex it is deemed to be according to this definition.

Structural complexity can be described in terms of a series of levels. At each level, what we refer to as knowledge exists in a different form.

These forms are summarized for each component of the problem space in Table 6.1. Although the level numbers are somewhat arbitrary, the particular levels presented capture the general flavor of the process. The most important thing to recognize about the figure is that gaining expertise in a particular task can be characterized as the process moving from higher levels to lower levels.

Table 6.1: Structural Complexity Levels

Level	State Space	Operator Space	Goal Space
1	Compiled knowledge in the form of chunks	Compiled knowledge in the form of automatized sequences	Fitness measured in terms of progress towards task completion
2	Related facts linked together into schemata sometimes referred to as objects or instances.	Operators organized into sequences, sometimes referred to as scripts or programs.	Task goals and sub-goals integrated into a single goal structure
3	Individual task-specific facts and relationships	Individual task-specific operators for knowledge acquisition and processing	Individual task goals and sub-goals
4	General assertions and models of problems in other domains.	General purpose operators, such as deduction, induction and abduction.	Basic drives and learned fitness estimators (such as the attractiveness of cash and something for "free"; Ariely 2007)

For the state space, this process involves moving from general knowledge (Level 4) to a set of largely disconnected task-related facts (Level 3). At this level, inconsistencies between knowledge elements are likely to exist (particularly where the underlying domain is complex). For example, a student of finance may be expected to hold seemingly inconsistent types of knowledge such as:

1. Efficient market theory, which hypothesizes that systematic outperformance of the market using only publicly available information is impossible (Siegel, 2009).

2. Capital markets structure, where the student learns that the equity investment management industry is huge, very well compensated, and largely premised on investor (and fund manager)

beliefs that a "smart" fund manager's investment strategy will outperform random guessing the market over the long term.

As internally consistent subsets of knowledge are applied together, a more comprehensively linked and consistent sets of relationships emerges (Level 2). With practice, these knowledge structures become chunked (Level 1). A similar process occurs in the operator space. We start with a collection of innate and learned operators that can be applied in many situations (Level 4), we then acquire individual operators specific to the task (Level 3) and, over time, we build common sequences of operators (Level 2). With practice, these sequences eventually become automatized (Level 1).

The goal space follows the same pattern. We start with generic fitness estimators (Level 4), move to distinct task-specific goals (Level 3) after which these become integrated into a single organized collection of estimators-of-fitness and subgoals (Level 2). Eventually, we no longer need to consciously consider our goals in order to guide task performance—the goal state equivalent of compiled knowledge. For example, the last time you made a routine trip to your office, you probably did not need to consider your driving-related goals along the way. If you tracked anything at all, it was probably how far you were from your destination.

The knowledge levels proposed have particular relevance to tasks performed on a rugged fitness landscape. Conceptually, they map to the landscape as follows:

- *Level 4*: Low structure task; no task specific knowledge.

- *Level 3*: General task knowledge; task-specific knowledge is fragmented, with facts and operators existing independently of each other; multiple goals mean that many peaks can potentially be reached.

- *Level 2*: Knowledge specialized to a particular peak; relevant knowledge and operators are linked together and consistent; a single problem space may support one or several distinct peaks, since not all instances of the task are the same.

- *Level 1*: Expert knowledge; because of its highly compiled nature, it is subject to the *paradox of expertise*, namely the more expert you become, the less well you are able to explain what you are doing.

Where a task is governed by a decomposable landscape, the distinction between Levels 2 and 3 is fuzzier, since separate knowledge for separate fitness peaks is not required. Nevertheless, some distinctions remain. In physics, for example, Level 3 knowledge could include independent observations about the behavior of electrostatic and magnetic phenomena. In Level 2, these become unified through experimental observations of the intimate relationships between the two and through mathematical expressions such as Maxwell's equations, which precisely define the relationship.

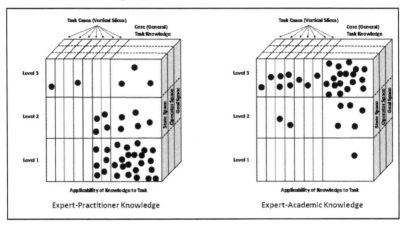

Figure 6.2: Practitioner versus academic expert knowledge (from Gill, 2008c), showing how practitioner task knowledge tends to be much more highly compiled, but potentially less broad, than academic knowledge.

This conceptual scheme has important implications for the informing business school. In applied disciplines that exist on rugged fitness landscapes, we would expect fundamental differences to emerge in the expertise of two types of experts: *practitioner experts* and *academic experts*. As illustrated in Figure 6.2, the practitioner expert, by virtue of applying knowledge repeatedly across a small set of fitness peaks, will tend to acquire lots of Level 1 and Level 2 knowledge related to a narrow subset of the entire domain. The academic expert, in contrast, will tend to seek out knowledge across a much broader set of peaks (or ignore peaks altogether, if the assumption of decomposability is maintained) but will tend to favor knowledge at Level 3, since fewer opportunities to apply the knowledge exist.

Naturally, we would expect the distributions of knowledge to reflect the nature of the discipline since the opportunities to practice vary widely across professions. In medicine, for example, faculty members often hold appointments that entail a mix of teaching, research, and clinical responsibilities. In education, the practice of teaching complements research on education (although not necessarily in the same specializations). Business faculty members, on the other hand, are typically not required to engage in practice-based activities. Thus, we would expect business faculty to be particularly prone to having different knowledge patterns than practitioners.

Storing knowledge

As suggested by the Chapter 5 (Figure 5.1) model of information processing, the path to long term storage is through working memory. Such storage is not automatic. In fact, most of what passes through our working memory is discarded without being saved. Overall, this is probably a good thing—since the alternative would be to remember what happened to us every minute of every day, creating a nearly insoluble search problem when it came time to retrieve a specific thought.

It is also worth noting that frequent exposure to a concept or object does not guarantee we will store it. As a demonstration, consider Figure 6.3 and imagine that it is the surface of your TV remote control. Now try to draw the layout of the buttons. How close have you come to the actual device?

Figure 6.3: Imagine this is the top of your TV remote control. Copy it to a piece of paper then attempt to draw the approximate layout of the buttons.

Considering the thousands of times that we have actively used (note *active use*, not just passive viewing) our remotes, it is amazing how poorly most of us are at recreating them[6]. A lot of this has to do with the manner in which we store knowledge. As was mentioned earlier, the cognitive system is full of different feature detectors. The visual system, for example, includes low level detectors for edges and motion, with stereopsis detecting differences between left and right eye views to estimate distances. At higher levels, we recognize familiar objects and use them to further calibrate our estimates of distance—without any conscious thought. When images, or any other form of knowledge, are stored, what is actually placed in memory is better thought of as a pattern of features abstracted from the contents of working memory as opposed to the actual image, block of text, or sequence of sounds that stimulated working memory. What specific features are saved will vary considerably across individuals and, much more significantly, across levels of expertise.

Experts already have a rich store of mental representations for the knowledge in their domain. When an expert encounters a particular image or collection of knowledge, he or she is likely to be able to find close analogs to it already present in long term storage. As a consequence, in storing that information the differences from the particular "base case" can be stored, rather than the entire case itself. We saw this effect very clearly in expert recall of chess board patterns; patterns from actual games were memorized with astonishing accuracy whereas recall for pieces randomly placed on the board was no better than for novices[7].

When the task performer is not expert, getting knowledge to move from working memory to long term storage in the manner that is desired is by no means trivial. Some important factors improving the likelihood include[8]:

1. *The amount of time the knowledge spends in working memory.* The longer we pay attention to the concept, the greater the likelihood that it will be stored.

2. *The number of relevant links to existing stored knowledge that can be established.* Knowledge that fits well with what you already know is accepted much more readily than knowledge provided in isolation.

3. *The number of relevant links with other items in working memory.* Nearly every mnemonic trick involves trying to link a particular concept (or image) with one or more other concepts or images.

4.   *Intensity of focus on the concept or on linked items in working memory.* If the concept itself evokes a strong reaction (e.g., interest, emotion) or is associated with a stimulus evoking such a reaction, it is much more likely to be retained[9].

5.   *Repeated exposure to the concept* (i.e., practice).

Meeting some or all of these conditions is not always easy. Practice, of course, takes time. Keeping a concept in working memory can be difficult; new stimuli are constantly competing to displace what is there. We may also develop stronger associations with the surface characteristics of a problem than the deep structure of the problem, an often-observed distinction between expert and novice problem solvers[10]. The mnemonics we use may prove as elusive as the concept we were trying to store when the time for recall arrives.

Some types of knowledge have built-in advantages in moving from working memory to storage. We are very good at detecting patterns[11]. What a pattern does, in essence, is to allow us to use part of the knowledge being stored as a cue for the remaining knowledge. Western music, for example, generally favors certain regular rhythmic patterns, chord progressions, and tones consistent with the key of the particular melody being played. As a consequence, it is relatively easy for us to remember a tune we like after a few repetitions. It would be much harder to remember a sequence of random notes[12]. Similarly, poetry—particularly poetry with rhythm and rhymes—is likely to be easier to memorize than prose. A particularly powerful form of knowledge is the story, since the narrative supplies links between the story elements that facilitate recalling the whole. Since stories prove to be particularly effective informing tools on many levels, we will postpone further treatment of them until the next chapter.

Another factor that can impact storage is emotion. Events or concepts acquired in the presence of strong emotion are more likely to reach long term storage than the typical day-to-day event. Emotion is not a necessary condition for storage, but it helps (Willingham, 2009).

Interest also plays an important role in storage. What interest really equates to, in practical terms, is the stickiness[13] of a piece of information in working memory. Per our model, the longer it sticks, the greater the chance of it making it into long term storage.

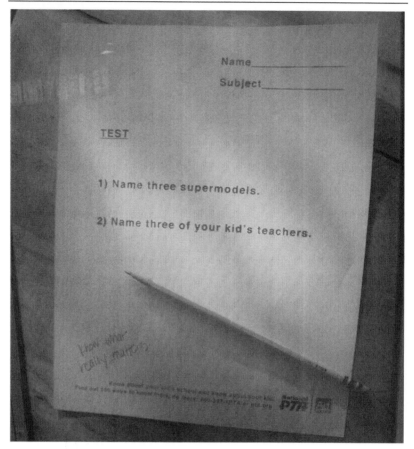

Figure 6.4: Message from the National PTA displayed at a local mall

Interest seems to arise from two forms. The first, which I will refer to as arousal interest, involves subjects that naturally acquire attention. A good sense of what generates this type of interest can be gained by looking at the contents of magazines at grocery store checkout counters—the very survival of these publications depends upon matching the general interests of the population. These popular topics map pretty well into the primary drives described by Lawrence and Nohria (2002): acquiring (wealth, power, politics[14]), bonding (sex, beauty, friendship, marriage, divorce, religion, social status, child-rearing, celebrity), defending (war, politics, personal injury attorney advertisements) and curiosity (aliens, "Believe It or Not!", supernatural, trivia). Arousal interest is not particularly goal directed and, in consequence, we end up acquiring a lot of general knowledge that floats around independent of any problems space. We are also not necessarily in control of these arousal interests, meaning that the knowledge we store is not always the knowledge that we think we should be storing. Every time I go to the local mall, I see an excellent reminder of this, which I photographed and included as Figure 6.4.

What can also make a concept "interesting" is its relationship to the individual's existing knowledge. Small anomalies that are inconsistent with the status quo but are not sufficient to call the entire status quo into question tend to produce peak levels of interest (Davis, 1971). For example, the fact that Stalin studied for the priesthood[15] is inherently interesting if you know anything about Stalin, since anti-religious, anti-humanistic proclivities were the hallmark of his later career. Interest is also generated by slight departures to expected patterns. What makes a particular piece of music "interesting" can be those times that the composer intentionally violates a rule (e.g., uses an accidental note or an unexpected chord) before returning to the well worn harmonic pattern. As individuals become more expert in a particular style of music, these departures need to become more frequent to generate expert interest. In the world of classical music, this has led to an "advancement" of the art such that many "important" new works seem to generate interest only to the expert's ear. To the rest of us, the composition seems little different from random noise.

The tight correspondence between successful storage and our ability to associate a concept with existing concepts means that the more we know about a subject, the easier it becomes to acquire a new concept. One implication of this is that storage is likely to be much more haphazard for Level 4 and Level 3 knowledge—when concepts are still largely disconnected—than it will be once task-specific chunks of knowledge have been acquired. For this reason, concrete facts and examples—particularly ones that allow links to existing knowledge to be formed (such as a sports analogy)—will tend to be easier to store than abstractions. Since abstract concepts tend to link only with other abstract concepts, building a system of concepts is extremely difficult before considerable expertise has been acquired. As Willingham (2009, p. 67) aptly puts it, "We understand new things in the context of things we already know, and most of what we know is concrete."

Existing knowledge can also interfere with storage, however. Consider some of previously mentioned heuristics employed in low structure task performance. To review: the representativeness heuristic causes us to assume that what we observe is similar to previously stored "representative" observations. The recognition heuristic causes us to weight information containing elements that we recognize more heavily than information consisting of unfamiliar elements. Both can distort what is stored by making assumptions about what is being observed or by causing the individual to stop attending more quickly than the information being stored warrants. Also worth noting is that there is little evidence that these particular issues decline with expertise; to the contrary, with a large set of beliefs about how the world works and representative examples to draw upon, experts may be more prone to these types of errors than novices[16].

We return to these issues in the next chapter, when we specifically consider informing processes.

Retrieving knowledge

Retrieving knowledge is actually a misnomer. It suggests that reacquiring a memory is similar to going to your bookshelf and pulling out a book that you previously read. Given how memories are actually stored, a better way of describing the process might be reassembling knowledge or recreating knowledge. For example, when we revisit a visual image, we use the same area of the brain that was stimulated when the original image was acquired. The same is true when we re-experience emotions. What we are doing, effectively, is attempting to reconstruct the original stimulus using the largely incomplete set of cues that we originally stored, supplemented by details provided by whatever representative examples that the stimulus originally invoked.

The retrieval process faces two challenges: locating the relevant knowledge in memory and properly reconstructing it. With respect to locating relevant knowledge, experts have a clear advantage. When knowledge is originally stored, the associated cues are likely to include relevant underlying principles, the so-called "deep knowledge" that educator's prize. When a situation calls for retrieving that knowledge, they recognize and cue the relevant underlying principle, resulting in the proper knowledge being retrieved. Novice performers, on the other hand, tend to be distracted by surface features, thus a word problem dealing with water is likely to be stored with a stronger association to water than to the underlying physical principle involved. When the next "water" problem then comes up, other problems involving water rather than the underlying principle are likely to be most accessible. Instructors, myself included, can be become quite frustrated when our students exhibit this phenomenon—why do they focus on the superficial aspects of a problem rather than the important ones? But the behavior is frequently not under their control. The chunked and automatized character of expert knowledge allows experts to associate knowledge with many cues when they store it and, as a consequence, retrieve it in many different ways. Novices do not have that luxury. Until they have practiced with basic concepts enough for some chunking to occur, they may be unable—not just unwilling—to store and retrieve the complex relationships that experts routinely deal with. Indeed, the earlier-mentioned observation that we have more concrete knowledge than abstract knowledge makes it almost inevitable that novices will associate new knowledge with the concrete aspects of a problem.

Our tendency to reconstruct memories incorrectly when we retrieve them is widely observed. Such errors can include missing knowledge we originally stored or, of particular interest, incorporating information in recall beyond what we originally stored. A typical experiment to demonstrate the latter phenomenon involves giving subjects lists of words to remember then asking them to recall whether a particular word was on the list. When the words are unrelated, the subject occasionally "remembers" a word that was not actually on the list. When the words on the list are related by some common theme, on the other hand, very different performance is observed. For example, the listed words might include (Reodiger & Gallo, 2003, p. 311):

> bed, rest, awake, tired, dream, wake, snooze, blanket, doze
> slumber, snore, nap, peace, yawn, drowsy

When later asked to recollect if "sleep" was on the list, subjects will typically perceive that it was at a much a higher rate than for unrelated words and be much more confident in their response. In free recall trials, the missing word was also judged to be on the list a high percentage of the time.

Another common problem of reconstruction is treating the ease of recall as a source of likelihood knowledge. We encountered this earlier in the availability heuristic, where we placed greater weight on memories that were easily retrievable. Another example of this can be found in a particular form of the representativeness heuristic known as the conjunction effect. Consider the following statement (Kahneman & Tversky, 1982, p. 496):

> Linda is 31 years old, single, outspoken and very bright. She majored in philosophy. As a student, she was deeply concerned with issues of discrimination and social justice, and also participated in anti-nuclear demonstrations.

Students were asked to rate the likelihood of the following two statements: (A) Linda is a bank teller, (B) Linda is a bank teller who is active in the feminist movement. The vast majority of undergraduate students (86%) rated the second statement as being more likely, as did half (50%) of the psychology graduate students tested. From a statistical standpoint, of course, it is impossible that (B) is more likely than (A)—even if all people with Linda's background are feminists, the probability of (B) would at best equal (A). In all other circumstances it would be less. From a recall standpoint, on the other hand, it would be much easier to retrieve the information on Linda with the cues *Feminist* and *Bank Teller*, than it would with either cue alone. Thus, the effect—also referred to as the *conjunctive fallacy*—can be considered another manifestation of availability.

There is much less evidence of a novice-expert difference in reconstruction errors during retrieval. Examples of the representativeness heuristic impacting recall (e.g., reasoning from a prototype rather from an observed observation; treating the conjunction of two events is more likely than the individual events) have been observed in many expert settings, such as psychological diagnosis (Teigen, 2003), investing (Glaser, Noth & Weber, 2007), and judges (Rachlinski, 2007)[17].

Directing processing

In the conceptual scheme used in this book, we view actual processing (i.e., thinking) as being directed by a problem space. Since we have already discussed low structure task performance in Chapter 5, we limit our attention here to two issues:

1. Choosing an appropriate problem space

2. Updating or replacing the problem space to reflect new knowledge

Choosing an appropriate problem space.

Over time, an individual will accumulate thousands of different problem spaces, each suitable for a particular set of task instances. The choice of what problem space to apply in a given situation therefore exerts a strong influence on task performance.

The process by which problem spaces are chosen is really a special case of memory retrieval. Features of the task setting serve as cues, and appropriate problem sets suggest themselves to the task performer through an estimate-of-fitness (utility). What experimental evidence makes very clear is that the context of a particular problem exerts a huge influence on decision-maker choices, much the way surface features impact recall in general. For routine (lower level) tasks, this process works to our advantage—we rarely choose the wrong problem space for tasks we have performed effectively in the past. For low structure tasks, the situation is quite different.

When a low structure task is encountered, one possible approach is to "borrow" a problem space from another domain and attempt to map it to the task, sometimes referred to as *learning by analogy* (e.g., Rumelhart & Norman, 1981; Jamieson & Hyland, 2006). Unfortunately, as it turns out, our ability to recognize appropriate analogies is imperfect. This assertion is supported by research in which isomorphic problems—problems with identical "deep" structures but very different surface forms—were created specifically so as to allow subjects to take knowledge from one situation and apply it to another. For example, in an experiment where various tasks were created so as to be identical to the "Tower of Hanoi" (a puzzle that subjects had previously learned to solve) the results were disappointing:

> In fact, any of the problems could have been solved by mapping it into the Tower of Hanoi problem and then solving the latter. No subject did this, and only two or three even thought of trying or noticed the analogy. The problems, then, were identical in formal structure, but different in their "cover stories". (Simon & Hayes, 1976, p. 478)

Another example that illustrates the impact of transferability across contexts was developed by psychologist Peter Wason (Johnson-Laird, 1985). The task is described as follows:

> You are given a pack of special cards, and you check that each
> card has a letter on one side and a number on the other side.
> The experimenter takes four cards out of the deck at random
> from the pack, and the rest of the experiment concerns only
> these four cards. They are laid out in front of you on the table,
> e.g., E, K, 4, and 7. The experimenter then states a general rule:
> If a card has a vowel on one side, then it has a number on the
> other side. Your task is to decide which cards you need to turn
> over in order to find out whether the rule is true or false.
> (Johnson-Laird, p. 181)

As it turns out, the majority of individuals get this wrong[18]. What is
particularly interesting about this exercise is what happens when you
put in a more familiar context. For example, you can play the game
with envelopes and stamps, and the rule:

> If a letter is sealed, then it has a 50-lire stamp on it.

Under these conditions, experimental subjects almost all get it right.
The same thing happens when you play the game with cards that have
"beer" or "coke" on one side, and a hypothetical person's age on the
other side, and you are asked to turn over enough cards to determine if
everyone is legal—i.e., if age is under 21, then the drink must be coke
(Willingham, 2009).

Even experts can, from time to time, use the wrong problem space. A
particularly popular example—described in both Ariely's (2007) *Predictably Irrational* and in Mlodinow's (2008) *The Drunkard's Walk*—
involves the television show *Let's Make a Deal*. In this show Monty
Hall, the quintessential game show host, would barter with members of
the studio audience (who often came dressed in bizarre costumes).
Some of the prizes would be minor (e.g., a can of tuna fish) while others would be outstanding (e.g., a new car). The highlight of each episode came when a lucky contestant was chosen to compete for the
grand prize, which would be behind one of three doors: Door Number
1, Door Number 2 or Door Number 3.

> Imagine yourself to be that contestant now. Just for the sake of
> fun, also assume that you watched the show for 10 days before
> and observed the following 10 day pattern:
>
> 2, 1, 3, 2, 2, 1, 3, 2, 3, 1

Based on the fact that 2 seemed due and since it seemed to appear more often than other numbers in the previous sample, you choose Door Number 2. Monty Hall then orders the contents of Door Number 3 revealed. It contains a 6-pack of Top Ramen noodles, valued at just under $1. Monty Hall turns to you and asks: "Do you want to switch doors?"

The question now becomes: As a rational academic, which should you do:

(A) Switch to Door Number 1,

(B) Stick with Door Number 2, or

(C) It doesn't matter, since neither choice affects your odds.

The answer, provided and explained in the Chapter 6 Notes[19], surprises most people. It certainly surprised the majority of people when it was published in *Parade Magazine*'s Ask Marilyn column. Of the 10,000 estimated readers who wrote in, 92% thought the answer given was wrong (it was, in fact, correct). This included about 1000 PhDs—with mathematics heavily represented—who wrote letters such as the following (composed by a member of the faculty at George Mason University):

> Let me explain. If one door is shown to be a loser, that information changes the probability of the remaining choice—neither of which has any reason to be more likely—to ½. As a professional mathematician, I'm very concerned with the general public's lack of mathematical skills. Please help by confessing your error and, in the future, being more careful (Mlodinow, 2008, p. 44).

What I remember about the first time I encountered this problem—which was while I was reading Ariely's (2007) *Predictably Irrational*—was the sense of frustration I felt as I attempted to figure out why the problem space I was applying was incorrect. It actually bordered on anger. What I subsequently found interesting is that when I present the problem to other colleagues who have not previously encountered it, I see in them the same simmering discontent bubbling up. We do not like to see our expertise contradicted, a subject to which I shall return shortly.

Given that even experts can sometimes apply the wrong problem space to simple problems *in their own domain of expertise*, it is reasonable to wonder if expertise can ever be transferred from one domain to another[20]. Building upon what I have already discussed, such transfer seems possible provided two conditions are met:

1. The patterns of the new task or problem to be solved are recognized, and

2. The knowledge in the problem space to be applied is relatively compiled (i.e., chunked representation, automatized procedures)

The second of these is particularly important because the surface characteristics of any new domain are likely to require a large amount of working memory—anything unfamiliar always does. If we then try to add a problem space that also requires attention, we will exceed our capacity limits. We see such a phenomenon occurring whenever we try to acquire new skills that build upon old ones. If the old skills are not mastered (and practiced), our ability to add additional skills is greatly hampered. For example, students who had automatized basic addition facts performed far better on multi-digit mental arithmetic (involving carrying and borrowing) than students who still had to think about the results of adding two digits (Cummings & Elkins, 1999).

To justify the two criteria—recognition and compiled expertise—it is helpful to return to the "Tower of Hanoi" example (Simon & Hayes, 1976). In the actual experiment, a small number of subjects recognized parallels between the Chinese Tea Ceremony and the Tower of Hanoi problem but nevertheless did not apply that knowledge to their actual problem solving. The obstacle here was that although they were familiar with the problem isomorph, they were not sufficiently expert at solving the isomorph—which they had just learned to solve as part of the experiment—so that they could handle both the problem itself and mapping it to the isomorph.

I inadvertently replicated the phenomenon I just described. Back in the late 1980s, I was simultaneously working on my doctoral dissertation (which involved characterizing tasks performed by expert systems) and developing an expert system. To give myself a much needed break, I decided to take my new bride Clare down to Walt Disney World, in Orlando. At the time, Disney's Epcot Center had a large building, sponsored by AT&T, known as the Communicore, attached to the Spaceship Earth attraction. The Communicore was, at the time, filled with interactive computer exhibits. After leaving the ride, I noticed that one was unoccupied. It involved moving things around according to a set of rules and as I tried to figure out what to do, I could only see one possible path. So I began moving the objects, according to a pattern that seemed oddly familiar. A few minutes later I was done. Upon the screen popped the message:

> You completed the game in 17 moves

> The minimum possible number of moves is 17.

I was (pleasantly) shocked by my performance, since I tend to be really mediocre at such tasks. But I then realized what I had just done: I had solved a variation of the 3 disk Tower of Hanoi problem—unlike Simon's experimental subjects. However, also unlike the experimental subjects, I had spent the previous 4 years working on tasks that required the same type of recursive thinking required by the Tower of Hanoi and had just finished writing a substantial program (15-20,000 lines of code) that incorporated these principles. And, of course, I'd also solved the specific Tower of Hanoi problem quite a number of times. Thus, the type of thinking required had become automatic for me, making it readily accessible in a novel situation.

Updating or replacing a problem space.

When we consider the process through which the problem space changes, there are two distinct cases that must be considered. The first is where the knowledge being added incrementally changes the problem space, without necessitating changes to existing knowledge. The second is where the knowledge conflicts with the problem space contents, requiring major changes or compete replacement.

As a general rule, we should be motivated to incrementally increase the knowledge in a problem space. There are numerous factors already discussed that would contribute to this motivation. Curiosity, for example, has been identified as a core human drive. Individuals with existing knowledge are also likely to find related information more interesting. As we have seen, the "interesting" represents small departures from what we know (Davis, 1971). Interest then promotes time in working memory which, in turn, promotes storage.

When a concept or novel problem space conflicts with existing knowledge, the situation is entirely different. The problem is so widespread that I refer to it as the *Law of Abandoned Expertise:*

> *We are extremely reluctant to accept new information that forces us to abandon any expertise we have already acquired.*

We have already mentioned an example of this in the history of science, where Kuhn (1970, p. 77) asserts:

> ...the act of judgment that leads scientists to reject a previously accepted theory is always based upon more than a comparison of that theory with the world. The decision to reject one paradigm is always simultaneously the decision to accept another, and the judgment leading to that decision involves the comparison of both paradigms with nature and with each other. (p. 77)

The problem of competing knowledge is also frequently observed, and goes unrecognized, in educational settings. For example, faculty members teaching an introductory physics course were disturbed by exam results that suggested their students were holding fast to their existing (Aristotelian) model of motion, despite their having been taught the more accurate Newtonian perspective (Halhoun & Hestenes, 1985, as cited in Bain, 2004). To counter this, the faculty conducted individual interviews with students, devised experiments to demonstrate the inadequacies of the student-held models, and conducted experiments that refuted Aristotelian notions in front of the students. They then asked the student to explain the results.

> What they heard astonished them: many of the students still refused to give up their mistaken ideas about motion. Instead they argued that the experiment that they had just witnessed did not exactly apply to the law of motion in question; it was a special case, or it didn't quite fit the mistaken theory or law that they held as true... The students performed all kinds of mental gymnastics to avoid confronting and revising the fundamental principles that guides their understanding of the physical universe. Perhaps most disturbing, some of these students had received high grades in the class. (Bain, 2004, p. 23)

The Law of Abandoned Expertise may be partially explained by reasons of ego (e.g., no one likes to be proven wrong) and by motivation (e.g., Why should someone pay me once I've conceded that my expertise is invalid?). The model of information processing presented in this chapter also suggests a strong cognitive basis may also exist. Information processing is often characterized as a tradeoff between applying existing knowledge and search, where search corresponds to what we normally refer to as thinking (e.g., reasoning, drawing new conclusions from existing knowledge). Experts excel at applying existing knowledge; when expertise is abandoned, we must rely more heavily on thinking.

Thinking is hard, however. Willingham (2009, p. 4-5) summarizes it nicely when he points out that thinking is *slow*, it is *effortful* and it is *uncertain*, further noting that "our brains are not designed for thought but for the avoidance of thought." It is the rare expert who would want to relinquish expertise—which tends to be fast, effortless, and reliable (within the expert's domain of experience)—for marginal improvements in performance. Thus, for such major restructuring of knowledge to occur, we need both evidence that what we are doing does not work well and that some other way of performing a task is *much* better. Just a little bit better will not justify the effort.

Bloom's Taxonomy of Skills

The most widely used conceptual scheme for learning is Bloom's taxonomy (Bloom et al., 1956), summarized in revised form in Table 6.2[21]. As a "reality check", we now compare this model to the problem space conceptual scheme that we considered.

The original Bloom's taxonomy was developed to classify different types of skills. Over time, however, it has frequently been applied to learning situations. The "critical thinking" movement, for example, tends to prize the higher levels—particularly evaluation (Level 6 of the original Bloom's taxonomy). What is implied by our problem space model, as well as by the taxonomy's original intent, is that problem solving typically requires skills from many or all of the six levels.

With that caveat in mind, it is certainly clear that the progression towards expertise that we have described will increasingly involve higher levels of Table 6.2. The disconnected facts and procedures that typify Level 3 of the problem space are well described by Levels 1-3 of the revised taxonomy, since facts and procedures acquired at these taxonomy levels tend to be specialized and may not even be "understood" (at the lowest level). Similarly, as facts become connected our ability to analyze and evaluate them (Levels 4 & 5 of the revised taxonomy) grows. Finally, the working memory demands of creativity make it likely that Table 6.2's Level 6 is most likely to be achieved only after a substantial amount of task knowledge and procedures have become compiled[22].

Table 6.2: A Revised Version of Bloom's Taxonomy, adapted from Krathwohl (2002, p. 215)

1. ***Remember:*** Retrieving relevant knowledge from long-term memory.
  1.1 Recognizing
  1.2 Recalling

2. ***Understand:*** Determining the meaning of instructional messages, including oral, written, and graphic communication.
  2.1 Interpreting
  2.2 Exemplifying
  2.3 Classifying
  2.4 Summarizing
  2.5 Inferring
  2.6 Comparing
  2.7 Explaining

3. ***Apply:*** Carrying out or using a procedure in a given situation.
  3.1 Executing
  3.2 Implementing

4. ***Analyze:*** Breaking material into its constituent parts and detecting how the parts relate to one another and to an overall structure or purpose.
  4.1 Differentiating
  4.2 Organizing
  4.3 Attributing

5. ***Evaluate:*** Making judgments based on criteria and standards.
  5.1 Checking
  5.2 Critiquing

6. ***Create:*** Putting elements together to form a novel, coherent whole or make an original product.
  6.1 Generating
  6.2 Planning
  6.3 Producing

Although the revised taxonomy does not articulate a specific role for the goal space, it does postulate meta-cognitive knowledge, which can serve the same role in guiding problem solving as preferences and generic goals do in the problem space conceptual scheme. What this all suggests is that the choice of a particular conceptual scheme for describing human information processing may be less critical than the user's comfort with that scheme. Had I chosen Bloom instead of Newell & Simon as the model to be employed, the conclusions would have been similar. This is how a conceptual scheme differs from theory. Whereas a theory is intended to describe how things "really" work, a conceptual scheme serves mainly to organize a collection of knowledge, to communicate knowledge, and to help identify those areas where more knowledge is needed.

Conclusions

The process of developing expertise consists of both acquiring new knowledge (learning) and practice. Key aspects of this process include the following:

1. As expertise grows we increasingly rely on knowledge that is compiled in form. As a result, our performance becomes smoother, it requires less effort, and it is more predictable in its outcome. Practice is every bit as essential as learning in the acquisition of this type of expertise. Moreover, owing to working memory limitations, it is impossible to acquire high levels of expertise in many domains without such practice.

2. Some of the same heuristics that interfere with low structure tasks also interfere with expert performance. Since experts generally know a lot, they can easily fall victim to such traps.

3. Where the underlying fitness landscape of a domain is rugged, practical and academic expertise tend to take on very different shapes. Practical expertise is likely to be clustered around highly compiled knowledge related to fitness peaks of interest. Academic expertise is likely to be more distributed across the entire landscape and may be much less compiled in nature—what business academics practice routinely are not the tasks associated with the domain being studied. Instead, their compiled expertise will tend to emerge in the skills associated with research, academic writing, and teaching.

4. We like being experts. When new knowledge threatens an individual's expertise it will be resisted. In order to even contemplate accepting such new knowledge, an expert must be convinced that existing knowledge is woefully inadequate AND

that the new knowledge offers substantially better performance.

Up to this point, we have paid little heed to how information being learned reaches the task performer. In the next chapter, we specifically consider how informing impacts the learning process. What this chapter and the previous chapter have made clear is: a) how much existing client knowledge the informer must contend with even when the client "knows nothing", and b) how seriously such knowledge can impact the client's ability or willingness to incorporate new knowledge.

Chapter 6 Foundational References

Anderson, J. R. (Ed.) (1981) *Cognitive skills and their acquisition.* Hillsdale, NJ: Lawrence Earlbaum.

Ericsson, K. A. & Smith, J. (Eds.) (1991). *Towards a general theory of expertise: Prospects and limits* (pp. 39-63). Cambridge, U.K.: Cambridge University Press.

Gill, T. G. (2008d). Structural complexity and effective informing. *Informing Science: The International Journal of an Emerging Transdiscipline, 11*, 253-279. Retrieved from http://inform.nu/Articles/Vol11/ISJv11p253-279Gill223.pdf

Kuhn, T. S. (1970). *The structure of scientific revolutions* (2nd ed., enlarged). Chicago, IL: University of Chicago Press.

Willingham, D. T. (2009). *Why don't students like school?* San Francisco, CA: Jossey Bass.

Chapter 6 Notes

[1] The choice of concept acquisition and practice as our two mechanisms for acquiring expertise is somewhat arbitrary. Rumelhart and Norman (1981, p. 335), for example, propose three qualitatively different forms of learning:

1. *Accretion:* the process of incorporating new information into existing schemata.

2. *Tuning or schema evolution:* The gradual process of refining existing schemata.

3. *Restructuring or schema creation:* The process by which new schemata are created. It may also apply to situations where existing

schema are radically reconfigured, as would be the case where an existing mental model is replaced by a new one.

In their model, accretion would correspond to expertise acquired through practice, while tuning and restructuring would correspond to what I refer to as concept acquisition.

² Back in the 1980s, when expert systems were in vogue, it was similarly argued that expertise at a job took 5 years to develop—which amounts to the same estimate, assuming a typical 2000 hour work year.

³ I vividly recall my first few minutes of driving instruction, given to me by my father. He had selected a dirt road for my first drive, since there would be no traffic to worry about. As I started to veer off the road, I still remember consciously trying to decide whether it would be better for me to brake or try to steer before I hit the tree that was slowly approaching. I admit that I do not recall what my father was yelling—though I seem to remember it being quite loud—so focused was I on making that important decision.

⁴ There is still some debate in the psychological community as to whether memories are actually lost or just cannot be retrieved (see Willingham, 2009, p. 42-43). For the purposes of task performance, it tends not to matter.

⁵ I have a vague sense that I may have learned the rule of thumb about remembering the material in the second-to-last course during my introductory psychology course at Harvard, taken during the 1972-1973 time period in order to fulfill my social science requirement. Unfortunately, all I really remember about that course, the only psychology course I took as an undergraduate, was that behaviorist theory dominated the field during that period (at least at Harvard). Much of our time was therefore consumed by learning the rules for effectively training pigeons and rodents. Sadly, I had forgotten all that knowledge by the time I acquired my first dog, so I never got a chance to apply it.

⁶ Our inability to recreate a remote control layout will, of course, be influenced by other factors, such as the degree to which a remote combines many functions and the detail orientation of individual operating it. The popular television series *Monk*, for example, is premised around a detective whose obsessive-compulsive tendencies are accompanied by an extraordinary ability to recollect details that others would overlook.

[7] I can also think of many examples from my own life where I have observed the ability to pick up small discrepancies accompanying high levels of expertise. When I served on a nuclear submarine, for example, the ship's captain would, from time to time, inspect the engineering spaces that were the responsibility of my department. I was continually astonished by the way he could instantly pick up on small details that I had overlooked. My undergraduate programming students, by the same token, are frequently amazed by my ability to zero on in a misplaced brace or semicolon in their code, often with only a fraction of a second inspection. This is certainly not the result of conscious thought on my part—the way my eyes sometimes move directly to a problem surprises even me. It is, instead, almost certainly the result of my experience; well over 20 years (and 10,000 hours) of frequent programming using languages in the C/C++/C# family.

[8] Most of these I selectively grabbed from Daniel Willingham's (2009) book *Why Don't Students Like School?* I found this book to be the best summary of the rules of cognitive science applied to learning that I have ever come across.

[9] How I tell right from left is a good example of the power of emotion and retention. For some reason, I have always had problem with the right/left distinction. Indeed, when my wife is driving she either questions me or ignores me every time I tell her to turn a particular way, since there is (at best) a 50% change I'll get it right. When I really need to know which is which, however, I have a foolproof way of remembering. Back when I was seven years old my mother enrolled me in a swimming class. When the attendant directed me to the pool, he pointed down a corridor and said: "Take a right, through the boy's locker room, to the pool". I walked down the corridor and, not knowing which way was right, took a left. Shortly thereafter, I found myself in the girl's locker room. Since that day, when I really need to know what direction is right, I peer down that very same corridor in my mind's eye.

[10] Jill Larkin (1981), for example, studied novice physics problem solvers and found that they tended to focus upon surface features (e.g., whether or not there was water involved) while experts immediately recognized the underlying physical principle.

[11] We are so "good" at detecting patterns that we frequently detect them where they do not, in fact, exist. This leads to a number of biases that we have already discussed, such as belief in "the law of small numbers". Nonetheless, pattern detection can be instrumental in moving concepts from working memory to long term storage, so we should be glad that we do it.

[12] As evidence of the difficulty of recalling random note sequences, I refer to the experiences of my father, who was a professional opera singer for many years. (He also taught economics at Harvard for many years, anticipating the reader's possible question with respect to discussions of his work in Chapter 16).

On one particular occasion, he performed in the world premier of a modern opera written by a well-known composer. The composer had chosen to depart from nearly all the normal western rules of rhythm and tonality and, as a result, my father found it nearly impossible to memorize. As it turned out, the same was true of nearly all the other performers. The orchestra, on the other hand, had the sheet music in front of them. Their only problem was keeping in synch with each other. As my father describes it to me, during the performances no one—neither performers nor audience—could tell if the opera was being performed as it was written.

[13] The term "stickiness" was introduced by Malcolm Gladwell (2000) in *The Tipping Point* and expanded upon by Chip and Dan Heath (2007) in *Made to Stick*. We will return to it, in depth, in Chapter 7 when we consider informing.

[14] Politics is a topic that falls under both acquiring and defending because political philosophies can lean in both directions. One philosophy is to keep government as limited as possible so as to preserve (defend) individual initiative. Another is to expand the role of government in order to ensure more equitable treatment of under-privileged members of society (acquire).

[15] I noticed the fact that Stalin studied for the priesthood in Willingham (2009, p. 45), where it was placed in a figure labeled "Material that is in the author's long-term memory even though the author didn't want to learn it and was in fact not all that interested in it." While I am reluctant to disagree with any of the insights in his book—which I consider to be

a marvelous synthesis of a large and unwieldy body of material—I would, in this case, argue that this particular fact is intrinsically interesting to those with any knowledge of Soviet-era Russia.

[16] Camerer and Johnson (1991), for example, suggest that representativeness may be one of the reasons that experts are often little better than amateurs at making predictions.

[17] While experts may be prone to make mistakes when they mix representative examples into their recall, we need to recognize that—on the whole—doing so provides experts with a major benefit since they do not need to acquire as much information. A particular example of this advantage sticks out in my mind.

Back in the mid-1990s, I was developing a series of case studies for use in my MBA classes at Florida Atlantic University. One of the cases was on a company called Galacticomm, the developer of the Major BBS—a phone-based electronic bulletin board system (very similar to today's course management systems in its features)—that I had acquired a few months earlier to use in my own programming classes. The company had 52 employees at the time and was run by a 21 year old CEO named Scott Brinker. I did a couple of days of case interviews with the company's managers then drafted a case study that I gave to Scott to look over and edit. When I met with him to discuss the case, the first words out of his mouth were (approximately):

> "I can't believe we told you all the things you included in the case."

As it turned out, what shocked him was the amount of (supposedly) confidential information I had included. When we went through the case, however, it became clear that most of what surprised him was content that I had never been told by the company. Rather, it represented my attempts to fill in the gaps of what I had been told based upon my earlier management and case-writing experiences (over a decade's worth).

[18] The correct answer to the E, K, 4, 7 exercise is that the E and the 7 need to be turned over in order to verify the rule. On the back of the E there must be an even number, on the back of the 7 there must not be a vowel.

[19] The correct answer is (A)—that you should switch to Door Number 1, since it will double your odds of winning. The most common answer, however, is (C)—that it does not matter.

It takes most people—and I definitely include myself in this group—quite a bit of time to achieve comfort with this particular solution upon first encountering the problem. The particular path to understanding I took involved asking the question: Does the fact that Monty Hall did not randomly choose what door to reveal make any difference to the problem? If he chose the door at random, then approximately 1/3 of the time he would reveal the grand prize before the contestant had a chance to switch. That, of course, never happens. In fact, he always reveals the door that has a lousy prize. What this therefore means is that we start with a 2/3 chance that the prize is behind one of the unselected doors. When he opens one of those doors, it does nothing to alter that 2/3 chance—since he will *always* reveal a door that does not have a prize behind it, and there will always be such a door (no matter where the prize is actually hidden). Thus, by revealing the Top Ramen, he has concentrated the 2/3 probability behind the remaining unselected door, Door Number 1.

A final note on my narrative: For this book I introduced some hypothetical prior data that was not in the original column. I specifically chose a history that would tell the reader nothing about the past (a 3-3 distribution is about as non-informative as you can get and a sample of 10 is highly unlikely to reveal any useful patterns, if such even existed). I did so to introduce a distraction from the core question—intended to trick the reader into thinking that I was setting up a (bogus) rationale for staying on Door Number 2. My variation was motivated by the fear that my readers would prove more adept at solving this problem than I was.

[20] If transfer of expertise across domains is impossible, it certainly does not bode well for transdisciplines such as informing science, whose very reason for being is premised upon taking expertise from one discipline and applying it in others.

[21] The original taxonomy, developed in 1956, also consisted of six levels similar in character to those of the revised version: knowledge, comprehension, application, analysis, synthesis, and evaluation. The revised

version (Krathwohl, 2002) was described by one of the original authors of the 1956 version.

[22] Theresa Amabile (1997), the well known creativity expert, asserts that creativity requires three sources: expertise, creative thinking, and task motivation. She points out that true creativity is rarely the product of wild, undisciplined thinking.

T. Grandon Gill
Informing Business
Santa Rosa, California: Informing Science Press.

Chapter 7

Complexity and Individual Resonance

Roadmap & Objectives: Having considered the mechanisms by which we process information (Chapter 5) and acquire expertise (Chapter 6), our next step is to look specifically at information acquired through informing processes. This chapter examines the processes that occur when one individual informs another and emphasizes the role that existing client knowledge (particularly the widely held heuristics of Chapter 5) can play in distorting that flow of information.

If the environment facing a typical business happens to be complex, then the informing business school must necessarily engage in *non-routine informing*. Such informing, involving changing and incompletely understood tasks, will constitute a core component of its interactions with both students and practice.

In this chapter, we examine informing processes and how the presence of complexity changes these processes. The central finding is that routine informing tends to be driven by the nature of the *content* being communicated and the *formal channels* in place. The presence of complexity, on the other hand, tends to require non-routine informing. Such informing tends to be driven by informer and client *relationships*. This distinction proves to be critical in Chapters 13 through 15, where we consider designs for informing.

Nearly any of us who are teachers recognize that there is substantial difference between what we teach and what our students learn. The material we teach may be highly rigorous. It may be relevant to the needs of our students. Even if it is not of direct interest, our course may be required or a prerequisite to another course they need to take. In spite of all this, what we communicate to students may never be received. Or, perhaps worse, what we intend our students to learn may be vastly different from what they actually learn.

In informing science, we use the term *resonance* to describe the state in which an effective communications pathway between sender and receiver has been established. We begin this chapter with a historical case study that illustrates a failure to achieve resonance on many different levels. We then consider a filter model that provides a conceptual scheme for recognizing the factors that interfere with individual resonance. We conclude the chapter by tying these findings into an existing framework, Chip and Dan Heath's (2007) SUCCESs model, for sticky communications.

A Case Study: Morison's Gunfire at Sea

Within the innovation literature, a widely cited example that highlights the challenges of achieving acceptance of an idea is presented in Elting Morison's *Man, Machines and Modern Times* (1966). The case study, summarized below, describes the obstacles experienced in attempting to convince naval authorities of the validity of a new way to fire the guns installed on U.S. naval vessels.

By way of context, achieving accuracy when firing shipboard guns has always been more problematic than achieving comparable accuracy with land-based artillery. The main source of the difficulty is the rolling of the ship, causing the angle of the gun's barrel to be continuously changing. As late as at the turn of the 20th century, individual gunners had to develop personalized approaches to compensating for the movement. Morison (1966, p. 21) describes the process as follows:

> First of all, the rapidity of fire was controlled by the rolling period of the ship. Pointers [gunners] had to wait for the one moment in the roll when the sites were brought on the target. Notice also this: There is in every pointer what is called a "firing interval"—that is a time lag between his impulse to fire the gun and the translation of this impulse into the act of pressing the firing button. A pointer, because of this reaction time, could not wait to fire the gun until the exact moment when the roll of the ship brought the sights into the target; he had to will to fire a little before, while the sites were off the target. Since the firing interval was an individual matter, varying obviously

from man to man, each pointer had to estimate from long practice his own interval, and compensate for it accordingly.

Another factor impacting accuracy involved the gun sights. Although telescopic sights were sometimes provided to enlarge the target, they were attached to the gun barrel and "recoiling with the barrel, jammed back against the unwary pointer's eye" (Morrison, 1966, p. 21). Thus, while useful in estimating target range, they were virtually never used during the actual firing process.

In 1898, an English officer—Admiral Percy Scott—developed an alternative approach to firing guns that involved continuous aiming. This approach involved three relatively minor changes to the physical equipment—changing the gear ratio on the guns, mounting a simulated target on the mouth of the gun, and changing the telescopic mountings so they did not recoil into the pointer's eye upon firing. More significantly, a major change to firing procedures was required: having the pointer continuously adjust the gun elevation so that it was always on the target. The results of this innovation were astounding:

> In 1899 five ships of the North Atlantic Squadron fired five minutes each at a lightship hulk at the conventional 1600 yards. After twenty-five minutes of banging away, two hits had been made on the sails of the elderly vessel. Six years later one naval gunner made fifteen hits in one minute at a target 77 by 25 feet at the same range—1600 yards; half of them hit in a bull's-eye 50 inches square. (Morison, 1966, p. 22)

In 1900, while serving in China, Scott met a junior U.S. naval officer, William S. Sims, who eagerly embraced the new approach and made the modifications necessary to institute the technique on his own ship. After a few months of practice, he demonstrated astounding improvements in accuracy, after which he began to communicate his findings with his U.S. Navy superiors in a series of 13 reports. Described by Morison (p. 22):

> Over a period of two years, he reiterated three principal points: first, he continually cited records established by Scott's ships, the *Scylla* and the *Terrible*, and supported these with accumulating data from his own tests on an American ship; second, he described the mechanisms used and the training procedures instituted by Scott and himself to obtain these records; third, he explained that our own mechanisms were not generally ade-

quate without modification to meet the demands of continuous-aim firing.

From an informing perspective, these messages demonstrated two things. First, the quality of the information was rigorously supported by multiple sources of the evidence. Second, the usefulness of the approach to the client (i.e., the U.S. Navy) was shown through outcome-based measures. Thus, the conditions of both rigor and relevance were clearly met. What transpired thereafter, however, illustrates how quality and usefulness may not be sufficient to ensure that effective informing takes place.

Morison (1966) described the Navy's reaction as taking place in three stages. During the first stage, Sims's reports were simply ignored. Indeed, after being filed away they were largely consumed by cockroaches—the 19th century analog to media failure. From an informing standpoint, this represents failure to attend to the channel. This failure of informing appears to have an underlying source that is mainly motivational in character: the individuals who received the correspondence had no particular interest in their contents.

After his initial efforts failed, Sims adopted a more strident tone in his reports and also began circulating them to other naval officers in the fleet. Described by Morison (p. 28-29):

> Aware as a result that Sims's gunnery claims were being circulated and talked about, the men in Washington were then stirred to action. They responded, notably through the Chief of the Bureau of Naval Ordnance, who had general charge of the equipment used in gunnery practice, as follows: (1) our equipment was in general as good as the British; (2) since our equipment was as good, the trouble must be with the men, but gun pointers and the training of gun pointers were the responsibility of the officers on the ships; and most significant (3) continuous-aim firing was impossible.

The third of these was based on experiments, conducted in Washington Navy Yard, where it was found that five men could not operate the gears fast enough to achieve the rate of changes in the gun barrel angle that were required to support continuous aiming. In his rebuttal to the last point, Sims pointed out that the fixed platform test was invalid; instead, the rolling of the ship provided momentum to the gun barrel that actually made continuous aiming much easier.

From an informing standpoint, the three elements of the response from Washington clearly illustrate a practical challenge to achieving resonance: the existence of prior mental models. The client belief that U.S. equipment could not be inferior to that used by the British made accepting Sims's premise much more difficult. The belief that the accurate gunnery could only be achieved through training and that the task was a ship's responsibility—rather than that of the bureau—caused the client to question the relevance of the information. Finally, knowledge of the existing test caused the client to question the veracity of the information. Conceptually, then, prior mental models distorted the information during the communications process. As a consequence, the client's interpretation of the message did not match the sender's intent.

Returning to the narrative, Sims's increasingly agitated tone ultimately led to the third stage: "name-calling". Described by Morison (p. 31):

> He was told in official endorsements on his reports that there were others quite as sincere and loyal as he and far less difficult; he was dismissed as a crackbrained egotist; he was called a deliberate falsifier of evidence.

In this stage, the principal obstacle to informing was less a matter of distortion resulting from prior mental models than of outright refusal to change existing models. There was no longer any desire to believe Sims; indeed the clients had an active interest in disbelieving him. Morison (1966, p. 36) further argues that a secondary but critical further source of resistance came from the implications that would necessarily result from the acceptance of the idea. Gunnery had always been perceived as an art rather than a science. As such, it has occupied a relatively low status position in the increasingly technological Navy. Sims's innovation would transform the nature of the task—increasing the status of gunnery with respect to other shipboard activities (such as ship handling) and prospects for promotion. In the context of an organization that had only recently made the transition from sail to steam and was still adjusting to its aftereffects, the motivation to accept the information that Sims was communicating was low indeed. This demonstrates that, in the informing context, failure to consider or accommodate the client's intrinsic motivation can lead to a complete breakdown of the informing process. When such motivational conflicts are present, message distortion is no longer the issue. The complete unwillingness of the client to modify existing mental models is the source of the problem. The described nature of the communication also indicates the important role that emotions can play in the informing context.

Ultimately, Sims broke the informing deadlock by writing directly to Theodore Roosevelt, then President of the United States. Roosevelt brought Sims back to the U.S. and assigned him to the post "Inspector of Target Practice," where he continued for six years. During that period, his innovation diffused throughout the Navy and he was ultimately acclaimed as "the man who taught us how to shoot." He eventually was promoted to Admiral and had a warship named after him (USS William S Sims, DE/FF-1059). This would be an example of a case where intrinsic motivation failed using a particular channel. As a result, an alternative channel was needed and considerable extrinsic motivational force had to be applied.

In summarizing this case from an informing standpoint, we can see three key elements of what we'll refer to as resonance. Even after rigor and relevance have been established, the content needs to be *internalized and made available for later recall*, something that did not happen for the early letters owing to lack of motivation on the part of the client. The amount of *distortion* between the sender's intent and the client's interpretation needs to be minimized, a failure evident in the first response received by Sims: a consequence of initial differences between sender and client mental models. Finally, the client must be *willing to restructure his or her mental models* to incorporate the content, another motivational issue that is also subject to significant emotional forces. If any of these prerequisites of resonance are not met, the informing can fail.

Single Client Resonance Model

In the naval gunfire case study, the barriers to informing seemed to cluster into two categories: issues relating to the client's existing mental models and issues relating to the client's motivation. In considering how informing impacts the client, we therefore need to synthesize the findings from the case just presented and the problem space model presented in Chapter 5.

Bias Filter Model

To organize the findings, I employ the conceptual scheme of a bias filter model (Jamieson & Hyland, 2006), which views incoming information as passing through a series of client filters. That model is augmented with three additional premises:

a) Because the problem space levels and forms of learning can be quite different in character, the nature of the filters that impact resonance may differ significantly across these levels. We therefore must consider each level separately.

b) The bias in the filter model can work in three ways: it can change information passing through the channel (including adding information not originally conveyed), it can inhibit specific information flowing through the channel, or it can amplify information disproportionately to competing information. All three filter actions produce distortion.

c) Unless otherwise stated, we may assume that the sender's intent is to convey information as accurately possible to the client. From time to time, however, we must also recognize that the distortion created by these filters may be intended by the sender, used as a tool for manipulating the client[1].

The model starts with the working memory-long term storage model introduced in Chapter 5. As illustrated in Figure 7.1, it then proposes that informing messages must pass through an attention filter to reach working memory. Once it reaches working memory, it must pass through a series of filters before it can ultimately become incorporated in the mental models we hold in long term storage. These filters include:

- *Information filters.* These distort the information as it is being held in working memory.

- *Cognitive filters.* These cause the message to be interpreted according the client's existing mental models.

- *Risk & time preference filters.* These weigh the consequences of the message in terms of uncertainty.

- *Motivation filters:* These examine the utility consequences of the message, perhaps rejecting it or modifying it if these consequences are unsatisfactory.

- *Visceral filters:* Modify or reject the message based upon other factors, such as emotions, arousal, or social pressures.

Before describing the filters of the single client resonance model in greater detail, a few comments must be made. First, although the attention filter is presented as being a gatekeeper to working memory, a failure to pay attention can be generated at any level. For example, we may decide to ignore a message that we are not motivated to attend to. As we saw in Chapter 6, however, the effect of not paying attention tends to be the same wherever it occurs: the message does not enter long term storage. Second, some filters are presented as operating at all three problem space levels (e.g., attention, information) while others are presented as being more active on higher levels (e.g., visceral factors, emotions). As we look at the filters, further justification for this depiction will be presented[2].

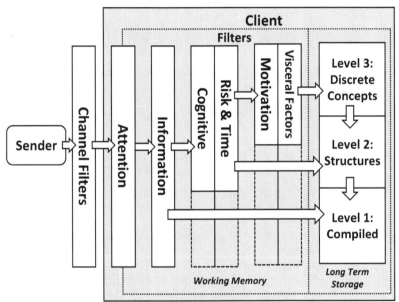

Figure 7.1: Single Client Resonance Model

In addition to the changes within the client system, we must explicitly recognize that additional filters exist that are best viewed as being a property of the informing channel. It should be self-evident that channel capabilities—such as media richness (Daft, Lengel, & Trevino, 1987), interactivity, time delays, and capacity limitations—can exert a powerful influence on the informing process. Suppose, for example, you were a sender whose goal was to inform the client about the emotional impact of the Mona Lisa. If you were employing a broadcast text channel—such as a list server—there would be significant limitations as to what types of information you could convey. To get around these you might choose to relate studies regarding the nature of that impact, describe techniques employed by da Vinci to achieve such impact, and you might even describe its personal impact on you. The nature of the informing process would change dramatically, however, were a richer channel available. You might choose to present a high-resolution picture of the work. You might show video clips of tourists being affected as they viewed the painting at the Louvre. You might also cite the previously studies as well, of course. Thus, the choice of channel—which may be a decision of the client, the sender, or a mutual decision—can exert a powerful influence on the nature of the informing message.

Client Filters

We now turn to the specific characteristics the filters. For many of these, all we will need to do is organize a number of the heuristics discussed in Chapters 5 and 6, as well as briefly previewing some time and risk findings that are covered in greater detail in Chapter 9. For the attention and visceral factors filters, however, some new concepts will be introduced.

Attention filters

Maintaining attention is a matter of balance. Although we exhibit a natural curiosity, which is to say we have a cognitive motivation for information seeking (Driver & Streufert, 1969) and variety (Hackman & Oldham, 1980), the drive for such stimulation is not unlimited. In fact, the cognitive demands of too much stimulation can lead to stress, or even panic (Streufert & Streufert, 1978), sometimes referred to as "information overload". As a consequence, the motivational character of information processing is generally plotted as an inverted-U, with desired arousal being an intermediate value that is not too great—leading to overload—but also not too low—leading to boredom.

Unexpected. We already discussed Davis's (1971) widely cited article regarding what is interesting. He emphasizes that research, in order to be interesting, must contain an element of the unexpected. Research whose sole purpose is to support an existing paradigm may be useful, but it will not be interesting. Davis further argues that a sender can also exceed the client's capacity to accept the unexpected, supporting the inverted U perspective. He asserts:

> Yet one must be careful not to go too far. There is a fine but definite line between asserting the surprising and asserting the shocking, between the interesting and the absurd. An interesting proposition, we saw, was one that denied the weakly held assumptions of its audience. But those who attempt to deny the strongly held assumptions of their audience will have their very sanity called into question. They will be accused of being lunatics; if scientists, they will be called 'crackpots'. If the difference between the inspired and the insane is only in the degree of tenacity of the particular audience assumptions they choose to attack, it is perhaps for this reason that genius has always been considered close to madness. (Davis, 1971, p. 343)

Distractibility. Another attention-related phenomenon that impacts informing, at the opposite side of the scale from information overload, is distractibility. Human cognitive systems are not like the single-process computers of the 1950s and early-1960s. They often attend to a number of tasks concurrently, at different levels of arousal. Focused attention can shift from task to task in the event that optimal arousal levels are not being achieved in the most highly attended channel. Indeed, distractibility is so common and significant in its impact that one of the most serious criticisms that a cognitive scientist can make against any proposed model of cognition is that it does not account for the phenomenon (Newell, 1990, p. 227).

An example of distraction's impact on attention can be found in teenage driving:

> A recent study found that a teenage driver driving alone was 40 percent more likely to get into an accident than an adult. But with one other teenager in the car, the percentage was twice that—and with a third teenager along for the ride, the percentage doubled again. (Ulene, 2007, as cited in Ariely, 2008, p. 102).

In this example, the informing channels that interfered with the task were unrelated to the task. It is also perfectly plausible that—in some situations—the informing activities of the task could interfere with other cognitive activities of the task. In an example that I have witnessed many times over the years, when a conference presentation is particularly engaging, the moderator often forgets to check the clock, thereby interfering with his or her assigned task of ensuring that subsequent presenters have a fair allocation of time.

Interference. Sometimes more than one message will simultaneously occupy the same informing channel. We refer to this specific type of distraction as interference. One of the earliest experimental demonstrations of interference, subsequently replicated in numerous experimental studies is the "Stroop Effect" (Stroop, 1935). As part of a typical experiment that demonstrates this effect, subjects will be asked to identify colors and words. They will then be given some words written in a color inconsistent with the word (e.g., the word "Green" will be printed in red) and will either be asked to read the word or identify the color. In both cases, it takes subjects much longer to do this task, and they are more prone to errors[3].

One business area where interference has been studied extensively is in the advertising industry, where senders pay large sums of money to inform clients using the same channels as program content. In one study (Lord & Burnkrant, 1993), researchers examined how the interest generated by program content interacted with the attention paid to commercials within the program. They found many levels of interaction between interest in the program, interest in the commercial, and use of an attention-grabbing device (audio beeps for the low involvement commercial relating to an oil product, a compelling visual image for the high involvement commercial involving drunk driving). The relationships they found were quite complex. For example, where program involvement was high, a high-involvement commercial combined with use of the attention grabbing device threatened to distract clients from the message. Low involvement commercials, on the other hand, benefitted from the high level of arousal carrying over from the high-involvement program. On the other hand, where program-involvement was low, a high-involvement commercial fared better and the attention grabbing device generally seemed warranted. The complexity of the results arising from this relatively simple stream of research suggests how difficult it can be to develop general principles for predicting how to format messages that garner optimal attention in the presence of interference.

Information filters

Information filters process incoming messages and, in the process, may distort those messages. We have already seen a good example of this in the representativeness heuristic, described in Chapter 5, where we conclude an entity is "representative" of a class of entities, and use that conclusion to fill in additional information about it.

A particularly compelling example of information filtering in practice is the implicit associations test (IAT)[4]. This test attempts to detect our unconscious associations with a topic based upon reaction time. For example, in one test that I took I was presented a series of words that could either be classified as "bad" or "good," and a series of images of faces that were either "fat" or "thin." Once I had some practice making that classification, the test then presented a set of both text and images where "thin"/"Good" and "fat"/"Bad" were associated with the same key, followed by a second set of text and images where "thin"/"Bad" and "fat"/"Good" were similarly associated. By measuring the differences in reaction time to these two sets, the test assessed if I was more comfortable classifying fat people with good or with bad[5].

More generally, information filters smooth out the incoming messages, both adding information that is unstated and skipping over the extraneous information. For example:

> Waiter, would you remove the
> the fly from my onion soup?

Unless you've seen these examples before, it is easy to miss the fact that the word "the" is repeated. Information filters do this type of processing all the time, and with little or no conscious involvement on our part. As a consequence, we expect such filters to be active at virtually all levels of expertise. For this reason, on the Figure 7.1 diagram, the filter is shown acting on all expertise levels.

Cognitive filters

Cognitive filters reduce ambiguity or shortcut problem solving. Many of these filters were described in Chapter 5. They are summarized in Table 7.1, along with the problems space levels on which they are likely to be most active.

Table 7.1: Examples of Cognitive Filters

Filter	Description (See Chapter 5 for more details)	Most Active Levels
Reasoning by analogy	Maps concepts from an unfamiliar problem space into a familiar problem space, using the familiar problem space to guide problem solving.	3 & 4
Abduction	When a correlation between a factor and an effect is observed, the assumption that the factor caused the effect is made. A common version is the illusion of control, where we perceive ourselves to have more control than we do.	3 & 4
Induction	Deducing rules from patterns. Can lead to the "law of small numbers," treating small samples as being more significant than is justified.	3
Anchoring	Using observed or arbitrary values as a basis for judging values on new observations. Includes attraction, similarity, compromise, and decoy effects.	3 & 4
Framing	Decisions influenced by how alternatives are presented; often based upon asymmetry between gains and losses.	3 & 4
Recognition	We are influenced by components of a problem that we recognize (e.g., celebrity endorsements) even though not related to the problem.	3 & 4
Social influence	We observe and identify with the choices we observe others making and weigh them heavily.	3 & 4
Availability	Weighting information based upon how readily accessible it is.	2, 3 & 4
Priming	Activation of cognitive elements by factors outside a task unconsciously influences decisions and values.	2, 3 & 4
Money and Price	We use price to estimate fitness and are strongly influenced by cash	2, 3 & 4
Projection	In predicting the behavior and reactions of others, we assume their mental models are like ours.	2 & 3
Choice heuristics	Shortcuts for choosing among many alternatives, such as satisficing. May lead to overreliance on specific attributes of failure to account for complex fitness interdependencies.	2 & 3

Although we originally framed these heuristics in terms of information processing, all are relevant to establishing a desired mental model in the mind of the client within the informing process. They represent the client's pre-existing knowledge and expertise, available even when no task-specific knowledge is present. Through the use of examples, we can set up the conditions for reasoning by analogy. Through the choice of observations we describe, we can set the stage for either valid or invalid induction. How we present a concept can either exploit, or be undermined by, phenomena such as framing and anchoring.

Most importantly, every single one of the Table 7.1 heuristics depends on prior client knowledge. What this means is that no two individuals in a group of clients will have precisely the same reaction to a particular informing process. This becomes very important when we consider how informing should be conducted—particularly so when the content domain is complex.

The third column of Table 7.1 indicates the cognitive levels at which we would expect the filters to be most active. Unlike information filters, which act at every level, we would not expect cognitive filters to have much impact at Level 1 (fully compiled knowledge). Expert performance has little need of shortcuts. By the same token, many of the heuristics near the bottom of table depend on pre-existing knowledge of relationships. Thus we would expect these filters to be particularly active at cognitive levels 2 and 3. The length of the "Cognitive" bar in Figure 7.1 is intended to this.

Risk & time preference filters

Much like the cognitive filters, the risk & time preference filters serve to establish preferences and provide processing shortcuts. Because failures to address risk properly and inadequate managerial time horizons have been so central to recent business crises, an entire chapter (Chapter 9) is devoted to the topic of the close relationship between complexity, risk, and time. For the sake of consistency, findings to be presented in that chapter are summarized in Table 7.2.

As was the case for the cognitive filters, we would expect these filters to be particularly active at the intermediate structure levels (Levels 2 & 3). At the compiled knowledge level (Level 1), preferences are likely to be built into whatever automatized decision rules are used and are therefore not likely to be consciously consulted (although, of course, heuristic preferences may have been employed in creating the compiled rules). Similarly, most of these rules require sufficiently well defined outcomes so that they would not apply well to low structure (Level 4) tasks.

Table 7.2: Examples of Risk & Time Preference Filters

Filter	Description (See Chapter 9 for more details)
Overvaluing low likelihoods	When likelihoods are very low, we tend to give them excessive weight. For example, we worry about very unlikely risks (e.g., plane crash) more than much more serious risks (e.g., car crash).
Undervaluing high likelihoods	We weight complete certainty (100%) much more than near certainty (e.g., 98%)
Overconfidence	We are more confident in our estimates of risks and ranges than is justified by reality.
Optimism	We tend to overestimate the likelihood of good events and underestimate the likelihood of bad events
Gambler's fallacy	We tend to assume that random processes *necessarily* produce random looking output.
Gain-loss discounting asymmetry	We appear to discount future gains and losses at different rates. For example, we might prefer a $10 gain now to a $15 gain in a year, while preferring a $15 loss in a year to a $10 loss now.
Exaggerated anticipation	We overestimate both the positive and negative magnitude of our anticipated feelings when considering future events.
Preference for escalating gains	Given the same total value, we tend to prefer a sequence of returns that rise with time over a sequence that declines with time.
Immediacy	We place a very high value on immediate rewards in contrast to slightly delayed rewards.
Hyperbolic Discounting	Rather than declining exponentially—as a "rational" discounting model would suggest—our actual discounting rates appear more hyperbolic in nature. A consequence can be that our preferences for between two rewards separated by a fixed interval can flip (for the first to the second) as the hypothetical choice is made more distant in time.
Presentism	Our expectations for how we will feel in the future are heavily colored by how we feel in the present.
Magnitude Effects	Our discounting preferences frequently change based upon the size of the amounts involved, with larger amounts being treated more rationally than smaller amounts.

Although these are generally presented as decision heuristics, their influence can, once again, be strong in informing contexts where the act as pre-existing estimates-of-fitness. For example, overconfidence and optimism could lead a client to reduce attention to familiar incoming information. Low and high likelihood effects could cause incoming information to be valued incorrectly. The variety of inconsistent preferences with respect to time can cause an informer's formulation of a model to be interpreted differently by a client. For example, a declining series of payments described by the informer might provoke a negative reaction in the client that was not anticipated.

Motivation filters

Keeping a message in working memory long enough for it to be reliably incorporated into long term storage is hard work. The motivation filter acts to determine whether this effort will be made. There appear to be two paths through the motivation filter: the intrinsic motivation filters and rigor-relevance filters. In both cases, motivation is closely tied to the concept of utility.

Intrinsic motivation

In Chapter 5, we first considered motivation for task performance. Building upon this, the intrinsic motivation to internalize a particular message can be grouped into three general categories (Gill, 1996):

- *Arousal:* The message captures an appropriate amount of attention—not too little; not too much—and, perhaps, stimulates one of our core drives: learning, defense, acquisition, and bonding.

- *Control:* The message contents provide us with better tools for exerting control over our environment.

- *Achievement:* The message provides us with tools that improve our ability to accomplish our internal goals or with which to measure that accomplishment.

Messages that stimulate intrinsic motivation do not necessarily need to be credible (e.g., we may choose to memorize a joke) or task-related, although they can be. What makes the motivation intrinsic is the fact that utility from this source is not tied to external rewards or recognition.

Rigor

The rigor-relevance filters involve two stages. Because this is information we intend to apply, we initially need to determine if it is rigorous (credible). There are at least three tests that can be applied in this regard. First, we can examine the credibility of the source. Such a test of rigor would be based largely upon the reputation of the source. Second, the internal consistency of the message can be examined—including its logic and the source of its factual content. Finally, we can check its consistency with our existing mental models. Messages found to be consistent with those models are deemed credible; those inconsistent can be ignored. An interesting demonstration of this can be found in research relating to the reasoning of historians (Tetlock, 1999). The study found that the historian's particular perspective played a highly significant role in determining his or her willingness to accept observations as fact[6]. This phenomenon is an example of the confirmation heuristic (also called *confirmation bias*) mentioned in Chapter 5. It also supports the previously mentioned *Law of Abandoned Expertise*, which states that experts will tend to resist any knowledge that is inconsistent with or undermines their existing expertise.

Relevance

The relevance filters determine the degree to which the message maps to something the client can use. This concept of usefulness closely relates to utility. Or, stated another way, our utility function for task-related information depends upon its expected usefulness.

The correspondence of the relevance filter to utility is important because utility, in turn, is heavily dependent upon the active goals of the client, an argument that I have presented at some length in a previous paper (Gill, 2008a). Thus, the key to ensuring a message passes through the relevance filter is relating it to active client goals. From the sender's perspective, this means instilling desired goals in the client may usefully precede the actual message in the informing process. This observation connects us to the large literature on *goal setting*.

By many measures, the field of management has had its greatest research success in the area of goal setting. The goal setting literature is huge (e.g., over 100 different tasks, involving over 40,000 subjects, have been studied; Locke, 2004, p. 124) and has successfully demonstrated, in many contexts, how individual goals are instrumental in establishing motivation. Some of the key findings of the research are summarized in Table 7.3.

Table 7.3: Important findings in goal-setting theory

Finding	Description	Example References
Specificity	Goals that are specific and difficult lead to better performance than a vague goal or no goal at all.	Latham & Locke, 2006, p. 332.
Commitment	Performance grows with goal commitment, especially for difficult tasks. Commitment tends to grow as progress towards a goal is made, sometimes referred to as the "escalating commitment effect."	Klein, Wesson, Hollenbeck, & Alge, 1999, p. 886 Jamieson & Hyland, 2006, p. 52
Proximity	People exert more effort to achieve goals where progress has already been made, referred to as the "endowed progress effect."	Nunes & Drèze, 2006, p. 510
Difficulty	Increased goal difficulty leads to increased motivation and performance for approach goals, provided the goal is achievable, but less so for avoidance goals.	Janssen & Van Yperen, 2004, p. 377
Participation	Goals provide an important motivation regardless of whether or not the individual has participated in setting the goals. In many cases, participation doesn't appear to matter.	Latham & Steele, 1983, p. 416

Given the important role played by the goal space in problem solving, as discussed in Chapter 5, the significance of goal setting in informing is not surprising. The technique does have its detractors, however. Interestingly, its weaknesses are seen to be a consequence of its strengths. In a recent article, for example, four researchers (Ordonez, Schweitzer, Galinsky, & Bazerman, 2009a) identified concerns that goal setting tended to promote narrow focus (i.e., specificity), produce dysfunctional behaviors in order to meet challenging goals (i.e., difficulty), and can undermine intrinsic motivation. In effect, what the researchers propose—drawing principally upon stories and anecdotal examples—is that the focused efficiency benefits gained from goal setting (which they do not dispute) come at the price of adaptability and learning[7].

Viewing the topic from a problem structure perspective, it is clear that tight goal setting may be appropriate where a highly structured and very specific mental model is to be conveyed to the client. Such models may be quite common in decomposable domains where effective known solutions exist. On rugged landscapes, however, highly specific goal setting can lead to a number of problems, many of which we have already observed. For example, it is often difficult to judge actual fitness on dynamic, rugged landscapes. Under such circumstances, specific goals will often be linked to estimates-of-fitness. Estimates-of-fitness tend to be imperfect, however, and may be subject to manipulation. For example, a manager's performance goals may be expressed in terms of sales volume, without attempting to measure the contribution or long term potential offered by the sales. A junior faculty member may be given a specific goal of 5 or more articles in journals whose quality ratings (another fitness estimator) are B+ or better in order to qualify for tenure, thereby eliminating any need for the ambiguous task of directly assessing the actual fitness of the articles themselves. Thus, complexity tends to undermine our ability to identify goals that avoid dysfunctional behavior—precisely as Ordonez et al. (2009a) suggested.

The four authors' views with respect to adaptability and intrinsic motivation are also consistent with the learning model presented in this paper. As we saw in Chapter 6, the progression towards expertise involves continuously replacing a vague multiplicity of goals with individual, task-specific goals. With that progression, however, comes increased focus on a specific peak and increased commitment to the particular goals (e.g., as occurs under the *Law of Limited Visibility*). As a consequence, it is quite reasonable to assume that both adaptability and learning behaviors will decline.

Given these observations, it is not surprising that Ordonez et al. (2009a) relied heavily on complex, real world examples as evidence, whereas controlled lab experiments were the source of many of the key findings of goal setting research. Presenting these findings in the context of informing, applying goal setting theory is probably a very effective way to inform a client about how to perform a particular task in a very specific way that is unlikely to change in the future. It may be much less applicable when the task is ill-structured and your role as informer is to help the client become informed about it, rather than simply conveying a specific mental model.

Visceral filters

Visceral factors include emotions and feelings—sometimes referred to collectively as *affect* within the psychology and management literatures—as well as drives (e.g., hunger, thirst, sex), moods, and pain (Loewenstein, 1996). These can play an important role in the informing process. Unlike performance, arousal, and control, however, many of the sources of visceral factors are not tied to the task-related content of the informing message or the task being performed.

Any separation between the visceral and motivation filters is likely to be one of convenience rather than reality. While I chose to concentrate on intrinsic motivation—in other words, aspects of the informing that satisfy the drive to learn and grow—in the motivation filter, we have already seen that other similar drives exist, such as the desire to acquire, to defend, and, in particular, to bond. These additional drives exert a strong motivational effect. For example, it has long been observed that teachers tend to favor attractive students (e.g., Salvia, Algozzine, & Scheare, 1977) and that students tend to rate attractive instructors more highly (e.g., Ambady & Rosenthal, 1993; Feeley, 2002). These suggest a tight relationship between desire to bond and motivation to learn. Like the motivation filter, these effects may exert their influence through widening or closing off the attention filter.

Visceral factors have the potential to impact virtually every aspect of the informing process, and a full treatment of the subject is beyond the scope of this chapter. Instead, we need to content ourselves with describing some of the mechanisms through which these factors, particularly emotions, may impact the informing process. Specifically, we consider:

1. Impacts of visceral factors on cognitive functions

2. Impacts of visceral factors on choice processes

3. Impacts of anticipated emotions and feelings

4. Impacts of social factors

Cognitive functions

Visceral factors have the ability to impact cognitive functions in many ways. Many of these resemble the task-related filters already discussed except that their source is extrinsic to the task. A number of the effects that have been observed are now described.

Emotions and information processing

Emotions can change the client's ability to process information. For example, a number of important emotion-related effects on information processing in the human cognitive system have been observed (Dolan, 2002):

- *Processing priority*: Emotion-laden information cues appear to get a higher priority when compared with other sensory and cognitive cues.

- *Enhanced memory of emotionally significant events*: Conditioning experiments support anecdotal evidence that when emotionally significant events (e.g., the Challenger disaster) occur, they enter memory more effectively.

- *Recalling past emotion-laden events can affect decision-making*: Specifically, when such states are evoked they can bias decisions either towards or against similar decisions, depending upon the emotions recalled.

Interference

As was the case with arousal related to information flows, visceral and emotional arousal can interfere with cognitive functions, including those related to informing. In the presence of strong arousal from visceral factors, individuals will frequently *and knowingly* act in ways that are inconsistent with their own long term self interest (Loewenstein, 1996). A rather graphic demonstration of the impact of such factors occurred in an experiment that examined how sexual arousal influenced decision-making and judgment (Ariely & Loewenstein, 2006). Subjects, in various states of physical arousal, were asked to rate their attitudes towards various questionable sex-related practices (e.g., safe sex, lying in order to get sex, continuing to pursue sex after a refusal). Uniformly, and highly significantly, their willingness to engage in questionable practices grew with their level of physical arousal.

The ability of visceral factors to interfere with informing was also amply demonstrated in the later stages of the naval gunnery case. In that example, anger became the dominating factor. By the time the process had degenerated into name-calling, it is doubtful that any informing was taking place, despite the fact that information was being communicated.

In considering the impact of visceral factors, a number of propositions are advanced that are particularly likely to be relevant in a client-sender context (Loewenstein, 1996, p. 278):

i.   We tend to become less altruistic than we would like to be when visceral factors intensify.

ii. When making decisions for another person, we tend to ignore or give little weight to visceral factors they are experiencing.

iii. Increasing the intensity of a visceral factor for ourselves and another person in parallel leads to a decline in altruism.

iv. When we experience a particular visceral factor, we tend to imagine others experiencing it as well, regardless of whether they actually are.

v.   People underestimate the impact of visceral factors on other people's behavior.

In the context of informing, this suggests that the sender will expect the client to be a rational party to the informing process even when the sender personally recognizes that visceral factors are influencing his or her own actions. The same would apply to the client's perception of the sender. Given the high potential for influence on cognitive processes of such factors, the failure to recognize their presence on either the client or sender side can present a serious barrier to informing. Like many other effects mentioned in this paper, this barrier could be considerably intensified in situations where channels of low media richness are employed. For example, discussion group trolling (Herring, Job-Sluder, Scheckler, & Barab, 2002) and email flaming (Alonzo & Aiken, 2004) both represent behaviors that interfere with effective informing. Both are posited to have a strong visceral component (e.g., Alonzo & Aiken, 2004). Experience also tells us that similar disruptive behaviors occur much less likely frequently when a media-rich face-to-face channel is used.

Choice effects

There are a number of visceral counterparts to the mental model effects of framing, anchoring, and choice strategies that have been observed. These seem to be particularly pronounced when emotions are involved, although we would expect that other visceral factors could exert a similar influence.

Emotional framing

Effects similar to framing may also be observed that have a distinct emotional component. We refer to these as emotional framing. One previously mentioned example involves the presence of money. Numerous experiments demonstrate that when money is involved, different preferences and behaviors are exhibited than if non-money equivalents are used and that such attitudes cross the line into non-economic contexts. As we saw, for example, individuals are found to be much more likely to cheat when money is not directly involved (Ariely, 2008). The influence of money can also explain, for example, the widely observed phenomenon that consumers spend more when using credit cards than when using cash—even consumers who pay their entire balances each month—and why such spending further increases based on the size of unused credit limits (Soman & Cheema, 2002).

Similar emotional impacts on rational decision making can be found in the phenomenon described as "auction fever" (Ku, Malhotra, & Murnighan, 2005). As noted in the article:

> In 1999, Chicago sponsored a public art exhibit of over 300 life-sized fiberglass cows that culminated in 140 Internet and live, in person auctions. Collectively, the cows sold for almost seven times their initial estimates. (Ku et al., 2005, p. 89)

The nature of the frenzy observed by the researchers caused them to attribute the unexpected valuations to competitive arousal, an emotional reaction to the auction process leading buyers to depart from intended behaviors. We will learn more about this type of herding behavior when we discuss information cascades in Chapter 8.

Although the second of these examples could be attributed to the unfamiliarity of the situation—how often do most people purchase fiberglass cows at auction?—the first example, credit cards being used more freely than cash, cannot. Thus, it is quite plausible that the impact of visceral framing may extend to routine, as well as non-routine, decisions.

Emotional anchoring

Similar to framing, anchoring can occur on an emotional level, as well as on a purely cognitive level. In politics, for example, candidates frequently attempt to draw parallels between their own background and those of other loved politicians, at the same time noting distinctions between themselves and other hated politicians. A particularly famous example of this occurred in the 1988 U.S. presidential campaign, during the vice presidential debate. In prior speeches one candidate, Senator Dan Quayle, had often identified similarities between his own background and that of John F. Kennedy, whose tragic death in office still evokes a strong emotional response in many Americans. His opponent, Senator Lloyd Bentsen, aware of these past comparisons, waited for Quayle to make a similar comparison during a televised debate. When Quayle did, Bentsen then offered the emotional response:

> Senator, I served with Jack Kennedy, I knew Jack Kennedy, Jack Kennedy was a friend of mine. Senator, you are no Jack Kennedy. (Commission on Presidential Debates, 2004)

That statement completely negated the attempted anchoring, as well as becoming the most famous rejoinder ever made during a vice-presidential debate (to be fair, not a terribly high bar to surpass).

Emotional impact on choice strategies

Emotions have been found to play a direct role in decisions involving choice. For example, individuals who are given a set of alternatives and attributes find it more difficult to make trade-offs of emotion-laden attributes for money than less emotion-laden attributes (Luce, Payne, & Bettman, 1999). There is also considerable evidence of the impact of emotional state on the perception of products and on the weighting placed on different product attributes (Adval, 2001). Viewed in the context of prospect theory—a cognitive model for evaluating uncertain and distant outcomes—emotions have been found to impact both perceived outcome values and the weight attached to uncertainty and time preferences when discounting (Rottenstreich & Shu, 2004). As a consequence, emotions can, potentially, distort the informing process in much the same manner as purely cognitive choice heuristics. This is particularly true in situations where the sender is not cognizant of the client's emotions, as would be the case where non-rich media are used as the channel (Daft et al., 1987).

Anticipated feelings

Emotions and feelings may be generated as a consequence of being informed. Where this is the case, the decision to engage in the informing process may be impacted by what the client expects to feel, rather than by what is actually felt. This effect may be amplified by the fact that anticipated feelings are often far greater than the actual feelings that are later experienced (Gilbert, 2007), in which manner they differ from most of the other visceral factors (which tend to be underestimated).

Procrastination

One example of how anticipated emotions can impact informing involves procrastination. If the anticipation of poor performance or failure is strong, a client may avoid attending to the informing system. Consider, for example, the following explanation provided by a distance learning student regarding her failure to attend to the course syllabus:

> What used to be a simple schedule and list of assignments, two pages at most, has become an intimidating document, often a dozen pages long, filled with mandatory administrative policies, honor codes, disability and religious accommodations, complex tables with Web links and even the occasional contractual agreement between instructors and students. Although I'm starting to learn about these things, I still have a strong flight reflex that leads me to avoid that which I cannot immediately understand and prevents me from actively seeking that which I do not want to know. (C. B. Gill, 2006)

Cheating

Cheating is another example of a behavior through which (desired) informing channels are not attended. One study that specifically examined the impact of anticipated emotions on willingness to cheat found that the anticipated elation associated with cheating was an important antecedent of willingness to cheat—much more so than anticipated regret (Sierra & Hyman, 2006).

Refusal to be informed

Anticipated emotions can also play a powerful role in the refusal to learn. One particularly common version of this phenomenon is those situations where the client perceives that by accepting the information, his or her mental models will become at odds with prevailing models in the social network. In the opening example of *Diffusion of Innovations* (Rogers, 2003, p. 1-5), a case study is presented of a Peruvian village in which existing mental models of health were based upon a dichotomy of "hot" and "cold," where "hot" was associated with illness and "cold" was associated with health. The attempts of a health worker to get the community to adopt the practice of boiling water to improve sanitation were largely unsuccessful. This was attributed to the fact that any individual following this practice would be at odds with the prevailing wisdom and behaviors of the community. Indeed, the two examples where the informing effort was successful were in the case of a woman who was already ill—and therefore expected to favor "hot"—and an outsider family, who had moved from another area where the hot-cold dichotomy did not exist.

Social factors

Many of the examples previously cited as evidence for the *Law of Abandoned Expertise* also have social components that amplify the task-specific effect of the proposed law. We saw this demonstrated in the example of the Peruvian village just presented. Similar examples closer to home are also readily available. The student who adopts models or behaviors at odds with his or her peers may be castigated. The scholar who is swayed by evidence that is contrary to existing paradigms may become isolated from colleagues. The middle manager who comes to believe in an unconventional idea, however strong the evidence supporting that idea may be, risks losing credibility and stature in the eyes of both employees and executives.

Conceptually, we can view the social factors that impact motivation to be informed as being somewhat parallel in structure to the intrinsic motivational factors that operate at the task level (Gill & Saunders, 1997). For example, the social constructs of power, dependence, and autonomy map well into control. Both performance and arousal can be viewed in a broader social context rather than being limited to the task itself. For example, the intrinsic benefits of mastery can easily translate into status in a social setting. The arousal experienced during many informing communications will likely have both an informational task-related component and a social component. Indeed, there is an entire category of job described as "emotional labor" (Morris & Feldman,

1996)—which includes many types of customer service activities—for which conveying proper emotions and engaging customers in a personal way are considered more important than the associated information-conveying function of the job. How much the emotional and social aspects of informing will impact the client's willingness to change existing mental models is likely to depend heavily on the context of the informing. Regardless, if we fail to take into account our client's perspective on the anticipated emotional and social consequences of both the informing process and of being informed, the likelihood that informing will be disrupted or distorted in some fashion is great.

The Unique Resonance of Stories

So where do *stories* come in? When it comes to informing, virtually everyone touts their benefits. Economists George Akerlof and Robert Shiller (2009) list them as one of the five "animal spirits" that drive economic behavior[8]. Business researchers Chip and Dan Heath (2007) propose that stories are a particularly sticky form of communication, as we later discuss. Cognitive psychologist Daniel Willingham (2009, p. 51) describes the human mind as being "exquisitely tuned to understand and remember stories." The *Harvard Business Review* uses stories and anecdotes as its principal—and, frequently, only—source of evidence (e.g., Rynes, Giluk, & Brown, 2007, p. 999) and has published articles on the value of story-telling (e.g., Guber, 2007).

There seem to be two general explanations as to why stories are so effective. The first is that, unlike other approaches to formatting a message, stories come with intrinsic built-in linkages that facilitate both storage and recall. Willingham (2009, p. 52) summarizes these as the four C's: causality, conflict, complications, and character. A good story is not a collection of random descriptions or relationships. It is formed so that elements interconnect in a way that the client can recognize. Just as chess experts cannot recreate a board where pieces are placed randomly, a story whose elements are entirely random is unlikely to be retained. We have also already seen that, within limits, humans exhibit an innate desire to understand (i.e., curiosity). Understanding, however, exists on a spectrum that ranges from making sense to complete empathy[9]. By incorporating action and characters, the story moves us further in the direction of empathy than disconnected facts ever could.

The other proposed reason for the effectiveness of stories is that they can, to a great extent, navigate their way through client filters. First, of course, a good story captures attention since we want to find out how it is resolved. Second, as part of the sense-making process, we tend to fill in missing elements with elements that make sense to us (e.g., what the characters or locations look like). These links to existing knowledge, as we just saw, encourage storage and retrieval.

Finally, the story format may mitigate the impact of the *Law of Abandoned Expertise*. If we consider the distribution of expert knowledge (recall Figure 6.2 in Chapter 6), there will always be a mix of core knowledge and knowledge of particular cases. Where a story contains lessons that disagree with core knowledge, it can always be filed away as a "special case." Moreover, a good story will contain insights into the goals (what the characters want), state (what the characters believe) and operators (what the characters do). Thus, the story presents a self-contained problem space that the client may view as being either generalizable or as an anomaly. Whether it requires changing existing knowledge is left to the discretion of the client.

Stickiness: A Unified Approach to Client Resonance?

In *The Tipping Point*, Gladwell (2000) introduced the notion of a "stickiness factor" as being one of the three principal laws of change, later illustrating the concept with examples from children's television shows, such as *Sesame Street* and *Blue's Clues*—where explicit changes to design were implemented to increase their effectiveness in informing preschool clients. The concept of stickiness has been further expanded into a six item framework (Heath & Heath, 2007), referred to using the acronym SUCCESs. The six contributors to stickiness are identified to be:

1. *Simple:* Messages should be as simple as possible.
2. *Unexpected:* Messages are more effective if they contain elements that the client cannot predict in advance.
3. *Concrete:* Concrete messages are more effective than abstract messages.
4. *Credible:* Message effectiveness increases with credibility.
5. *Emotional:* Messages with emotional content are more effective.
6. *Stories:* Stories are among the most effective form of message.

Stickiness has much in common with resonance. In particular, it emphasizes that the form of a message—as opposed to its specific content (i.e., quality, usefulness)—can exert a major influence on whether or not effective informing occurs. As an informal test, it is therefore useful to consider the degree to which the Single Client Resonance Model, presented earlier in Figure 7.1, maps into the SUCCESs framework. Remarkably, they not only seem to correspond quite well but also in the same sequence as the application order as the resonance filters.

Messages that are *simple* and *unexpected* both stand the best chance of penetrating the *attention filter*. Simple reduces the likelihood of cognitive overload; unexpected makes them interesting (Davis, 1971). *Concrete* messages reduce the likelihood of distortion passing through the *cognitive filter*. The less a message is subject to interpretation, the lower the chance that representativeness and confirmation biases will transform the message into something that the client perceives to be already known. *Credibility* should reduce interference from the *risk & time preference filters* and should also help *motivate* the client. Naturally, the *emotional* content of the message maps to the *visceral filters* and we have already discussed the power of stories.

Given the elegance and simplicity of the SUCCESs model, along with its correspondence to the filters of the single client resonance model, why should we bother with more involved conceptual schemes? The justification involves an important difference in purpose. The SUCCESs model is particularly focused on situations where an informing process targets many clients in parallel, as is the case with mass media. For this reason, it is designed to encapsulate the general principles that apply to all clients. In this respect it performs admirably; there is not a single element of the SUCCESs model that does not apply to almost any real mass communication situation.

The *Single Client Resonance Model*, on the other hand, is intended to model informing systems, particularly those existing on a complex landscape. In such systems, we are much less likely to have a complete understanding of the task to be performed and—in many cases—a reasonable sense of the mental models of the individuals who will be performing that task. As a consequence, it can (and needs to) address many issues that may vary on an individual client basis. With increasing sender-task-client-specificity comes the need for increasing comprehensiveness in what we consider. Given the inherent nature of the general informing system—requiring the melding of the needs of the sender, the technologies that support the channels, and the client—it is doubtful that a general set of principles as compact as the SUCCESs model will ever be developed. If, as researchers, we are ever going to contribute to the general understanding of these systems, we must accept that the complexity of the activity that we have chosen to investigate will prove an ever-present and formidable obstacle.

Conclusions

For about half a century academic researchers in business—and other disciplines as well—have been debating whether our research should be focusing on rigor or relevance. In engaging in that debate, many of us lose sight of the fact that our approach to informing our clients is likely to be every bit as important as the quality (rigor) and potential usefulness (relevance) of what we have discovered. This realization needs to be the centerpiece of any serious effort to inform business.

Even if we were to understand all the ins-and-outs of informing a single client, however, the problems of informing business would not be solved. What we need to recognize is that few complex ideas are transferred to a group of clients through a direct, one-way informer-to-client channel or through multimedia. Such direct approaches may succeed with a few clients within a population, but usually not with very many. In fact, experience tells us that client-to-client informing processes dominate the diffusion of innovation. Thus, if we want to convey complex ideas, we need to understand these peer-dominated processes. The role of client networks in non-routine informing is therefore the subject of the next chapter.

Chapter 7 Foundational References

Gladwell, M. (2000). *The Tipping Point*. New York, NY: Back Bay Books.

Heath, C., & Heath, D. (2007). *Made to stick*. New York, NY: Random House.

Jamieson, K., & Hyland, P. (2006). Good intuition or fear and uncertainty: The effects of bias on information systems selection decisions. *Informing Science: The International Journal of an Emerging Transdiscipline, 9*, 49-69. Retrieved from http://inform.nu/Articles/Vol9/v9p049-069Jamieson60.pdf

Morison, E. (1966). *Man, machines and modern times*. Cambridge, MA: MIT Press.

Chapter 7 Notes

[1] In their 2008 book *Nudge*, economists Richard Thaler and Cass Sunstein specifically recommend designing public policies in such a manner that our biases and heuristics be exploited in policy design so as to "nudge" us towards the most individually or socially beneficial decisions.

[2] The other aspect of Figure 7.1 that must be viewed with suspicion is the precise ordering and grouping of the filters. The filters are portrayed as operating in a sequence largely because it is convenient to think of them working in this way. Indeed, where I couldn't come up with a logical reason for one operating before the other, I divided the bar and put both filters in it. For example, the motivational and emotional consequences of a message probably *should not* be weighed until the message contents are understood, but I could not make a judgment as to whether emotion or motivation would be applied first. Since the brain generally does everything in parallel and abhors strict sequences, it would be silly to assume that such a logically designed ordering of filters actually exists. The purpose of a conceptual scheme, however, is primarily to help us organize and systematically consider knowledge related to a given phenomenon. For this purpose, a logical ordering is likely preferable to a random collection of filters.

[3] I particularly liked Willingham's (2009, p. 62) anecdotal example of interference:

> Another teacher once told me she wore a toga to class on the first day she began a unit on ancient Rome. I am sure that got her students' attention. I am also sure it continued to get their attention—that is, to distract them—once the teacher was ready for them to think about something else.

[4] I first encountered the test in Malcolm Gladwell's (2005) *Blink*. I was able to access it at https://implicit.harvard.edu/implicit/

[5] In my case, it turned out that I was moderately inclined to group fat with good—moderate automatic preference for fat—which certainly came as a surprise to me. (FYI, I am fat but not because I particularly prefer to be that way.) Gladwell (2005, p. 84), on the other hand, re-

ported getting moderate automatic preference for whites on the race IAT, despite the fact that he describes himself as half black.

[6] I first encountered the Tetlock (1999) article when it was mentioned in Taleb's (2007) *The Black Swan*. The study was a quasi-experiment which attempted to test the importance of a historian's personal perspective on his or her willingness to accept facts. The first set of tests involved giving experts in different regions (e.g., the Soviet bloc) alternative histories (based on divergences from what actually happened at key points in time) and having them rate the likelihood of different counterfactuals (i.e., things that did not occur in fact, but which might have occurred) that contributed to the divergence. The second set of tests involved taking the earlier published predictions of historians—Tetlock reported having collected over 5000 of these—and examining the subsequent beliefs as to why the predicted event did, or did not, occur. What the study found was that historians were very skeptical of counterfactuals that were inconsistent with their belief system. When their predictions proved consistent with what actually happened, they strongly attributed the result in a manner consistent with their perspective. When results unfolded differently, they tended to attribute that result to factors such as bad timing, claim that their prediction nearly happened, or questioned the validity of the experimental protocol in general. In an interesting side note, the overall accuracy of the predictions of the expert historians of future events proved to be little better than random guessing.

[7] The full exchange between the researchers questioning goal setting and its proponents (Edwin Locke and Gary Latham, the two researchers most influential in the development of the field) is more or less captured by the titles of the articles, which appeared in the following sequence:

1. Goals gone wild: The systematic side effects of overprescribing goal setting (Ordonez, Schweitzer, Galinsky, & Bazerman; 2009a)

2. Has goal setting gone wild, or have its attackers abandoned good scholarship? (Locke & Latham, 2009)

3. On good scholarship, goal setting, and scholars gone wild. (Ordonez, Schweitzer, Galinsky, & Bazerman; 2009b)

4. Science and ethics: What should count as evidence against the use of goal setting? (Latham & Locke, 2009)

What we observe here is a shift in the argument to focus on the rigor filter, then the emotion filter—much as we saw in the naval gunnery case study. We also see clear evidence of the intensity that can accompany the Law of Abandoned Expertise.

[8] The five "animal spirits" identified by Akerlof and Shiller (2009) are: confidence, fairness, corruption, money illusion, and stories. These, they argue, lead to behaviors that undermine the assumption that people rationally pursue their economic interests.

[9] The "making sense" to "complete empathy" spectrum was proposed by Roger Schank (1986) in his book *Explanation Patterns*. The central theme of this book is that understanding is largely equivalent to being able to explain. I personally find this somewhat more convincing than Willingham's (2009, p. 68) "Understanding is memory in disguise" but both descriptions capture the fact that the feeling we get of "understanding" is probably more mechanical than we perceive it to be. I "understand" the multiplication tables because I am so familiar with them that the associated rules "feel" right.

Chapter 8

Non-Routine Informing and Networks

Roadmap & Objectives: In Chapter 7, we presented informing from the perspective of a single informer communicating with a single client. An alternative pattern, however, would involve one or more informed clients communicating with other clients. This mechanism would involve a somewhat different scenario, as we may reasonably assume that informed clients have a better understanding of the pre-existing mental models of uniformed clients than would be the case for external informers. This would be particularly true when non-routine information is being conveyed. This chapter considers the mechanisms by which information flows from an individual to and within a group and also examines how the routineness of the informing situation impacts this overall process.

Given the number of filters that could potentially interfere with non-routine informing described in Chapter 7, it seems remarkable that such informing ever takes place. Actually, this observation is closer to the truth than we might care to believe. In fact, if the domain about which we are communicating is complex, our best prospect for informing mandates an informer with highly reliable insights into the expected nature of those filters. It stands to reason, therefore, that some of the most reliable informers would be individuals very similar in characteristics to the client. In other words, the most plausible informer would seem to be another client.

In this chapter we further explore non-routine informing in the context of client-to-client informing networks. What becomes apparent almost immediately is that these networks of peers are responsible for the lion's share of complex informing that takes place. The process is not without some structure, however. Within any given population there are likely to be some individuals who are unique in their characteristics: individuals highly receptive to innovation, incredibly well networked, or unusually effective communicators. Informing strategies that leverage these individuals stand a particularly good chance of succeeding.

Networked communications also impact the overall behavior of the system. The social influence motivators that cause us to care what our neighbors are doing can lead to information cascades in which the system virtually stampedes to adopt a particular perspective. This behavior can be further exacerbated by the manner in which these networks develop. Far from being random, the degree of connectivity between network participants tends to gravitate towards a power law distribution. This means that a small number of participants become disproportionately connected and can exert an extraordinary influence on system behavior. The importance of these observations later becomes clear in Chapter 9, when their implications for the dynamics of business systems are considered.

The Complex Informing Problem

If there is a common theme to the various filters described in the previous chapter, it is their dependence upon the prior knowledge and emotional state of the client. It is hard to exhibit confirmation bias or the *Law of Abandoned Expertise* when your mind is completely blank on a particular subject. Where prior knowledge and emotional state become particularly problematic, however, is when the informer's goal is to inform an unfamiliar client or group of clients. In these cases, client mental models may be largely unknown to the sender, as would be the specific obstacles such models may present.

I can illustrate these potential challenges with an example from my own experience. Back in the mid-1980s, I was employed as an agribusiness consultant. During that period, my particular expertise was developing computer models of business problems. One such problem was brought to my firm by the *Long Island Duck Farmer's Cooperative*, whose manager approached us desiring to upgrade the organization's production facilities. Because the project was a small one, I assigned a research assistant to determine the costs and built a small spreadsheet-based model. We then proceeded to Long Island to make our presentation.

I invited the research associate to make the presentation to the 17 member cooperative. Very soon after the presentation started, however, considerable hostility from the audience began to surface. Every cost we proposed was questioned, every assumption debated. The situation became so tense that I took over the presentation. A couple of members of the audience—consisting of farmer-owners—seemed sympathetic. The rest seemed positively determined to take apart everything we said.

Eventually, after what had become one of the longest afternoons of my life, the meeting came to an end. At that point, the manager and two of the members met with us, mainly to commiserate. At that time they mentioned some facts of which I had previously been unaware[1]. Duck farms on Long Island happened to be located on some of the priciest land on the entire U.S. east coast. Moreover, as agricultural land, owners of these farms received a huge tax break. Thus, only two of the seventeen members were committed to expanding their production (I leave it to the reader to guess which two). The others had a strong interest in preserving the status quo. Indeed, given how small existing production was on some farms, I freely speculate that members may well have been concerned that their low tax status would be called into question in the absence of the convenient excuse that they were limited by the cooperative's existing production capacity. Needless to say, had I known the mental models in place, I would have rethought the entire presentation. I am sure that the topic "economics of land development for condominiums" would have gone over brilliantly.

What becomes clear from this example is that there must be (at least) two distinct dimensions to informing fit, illustrated in Figure 8.1. The first is the structure of the model we want to convey. Where that model is first year physics or the cost of the factory, it will tend to be high. Where that model is a collection of thoughts about how to appreciate 18th century French literature, it is likely to be far lower; we probably do not have a clear model in mind that we want to convey. The second dimension is our knowledge of existing client models. Do we know the client's background in the subject of concern? Are mental models inconsistent with what we are attempting to communicate in place?

Because the two dimensions of Figure 8.1 obviously interact, we have a "fit" problem that, by its very nature, is likely to exhibit ruggedness (i.e., multiple fitness peaks). Where both types of structure are high, we have routine informing. I choose the term "routine" because it is hard to imagine how both dimensions could become high without repetition of the process. At the other extreme, we have low structure informing. This will necessarily be an exploratory process of interaction between informer and client. The large region in the middle, labeled non-routine informing, represents the case where knowledge is somewhat imperfect on one or both sides.

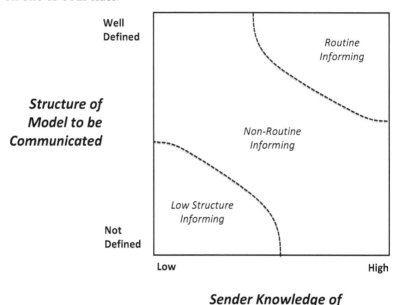

Figure 8.1: Structure of informing processes

In the absence of clear knowledge of client mental models, we are necessarily in the non-routine informing zone, regardless of how well we know what we want to convey. That leads to a critical question: How can you inform a community of clients, particularly if the topic is complicated? Most likely, the process will need to begin with a two-way, low structure informing process with a very small number of clients—perhaps even one. Through interaction, you can gain a sense of the individual's existing knowledge and state of mind. After that, however, the informed client(s) can become instrumental in informing the rest of their community. Particularly if the community is relatively homogeneous, these informed clients will have a far clearer picture of the remaining clients than you ever will.

Diffusion Models

As it turns out, the reasoning that clients would be particularly effective at informing other clients is not misplaced. In fact, client-to-client informing appears to play the dominant role in many knowledge diffusion processes. This contention is supported by the huge literature on the diffusion of innovations (as of 2003, an estimated 5200 publications on the subject; Rogers, 2003, p. xvii). The seminal book in the field, *Diffusion of Innovations* (now in its 5th edition), was written by the late Everett Rogers, a researcher whose pioneering studies of diffusion were conducted in the 1950s after patterns started to become apparent in the adoption of farming technologies during the 1930s and 1940s. Some of the key findings from this research stream, as summarized by Rogers, are as follows:

- Certain characteristics tend to make some innovations easier to diffuse than others. Examples of these are simplicity, compatibility with previous models or ideas, relative advantage compared to previous ideas, trialability (the ability to try out the innovation prior to adopting it), and observability (Rogers, 2003, p. 222). Ideas lacking these characteristics take much longer to diffuse.

- Diffusion does not occur immediately but, instead, through a gradual process of adoption within the client community. Two forces that are particularly important for this process are mass media (i.e., any communication where a single sender provides information to multiple clients concurrently) and interpersonal communications within the client network. In general, mass media communications are more important in the earlier stages of communications, while interpersonal communications dominate later stages (Mahajan, Muller, & Bass, 1991, cited in Rogers, 2003).

- Diffusion processes often have to reach a "critical mass" after which diffusion starts to take off at a very rapid rate (Rogers, 2003, p. 349).

- Individuals within client communities are not homogeneous. Rather, they exhibit different characteristics with respect to their willingness to adopt innovations. These may be modelled in terms of thresholds (Rogers, 2003, p. 355). Idealized categories of adopters are often classified as: innovators, early adopters, early majority, late majority, and laggards (Rogers, 2003). Individuals may also exhibit different degrees of influence on other clients in the community (e.g., opinion leaders; Rogers, 2003, p. 300), awareness of the social nature of the community (e.g., key informants; Rogers, 2003, p. 310), and willingness to venture outside of their community and cumulative past experience (innovators; Rogers, 2003, p. 282).

Because mass media, when used to convey complex ideas, generally influences only the most receptive portions of the client community (e.g., innovators), we can expect that interpersonal client-to-client communications will play an increasingly critical role in idea diffusion as the complexity of the idea grows and in informing the less receptive members of the client community.

Small World Network Model

Diffusion models are generally specified in terms of information moving out into a community. Network models, on the other hand, view multiple clients as a network of connected entities, sometimes referred to as a topology. A particularly common type of network model is called the small world model (e.g., Watts, 2003). In this topology, closely linked sub-communities are joined by infrequent links between communities, as shown in Figure 8.2. It was developed primarily to explain a commonly observed phenomenon in human networks, popularly referred to as the "six degrees of separation"

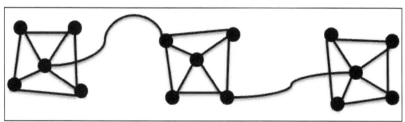

Figure 8.2: Small world model (Watts, 2003), showing tightly connected clusters tied together by a small number of cross cluster links.

The six-degrees phenomenon was first identified by social psychologist Stanley Milgram[2] (Travers & Milgram, 1969), who was a virtual dynamo in the production of interesting psychological experiments. In the

1960s, he gave 296 volunteers in Boston and Omaha letters intended for a particular individual (the target was a stock broker in Sharon, Massachusetts). Participants were given general information about the target but they had to abide by the following rules:

- They could send the letter only to people that they personally knew. Those people could, in turn, participate in the experiment.

- They had to fill out a roster (to prevent individuals from receiving the same letter later in the chain).

- They had to send in a card giving some information about themselves.

While a substantial number of the letters did not get delivered, many (64) did and the mean length of the chains was 5.2—with the Boston chains (mean 4.4) being only slightly shorter than the Nebraska chains (mean 5.5).

The experimental results were surprising since it had previously been assumed that because people in a given community tend to know the same people, any route to the target would necessarily be very long and convoluted. Instead, it appeared that 6 steps were generally enough. Moreover, the actual results seemed likely to be far from optimum, since the experiment's rules required that the volunteers guess who among their acquaintances would most likely know the target. Thus, 6 steps seemed to represent an *upper bound*.

The explanation for the small world phenomenon that emerged is as follows. Although we tend to exist in closely linked communities, we are normally situated in several such communities. For example, there is our work community, our job community, and perhaps church, alumni, and hobby communities as well. Because each of these networks is linked based upon different criteria (e.g., who you live near vs. who you work with), information can leap from community to community and, in process, move great physical distances quite rapidly. For example, the target's alma mater, graduation date, and home town were included in the profile in addition to his or her profession. If you happened to know anyone matching those items, this person would be a logical choice for the next link in the chain.

Tipping Points

The *Tipping Point* model (Gladwell, 2000) further synthesizes the findings of diffusion and network topology research into a series of general principles that guide the flow of information in networked human systems. The concept of "critical mass" in innovation theory is restated in terms of *tipping points*. As these points are reached, the level of communication of a particular idea within a social system suddenly jumps dramatically. Gladwell organizes his findings into four central themes:

1. *The Law of the Few* (Gladwell, 2000, p. 30): Three types of individuals play a particularly crucial role in the diffusion of information within social systems. *Connectors* maintain active communications links with an unusually large number of individuals within and outside of the immediate social network. For example, given a random set of last names from a phonebook, a connector might be able to identify personal connections with 3-10 times as many names as the average individual. *Mavens* act as sinks for information, gathering information from many sources and willingly sharing it with others in the community. *Salesmen*, whom we will refer to as *Persuaders*, are unusually adept at convincing other individuals to adopt a particular product or idea.

2. *The Stickiness Factor* (Gladwell, 2000, p. 30): As mentioned in Chapter 7, certain characteristics of a communication (e.g., simplicity, unexpectedness, concreteness, credibility, emotional impact, story setting; Heath & Heath, 2007) make it particularly likely to resonate with a client.

3. *The Power of Context, Part I* (Gladwell, 2000, p. 133): Small aspects of the decision-making setting can exert a huge influence on overall decision-making.

4. *The Power of Context, Part II* (Gladwell, 2000, p. 169): The effective size of a social community is limited to roughly 150 participants. Beyond this point, there is insufficient cohesion for consistent messages to be shared among all members.

Common to diffusion models, the key participants involved in moving information within the client community are, themselves, members of that community. The only exception to this is connectors, who often serve the role of connecting disparate communities together. In my own research I explored the impact of these participants on the speed of diffusion using spreadsheet simulation models. My results were consistent with Gladwell's model; a diversity of participants led to faster spread of information than was achieved by a homogeneous group (Gill, 2008c).

Information Cascades

A particularly pronounced version of the "tipping point" phenomenon is known as the *information cascade*. The theory of cascades (also referred to as informational cascades) was originally developed to explain rapid changes in behavior within a group, as are often observed in fashion, financial markets, science, and medicine (Bikhchandani, Hirshleifer, & Welch, 1992). In addition, it can be used to explain consistencies in behavior that are not necessarily rational, such as tendencies of employers to discount applicants with a long stretch of unemployment, perceived as evidence of rejection by previous employers (Kubler & Weizsacker, 2003) or for the tendency of a paper rejected by one journal to be rejected by subsequent journals (Bikhchandani et al., 1992). Prior to cascade theory, explanations of such behavior included (Bikhchandani et al., 1992, p. 993):

(1) sanctions on deviants,

(2) positive payoff externalities [meaning that consistency of adoption leads to higher overall payoffs, as might occur when everyone adopts the same communication standard],

(3) conformity preference, and

(4) communication [such as occurs when prior adopters extol the benefits of their choice].

Although these explanations certainly help account for rapid adoptions of a particular behavior, they are not particularly useful in explaining why behaviors might suddenly shift.

The basic concepts behind an information cascade are straightforward. In the simplest case, assume that that multiple individual clients are each faced with making a choice between two alternatives. In order to make that choice, two sources of information are available:

1. Private information, including information from direct observation by the individual client of the alternatives.

2. Public information regarding what previous clients have adopted each alternative.

If the clients start to use public information in preference to private information, then very quickly those clients will gravitate towards the same alternative, leading to the cascading or herding phenomenon. One of the two original formulations of the model also extended the analysis to include choices between many options (Banerjee, 1992).

Experimental studies have found that information cascade behaviors are relatively easy to produce (e.g., Anderson & Holt, 1997). They also demonstrate that even when subjects are aware of the information cascade phenomenon, they will often fail to recognize that a cascade is taking place and therefore tend to be overconfident in their judgment regarding the suitability of a choice (Grebe, Schmid, & Stiehler, 2008).

The information cascade model often incorporates heterogeneity among individual clients. Threshold models, for example, assume a process where individuals do not join the cascade until a certain level of adoption has been reached. There is certainly anecdotal evidence that some individuals have a particular susceptibility to cascade phenomena such as bubbles and fads. For example, during the peak of the tulip bubble that occurred in Holland in the 17th century, another bubble—known as "Conchylomania", the collection of sea shells—was also in progress. One collector who died during that period had enough tulips to fill a 38-page inventory. That was not the only item he collected, however:

> ...he also had 2,389 shells, and considered them so precious that, a few days before his death, he had them put away in a chest with three separate locks. The three executors of his estate each got a single key, so they could show the collection only when all three of them were present. (Conniff, 2009, p. 46)

In another example of heterogeneity, experts can play an important role in information cascades. In a cascade situation, where all participants make a decision based upon what other participants have chosen, the state-of-the-world has little influence on behavior. Including just a few experts—who base decisions on the state-of-the-world rather than on the behavior of other agents—can lead to changes in the system when exogenous events occur (Bowden & McDonald, 2008). Similarly, information cascades can be influenced by opinion leaders, who are not necessarily experts, which implies that cascade phenomena can sometimes be inhibited by aggregating information so that details—such as who voted for a particular proposition in a meeting—are hidden (Arya, Glover, & Mittendorf, 2006)[3].

Where an information cascade can become particularly pronounced is where client adoptions themselves become a source of fitness. For example, some bookstore chains aggressively discount best-sellers. As a result, sales figures not only provide a source of adoption information, they also can directly impact fitness itself (by leading to higher discounts for the most popular books). Similarly, the fitness of a film experience is likely to be enhanced by the individual's ability to talk about it with other people (satisfying both learning and bonding needs); the more people who see the film, the greater the number of opportunities for such discussions. This type of positive feedback loop tends to make "the rich get richer."

Positive feedback from estimates-of-fitness has also been proposed as an explanation for economic bubbles and busts (Stix, 2009). As the stock market indexes (an estimate-of-fitness of the underlying economy) or housing sale prices (an estimate-of-fitness for the housing market) rise, confidence builds, encouraging us to buy more. Seeing our neighbors do the same contributes to the exuberance. Soon, whatever economic forces drove the initial rise are forgotten, and the rise continues based on pure positive feedback alone[4]. Finally, something occurs—large or small—that undermines our confidence. At this point, our generic motivation to defend kicks in. We find ourselves experiencing anxiety. Even faster than the market rose, the stampede to exit (which also builds on itself) causes the bubble to burst.

It is important to note that the information cascade is not, in and of itself, an informing phenomenon. The type of "information" that cascades can offer is very limited—certainly not the highly complicated ideas associated with diffusion. What mainly gets impacted through the cascade phenomenon is the motivation filter; in fact, if they were not already named, I believe "motivational cascades" would be a much better description. We must not underestimate the importance of motivation, however. As a consequence of such cascades, we may be induced to read a long book, take a particular course, see a particular film, attend a particular university, or apply a particular treatment to our crops. In other words, a cascade can be the trigger that initiates a long and involved informing process.

The Ubiquitous Power Law

The positive feedback "rich get richer" loop just described for information cascades turns out to be a fairly common phenomenon. It usually happens in the presence of two competing forces:

1. Forces that tend to oppose the development of size or momentum. In the case of a book or film, for example, the continuous stream of activities that compete for our attention makes it hard for any book to get a lot of readers. We'll call these the *forces of entropy.*

2. Forces that tend to encourage size or momentum. In the case of a book, this might include the ability to discuss it with others (which grows with readership or viewing) and economies of scale (e.g., discounts that result from high volume). We'll call these the *forces of cohesion.*

In the competition between these forces, entropy is usually the winner. What that means is that elements relatively small in size or momentum dominate the landscape. Every once in a while, however, conditions become just right to allow the forces of cohesion to coalesce to create larger elements. What is particularly interesting about this type of process is that it frequently generates a distribution that we have seen before: the power law.

The core relationship associated with the power law is:

$$F(x) = ax^K$$

Taking the logarithm of both sides, we get:

$$Log (F(x)) = Log (a) + K Log(x)$$

This leads to the characteristic signature of a power law, a straight line (of slope K) on a log-log plot. In real world systems, however, you will never get a pure power curve. System limitations necessarily put an upper bound on size (e.g., the sum of all assets place an upper bound on wealth, celestial bodies that get too large turn into stars when their own gravity becomes sufficient to induce fusion). Random variations (including measurement error) also distort the curve at the lower end. Wealth, for example, can potentially be negative but it is not clear what that means from a practical standpoint since bankruptcy can be used to repudiate debts. In the case of celestial bodies, it is hard to get smaller than an atom. Thus, a typical power law plot of observations will look something like that of Figure 8.3. What is important to remember about the plot is that the axes are logarithms. In other words, if Figure 8.3 were plotted in base 10 logarithms, the six dots in the power law region would represent size differences of 10^6 (a million). It is not unusual, however, for actual power laws to operate over much larger regions.

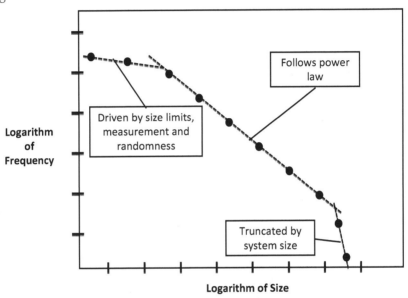

Figure 8.3: Typical observed power law plot

A typical power distribution follows a ratio formula like the familiar 80/20 rule[5] first noticed by Alfredo Pareto in his studies of European economies in the 1800s (Watts, 2003). Observed variations of the power law have been described under a variety of names, such as Pareto distributions (e.g., wealth), Zipf's Law (e.g., word usage, city size) and the Gutenberg-Richter law (e.g., earthquakes). When we are talking about a size distribution, what we normally are plotting is the log of the size against a frequency measure, such as the number of observations of that size we expect to observe during a particular time interval[6].

A representative set of observed power law examples is presented in Table 8.1[7]. The fact that book sales made the list—as well as being used as an example of information cascades—proves to be very significant in Chapter 9, where we consider how we perceive the future. What it suggests is that cascade phenomena are likely to exhibit a power law relationship in their intensity. That, in turn, means that very large events are likely to be inevitable in any system that exhibit cascades.

Table 8.1: Some examples of phenomena that follow power laws

Entity	Forces of entropy	Forces of cohesion
Asteroids	Existing kinetic energy; breakups upon collision	Gravitational attraction
Book sales	Alternative sources of information; competition	Opportunities to share interests; economies of scale
Cities	Scarcity of resources such as food and water; lack of living space	Opportunities for efficient commerce
Companies	Competition; market saturation	Economies of scale, name recognition
Earthquakes	Movement of tectonic plates	Roughness of plate edges
Learning	Forgetting, competing demands for attention, boredom	More linkages make long term storage more efficient
Sexual partners	Jealousy, exhaustion	Allure of the in-demand partner
Wealth	Economic volatility, taxes, earning ability	Opportunities are attracted to wealth
Weblog links	Competition; diversity of topics	Most popular are easy to find
Word usage	The need to express a diverse set of concepts	Familiarity makes words easier to retrieve

What truly distinguishes a power law relationship from other types of distribution is the fact that it is scale free. What this means is that as you step back from it, its shape tends to appear the same. For example, if you look only within the top 20% of an 80/20 distribution, you'll find it is also divided up 80/20 (which would represent 64% and 16% of the original values). Similarly, if you were to be given an outline of many coastlines—Norway being the most commonly used example—and no scale were provided, it would be nearly impossible to tell by the shape if the perspective were drawn from a few hundred yards up or a few hundred miles up.

One important, and somewhat frustrating, aspect of power law relationships is that they are hard to estimate. There are three reasons for this. First, you need a lot of observations in order to capture enough data to develop a good estimate of the exponent (the slope of the log-log line). That is because the large, crucially important events that are characteristic of a power law are quite infrequent. Second, in many power law situations, the vast majority of observations (numerically) come from the range dominated by effects like measurement error—such as the problems we described in categorizing negative wealth—and randomness. Within that range, behavior may be more usefully modeled using other tools. Third, it is fairly common for observations to be generated by different processes, in which case more than one power law may be involved. Such appeared to be the case for asteroids, for example, based upon my cursory web search. As a consequence, the assertion that a particular relationship follows a power law can nearly always be disputed and alternative explanations—such as abnormal outliers—proposed. In Chapter 10, during our discussion of rigor, it becomes clear why this dispute is so important. For now, however, we turn to the implications of power laws for informing networks.

Scale Free Networks

When communications patterns are considered in the abstract, it is relatively easy to posit benefits for both centralized and decentralized structures:

- *Centralized*: When communications come into a hub—which might be a piece of equipment or a person—it is relatively easy to get from one place to another. Also, the hub can serve as a clearing house of knowledge, making a particular piece of information easy to find. On the other hand, all the incoming and outgoing traffic places large demands on the hub—leading to stress and rapid drops in performance—and the entire network is vulnerable when a hub fails.

- *Decentralized*: When entities communicate peer-to-peer, relaying traffic when a direct connection cannot be made, the system is very robust and can also handle increasing loads without degrading rapidly. On the other hand, large amounts of time can be wasted in the process of relaying traffic and knowledge can be very hard to find.

These types of issues would be familiar to any student who has taken a data communications or database class. They also seem very reminiscent of the forces of cohesion and forces of entropy that seem to predict the likely existence of a power law relationship.

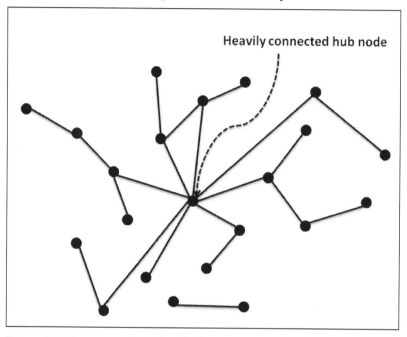

Figure 8.4: Representation of scale-free network with emergent heavily connected hub node.

As it turns out, this speculation is borne out by actual networks. In the scale free network model, connection densities of nodes are governed by a power law. Such a network naturally evolves under circumstances where new nodes gravitate towards connections with existing nodes that are highly connected ("the rich get richer", Barabasi, 2002, p. 79). As networks grow large, this will naturally lead to the emergence of hub nodes that play a particular influential role in enabling communications across the system, as illustrated in Figure 8.4. Barabasi and his colleagues demonstrated that the Internet and World Wide Web map very well to this pattern, both in terms of router[8] activity and links between sites.

When we talk about social networks, what we see is precisely the same pattern played out in connectors (who exhibit an unusually large number of communications links to other people) and mavens (who amass unusually large and diverse stores of knowledge). This type of clustering is seen in many types of affiliation networks, such as corporate directors, which appear to follow a small world model (Watts, 2003). There is also evidence that knowledge of such clustering can be exploited to improve the effectiveness of informing processing. In a widely repeated example (e.g., Gladwell, 2000; Rogers, 2003), in 1775 two men left Boston, Massachusetts on horseback, following separate routes to alert the surrounding communities of British troop movements. One of them was Paul Revere, a classic connector in Gladwell's terminology, who was the hub of many of the most significant social and civic activities in the greater Boston area. Not only did he succeed extraordinarily well, rousing the members of every community he visited, he ended up being immortalized in a famous poem by Henry Wadsworth Longfellow. The other, William Dawes, rode 17 miles through communities of similar population yet was unable to rouse anywhere near the same level of support. He is now mainly known for being so ineffective by comparison to Revere.

Conclusions

In the previous chapter, we were particularly concerned with the challenges presented by low structure informing—where neither what the client knows nor the precise knowledge we want to convey is well defined. In such situations, effective informing is likely to occur only through intensive engagement between a motivated informer and client. At the other extreme, routine informing, both what is to be conveyed and pre-existing client models are well understood. For these cases, highly structured communications systems—such as information systems or mass media—will probably do the trick.

The central focus of this chapter has been the non-routine informing process, slightly more structured than low-structure but much less well defined than routine. Such a scenario probably describes most of the situations where we are informing business. The principal conclusions are as follows:

1. Non-routine informing is vastly more likely to take place through established personal relationships than through broadcast channels, such as mass media. Within any large group, there will likely be a few who can be reached through impersonal efforts (e.g., the mavens), but they will be in the minority.

2. An important type of informing that may take place through broadcast channels is communications reflecting the degree to which a community has been informed or has adopted a particular mental model. This type of informing can be very significant because social influence can strongly impact the motivation filters of individual clients. In doing so, it can lead to sudden shifts in the community's knowledge or behavior, referred to as information cascades.

3. When an outsider informs a group with a non-routine message, peer-to-peer processes, a.k.a. "word of mouth" will account for a much larger share of informing than the direct efforts of the outsider.

4. Within communities of shared knowledge and values, considerable variation in the degree of connectivity associated with a particular individual is likely to exist. This is an emergent property of complex networks of all sorts, and is observed in human networks as well. Highly connected individuals, known as connectors, may exhibit more connectivity by an order of magnitude or more. Informing these individuals can significantly increase the rate of information diffusion through a community.

In developing the theory for items (2) and (4), we also noted that a particular type of distribution—the power law—is often observed. This distribution turns out to play a very important role in both Chapter 9 and 10, since it exerts a profound impact on our ability to accurately forecast the future.

Chapter 8 Foundational References

Barabasi, A. L. (2002). *Linked.* New York, NY: Plume.
Gladwell, M. (2000). *The Tipping Point.* New York, NY: Back Bay Books.

Rogers, E. M. (2003). *Diffusion of Innovations* (5th ed.). New York, NY: Free Press.

Taleb, N. N. (2007). *The Black Swan.* New York, NY: Random House.

Watts, D. J. (2003). *Six degrees: The science of a connected age.* New York, NY: Norton.

Chapter 8 Notes

[1] A news story detailing what was going on at the cooperative at around that time was published by the Los Angeles Times (Hillinger, 1986).

[2] My original acquaintance with the Milgram experiment is based largely upon the account written by Duncan Watts (2003), in *Six Degrees* and a similar account appears in Galdwell's (2000) *The Tipping Point.* Milgram's most famous experiment was not related to the six degree concept. Rather, it was an experiment where subjects willingly administered shocks (they thought) to volunteers at the instruction of a lab assistant.

[3] A number of criticisms and limitations have been identified with respect to the pure information cascade model. For example, in some experimental simulations, temporary cascades are more common than extended cascades (Goeree, Palfrey, Rogers, & McKelvey, 2007), a phenomenon not predicted by the basic model. When allowed to pay for private information, experimental subjects have been found to pay more than an optimal amount in early stages of play, preventing cascade formation in some cases (Kubler & Weizsacker, 2004). Improvements in decision making with payoffs, an effect not predicted by the model, have also been observed (Anderson, 2001). In field settings, cascades do not always appear as expected. For example, motion picture revenues are better modeled with an extension that allows individuals to report quality to each other (De Vany & Lee, 2001). Social groups and collective knowledge may also play a larger role in decision consistency than is credited by cascade models (Shiller, 1995). Despite these qualifications, however, cascade behaviors are widely observed and are to be expected in situations where individuals employ the social influence heuristic and therefore weigh what others do in their own decision-making.

[4] We would not expect all types of assets to experience positive feedback bubbles, since the availability of solid fitness estimates outside of

price should tend to add stability. Asset classes most likely to be susceptible to bubbles of this type will therefore tend to lack other estimates-of-fitness that could be used as a basis of comparison to the estimate provided by price. Characteristics that could contribute to such a shortage of estimates might include:

- Intrinsic fitness that is highly subjective except by comparison to other assets of the same class (e.g., artworks, tulips, fiberglass cows, residential homes in built-out areas)

- Fitness that is very hard to estimate or highly dependent upon other hard-to-estimate conditions, such as the future economy (e.g., company stock prices, commercial real estate, South Sea real estate)

- Fitness that varies significantly across different groups of customers or which interacts with other assets (e.g., commodities, such as oil, may be required in order to keep other productive assets—such as your car—operational)

[5] The ratio of a power law is not necessarily 80/20. The actual values will be determined by the exponent. For example, John Burry Jr., as chairman and chief executive officer of Cleveland-based Blue Cross & Blue Shield of Ohio, conducted a Pareto analysis of medical expenses (Burry, 1992) and found over 2/3 of all expenses were the result of 10% of the subscribers. The top 1% was accountable for 31% of all expenses and the top 50 people, in terms of expenses, cost more than the bottom 75,000.

[6] Benoit Mandelbrot, for example, plotted the percentage variations in the price of cotton and other commodities and found that they followed the basic power law pattern (Bak, 1996), with large variations being much scarcer than small variations. A similar distribution was observed when the length of the coastline of Norway within equal size boxes was estimated. This type of scale free manifestation of the power law—proven to be extremely common in nature—has given birth to the science of fractal geometry, now used extensively in computer generated art because the underlying mathematics are quite simple yet the results produced can be extremely realistic.

[7] The purpose of the power law examples in Table 8.1 was to illustrate the diversity of phenomena following the distribution. The original discovery of the power law distribution was made in the area of wealth by Alfredo Pareto (Watts, 2003). The sexual partners reference came from Barabasi (2002, p. 137). The weblogs article came from a contribution to a mailing list made by Clay Shirky (2003). Earthquakes are discussed extensively by Per Bak in his book *How Nature Works* (1996). The learning curve was discussed in Chapter 6. The power law distribution in word usage became known as Zipf's Law, after the Harvard linguist who discovered it (Taleb, 2007). He also pointed out the distribution of city sizes (Bak, 1996). The power law of company sizes was mentioned by Mauboussin (2008, p. 230) and in numerous other places. I looked up asteroids myself on the Internet, since they seemed like a likely candidate and, sure enough, power laws describe them too. The point here is that nearly any object that experiences both entropy and cohesion seems likely to display a power law over some of its range.

[8] In a communications network, a router connects to multiple sources (including other routers) and relays information between them, serving as a kind of information post office.

Chapter 9

Complexity and Time Horizons

Roadmap & Objectives: Chapter 8 showed how peer-to-peer communications provide a particularly important pathway for non-routine informing. As the expansion of large peer-to-peer networks is facilitated by technology and globalization, however, we fundamentally alter the complexity characteristics of our business systems: increasing the number of entities, their degree of interaction and the rate at which they change. This chapter explores the relationship between complexity and individual time horizons, presenting arguments that as complexity grows, time horizons will tend to shrink even where such shrinkage works against individual and societal best interests—making the lengthening of time horizons an important social priority.

When the crisis of confidence in business was introduced in the first chapter, I commented that many of the failures in business practice that have recently been observed can be characterized as failures to recognize the long term consequences of actions. Bubbles always burst; a manufacturer cannot operate at a cost disadvantage forever; Ponzi schemes inevitably collapse. Even when those consequences should have been obvious, however, well-educated managers and investors apparently ignored them. Thus, understanding the role of time horizons in decision making and informing is a continuing priority in this book.

Time horizons prove to be related to complexity in two important ways, both of which are discussed in this chapter. First, complexity can be a major contributor to the uncertainty of the future. Such uncertainty naturally leads to discounting, or even ignoring, future consequences that seem to defy prediction. Second, as technology and globalization increase the number and variety of individuals and entities that we interact with, the complexity of the global informing network naturally grows. A side effect of this growth is increased prevalence of characteristic system-wide behaviors such as *punctuated equilibrium* that further increase the unpredictability of the future, and the challenge of maintaining a long-term perspective.

Time Horizons

Closely related to the concept of discounting, a time horizon refers to the distance into the future that an individual considers when making decisions in the present. As a general rule, we would expect three factors to be particularly influential in determining a rational decision-maker's time horizons:

1. *Preference:* How far into the future we consider will depend somewhat on our preferences for present versus future gratification. Implied by this is that if you cannot identify with your future self[1] or your posterity, then it is unlikely you are going to engage in behaviors that postpone present gratification for the sake of your (their) future benefits.

2. *Uncertainty:* Our ability to forecast the future influences our ability to consider it. If the future seems very uncertain, our ability to incorporate it into our decision-making is quite limited.

3. *Controllability:* Even if the future seems relatively certain, our willingness to consider it in our decision-making will depend on our ability to affect it (at least from the perspective of the direct or indirect part we will play[2]). As we have previously seen, control is a strong intrinsic motivator.

There is little consensus regarding what constitutes short and long term thinking (Brier, 2005). There is, however, a widespread consensus that our time horizons are too short[3]. Frequently mentioned evidence of this phenomenon in the U.S. includes inadequate savings rates, mediocre educational performance (with respect to other countries), insufficient research and development (R&D), looming deficits, large out-of-wedlock birth rates, and countless other indicators.

Risk and Uncertainty Heuristics

One of the greatest impacts of time is its natural, some might say inevitable, tendency to generate uncertainty. Time, however, is not the only source of uncertainty; randomness can also be one, as can *pseudo-randomness*, defined earlier as unexplained variability generated by a process that we do not fully understand.

Within the decision sciences, it is common to distinguish between risk and uncertainty. Risk is present when the level of randomness can be precisely quantified in probabilistic terms. For example, the probability of rolling 3 on a (fair) six-sided die is 1/6. Uncertainty is present when we do not have a precise probabilistic estimate of the odds of a particular outcome. In considering the two, however, it is important to recognize the following:

> *In a complex environment, there are very few activities properly described by* **risk** *outside of gambling*[4].

To explain this assertion, consider the probabilistic sounding finding relating to coffee drinking first used as an example in Chapter 3:

> Men who had six cups per day or more experienced a reduced risk for type II diabetes of 54%.

Given that this involved a study of over a hundred thousand people over a period of 15 years, you could easily argue that we have a sufficiently accurate estimate of the probabilities involved so as to make the uncertainty vs. risk debate academic[5]. Unfortunately, landscape ruggedness makes the distinction much more meaningful. Assuming you happen to be a coffee guzzling man who does not already have type II diabetes, consider just a few of the possible confounding factors:

1. If you discover you have some other terminal disease, the efficacy of coffee in reducing diabetes risk is likely to be moot—since it is very unlikely you will live long enough to contract it.

2. Diabetes risk increases with weight and inactivity. How likely is it that the same 54% reduction holds across all weights?

3. Susceptibility to diabetes, like most diseases, almost certainly has some inheritable component. How likely is it that the 54% holds across all genetic predispositions?

These are examples of precisely the type of interactions that we'd expect in a complex system. Taken together, what appears to be a "solid" risk number is, at best, a guesstimate of uncertainty when applied to a particular individual's situation.

A central theme of this book has been to argue that complex processes are much more common in business than decomposable processes. It would therefore be reasonable to conclude that uncertainty is much more common than risk. An interesting piece of supporting evidence for this conclusion comes from the history of science. Much elementary probability theory is mathematically straightforward; the algebra necessary to perform the necessary analysis was in place by the time of the ancient Greeks. Despite this fact, the first book on probability theory was not created until the early 1500s, written by Gerolamo Cardano and not published until after his death in 1576. Even as late as the 18th century, what would be considered elementary errors today could be found in the published work on probability[6].

Given that true risk is rarely encountered in the natural world, it is not surprising that the heuristics we employ tend to be very bad when it comes to addressing risk in a "rational" manner. Similar to the heuristics presented in Chapter 5, the pre-existing knowledge incorporated into these heuristics can influence our ability to inform (as described in Chapter 7), as well as exerting an influence on our time horizons. Consider some of the examples that follow.

Example 1: *We vastly overvalue the impact of very small risks*. At very low levels of likelihood, our focus tends to drift towards the consequences rather than the risks involved. For example, when individuals consider playing lotteries, they tend to concentrate on the payoff rather than on the likelihood of winning (the rational decision-maker would concentrate on the product of the two).

Example 2: *We treat complete certainty very differently from very high certainty*. For example, faced with choice between a 100% probability of a payoff and a 99% probability of a payoff, we are willing to sacrifice a great deal to get the extra 1% likelihood.

The inconsistencies that can result from Examples 1 and 2 were demonstrated by Daniel Kahneman and Amos Tversky (1979, p. 267) in an experiment where subjects were given two choices:

Choice 1:

 a. A 50% chance of winning a 3 week tour of the U.K., France and Italy.

 b. A 1 week tour of the U.K.

Choice 2:

 a. A 5% chance of winning a 3 week tour of the U.K., France and Italy.

 b. A 10% chance of winning a 1 week tour of the U.K.

For Choice 1, 22% chose the first option, while 78% chose the second. For Choice 2, however, 67% chose the first option, while only 33% chose the second. Based upon a "rational" choice scheme, the same choice should have been made in both cases since the odds remained in the same ratio (50%-100% vs. 5%-10%).

Example 3: Gambler's Fallacy. We assume that random processes necessarily produce erratic looking results. For example, if asked to order the following three coin toss sequences by their likelihood (assuming a fair coin), most uninitiated individuals would chose 2, then 3, then 1:

1. HHHHHHHHHH

2. HTTHTHHTHT

3. HHHHHTTTTT

In fact, any specific sequence is as likely as any other, so their likelihood is identical.

Example 4: We tend to be overconfident with respect to our abilities both to estimate and to control probabilities. On the estimation side, when asked to establish range brackets for estimates, we usually choose bounds that are too narrow. This problem was first demonstrated at Harvard Business School, where MBAs were given a variety of obscure data points to estimate and were asked to specify ranges that were 98% likely to contain the actual values—meaning that they should have been wrong about the value being outside the range about 2% of the time. The actual error rate was closer to 45% (Taleb, 2007)[7]. A sample test is provided in Figure 9.1[8].

Self-Test of Overconfidence	90% Confidence Interval	
	Lower	Upper
1. Martin Luther King's age at death	——	——
2. Length of the Nile River (in miles)	——	——
3. Number of countries in OPEC	——	——
4. Number of books in the Old Testament	——	——
5. Diameter of the moon (in miles)	——	——
6. Weight of an empty Boeing 747 (in pounds)	——	——
7. Year in which Wolfgang Amadeus Mozart was born	——	——
8. Gestation period of an Asian elephant (in days)	——	——
9. Air distance from London to Tokyo (in miles)	——	——
10. Deepest known point in the ocean (in feet)	——	——

Figure 9.1: Test of overconfidence, originally published in Russo & Shoemaker (1989) and included in Lo (2005, p.4).

On the control side, individuals seem to believe that they can exert some special control over obviously random processes, a special case of the *illusions of control* previously mentioned in Chapter 5. For example:

> ...people bet more money on games of chance when their opponents seemed incompetent than competent—as though they believed they could control the random drawing of cards from the deck and thus take advantage of a weak opponent. People feel more certain that they will win the lottery if they can control the number on their ticket, and they feel more confident that they will win a dice toss if they can throw the dice themselves (Langer, 1975, and Dunn & Wilson, 1991, as cited in Gilbert, 2007, p. 22)

Example 5: Optimism. We tend to overestimate the likelihood of positive events and underestimate the possibility of negative events (Weinstein, 1980). For example, in his MBA class Richard Thaler asks students to identify what decile (top 10%, 20%, 30%, etc.) they expect to be in when they complete the course (Thaler & Sunstein, 2008, p. 31-32).

Only 5% expected to finish in the bottom 50% and more than half the class predict they will be in the top 2 deciles[9].

Table 9.1: Optimism among students (adapted from Weinstein, 1980, p. 810)

Students thought odds much higher for themselves	Students thought odds much higher for other students
1. Like postgraduation job	1. Having a drinking problem
2. Owning your own home	2. Attempting suicide
3. Starting salary > $10,000	3. Divorced a few years after married
4. Traveling to Europe	4. Heart attack before age 40
5. Starting salary > $15,000	5. Contracting venereal disease
6. Good job offer before graduation	6. Being fired from a job
7. Graduating in top third of class	7. Getting lung cancer
8. Home doubles in value in 5 years	8. Being sterile
9. Your work recognized with award	9. Dropping out of college
10. Living past 80	10. Having a heart attack

We are particularly optimistic when estimating our own odds compared with the odds of others. In the late 1970s, psychologist Neil Weinstein (1980) surveys students, asking them to estimate the likelihood of various events happening to them, versus others. The top ten positive and negative results are summarized in Table 9.1. 19 of the 20 results represented statistically significant differences[10].

Future Preference Heuristics

Future preference heuristics refer to the choices that we make regarding the future in the absence of uncertainty. It is, of course, debatable that we can (or should) ever fully separate uncertainty from our thoughts about the future. Events could always intervene that render "certain" events impossible or irrelevant. There is also some biological evidence that delayed and uncertain outcomes employ a great deal of common circuitry in the brain (Politser, 2008, p. 54) and that our perceptions of differences in distant time are fuzzy (Gilbert, 2007, p. 107), much fuzzier than would be implied by the computations entailed in neoclassical discounting models.

The "reference" model for rational discounting is generally taken to be Samuelson's (1937) discounted utility model. Under this model, preferences are discounted by some constant rate over time—leading to an exponentially declining weight being applied to each period, reflecting future preference. This particular model has the virtue of being mathematically tractable and also allows distant preferences to remain consistent over time (as opposed to shifting occasionally as they draw closer, which invariably happens with other mathematical forms). As a result of its mathematical and logical consistency, Samuelson's model was almost universally adopted among economists and remains so to this day. Interestingly, Samuelson himself specifically warned of the arbitrariness of assuming that individual preferences actually behave this way (Loewenstein, 1992).

Example 1: Gain-Loss Discounting Asymmetry. According to the reference model, we should discount gains and losses similarly. This often does not appear to be the case, however. This allows for the creation of framing problems (see Chapter 5) of a particular type, where one frame involves choosing between present and future consumption while the other involves viewing the problem as one of delaying gratification from the present to the future. An example of such a tradeoff is now presented (Loewenstein & Prelec, 1992, p. 135-136):

Version 1:

> Suppose you bought a TV on a special installment plan. The plan calls for two payments; one this week and one in 6 months. You have two options for paying:
>
> A. An initial payment of $160 and a later payment of $110
>
> B. An initial payment of $115 and a later payment of $160

Version 2:

> Suppose you bought a TV on a special installment plan. The plan calls for two payments of $200; one this week and one in 6 months.
>
> Happily, the company has announced a sale that applies retroactively to your purchase. You have two options:

C. A rebate of $40 on the initial payment and a rebate of
$90 on the later payment

D. A rebate of $85 on the initial payment and a rebate of
$40 on the later payment

As is nearly always the case in framing problems, the pairs of options
are actually identical (A & C, B & D). Despite this, 54% preferred A
over B, while only 33% preferred C over D. The first is presented in
terms of a simple choice: take the cost now or take it in the future. We
generally choose to get the pain over with. The second involves delaying gratification. That is something we do not like to do.

Example 2: Exaggerated Anticipation. We tend to over-estimate how both
pleasant and unpleasant events will affect us in the future (Mitchell,
Thompson, Peterson, & Cronk, 1997). In addition, when recollecting
the memory at a later date, we appear to be more influenced by our
original anticipation than by what we actually experienced.

Psychologist Daniel Gilbert (2007, p. 209-210) describes an experiment
demonstrating this phenomenon in the context of the 2000 U.S. presidential election. By the end of election night, in November, it became
clear that the election was so close that neither candidate, George W.
Bush or Al Gore, would be certified until after a lengthy recount. A
team of researchers then rushed out to interview both Bush and Gore
supporters. Among the questions they asked was "how happy will you
feel if Bush is determined to be the winner." Bush supporters, naturally,
expected to be elated. Gore supporters, in contrast, expected to be
severely depressed. When the actual day came, in December, both sides
experienced a much more muted emotional impact. However, when
later interviewed in April of the following year (2001), they recalled
having experienced much greater emotion in December than they actually reported at the time.

An interesting variation of the phenomenon can be found in the anxiety experienced by students reported before, and recalled after, an
exam. What investigators found was that students who did better than
expected reported experiencing greater anxiety than they reported at
the time, while students who did worse reported feeling less anxiety
(Dewhurst & Marlborough, 2003). One explanation of this can be presented in terms of the students' desire to demonstrate control. High
anxiety would tend to lead to more studying, justifying the higher than

expected grade. Low anxiety would lead to low studying, justifying a lesser grade[11].

Example 3: Preference for Escalating Gains. We often exhibit a preference for a series of escalating gains over time, as opposed to level or declining gains. Assuming any discount model (with a positive discount rate), such a preference would be considered irrational. For example, Loewenstein and Sicherman (1991) found that 83% of respondents preferred a five-year salary profile that gradually increased from $23,000 to $27,000 to one that gradually decreased from $27,000 to $23,000. Some research suggests that this is a rational response to an underlying preference for improving conditions (Becker, Grossman, & Murphy, 1992).

Interestingly, there seem to be a number of confounding factors that can interfere with this preference. For example, Frederick and Loewenstein (2008, p. 229) describe an experiment in which students were given a hypothetical choice involving a sequence of restaurant dinners. The two establishments were a highly rated French restaurant and a lesser-rated Greek restaurant. The options were as follows:

A. You get free dinner for two at Cafe Matisse on the last Friday of this month, and free dinner for two at Zorba's Grill on the last Friday of next month.

B. You get free dinner for two at Zorba's Grill on the last Friday of this month, and free dinner for two at Cafe Matisse on the last Friday of next month.

What is interesting is that while most students indicated they preferred Option A (51%), most also indicated that they would pay more for option B (63%). This is another example of the peculiar impact that money can impart to transactions, first noted in Chapter 5.

Example 4: Immediacy Effect. With respect to the timing of rewards and punishment, the immediate is considered quite different from the delayed. This is inconsistent with the reference model because it means that preferences can switch. For example, we might prefer $100 now to $120 three days from now. At the same time, we may also prefer $120 33 days from now to $100 30 days from now (Frank, 1992).

Example 5: Hyperbolic Discounting. In the reference model, rational discounting occurs exponentially, leading to the mathematically desirable property that preferences do not suddenly shift as they draw closer in time. Hyperbolic discounting, advocated most visibly by psychiatrist George Ainslie (2001) in his book *Breakdown of Will,* represents an attempt to create a curve that more realistically depicts what actually happens. Unlike an exponential curve, the hyperbolic discounting curve causes differences in timing to become much more heavily weighted as they approach the present. For example, you might prefer $500 in five years to $400 in four years, yet still prefer $400 tomorrow to $500 in a year. His model also allows for the possibility that different goods may be discounted at different rates, with money being discounted most closely to exponentially (Ainslie, 2001, p. 100). The key feature of his model is the way it causes short term options with less desirable long term consequences to become more attractive as they draw nearer. He uses this to explain a variety of phenomena, ranging from addictive behaviors to the sudden desire for epidural anesthesia among women in labor who had previously decided that they intended to pursue a fully natural child birthing experience.

Another less-discussed aspect of hyperbolic discounting is that it tends to reduce the degree to which the very distant future is discounted, since a hyperbola asymptotically approaches 0 more slowly than an exponential curve. This could be part of the explanation for our willingness to consider the very distant future. For example, the U.S. Nuclear Regulatory Commission recently began revisiting the impact of nuclear waste disposal employing a one million year time horizon, as opposed to its original ten thousand year horizon (Summers & Zeckhauser, 2008). Under the reference model, it is doubtful that the discounted utility of any catastrophic damage a million years from now could exceed a penny under any reasonable discount rate; even more amazing when we recall that the recorded history of humanity is barely 6,000 years old.

Example 6: Presentism Effects. Our expectations for how we will feel in the future are heavily colored by how we feel in the present. Daniel Gilbert (2007) describes the phenomenon under the general heading of *presentism.* An experiment demonstrates the phenomenon (Read & Loewenstein, 1995). Subjects were asked to come into a lab for several weeks and were told they would be given a snack each week. On their first visit, however, they were also required to identify what snack they would be getting for *each* of the subsequent weeks. Most choosers selected a substantial variety—which is what would have made sense if they were going to consume all the snacks (or part of them) in one sitting. In subsequent weeks, they were then asked if they wanted to change their mind about the snack they received (although the snack they were actually given did not change). The mean variety of the revised choices was significantly lower than that of the original simultaneous choices. Of the 84 participants, 37 indicated that they would have changed their mind at least once, with 31 (84% of the 37) choosing in the direction of less variety. In other words, when subjects were selecting, they did so while imagining what if would be like to consume them all in the present, even though they were being asked about intervals in the future.

Example 7: Magnitude effects. The magnitude of a reward can affect the degree to which discounting occurs (just as it can also impact risk preferences). For example, in one experiment with students, indifference was found for the following combinations (Loewenstein & Prelec, 1992, p. 121):

- $15 now or $60 in a year

- $250 now or $350 in a year

- $3000 now or $4000 in a year

In other words, as the amount gets smaller, the ratio becomes larger. In the real world, this would be consistent with the observed phenomenon of payday loans, small loans that need to be paid back when the borrower gets his or her next paycheck, often at effective annualized interest rates that exceed several hundred percent.

One contributing explanatory factor that I have proposed in the past (Gill, 2008a) has to do with the ability to visualize how the money could be used. For small amounts, it may be relatively easy to imagine how it could be used now —a lunch, a desired article of clothing, etc.— while nearly impossible to envision for the future. Who can precisely imagine how they would spend $60 a year from now? Presumably, such expenses motivate many payday loans. As the amounts grow larger, however, envisioning future big ticket purchases would be easier, while ascertaining how the large unexpected windfall would be applied in the present would become less clear. Both would reduce the psychological cost of delaying, making it natural to discount at a lower rate.

Time Horizons and Control

The dozen examples of risk and time preference behavior described may seem like a bit of a hodge-podge. Indeed, some seem downright contradictory. For example, we view 99% chance as being very different from 100% while, at the same time, treating 0.00001% as being very similar to 0.000001% in buying lottery tickets. Despite these surface incongruities, however, nearly all of them can be seen as having potential implications for control. For example, they may:

- *Represent our attempt to find a pattern that we can then exploit.* A good example of this is our tendency to see patterns as part of the gambler's fallacy.

- *Be consistent with our belief that we exercise more control over the environment than we actually do.* The way we account for very small probabilities would be an example of this, as would our tendency towards overconfidence.

- *Reflect our desire to exert control.* The great weight we place on the difference between near certainty and certainty is an example of this, as would the high weight of the near futures assumed by hyperbolic discounting.

- *Afford us the opportunity to exercise control.* The differential weight we place on immediate versus delayed actions would is consistent with this. I have also speculated how small payouts may provide more immediate opportunities for control than larger payouts.

- *Describe a future consistent with being in control.* Optimism and our preference for escalating gains, particularly in wages, would be examples of this.

- *Indicate our preference for being in control versus being out of control.* The asymmetry between gains and losses would be a good example of this, since we tend to attribute gains to our own efforts and losses to external effects, a phenomenon referred to as *self-serving bias* (Mirels, 1980)[12].

Since presentism and exaggerated anticipation both involve projecting what we feel in the present (where we *can* exert control) into a future (where we cannot directly exert control), they could also be treated as having a control component. These control implications of all 12 risk and time preferences are summarized in Table 9.2.

Table 9.2 Control Implications of Risk and Time Preferences

Preference	Description
Overvaluing low likelihoods	Consistent with our sense of personally controlling things that we probably do not, the *illusion of control*.
Undervaluing high likelihoods	Eliminates any chance that the outcome of our choice will not be under our control.
Overconfidence	Belief that we are more in control of a situation than we actually are.
Optimism	Vision of a future in which we are in control.
Gamblers fallacy	Detection of patterns affords the opportunity to control outcomes. Patterns we cannot discern do not.
Gain-loss discounting asymmetry	Self-serving bias suggests that losses are accompanied by loss of control, adding to the negative impact that makes loss values seem more serious than gain values.
Exaggerated anticipation	Pre-and post event recollections are subject to the illusion of control, magnifying their potential impact[13]. For example, students appeared to realign their recollections of anxiety consistent with their being in control of the outcome.
Preference for escalating gains	In most situations, an escalating series of payments is more consistent with an individual being in control than a declining series. This is particularly true in the future wages domain, where many of these studies were conducted.
Immediacy	We can control the present but we cannot directly control the future. Thus, immediate rewards (and punishments) offer the benefit of allowing control to be exerted at once.
Hyperbolic Discounting	The closer that an option gets, the greater the sense of control we have of it, leading to the higher rate of discounting during the periods in close proximity to the present.
Presentism	We assume that the control we exert in the present will be similar in its future impact.
Magnitude Effects	We have a greater relative sense of control for small amounts now vs. the future.

Harvard psychologist Daniel Gilbert (2007, p. 20-21) makes a point of emphasizing how important the feeling of control can be with respect to prospection (imagining the future). He asserts the following:

> ...people find it gratifying to *exercise* control—not just for the futures it buys them, but for the exercise itself. Being effec-

tive—changing things, influencing things, making things happen—is one of the fundamental needs with which human brains seem to be naturally endowed, and much of our behavior from infancy onward is simply an expression of this penchant for control...

He goes on to cite a study (Rodin & Langer, 1977), performed in a nursing home, where each resident was given a plant. Half the residents (the high control group) were told they would have complete responsibility for taking care of their individual plant. Half (the low control group) were told a staff person would take care of it, and they would not have to concern themselves with it. At the end of the 6 month study, 30% of the low control group had died compared with 15% for the high control group. This confirmed an earlier study (Langer & Rodin, 1976) where residents given greater responsibility seemed to do better in nearly every respect.

The impact of control upon time horizons is very significant because a complex system tends to produce an environment where long term control can be very difficult to achieve. In consequence, the easiest domain over which to exert control is the short term. Why this is the case, and the key role that informing plays, is the subject of the next section.

Complex System Behaviors and Informing

In Chapter 3, we saw how discontinuous change—the result of the need for peak-to-peak adaptations—and punctuated equilibrium were typical behaviors in complex adaptive systems. In Chapter 4, we then saw the strong consensus[14] of business researchers that these types of behaviors are generally observed in the business environment; indeed, they are frequently dominating characteristics. Finally, in Chapter 8, we saw how some very simple underlying principles—a tendency towards disorder pitted against a "rich get richer" fitness profile—naturally leads to institutions and informing networks that follow a power law in size distribution; cities, companies, contact networks and the hubs on the internet being just a few examples.

What is interesting about the complex system behaviors is just how universal they appear to be. When George Zipf started seeing power law distributions everywhere he looked, he imagined them to be a phenomenon of social systems (Mauboussin, 2008, p. 230). As it turns out, however, they were much more general. As we saw in Chapter 8, they appear in physical and biological systems as well. Events such as earthquakes and species extinctions—as well as the behavior of stock (Taleb, 2007) and commodity prices—follow the pattern very nicely (Bak, 1997).

Even where a power law does not exist, or has not been verified, discontinuities in nature abound. Aside from the obvious birth and death—abrupt in the majority of cases—and analogous distinct business events—e.g., incorporation, acquisition, initial public offering, bankruptcy, dissolution—we find that many natural systems operate off of triggers or thresholds. We saw that with respect to information cascades in Chapter 8. There are similar biological analogs. Bacteria, for example, sometimes employ a recently discovered "quorum sensing" mechanism to trigger sudden attacks. Each bacterium sends a small number of special molecules into the surrounding environment. They also detect the concentration of molecules, refraining from any attack on the host organism while the concentration is low. Once the molecule concentration reaches a threshold level, the situation abruptly changes. Knowing that there are sufficient neighboring bacteria to sustain the infection, the attack on the host organism suddenly begins. Researchers believe this phenomenon helps explain the virulence and sudden onset of conditions such as food poisoning, pneumonia, and cholera (Naik, 2009).

All this is important because economic systems are, at their core, informing systems. It is true that physical and services goods are produced and moved from place to place. Nevertheless, without information to guide them, the entire system would come to an abrupt halt. What I therefore argue is that trends impacting the underlying complexity of the economic system structure can be expected to produce changes in the overall behavior of the system. Of particular interest in this case is the size and frequency of the discontinuities that punctuate periods of equilibrium.

To understand the main effects of informing structure on system behavior, let us consider the core features of a routine informing system network. The use of the term *routine* here is important because most business networks, on a day to day basis, conduct far more routine informing activities than non-routine or low structure informing activities. Such a system can be viewed as having three fundamental properties—closely related to the objective complexity properties we used throughout the book:

1. *Size*. Number of elements in the system

2. *Reactivity*. How fast elements react to signals from other elements—this is essentially a speed of interaction term

3. *Connectivity*. Degree of connectivity between elements

Now consider the likely effects of changing these on the typical power curve plot introduced in Chapter 8 and repeated below as Figure 9.2. If you recall, there were three regions of the curve. In the top region, size—in this case, event size—is driven by randomness or pseudo-randomness and other features. In the bottom region, effect size is limited by the total size of the system (e.g., you can't have a fjord larger than the size of Norway). In the middle, we have the region that follows the power law.

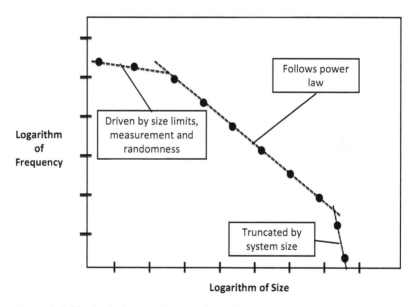

Figure 9.2: Typical observed power law plot

Increasing Size

Using this model, the direct effect of raising the number of elements in the system is straightforward. It lengthens the right hand side of the curve—meaning that larger effects *can be* encountered before they are truncated. There is no obvious reason that size alone would cause events to be more frequent, so these mega-events would be very unusual, but they would nonetheless be possible. Globalization, independent of any other changes, leads to such an effect. For example, the Black Death that killed half of Europe appears to have spread as a result of a trade with the Far East that had not existed prior to the expeditions of Marco Polo. Without the trade connection, the infection could not have spread.

Increasing Reactivity

The main effect of increasing reactivity is to compress the time axis. A game of chess where players are given only 10 seconds per move will play out a lot more quickly, on average, than a game without time limits. The way this would change the power law portion of the curve is to move it upwards. In other words, barring additional assumptions[15], increasing reactivity would tend to make large, infrequent events occur more frequently because all events occur more frequently. Just as globalization resulted in increasing system size, technology—and particularly information technology—can serve to increase reactivity. The effect occurs through two mechanisms. One involves increasing the speed at which routine communications can take place. First, we increased the speed of the mail, with better roads and later railroads. Next, we developed the telegraph as an alternative to mail or personal travel. Next the telephone was developed, providing a much broader range of communications options. Then radio and television provided a rapid one-way communications tool. Finally, computers and the Internet allowed us to exchange routine information faster than was ever previously possible.

The other dimension of reactivity is decision time. Here computer technology plays a particularly important role. Credit card approvals, for example, once required human intervention for many cases[16]. Now, the vast majority are handled automatically. Computer systems approve tax returns and mortgage applications based on complex sets of rules. Companies exchange purchase orders generated and processed automatically at both ends by complex enterprise requirements planning (ERP) systems. These systems also serve to reduce the average size of orders that can economically be processed. Hence, we see the development of a publishing on demand industry—where a company can make money on print runs of only one or two books.

If we assume that increasing reactivity *only* serves to speed up the pace of everything, there would seem to be no motivation for innovations along those lines. After all, who would want to adopt a new technology just to become more harried? What these examples suggest, however, is that increasing reactivity may also serve to impact the pre-power curve region; enlarging it and making it better behaved. If our children have cell phones, the logistics of getting everyone to meet become simpler. If companies are in more continuous contact with suppliers, they can reduce both order size and the amount of expensive inventory they keep on hand. Less planning is required for a trip when the individual can take along a laptop that allows frequent communications and updates from the office to continue uninterrupted. In other words, *the benefit that justifies being subject to increased frequency of large discontinuities is improved ability to manage short term behaviors.*

To illustrate the assertion I just made, consider the bullwhip effect (Lee, Padmanabhan, & Whang, 1997), well known to students of operations management. The problem occurs in supply chains—networks of suppliers associated with the same product, starting from raw materials and going all the way to the finished goods[17]. The basic problem is as follows:

- In order to avoid running out of a particular product, component, or raw material, it is generally advisable for a company to keep a certain amount of overstock (sometimes called safety stock) on hand. The amount of overstock depends on the perceived accuracy of the forecast demand.

- Each company in the chain forecasts its expected demand to its suppliers, either directly or through orders. These forecasts not only include what it needs for production, but also what it needs for overstock and, occasionally, a bit extra (since it is cheaper to have a supplier hold inventory than for the company to do it).

- As a consequence of this process, the margin of errors in the forecast grows as you move up the supply chain, meaning that by the time you reach the upstream (raw materials) end, the accumulated error is huge, as is the corresponding need to hold safety stock.

The overall effect of this structure is that small changes in demand at the consumer end of the chain are amplified to produce huge swings at the raw materials and production equipment manufacturers end; thus the expression "bullwhip effect"[18].

The treatment for the bullwhip effect is to work with smaller orders and to share forecasts more efficiently throughout the supply chain. This allows entities throughout the chain to react more quickly to changes and reduces the magnitude of the swings. One of the true pioneers in the retail implementation of these policies is Walmart. As early as the 1980s, the company began requiring suppliers to connect with them electronically. They were also early adopters of barcode technologies, allowing them to track demand on a minute by minute basis, if desired. Their ability to react quickly and to order efficiently were both key elements of a strategy that ensured they were always the lowest cost competitor. That strategy resulted in their becoming the largest retailer in the world.

The net effects of increasing size and reactivity on a hypothetical size-frequency curve are illustrated in Figure 9.3. From an overall behavior standpoint, the net expectation is that we will have a larger frequency and percentage of small, manageable events. The price we pay is a greater frequency of large power law events (as a result of the overall reactivity-induced speed up) and a greater potential for very large events as a result of system size. Viewed in terms of punctuated equilibrium, the periods of order may even prove to be more orderly as a result of the continuous flow of information. Thus, an idea like rapid computer-controlled automated trading (sometimes referred to as flash trading) is not necessarily a terrible development, although if widely adopted the time compression effect could lead to increased frequency of the occasional very large discontinuous events along the power law range of the curve.

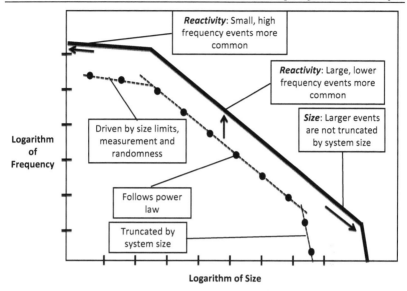

Figure 9.3: Hypothetical power law (in solid black) after system size and reactivity is increased

Increasing Connectivity

It would be tempting to assert that increasing connectivity will have the same effects as increasing size and reactivity on our hypothetical behavior[19]. In a randomly connected network with no "rich get richer" effect, it is relatively easy to argue either way. Consider the "choosing between alternatives" problem and assume that knowledge of alternatives flows to the decision-maker along network connections. More connections would tend to retard the decision making process if we use an exhaustive consideration of choices decision process. That would reduce reactivity. On the other hand, more connections would also mean that acceptable options would reach us faster, on average. Thus, if we are satisficers, we might react in less time.

If we assume connections are distributed according to the "rich get richer" model, as they are in so many other self-evolving (as opposed to designed) networks, the predictions of impact seem somewhat less ambiguous. Where power laws are concerned, a greater average probably signifies a more steeply sloped curve, since highly connected nodes play a disproportionate role in determining the average[20]. With greater connectivity, we would expect that a greater percentage of nodes would have the ability to impact network as a whole. In effect, these nodes increase the slope of the power law curve, making calamitous events (on the negative side) more likely. The "too big to fail" rationale, often used to justify government intervention in private industry, reflects our concerns regarding the emergence of such highly connected nodes.

In summary then, factors that increase the size, reactivity, and connectivity of a networked informing system—such as globalization and increasingly powerful information technologies—can be expected to increase the magnitude and frequency of discontinuous events within the system. The motivation that drives these changes to the system, however, may be an improvement in our ability to tune our activities during the period between discontinuities. These two conclusions have important implications for the time horizons of individuals participating in such systems.

Complex System Behaviors and Time Horizons

Earlier in the chapter, I commented that there has long been a nagging question of what constitutes "short" and "long" time horizons (Brier, 2005). The punctuated equilibrium model just presented suggests that a process-oriented, rather than temporal, definition may be appropriate. Short time horizons emphasize activities up to the next major discontinuity. Long time horizons involve the considering the possible futures that may exist after one or more discontinuities. The occurrence of these discontinuities cannot be predicted with any accuracy as of yet; the inherent unpredictability of punctuations is a fundamental characteristic of complex systems as we understand them today. That means time horizons are better described in terms of what assumptions we make about the future rather than upon how long into the future we appear to be looking. Projecting a current trend ahead for 50 years would therefore be considered an example of short time horizons. Planning what you would do a year from now given several alternative major shifts in the environment that *might* occur would represent long term thinking.

The principal motivation for distinguishing short and long time horizons based upon discontinuities is that this distinction translates into both informing and problems solving differences. The information technology networked informing system described in the previous section is dominated by routine informing. Well structured information and decision logic is what technology handles best. The discontinuities, however, require non-routine and often low-structure informing processes[21]. When airlines were deregulated, nearly all the old rules regarding how to compete had to be thrown out. Thus, informing in such systems demands more than simply riding out a discontinuity. It may require completely rethinking how the environment is behaving and adjusting actions accordingly. Sometimes a stock market crash presages a complete change in the economic world, as it did after October 1929. Sometimes, the world pretty much reverts back to its old behaviors as if the crash never happened, as was largely the case after October 1987.

Beyond informing, short term thinking involves a philosophy of tuning to the current environment, rather than boldly thinking about new approaches. Many of the technical tools employed by business analysts serve these tuning needs. This relationship was recognized in the Hayes and Abernathy (1980, p. 5) article mentioned in Chapter 1. To repeat what they asserted:

> ...during the past two decades American managers have increasingly relied on principles that prize analytical detachment and methodological elegance over insight, based on experience, into the subtleties and complexities of strategic decisions. As a result, maximum short-term financial returns have become the overriding criteria for many companies[22].

Also, as we have already seen, focusing on tuning existing systems to make them react more quickly and in smaller increments—the Walmart information system example—can help us manage day-to-day activities more efficiently. The problem is that if we become too dependent upon these systems for all our informing needs, we may not have the non-routine and low structure informing capability available to react to discontinuous change when it finally occurs. This was the central conclusion I came to in my study of *Batterymarch Financial Management* and *Mrs. Fields' Cookies*, two companies that did an absolutely astounding job of tuning to their environments to promote rapid growth and then, even more quickly, suffered disastrous reverses when the environment changed (Gill, 1995a).

What we have therefore seems to be a paradox. Our need for long time horizons is growing. Not only are globalization and information technology increasing the rate at which system discontinuities must be addressed but, in most of the world, life spans are increasing. Thus, someone born today with an 80 year life expectancy can anticipate experiencing dozens of major system disruptions contrasted with someone born in the Middle Ages—with a life expectancy in the mid-20s and a vastly less complex informing environment—who might go through life without even seeing even one such transforming event.

The paradox is that *the very technological forces that create the need for longer time horizons are also working to increase our motivation towards short term thinking by giving us greater opportunity to exert more effective control over the pre-discontinuity environment.*

White Swans, Grey Swans and Black Swans

Anyone who has ever worked with systems quickly recognizes that although the concept of "system" sounds good on paper, determining the actual boundaries of any real world system—such as an industry—tends to be quite tricky. Up to this point in the book, I have ignored this unfortunate feature of reality. In this section I attempt to consider how interaction between systems impacts our models.

To keep things simple, let us limit ourselves to considering three basic system relationships: overlapping systems, sub-system/super-systems, and co-evolving systems. The overlapping system relationship exists where an entity is a member of more than one system. We saw an example of that in Chapter 2, where a faculty member participates in both the disciplinary and institutional systems. The sub-system/super-system relationship, illustrated in Figure 9.4, exists when one system is a component of another system. For example, a company acts within an industry or more than one industry (in which case an overlapping relationship also exists). The co-evolving relationship exists when different systems (fitness landscapes) within a larger system impact each other. The supplier and customer relationships within a particular industry represent typical business examples.

Naturally, these system relationships get very messy in the real world. For example, a vertically integrated company may have overlapping relationships with several industries while a company participating in one of those industries may have co-evolving relationships. Thus, any attempt to assert the conceptual scheme just described is easy to apply should be greeted with considerable suspicion. For our purposes, however, what really counts is the expert's perspective of what is within a particular system versus what is outside of that system. Simplified to the extreme, we come up with relationships resembling those of Figure 9.4.

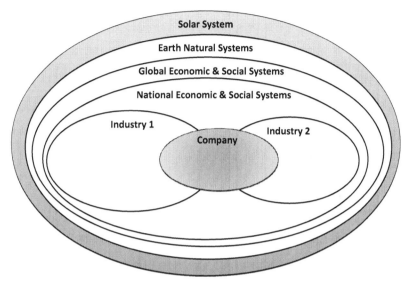

Figure 9.4: Some simple sub-system/super-system relationships. Also illustrated is an overlapping system relationship in which a company participates in more than one industry

This brings us to Nassim Nicholas Taleb's (2007) swan families. When we participate in a system operating in the region between discontinuities, we are dealing with *white swans*. For as long as this period lasts, *a duration that cannot be predicted*, events are generally well behaved and may even come close to following standard patterns of variability, such as the Gaussian (normal) distribution. By virtue of the system's complexity, however, it will—from time to time—produce events in the power law range[23]. These roughly correspond to Taleb's *grey swans*. They are called grey because their timing is unpredictable but the very fact that you have a system consisting of many interacting elements makes their eventual presence inevitable. What we may be able to impact is their frequency through changing system characteristics. Thus, it would be a mistake to call them entirely unpredictable—once again, it is only the precise timing and size of an individual event that defies prediction.

Black swans arise when discontinuous events from outside the system being considered impact the system. Their defining feature is that no matter how hard you look *within* your specific system, you will *never* be able to predict them.

Are black swan events important? The best answer would seem to be that they can be, and often are. For example, black swans likely accounts for our existence. About 65 million years ago, an asteroid collision appears to have wiped out the dinosaurs, paving the way for mammals to evolve. That represented a solar system event impacting the earth natural systems. According to another theory, the extensive period of cold that followed a volcanic eruption about 70,000 years ago near Indonesia may have resulted in a near extinction of the human race, producing a high degree of genetic similarity across the human race (Ambrose, 1998). This is an example of the earth's natural system impacting the global human social and economic systems[24]. Recently, the global credit freeze demonstrated how international markets could exert an influence on local businesses everywhere.

The frequency with which economic black swan events influence entities is likely to grow with globalization, which offers a pathway through which such influence can travel. And, to avoid sounding too negative, we would do well to recall that positive black swan events can be generated in the same way that negative ones are. As a result of the disruption they produce, opportunities are created. While it is well and good to pity the poor dinosaurs, we would not exist today if that asteroid had not cleared the way for our evolution. Positive or negative, black and grey swan events are inevitable when complex systems are present and can interact. Thus, building the skills to adapt to the challenges and opportunities that they present is crucial. To quote an oft-used phrase: "A crisis is a terrible thing to waste."[25]

Conclusions

The goal of this chapter has been to present the relationship between time horizons and informing. The underlying model employed is that of a complex system whose characteristic behavior is one of punctuated equilibrium—a model whose qualitative behaviors strongly resemble those of competitive environments as described by many researchers. Unfortunately, we have many heuristics and preferences that are ill-suited to the type of environment that we are now facing. Understanding how they affect our decision-making, and how to counteract them, is therefore a matter of considerable importance.

The core arguments presented are as follows:

1. The control that we can predictably exercise at any given time is likely to be much greater in the pre-discontinuity period than over a period that includes one or more discontinuities (i.e., the long term).

2. A variety of forces, most notably globalization and technology, are continuously reshaping that environment.

3. Globalization is increasing the size of the systems in which we participate. That has the potential effect of making discontinuities larger.

4. Technology tends to increase the rate at which we can react to information. In doing so, it tends to compress time—potentially increasing the frequency at which discontinuities are experienced.

5. Technology also tends to increase our control over the periods between major discontinuities. The motivational influence of this effect is to encourage us to focus our attention on this orderly period rather than attempting the much less structured process of analyzing what the world could be like after a discontinuity and how to manage for it. This effect is probably compounded by the analytical techniques that we teach.

The net effect of this is to suggest that while the actual need for long term thinking is growing, our success in creating informing systems is actually working to make us more shortsighted in our decision-making. This leads to the following assertion:

> ***A principal goal of an informing business school should be to help its students and managers better cope with complexity without becoming myopic in their time horizons.***

Thinking back to Priority 3, presented in the Preface, this conclusion implies that we might be better off paying more attention to the extraordinary and correspondingly less to the ordinary conduct of business.

Chapter 9 Foundational References

Bak, P. (1996). *How nature works: The science of self-organized criticality*. New York: Copernicus.

Gilbert, D. (2007). *Stumbling on happiness*. New York: Knopf.

Gill, T. G. (1995a). High tech hidebound: Case studies of information technologies that inhibited organizational learning. *Accounting, Management, & Information Technologies, 5*(1), 41-60.

Hayes, R. H., & Abernathy, W. J. (1980). Managing our way to economic decline. *Harvard Business Review, July-August,* 67-77.

Taleb, N. N. (2007). *The Black Swan.* New York, NY: Random House.

Chapter 9 Notes

[1] A famous song "My Generation" from the 1960s, performed by the rock band *The Who,* included the line "I hope I die before I get old." If you really feel that way, then all sorts of myopic behavior—such as drug and alcohol abuse—make sense. A similar conclusion would follow from a popular statement of the time: "Never trust anyone over 30."

[2] A survivalist, for example, may believe the country or world is going to degenerate shortly into chaos and that there is nothing that he or she can do about that fact. Nevertheless, he or she may stockpile food and weapons so as to increase the likelihood of survival when the apocalypse arrives.

[3] The concern with temporal myopia was particularly rampant in the late 1980s, when comparisons of the short time horizons in the U.S. with the much longer perspectives of the Japanese filled both the business press (e.g., Dertouzos, Lester, & Solow, 1989; Jacobs, 1991) and the popular culture, though novels such as Michael Crichton's (1992) best-seller *Rising Sun.* The furor for the subject died down somewhat over the next decade as it became clear that the very factors that were supposed to ensure Japanese success—most notably the tight, non-competitive relationships that existed between Japanese banks and companies—proved to be significant contributors to Japan's "dark decade", a recession beginning in 1990. Competing concerns of global warming and massive deficits in the U.S. appear to be renewing interest in the topic. For example, a recent issue of the *Journal of Risk and Uncer-*

tainty featured an issue devoted to these topics (Zeckhauser & Viscusi, 2008).

[4] Giving credit where credit is due, I would have to attribute my recognition of the scarcity of true risk processes to Nicholas Taleb's (2007) *The Black Swan*. To the extent that I am offering anything additional here, it is by pointing out that the degree to which the truth of the statement is magnified by complex landscapes. I suspect, however, that if I looked close enough, I could find that implied in some of Taleb's arguments.

[5] Philosophers and some statisticians will, of course, argue that estimates of probabilities developed from observations will *never* amount to the same thing as the actual underlying probabilities. As a practical matter, however, the error of the estimate will become small enough so that to quibble about the distinction will serve only to cause us to lose sight of the "big picture". *This reasoning applies, however, only when the underlying distribution is decomposable.*

[6] Leonard Mlodinow (2008) provides an engrossing narrative on the development of probability theory in his book *The Drunkard's Walk*. He reports that a famous 18th century French mathematician, Jean Le Rond d'Alembert, reasoned that since the number of heads that can appear in two coin tosses is either 0, 1 or 2, the probability of each outcome must therefore be 1/3. (Of course, the actual probabilities are 25%-50%-25% for 0, 1 and 2 respectively).

[7] When I read about the experiment in Taleb's (2007, p. 139) *The Black Swan*, I remembered participating in a demonstration of the effect when I was doing my first year MBA at HBS. I seem to recall making 10 estimates and getting 2 of them wrong, which mortified me at the time. Based on Taleb's reported 45% number, however, I now discover that I was one of the humble ones…

[8] The answers to the self-test in Figure 9.1 are as follows (Lo, 2005, p.34):

1. Martin Luther King's age at death: 39 Years
2. Length of the Nile River (in miles): 4,187 Miles
3. Number of countries in OPEC: 13 Countries
4. Number of books in the Old Testament: 39 Books
5. Diameter of the moon (in miles) 2,160 Miles

6. Weight of an empty Boeing 747 (in pounds): 390,000 Pounds
7. Year in which Wolfgang Amadeus Mozart was born: 1756
8. Gestation period of an Asian elephant (in days): 645 Days
9. Air distance from London to Tokyo (in miles): 5,959 Miles
10. Deepest known point in the ocean (in feet): 36,198 Feet

[9] I recall a similar optimism in my 1982 MBA class, although I believe only 75% or so thought they would end up in the top half of the class. As a side note, the fact that many of these experiments have been around for three decades or more and only now are they starting to impact economic thinking in a meaningful way tells us something about the pace of change in academic research. This will be revisited in Chapter 10.

[10] In the Weinstein study, the only event (out of 42) that significantly varied from the rule was "being injured in an automobile accident", where students thought their own likelihood to be higher ($p < 0.05$). They also thought that they were somewhat *less likely* to marry someone wealthy, but the finding was not statistically significant.

[11] This explanation of the findings of the lower score/lower recalled anxiety and higher score/higher recalled anxiety is somewhat different from that provided by the study's authors. They are not necessarily inconsistent, however. Mine simply hypothesizes that the students might have in mind the mental model:

anxiety level → level of studying → score

This would imply students viewed they exerted control over the test through studying, rather than merely through worrying about it. The authors of the study did suggest, "The tendency of underperforming students to underestimate how anxious they had been before the exam (thereby downplaying its importance) can thus be seen as an attempt to dissociate themselves from the negative outcome" (Dewhurst & Marlborough, 2003, p. 700). This assertion has a similar flavor, since most of us are less likely to study very hard for an unimportant test.

[12] The finding that we tend to attribute success to ourselves and failure to outside forces has some significant interactions. When expressed as a general principle, it holds for men but is much less pronounced for women. When stated in terms of social outcomes, however, the reverse is true—the effect is much more pronounced for women. To muddy

the waters further, for academic outcomes the effects were pronounced and quite similar across sexes (Mirels, 1980). The fact that the experiment was conducted on students—whose greatest experience with success and failure was likely to be in the academic domain—likely influenced that last of these results.

[13] With respect to the magnifying aspect of control, Hackman and Oldham (1980) actually view their control motivator (autonomy) as being multiplicative with respect to its motivational effect on arousal (variety) and achievement (significance and identity).

[14] "Strong consensus" is an expression that I do not use lightly. While my usual rule of thumb is that in business research you can always find someone who has said practically anything, I have yet to find any serious (or even casual) writer who argues that discontinuities in the environment or business behaviors do not occur, and that gradual changes are much more important than sudden shifts. In fact, the closest I can come is a statement from Charles Handy (1990, p. 5)—a very strong proponent of discontinuities—who asserts:

> The changes are different this time: they are discontinuous and not part of a pattern; such discontinuity happens from time to time in history, although it is confusing and disturbing, particularly to those in power.

This would seem to imply that, in the past at least, there have been entire eras characterized by what Handy refers to as continuous, "comfortable change." My own suspicion is that it is the fact that such change took place in the distant past that makes it appears comfortable. Consistent with the arguments in this chapter, I would gladly concede that the frequency and magnitude of such discontinuities are likely to have increased in recent decades as a consequence of fundamental (and discontinuous) changes to our informing systems.

On the other hand, it is very common for theory—particularly in the areas of economics and finance—to assume that such sudden changes are not material. That is the core of the grey and black swan arguments presented later in this chapter and in Chapter 10.

[15] When developing computer models, seemingly small assumptions can dramatically change system behaviors. Thus, the ideological preferences of the modeler tend to play an important role in the outcomes

predicted—a subject I return to in Chapter 16. I describe reactivity as increasing event frequency since I would be hard pressed to design a model where it would not.

16 An example of such a system is the Authorizer's Assistant, developed by American Express in the mid-1980s and one of the systems I researched while writing my dissertation.

17 In agribusiness, these are referred to as commodity systems, where they have been studied since Ray Goldberg (see Chapter 15) refined the concept in the 1950s.

18 I saw a graphic demonstration of the bullwhip effect in 1981, when I was working a summer job (between my first and second year MBA) for a company called GCA. The company made wafer-steppers, a piece of equipment used for creating integrated circuits images on silicon disks known as wafers. As a consequence of the exploding growth in the use of integrated circuits, their business was booming and they had an 18 month backlog of orders. The hired me, along with my brother Geoffrey Gill, to develop a computer-based production model they could use to ramp up production.

In designing the model, it was relatively easy to come up with assumptions necessary for growing production (e.g., training assumptions for each workstation, productivity and capacity estimates). It was much harder to model costs associated with decreases in production, since layoff policies and other errors were not mechanical. When I asked about this, the assured me that it was unnecessary to include such assumptions because the only foreseeable environment was rapid growth.

Just two months after I returned to finish the second year of my MBA I got a phone call. In that period, 18 months of back orders had become excess inventory and they asked me to walk them through the changes to the model that would be necessary to incorporate production reductions into its forecasts.

19 I used to believe that increased connectivity, though increasing complexity, would necessarily increase size and frequency of discontinuities. In some situations, this may be true. In many others, however, it drives the system into chaotic behavior for which no recognizable patterns exist. There do not, for example, seem to be any simple, generalizable rules that I could glean from my readings on the behavior of cellular

automata (Wolfram, 1994) or in my own work with neural networks, both of which have attributes that map to the size, reactivity and connectivity properties very nicely.

[20] As an illustration of the impact of outliers on a power curve average, recall the Chapter 8 footnote regarding Blue Cross & Blue Shield of Ohio (Burry, 1992), where the most expensive 50 patients collectively cost more than the least expensive 75,000.

[21] With respect to analyzing post-discontinuity behavior, complex adaptive systems differ from complex physical systems such as tectonic plates and piles of sand. Discontinuities do not change the characteristic behavior of the physical systems in any meaningful way; the sand piles up after the avalanche pretty much the same way it did before the event. Complex adaptive systems, on the other hand, can fundamentally change their behavior after a discontinuity. Life and ecologies forever changed, for example, after the asteroid collision wiped out the dinosaurs.

[22] Interestingly, using my proposed definition of short and long term thinking, Hayes and Abernathy were themselves more than slightly guilty of taking a short term perspective. Stagflation had put U.S. managers in the doldrums and they therefore used Germany and Japan as their models. In retrospect those two countries were bad choices, experiencing overall growth rates much lower than those of the U.S. in subsequent years. The authors proposed that the close relationships with suppliers cultivated in those countries was a source of their strength; in reality, excessively close relationships with suppliers of capital in Japan (the banks) and labor in Germany (the unions) are widely attributed to be key sources of their lackluster performance. The authors criticized the imitative, rather than innovative, approach to design pursued in the U.S., yet today the design element of processes is frequently conducted in the U.S.—even offshored to us by foreign manufacturers. The authors pointed out that our relatively low percentage of corporate R&D funding (relative to other countries) would naturally cause us to lose the innovation edge; in doing so they missed the huge impact that both the entrepreneurial activities of startups and our relative freedom from regulation and price controls (e.g., in the drug industry) would have over the intervening decades.

None of this is intended as a criticism of Hayes and Abernathy's article, which I believe was correct in many of its key fundamentals. Rather, it illustrates the inherent risk in predicting existing trends into the future, rather than putting forward a broad range of alternative possible futures. Existing trends are likely to serve as useful predictors only until the next major discontinuity occurs.

[23] Assuming a system will follow a single power law is, of course, an oversimplification because several power law relationships—such as connectivity of nodes and asset distribution—could potentially impact a system. The important fact to recognize is that big events outside of the orderly range will occur frequently enough to be very material in their impact.

[24] From time to time, U.S. broadcasters such as the History Channel run episodes on "Mega Disasters" that detail threats from sources such as asteroids, volcanoes, and tsunamis. What becomes clear is that, while the possibility of such threats is remote, they have—from time to time—altered the course of natural history. Moreover, it is clear that they will also do so in the future. For example, when the caldera volcano that sits under Yellowstone National Park erupts, there is a good chance that it will render much of North America uninhabitable. There is a side of a volcanic mountain in the Canary Islands that could collapse into the ocean (as it may have done into the past) that could trigger a tsunami that would engulf much of the U.S. East Coast. I missed the episode on the threat of locust swarms, but I'm sure it would have made my skin crawl. These shows would be quite alarming were it not for the scientists brought in to describe the threats, doing so with such visible relish that it is hard not to think of the threats as "cool".

[25] New York Times columnist Thomas Friedman attributes the phrase "A crisis is a terrible thing to waste" to Stanford economist Paul Romer.

T. Grandon Gill
Informing Business
Santa Rosa, California: Informing Science Press.

Chapter 10

The Question of Rigor

Roadmap & Objectives: Chapter 4 argued that business environments are complex; Chapter 9 argued that they are likely to become more so. This chapter presents arguments that by failing to account for the possible complexity of the business landscapes we study, we vastly overestimate the rigor of our research findings.

In the first chapter of this book, we encountered the widespread belief that business schools are producing a large amount of research that is entirely irrelevant to practice. We also found concern that the theories we are teaching to students may actually be contributing to the questionable ethical climate of business today. What we did not see, with some important exceptions[1], were serious objections raised with respect to the rigor of our research. The current situation represents a huge departure from 50 years ago, when the Ford Foundation (Gordon & Howell, 1969) and others savaged business schools for their weakness in this area.

The present chapter presents the argument that business research is far less rigorous than we generally believe it to be. We have cultivated the appearance of rigor; of that there can be no doubt. But if you look closely at the assumptions underlying our research, cracks appear. These cracks are so serious that we would do well to rethink our entire philosophy—the topic of Chapter 13.

The bulk of the arguments I present are based on a key assumption: that the domains we are researching are complex adaptive systems. Paradoxically, this very assumption ensures that any broad assertion such as "our research is not rigorous" is destined to fail ingloriously in some examples. Research itself is, after all, a process existing on a rugged fitness landscape, meaning that the nature of the product will end

333up being so diverse that many—and perhaps even most—finished products of that process will violate any general rules that might be proposed. With this in mind, I focus my attention on three areas that I believe warrant particular attention: construction of theory-of-fitness, empirical testing of theory-of-fitness and the quality control process we apply to determine the fitness of research (and researchers).

What is Rigor?

In writing this chapter, I discovered that while a great many researchers discuss the subject, very few of them are precise in what they mean by "rigor". The definition I choose to adopt is based on the following:

> By scientific rigor, we refer to the process of systematically studying a phenomenon, using an appropriate design and methods for the problem, and often including the development or testing of theory. It is more than this, however, involving an attitude of curiosity about the way the world works, with the attendant risks of having one's hypotheses proven incorrect. (Allison & Rootman, 1996, p. 334)[2]

The key elements that I extract from the definition are as follows. In order for research to be rigorous it must:

1. *Be systematic in its inquiry.* In the case of research intended to build theory, this implies that determining the boundaries of what we observe is as critical as understanding the phenomenon within those boundaries. In the case of research intended to generate detailed observations (upon which theory might later be based), this further implies attempting to gather all information that could be relevant to the phenomenon being observed.

2. *Employ appropriate design.* To be appropriate, a design must ensure that the methods being employed are not prone to either errors of commission (where a false relationship is detected, commonly referred to as Type I error) or omission (where a significant relationship is omitted, known as Type II error).

3. *Ask challenging questions.* If you know the answers to your questions in advance, then there is little risk that your hypotheses will be proven incorrect. If there is no doubt of the outcome

of your research before you conduct it, then whatever tests are performed cannot be considered particularly stringent.

There are, of course, many other ways that rigor can be defined. Nevertheless, these three characteristics are certainly important aspects of research quality *and* none of the three naturally fit into our notions relevance or resonance. If we believe they are worth consideration in judging our research, it is within the characteristic of rigor that they belong.

Constructing Theory-of-Fitness

Building upon Chapter 3, research that develops theory-of-fitness is easy to recognize. It can nearly always be translated into a functional form, with some desirable outcome on the left hand side. When drawn, it appears as a series of boxes with nicely organized arrows—proceeding mainly in a single direction if decomposability is assumed (as it usually is). When tested, statistical approaches—and particularly multivariate approaches—are preferred since few examples of real-world fitness depend on a single variable.

This book is full of arguments as to why attractive theory-of-fitness can never arise when the landscape being studied is rugged. These will not be repeated here. The question that we will instead consider is how seemingly sensible approaches to developing our theory can lead to results lacking in rigor. The focus will be on four areas: 1) the way we create theory in conjunction with acquiring observations to support our theory, 2) the problem of poorly considered boundary conditions, including limits to applicability and underlying assumptions, 3) the impact of disciplinary silos, and 4) a preference for theory that may have evolved because early researchers became well known by approaching research from this perspective, a social phenomenon sometimes referred to as the *Matthew Effect*.

The Rigor of Theory Creation

There can be little doubt that the creation of theory is considered to be the pinnacle of the researcher's craft in many business related fields, such as management (Hambrick, 2007). Without attempting to delve too deeply into the philosophical implications of theory and its construction, it is not too farfetched to characterize the process as involving three parts:

1. Identifying an interesting or important phenomenon to explain; one for which existing explanations are absent or appear to be inadequate.

2. Identifying a set of assumptions and attributes that are deemed relevant to that phenomenon.

3. Constructing and justifying a system of logical or empirically tested arguments to explain how the assumptions and attributes (item 2) explain the phenomenon (item 1).

Theory creation does not end the theory-building process. It omits the critical validation stage, where predictions resulting from (item 3) are tested against new observations of the phenomenon (item 1). But it is a good start.

In most cases, a theory does not justify a phenomenon in any fundamental way. Rather, it presents an explanation for a higher level phenomenon in terms of lower level, and often unexplained, phenomena. For example, when Newton developed his theory of gravitation, he could not explain *why* matter attracts other matter—even physicists today cannot explain that convincingly. What he found, however, is that if you do assume that such an attraction exists and that it varies according to an inverse square law, you can explain a lot of previously unexplained phenomena[3], such as the motion of the planets. When Darwin developed the theory of evolution, he did so without any knowledge of the mechanics of genetics, meaning he had no scientific basis for explaining the transmission of traits through successive generations. What he was aware of, on the other hand, was a long history of animal breeding that had allowed different breeds of livestock and pets to flourish, thereby demonstrating that traits could be inherited. A biologist commenting on the subject once remarked: "Darwin didn't know 99 percent of what we now know [but] the 1 percent he did know was the most important part" (Hayden, 2009).

Oddly enough, a desire for relevance is likely to lead us towards theory-of-fitness in our theory building efforts. To illustrate this, consider the following two (whimsical) propositions:

1. Individuals who favor earth tones prefer to eat more at lunch than supper whereas people who favor blue prefer a larger supper.

2. Individuals who favor earth tones perform better at creative tasks than individuals who favor blue.

Which proposition would you prefer to investigate as a researcher? Probably the latter, since it seems like the type of information a manager might want to know. Would this research choice be universally true? Absolutely not! If you happened to be targeting the food service business, the first might help you improve the fitness of the décor in a restaurant trying to attract a lunchtime crowd. In either case, however, the relevance is tied to what we expect to be most conducive to improving the fitness of our intended audience.

The problem is, of course, that rugged fitness landscapes resist attractive theory-of-fitness by their very nature. But their diversity also leads to another characteristic: *excepting those attributes that are actually decomposable, you will nearly always be able to find some region of the landscape where a particular characteristic leads to fitness.* This is not a mystical conjecture. Rather it is almost a matter of definition—if an attribute always contributes to fitness or always works against it, we might as well treat it as decomposable or nearly decomposable. Clusters of attributes may also be decomposable from other clusters in a rugged landscape—meaning that once the cluster's effect is determined, it will act consistently across the entire landscape[4].

The implications of the rule just described are as follows: *if you research a rugged fitness landscape long enough, you will be able to find examples supporting nearly any previously unrecognized simple (single variable) fitness relationship you might care to propose.* Implicit in this assertion is the likelihood that material decomposable single variable relationships will not fall into the "previously unrecognized" category, since they will be easy to detect.

This observation presents a singular threat to the rigor of any theory-of-fitness we might care to propose. What it means is that if we create a theory-of-fitness relating to a rugged landscape we will be able to find at least some examples supporting virtually any simple proposition associated with that theory. We simply need to gather a large enough cross sectional collection of examples. Assuming we are dealing with a complex adaptive system, the landscape will also be continuously (and, more significantly, discontinuously) changing. If we do not lock ourselves to a particular point in time, we further increase the odds of finding what we are looking for[5]. The "systematic" element of rigor is the key remedy to this threat. In constructing theory, it is insufficient to limit yourself to evidence supporting the theory. An active effort to identify and present the competing case is also required. This assertion brings us to the issue of theory boundaries.

Theory Boundaries

In hard science fields like physics, the key to solving most applied problems is to specify the appropriate boundary conditions. If you are interested in the shape of a microwave signal, for example, you need to know the shape of the waveguide inside of which it is generated. In business theory, the corresponding boundary conditions consist of two components: 1) the domain of applicability for whatever theory is being proposed or tested and 2) the form of the underlying assumptions and initial conditions being used. We now consider how these can impact rigor.

Domain of applicability

In a decomposable landscape, the expected domain of applicability will tend to be the entire landscape. Thus, the issue of boundaries can be casually tossed out as a direction for future research. Little danger that such a direction will be pursued, however; we do not even test most of our theory[6], much less study its boundaries.

In a rugged landscape, rigor can be achieved in two ways. The first is through developing a comprehensive ugly theory, that non-compact description accurately characterizing fitness across the entire landscape; time consuming to construct, very hard to test, nearly impossible to communicate. The second approach is to develop attractive local theory *and* clearly specify the boundaries over which that theory extends. The boundaries of such theory are an integral part. If they are omitted then the theory is not rigorous. It is actually misleading.

Applicability problems are not just limited to cases where we attempt to apply our theory outside of its domain (we later refer to these as Type I errors). They can also result from failing to recognize that processes outside of the theory we present can also impact fitness (later called Type II errors). These errors are a consequence of the tunnel vision that can result when we become too focused on the relationships described in our theory, thereby ignoring other paths to fitness. Taleb (2007) repeatedly emphasizes this threat and provides a marvelous example. He attended a conference on uncertainty held at a casino. He felt compelled to remark upon the irony that the venue chosen for discussing uncertainty was one of the few places on earth where reasonably reliable probabilities could be computed. When he brought this up, the casino management was surprisingly in accord with his observation. The manager then talked at length about the measures they employed to reduce a threat to fitness to which they could not attach odds: the problem of cheaters. While Taleb did not describe the specific techniques employed, from his comments ("I felt transported into a James Bond movie"; Taleb, 2007, p. 129-130) one can easily imagine scenes from recent cinematic blockbusters such as *Oceans 11, Oceans 13* or *21*, including advanced surveillance and monitoring of bodily functions. But that was not moral of the story. The salient aspect was that the actual experienced loss owing to cheating was negligible. The casino had, however, experienced some losses and threats to fitness so serious that they could have put the entire operation out of business. These consisted of:

1. A tiger that mauled one of the performers in the *Siegfried and Roy* show ($100,000,000).

2. A disgruntled contractor who plotted to blow up the casino (a plot that was, fortunately, foiled).

3. A failure of an employee to file appropriate IRS forms documenting gambler winnings (which threatened their gaming license and led to a large, undisclosed fine).

4. A kidnapping of the casino owners daughter, which led him to dip into the casino's funds in order to get the necessary cash (again, violating gaming laws and putting their license in jeopardy).

All of these events fell outside of the prevailing fitness models. But if these alternative paths to fitness (or destruction of fitness) are ignored, the rigor of the remaining theory for assessing casino fitness is questionable. Theory-of-fitness needs to be systematic in order to be rigorous. Theory fragments used to describe a rugged landscape do not meet this standard *unless* they identify alternative sources of fitness and risks to fitness originating from outside of the boundaries of the theory. Furthermore, even well delineated theory-of-fitness is not particularly useful unless the relative importance of the alternative forces is estimated in some meaningful way. To the contrary, such fragments may actually do harm by focusing the individual's attention exclusively on the system under study. This is at the heart of Ghoshal's (2005) concerns regarding management theory. It is not that the market value of a firm or an individual's financial compensation package should be ignored in our understanding of fitness. The danger is when theory encourages you to focus on these specific considerations to the exclusion of other factors that can impact fitness.

Theory based on lab experiments is particularly vulnerable to rigor concerns. In developing theory from this source we not only have the question of generalizability, we also make assumptions about what does and does not interact by pulling the phenomenon being tested out of its natural landscape. Then, to add insult to injury, we have more than likely performed the experiments on a very non-representative population: undergraduate or graduate students[7]. Taken together, experimentally-grounded theory should require a warning label[8].

In their book *Super Freakonomics*, University of Chicago economist Steven Levitt and journalist Stephen Dubner (2009, p. 108-110) describe a series of variations on a widely cited lab experiment that illustrate how sensitive such results can be to small changes. The original experiment, a game called *Ultimatum*, involves a pair of participants unknown to each other. One (the giver) is provided an amount of money and is instructed to offer the other (the receiver) as little or as much of it as he or she chooses. The receiver can then accept or reject the offer. If accepted, the transaction is performed. If rejected, neither gets anything.

If the *Ultimatum* game were played according to traditional economic theory, the person in charge of the money would offer the other a pittance. That is not what happens, however. In a result widely replicated across cultures, offers of 50-50, 60-40, or 70-30 are much more common. Given our earlier discussions of utility in Chapter 5, this is not so surprising. An insultingly low offer might activate "defense" goals relating to fairness on the receiver side. The giver, through the process of empathy, would be able to predict such a reaction. It is therefore prudent not to risk insulting the receiver with too low an offer.

The next variation of the game is called the *Dictator* version. It is the same as the original version, except that the receiver no longer has any say in the matter, the division is entirely in the hands of the giver. Without fear of rejection, economic theory would definitely predict that the giver would keep all the money. What the original experiments found, however, was very different. When given a choice of a 50-50 or

90-10 split in favor of the giver, three out of four givers chose a 50-50 split. When given complete freedom as to what percentage to give away, givers averaged 20%. These results have been widely cited as evidence that we are "hardwired for altruism" (Levitt & Dubner, 2009, p. 110).

The next variation involved the same basic *Dictator* setup with one minor change: both giver and receiver were given sums of money for participating but the giver (a.k.a., the dictator) was given additional money *and* was also allowed to take up to $1 from the receiver. This setup led to a substantial change in behavior, with over 20% of the givers choosing to take $1 and almost 45% choosing not to give or take anything (List, 2007, p. 488). This compared with over 70% of givers choosing to give at least something in the original *Dictator* version, which was the same except for the ability to take. Thus, the addition of one additional option (the ability to take $1) profoundly changed the dynamics of the game. Such a result would not be unexpected in the rugged utility model proposed here; having a "take" option can easily change how alternatives are framed, with neither giving nor taking being preferred as a result of the compromise effect (discussed in Chapter 5). What we conclude, however, is that the cause of rigor would not have been well served by attempting to generalize from the theory fragment based on either of the original *Ultimatum* and *Dictator* findings.

Good reasoning, bad assumptions

No matter how impressive the logic or mathematics, a theory cannot be rigorous without justifying the quality of the assumptions and initial conditions upon which it is built. Where underlying assumptions are flawed, those flaws will be incorporated in the resulting theory. Where the underlying assumptions are known to be flawed, then a question of rigor needs to be raised. You are not being systematic in your inquiry if you do not.

The disciplines of economics and finance are currently experiencing considerable turmoil in this area because research and recent events have come together to make us question some of our most cherished assumptions. On the behavioral side, the discipline faces an increasing stream of criticism for its failure to incorporate repeatedly observed behavioral anomalies (such as those reported in Chapters 5 and 9) into its mathematical models of decision-making. In a recent article in the *Harvard Business Review*, Dan Ariely (2009) asserted:

> We are now paying a terrible price for our unblinking faith in the power of the invisible hand. We're painfully blinking awake to the falsity of standard economic theory—that human beings are capable of always making rational decisions and that markets and institutions, in the aggregate, are healthily self regulating[9].

The empirical research upon which this assertion was based, however, has a long history—as we have seen. Many of the preference findings have their origins in the 1970s and have been widely known in the academic community since the 1980s. A decade ago, Thaler (2000) called for a transition from *homo economicus* to *homo sapiens*. These calls have simply been ignored in mainstream econometrics. Most likely, this is because the observed behaviors make the type of mathematical models whose elegance is prized by economists nearly impossible to construct.

Another good example of this phenomenon can be found in the faith that economists place on relatively stable processes, whose error terms can be described reasonably well by Gaussian distributions. Many of the most widely used models of finance, such as the capital asset pricing model (CAPM) and portfolio theory, are rendered either invalid or useless if their parameters are not reasonably stable over time (e.g., beta in the CAPM model, correlation coefficients in portfolio theory). Unfortunately, such stability can be adversely impacted by either process changes—such as would be typical in the dynamics of a complex system—or by grey and black swan events (as discussed in Chapter 9). The problem is that correlation coefficients are notoriously unstable and a lot of financial processes tend to generate power law distributions. The latter observation was published by Benoit Mandelbrot (1963) in the early 1960s with respect to cotton prices. Nassim Nicholas Taleb (2007, p. 266) reports a similar finding more broadly, with an important caveat:

> My colleagues and I worked with about 20 million pieces of financial data. We all had the same data sets. We knew the data revealed a fractal power law, but we learned that one could not produce a precise number. But what we did know—that the distribution is fractal and scalable—was sufficient to operate and make decisions[10].

In other words, their conclusions suggested a result that would, all at once, threaten economic orthodoxies *and* be hard to quantify precisely. As we have seen, such is typical for observations from a power law process. Moreover, if we accept the likelihood of process changes resulting from adaptation, as would be expected in such a system, getting a precise measure of underlying distributions is likely to be impossible. This is not a desirable property in terms of potential for academic publication.

All of this could be forgiven if academic economists and finance experts were good at making predictions—which represents the truest test of theory. Regrettably, they are not. In Tetlock's (1999) study of expert prediction discussed in Chapter 7, for example, economists consisted of about a quarter of the sample. Error rates were high and largely unaffected by the amount of professional training or occupation (Taleb, 2007, p. 151). In another study (De Bondt, 1991, p. 90), examining how well economists predicted stock market indices based on over 5000 predictions, the group performed even worse than a simple strategy of always predicting the market would rise over the next 7 or 13 months. The study's findings included the following:

> Significantly less than half of the seven- and thirteen-month forecasts [of the economists] are false: 47.4% (p < 0.01) and 45.9% (p<0.0001)... Even a naïve observer of history—who remembers only that the market rises more frequently than it falls—would easily beat the economists' forecast performance by predicting an increase 100% of the time... the error rate of this strategy is 32.9% for seven month forecasts and 34.3% for thirteen month forecasts...

> The average error (AVE) of the economists' seven-month forecasts is 6.1%, and their mean absolute error (MABE) is 21.1%...By way of comparison, a forecaster who guesses that stock prices always rise at the same rate—say, the arithmetic average rate of capital appreciation on stocks between 1926 and 1951, i.e., 5.47% per year according to Ibbotson Associates—would make an average error of 3.4% and a mean absolute error of 17.3%. For the thirteen-month forecasts, the errors of the naïve strategy amount to, respectively, 1.7% and 12.7%. Again, these numbers compare favorably with the economists' thirteen-month average error of 4.1% and mean absolute error of 15.1%.

A model that yields good predictions from bad assumptions probably has its place[11]. But can a process that generates weak predictions from questionable assumptions really be considered rigorous?[12]

Impact of Disciplinary Silos

Disciplinary silos exist when functions engage in research and teaching activities independently of each other. While they would make sense on a landscape where functional activities can be conducted independently of each other—such as a decomposable landscape—the rationale for their existence where functions are interdependent is murkier. These silos can be observed at most leading business schools and have already been criticized for their tendency to produce an environment where cross-functional learning is minimized (Navarro, 2008). But the type of specialization that leads to silos can also seriously endanger the rigor of our research.

The particular threat to rigor presented by disciplinary silos is the evolution of parallel and inconsistent assumptions. This evolution is another example of failing to be systematic, compounded by a reluctance to challenge ourselves. In my own transdisciplinary research activities, I am constantly struck by such inconsistencies. Take, for example, the concept of utility. As I pointed out in a review of the topic (Gill, 2008a), the concept—first introduced by economists—is closely related to motivation, since both are presumed to guide an individual's action. When the utility and motivation literature are contrasted, however, it is as if they were constructed on different planets. Psychologists, such as Daniel Kahneman, have spent decades demonstrating that our preferences are inconsistent and easily manipulated. Economists, in contrast, treat utility as a function of consumption and savings and assume rational tradeoffs. Researchers in management argue that the most important forms of motivation are intrinsic; the goal setting research stream does not necessarily disagree, but argues that specific external goals drive the process. Finance, on the other hand, views motivation in terms of agency theory (Jensen & Meckling, 1976), with the agent's motivation largely derived from compensation.

I find a similar situation exists in the concept of informing. In the study of leadership, the characteristics of the sender tend to be emphasized. In marketing, the greater emphasis is placed on channels. In MIS, we have come to view the user (client) as driving the process. Contrast these views with that of finance. It is only a slight exaggeration to say that the efficient market hypothesis implies that informing is no issue at all; indeed, taken to an extreme, by the time I finish typing this paragraph, the market has already become aware of my thoughts and adjusted for them.

Even within disciplines—such as economics—different schools that rarely talk to each other have emerged. You have the traditional Marxist, Keynesian, Chicago, and Austrian schools—just to name a few. On top of that you have the behavioral economists, the neuro-economists, and the evolutionary economists. All these groups employ different assumptions about how human beings and the world work. Moreover, their efforts to integrate their views are far exceeded by the forces that increase their specialization, such as narrowly-focused journals.

The needs of rigor are rarely well met by wearing blinders. Specialization provides a convenient means for keeping our assumptions from being challenged. So long as we cluster around those who agree with us, our relationships with colleagues will remain very collegial. If, however, we are interested in the truth, we should relish the discovery of differences and strive to understand them. Sometimes, the result will be reconciliation[13]. In other cases, one assumption will simply prove to be a better fit with reality than the other. But as long as we do not seek out these differences, we are underperforming in our search for better understanding.

The Matthew Effect

The final threat to theory rigor comes from an excess of incentive to create and test theory in most of the business disciplines. This threat falls into the "appropriate design" aspect of rigor and has two effects. First, it drives out useful research that is not theory based, since prestigious outlets have limited capacity—a key contributor to what makes them prestigious. Second, it gives us the incentive to cast our findings in terms of theory, even when it is not necessary or appropriate to do so.

To justify the threat of over emphasis on theory-of-fitness development on a rugged landscape, we begin with the assumption that there is a wide set of theoretical propositions floating around that could either be studied or used to support other propositions. It should be clear that the distribution across possible propositions is likely to be far from uniform. In fact, each proposition comes with a built-in estimate-of-fitness: who said it and where it was said. Few of us—myself included—can resist adding "Nobel Laureate" or "Stanford Professor" to the name of someone we are citing as a method of adding credibility. In the absence of personal credibility, it is sadly true that something said in a discipline's top journal—such as *MIS Quarterly* or *Academy of Management Review*—has vastly greater assumed credibility than a similar statement made in *Informing Science: The International Journal of an Emerging Transdiscipline*, the journal that I edit. The potential obstacle to rigor that this presents is sometimes specifically referred to as the "Matthew Effect" (Merton, 1968) although, by now, it should be familiar to readers as being a typical consequence of the information cascade that can result from using estimates-of-fitness to guide behavior[14].

In the case of an academic career, the effect works as follows. An individual who gets a particularly prestigious academic posting or early successes in a top journal gets a lot of positive feedback and, as a result, tends to work harder. By virtue of these efforts (and their initial success), that work is reinforced. That leads to even greater effort and perquisites, such as greater access to funding and reduced teaching load, that further increase productivity. And the cycle continues… If this cycle sounds suspiciously like the type of process that generates a power law distribution of individual citation, it does (Gupta, Campanha, & Pesce, 2005)[15]. The same effect can occur for journals, where high impact factor—the current gold standard for estimating journal fitness—would naturally tend to reinforce itself.

The obstacle to the rigor of ideas that this process presents is a familiar one to science. Once an idea gains traction, it can be very hard to dislodge. In the case of many areas of business research, that idea is the belief that we are moving towards theories that will be useful in describing the broad business environment. Bolstering that assumption are the most successful researchers and the publication standards of each discipline's top journals.

Evidence for the second point, the journal standards, is easy to come by. For example, *MIS Quarterly*, the most highly ranked journal in MIS, requires authors of research articles to "ground their work in theory." The *Academy of Management Review (AMR)*, the most highly ranked journal in management, only considers theory pieces. Its sister journal, the *Academy of Management Journal (AMJ)*, shares the leading position with AMR but does not *strictly* require theory. What has evolved in practice, however, brings us to the first point—what top researchers actually choose to publish.

Researchers Colquitt and Zapata-Phelan (2007) published a study of the distribution of AMJ articles by category for selected years (3 year intervals). These categories, illustrated in Figure 10.1, identified the level of two types of theoretical contribution made by articles: theory-building and theory-testing. As suggested by the chart, the lowest theory category is the *reporter*. In the years 1963, 1966 and 1969, roughly 75% of all articles were classified as reporter articles. On the other hand, in 2002, 2005, and 2007 *not a single reporter article* was published (recall that AMJ is the journal that *allows* non-theory articles, at least in principle). Instead, roughly 75% of the articles were about evenly divided between the *qualifier* and *expander* roles.

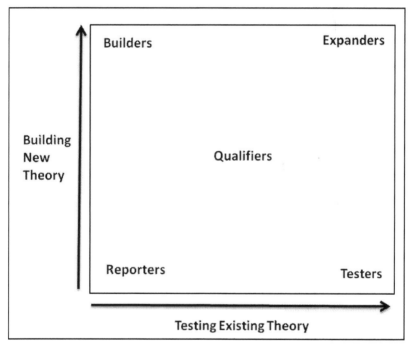

Figure 10.1: Theoretical contributions of empirical research, from Colquitt and Zapata-Phelan (2007, p. 1283)

Of all the research categories, those that combine theory-building and theory-testing run the greatest risk of being "rigor-challenged", since theory-testing and theory-building can iteratively take place in a manner that pretty much guarantees that whatever theory is proposed is justified. Jason Colquitt[16] points out, however, that expanders and qualifiers normally combine tests of *existing* theory with building of *new* theory, so the risk of mixing testing and construction may be less severe than it first appears. Theory builders, on the other hand, may employ techniques such as *grounded theory* (the construction of theory based upon the researcher's observations) that runs such a risk. The risk is particularly great in a research environment where only a tiny fraction of the theory that is constructed is ever tested, such as management (Hambrick, 2007).

Given the evolving preference of business academic journals towards theory, it is hard to imagine that any sensible, career-minded researcher would target publishing anything but theory-based research. This being the case, however, we should not attach any particular significance to the fact that nearly all top journal research is grounded in theory.

Statistical Rigor in Empirical Research

Chapter 4 presented an argument that presence of statistical significance in empirical research results was not necessarily inconsistent with a rugged fitness landscape. I will now make the case that the manner in which we employ statistics often threatens the very rigor that we are hoping to demonstrate. Three separate arguments are presented:

1. The cult of statistical significance
2. The illusions presented by an adaptive landscape, and
3. The dangers of assumed normality

The principal target of this analysis will be the use of statistical techniques to test existing theory-of-fitness. Virtually all these problems are magnified, however, when the researcher combines theory building and theory testing, as was previously noted in our discussions of the expander, qualifier, and theory builder research roles.

The "Cult of Statistical Significance"

Economists Stephen Ziliak and Deidre McCloskey (2008) wrote a marvelous history and critique of statistical methods called the *Cult of Statistical Significance*. The overarching theme of the book is that we would be producing much better, and more useful, research if we concentrated on identifying substantive significance—e.g., economic significance, clinical significance, epidemiological significance—rather than on statistical significance. We will now explore three of the many specific threats to rigor that the authors raise.

To set the stage, imagine that you have a theory that relates A to B; two boxes on a diagram. What you are interested in determining is whether or not your observations justify drawing a line between the two boxes. The way most business researchers today would make that decision would be to examine the data and determine: a) if the pattern supports the existence of the relationship, and b) the relative likelihood that such a pattern could have occurred by chance in the absence of any relationship. Typically, we accept our hypothesis that the line should be drawn if that likelihood (item b) is less than some value, such as 5%. This type of test, popularized by Ronald Fisher in the 1930s, has emerged as the gold standard of empirical research in business. But is the approach rigorous?

Powder Puffs: Unrealistic competing hypotheses

If we accept that challenging our own findings is an important aspect of rigor, then hypothesis testing should always be conducted with respect to competing plausible hypotheses, not with respect to the "null" hypothesis of no relationship. Ziliak and McCloskey (2008, p. 250) call this the distinction between *hypothesis testing* and *significance testing*.

The rigor issue accompanying significance testing is that it allows you to get away with constructing tests that offer absolutely no useful information, after which you can then claim that the tests support your particular theory. Where is the challenge of that?

To illustrate this, I will use an example from my own research area, MIS. One problem that has continuously vexed both academics and practitioners in my field is the fact that we often spend a lot of money building information systems that never get used. For example, in a comprehensive early study of the decision support systems (DSS) research stream (Keen and Scott Morton, 1978, p. 196), the contributors to DSS success were found to be:

- Top management support
- A clear felt need by the client
- An immediate, visible problem to work on

- Early commitment by the user and conscious staff involvement
- A well-institutionalized OR/MIS or MIS group.

In what possible universe would these characteristics fail to contribute to success (fitness) of a system?

The trail does not end there, however. One of the most successful streams of MIS research is referred to as the technology acceptance model (TAM) [17]. There have been several hundred articles (and dozens of dissertations) focused on testing or refining the model in the past decade alone; well over a thousand articles mention it. The originator of the model describes it as follows:

> TAM posits two particular beliefs, perceived usefulness and perceived ease of use are of particular relevance for computer acceptance behaviors (Davis, Bagozzi, & Warshaw, 1989, p. 985)[18]

Compared to *usefulness* → *intention to use*, even hypothesizing *top management support* → *intention to use* seems challenging. I refer to significance testing of propositions such as these as *powder puff tests*. The propositions themselves I refer to as *low hanging fruit*, since even in the most complex environments, we would expect some attributes to have a strong main effect; which is to say that they are generally true except, perhaps, in isolated cases[19].

All of this might be classified as a problem of relevance—you can imagine a manager rolling his or her eyes after learning the MIS field has invested hundreds of thousands of high priced researcher-hours attempting to demonstrate that relationships such as these exist—but the problem has serious implications for rigor as well. Once we start accepting powder puff tests as support for hypotheses, a number of subsequent rigor issues surface.

First, we start to imagine that extremely low p-values (very high significance, such as $p < 0.001$) are somehow more meaningful than higher values (e.g., $p < 0.05$). That sets us on a relentless drive to gather more observations for each of our powder puff tests, an easy and mechanical way to achieve higher significance. Assuming that we have limited resources, engaging in that relatively meaningless pursuit will then keep us from doing something informative.

Second, we will make the mistake of believing that a successful powder puff test actually provides meaningful support for whatever theory we proposed. A theory that is marginally nonsensical will always perform well against complete and utter nonsense (which describes many, and perhaps most, null hypotheses). That does not make the marginally nonsensical theory any more likely. Recalling an earlier example, when you choose door Number 1 and Monty Hall then reveals a stuffed capybara behind Door Number 2, it does not change the likelihood that the real prize is behind Door Number 1.

Third, when we accept powder puff tests as meaningful, researchers are drawn to them like bees to honey. The reason for this is simple. Empirical research demonstrating statistical significance is much easier to publish than pure theory building research. But complete non-significance in one's findings is a serious barrier—I cannot recall ever having seen a publication where all the significance tests failed, although there is probably an article or two floating around[20]. Thus, if you are a researcher concerned with your career, it makes sense to include some low hanging fruit to test among your hypotheses. Over time, this practice becomes widespread and institutionalized to the extent that we do not even recognize that we are doing it; recalling Chapter 6, automatized activities are the hallmark of true expertise. Ziliak and McCloskey (2008) refer to this as "trained incapacity", which is just another variation of the Matthew Effect[21].

Finally, and this is the most serious impact, finding support for powder puffs tends to reduce your motivation to seek out realistic, interesting theories[22]. Instead, it tends to encourage the development of simple, incomplete theories that can be tested mechanically. Assuming decomposability also makes the task much easier, since it allows you to produce your theory in chunks, rather than in the complete (and ugly) form that a rugged landscape would demand. As an illustration of this effect, contrast the two sets of findings on information systems acceptance presented earlier. The first made no reference to system usefulness—a totally ridiculous omission. The original TAM had no provisions for organizational context and support—equally ludicrous (but understandable since the initial tests were conducted using student subjects).

The sensible rejoinder to the arguments I have presented is that what seems obvious to me may not seem equally obvious to everyone. Thus, rigor demands we test every assumption, no matter how straightforward it seems. I completely agree with that statement. In fact, on a rugged landscape, I would be willing to bet that I could find a violation of almost any low hanging fruit proposition, no matter how unequivocal its support from significance tests might be. In Chapter 11, for example, I mention a case that I observed where the usefulness and ease of use of a system actually led to user resistance. I can also think of another example where the support of a business owner for a system may have actually hurt its chances for success; his motivation was perceived to be self serving, rather than being in the best interest of the company's stakeholders as a whole. The problem is that you do not find examples like these by using statistical significance tests. You need to look for them in the field and you need to be a sufficiently skilled observer to recognize them when they are encountered.

When to draw the line: Type II error

Returning to this section's original question, deciding whether or not to draw a line between boxes A and B, the decision to draw a line when—in fact—the relationship does not exist is an example of Type I error, an error of *commission*. It is precisely to counter that form of error that significance testing was developed.

There is, however, another form of error: Type II error. This error occurs when a relationship exists—a line between the boxes *should* be drawn—but we conclude that it should not; an error of *omission*.

It stands to reason that excessive zeal in defending against Type I errors necessarily leads to an increased likelihood of Type II errors. Thus, any truly rigorous investigation needs to balance the possibility of both types of error. Not doing so results in a failure to be sufficiently systematic. Such a failure can lead to serious consequences. Ziliak and McCloskey (2008, p. 28-29) specifically mention the case of Vioxx, a painkiller developed and marketed by the drug company *Merck* that was later found to increase the likelihood of heart attacks and stroke materially. During its early trials, 5 heart attacks were encountered in the trial group using Vioxx, compared with 1 in the control group using another drug. Given baseline heart condition rates, however, this difference did not achieve the necessary 5% significance to "prove" the risk was genuine. As a consequence, the drug was approved. It was later discovered that three more deaths occurred than were originally reported, a finding whose source was the family of the victims. This was, of course, fraud and had nothing to do with the rigor of the statistical tests employed. Ziliak and McCloskey (2008, p. 29) infer, however, that the decision to underreport was likely made to ensure that the statistical significance of the finding remained below the threshold.

There is a test that can be used to determine the likelihood that an effect of a given size will be ignored, thereby leading to a Type II error. It is known as a power test. In order to conduct such a test, you need to have reasonable estimates of three things:

1. The size of the effect you are trying to detect

2. The variability of outcome being predicted (i.e., fitness values)

3. The level of variability in the value being considered in the sample (i.e., the independent variable)

In the Vioxx illustration, for example, (1) might be death vs. non-death, (2) would be the variability of death rates in random samples of equivalent size, and (3) might be based upon the ratio of Vioxx to non-Vioxx treatments. Without going into the mechanics, the power test can then give you information regarding either (a) the number of people needed in the trial to guarantee a certain likelihood that the effect size will be recognized (information often used in research design), or (b) the likelihood that you will find (or miss) an effect of the specified size given (1), (2) and (3); information that tells you the likelihood of committing a Type II error.

Reported power test results are relatively rare in business research, although the situation has improved slightly in economics[23]. There are two reasons, in particular, why I suspect power tests may remain unpopular. First, the results would tend to undermine our assertions of rigor. For example, crude power estimates of existing research in psychology have found likelihood of detection values of 21%, 50% and 84% for small, medium and large effects respectively (Ziliak & McCloskey, 2008, p. 137). This is not good news if 5% is our gold standard, since it suggests that we are very biased in favor of rejecting effects that are actually present.

The second problem with power tests is that in order to construct a meaningful effect, you need to establish clear criterion for what magnitude of effect is considered substantively significant. This leads to a number of challenges. First, it requires a substantial amount of knowledge of the behavior of the domain being studied; it is an expert judgment. Making such judgments could prove to be a formidable obstacle in disciplines where observations are pulled from financial data repositories and researchers have little or no practical experience in the industry being studied. Second, it is nearly impossible to determine objectively for some of the most common types of survey questions, for example those constructed using a Likert scale. Third, and perhaps most unsettling for research where data has already been gathered, once you have distinguished between those effects that are substantively significant and those which are not, as required by the power test, what do you do when you detect statistically significant effects that are much smaller?

Consider the following illustrative example of the rigor problem raised by incorporating substantive significance. Let us imagine a hypothetical "best practice" case, where you actually do a power test analysis to determine your sample size. Suppose then you have just encountered a theory that Ipod ownership increases income[24]. You then decide that an income difference of $1,000/year is the meaningful cut point for power testing *and*, based on your estimates of the likelihood of Ipod ownership and variability of income, you decide that a sample size of 100 is needed to generate the necessary power at the 5% significance test level. What do you do when you discover a $p<0.01$ value for your Ipod effect with an average income difference effect estimated to be $250? Do you accept it, drawing the line between Ipod and income despite the fact that you previously decided that anything below $1,000 was not worth detecting? Or do you choose not to draw the line based upon the fact that the effect is not substantive? Would it make a difference that choosing not to draw the line increases your risk of rejection by a top journal?

But the situation gets even worse. Unless our cut points for small, medium and large effects are very close together, detection of a small effect at a high level of statistical significance virtually guarantees that the effect is not large. The reason is simple. For a small effect to be significant, the error in the estimated coefficient must be low. Since most of our significance tests assume an error distribution around our estimate that is close to normal, the likelihood of the value being double our estimate as about as low as the likelihood of it being 0. Or, returning to our example, if $p<0.01$ for our estimated income effect of $250—meaning the likelihood that observations where an effect was not present could produce that average was less than 1 in 100—then it also follows that the odds of the effect being greater than $500 are equally low. This is another reason why rigor would argue that we should not draw the line if $1000 is what we are concerned about. In fact, in a roundabout way, we have returned to the issue of powder puff hypotheses. Rather than testing for any effect (our estimated value versus 0, the null hypothesis), we should really be testing against our threshold for substantive significance ($1000 in our example). That would, of course, make our Type I error rate much lower. Unfortunately, it would also make our Type II error rate much higher. The intrinsic challenge we face is that there is no mechanical technique that we can devise to balance between the two types of error. As a result, we are hugely dependent upon the researcher's judgment in trading off the two. But it was precisely the desire to eliminate such subjectivity from the hypothesis testing process that led to our preoccupation with Type I error.

It is easy simply to ignore Type II errors. But doing so is not rigorous. The interesting thing about both the Type II error and competing hypothesis problems is that, unlike nearly all the other issues discussed in the book, they are not a consequence of a rugged fitness landscape. In fact, they can be problems even where the landscape is fully decomposable. Later in the chapter, however, we will see that a rugged fitness landscape is likely to increase the likelihood of small, highly statistically significant results being detected at much lower than expected sample sizes. That greatly magnifies the threat to rigor presented by statistical tests.

Theory fragments: High tolerance for randomness

The last of the Ziliak and McCloskey (2008, p. 245) threats to rigor that we consider involves our willingness to accept randomness as an explanation for what we cannot explain in our models. It is inspired by a quote from William Sealy Gosset[25] in a letter to Egon Pearson:

> [O]bviously, the important thing... is to have low real error, not to have a "significant" result... The latter seems to me to be nearly valueless in itself... You want to be able to say not only "We have significant evidence that if farmers in general do this they will make money by it," but also "we have found it so in nineteen cases out of twenty and we are finding out why it doesn't work in the twentieth." To do that you have to be as

sure as possible which is the 20th—your real error must be small.

The problem that Gosset describes goes hand-in-hand with over-reliance on significance testing, particularly in a multivariate environment such as regression analysis or structural equation modeling. Often we find ourselves in a situation where we appear to have estimates of individual effects (e.g., coefficient values) of high statistical significance while our overall model does not do a very good job predicting (e.g., R-square much less than 1, which would signify a perfect fit). We therefore attribute the unexplained error that remains either to randomness or to relationships that we have yet to capture.

The seriousness of this problem depends upon your assessment of the landscape you are observing. If the landscape is believed to be decomposable, then you can make a plausible argument that the problem is not very serious. What you are, in effect, testing is a theory fragment. Naturally, you would not expect such a fragment to describe the process properly—a full description would require that you combine a whole bunch of theory fragments, such as combining a fragment considering organizational considerations and one describing individual considerations in the decision to use an information system presented earlier. But, the very fact that the landscape is decomposable means that the fragment you do know is likely to be largely unaffected by the fragment you do not know; what starts significant stays significant. So any variation attributable to the latter fragment can be treated as randomness without impacting rigor. Viewed in graphical terms (see Figure 10.2), those elements we include represent discrete pieces of the overall decomposable fitness bar whose contribution and be measured meaningfully.

Where the landscape is rugged, the threat to rigor is much greater. Theory fragment results will not carry over to the landscape as a whole unless the variables in your fragment happen to be completely decomposable, as a group, from the rest of the landscape. If they are not, their values and significance will change when observed in real world contexts. Worse than that, the individual variable estimates will not even be meaningful since variables act in concert, through interrelationships, rather than individually. Fail to accurately include *any* of the X variables in the interacting bar of Figure 10.2 and major changes to fitness can result. Claiming that some "percentage of variance" is explained by our measured variables simply makes no sense.

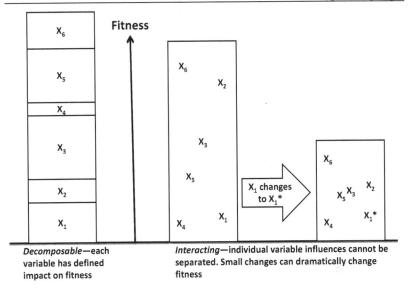

Figure 10.2: Decomposable versus interacting contributions to fitness (originally presented as Figure 3.2)

Additionally, our demand that researchers provide plausible explanations needs to be weighed against the danger that researchers will be motivated to make-up such explanations (often unintentionally). Taleb (2007) warns of the narrative fallacy. Anyone who has read a researcher's explanation as to why a particular variable "probably" did not achieve expected significance and sign or as to why the research results presented should be of compelling interest to managers has likely observed this process in action. Often, the researchers themselves are not to blame; reviewers and journal policy may force the decision by requiring such statements[26].

On balance, it probably makes sense to leave error unexplained in a decomposable world. Where the landscape is rugged, however, unexplained error means that variables contributing to important interactions are likely missing. Since the values of these unspecified variables can impact the entire effect, not just the unexplained portion attributed to "randomness", stating a partial relationship as if it were fact can prove very problematic. Recall what can happens to a cake when you judge its fitness based on major ingredients and ignore the small ones, such as baking powder.

Migration towards Fitness

In Chapter 4, we considered how it could be possible for statistically significant main effects to mask more important interaction effects. The example considered was the combinations of ice cream vs. roast beef and fudge sauce vs. gravy. This argument would apply even to random block trials, provided you were not looking for interactions. Of course, in most properly designed trials of this sort you are looking for interactions, so it could be argued that the problem is not that serious.

Where the threat to rigor grows is when a multivariate tool, such as multiple regression analysis, is used to analyze observations gathered from a fitness landscape. In this situation, entities are not randomly assigned to blocks. Instead, we count on the individual coefficient values to act as our controls, separating the effect of each.

Unfortunately, on such a landscape we would expect entities to migrate towards local fitness peaks. The consequence of such migration will be that spurious statistical significances likely emerge, even with a relatively small number of observations. I base this assertion on some experiments that Terry Sincich, a statistician, and I ran using simulated fitness landscapes of known complexity that we created (Gill & Sincich, 2008). The experiments were designed as follows:

1. Using a combination of randomization and formulas, we created simulated NK fitness landscapes for a number of different N values (e.g., 6, 8, 10 and 12).

2. We placed entities on the landscapes and allowed them to migrate towards local fitness peaks. Naturally, the assumption that such migration would occur makes sense only where the domain of study is theory-of-fitness on a complex landscape with adapting entities.

3. While the migration was occurring and after it was completed, we treated each entity as an observation.

4. We performed multiple regression analysis on these observations and examined the resulting significance patterns.

What we found was unexpected[27]. For orderly (i.e., decomposable) landscapes, our analysis allowed us to reconstruct the formulas used to generate the landscapes perfectly—hardly surprising. For chaotic and complex landscapes, however, the results were quite different. Instead of finding no statistical significance where random numbers were used, we found many high significance values that would have suggested that important decomposable relationships were present. These relationships persisted even when only partial migration was allowed (i.e., many observations had not yet reached peaks) and when a variety of random observation error terms were introduced to fuzzy up the regressions.

Once we observed these results, it was relatively easy to explain what caused them. As observations began to cluster around the fitness peaks, the underlying statistical assumption of observation independence were violated. As a result, computed coefficient significances became meaningless[28].

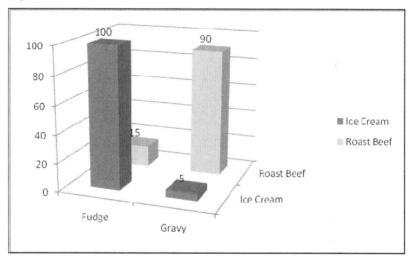

Figure 10.3: Fitness levels for ice cream vs. roast beef and fudge vs. gravy

This effect can best be illustrated through a simple example. Suppose we have set of observations from our ice cream vs. roast beef and fudge vs. gravy example. Further suppose, according to some arbitrary scale, that the fitness of the various combinations is as follows:

- Ice cream & fudge: 100
- Ice cream & gravy: 5
- Roast beef & fudge: 15
- Roast beef & gravy: 90

This fitness profile is illustrated graphically in Figure 10.3.

Now, assume that we are unaware that the interactions between the variables exist and are not looking for them. If we happened to get a perfectly balanced sample of 100 observations (25 subjects in each of the four combinations) and performed a multiple regression on the two variables (Roast beef=0, Ice Cream=1 and Gravy=0, Fudge=1) you would get a very low R-square (indicating a poor model fit), an Ice Cream coefficient of close to 0 (since ice cream and roast beef both sum to 115 and the number of subjects in each treatment is equal) whereas the Fudge coefficient would be estimated as 10 (since fudge fitness is, on average, 10 points higher than gravy). This will be true even if you add some random error to the fitness values, to account for the fact that peoples tastes differ slightly and there is likely to be measurement error[29]. Naturally, no one would ever take such a model seriously, since it demonstrates neither good overall fit (R-square) nor significant coefficient values.

The assumption of 25 observations per block is extremely unrealistic if we assume the observations are being drawn from a fitness landscape, however. A much better assumption would be that individuals on this landscape would gravitate towards the high fitness combinations (ice cream & fudge, roast beef & gravy). I therefore arbitrarily assume that instead of 25-25-25-25, we instead had 50 choosing ice cream & fudge, 40 choosing roast beef & gravy, 3 choosing ice cream & gravy and 7 choosing roast beef & fudge[30]. Under these circumstances, the results of the regression of the observations against fitness change dramatically. Specifically, with no assumed error in fitness, I computed the following coefficient values:

- R-square: 0.15 (not a great fit, but definitely not random)
- Ice Cream: 31.9, p=0.000131 (a highly significant result)
- Fudge: -20, p=0.0137 (also quite significant)

The problem with these results is that they are entirely meaningless in any practical sense (representing the program determining the best fit for a line between the two main peaks, adjusted for the 10 non-peak observations). And, of course, you would never be tempted to apply regression to an obviously interacting landscape such as the ice cream/roast beef problem I just described. But Terry Sincich and I demonstrated the same effects in much more complex 6, 8, 10 and 12 variable cases with thousands of simulated observations.

In addition, under the research protocol, at the outset I provided Sincich—who teaches our doctoral statistics course and has published some very successful statistics textbooks—simulated data that I had created using the fitness landscape model. I then asked him to see if he could figure out the underlying process I employed to generate the data. Aside from noticing some departures from normality in the error terms, he did not find anything particularly unusual about the data set and certainly did not guess that it had been generated from a fitness landscape. And that is the true threat to rigor: if you are not looking for this phenomenon, you are unlikely to notice it. What you will notice is significance values at a level that provides an optimistic prognosis for publication.

Long Tails

Since we previously considered the impact of power law influenced processes on theory, that subject does not need to be revisited here. The particular problem that needs to be considered with respect to empirical theory testing relates to the question of outliers. In any power law process, these outlier observations will have a disproportionate impact on fit. For example, the average individual net worth graduates of Harvard's Class of 1977 is probably about $20 million higher than the average net worth of Harvard's Class of 1976 (my class). Why? Bill Gates is officially a member of the Class of 1977[31].

The interesting thing about long tail observations is that a reasonable case can be made both for excluding them and including them. On the "exclude" side, grey swans and particularly black swans tend to be one-of-a-kind observations and therefore do not help us understand the day to day processes we are trying to model with our theory. On the "include" side, these swans frequently make a huge difference (witness the Bill Gates example) and, in the case of events, are often far more significant than years of "day-to-day" activities. Thus, some observers—such as Taleb—suggest that we would be better off if we concerned ourselves *only* with black swans.

The threat to rigor the long tail represents is, in fact, the considerable discretion that the investigator has in choosing to include or exclude these observations or events. Where the object of the research is to empirically test a theory, the natural tendency would be to choose based upon whether or not you believe the theory to be true or false. Where that happens, however, rigor is potentially compromised.

Given the concerns presented by theory fragments, migration towards fitness and long tails, rigor would demand that researchers justify decomposability assumptions where made. Such justifications are rare[32]. To understand why, we turn to the topic of quality control in our research.

Quality Control of Research

In order for our research to be rigorous, we need some form of quality control. In business research, we would expect this to be a particularly important role for academic journals, since they act as gatekeepers for the research that enters our literature. To ensure novel ideas are carefully vetted, we employ the process of *peer review*. To validate existing ideas, we can *replicate* existing research. Let us now consider how well each process is working.

Anonymous Peer Review

Detecting problems in research rigor is supposed to be the particular strength of the anonymous peer review process. The likely benefits of peer-review of some form are self evident. There is, however, an additional rationale for requiring anonymity. A particularly compelling example comes from the domain of music. In *Blink*, Malcolm Gladwell (2005) describes the case of trombone auditions for the Berlin Philharmonic in 1980. At the time, such auditions in Europe involved each performer getting on stage and playing a piece. In this case, however, performers were asked to audition behind a screen because a relative of one of the orchestra members was auditioning. As a result of this process, their choice was a woman—much to the shock (and, sadly, dismay) of the judges. As it turns out, the trombone was considered to be a "masculine" instrument so the orchestra leaders were upset. For the next decade and a half, the musician was forced to endure attempts to demote her for specious reasons, to receive pay that was far below equivalent to her male colleagues, and to undergo frequent testing to demonstrate that she could do the job. All because her work was judged according to an irrational prejudice. In fact, Gladwell (2005, p. 250) reports that, "In the past thirty years, since screens became commonplace, the number of women in top U.S. orchestras has increased five-fold." Viewed in this light, the case for anonymous peer review would seem to be indisputable.

Unfortunately, the practice may not live up to the justification. We begin by describing one of the most famous case studies in the area of peer review. We then consider some of the weaknesses that have been identified in the process, and conclude with an often overlooked strength.

The Ceci and Peters study of peer review reliability

Perhaps the best known study of the peer review process was conducted by Stephen Ceci, and Douglas Peters, at Cornell University and at the University of North Dakota respectively (at the time the study was published). It is well worth close consideration.

The study began when the authors chose 13 recently published papers that had appeared in 13 top psychology journals that were non-blind in their review processes. Articles were selected specifically on the basis of having authors with prestigious institutional affiliations. Their secretary retyped the articles, creating figures matching those in the articles, with three changes:

1. Some slight rewording, such as the use of the passive voice, was done to foil computer identification

2. The original authors names were replaced with fictitious names that were unknown to psychology

3. The original author institutional affiliations were replaced with institution names that sounded as if they were low status (e.g., Tri-Valley Center for Human Development) but which actually did not exist.

Once the articles had been retyped, the study's authors *sent them out to the same journals that had originally accepted and published them*, with routine cover letters. Neither the editors nor the reviewers knew about the experiment.

The results of the experiment were as follows:

•   Only 3 of the 13 manuscripts were identified as duplicates of previously published work.

- 9 of the 10 undetected manuscripts "were recommended for rejection resoundingly." In other words, the editors and reviewers were in full consensus.

- Of 20 reviewers recommending rejection, not one suggested that it might be possible to rewrite the manuscript so as to make it suitable for publication.

Based on the authors' estimates, in order for the original 10 manuscripts to have been published, they would have needed at least 16 favorable reviews. This contrasted with the 2 favorable reviews that were actually received—a huge indictment of the reliability of the review process.

Subsequent to the study's publication, but before the study's results became widely known, Scott Armstrong (mentioned later in this book for his replication studies) polled 21 full professors to get their assessments of what results they would have expected from the protocol. Their reported expectations "greatly overestimated the number of duplications that would be detected by reviewers and greatly underestimated the number of undetected manuscripts that would be rejected" (Ceci & Peters, p. 46).

The study's repercussions were nearly as disturbing as its results. To quote the authors:

> ...several editors who had not been directly involved with our study wrote scathing letters calling into question our professional ethics because of our use of deception (which, according to our national code of ethics, requires a careful cost-benefit analysis before employing). Actually, we had given serious consideration to alternative, nondeceptive means of examining per review but we ended up rejecting them. There was simply no experimentally sound way to study the issue we were interested in without using some form of deception...

> Other negative repercussions included several threats to professionally censure us and threats to reject the work of our colleagues, supposedly because they had been part of a department that approved such ethically bankrupt research...

> We received criticism of a different sort from colleagues and friends...Had we not irresponsibly played into the hands of

those desiring to reduce social science research training and support? (Ceci & Peters, 1982, pp. 46)

The story has a somewhat happier ending. After being rejected by two journals—"replete with personally insulting, ad hominem reviews"— they found a publisher. As the findings became broadly known, the authors received over a thousand letters, every single one of which was complimentary, expressing appreciation for their efforts.

Reviewer expertise

The first area that the Ceci and Peters (1982) study highlights is the expertise of reviewers in assessing the quality and currency of submissions. Their finding is, of course, troubling on that dimension. It is, however, largely to be expected and very consistent with my own observations as an editor. For maximal rigor, it would be desirable to match reviewer expertise closely to the subject matter of a particular paper. Typically, the editor in charge of that process—as I have been at two journals—is not particularly well-versed in either, however. As a result, the matching process tends to be relatively arbitrary, driven by a small number of keywords in the database. To address this problem, some journals request that authors suggest their own reviewers. The potential for conflict of interest in this protocol should be relatively self-evident.

The other expertise-related concern occurs where a reviewer's expertise conflicts with that of the piece being reviewed. Such conflicts invariably occur in a complex landscape, owing to the diversity of phenomena such a landscape can accommodate. Peter Berkowitz (2010, p. A13) summarized the problem nicely in a Wall Street Journal editorial:

> ...the peer review process violates a fundamental principle of fairness. We don't allow judges to be parties to a controversy they are adjudicating, and don't permit athletes to umpire games in which they are playing. In both cases the concern is that their interest in the outcome will bias their judgment and corrupt their integrity. So why should we expect scholars, especially operating under the cloak of anonymity, to fairly and honorably evaluate the work of allies and rivals?

Reviewer consistency

A second area highlighted by the Ceci and Peters (1982) study is the problem of consistency. Some particularly useful additional research in this area was done by William Starbuck (2003, 2005), who was the editor of the highly rated *Administrative Science Quarterly (ASQ)*, a top management journal. He compared reported various measures of inter-rater review correlation (the degree to which reviewers agree with each other) for different journals in the fields of management, sociology, and psychology. The coefficient was 0.12 for the *ASQ*, statistically significant as a result of the 500 articles considered but representing virtually no consensus in practical terms. He compared this with similar measures for other journals in the fields of psychology and sociology. In these other fields, the measures were substantially higher on average—but the range was large, typically between 0.16 and 0.50 (Miller, 2006)[33]. Based upon Starbuck's assumptions regarding the possible range of actual correlations to the underlying value of the manuscript, he estimated that between 29% and 77% of the articles published in a top tier journal are not in the top 20% in terms of actual underlying value, with a midpoint estimate of 57% (Starbuck, 2005, p. 197). This would suggest high levels of both Type I and Type II errors.

I would make two observations on these findings. The first would be my complete agreement with respect to the likely variability in reviews. As a rough estimate, I have served as editor for about 60 papers and book chapters. During that time, I have almost never seen complete consensus either for or against a submission[34]. More often than not, significant differences in reviewer opinions exist. Also, reviewers themselves have quite different average standards. As Eli Cohen, founder of the *Informing Science Institute*, is fond of reminding its journal editors, some reviewers never see a paper that they like, others never see one that they don't like.

The second issue that Starbuck's (2005) statistical analysis, in particular, raises is the question of the "underlying value of a paper." Value in this context is, of course, closely related to, if not synonymous with, fitness. The challenge becomes determining what is meant by "value."

One way we might define value would be in terms of how effectively the paper communicates its ideas over its life, closely aligned with the concept of resonance. The parallel I see is with assessing relative fitness of a college. The problem here is that, as we saw in Chapter 3, it really does not make sense to describe the fitness of a college without reference to a particular student—since the fitness function for instruction involves both informer and client characteristics, the theory fragment describing college fitness alone is of no particular use. Similarly, you cannot assess the communications fitness of an article without knowing its reader[35]. The reader new to the topic may be inspired by the submission's clarity; the familiar reader may chide its unnecessary repetition of facts everyone already knows. What of the manuscript that espouses a theory so breathtakingly wrong that it serves as the catalyst for a new theory that is vastly improved? Or the manuscript that stretches the ethical envelopes in order to tell us something that we ought to—but may not want to—know? We saw the huge variation in reaction to Ceci and Peter's (1982) experiment. What is the underlying fitness of that research?

Why this is important is that the reason for the wide variation may not be reviewer capriciousness or inattention, attributes that can conceivably be altered with sufficient screening and training. Instead, reviewers may be evaluating the submission from entirely different positions on the fitness landscape, a direct consequence of their individual differences. Starbuck (2005) refers to something similar with his term *shared value*. For this reason, diversity of opinion could be a healthy reflection of the fact that we have yet to become numbingly of one mind in our thinking.

Conservatism of expert reviewers

Communications fitness, as just discussed in the context of reviewer consistency, is not the only plausible candidate for what we mean by a paper's "value." An alternative, and to my mind more intellectually satisfying, view of fitness might be *the paper's potential to produce large and legitimate changes to prevailing mental models*. The size of the potential changes then becomes a proxy for relevance; legitimacy a proxy for its rigor[36]. Starbuck's (2005) concept of *true value* seems to map most closely to this perspective, which he describes in terms of its underlying potential to create a new consensus among social science thinkers.

Based on the conceptual scheme presented in Chapter 7—most particularly, the *Law of Abandoned Expertise*—we would expect targeting size and legitimacy to produce an interesting phenomenon. Our most acknowledged experts, frequently serving as editors and reviewers for elite journals, are undoubtedly in the best position to assess legitimacy; they have built their successful careers on the basis of defending it. They are, however, collectively likely to be the worst possible group when it comes to assessing findings requiring "large" changes to mental models. After all, their very success means that they have a great deal invested in the status quo. Reviewers with much less expertise, on the other hand, should be far more likely to miss legitimate questions of rigor while, at the same time, be less resistant to radical ideas, having much less invested in the status quo. Simply stated then, we would expect large ideas to be much more likely to find a home in low prestige or brand new outlets—along with a great many more half-baked ideas. The world being the complex place that it is, there will of course be exceptions; not every expert shares the same mental models[37], nor are all of us who could be called experts confident of the legitimacy of our so called "expertise." Nevertheless, on purely theoretical grounds we would expect this pattern to be strong enough to be detectable.

The most widely known research on the topic of publication difficulties was conducted by Juan Miguel Companario (1993), who examined narratives of authors relating to the difficulties they had getting works published that were later highly cited. The source he used was *Citation Classics*®, a magazine that presents author commentaries on their highly-cited published research and includes a specific request that they describe any difficulties they had in performing or publishing the research. Approximately 6% of the commentaries described such problems, a result that many researchers suggest demonstrates that reviewer conservatism exists (e.g., Pfeffer, 2007).

Personally, I am not entirely convinced by the evidence that reviewers at prestigious journals necessarily resist new ideas. In the first place, the 6% value is not all that large. Second, it suggests citation count to be a strong indicator of novel ideas. The citation count-impact relationship (in management research, at least) appears to be somewhat contradicted by a study in which the sources of citation counts were analyzed (Judge, Cable, Colbert, & Rynes, 2007, p. 510). Significant path coefficients in the total model, in descending order of significance, were as follows:

- Journal citation rate (0.28)

- Number of references cited in the article (0.26)

- Whether or not the article was a meta-analysis (0.17)

- Presentation clear and readable (0.16)

- *Exploration research plot (0.15)*

- Highest prestige of author affiliation (0.14)

- Subjective prestige of journal (0.14)

- Length of article (0.10)

- Year of publication (-0.10)

- Top-tier publications of authors (0.08)

- Article first in the issue (0.07)

These results are confirmed by the authors' finding that "idea" appeared to explain less than any other classification category they used when looked at independently (Judge et al., 2007, p. 502)[38]. Thus, highly cited research is not necessarily novel research.

Considerably more convincing is Jeffrey Pfeffer's (2007) list of important ideas that originated outside of top tier journals, either in books or in less prestigious journal outlets. Supporting this, his assertion that among the 50 most important management innovations described in the recent *Giant Steps in Management* (Mol & Birkinshaw, 2008), not one had its origins in academia. And his evidence that books by managers and consultants tend to be much more widely read and cited than those by academic researchers (Pfeffer, 2007, p. 1336). Collectively these suggest that the elite vs. non-elite journal issue may just represent the tip of the iceberg. It may be the very fact that we are encouraged to view our research in terms of what can be conveyed in an academic journal article that is the true source of conservatisms that represents a threat to rigor. To meet the inherent limitations of the journal article format, it is much easier to focus research on the development of theory fragments. Unfortunately, these do not fit a complex world very well.

Anonymity of peer reviews

The Ceci and Peters (1982) experiment provides yet another good reason why anonymity is warranted. That name and institutional affiliation had a huge impact on acceptance rate is indisputable. The authors went on to do another study specifically addressing the question of the effect of anonymity (Ceci & Peters, 1984). In a study where they asked reviewers to guess author identities on blinded papers, they found that the reviewers were able to guess correctly about 36% of the time, while another 8% guessed incorrectly. Interestingly, the rate of correct guesses was about half of that predicted by the respondents prior to the experiment. Subsequent research, particularly in the field of medicine, seems to confirm these estimates, except the reported values are often higher and may also grow with the experience of the reviewer (Newcombe & Bouton, 2009). That later body of research also suggests, however, that the practical effect of being able to guess author identities is not that material.

I believe it is possible to reconcile these seemingly conflicting findings by understanding how many journals handle blind peer review. In most, but not all, journals in my field, reviewers do not know the identities of the authors. The associate editor may or may not know the authors. The senior editor or editor-in-chief, on the other hand, does know the author identities. For that small percentage of papers were everyone is in full accord, blinding probably makes no difference since the decision is straightforward. At *ASQ*, for example, Starbuck (2003) found that total percentage to be in the range of 30% (about 6% unanimous accept, about 25% unanimous reject). Where the reviews are split—the most common condition—the decision gets escalated. When I was an associate editor for the *Decision Science Journal of Innovative Education*, for example, I would estimate that split decisions accounted for well over half of the 21 articles I reviewed in 2008, consistent with Starbuck's estimate. I knew the identity of the authors in all of those cases. Thus, while reviews were made under blinded conditions, the actual decision was not.

Rigor benefits of peer review

Given all the arguments I have presented suggesting the inherent unreliability of peer review, it may come as a surprise that I am a huge fan of the process. It can be—and often is—the noblest thing we do as academic researchers. We invest our time on this task with little or no chance of professional benefit. It can get very uncomfortable when we are forced "go negative." When we are helpful to authors, our contribution gets—at best—generic acknowledgment. In other words, we take on this extra-curricular, unpaid "grading" assignment for no other purpose but to advance our discipline and assist our colleagues.

The problem seems to be that peer reviewing consists of two components: serving as a gatekeeper and mentoring authors. Ironically, even researchers strongly in favor of the process often seem to underplay the latter aspect. Consider the following paragraph in support of peer review written by William Starbuck (2003, p. 345), whose "Golden Rule" is that the reviewer is always right:

> The central purpose of my Golden Rule is to compel me to regard reviewers' comments not as judgments about the value of my research or the quality of my writing, but as data about the potential audience for my articles. If a reviewer interprets one of my statements in a different way than I intended, other readers, possibly many other readers, are likely to interpret this statement differently than I intended, so I should revise the statement to make such misinterpretations less likely. If a reviewer thinks that I made a methodological error, other readers, possibly many of them, are also likely to think that I made this error, so I should revise my manuscript to explain why my methodology is appropriate. If a reviewer recommends that I cite literature that I deem irrelevant, other readers are also likely to think that this literature is relevant, so I should explain why it is irrelevant. In general, I should attend very carefully to the thoughts of anyone who has read my words rather carefully… Good data about readers' reactions are hard to obtain, and good data can never be wrong.

Now compare this with some comments made by Jeffrey Pfeffer, echoing comments made by Bruno Frey (2003) in an article titled "Publishing as prostitution? Choosing between one's own ideas and academic success":

> …the editing and reviewing process tends to distort or suppress the original insights and points of view of researchers even if they get their work published… Editors and reviewers, in positions of power, have a tendency to engage in coproduction, to "help" an author write the paper they want to see or the paper they might have written had they done the particular study. As Frey argued, "Authors only get their papers accepted if they intellectually prostitute themselves by slavishly following the demands" (2003: 205) of people who have no property rights to the journals or, for that matter, to the works they print. The process that Frey so eloquently described and that

most readers of this article will have lived through almost assuredly curtails innovation and results in a conservative and homogenizing bias in the publication process. (Pfeffer, 2007, p. 1339)

What amazes me about these two paragraphs—one justifying the process and one condemning it—is their common thread. In neither case does the respective author appear to contemplate even the remotest possibility that he may have made an actual error in his research that a reviewer might pick up.

Here I am forced to admit that my own research exists on a plateau far below the exalted heights apparently occupied by these colleagues. That will become obvious in the next chapter[39]. Moreover, I cannot think of a single article that I have published that did not benefit substantially from serious review criticism; where I get into trouble is when I get favorable but cursory comments.

Thus, my own experience has been that peer review can contribute greatly to rigor—but only when reviewers view themselves as mentors rather than as gatekeepers. Moreover, my strong sense is that in this regard, business research is actually improving substantially. Whereas the rejections I received on my early submissions tended towards making me wish to change occupations, my more recent rejections from elite journals have been quite useful in their commentary and written in a tone that suggested the reviewers actually wanted to help me improve my work. I will concede, however, that such helpfulness could, in some case, constitute a threat to rigor since it can also serve as a gentle social nudge to present ideas in a manner conforming to existing paradigms.

My main complaint with respect to the rigor of peer review comes from attempts to maintain the appearance of anonymity where it does not actually exist. Where we can truly keep the process anonymous, I can see *some* potential benefits. But with editors rendering split decisions and the "problem" of self-citations or distinctive writing styles identifying the author, I believe the actual amount of peer review that is truly anonymous is very limited.

The price in lost rigor we researchers pay for the appearance of anonymity can be very high. In my main research area, which nowadays mainly covers informing and education, a large percentage of studies are action research, meaning that at least one researcher is an actual participant in what is being researched. It is very rare to find a classroom study, for example, where the instructor is not an author of the resulting paper. Achieving anonymity therefore requires disguising course numbers, institutional affiliation, project names (where applicable), past studies on the same course (where applicable) and the names of any colleagues. With today's search technologies, virtually any of these pieces of information could reveal one or more of the researcher's identities. The massive amount of disguising required to achieve anonymity in such research actually interferes with the reality of the study. For this type of research, I believe that threat to rigor far exceeds whatever benefits are conferred by anonymity. To make the problem worse, in Chapter 13 I present the case as to why more action research should be encouraged if our true goal is to inform business.

Replication Research

On a fully decomposable landscape, we would expect the findings of field studies to replicate well if our research methods are rigorous. On a complex landscape, we would expect far less agreement unless the theory is systematically specified because behaviors in one domain are unlikely to match those in other domains. Thus, replication research represents not only a critical quality control activity but can also provide insights into the shape of the underlying landscape.

Unfortunately, replication research has not lived up to its promise. To begin with, a great many top business journals explicitly refuse to publish it. Possibly this is because it would crowd out novel theories. The other possibility is less appealing: when replications are performed, they are—more often than not—inconsistent with the original study being replicated, thereby casting a negative pall on the overall rigor of our research.

Owing to the lack of replication research published, care must be taken in drawing any conclusions. What little evidence is available clearly supports the possibility that our research does not replicate well. Most of that evidence comes from the unflagging efforts of Raymond Hubbard, who first began publishing on the subject in the early 1990s. Consider first his study of research in the finance area:

> Replication is rare in the finance literature. Of the 1,028 papers sampled from four major finance journals, only one was a replication. Only 5.3 percent were replications with extensions, and they accounted for merely 4.3% of journal space devoted

to research reports. Published replications with extensions typically produce results that conflict with original studies; of the 54 extensions published, 60 percent conflicted with the earlier results and only 20 percent provided full confirmation. (Hubbard & Vetter, 1991, p. 70)

One might argue, of course, that finance—being particularly focused on developing estimates-of-fitness instead of theory-of-fitness--is a special case; as we have previously noted, the field is not renowned for its ability to make accurate predictions, yet its findings diffuse well enough nevertheless. As it turns out, however, nearly identical results (along with a nearly identical abstract) were found in the case of marketing:

> Replication is rare in marketing. Of 1,120 papers sampled from three major marketing journals, none were replications. Only 1.8% of the papers were extensions, and they consumed 1.1% of the journal space. On average, these extensions appeared seven years after the original study. The publication rate for such works has been decreasing since the 1970s. Published extensions typically produced results that conflicted with the original studies; of the 20 extensions published, 12 conflicted with the earlier results, and only 3 provided full confirmation. Published replications do not attract as many citations after publication as do the original studies, even when the results fail to support the original studies. (Hubbard & Armstrong, 1994, p. 233)

And if this is insufficient evidence, they found a similar trend in other disciplines. Overall, only 6% of studies were replications. In accounting, 50% of the results conflicted. In economics, 61% conflicted. Only management bucked the trend, with 14% of results conflicting. Even there, however, less than half of all replications fully supported the results of the original paper (Hubbard & Vetter, 1996). Sadly, the situation has not improved. In fact, since the time of the original studies, the rate of replication research appears to have been reduced by at least half (Evanschitzky, Baumgarth, Hubbard, & Armstrong, 2007).

If we are truly concerned with rigor, replication research should be held in high esteem. Such is the case in most of the physical and even the life sciences (recall how many times coffee has been studied). Of course, if we are routinely assuming decomposability where the assumption is not warranted, then maintaining the appearance of rigor demands we avoid the inconvenient findings that most replications will report. The question then becomes one of values. Which is more important to us, rigor or its appearance?

Conclusions

Rigor is where today's academic business researchers generally consider themselves to be strongest; most will concede that we could do better in the areas of relevance and resonance. In this chapter, I have argued that rigor is a much bigger problem than we make it out to be. Among the problems identified are the following:

- We are obsessed with the creation of theory fragments to describe an environment where such fragments are probably not a good fit. We solve this problem by empirically testing very little of our theory.

- We hold theories that are wildly inconsistent with each other. We manage this by establishing disciplinary silos and "schools" within disciplines that do not talk to each other and therefore do not need to confront these inconsistencies.

- We have become so obsessed with constructing theory that we have lost all interest in publishing the research findings of the skilled observer.

- We employ a variety of statistical techniques whose implications we do not fully understand in a manner that almost guarantees the success of our efforts and then congratulate ourselves when we find significant values; to avoid embarrassment we take care not to replicate our finding and, if we do, we make sure the results are published in journals of sufficiently low stature so that there is little danger anyone will attend to them.

- Our standard for determining what is good and bad research is so inconsistent that we actually model publication acceptances as random processes (e.g., Starbuck 2005; Glick, Miller, & Cardinal, 2008).

In the next chapter, I present (and sharply criticize) some of my own prior MIS research as a case study in the hope of making these conclusions more concrete. After that, we enter the portion of the book where solutions are proposed.

Chapter 10 Foundational References

Evanschitzky, H., Baumgarth, C., Hubbard, R., & Armstrong, J. S. (2007). Replication research's disturbing trend. *Journal of Business Research, 60*(4), 411–415.

Gill, T. G., & Sincich, A. (2008). Illusions of significance in a rugged landscape. *Informing Science: The International Journal of an Emerging Transdiscipline, 11*, 197-226. Retrieved from http://www.inform.nu/Articles/Vol11/ISJv11p197-226GillIllusions.pdf

Pfeffer, J. (2007). A modest proposal: How we might change the process and product of managerial research. *Academy of Management Journal, 50*(6), 1334-1345.

Taleb, N. N. (2007). *The Black Swan.* New York, NY: Random House.

Ziliak, S. T., & McCloskey, D. N. (2008). *The cult of statistical significance.* Ann Arbor, MI: University of Michigan Press.

Chapter 10 Notes

[1] Both Ziliak & McCloskey (2008) and Taleb (2007) are recent notable exceptions to the general complacency regarding the rigor of business research; the former focusing on the empirical side with the latter attacking the rigor of much of our theory.

[2] As often seems to be the case, I find myself moving far afield to acquire a needed definition or evidence; my definition of rigor took me to the journal *Health Promotion International,* published by the Oxford University Press. It happened to top the list on Google Scholar when I searched for the term "rigor." I rejected the dictionary definitions I looked at because they were too focused on rigor mortis and the effects of cold; Webster's definition of logical rigor consisted of: "strict precision." Ironically, the first three definition of rigor it provided was: "(1) : harsh inflexibility in opinion, temper, or judgment : severity (2) : the quality of being unyielding or inflexible : strictness (3) : severity of life : austerity b : an act or instance of strictness, severity, or cruelty". I felt that stacked the deck against me—if being unyielding and inflexible are

really what we mean by rigor, then we are probably doing it better than I care to concede.

Wikipedia failed me as well. Its principal definition of intellectual rigor consisted of "no suspicion of double standard be allowed: uniform principles should be applied. This is a test of consistency, over cases, and to individuals or institutions (including the speaker, the speaker's country and so on)." I will address the question of double standards when I consider review processes at the end of the chapter. Defining rigor entirely in terms of consistency, however, strikes me as being very limiting. By that standard, all scientists should strive to become obsessive compulsives. Later in the article, Wikipedia does (did) go on to say, "It can also degenerate into pedantry, which is intellectual rigour applied to no particular end, except perhaps self-importance." No argument here.

[3] Planetary motion before Newton could be, and frequently was, explained in terms of God's or "the gods'" will. Scientists hate such explanations since they can be used to justify anything and cannot be used for prediction by anyone but demagogues (or demi-gods).

[4] For example, one way to create an NK landscape is the button and string method (Bak, 1997). Imagine you start with a series of buttons, which represent attributes, and strings, which represent interdependencies. Starting with no strings, you have a fully decomposable landscape. Then, at random (or in some non random way), you begin connecting individual attributes together—representing interrelationships affecting fitness. If you stop before every button is connected, you will probably find some buttons that are not connected to anything. These are fully decomposable attributes. You will also find networks of buttons that contain some number of buttons: 2, 3, 4, etc. These networks contribute to fitness independently of each other. In fact, using this model, you will always have some decomposable networks until the landscape reaches N,N-1 (chaotic) status.

[5] Another way of stating the proposition about relationships between attributes and fitness is "for anything you say, you can almost always find someone who said it before you." I first developed a suspicion that this was true while I was doing my doctorate. At that time, I exhibited a marked tendency to propose my own conceptual schemes and then incorporate them into the term papers I was writing. My mentor in this

process, the late Jim McKenney, castigated me for this tendency. He explained that reviewers would "take me apart" for doing so. When I revised the papers, I then visited the library and searched for researchers who had said pieces of what I was proposing in the past. I then rewrote the papers to make it appear as if I was building on that past research—thereby transforming what I had done from "making it up as I go along" to synthesis. At the time, I took the fact that I could always find such supporting statements as evidence that I possessed some heretofore unsuspected (by me or by any who knew me) gift of insight. What I now consider vastly more likely is that I simply had spent enough time looking for something that was not really that hard to find. And today, with Google search and library databases accessible through the Internet, the process has gotten that much easier.

[6] Hambrick (2007) cites an article (Kacmar & Whitfield, 2000) reporting that only 9% of the theories articulated in the prestigious *Academy of Management Review* are actually tested.

[7] The fact that subjects *volunteer* to take part in the experiment also influences the sample and can profoundly impact results (Levitt & List, 2007).

[8] Having made such a strident statement about experiments, it might seem somewhat inconsistent that I have described dozens of them in this book—most of which were conducted using students. The fact is, I am a fan of well designed experiments provided that they are used in an appropriate context. In this book, as an example, a great deal of analysis involves: 1) what happens to individuals facing novel situations, and 2) coming up with techniques for informing students. Oddly enough, nearly all the experiments described fit these two criteria. In addition, nearly all the experiments seem to exhibit considerable face validity, meaning that most of us can identify with the results obtained (or at least I could). By describing the experiments themselves, rather than just presenting the findings, my intent was to let the reader arrive at his or her own conclusions.

[9] While I am very sympathetic with Ariely's (2009) complaints about economic theory, I also believe that he is committing a supreme act of abduction (what Nassim Nicholas Taleb might refer to as the "narrative fallacy") by asserting that the recent economic crisis is a consequence of "our unblinking faith in power of the invisible hand." The "invisible

hand" can be viewed as a theory-of-process and happens to be one of the inspirations for Darwin's theory of evolution. Rather than being a failure of the invisible hand, a counter-argument can be made that the recent global financial crisis was, if anything, the consequence of a lack of faith in the invisible hand since a major contributing factor was a government policy intended to artificially encourage widespread home ownership in the U.S. through encouraging Fannie Mae to make risky loans. Such arguments inevitably turn into ideological debates that can never be settled since the complexity of the global economic system guarantees that evidence for the position of both sides will be plentiful.

From a complex systems standpoint, the recent crisis would be an example of precisely the sort of large discontinuity predicted to arise from time to time according to the power law. In the final chapters of this book, I pursue this issue further.

[10] It is worth noting, with respect to Taleb's (2007) assertion that a rather fuzzy view of how financial data mapped to a power law "was sufficient for us to operate and make decisions," that he was a practicing trader at the time.

[11] According to a number of sources (e.g., Taleb, 2007 and an unpublished paper I read by Colin Camerer), Milton Friedman made the assertion that it is okay to produce good predictions from bad assumptions.

[12] As an interesting side note, the natural tendency of an economist to put faith in the ubiquity of the Gaussian distribution probably cost economist Lawrence Summers, currently the Director of the White House's National Economic Council, his job as President of Harvard University.

The incident was a result of a misunderstanding of the relationship of intelligence to the bell curve (i.e., the Gaussian). It involved a comment that he made regarding the relative intelligence of men and women in the sciences. Widely misreported by the press, he did not assert that men were better at the sciences than women. What he asserted was a widely accepted finding that men typically have a higher standard deviation with respect to their math and science aptitude scores than women. Eyeballing the SAT data for 2004 and 2009—available on the College Board web site (http://professionals.collegeboard.com/data-reports-research) the difference looks to be about 6% higher for men. Because these scores are normalized, however, a result that could be more informative is scores on the U.S. Armed Forces Qualifying Test, where the standard deviation for men was almost 20% higher on the science aptitude portion (Deary, Irwing, Der, & Bates, 2007).

Under the Gaussian assumption, the implications of such a difference in variance were actually far more disturbing than any small difference in average aptitude would have been. The reason for this is that universities such as Harvard are very selective in recruiting science faculty—the context in which the comment was made—and would normally recruit faculty *only* from individuals several standard deviations above the mean. Assuming science ability is distributed normally, 4 standard deviations or more from the mean contains only 0.0032% of the population, meaning that you would find only about 100,000 men in the world meeting that criteria (0.000032 * 3 billion). If men had a 20% higher standard deviation, however, you would have to go out nearly 4.8 standard deviations to get women with the same raw ability. At 4.8 standard deviations or more away from the mean, you have less than 1 in a million odds, so the pool of equivalent women would less than 3,000. Thus, *making the argument from an economist's perspective of assumed normality*, what he was saying was sensible. In fact, if Harvard had anything over 3% (3,000/103,000) women among its science faculty, he could argue that he had been very successful in recruiting them. This rather self-congratulatory model was probably what motivated the comment in the first place.

The weakness in the argument is the assumption of normality. It is an easy mistake to make because intelligence measures such as IQ are frequently normalized—which is to say forced into a normal distribution by adjusting cut points. It is, however, very unlikely that the distribution of scientific ability follows anything remotely like a normal distribution when you approach its outer reaches. In fact, as we saw in Chapter 6, expertise is one of those processes where the rich get richer—the reduced working memory load of expertise makes it easier to accumulate additional expertise. As a result, it would be surprising if the power law did not make an appearance at some point in the distribution (a fact that would be hidden by the normalizing of the distribution). In fact, even if we made the unjustified assumption that scientific ability is the direct product of general intelligence, intelligence tests themselves are woefully ill-suited to the task of measuring very high intelligence. Not only can intelligence scores be increased with practice (Willingham, 2009) but interpreting scores at the high end is far from standardized—particularly given the fact that they are normalized to 100 each year and scaled such that the standard deviation is always 15. For example, according to the *Guinness Book of World Records*, the world's highest recorded IQ is 228 and belongs to Marilyn vos Savant (a woman!), author of the "Ask Marilyn" column mentioned in Chapter 6 (Mlodinow, 2008, p. 43). Currently, the mean U.S. IQ is about 115 when scaled according to raw scores of an older test (Willingham, 2009, p. 137; supplemented by an explanatory email he sent to me) and the standard deviation is 15. That would make her score about 7.5 standard deviations above the mean, giving it a likelihood of about $3 * 10^{-14}$. Given that the population of the world is in the neighborhood of $6.7 * 10^9$, the expected likelihood of her existence would be about 1 in 5000.

[13] As an example of reconciling views, I have proposed that different forms of utility dominate at different levels of expertise, meaning there is some merit in nearly all the perspectives. The price for that reconciliation is that you need to know the individual's level of expertise before becoming too engrossed with his or her preferences. If I were planning to demonstrate a simple framing effect to a class, I would do well not to solicit the preferences of Dan Ariely (or even myself). Once you have seen a few hundred framing problems, your preferences could not help but shift towards the "rational" model.

[14] The "Matthew Effect" is not limited to academic situations. In *Outliers*, Malcolm Gladwell (2008) presents numerous examples, including professional hockey and music where a similar feedback loop is observed.

[15] I would hate to misrepresent myself as being a regular reader of the *Brazilian Journal of Physics*, which happens to be where I found an article relating power laws to scientific citation counts. I offer this in support of what I stated in a previous footnote, where I claimed you could find support for anything. As I was writing the paragraph on the "Matthew Effect" it occurred to me that the publication process I was describing was exactly the sort of process that would lead to a power law, so I did the search "citation power law" and the article popped out near the top. There is, however, evidence that the same phenomenon applies to

business related fields. For example, in management the distribution of citations in one study was found to be "2 percent of the articles had generated no citations, 53 percent had been cited 20 times or less, and 8 percent had been cited more than 100 times" (Judge, Cable, Colbert, & Rynes, 2007, p. 495). The large tail at the 8% end certainly has the flavor of a power law distribution.

[16] Jason Colquitt was kind enough to comment on my references to his research in a draft provided to him during the review process for this book.

[17] I recently did a count of articles on ABI/Inform referring to the technology acceptance model between 1991 and 2008. 391 articles referred to it in the title or abstract; the count was 1351 if references in the text were also included. These were gathered in my research for an *MIS Quarterly* piece in which Anol Bhattacherjee (my co-author) and I respond to a prior article by Baskerville and Meyers on fashions and fads in MIS research.

[18] In defense of the original TAM paper (Davis, Bagozzi, & Warshaw, 1989), its authors set up the paper so as to compare TAM with an alternative explanation, the theory of reasoned action (TRA), which posits that our behavior results from an intention to behave, and that our intention to behave is the joint consequence of our attitude towards the behavior and subjective norms (roughly equivalent to the perceived attitudes of those around the individual towards the behavior). Thus, the authors did attempt to engage in hypothesis testing using competing hypotheses. They did so, however, by comparing each of the two theories with the null hypothesis (e.g., testing if usefulness impacts intention to use and if attitude appears to impact intention to use). The complaint I would make about this approach is that choosing a theory based upon comparing the results of two powder puff tests is little more rigorous than accepting a theory based upon one.

[19] The problem of researching "low hanging fruit" propositions is that it would be rare to find one that is of major substantive significance that is also unknown. That is likely to impact the relevance and resonance of the resulting research, but not necessarily its rigor.

[20] The fact that non-significance is treated as being much less publishable than results showing significance is, in itself, an indictment of

rigor. One reasonably well known study (Hubbard & Armstrong, 1992) that did look at publication of marketing research in which the null hypothesis was not rejected found a systematic bias against such research, but also found that about 8% of the studies in top marketing journals reported non-rejection of the null hypothesis. The authors also reported that the rate had been dropping substantially over time—with the 1980s rate being half that of the 1970s.

For the purposes of comparison, the 8% rate reported for marketing was far worse than the rate for medicine (about 15%) but substantially better than some estimates for psychology—coming in as low as 4% (Armstrong & Hubbard, 1997). Part of this latter discrepancy may be explained by the fact that marketing research, as well as business research in general, tends to rely heavily on multivariate techniques, allowing multiple hypotheses to be tested at once, whereas psychology more often employs experimental techniques that manipulate one or two variables. The practical consequence of multivariate analysis is that *some* hypotheses may be rejected, while others are not. The authors reported classifying a paper as not rejecting the null hypothesis if either: a) the dominant hypothesis was not rejected, or b) a majority of the null hypotheses were not rejected. This would cause papers to fall into that category that were either attempts to present an alternative theory or in which some hypotheses were rejected. Once again, there may be some widely known empirical business papers in which no statistically significant results were reported, but I am not familiar with them.

[21] Both "trained incapacity" and the Matthew Effect were described by sociologist Robert K. Merton, who picked up the former phrase from famous economist Thorstein Veblen (Ziliak & McCloskey, 2008, p. 238-239).

[22] The problem of "undue inattention" has sometimes been referred to as Type III error (Ziliak & McCloskey, 2008, p. 246).

[23] Ziliak and McCloskey (2008, p. 81) found that 4% of the empirical studies published in the American Economic Review discussed the power of tests in the 1980s, whereas 8% did so in the 1990s. Of these articles, the number actually looking at the power function itself rose from 17% in the 1980s to 44% in the 1990s.

[24] In a survey of my HBS Class done for their 25th reunion in 2007, I found that Ipod owners had an average net worth of $2,360,000 more than non-owners, at a high level of statistical significance. With this and other meaningless—but rigorously computed—statistics, I attempted to amuse my classmates for over 40 minutes during our reunion dinner. Sadly, what I found was the likelihood that any particular subgroup would underperform the class as a whole financially was extremely well predicted by my membership in it. But I went out and purchased an Ipod anyway, just to be on the safe side.

[25] Gosset was, in fact, a brewer employed by Guinness whose initial research in statistics was published under the pseudonym Student. He was responsible for the Student's T test—the very test used to assess the significance of coefficients in multiple regression models. Ironically, he did not see much practical use for significance testing. He was much more interested in the economic value of applying statistical techniques. As Ziliak and McCloskey (2008) describe it, that attitude often put him in conflict with Ronald Fisher, whose advocacy of significance testing was unswerving.

[26] I admit to personal bias in suggesting that the narrative fallacy may frequently be forced by reviewers and policy. When I submitted an early draft of my dissertation, the first chapter asserted, on the very first page, that the topic was unlikely to be of interest to executives, but was of potential value nonetheless. It turned out that my candor was contrary to Harvard Business School's policy, however. During the succeeding two months, I rewrote that chapter—from scratch—precisely seven times. Each time, I further refined my totally ludicrous claims that executives should be interested in how to map the characteristics of a task into an appropriate expert system development tool. While I am not sure whether the exercise enhanced my research skills per se, it certainly taught me the potential value of rhetoric, distraction, and contorted prose in research writing.

[27] That the results were unexpected is not an exaggeration. When I originally laid out the simulation, I was anticipating no coefficient significances beyond the coincidental. The simulation had originally been set up so I could verify Kauffman's $2^N/(N+1)$ formula and find out how entities distributed themselves across the peaks after migration.

The decision to run a regression on the post-migration entities was purely an afterthought, likely the result of too much time on my hands.

[28] You can achieve the same effect by copying the same set of observations multiple times then applying multiple regression again. When you compare the results, the coefficients will be roughly the same, yet their significance will appear to be much higher.

[29] I have tried to make the migration to fitness regression experiment simple enough so that it could be replicated by any interested reader with a spreadsheet and basic knowledge of regression. The experiments in my paper with Terry Sincich (2008) were considerably more sophisticated and exhaustive.

[30] The specific combinations that I chose among the ice cream, roast beef, gravy and fudge values are largely arbitrary. The results begin to emerge as soon as the collections become unequal. In the two variable case, it is important to leave some entities in the low fitness boxes, otherwise the independent variables become linearly dependent and the regression ceases to be computable. As the number of variables grows, however, this becomes less and less of an issue, as the number of peaks typically grows faster than the number of variables (e.g., Kauffman's $2^N/(N+1)$ formula for estimated peaks on an NK chaotic landscape).

[31] At Harvard, you remain a member of your class even if you drop out, as Bill Gates did, unless you are expunged—which is very rare indeed.

[32] In reviewing a recent submission to a top-tier MIS publication, I raised the question of assuming decomposability with respect a to regression analysis performed on a fitness landscape. It was quite clear from the revision remarks that the author(s) did not understand my comments, since their response involved performing tests for multi-colinearity between explanatory variables—which has almost nothing to do with decomposability. The editor meanwhile suggested that my recommendations relating to this specific concern could safely be ignored in the revision, as they reflected personal preference as opposed to actual concerns relating to rigor.

In truth, I was almost relieved by the response. I felt the particular contribution had done a good job conforming to existing norms of research and, on a purely personal level, it therefore seemed unfair that their career prospects should be impacted by the unhappy accident of having me as a reviewer. It was I who was suddenly changing the rules of the game. Of course, the very fact that I frame our research as a game is not necessarily the best testament to its presumed rigor.

[33] Direct comparison of the reported correlations between reviewers is somewhat difficult as a number of different measures are reported (e.g., product-moment correlations, intraclass correlation, Kappa values), but the results are qualitatively similar.

[34] The lack of complete consensus against a submission is somewhat illusory. At all the journals where I have served, the editor-in-chief (including myself, for *Informing Science*) intercepts obviously unsuitable pieces and returns them to the author unreviewed. Many of these submissions would have resulted in a unanimously negative consensus.

[35] Usual disclaimer: unless the landscape is nearly decomposable.

[36] In psychology, what I refer to as size and legitimacy are sometimes distinguished in terms of being *impact* and *quality* (Gottfredson, 1978), although the former clearly incorporates a communications resonance component as well.

[37] The fact that not everyone shares the same ideas would be characteristic of what is referred to as a "weak paradigm" field (Glick, Miller, & Cardinal, 2007). Naturally, complex landscapes will tend to favor the development of weak theory-of-fitness paradigms, for reasons that should be self-evident.

[38] While my own negative views regarding the limitations of structural equation modeling on an obviously rugged fitness landscape should be pretty clear by now, what the results on citation count suggest is that the novelty of the research exerts a relatively low main effect.

[39] I can think of at least three instances where reviewers saved me from embarrassment. In one case, I became so engrossed in the minute details of the project that I lost sight of the fact that it was almost entirely pointless (*Management Science*). In another case, I was applying a statistical technique on a sample that was just too small for it to be valid (*MIS Quarterly*). In another case, I submitted an article before it was truly ready—one that I refined and which later became the core of this book (*MIS Quarterly*). In all three cases, my annoyance with myself was balanced somewhat by my gratitude to the reviewers.

Chapter 11

A Research Case Study

Roadmap & Objectives: In Chapter 10, I cast aspersions on the overall rigor of business research—conceding that there might be some exceptions. The reader might reasonably suppose that I would include my own past research among those exceptions. To remedy that misconception, in this chapter I use my own research as a case study whereby the potential threats to rigor presented by complexity can be exposed.

In the previous chapter, I made the case that our research was not as rigorous as we perceive it to be. A considerable amount of the evidence presented was based on summary data collected over a large number of papers or submissions. There is a certain irony in this, however. After all, much of the chapter presented the threats to rigor that can result from applying statistical methods to a complex domain. In this chapter, I therefore take the complementary approach. I profile the conduct of an actual research project—a successful one by prevailing standards—as a case study.

The research project that I profile is one of my own, conducted shortly after I had joined Florida Atlantic University (FAU). It involves a study that I conducted that examined the factors driving expert system success. Within the chapter I consider the motivation for the project, the design and conduct of the research, and the subsequent impact of the research on my life and career. The treatment contains a certain amount of biographical background because I do not believe the topic of how research proceeds can truly be understood without such details. I have also omitted some names, excepting in cases where the parties involved actively encouraged me to include them. The central question posed by the chapter is a simple one:

Would I submit the same research for publication today, given what I now believe?

Being that the research I am profiling is my own, my objectivity in reporting it is, and should be, immediately suspect. I try to stick to the facts as much as possible as the narrative proceeds. There will be times, however, when I necessarily rely on my recollection of my past feelings. The conduct of research is, by its very nature, driven by personal as well as scientific motivations. Perhaps I am unique in the degree to which non-scientific motivations have driven me in the past and continue to drive me. I am inclined to doubt it, however.

Background

To establish the context of the research case, I begin with some background details. Prior to beginning my doctorate in 1986, I had just spent three years working as an agribusiness consultant at a firm that had been founded by Dr. Ray Goldberg, the George M. Moffett Professor of Agribusiness at Harvard Business School. While working there, I had taken my rudimentary knowledge of computer modeling (acquired during a summer job between my two MBA years in 1981) and built it into a full-fledged modeling and simulation practice. Without the benefit of any formal training, I had developed a diverse set of models that included studies of high fructose corn syrup production plants, citrus prices, soft drink syrup distribution, duck processing, pesticide application, and restaurant home delivery effectiveness. These models had been quite profitable for the firm where I worked (generating about $250,000/year in average billings) and had led to three promotions within my first 18 months. They were, however, becoming an increasing source of unease to me—precisely because I had no formal training in the area and was therefore relying heavily on my intuition and self-taught programming skills. I had this nagging suspicion that there was more about computer modeling that I needed to know.

In mid-1985, I made the decision that I would return to school for my doctorate. There were two main sources of motivation for this decision. First, I felt it would be an opportunity to develop my computer skills. Second, it would afford me the opportunity to teach, a vocation that I have always felt called to. Since childhood, I envisioned myself becoming a high school teacher in later life, once I had become financially secure. I just decided to move the timetable up. Being a college professor, I decided, would be almost as good[1], and I felt I could probably make ends meet on a professor's salary.

Notably absent from my motivation was a passion for business research. What I felt at the time was not so much disdain as it was indifference. If you wished to distance yourself from the world of theory and academic journals, there was no better place to do your M.B.A. than Harvard in the early 1980s. That program consisted of just under 900 case discussions and, in my case, perhaps as many as 50 lectures (i.e., roughly 5% of my class time). The conceptual schemes each of us employed in analyzing cases were mainly of our own invention; the closest we ever got to academic writing was the *Harvard Business Review*, which we considered far too pedantic in its tone.

The closest I had come to research before entering the program was case writing for the agribusiness program. These were done largely at the behest of Ray Goldberg, who had dismissed his research assistant one particular year and therefore needed some help filling the gap. By the time I started the doctoral program, I had written several HBS cases and a technical note and had exhibited some talent for the activity[2]. Thus, to the extent I had any idea of what research was, it was based around case studies. In fact, as of the day I officially started my D.B.A., I had never read, or even looked at, a single academic journal article relating to business.

My choice of classes serves as a clear indicator of the direction of my motivation[3], with less than 1/3 of my course work being directly related to business research—compared with over 50% taken in the computer and cognitive sciences field at Harvard's GSAS and MIT's Graduate School of Engineering. This balance did not go unnoticed by my HBS advisors, nor was it discouraged. To the contrary, it was applauded[4]. Thus, I had no concern about selecting a highly technical dissertation topic.

Expert systems, the topic I settled upon, are a type of computer application where the knowledge of human experts is encoded into rule-like forms in order to perform tasks that would otherwise be very hard to program. My interest in expert systems developed as a result of both my course work and some teaching case studies of operational systems that I wrote with Dr. John Sviokla—a newly appointed assistant professor at the time. With my interest in building things, I quickly became enthused by the broad array of tools available for constructing such systems. I decided that how the underlying characteristics of a task determine the most appropriate tools for constructing a corresponding expert system would be an interesting topic to study. Having no particular reason to disagree, my dissertation committee approved.

Starting in the fall of 1988, I began visiting companies while, at the same time, doing a longitudinal study of the development of a large system under development by a local startup firm that had been founded by MIT faculty members. With a $10,000 research travel and expense budget (more than my department's entire annual T&E budget at FAU) I could go practically anywhere. During the early stages of my investigation, I travelled to California to visit AI tool makers, to Houston to watch an expert gate scheduling system being implemented, and to numerous sites along the U.S. East Coast to meet with system managers and developers. I learned a great deal from these conversations and observations but a gnawing discomfort remained: I had never actually built a commercial expert system.

To me, the notion that I would shortly be teaching about something I had never done in practice made me very uncomfortable. I was also sufficiently enthusiastic about the technology so I imagined that I might make some money with my ideas. I therefore concluded that I needed to build an expert system. In order to free up the time to do this, I spent the summer creating a monstrosity of a first draft of my dissertation[5] that I gave to all my committee members, explaining to them that they had about 6 months to read it because I was going to turn my attention to system building .

The actual project took nine months, leading to the creation of the College Expert™ (see Chapter 3). The system grossed almost $1000 in royalties before expenses, giving me practical exposure to the challenges presented by third world wages. It also gave me irreplaceable insights into the underlying nature of the problem I was studying. Along with the skills it imparted, I acquired a firm conviction that I had chosen as a dissertation topic a problem that wasn't. Developers were doing a perfectly good job of choosing the right tool without my help. In fact, about the only interesting insight I found was a pattern I noticed when I classified all 13 systems I had investigated in a table with two dimensions: "Were procedural activities transferred to the system (yes/no)?" and "Did the user have any discretion in performing the task when the system was being used (yes/no)?" What I noticed was that although I had systems in all four quadrants, the only quadrants where I had operational systems were in the yes/yes and no/no quadrants—all the other systems never made it past the prototype stage. Since the yes/yes quadrant would seem to have a positive motivational character and the no/no quadrant would be expected to have no motivational impact whatsoever, it occurred to me that motivation might serve as a useful predictor of expert system use. Since this had nothing to do with my topic, I gave it a page or two in my "directions for future research" section and filed it away for later reference.

When I returned to the dissertation in earnest, in Fall 1990, the only feedback I got on my original draft was to bring it down to 250 pages, which is all the feedback that I deserved. I cut the beast down unmercifully, turned it in, and began my job search. My particular goal in choosing an institution was to find a school where my teaching would be given at least as much weight as my research. Based on that criterion, I ended up selecting the Decision and Information Systems department at FAU headed by Carol Saunders. In retrospect, it proved to be a nearly perfect fit with what I was looking for. That choice did, however, precipitate a rather uncomfortable 10 week period (described in an end note to the previous chapter) during which I was required to rewrite the first chapter of my dissertation seven times. What I had failed to realize at the time was that a career decision that made perfect sense to me might also cast a negative light my HBS department and its chair, who were being judged according to the prestige of institutions hiring their newly minted doctorates.

The Project

I joined FAU in fall of 1991. Since I had concluded that my dissertation topic was entirely unneeded and unwanted, it was incumbent upon me to find some new topic to research. Fortuitously, FAU's College of Business initiated a competitive program for summer stipends that year, so I proposed a research project where I would look at the relationship between motivation and expert system use. In this section, I outline the actual conduct of the research itself, then critique it according to what I now believe about research on a rugged landscape. After this analysis is complete, I turn to the portion of the research that was outside of my control: the review process.

The Conduct of the Research

The research project began in the early summer of 1992. Data gathering was completed by late August of that year, I performed my data analysis in September and October, and my initial draft write up was completed by November.

The research model

The research design involved taking a list of "successful" expert systems published in 1988 and doing a phone survey to determine both the characteristics of the task each was performing and their apparent fitness (measured in terms of longevity). Fortunately for me, my proposal was funded. Equally lucky, a good friend and research colleague of mine, Mark Keil, suggested that I consider using a questionnaire developed by management researchers (Hackman & Oldham, 1980) that could be adapted to assess the intrinsic motivation associated with a task change. Thus, that portion of my questionnaire was based upon an existing model and incorporated questions designed around a validated instrument.

In designing my research model, I could not employ Hackman and Oldham's tools directly for two reasons. First, their tool was intended to measure the motivational character of a particular job, whereas I was interested in how work changed as a consequence of performing it with an expert system. Second, from my dissertation field work I already knew that expert systems could introduce changes at two levels: they could change how a user performed a particular instance of the task, and they could change the mix of task cases that the performer encountered. For example, when American Express introduced its Authorizer's Assistant to help automate credit card approvals, the system approved a large number of transactions that had previously involved a customer service agent. It then routed the remaining transactions to the customer service agent, displaying the data it considered relevant and making a recommendation that the agent could override. In other words, it made the difficult cases easier for the customer service agent while, at the same time, it greatly increased the average difficulty of the case mix presented to the agent.

To keep my model as simple as possible, I assumed that changes to the "typical" task and to the mix of tasks both contributed to motivation and that the effects were additive—in other words, decomposable. I also grouped the intrinsic motivators into three categories that seemed to capture the spirit of the motivation literature: control, arousal, and achievement. The resulting model is illustrated in Figure 11.1.

One component of the Hackman and Oldham (1980) model that I omitted from my research model was *feedback*. While feedback is frequently associated with intrinsic motivation, its effect on motivation would clearly not be additive. Rather, it would tend to amplify both positive signals and negative signals. As a result, it would be very hard to significance test. Thus, while I included feedback related questions in the questionnaire, I happily discarded them during the later data analysis. Interestingly, Hackman and Oldham (1980) also treated their control motivator, autonomy, as an amplifier as well in predicting a job's motivation potential. There was, however, plenty of other motivational literature that viewed control as intrinsically motivating independent of other effects[6]. Thus, my model generally conformed to existing theory.

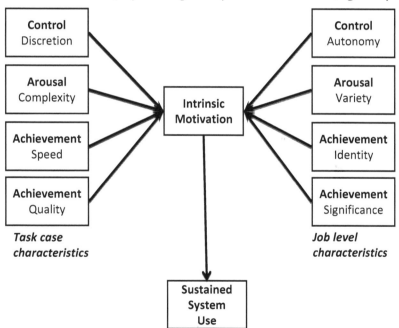

Figure 11.1: Intrinsic motivation for task change used in Gill (1996)

The Research Method

The systems I surveyed were drawn from a published list of 111 commercial expert systems in the trade book *Expert Systems: Tools and Applications* (Harmon, Maus, & Morrissey, 1988), of which 97 were U.S. based. Based on my own knowledge of the field, acquired mainly during my dissertation research, I knew that some had been abandoned and, presumably, some remained in use. Thus, I decided that system status would be a reasonable measure of fitness. Rather than sampling selectively, I decided that the entire list of U.S. systems would be examined.

The approach to data gathering occurred in two stages. It began with library research on each of the individual systems. I acquired the able assistance of three undergraduates—Chuck Taffinder, Martha Griffith, and, especially, Allyn Rodriguez—who joined the project for course credit, and to whom I remain indebted to this day. Together, we combed the library for references on each of the systems, creating a folder for each one.

The conduct of the actual interviews is one aspect of the research with which I remain comfortable to this day. Expending nearly 300 hours of phone time[7], I was able to obtain usable responses—from a user, developer, or manager of the system—for 81 of the 97 systems on my list. The average time I spent on each phone interview was roughly 45 minutes, but ranged from 10 minutes (for systems that were never completed) to over 2 hours. The interview protocol included both Likert-scale variables and free form answers (see Gill, 1995b, for the actual instrument employed). Most of the phone time was actually spent attempting to locate suitable participants; although the Harmon, Maus, and Morrissey (1988) book included contact information for many of the systems, nearly five years after the fact relatively few entries were still accurate. For several systems this process took days, particularly in light of the fact that email and web pages were virtually non-existent in the commercial world at that time. I kept a large status chart on the wall upon which I marked my progress.

In preparation for each interview, I wrote up a preliminary description of what each system did—based upon the public descriptions we were able to find in the first phase of the project—and tentatively scored where I thought the system would end up on the task change portion of the questionnaire. During the course of the actual interview, if a respondent provided a value substantially different from what I had anticipated, I would ask about the response. In most cases, the explanation led me to better understand the precise nature of the task change brought about by the system; in some cases it turned out the respondent had either misinterpreted the question or did not understand it, in which case he or she was given the opportunity to revise the response.

The study's response rate exceeded 80% (81 out of 97 systems) and many of the missing 17 systems may not have existed. I am convinced that the reason for this very high rate was the preparation. As soon as a suitable respondent was on the line, I would detail what we already knew about the system. This distinguished me from the typical survey call. Another factor that may have contributed was the fact that my sample consisted entirely of systems whose participants had been positively disposed towards publicity in the past.

After a respondent agreed to participate, the interview protocol involved first asking the scored questions and then collaboratively modifying the draft write-up, prepared prior to the interview, to ensure its accuracy. Subjects were also encouraged to make general comments about their system and the industry in general; many were also eager to hear my own comments. It was from their comments, for example, that I began to develop a clear sense of the decline in stature that artificial intelligence and expert systems were experiencing in the commercial sector, a theme that I used to lead off the subsequent write up of the research.

Survey results were entered into a database. After each interview, respondents were mailed copies of their free-text responses, printed from the database, and were offered the opportunity to make corrections. I recall that a few came back with minor edits, but no substantial changes were received. At the end of the research, I developed a database program that allowed users to access the data in summary form and to look up system information. This program was sent out to all respondents on a floppy disk. Several wrote thank you notes in response.

Data analysis

As is fairly typical in multivariate data analysis, the rough results (just taking nearly all the variables and regressing them in raw form against use) did not yield spectacular results. But, as I refined the analysis by eliminating variables of negligible significance and focusing on the model variables, clear patterns began to take shape. Because of the discontinuous nature of the dependent variable (long term usage), I used an ordinal probit model as well as linear regression to test the model, with the two approaches yielding similar results—although ordinal probit showed slightly higher significances. The regression version of my final model had an R-squared of 0.32—meaning that the model appeared to explain 32% of the variation in long term usage—and of the four Hackman and Oldham variables, all but "Job Significance" exhibited statistical significance at the 5% level or greater.

Write up

Based upon the results I had obtained—both statistically significant and consistent with my model—by Fall 1992 I was feeling quite elated. As I wrote the draft of the paper, it quickly became clear that I had too much material for a single article. I therefore broke the paper into two separate papers, the first addressing the broad question of which was more significant in predicting system success: technical factors or other (e.g., managerial) factors. Its central theme was the huge role played by non-technical factors in systems success. Among its key findings was that inadequacies in system task performance for technical reasons was cited as an important limitation of system success for only about 10% of the systems examined.

The second paper focused on the topic of motivation. Its purpose was specifically to describe and then test the proposed model (illustrated earlier in Figure 11.1) using multivariate statistical techniques.

Rugged Landscape Critique

Prior to describing the review process, I now consider the research in light of the earlier chapters of this book. As presented at the outset of the chapter, the question is: Believing what I now believe, would I be able to submit the same papers in good conscience?

The model

Were I to review my research model today, I would immediately notice that I was trying to construct attractive theory-of-fitness on what was very likely a rugged landscape. Since I had never even heard of a rugged landscape in 1992, the thought never even occurred to me at the time.

Rather, I proceeded on the belief that the phenomena I was observing were largely decomposable. Should substantially more complex relationships exist, I assumed the tools I was using would, to a great extent, protect me from Type I error by reporting no significance. This belief was consistent with all that I had been taught.

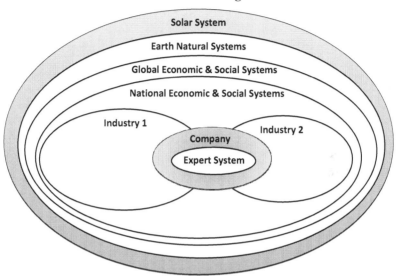

Figure 11.2: Sub-system/super-system diagram for expert system adoption and use

As I look back upon the process while writing this chapter, I also realize that the decision to split the paper into a general paper and a motivation-specific paper helped enable the process. While that decision had been based entirely on the length of the write-up, it also reduced my need to address—actually, even to recognize—certain logical inconsistencies between the two papers. In the first paper, I clearly identified the huge number of forces impacting system use. For example, 38 systems in the study had been completed and had demonstrated the technical ability to perform the task, yet were no longer being used. Within this group, I found 10 quite different principal explanations from respondents for non-use (Gill, 1995b, pp. 64-66). Viewed in the context of the sub-system/super-system diagram first presented in Chapter 9 (shown in Figure 11.2), among these 10 effects were at least six that had nothing to do with task change motivation. These included company forces (e.g., cost, misalignment with company computing environment, loss of key personnel, inability to find an organizational supporter), industry forces (e.g., change in industry outlook), and even national forces (e.g., potential legal liability). By partitioning the research into two separate papers, it became much easier to develop the motivation theory fragment without confronting the broader findings. You may notice that this is exactly the type of problem I described as arising from departmental silos.

With respect to the second paper, my obvious first concern would be that I had no basis for assuming that the motivational components I identified were even remotely decomposable in their contribution to fitness. In my defense, I would suggest that Hackman and Oldham's (1980) own proposed *motivating potential score*, which involves adding significance, identity, and variety, then multiplying the result by autonomy and feedback, seems even less plausible than my own approach. Here, once again, my presumption was that non-decomposable relationships would *reduce* coefficient significance by injecting pseudo-randomness into the process. Thus, if significance was detected, that would be evidence that my simpler model was supported. Of course I now know that this is not necessarily true. In fact, in a complex adaptive landscape, the better assumption is that migration to fitness peaks will actually produce spurious significances, as shown by the simulations I did with Terry Sincich (Gill & Sincich, 2008).

A second factor that, perhaps, should have given me pause but did not was what I had actually seen when observing two expert systems as part of my dissertation—one outside of the sample and one included in it.

The outside system that I had studied was an airport gate scheduling expert system. This system automatically accessed information from the airlines reservation system—which was quite a trick in those pre-commercial Internet days of the late 1980s—and provided its users, experienced gate schedulers, with a graphic user interface (also unusual at the time) that allowed them to drag and drop gate assignments, information that would then be displayed on airport monitors. The system was quite sophisticated and incorporated information such as jet type, gate capabilities, gate location, and number of passengers involved in connections between different flights.

Manual gate scheduling was an important, yet often tedious, highly skilled task that was also well paid. This system simultaneously allowed the task to be performed more effectively, with less tedium, and with less training. By job enrichment standards, therefore, users should have been highly motivated to take on the system. Based on my own observations, however, there was considerable resistance to the system and, ultimately, it was abandoned after operating successfully for a short period of time[8]. An important source of resistance appeared to be fear of job loss; in fact, one of the schedulers asked me (in confidence) if that was the ultimate goal of the system while I was observing it in operation. While the developers and management took great pains to reassure users that the system was a support tool, rather than a replacement for them, the fact remained that it took a very difficult job that required years of practice and made it much easier both to learn and to perform. It is therefore easy to imagine that it would have ultimately impacted the pay prospects of the job in the future—and not in a positive way. Had the gate scheduling activity been a minor (nonsignificant) portion of the user's job, we can reasonably expect that a tool that made the activity less tedious would be appreciated. It was the very significance of the activity—combined with its attractive qualities—that made the system a threat. In other words, significance appeared to interact with the other sources of motivation—intrinsic and extrinsic.

The system within the sample was one of the best known expert system success stories, *Digital Equipment Corporation*'s (DEC) XCON. This system allowed for automated configuration of DEC's VAX computer line at a time when it was becoming increasingly difficult to accomplish such configuration by hand. I was quite familiar with the system and its history since it had been the subject of my advisor John Sviokla's dissertation and because I had quite a number of contacts within the firm. The particularly distinguishing aspect of the system was the fact that it had allowed DEC to continue a strategy of customizing its systems for each customer, a service in direct contrast to its main competitor IBM's approach of selling a series of standard models. As a result, the benefits of the system were viewed as being highly strategic to the company.

What my particular model did not capture was the fact that the development of the system had been a highly political process within DEC. Prior to XCON's completion, there had been a strong movement within the company to adopt greater standardization of its product line. In part this was a result of the increasing error rate in manual configurations. There was, however, also a belief that standardization might make sense in view of where the industry was heading. To shelter the system's developers from this political battle, the early stages of the system's development were conducted using a skunkworks approach: a project group whose reporting relationships were obscure, even to the members of the group itself (Leonard-Barton & DeLacey, 1987).

The conceptual problem that XCON presents is that it now strikes me as inconceivable that the political forces affecting use did not interact with the motivational forces. The instrument I used, however, was far too crude to pick up on effects such as these, however. Once again, I assumed that while observations such as this one might reduce observed significances by adding randomness, they would not generate spurious results. I am much less confident of that now.

My final reason for suspicion regarding my model is the fact that during the extensive phone interviews I conducted, not one of the managers or developers I spoke to mentioned anything related to intrinsic motivation as a reason for system success or failure. At the time, I thought this was a good thing. One of the most common problems I have with academic business research is its tendency to spend a lot of time researching the obvious—the low hanging fruit of Chapter 10. Here, then, was a model that explained 32% of all the variation in system use that managers were unaware of. The unasked question was: How could such an important economic influence have been overlooked?

Data analysis

Beyond the questionable nature of the decomposability assumed in my model, the data analysis conducted in the paper could be taken as a textbook case of many of the traps that Ziliak and McCloskey warn about. For example:

- I had my share of powder puff tests. Would anyone ever anticipate that a system's technical performance *would not* influence system use?

- I had my share of variables whose practical impact was very hard to discern, being items whose units were agree/disagree on a five point Likert scale.

- My tolerance for randomness outside of my explanatory theory fragment was high in my statistical analysis. To be fair, I somewhat compensated for this through my qualitative data gathering efforts, allowing me to supplement my quantitative analysis with a series of narrative observations.

As a weak defense, Ziliak and McCloskey assert that nearly all researchers in economics and business engage in similar practices. Indeed, the authors admit to having fallen prey to some themselves in their early days. But once again recall the question I am trying to answer: "Would I submit the same research today, given what I now believe?"

Beyond my newly awakened concerns regarding specific practices, I have a broader general concern about the data analysis I conducted. As we saw in the previous chapter, being able to demonstrate statistical significance seems to provide a huge advantage when it comes to getting empirical research published. I am an organism tuned by millions of years of evolution to adapt to the highest fitness I can. I have been trained to exploit the capabilities of a very flexible toolbox with which to analyze any data I happen to acquire. Even though I did absolutely nothing that I felt—at the time—was inappropriate, the fact remains that I reached a high fitness peak—two sole-authored articles in my discipline's most prestigious journal. Is this because I was lucky enough to happen upon the truth, against great odds? Or is it more plausible that my training allowed me to assemble what was necessary for publication out of whatever raw materials (data) happened to be at hand—without even being consciously aware of what I was doing?

What I can say is that some of my variables gave me considerable wiggle room, more than I realized at the time. For example—and this was specifically stated in the published motivation-focused paper (Gill, 1996)—my arousal variables (complexity and variety) were based on a model that assumed we try to keep arousal within reasonable bounds—both too little and too much perceived complexity is bad. What this means is that large changes in either direction would be demotivating, while a small change could be motivating either way (depending upon whether you were stressed by the task before the expert system was implemented). While Hackman and Oldham (1980) propose *variety* as being motivating, I could have viewed statistical significance in either direction as being consistent with my model (as well as no significance at all).

To balance these concerns, I did provide examples—based upon detailed interviews and, in many cases, direct observations—to support every statistical relationship that I had identified. Thus, there is absolutely no question in my mind that the relationships I described do exist *under some circumstances.* From a rigor standpoint, I therefore might have been better off simply focusing on these descriptions. Along with this, of course, I would have needed to determine and describe *the boundaries of the domain over which the effect was likely to be observed*, something I did not attempt to do in either original paper. Had I chosen the purely qualitative approach, however, I suspect that the odds of my research finding its way into MISQ would have been negligible.

The Review Process

The process of creating the research was largely under my control. The actual review process, on the other hand, was much less so. I now describe the process for each paper, completing the section with my observations.

The First Paper

By the time I had divided up the two papers, it was early 1993. I submitted the first to *MIS Quarterly* at that time. The paper was classified as an "application piece", which—based on the journal's 1993 procedures—meant that it was assigned to two academic reviewers and two practitioner reviewers. About three months later, I got the results back. Both academic reviewers had recommended outright rejection, one practitioner reviewer had recommended more or less immediate acceptance, and the other was positive, but recommended I make some significant revisions. The associate editor seemed to be leaning strongly in the direction of rejection. The senior editor, however, decided I should be given a further chance. Coincidentally, he had been a visiting scholar at Harvard while I was a doctoral student. In the end, I received a rather foreboding letter indicating that I would be allowed to revise and resubmit, but that the overall likelihood of success was not particularly promising.

I found the substance of the reviewer comments, even those disputing the fact that my manuscript had any value whatsoever, to be quite illuminating. I set about to address all of them, producing a massive "response" document in which I detailed all that I had done, and sent the revised paper back. The outcome of this round was that one of the practitioner reviewers felt he might have been too enthusiastic in the first round, the other bought off on all the changes, one of the academic reviewers felt that I had made progress, and the other, the most negative of all the reviewers, dropped out. Once again, I responded to all the suggestions—which were now more along the lines of tuning as opposed to full scale rewriting—and the paper was subsequently accepted.

The Second Paper

Once the first paper had been accepted, I immediately submitted the second paper. The same senior editor was assigned to it, but the outcome was different. By this point in time, MIS Quarterly had changed its review process such that only academic reviewers were assigned to the paper. I do not recall the precise score the paper received, but it was sufficiently negative that the result was outright rejection. In the rejection letter, however, the senior editor indicated that I could—after a thoughtful rewrite—resubmit the paper for a new set of reviews.

Once again, I found the reviews very helpful (despite their tone and conclusions) and, being one who could never turn down an invitation, I resubmitted the revised version as a new paper. The new version, once again under the same senior editor, received academic reviewer comments that were considerably more positive—major revisions across the board—and so, after one more round of revisions, the paper was accepted.

Comments on the Review Process

It should be clear that my own experiences helped to shape my analysis of peer review as presented in the previous chapter. Most significantly, I found the comments of every *MIS Quarterly* reviewer to be very useful, even when their tone was not one that I would have chosen in writing my own reviews. I also experienced the inconsistency in reviews described in the literature. This was true to some degree with respect to scores (e.g., on the first paper) but the phenomenon was particularly pronounced with respect to comments[9].

With respect to the effective anonymity of the peer review process, I certainly have my doubts based on my own experience. As a deciding editor (whatever the official title), I have been faced with many close decisions after the first round of reviews. Familiarity with the author—even to the extent of having seen a presentation at a conference—is not something I would, or could, ignore in such cases[10]. While most of my publications have been in the education and informing areas[11], on eight occasions, I have personally submitted to top-tier mainstream MIS or management journals because I felt the subject matter warranted it. Including the two papers just described, I have had three acceptances and five rejections. As it happens, I knew the deciding editor in the case of all three acceptances. In the case of all five rejections, I did not. I am not claiming this process is unfair; I respect the process and accept the decisions made in all eight cases (finding myself disagreeing with only two of them). But I would not be inclined to use my experience as evidence of the anonymous nature of our decision processes.

Conclusions

Research is personal, so I think it would be useful to have more people discussing their experiences during the process. I do so here with some trepidation, since not everything that I have described casts me in the most favorable light. But I do not believe that we can reform the business research process unless we are open and honest about what actually takes place.

I opened the chapter with a question:

> *Would I submit the same research for publication today, given what I now believe?*

The answer is, regrettably, no. Were I to conduct the project over again, to square with my beliefs I would necessarily start with the assumption that I was investigating a rugged fitness landscape and would modify my goals and methods accordingly.

What I can also say, with considerable certainty, is that I would cheerfully pay a great deal of money *not* to be able to communicate these misgivings to my past self back in 1993—when I started analyzing my data. Had I been able to convince myself of the weaknesses in rigor that I have presented here, I certainly would not have written the two articles that were accepted by *MIS Quarterly;* I doubt the articles that I would have written in their place would have been acceptable to any top-ranked journal. That, in turn, would have likely meant denial of promotion and tenure at Florida Atlantic University. That denial would have guaranteed my departure from academia. I have no idea what I would be doing now. I doubt that I would be as happy. As it turned out, I vastly underestimated the pleasures and freedoms offered by an academic career when I started down that path in the mid-1980s.

If other business academics feel the same way about their careers (and I'm sure they do) then as long as theory fragments and statistical significance remain the currency of publication, we can expect them to be ubiquitous in our research. In Chapters 13 through 15, I present some alternative approaches to research that we might want to consider pursuing.

Chapter 11 Foundational References

Gill, T. G. (1995b). Early expert systems: Where are they now? *MIS Quarterly, 19*(1), 51-81.

Gill, T. G. (1996). Expert systems usage: Task change and intrinsic motivation. *MIS Quarterly, 20*(3), 301-329.

Chapter 11 Notes

[1] In the context of a college professor being "almost as good" as a high school teacher—which is really the way I felt—it may be worth noting that I grew up as the son of a tenured Harvard faculty member who was also the Master of Leverett House (an undergraduate complex similar to an Oxford college), meaning that for the first 16 years of my life, I lived in Harvard housing and among Harvard faculty. Familiarity breeds contempt, as the saying goes.

[2] For example, the second case I ever wrote, on the subject of Cape Cod Potato Chips was subsequently used as the first case discussion in the HBS Agribusiness course for well over a decade.

[3] Excluding dissertation credits and non-credit seminars, my doctoral program consisted of 50 credits. Of these, 26 were in computer or cognitive science (20 at Harvard's Graduate School of Arts and Sciences, 6 at MIT), 8 were in statistics, and only 16 were in topics related to business research at HBS.

[4] I will relate one specific incident to support the assertion that my peculiar choice of course work was viewed positively. In spring of 1988 the department chair, the late Jim McKenney, brought me into his office as announced that he had recently visited with Derek Bok, then

President of Harvard, who had agreed with him that I should be nominated to become a Harvard Junior Fellow. Although I had never heard of the Harvard Society of Fellows, he assured me that it was quite an honor and that I was—to the best of anyone's knowledge—the first doctoral student from HBS ever to be so nominated. He then explained to me that the position, were I to be accepted, would involve five years of doing nothing but research at Harvard. I seem to recall having said something like "Go five more years without teaching, why on earth would I want to do that?" It is possible that I may have even filled out an application—in which case I must have been turned down. The very fact that I do not recall suggests how low I viewed the likelihood of it proving to be a good fit.

5 When I use the term "monstrosity", I refer to the fact that it was just shy of 1100 pages long and explored not just the paths of reasoning leading to my conclusions but also every other path anyone had ever considered and, quite probably, a fair number of paths that no one in their right mind would ever consider. I still feel some regret for the senseless slaughter of trees that making five copies of it entailed.

In my defense, the reason that I did not finish the dissertation prior to creating the system—which would have been the sensible course of action (and what I would have preferred to do)—was an example of the law of unintended consequences. As part of its relatively generous doctoral student stipend package, HBS had given me upwards of $50,000 in loans that would be forgiven so long as I took an academic position immediately upon graduation. Failure to do so would mean the entire balance had to be paid back. Thus, I needed to ensure that I did not graduate until I was ready to start working as a faculty member.

6 To return to an earlier quote, psychologist Daniel Gilbert's (2007, p. 20) *Stumbling on Happiness* asserts, "People find it gratifying to exercise control, not just for the futures it buys them but for the exercise itself. Being effective—changing things, influencing things, making things happen—is one of the fundamental needs with which human brains seem to be naturally endowed, and much of our behavior from infancy onward is simply and expression of this penchant for control."

7 300 hours of phone time is a rough estimate based upon the fact that just one of the monthly phone bills was over $2000. I know this because Carol Sunders relayed this fact to me, also mentioning that I

had—in that single month—exceeded the entire department's phone allowance for a semester. That she passed on this news with an amused look rather than as a condemnation served to further confirm my belief that I had been uncharacteristically wise in my choice of department.

[8] The official explanation for the abandonment involved the financial situation of the airlines involved (Gill, 1991). The system was not that expensive, however, with the lease payments on the hardware being the major cost. Thus, one may reasonably conclude that user reaction played an important role.

[9] One particularly amusing example of inconsistent comments was encountered in my first paper. In this case, an academic reviewer argued that the fact I was looking at systems that were five or more years old made my findings irrelevant while a practitioner reviewer complemented the research for its relevance.

[10] I recall one case where I recognized an author who had given a lively and informative conference presentation that I had happened to attend. The manuscript, however, had extracted and removed all the best qualities of the presentation leaving only a dull shell that all the reviewers (and I) hated. Realizing its potential, however, instead of rejecting the submission outright, I offered the authors the opportunity to resubmit with the specific caution that they needed to bring back the qualities that had made their presentation so engaging. They did, and the paper ended up being accepted and published.

[11] Because education and informing tend to be considerably less competitive with respect to publication the business disciplines, a high success rate publishing in these areas does not represent a particularly strenuous test.

Chapter 12

Complex Informing: A Synthesis

Roadmap & Objectives: In Chapters 3 through 11, the book has followed two distinct paths; one exploring the rigor of our research and one exploring the effectiveness of our informing efforts. Since the two streams are influenced by the same source, complexity, it is useful to bring them together. This chapter therefore summarizes the key findings of the preceding chapters in 15 propositions that can be conveniently referenced in the chapters that follow and, for the most part, are applicable to both research and education.

Up to this point in the book, there have been two objectives: to identify the crisis currently being faced by business schools (Chapters 1 and 2) and to set forth a conceptual scheme, largely driven by the nature of complexity, that can help us better understand how to address this crisis. For the remainder of the book, the goal is to outline both a general philosophy for increasing the impact of our research and teaching and to make some specific proposals—a sampling rather than a comprehensive list—that would be consistent with that philosophy.

This chapter is intended to be short. Its purpose is to take the lengthy analysis conducted in Chapters 3 through 11 and condense them into a compact set of generalizations that, in turn, suggest some guidelines for informing business. I have divided these generalizations into five areas:

1. Rugged Landscapes

2. Adaptation

3. Learning

4. Informing

5. Behavior of Complex Systems

I have also intentionally limited myself to three observations in each area. By doing so, my objective has been to create a list that is manageable enough to be applied in the subsequent chapters. In writing the generalizations, I have tried to be as straightforward as possible, ignoring nuance even at the risk of sometimes overstating the point. To placate the academic reader, I have restated the observations as more precise and carefully measured propositions in the footnotes.

The purpose of this chapter is not to defend these generalizations— Chapters 3 through 11 should have served that role. Comments and examples are presented after each one, however, so as to improve their resonance by acting as reminders of what was previously presented.

1. Generalizations on Rugged Landscapes

The concept of a rugged fitness landscape is the core upon which this book is based. The multiple peaks and non-decomposability of such landscapes should be familiar by this point. The observations therefore are most directly concerned with our ability to estimate fitness.

1.1 Ubiquity of Estimates-of-Fitness

> *Observation 1.1:* We depend on fitness estimates because "real" fitness is almost always impossible to know.[1]

Getting philosophical for a moment, in order to determine the "true" fitness of an entity's choices, you would need to know the future. Foreknowledge of a major black swan could completely change your estimate. Heavy drinking, for example, is something I regard as highly detrimental to both my personal fitness and to the fitness of my children (through the example I would be setting). Therefore, I choose not do it. Were I to discover, however, that a large asteroid was going to collide with earth and destroy all life in six months, I imagine that heavy drinking would become part of my daily regimen and that I might well encourage my wife and (underage) boys to indulge in the activity as well.

Not only do we need to depend upon estimates in order to assess the fitness of our behavior, we also frequently employ more than one estimate-of-fitness in novel situations. Our sense of fitness, as determined by "utility", can therefore be skewed by what particular estimate we are attending to. That is the basis of the wide range of inconsistent behaviors, such as framing, that were described in Chapters 5 through 9. For this reason, I introduce the notion of a *dominant estimate-of-fitness*, representing that particular estimate or consistent combination of estimates that guides an entity's behavior. That particular concept becomes relevant only after the entity has started to develop a model of the landscape. While the landscape's structure is completely novel, we have seen that utility bounces around too much for any particular view of fitness to be considered dominant.

1.2 Limited Visibility

> *Observation 1.2:* We perceive the world based upon the peak we are pursuing; we choose that peak based on our dominant estimate-of-fitness[2].

This is a variation on the *Law of Limited Visibility*, presented in Chapter 3, where the impact of college ratings was discussed. The critical point here is that how you estimate fitness is likely to have a huge impact on how you model the landscape. For example, if the fitness of an elementary school is estimated using test scores we can then expect its principal to start modeling fitness in a manner heavily weighted towards those activities that are believed to improve test scores. Over time, he or she is likely to come to believe that fitness and test scores are nearly synonymous.

1.3 Importance of Boundary Conditions

> *Observation 1.3:* Coming up with a theory that works somewhere is easy; figuring out where it applies is hard.[3]

Stated another way, almost any proposed compact relationship between variables is likely to hold somewhere on a rugged landscape. Thus, the act of verifying that such a relationship exists does not provide us with much useful information. Rigorous information regarding when and where we can expect to see that relationship hold, on the other hand, is likely to be very useful.

This observation was a central point made in Chapter 10 during the discussions of rigor. Between low hanging fruit (i.e., strong main effects) and rules learned through adaptation, an entity tuning to a particular peak on the landscape is likely to have a pretty good idea of how fitness behaves in that region. What the entity will likely lack is a clear idea of the degree to which that model is applicable in different regions of the fitness landscape. For example, a common explanation for the frequent failure of business school deans hired directly from industry is that they attempt to apply the same rules that they learned in a corporate setting to the academic setting (Dahringer, 2003).

2. Generalizations on Adaptation

The next group of observations deals with the adaptation behaviors commonly associated with entities on a rugged fitness landscape.

2.1 Estimates-of-Fitness and Unfreezing

> *Observation 2.1:* Change a person's dominant estimate-of-fitness and changes to behavior will surely follow.[4]

This generalization emerges from several sources. In Chapter 5 we saw how fitness evaluators can be among the most important components of a general problem solving system. In Chapter 7, we considered the well-documented power of goal setting in directing task performance. In Chapter 8, we explored the ability of fitness estimates to induce information cascades. In Chapter 6 we saw how resistant students can be when it comes to relinquishing their existing mental models—the same observation made by Kuhn with respect to the paradigms of entire disciplines. Collectively, these lead to the conclusion that transformation—as opposed to incremental change—is most likely to be initiated by changes to how we estimate fitness as opposed to attempts to change our models in the absence of changing our perception of fitness.

This view is also relatively consistent with a widely used model of behavioral and organizational change originally proposed by Kurt Lewin and later adapted by Edgar Schein (1999) that asserts change follows a pattern of:

Unfreezing → Moving → Refreezing

The implication of the model is that change will not occur unless the status quo is disrupted through unfreezing. In order to achieve unfreezing, our existing sense of fitness must be disconfirmed. Schein (1999, p. 60) describes this, in terms familiar to evolutionary fitness models, as follows:

The disconfirmation must arouse what we can call "survival anxiety," or the feeling that if we do not change, we will fail to meet our needs or fail to achieve some goals or ideals that we have set for ourselves.

Zand and Sorensen (1975, p. 535) elaborate on this, emphasizing the same social influence factors that were previously described in both Chapters 5 and 8. Specifically, they assert the following:

> Disconfirmation is feedback that one's present behavior is in-effective or not as effective as it might be with reasonable additional effort. The feedback may vary in source, form, and method of transmittal; for example, (a) objective measurements of physical production showing that one's intended level of production was not attained; (b) social comparison showing that one's performance is inferior, in objective or qualitative measurements, to that of another comparable unit; (c) information from important others, such as superiors, peers, or subordinates, indicating that one's intended effects are not being attained; (d) criticism from important others emphasizing that one's behavior is seriously deficient compared to highly valued, ideal behavior.

While it would probably be a stretch to assert that all transformational change is initiated through changes to estimates-of-fitness, discontent that arises solely from the low fitness produced by a behavior is often insufficient to produce change. If it did, the inability of disciplines such as economics and finance to make predictions significantly better than random guessing (and sometimes worse)—described in Chapter 10—would have led them to abandon their theories. That leads to the next generalization.

2.2 Adaptation towards Dominant Estimate-of-Fitness

> *Observation 2.2:* As long as our dominant estimate-of-fitness does not change, we cling tenaciously to the peaks we have chosen (even if they are not very fit)[5].

As I was writing this chapter, I happened to watch a TV show detailing the gang situation in Oakland, California[6]. The show described a particular city with one of the worst gang problems in the U.S. During the year profiled, over 100 people had already been murdered as a consequence of gang-on-gang violence.

The problem in Oakland was exacerbated by the existence of three major gangs, who were in constant conflict. What particularly impressed me about the episode, however, was one of the gang members they profiled. That individual, who had previously been shot by another gang and was in a wheelchair, was surprising in two ways. First, he had an extremely clear vision of what constituted fitness according to the particular peak he was seeking. Second, he readily conceded that the goals he was pursuing were likely to get him killed.

Naturally, one might dismiss comments in a TV interview as bravado. But the episode continued by showing him driving an old passenger van into the territory of a competing gang so as to intentionally provoke the members of that gang. He asserted that doing so was necessary in order to maintain the stature of himself and his gang. Certainly, the excursion offered no prospect for material gain. Once again, perhaps the "danger" of the trip was exaggerated. That seems unlikely, however. In the course of making the run, the van overheated and broke down while it was in the competing gang's territory; it was quite clear that the occupants feared for their very lives once they determined that they had been observed by a passing car. Perhaps even more convincingly, later in the episode the rival gang drove by the individual's home and pumped over a dozen bullets into that same van. Although no one was killed in that particular encounter, that non-fatal outcome was the exception rather than the rule given Oakland's crime statistics.

Throughout this book, I have presented examples questioning the validity of the estimates-of-fitness, such as publication and citation counts, that we use for assessing the fitness of our research activities. What I hope to convey by this example is that being strongly attached to a particular estimator does not necessarily imply that the estimator is a good one.

2.3 Stability of Local Peaks

> *Observation 2.3:* Once expertise has been acquired during periods of stability, we will resist any efforts to make us relinquish it unless forced to do so by our environment[7].

This generalization is, in effect, a restatement of the *Law of Abandoned Expertise* first mentioned in Chapter 5. The important refinement offered here is the notion that the attachment to a particular model or set of models grows over time during periods of order. The corollary to the rule is the oft repeated "a crisis is a terrible thing to waste" (see the end of Chapter 9)—another way of saying that during the course of or immediately after a large discontinuity is generally the best time to implement transformational change.

3. Generalizations on Learning

The observations in this group principally address the form of the knowledge we hold. Of specific interest is compiled knowledge, which is to say memory that is chunked and procedures that are automatized, as discussed at length in Chapter 6.

3.1 Attenuation of Knowledge and Skills

> *Observation 3.1:* If we do not practice something, we forget it[8].

This phenomenon was illustrated by the large difference in algebra performance between individuals who had just had algebra contrasted with those who had taken subsequent math courses. In practical terms, it means that if you are concerned with long term outcomes, a small amount of content and a large amount of practice will have a greater impact than a large amount of content and small amount of practice.

3.2 Existence of Compiled Prerequisites to Learning

> *Observation 3.2:* There are many advanced concepts we simply cannot learn until we have become practiced at the basics[9].

This phenomenon was a consequence of working memory capacity. What it highlights is the importance of identifying desired core skills and ensuring that they are sufficiently practiced prior to introducing higher level skills.

3.3 Barriers to Generalization of Knowledge

> *Observation 3.3:* Do not expect to be able to transfer skills from one problem to another until those skills are practiced[10].

This phenomenon has been demonstrated many times in problem isomorph studies, such as the Tower of Hanoi problem discussed in Chapter 6. Similar to observation 3.2, it is a result of our working memory limitations; an unfamiliar situation takes up so much space that we cannot concurrently apply an unpracticed problem solving approach. For example, in the studies described there were some subjects who identified parallels between the problems they were given (e.g., Chinese Tea Ceremony and Tower of Hanoi) yet still failed to apply the rules learned in one to the other.

The practical implication of this is that the specific skills that we teach are unlikely to be applied generally unless: a) they are practiced, and b) they are employed in many different contexts.

4. Generalizations on Informing

The observations on informing are specifically focused on non-routine and low structure informing situations (see Chapter 8), since routine informing generally represents the end-point of an adaptive process and, once established, tends to be reasonably effective. In addition, since student and practitioner mental models are typically not completely known prior to commencing informing, nearly all academic informing falls into our definition of non-routine—despite the fact that we may teach a class or give the same presentation on a regular basis.

4.1 Diffusion of Estimates of Fitness

> *Observation 4.1:* We love rankings and other estimates-of-fitness—especially if we believe our actions can affect them[11].

Particularly in situations where behaviors have yet to become routine, a good estimate-of-fitness will always be welcome and will diffuse quickly. Since we are strongly motivated by control (see Chapters 5 and 9), estimates-of-fitness that can be impacted through voluntary behaviors are particularly likely to diffuse. Fashions are a good example, as are the wide range of ranking schemes that we frequently use to guide our behaviors, such as grades and journal ratings.

4.2 Estimates-of-Fitness and Peer Informing

> *Observation 4.2:* Most of our complex ideas are initially acquired from people we know or people we observe[12].

Social influence works in two ways. First, by observing our peers we can judge how they attempt to maximize fitness. In agriculture, for example, seeing your neighbor's yield exceed your own provides a great incentive to ask what the neighbor is doing differently. Second, it helps fulfill an underlying drive to bond (see Chapter 5) through conforming to social norms. Thus, study after study finds that peer-to-peer processes in the client community dominate knowledge diffusion processes. In the specific context of business, for example, Davenport and Prusak (Davenport, Prusak, & Wilson, 2003) emphasize the role of *idea practitioners* within organizations in ensuring knowledge gets transferred. In agriculture, it was the agents of the cooperative extension service (Rogers, 2003).

In many cases, technical content will still involve external informers, such as schools. Such informing is facilitated once the appropriate estimate-of-fitness has been established to motivate the acquisition of such content.

4.3 Power of Stories

> *Observation 4.3:* If you want someone to listen and learn, tell a story[13].

In Chapter 7, the unique resonance of stories was analyzed. They promote attention by incorporating suspense. The narrative form promotes recall by offering internal linkages within the content as well as linkages to what the listener already knows. They do not threaten existing knowledge the way that abstract rules might, since they can always be treated as a special case rather than as an effort to undermine what is already known.

5. Generalizations on Complex System Behavior

The common thread of the observations in this group is the nature of punctuated equilibrium and its effects upon entities existing on a particular fitness landscape. As a starting point, we assume the punctuated equilibrium that appears to be ubiquitous in such systems (see Chapter 9). This behavior is characterized by periods of orderly, predictable behavior interrupted by discontinuities during which behaviors can change suddenly and radically.

5.1 Punctuated Equilibrium and Fitness

> *Observation 5.1:* In complex systems, rules are stable only between discontinuities—and discontinuities may permanently change these rules[14].

This more or less follows directly from our definition of punctuated equilibrium. In practical terms, it means that we can develop rules for efficient behavior during orderly periods but may need to abandon those rules when major discontinuities occur. Where a complex adaptive system is likely to differ from complex systems in general is with respect to what happens after a discontinuity. In a non-adapting system, behavior reverts to its former pattern. For example, when you drop grains of rice on a pile, from time to time a sudden avalanche occurs. After the avalanche, however, if you continue to drop grains of rice on the pile, the process behaves pretty much the same way it did before the avalanche. In adapting systems, however, behavioral changes in the individual entities making up the system are likely to occur so the rules of post-discontinuity system behavior may be quite different from behavior prior to the discontinuity.

5.2 Unpredictability of Discontinuities

> *Observation 5.2:* The size and timing of discontinuities cannot be predicted in a complex system. What we can predict with considerable certainty is that, eventually, a jolt will come along that is large enough so that we will really regret not having prepared for it[15].

In Chapter 9, we pointed out that many systems exhibit a pattern of discontinuity that follows a power law. Unfortunately, most systems are unlikely to follow a pattern that precise—even if the system itself generates discontinuities of that sort (e.g., Taleb's grey swans) it is also likely to be impacted by discontinuities in co-evolving systems or supersystems (e.g., Taleb's black swans) that are discontinuous according to different power laws.

What can be said about all these effects, however, is that they have very wide tails. In other words, discontinuities will eventually exert effects that are sufficiently significant so that to ignore them invites disaster.

5.3 Adaptability and Survival

> *Observation 5.3:* If you want to survive on a complex landscape over the long term, you must acquire a diverse set of skills and cultivate adaptability[16].

This observation is based on an evolutionary argument. What it asserts is as follows. In any complex adaptive system, we can eventually expect a discontinuity (either a grey swan or a black swan, using Taleb's terminology) that is of sufficiently great magnitude so as to threaten the existence of virtually every entity. Such a threat is magnified when entities employ a strategy of focused efficiency, where all their activities are tuned towards a single goal or fitness peak.

There appear to be two strategies for avoiding extinction. The first is *diversity*. Where entities are spread across a broad range of fitness peaks, covering most of the landscape, it is reasonable to expect that some entities will be located at or near peaks where fitness is less affected or even improved. In Chapter 9, for example, I mentioned the case of the asteroid 65 million years ago that wiped out the dinosaurs but paved the way for mammals to become dominant. One theory is that species that burrowed or spent much of their lives underwater (e.g., crocodiles) were most likely to survive the asteroid's impact and the period that followed. Since dinosaurs were dominant at the time, mammals were small and particularly likely to fall into the burrower category. Thus, the particular fitness peak they occupied was fortuitous.

The other approach to avoiding being wiped out by a major discontinuity is to be highly adaptable. But adaptability always comes at a price. For the human species, it meant evolving a brain that requires a lot of energy, enclosing it in a skull so large that it makes the birth process agonizing, and requiring that our young experience a long period of dependency almost guaranteed to give the concerned parent grey hairs. For the individual, it means giving up immediate employment in favor of a period of skill acquisition—often in the form of formal education—intended to develop the adaptability necessary for a changing world. The idea that a tradeoff between adaptability and focused efficiency nearly always exists is revisited many times during the remainder of this book.

Conclusions

I have chosen to characterize the generalizations made in this chapter as observations, as opposed to hypotheses for three reasons. First— believing in complexity as I do—I seriously doubt that they represent "universal truths". Rather, I believe them to be true much more often than not, which is sufficient for my purposes. Second, using the term hypothesis would suggest that I am trying to present a theory. In Chapter 10 I tried to be very clear on this particular point: *a theory is not rigorous unless its boundaries are clearly specified.* Furthermore, as I pointed out in Observation 1.3, determining those precise boundaries is generally a lot harder than describing the behaviors within them. Thus, what I have proposed remains a conceptual scheme—albeit a powerful one. Finally, as soon as you describe a statement as a hypothesis, the next thing you are expected to do is test it and—in most academic endeavors—that is where the process ends. Testing these observations is not my goal, however. Chapters 3 through 11 were written specifically to justify them (although additional replications would certainly be welcome). What I really want to do with these observations is to put them to work!

In presenting the next three chapters, I chose an organization that should be readily discernable: informing ourselves (research), informing our students (education) and informing practice (impact). What will quickly become clear, however, is my belief that the three types of informing cannot sensibly be considered independently. This philosophy becomes evident when it comes to the recommendations that I make. There is not a single one that could not easily be moved to one of the other two chapters. Many would be at home in all three. I believe that this overlap is more than a coincidence. Rather, I believe the opposite: if a recommendation does not make sense in at least two of the three categories of informing, then it probably does not make sense at all. In other words, they are not decomposable!

Chapter 12 Foundational References

Kauffman, S. A. (1993). *The origins of order.* Oxford, UK: Oxford University Press.

Rogers, E. M. (2003). *Diffusion of innovations* (5th ed.). New York, NY: Free Press.

Taleb, N. N. (2007). *The Black Swan.* New York, NY: Random House.

Willingham, D. T. (2009). *Why don't students like school?* San Francisco, CA: Jossey Bass.

Chapter 12 Notes

[1] *Proposition 1.1:* The underlying "true" fitness of a rugged landscape can almost never be observed directly; it will almost always need to be estimated.

[2] *Proposition 1.2:* An entity existing on a rugged landscape will exhibit a model of fitness that is heavily influenced by the particular peak to which it is adapting; the choice of peak will, in turn, be heavily influenced by its dominant estimate-of-fitness.

[3] *Proposition 1.3:* Knowledge of the boundaries over which a particular model of fitness applies is generally harder to obtain than the actual model itself; that knowledge is also generally more valuable.

[4] *Proposition 2.1:* The most effective way to begin transforming an entity's routine behavior on a rugged fitness landscape is to change its dominant estimate-of-fitness.

[5] *Proposition 2.2:* Once an estimate-of-fitness becomes dominant, an entity will begin adapting to achieve fitness according to that estimate no matter how low its "true" fitness is.

[6] The specific episode I refer to was titled *Gang Wars: Oakland II* and it aired on 21 September 2009 at 9 PM on the Discovery Channel. I could find no permanent link to it on the web, although sections of it were posted on Youtube.com. There was some dispute on Internet blog sites regarding the accuracy of the show's estimate that the city had 10,000 gang members (some felt that 2000-3000 was more reasonable). I did, however, confirm some of the statistics in the episode using public web sites such as:

http://www.cityrating.com/citycrime.asp?city=Oakland&state=CA

From those sites, it is clear that the city does indeed have a serious crime problem, with a murder rate roughly 3.5 times the U.S. national average and currently has well over 100 murders/year, a figure that has risen dramatically in recent years, consistent with the show's assertion.

[7] *Proposition 2.3:* Once a rugged fitness landscape has been stable for a sustained period of time, adapting entities on that landscape will believe that they have attained a peak or are close to one according to their

dominant estimate-of-fitness; they will therefore see little or no value to acquiring new models.

[8] *Proposition 3.1*: Knowledge and skills that have become compiled will attenuate much more slowly than knowledge and skills that have not been.

[9] *Proposition 3.2*: Higher levels of knowledge and skills often cannot be attained until specific lower levels have become compiled.

[10] *Proposition 3.3*: Generalization of knowledge acquired in one domain to another domain is unlikely to occur unless much of that knowledge is compiled.

[11] *Proposition 4.1*: Estimates-of-fitness tend to diffuse more rapidly than complete mental models; those estimates that incorporate behaviors or choices under the entity's control tend to diffuse most rapidly of all.

[12] *Proposition 4.2*: Estimates-of-fitness tend to be acquired from peers; where the estimate contains social influence components, the importance of the peer-to-peer channel is further amplified.

[13] *Proposition 4.3*: Stories diffuse more rapidly than abstract concepts; they are a principal mechanism through which estimates-of-fitness and knowledge of new fitness peaks diffuse.

[14] *Proposition 5.1*: In complex landscapes exhibiting punctuated equilibrium, discontinuities can lead to unpredictable changes in the fitness landscapes governing the entities on that landscape, whereas changes to fitness during orderly periods tend to be more gradual and predictable.

[15] *Proposition 5.2*: The timing of discontinuities in complex adaptive system behavior cannot be predicted nor can their magnitude; the only thing that can be asserted about these discontinuities is that the variability in their magnitude is sufficiently large so that, from time to time, the entire behavior of the system will be completely disrupted.

[16] *Proposition 5.3*: Entities existing within complex adaptive systems adapt to reach the local fitness peaks of the corresponding rugged landscape and thereafter exhibit a preference for tuning themselves to those peaks; entities that surviving a large discontinuity will be those whose original fitness peak is close to a corresponding peak in the post-discontinuity landscape and those with the ability to adapt rapidly.

Chapter 13

Informing Ourselves

Roadmap & Objectives: Chapters 13 through 15 focus on offering recommendations to improve our informing—including the manner in which we inform ourselves. This chapter proposes that we could be more impactful in our research if we focused on the relationships created by such research—including relationships to practice and to researchers in other non-business disciplines—instead of narrowly emphasizing the publications we generate.

"Informing ourselves" refers to the nature of our research. Since Chapters 10 and 11 set forth the argument that our research was not as rigorous as we perceive it to be, it is convenient to make rigor the central focus of this chapter, placing greater emphasis on relevance and resonance in the subsequent two chapters. For this purely organizational reason, our focus becomes the nature of rigorous research on a rugged landscape.

To say the chapter focuses strictly on rigor would be a misstatement, however. What we are really after is research with impact. Rugged fitness landscapes tend to produce findings that are specific and transitory in nature. Simply ensuring that these findings are developed in a rigorous manner will be deeply unsatisfying—which is to say, not unlike what we have today. If we truly want to improve the impact of what we are doing, considerations of resonance, in particular, need to be incorporated into every research design decision that we construct.

The organization of the chapter is based around some of the threats to rigor identified in Chapter 10. The specific areas considered include: getting over our preoccupation with theory, reducing the silo mentality, appropriate gathering and analysis of data, sensible quality control, and better assessing our research contributions. I begin, however, with some general comments regarding the importance of unfreezing.

We Need to Get Over Ourselves

Lewin and Schein (1999) assert that before a change can occur, unfreezing must take place. That process requires two components: disconfirmation—accepting that our existing model is not working well—and an alternative means of estimating fitness [2.1][1]. The disconfirmation process will require that we "get over ourselves."

We Are in Worse Trouble Than We Think

On the surface, business faculty—particularly tenure earning faculty at a research university in the U.S.—would seem to have it made. Consider how we, as a group, compare with faculty from other disciplines. At my university, a fairly typical of a large research university, the comparison would look something like the following:

- Our pay is much higher than the pay of faculty doing similar work, such as faculty teaching sociology, psychology, or industrial engineering.

- We are not held accountable for acquiring external grant support, unlike our colleagues in medicine, education, the physical sciences, and engineering.

- We have far lower teaching loads than our colleagues in the liberal arts.

- We are not required to engage with the local practitioner community—accounting being a possible exception to this—unlike our colleagues in education and social work.

In other words, we benefit from all the privileges of being an academic researcher, face far fewer specific demands, yet we still get paid more. Furthermore, the nature of our research makes its true fitness nearly impossible to determine [1.1]. As a result, we have fine tuned our estimate-of-fitness to the extent that at most research universities, top-tier publications and citation counts are all that *truly* matter when it comes to promotion and merit determination. And, not surprisingly, we have become pretty good at racking up fitness points according to this metric[2]. But the unintended consequence of this highly specialized focus is that we now have few strong allies among either the non-business disciplines in our institutions or in the local practitioner community. While both may pay lip service to the research we are doing, we have given neither group a compelling reason to stand up for us should our activities be threatened or curtailed.

I believe that our favored estimate of fitness makes us too focused and threatens our very survival in the long term [5.3]. As I mentioned in Chapter 2, as long as a steady stream of students want to study business, we are probably safe. But, there are many threats that could, very quickly, disrupt our landscape. Should events such as the recent disruption in the financial community tarnish the image of business schools, enrollments would drop and faculty members, particular junior faculty, would find their position far less secure. Should non-traditional approaches to business education that are not coupled with research—such as those pioneered by the rapidly growing *University of Phoenix*—gain greater traction[3], we could see the same thing happening. Global competition could also lead to a discontinuous transition in demand should the U.S. model lose its luster. Assuming that such discontinuities will not occur is naïve [5.2]. In fact, as mentioned in Chapter 1, we saw precisely such a massive disruption (favoring research in that case) take place in the late 1950s precipitated by a set of critical reports such as the one published by the Ford Foundation (Gordon & Howell, 1959).

Our Current State of Comfort Grants Us Serenity...

The highly comfortable position that we currently occupy [2.2] has given us nearly infinite patience in our wait for the important research discoveries that we expect will, at some point in the future, transform and improve business practice. But are we being realistic in expecting those discoveries will ever be made? Noted expert on the capabilities of experts, James Shanteau (1992, p. 259), lists 10 task characteristics that typically to lead to poor predictive performance by experts:

1. Dynamic (changeable) stimuli
2. Decisions about behavior
3. Experts disagree on stimuli
4. Less predictable problems
5. Few errors expected
6. Unique tasks

7. Feedback unavailable
8. Subjective analysis only
9. Problem not decomposable
10. Decision aids rare

Of these 10 characteristics, at least 7 apply to virtually every business problem that is characterized by a rugged fitness landscape: dynamic stimuli, decisions about behavior, experts disagree, less predictable problems, unique tasks, feedback unavailable, and problem not decomposable. Many business situations involve all 10. This profile is substantially worse than that faced by the physical sciences in its pre-theory days. It is also worse than the profile faced in the life sciences; at least bacteria do not change their minds. Until we observe a discipline—and just one would be all that it would take!—having the same characteristics that has nonetheless successfully built a theory that demonstrates good overall predictive performance, we should at least consider the possibility that none will ever exist and develop our portfolio of research accordingly. That does not mean we have to stop searching for that holy grail of rigorous, compact, and generalizable theory. It merely means that we need to cultivate a diversity of research that includes a substantial fraction of activities that could be immediately useful to practice or our students.

We Do Not Agree on How to Solve the Problem

Many individuals and organizations have identified the problems with our research and education—Chapter 1 offered just a brief summary of extensive literature discussing our many perceived weaknesses. Unfortunately, simply demonstrating that a particular approach to fitness is not very good will not, by itself, promote movement [2.2]—just ask the gangs at war with each other in Oakland, California. Equally disturbing, there is no consensus on how to go about solving the problem.

AACSB's perspective

The uncomfortable feeling I get is that the business researchers, on the whole, do not fully grasp the source, magnitude, or the actions that might help to solve our research problem. My own views on this matter were strongly influenced by AACSB International's (2008) recent report on how we might improve the impact of our research. Their very first, and least incremental, recommendation was as follows:

Recommendation #1: Extend and augment AACSB International accreditation guidelines to require schools to demonstrate the impact of faculty intellectual contributions on targeted audiences. (AACSB, 2008, p. 29)

On the surface, this recommendation seems like a very promising step—demand that institutions demonstrate their research has impact!

Table 13.1: Impact of Mission Characteristics on Impact Expectations: Examples

Characteristic	Model A	Model B	Model C	Model D
Scholarship Emphasis	Scholarship emphasizes learning and pedagogical research and contributions to practice	Scholarship emphasizes contributions to practice and learning and pedagogical research	Scholarship emphasizes contributions to practice and discipline-based scholarship	Scholarship emphasizes discipline-based research and contributions to practice
Doctoral Program Emphasis	No doctoral program		Doctoral program that emphasizes practice and/or places graduates in teaching focused schools or industry	Large doctoral program placing graduates in research focused schools
Weighting of Impact: Expectations	Teaching - Higher Practice - Moderate Theory - Lower	Practice - Higher Teaching - Moderate Theory- Lower	Practice - Higher Theory - Moderate Teaching - Lower	Theory - Higher Practice - Moderate Teaching - Lower

Excerpted from Table 2 (p. 31), AACSB, "Final Report of the AACSB International Impact of Research Task Force", *AACSB International*, 2008, Accessed on 5/27/08 at http://www.aacsb.edu/resource_centers/research/Final/Impact_of_Research_Report-FINAL.PDF

The problem surfaces when they subsequently explain the recommendation using a table to qualify what they mean by "target audiences." That table, summarized in Table 13.1, contains an embedded estimate-of-fitness that sends chills up my spine. Reading from left to right, it should be obvious that institutional prestige (and salary) grows from Model A to Model D. Equally obvious, the importance of discipline-based research and theory creation grows correspondingly. If there were a Model E, it would consist of nothing but theory! This estimate-of-fitness should remove any doubt as to where a researcher who is seeking professional stature should concentrate. Only theory-builders need apply. And heaven help those of us who do pedagogical studies.

Pfeffer's recommendations

Jeffrey Pfeffer's thoughtful synthesis of the weaknesses of business research heavily influenced my own views on the subject, presented in Chapter 1. He also offers what I perceive to be the most useful starting point with respect to where we need to go in our research. He recognizes, for example, our extreme weakness in communicating our findings to practice and suggests we look at innovation research to help us in our efforts to improve the situation (Pfeffer, 2007, p. 1341). He then suggests we look to medicine, engineering, and education as exemplars of disciplines that are more effective in their efforts to communicate their ideas to practice. Interestingly, these disciplines do not necessarily regard themselves as paragons of diffusion. Medicine is constantly lamenting its weakness in getting research to practice—it even has a journal, *Implementation Science*, devoted to nothing but that topic. Engineering reports a similar problem[4]. Where these disciplines differ sharply from business is in the degree to which researchers are embedded in the practitioner community. A large percentage of medical school faculty members maintain a clinical practice as well as an academic position. Many times engineering academic research flows to practice through faculty members founding or becoming affiliated with startup companies; the specific individual Pfeffer uses as a "best practice" example, a founder of *IDEO Product Development* and a professor at Stanford University, fits that category. We return to this dual role concept frequently as the recommendations are developed.

Pfeffer's use of education as an example of effective diffusion, however, provides a clear case for why "what" you are diffusing needs to be considered in parallel with "how" you are diffusing it. Using the 10 Shanteau (1992) criteria presented earlier in the chapter, education seems pretty comparable to business in terms of the task characteristics. It also provides the opportunity for a type of natural experiment. Public education almost universally requires at least some certification from a college of education, and the vast majority of teachers actually have an education degree. There is also plenty of evidence that educational theories do diffuse to public school districts[5]. Private and parochial schools, on the other hand, are not similarly constrained and are much more likely to have teachers whose background does not include an education degree and whose expertise in education theory is therefore likely to be much lower. Which, do you suppose, exhibits the higher academic performance? To me, this "experiment" forcefully suggests the danger of excessive reliance on theory fragments in a complex environment[6].

Medicine, public education, and many branches of engineering also meet Rakesh Khurana's (2007) strictly defined notion of a profession, which is to say an occupation that has well defined educational requirements, a shared code of conduct, and specific certification requirements. Professions of this type can effectively *require* a certain degree of diffusion of ideas through their education and certification standards. Khurana goes so far as to argue that we should require the same of business (or, at least, of certain sensitive business positions). The concern I would have about embracing this professional model too enthusiastically for business—as Khurana suggests we should do—is its potential impact on adaptability. I return to this subject in Chapter 16.

Pfeffer's recommendations go on to advocate academic-practitioner collaborations. These I applaud wholeheartedly for reasons that will soon become abundantly clear. Such arrangements will be discussed at some length in Chapter 15, as will another of his recommendations: recruiting non-traditional faculty members.

About half of the space Pfeffer devotes to recommendations involves journal policies and evaluation. Here, he makes a qualified suggestion that involves weighing raw citation counts more heavily. That, I believe, would have an extremely deleterious effect on research impact since it would further reinforce an estimate-of-fitness that naturally increases the more that we, as academics, focus on each other. Not an auspicious behavior if the goal is to encourage greater impact on practice. I have no particular objection to his remaining suggestions. I simply do not believe that they would have more than a peripheral impact on practice. My justification is simple: complex ideas are much more likely to diffuse through face-to-face contacts than through mass media channels [4.2] such as journal articles.

My prognosis: Building informing networks

All of which leads to a central point that I will continually emphasize in this chapter and those that follow:

> *The impact of your research on a particular community will generally be more affected by the network of personal relationships that you have available to you than by the actual content.*

If we did not believe this to some extent, we would not have so many academic conferences. But this also leads to a second, equally important corollary:

> *Research activities that serve to build enduring personal relationships from a discipline to a targeted audience are likely to be as beneficial to the discipline as "great ideas". They should therefore be equally rewarded.*

This philosophy guides nearly everything I propose. It implies a far more radical rethinking of how we conduct and disseminate research than proposed by either the AACSB or Pfeffer.

Theorist vs. Observer

The somewhat negative portrayal of business research presented in Chapters 1, 10 and the previous section might lead to the conclusion that I see no role for business research activities. Nothing could be farther from the truth. From the very beginning of this book, I have asserted that business today faces major problems. Indeed, the shoddy practices of a few and the short-term thinking of many have driven confidence in U.S. business to its lowest levels in decades. What affects business affects our students. What affects our students affects those of us who teach them. Through our research we can become part of the solution, part of the problem, or completely irrelevant. I will refer to research that is part of the solution as *impactful* research.

The challenge is that research is not a homogenous product like a sack of flour that can be dispensed and paid for by the cup. Every research project has its own distinct characteristics. These characteristics can be either harmonious with the domain being studied or very much out-of-synch. Thus, it makes sense to carefully consider the nature of the research we intend to conduct.

The Qualities of Impactful Research

Given the rugged nature of the typical fitness landscape facing today's organization, I would propose that impactful research will nearly always be imbued with three qualities:

1. It will improve our understanding of the fitness landscape facing one or more business entities.

2. It will generate resonant forms of expression, such as stories, that will facilitate its diffusion.

3. It will build or maintain face-to-face channels through which its findings and future research can diffuse.

Of these, the first embodies the qualities of rigor and relevance. The remaining two are particularly focused on resonance. The problem with research whose central goal is to create theory or theory fragments is that it is often of limited value in meeting the first objective (discussed ad nauseum in Chapter 10) and will not necessarily be of any value in meeting the remaining two objectives.

Revisiting the Reporter Role

In Chapter 10, we discussed the different research roles introduced by Colquitt and Zapata-Phelan (2007). In their research, they found that the role of "reporter", which is to say the observer who does not attempt to build theory, had virtually disappeared from top management journals. In a stable decomposable landscape, that would make sense; we would expect roles influential in the development and refinement of theory—e.g., builders, expanders, and testers—to grow in emphasis since the emerging theory is likely to be attractive. On our dynamic rugged landscape, we would expect these priorities to be reversed. Since such a landscape is likely to produce ever-changing ugly theory under any circumstances, those roles that seek out and describe interesting areas of the landscape—in other words, the reporter—should be of greatest value.

Detailed individual observations, as opposed to averages taken from large collections of more superficial individual observations—a description that fits most surveys—make more sense when the landscape is rugged. When you are driving down a flooded street, the fact that the average water depths is three inches is not what destroys your engine. It is that one 3 foot trough in the middle. In fact, practitioners are likely to be extremely unimpressed with average values. If they have been adapting on the landscape for a significant period of time, they are likely to believe that they are pretty close to the particular peak [2.3] they have chosen to pursue. Telling them that they are not based upon averages taken from observations distributed across many peaks will tend to provoke resistance—well justified resistance, more often than not.

Another reason that in-depth observations are preferable is that they can help determine whether or not a particular entity is at or close to a fitness peak. Where the entities on the landscapes being modeled are individuals, groups, or organizations, we would anticipate evidence of conscious migration towards higher fitness will be present in past behavior. The reporter may well be able to assess proximity to a local peak by examining the nature of the search process through which the entity reached its current fitness state. Longitudinal investigation of entity fitness—even if acquired through examination of archival data, interviews, and other sources rather than through direct observation—may be extremely valuable.

The skills of a good reporter are those of the expert observer. Not only are the attributes that must be observed likely to be numerous, many will prove difficult to observe directly, such as those relating to participant motivation. Accumulated experience with landscapes similar to the one being observed would be a major plus; it can literally be impossible to see important details if you are inexperienced in similar settings [3.2].

The reporter would benefit from experience in interpreting opinions, as well. While we would like our research to be as objective as possible, the subjective opinions of individuals on matters such as causality may be the single most valuable source of insights in complex and dynamic situations. Direct observational research cannot rely on statistics to lend an air of credibility. The researcher becomes uniquely responsible for deciding what to observe and interpreting those observations.

Another aspect of reporting that differs between decomposable and rugged landscapes is the nature of what the research is trying to accomplish. In Chapter 3, we observed that on the continuum from science to art, the emphasis of research shifts from understanding the fitness function (science) to exploring techniques whereby fitness can be improved (art). That shift, however, becomes evident long before we reach what would normally be considered arts. Looking at fields such as evolutionary biology and genetics, we see at least as much interest in investigating how migration towards fitness takes place as we do in understanding the fitness function itself. Indeed, the process of migration towards fitness is central to much of the landmark research in these domains, from Darwin's original work to Kauffman's (1993) NK landscapes and Holland's (1992) genetic algorithms. Thus, the reporter surveying the rugged landscape needs to be attuned to identifying those characteristics that lead to fitness in a particular region of the landscape, to determining the boundaries of that region [1.3], and to identifying those techniques that can be used to search for states of higher fitness and to transition to those states. The types of theory-of-process findings that may result from the last of these could be of equal, or even greater, value than what has been observed with respect to fitness.

Returning to the three characteristics of impactful research, the results reported by a skilled observer are a likely to be:

1. As rigorous as the reporter's skill allows, with relevance determined by the nature of the situation being observed

2. Resonant in form, since such research nearly always develops into a story, otherwise known as a case study

3. The basis of a pathway through which research can diffuse, since such research nearly always requires on site observations that foster the development of close ties to participants.

In other words, reporter research is uniquely positioned to generate results with impact potential. In Chapters 14 and 15, we further discuss the types of specific activities and projects that can both utilize and build reporting skills.

The Three Dimensions of Focus

The threat posed by disciplinary silos was discussed in Chapter 10. To summarize, silos can interfere with rigor by promoting tunnel vision. Tunnel vision, in turn, means that inconsistent perspectives can emerge without challenge so long as they exist in separate disciplines (or even distinct schools within disciplines).

The problem with castigating silos is that they also make sense. The days of Benjamin Franklin, when a single individual could stay relatively current in nearly all areas of intellectual progress, are long since past. With knowledge accumulating at an alarming rate, it is only sensible that we specialize.

I have also observed that efforts to break down silos often fail. At my university, for example, my department, Information Systems & Decision Sciences, is housed in the Communications and Information Sciences (CIS) building. In the same building are the Communications department and the School of Library Science. The theory behind this arrangement was that since we share similar problems and a strong interest in technology, housing us together would lead to synergy. Regrettably, the extent of our interdisciplinary collaboration has generally been limited to nodding politely as we pass each other on the way to the communal rest rooms[7]. When I visited Northern Arizona University several years ago it was, at the time, the largest business school in the country without formal departments; the object, once again, being to promote collaboration. What the faculty there told me, however, was that the absence of formal structures did not prevent informal structures—virtually indistinguishable from departments—from forming.

The Three Dimensions

In reality, then, breaking down disciplinary silos is one of those ideas that sounds great on paper but is likely to be very hard to implement in practice. What I would therefore propose is rather than eliminating silos, we should simply encourage researchers to participate simultaneously in three distinct types of specialization:

1. Disciplinary specialization
2. Landscape specialization
3. Transdisciplinary specialization

The *disciplinary specialization* would resemble what we have today. Whether it is imperfect or not is beside the point. It exists, it makes some sense, and the energy that would be necessary to break it down would not justify the effort. Enough radical ideas are being advanced in this book so that there is little point in proposing unnecessary fights.

The *landscape specialization* would involve identifying a particular fitness landscape, most likely an industry or type of business (e.g., family businesses, technology startups), and focusing research on that particular domain. Critical to the landscape specialization would be that the objects of study should not be limited to the discipline specialization. A marketing researcher should not choose "marketing departments" as the landscape of interest. Instead, a suitable landscape should offer the potential for research across most or all business disciplines. Thus, a finance researcher specializing in medical services might encounter issues with the information systems being studied. At that point, he or she could then collaborate with an MIS faculty member having the same landscape specialization.

The landscape specialization offers two particular advantages. First, it naturally promotes cross departmental collaboration since virtually no real business problems exist entirely within the boundaries of a single function, another way of saying that they are complex. Second, such a focus will, over time, promote the accumulation of genuine expertise of a kind that will make the researcher a more effective reporter and will also be respected by practice. A consequence will be that establishing the linkages required for such research will become much easier over time. In Chapter 15, I use the agribusiness program at Harvard Business School as an exemplar of how effective the accumulation of landscape knowledge can be.

Many researchers have, at least informally, developed a landscape focus in their research. The *transdisciplinary specialization* is quite different. Its purpose is to promote research activities across a much broader range of disciplines than the other two specializations. Specifically, a transdiscipline tends to be unified by a particular activity or problem that is studied by many disciplines—across many colleges—that may view the activity or problem in different ways. This book, for example, represents a transdisciplinary effort on my part. Its unifying topic is informing. The concepts I incorporate include contributions drawn from management information systems, psychology, sociology, evolutionary biology, economics, statistics, organizational theory, communications, education, philosophy, and quite a few additional sub fields.

There are numerous transdisciplines that have emerged over the past two to three decades, some examples of which are presented in Table 13.2. Common to all is a general area of interest and an extremely broad range of disciplines that are actively studying the topic. Most also have an organizing body that holds conferences and/or workshops and that sponsors publications, such as the *Informing Science Institute*, the *Cognitive Science Society*, the *Santa Fe Institute* (complexity science),the *Decision*

Science Institute and the recently founded *World Society of Motivation Scientists and Professionals.*

Table 13.2: Examples of Transdisciplines

Name	Focus	Typical fields contributing
Informing science	Processes through which informing occurs.	Management information systems, psychology, sociology, economics, communications, education, library science, computer science, philosophy
Network science	Formation and behavior of networked entities.	Computer science, sociology, connectionism, psychology, engineering, mathematics
Cognitive science	Mechanisms of human cognition.	Psychology, artificial intelligence, philosophy, education, linguistics, neuroscience
Complexity science	Behavior of complex systems, particularly complex adaptive systems.	Physical sciences, biology, sociology, economics, neural networks, physics, engineering, computer science, genetics
Decision science	Rational and heuristic decision making.	Nearly all business disciplines, computer science, education, psychology, sociology, mathematics, statistics, economics
Design science	Creating innovative artifacts	Engineering, business, information technology, medicine
Sustainability science	Behavior of human-environmental systems	Geology, meteorology, economics, sociology, government, engineering, medicine
Motivation Science	Human motivation in many contexts	Business, counseling, health care, and athletics

The particular benefit of a transdisciplinary specialization is that, properly implemented, it virtually forces a researcher to experience different perspectives on the same area of focus. This makes it hard for contradictory views to evolve without the need to confront differences—the greatest threat to rigor presented by silos. Unfortunately, my own observation is that transdisciplines can easily develop their own silos—consisting of a particular component discipline's approach to a problem—once the membership of the transdiscipline becomes too large[8]. Because the entire benefit of the transdisciplinary approach is premised on the researcher's exposure to very different approaches to the problem, some formal mechanism for ensuring such exposure takes place is warranted. The *Santa Fe Institute*, for example, offers a variety of workshops, research fellowships, and programs specifically intended to ensure a broad perspective to complex systems is developed.

Acquiring the Three Dimensions of Focus

The discipline and landscape dimensions of research focus can be acquired through a mixture of education, incentives, and recruiting. The transdisciplinary dimension, on the other hand, would require considerable rethinking with respect to how we develop and reward our researchers. For this reason, we consider discipline and landscape focus together, and then look at transdiscipline focus separately.

Acquiring disciplinary and landscape expertise

The acquisition of disciplinary focus is largely determined by the individual's choice of doctorate. Whether this occurs before or after landscape focus is established depends upon the individual's career path. Where the individual joins a doctoral program right out of an undergraduate or master's degree program, choice of landscape is likely to occur after the doctorate is received, during the course of his or her first academic posting. Where a doctoral candidate is recruited out of industry with 5-10 years of experience, on the other hand, it would make sense for the individual to come into the program with a landscape already identified. In that case, choice of discipline may well occur subsequently.

Whereas it makes sense for choice of discipline to be made by the individual, choice of landscape should be heavily influenced by the business school employing the individual. Particular industries and types of business are not uniformly distributed around universities. A university in Florida might want to encourage research into tourism; one located near the Quad Cities on the Illinois/Iowa border might want to emphasize heavy manufacturing. Switching the two would limit research opportunities in both cases. Furthermore, the benefits of landscape focus—encouraging collaborative activities across business disciplines—would be reduced if a researcher chooses a landscape that is of no interest to researchers in other disciplines at the same institution. Setting priorities for "landscapes of particular interest" at a school would therefore make sense. What this means is that recruiting of more senior faculty members and of junior faculty members with industry experience would heavily weigh landscape focus as well as the candidate's discipline[9]. Newly minted faculty members without industry experience, on the other hand, should expect to find themselves strongly encouraged to focus on a particular landscape or choose from a small set of options[10]. Although a researcher's choice of appropriate landscapes might be limited, a school's targeting of particular landscapes focus could offer the researcher broader options for demonstrating fitness than are currently available. A school focusing on tourism, for example, might view articles in a hospitality trade journal—publications that would normally be ignored at a research university—as meaningful contributions to the school's mission during merit, promotion, and tenure decisions. Indeed, not doing so would constitute a failure of common sense[11].

Acquiring transdisciplinary expertise

Transdisciplinary expertise is, at the present time, hard for the individual to obtain and is rewarded inconsistently, if at all. It is hard to obtain because it requires knowledge of diverse fields that tend to view the world in very different ways[12]. Many of these fields also require technical expertise that is not achieved through casual inspection. It is rewarded inconsistently because its quality is often very hard to evaluate. The journals that publish it are not mainstream, the reviewers assessing it are generally unversed in key aspects of what is being argued, and the researchers themselves frequently find themselves at the far edge of their comfort zone—or beyond it (if I can be considered a representative example).

Weighed against these challenges must be the potential benefits of transdisciplinary research. Whereas landscape specialization can be used to build relationships with other business disciplines and with practice, transdisciplinary research builds research relationships that span the entire university. Transdisciplinary topics tend to be important. Otherwise, why would so many different disciplines be studying them? Finally, transdisciplinary topics tend to be of a type where any likely solution will require mustering many different types of expertise. What serious environmental sustainability question, for example, could be addressed without the physical sciences, engineering, business, and government being involved? By getting disparate groups involved in researching a problem, you have also collected the individuals most likely to be able to chart out a plausible solution.

Transdisciplinary professorship

Top universities have already recognized the importance of being able to work across disciplines. At Harvard, for example, the highest academic honor is to become a University Professor. As described by *The Harvard Crimson*:

> The title of University Professor was created in 1935 to honor individuals whose groundbreaking work crosses the boundaries of multiple disciplines, allowing them to pursue research at any of Harvard's schools. (Vittor, 2004)

Typically there are about 20 Harvard faculty members with the University Professor appointment at a given time.

In line with this approach, a plausible way for a university to incentivize transdisciplinary scholarship would be create a new academic rank, above that of professor, specifically intended for individuals who have demonstrated significant transdisciplinary contributions. The career timing of such a rank would make sense. Transdisciplinary scholarship would tend to be particularly effective once an individual has already achieved substantial success within a discipline, since the ability to generalize techniques to across problems tends to grow with practice [3.3]. Entering a transdisciplinary career phase could also re-energize professors whose existing stream of research has become routine, a condition likely to develop after a long period of success [2.3].

Transdisciplinary doctorate

Acquiring the necessary skills to become an effective transdisciplinary researcher will not be easy. Even where the individual is able to acquire such skills independently, he or she may still lack the relationships through which impactful informing is most likely to occur [4.2].

Interdisciplinary doctorates do exist at many institutions. They have the reputation of being weak in placing graduates, however. This is hardly surprising, given the departmental focus of most faculty hiring. The transdisciplinary doctorate proposed here would differ from existing programs in three important ways:

1. Admission would be limited to those who already had senior faculty status (e.g., professors, senior tenured associate professors) and were not actively seeking employment.

2. Participants would already have a substantial research record within their discipline.

3. The program would be designed specifically so that candidates could continue their existing employment while pursuing it.

Streamlined requirements for such a doctorate would make sense given that the socialization and instruction in research methods that normally play an important role in grooming doctoral candidates for their first position would be far less necessary for the transdisciplinary candidate. Instead, the program would emphasize the development of research relationships across the colleges of the university through course work and collaborations on research papers. Dissertation requirements might also be modified; rather than being used to demonstrate the candidate's ability to perform individual work—presumably already demonstrated by his or her first doctorate—collaborative efforts by candidate and committee might be encouraged, designed to demonstrate ability to work effectively across disciplines.

A variety of incentives could be offered to attract faculty members to such a program, such as the previously proposed establishment of transdisciplinary professorships and course release time granted while participating in the program. Based upon the tiny sample of faculty members I have spoken to, I suspect that large research universities would find plenty of applicants among their own ranks. Implemented on top of existing doctoral programs, as they would almost certainly be, their incremental cost would be modest since most course work would already exist.

Three Dimensions and Small Worlds

Before leaving the topic of the three dimensions of research focus, it is important to re-emphasize a key goal that is easily lost in the discussion of content. The key value of the approach is not content-related. It is the construction of a network of enduring relationships.

In Chapter 8, one of the network models presented was the "small world" model, wherein individuals were viewed as members of closely knit networks that mainly communicated internally. Because individuals simultaneously belong to several networks, however, it is sometimes possible to move ideas quickly across great distances through individuals who linked together different networks. Viewed in this light, the motivation for the three dimensional focus of research is to actively encourage researchers to engage with three distinct networks: the discipline, the landscape, and the transdiscipline. As illustrated in Figure 13.1, this greatly increases the number of cross-community linkages in which the researcher can participate. This design should allow research to diffuse more quickly and, perhaps, increase the complexity of problems that we can address successfully. It also encourages diversity in research approaches, which could be the key to survival if we, as business academics, should ever be called to task for our lackluster impact.

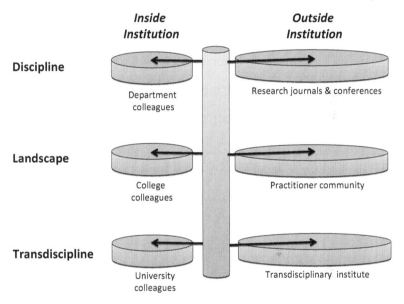

Figure 13.1: Small world view of the three dimensions of focus research model

Changing the Form of Refereed Journals

The refereed journal has proven to be a robust channel for communications between researchers. Our enthusiasm for the medium, however, has—if anything—reduced the impact of our research. It is a channel that practitioners attend to very little, if at all. Therefore focusing on it distracts us from informing the practitioner community. The length restrictions imposed by the article format encourages the creation of theory fragments, since more systematic descriptions of a landscape would take up too much space. The review process tends towards the conservative: accepting the incremental and resisting the transformative. While there will always be a role for refereed journals, we need to wean ourselves from overreliance on them.

The End of the Print Era

One factor that may help us move away from overspecialization on journal content is the strong forces impacting the publishing world. These forces both foretell the demise of printed journals and, at the same time, make alternative informing channels much more practical.

Forces aligned against printed journals

The era of the printed business research journal seems to be coming to an end. There are a number of reasons for this. First, the economics of hard copy are changing rapidly. In the past, libraries tended to subsidize other readers by paying subscription rates that were, relatively speaking, huge. Today, however, the same journal can usually be acquired, at a much cheaper rate, through commercial database bundlers, such as ABI/Inform. Libraries with large budgets have often chosen to acquire both; libraries with large budgets are becoming extinct[13]. Thus, we can expect online copy to become dominant to the point where printed copy does not make sense at any price.

Up to this point in time, the unfavorable economics of paper have, to a great extent, been balanced by declines in the remaining costs of production. It is vastly less expensive to prepare an article or book for printing than it was a few decades ago, when manuscripts were submitted on typewriter paper with hand-drawn graphics. Before that, there was the large added cost of typesetting. Printing technology has also reduced the price of short runs dramatically. In preparing this book, for example, I discovered it was cheaper to print 20 bound copies than it would be to get them copied locally. This is one of the main reasons that the mythical "paperless office" has failed to materialize—the cost of printing has fallen almost as much as the cost of alternatives to hard copy. But we seem to be reaching the limits of savings from that source.

Beyond simple economics, electronic copy also has the advantage of being much easier to search. This is not only true online, but also on the individual's personal computer. Using tools such as Google Desktop I can, for example, search for terms in most of the thousands of PDF and MS-Word files that I keep archived on my notebook.

Advances in technology also make electronic copy much easier to read in its native form. I use a Tablet PC, for example, which allows me to read articles a page at a time, inking comments as I would on paper, with the convenience of reading a book. I recently gave my wife Clare a *Kindle DX* for our 20th wedding anniversary. Using that, she can read and highlight PDF files directly at roughly the same clarity as the printed page using a device thinner and lighter than a typical book. Just before this book went to press, Apple's *iPad* sold several hundred thousand units during the weekend when it was first released.

There is also increasing environmental pressure that works against printed copy. Paper is made from trees: a carbon sink. The ever-increasing space requirements of physical manuscript storage demand energy-intensive climate control. Picking up printed copy may involve an extra trip to the campus. Would shifting to electronic formats save the planet? Very unlikely. On the other hand, many of the same academic researchers who would fight to the death, or at least talk to the death, to preserve their right to paper versions of their favorite journal might meekly submit to the "green" argument, even if the gesture were to be largely symbolic.

Rise of alternative channels

The shift to online format is important is because it fundamentally changes the balance between "elite" and "non-elite" journals while, at the same time, opening up other non-journal informing channels. Publically available academic search tools, such as Google Scholar, attempt to present results using both estimated relevance and citation count as their principal sorting criteria. For general searches, the citation count weighting more-or-less ensures that prestigious journals maintain the advantage they always had. As searches become narrower, however, articles from specialty journals and less highly ranked journals become visible in a way they never did before. Thus, these new journals will be able to compete in a manner that was simply not possible in the past. A reference to an obscure journal not held in your library's print collection could be ignored easily; given the low probability it would be useful, the effort of acquiring it was not warranted. When a search engine places that reference on the first page and includes a link to the associated PDF, it is much harder to justify not taking a look at it.

Not only does search technology make less prestigious journals more accessible, it also opens up entirely new channels for informing. In writing this book, for example, I have been absolutely astonished at how useful Wikipedia can be[14]. I have similarly found individual blogs to be a useful source of opinion and feedback. Later in the chapter, I discuss how these could redefine the way we assess research.

Anonymous Peer Review

C. Chet Miller (2006) paraphrased Winston Churchill to the effect: "Anonymous peer review is the worst form of research assessment except for all those others that have been tried." In Chapter 10, we saw some obvious deficiencies in the process, including the following:

- Inconsistency

- Conservatism, in the form of strong preference for existing paradigms and hypotheses

- Failure to be truly anonymous

I also admitted, at least for my own part, that the mentorship aspects of peer review can be quite beneficial. Moreover, in a trend that I consider truly positive, journals have made constructive reviewer feedback an increasing priority.

Had business research been transformative in its effect—as research has been in some of the sciences—I would probably be urging us to continue doing what was working. Based upon what I have seen, however, the principal success of business research has been its ability to generate citations from other business researchers. Anonymous peer review, particularly when its gate keeper aspect is emphasized, tends to foster this process by encouraging authors to cite the works of others indiscriminately, based on the high likelihood that some of them will be reviewers. It also encourages reviewers to react positively to manuscripts in which their own work is cited, since citation counts are often used as an estimate-of-fitness for research quality. Thus, we have the very sort of positive feedback that tends to lead to phenomena such as information cascades. Elite journals would be particularly prone to the process, since their authors and reviewers tend to be drawn from a tightly knit circle of top researchers within each discipline.

Pressures on anonymous peer review

There are a variety of pressures that may lead us away from anonymous peer review that emphasizes the gate keeper role. The most important of these forces is globalization. Regrettably, the easiest basis upon which an anonymous reviewer can reject a paper is on the grounds that it poorly written or does not conform to the standard research format. Too often, I see reviewers take that easy route. This creates a patently unfair advantage for researchers whose native tongue is English, as well as an advantage to those who have been trained in the U.S. and follow U.S. norms. Jeffrey Pfeffer (2007, p. 1340) describes the process as the "Americanization" of research.

In the long run, the relative influence of U.S. researchers and institutions will necessarily decline as countries such as India and China develop an increasing number of sophisticated institutions of higher education. It is extremely unlikely that researchers from these nations will continue to participate in a process that places them at a disadvantage. One outcome could be that native language journals will emerge to the extent that research becomes completely fragmented. That would tend to flip the advantage in the opposite direction—deservedly so—since the multilingual researcher will be able to take ideas from one fragment and repackage them for publication in the other. How would I know if a novel concept I read about in an English language journal is actually widely discussed in the Chinese journals? As today's gate keepers are increasingly bypassed, their relative importance cannot help but suffer.

Another significant pressure on the process would occur if the earlier recommendations of this chapter and the chapters that follow were to be implemented. The most impactful research category of all tends to be action research—research where the researchers actively participate in the process being described. How can such research fail to impact practice, at least at the local site where it was conducted? In business education research, we already see a great deal of this type of research, since it would be unusual to find a classroom study where the instructor is not an author. As mentioned in Chapter 10, however, a manuscript can pay a heavy toll for maintaining anonymity for this type of research[15].

Anonymity can even threaten the credibility of reporter research. Analytical research—both theory building and empirical—can rely on logic, mathematics, or statistics to support conclusions. Thus, whether the investigator is a disciplinary luminary or a doctoral student can, in theory at least, be discounted. Observational research, on the other hand, depends heavily on what the observer sees and reports. That will depend heavily on the skills of the observer [3.2] and is unlikely to be precisely the same for any two individuals. Thus, awareness of the background of the observer is useful information. Anonymity forces us to give up that information. If the role of the reporter grows, as I proposed it should earlier in the chapter, we can expect this unnecessary loss of information to become an increasing concern.

Forces favoring mentorship

The forces that favor mentorship in the review process overlap the forces working against the gate keeper role. Reviewers and editors will, from time to time, take an active role in helping authors for whom English does not come naturally. Anonymity works against this process, however, since it often involves a considerable amount of back-and-forth exchange. Keeping reviewer identities anonymous also prevents credit for such efforts from being given in a meaningful way. Offering heartfelt thanks for help provided by "an anonymous reviewer"—as is often done in journals today in the "Acknowledgments" section of a published paper—is rather impersonal given the depth of assistance that I have seen rendered in some cases.

Increased emphasis on transdisciplinary scholarship also favors an increased mentorship role. If my own experience in the informing science transdiscipline is anything to go by, the effort to view problems from new perspectives frequently requires us to delve into areas where our familiarity is limited. The reviewer with strengths in areas where we may still be experiencing some confusion can be a valuable asset. That is true, however, only if they happen to view mentorship as an important part of their role as reviewer. If they perceive themselves to be a gate keeper, they will more likely to serve as an immovable road block.

Forces favoring no review at all

A final approach to the peer review process would be to abandon it altogether, allowing articles to be published after a modest editorial review to prevent spam and obviously inappropriate content. That is the philosophy of the Social Science Research Network (SSRN) and is proposed by Pfeffer (2007, p. 1342) as a reasonable solution. The ability of tools such as Google Scholar both to catalog articles and keep track of citations to an article (allowing its fitness to be estimated) makes this a plausible approach. As previously noted in Chapter 10, however, I place more value on the mentoring aspects of the review process than some others do, such as Pfeffer. Thus, I feel that peer review should continue, despite its obvious imperfections.

Changing Our Research Estimate-of-Fitness

Even if the suggestions I have made regarding impactful research make sense to the reader, it is extremely unlikely that we will see them implemented if we do not change how we estimate the fitness of our research [2.2]. Thus, even though I believe that journal articles will never exert a strong impact on students or practice, their disproportionate current influence on academic careers cannot be ignored in designing an informing business school.

Presently, there are four ways that business research productivity is routinely evaluated:

1. Number of publications

2. Number of publications in "suitable" journals

3. Number of citations to published works

4. Quality of the ideas and impact of research

I include the last because some institutions claim that to be the criteria they use. I am forced to admit, however, that I have not actually seen concrete evidence of it being applied in recent years[16].

With the exception of the last (as a matter of definition) these measures do not do a very good job of assessing or predicting impact. To illustrate just how bad a job they can do, I return to a favorite target of this book: my own past research. I then consider ways in which our estimate-of-fitness might be improved.

The Folly of the Three Measures

The inherent weaknesses of the approaches by which we estimate the fitness of our research started to become glaringly apparent to me during one afternoon in 1998, while I was an Associate Professor at Florida Atlantic University.

A strange afternoon in 1998

I had just finished interviewing a job candidate, Dr. Yogesh Malhotra, when another faculty member, Dr. Ron Dattero, came running by my office yelling:

"We're 32! We're 32!"

I had no idea what he was talking about. But he seemed determined to speak with me, in particular. I raised my eyebrows to Dr. Malhotra, signifying I did not know what was going on. Then I let Ron explain.

It turned out that *Decision Line* had just published an article ranking MIS research departments. Florida Atlantic University's department had come in at 32nd in the world over the 5 year period covering 1993 to 1997, inclusive. Ron wanted to speak with me in particular because Harvard, my alma mater, had come in at number 50. Imagine my chagrin...

Later, although I cannot recall if it was in the same afternoon, he relayed some information to me a bit more sheepishly. It appeared that my two *MIS Quarterly* articles (see Chapter 11) had contributed roughly three quarters of the department's points[17]. Part of his sheepishness may have stemmed from the fact that just over two years earlier, he had chosen to abstain on my tenure vote because, despite the fact that I had one published MISQ article and one accepted, I had not met the '5 refereed publications in 5 years' standard that the department formally applied[18].

It gets better... Later, when I looked at the article, I realized something even more astonishing. Departments were ranked by productivity score:

Pages * Journal quality factor / Percent authorship

The authors on the list were ranked by number of papers (Im, Kim, & Kim, 1998, p. 10). Had they been ranked by productivity factors, the same as departments, *I would have been the 15th most productive MIS researcher in the entire world during the 1993 to 1997 period.*

It is my hope that the sheer lunacy of such a proposition will convince the reader that estimating research fitness by journal rankings is not a robust metric. There are two key factors that led to my purported luminary status: a) I worked alone on the project (reducing the formula's denominator) and b) I tend to be long-winded (bloating its numerator with large page counts). Personally, I am not sure that it is in the best interest of research quality to reward richly either of these two dimensions of "quality".

The citation count approach

So, does citation count work much better as an estimate-of-fitness for research? Not much, at least in my case. To understand why, let us look at the two articles that I wrote in 1995 and compare their actual impact (as best can be determined) as contrasted with their citation counts. The first article of mine to come out that year was "High tech hidebound: Case studies of information technologies that inhibited organizational learning", published by *Accounting, Management & Information Technologies* (Gill, 1995a; henceforth, the "AMIT article"). The second was "Early expert systems: Where are they now?" (Gill, 1995b; henceforth the "MISQ article").

Using raw citation counts, the MISQ article comes out the clear winner. As of the time I wrote this paragraph (29 September 2009), it had 81 citations in Google Scholar, whereas the AMIT article had 47. Even more critically, the MISQ article had 43 citations in Thompson/ISI's Web-of-Science. What makes this critical is that journal impact factors are computed using the Web-of-Science database and, internationally, many countries will not accept publications for purposes of merit, promotion, and tenure unless they are listed in this database. Unfortunately, because AMIT is not one of the journals currently listed in Web-of-Science, it is essentially invisible.

If you look more deeply, however, quite a different picture emerges. We begin with the MISQ article. A citation count of 81 sounds great but, if you compare it with other MISQ articles published around the same time, it is a bit of a laggard[19]. MISQ, as it turns out, is a citation generating engine. Unfortunately, for citations to be generated, you need to be researching a topic that others are looking at. As it turns out, my second article in the series (Gill, 1996) was the last MISQ article to be published with expert systems in the title (11 were published overall). What this would seem to suggest is that the actual number of citations might have been higher if I had chosen a topic that was not near the end of its shelf life.

I am not entirely speculating in making this last comment. When I actually looked at why my article was cited, what I discovered was that the most common reason—by far—was to reference some introductory comments I made about the decline of standalone artificial intelligence. These comments had very little to do with the subject matter of the article; they were added principally to motivate the reader's interest in the topic. Yet those comments seem to be the principal source of the article's interest to other researchers. By the end of 1995, with the acceptance of the second article, my own research into expert systems ended as well.

The AMIT article presents a very different story. To begin with, the research was the starting point for nearly all my later research into time horizons and complex systems behavior; its impact on me is indisputable. In addition, nearly all the citations that I looked up actually referred to the research in a context relating to its key findings. In some cases, the article appeared to have had a profound influence on the entire piece.

Which brings us back to the subject of Dr. Yogesh Malhotra, the individual that I was interviewing that afternoon in 1998. The interview was particularly memorable because I have never before encountered an applicant who first greeted me by saying:

> "I want to shake the hand of the man who wrote 'High-Tech Hidebound'!"

I originally assumed this was just a case of shrewd interview preparation. But I later concluded he was actually being sincere. In fact, he had referenced my article on numerous occasions, had run a seminar under the "High-Tech Hidebound" title, and had titled a chapter "From Information Management to Knowledge Management: Beyond 'Hi-Tech Hidebound' Systems" in a book that he edited (Malhotra, 2001).

The story does not end there, however. In Chapter 2, I mentioned that the AACSB report on research impact had identified two areas of MIS research that had exerted impact on practice. One of these was the Bass diffusion model—which had been developed by a marketing professor. The other was described as follows:

> In information systems, the research of Malhotra has helped companies to understand why knowledge management systems fail...(AACSB, 2008, p. 19)

This happened to be the central theme of my AMIT article, as well. While my suspicion lingers that alcohol might have been involved in AACSB's efforts to find areas of MIS research impact, the haphazard chain of linkages I just describes suggests that my AMIT article did have an impact on the formative stages of the knowledge management field. Oddly enough, I did not make this discovery until I began asking myself the question—for the purposes of this very book—of how impact might more effectively be measured.

Table 13.3: Levels of Citation

Type	Description
Fundamental	The source being cited was fundamental to the researcher's understanding of the topic and contributed significantly to its form. Normally, such a reference precedes the actual research or causes it to become redirected in a major way.
Incremental	The source provides incremental understanding and results in significant changes to the research or analysis.
Supporting	Used to support or justify a statement so that the author does not need to.
Clarifying	Provides a reference that can be examined to clarify what is being said.
Obligatory	Cited not because it was particularly important but because the researcher feels obligated to make the reference. Seminal contributions to a field are often cited in this manner, as are articles that might be authored by potential reviewers. These citations often have not even been read by the author and frequently appear as one of a list of citations.

In fact, citations can mean many things. For my own use, I classify them into five categories, such as those shown in Table 13.3. The citations that *really* matter are the fundamental ones, with incremental ones being of value as well. The remaining three levels are necessary if your work is going to make it through review, but don't really affect the research conduct or results to a great degree. At most, they impact how the research is worded.

Beyond the question of citation level, there are a variety of factors that can impact citation count that are not necessarily a result of the quality of the research or its level of impact. Popularity of the topic being researched is an obvious one. Another is the type of research: meta-analyses and research that incorporates many references tend to garner many more citations (Judge, Cable, Colbert, & Rynes, 2007). And, the big one, publishing in a prestigious journal outlet.

All of this might be viewed as acceptable error but for the fact that big decisions, ones that profoundly impact the life of the researcher, are made based upon estimates of research fitness. That means how we estimate that fitness will have a big impact on the type of research we do [2.1]. The overriding problem with citation count is that it directs researchers towards a very specific goal: *being cited by other researchers*. This goal would seem, in many ways, to be the exact opposite of, or at least irrelevant to, what we would want to see our researchers striving towards if we care about impact.

Measuring Research Impact

An easy-to-acquire estimate-of-fitness for research impact is an unlikely prospect. If we believe such impact is important, we will need to work at measuring it. Without a means of measurement, there is little hope that we will seek out impactful research projects purely on altruistic grounds.

Impact of research on researchers

The impact of an individual's research on other researchers is the easiest area to demonstrate. I attempted a crude version of that very process when I contrasted my MISQ and AMIT articles. Using tools such as the Web-of-Science and Google Scholar, identifying articles that cite your own work is straightforward. By going to those articles and looking at the context in which you were cited, it is relatively easy to identify the level of citation according to Table 13.3. Moreover, the classification that you make can be documented by block quoting the actual citation.

Naturally, this process would be excruciatingly tedious for those rare individuals with papers garnering thousands of citations. They might, therefore, choose to limit themselves to classifying how their work was used in papers that had similarly large numbers of citations. Or they might choose to ignore the justification process entirely; once you become a "household name" in your discipline, there likely to be minimal career benefit to such undertaking such activities. There may be some personal benefit, however. I think a researcher can learn a great deal through understanding what portion of his or her work is used and what portion ignored.

If research impact is valued, the objectivity of this process could be further enhanced by journals in two ways. First, online commenting could be enabled and archived for all articles. This would provide readers with a tool for reporting the degree to which the research has impacted them. It would also provide a post-publication mechanism for discussing the rigor of the article. A number of journals and magazines, such as eLearn, already allow such commenting. Given today's growing movement towards digital publication, I would recommend that it become universal. I would also suggest that these comments should be linked to each article's abstract, which is to say freely available even in journals that charge for online access.

Even as we wait for journals to begin universally allowing us to comment, I would propose that we should be searching blogs and other public web sources for evidence of impact. While looking for an example of how blogs might help us better understand how our research impacts others, I came across a posting by Alison Ruth (2007), of Griffith University in Australia, which began:

> I was reading (rereading for the umpteenth time) Grandon Gill's 5 (Really) Hard Things about Using the Internet in Higher Education. It's from eLearn Magazine published early last year. There are some interesting points that I'd like to think about, because I'm sure many of us are overwhelmed by the changes in what we do.

She then spent well over a page detailing both her agreement and disagreement with the specific points that I had made (mainly disagreed, I might add). But that did not matter to me. According to Google Scholar that particular article had been cited exactly once—and that was by me. I had come to suspect that what I had written was entirely invisible.

Yet here was someone I never met who had spent a great deal of time thinking about what I had written. I cannot even get my students to do that, and I grade them! I would gladly exchange 100 casual references for one such indication of real impact. I would also add that if we judge the impact of our research solely based upon it being cited by other researchers, we are missing that huge segment of our potential audience that does not routinely publish.

A second technique for increasing the reliability of impact measures is implicitly suggested by Juan Miguel Companario'a (1993) article on research difficulty, where he used the authors' own reflections in *Citation Classics*®. I see little reason why such reflections should be limited to the classics. Instead, once an article is accepted by a journal, the authors should be required to write a short essay on the process they experienced in conducting the research and getting it published. As part of that, they should specifically identify their foundational and incremental references[20]. I believe these essays would be highly instructive to other researchers. They might also highlight the role played by non-academic authors—such as Malcolm Gladwell, whose writings have obviously played a foundational role in forming many of my ideas—in the research process. I tried to do this with my list of (no more than five) references included at the end of each chapter of this book.

Because search engines have become very good at picking up this type of commentary, were research comments and research reflections to be hosted on journal sites, they would rapidly diffuse to the broader audience of scholars with limited formal publications.

Impact on students

Impact on students tends to be felt locally, at the researcher's own institution. At one of my universities, the annual self-evaluation form that we had to fill out included an item where we were asked to detail something along the lines of:

> *Evidence that your research is being incorporated into the courses you teach.*

I am not at all sure if anyone paid any attention to what was written in response. If we want our research to impact students, questions like this should always be asked and weighted heavily.

Other items that should be given a heavier weight than might be typical in top U.S. research universities include:

- *Textbook authorship*: Like it or not, textbooks are a major informing channel through which our research can flow. The authors of such textbooks are likely to have far greater impact on our students than the "top" researchers who view textbook authorship as a pedestrian activity. Synthesis, of the sort required to write a good textbook, is valid a form of research.

- *Textbook citations*: Having one's research cited and discussed in a textbook vastly increases the likelihood that it will not be invisible to students—who are very likely to become practitioners.

- *Teaching case study development*: Discussed in much greater detail in Chapter 15, the teaching case study represents the intersection of informing students, practice, and other researchers.

- *Pedagogical research*: Pedagogical research—an activity existing entirely on the dreaded left hand side of AACSB's example institutions chart presented in Table 13.1—is likely to be the most impactful research that is routinely conducted by a faculty member today. Why? Because such research is generally conducted in the context of a classroom by individuals who will make decisions based upon the results.

- *Involving students in research projects*: Interestingly, this is an area where a lot of institutions seem to be placing greater priority[21].

Institutions might also encourage instructors to blog about their use of research in their courses. Not only would this provide evidence of their own commitment, it would also offer evidence to other researchers whose findings were found to be useful.

Impact on practice

Chapter 15 is largely devoted to the subject of how research can impact practice. Measuring this is likely to be particularly tricky, since businesses will not necessarily wish to see specific examples of impact published. Similarly, while publication in practitioner-focused journals and magazines is laudable, and should be encouraged, such publications are unlikely to exert a major impact. Practitioner-focused books may be a more effective channel for reaching a small fraction of the audience, as is discussed in Chapter 15. Nonetheless, for complex research findings to diffuse broadly, face-to-face interactions will likely be required [4.2].

As a proxy for research's direct impact on practice, it would therefore make sense to focus on face-to-face channels rather than on some measure of citations by other researchers. I would consequently propose that we should be attempting to measure the individual's network of connections to practice when actual impact data is not available. Connection measures might include:

1. Number of active research projects involving practice

2. Number of case studies of local organizations developed by the researcher

3. Degree of active participation in local business service organizations

4. Degree of participation in alumni organizations

5. Number and magnitude of consulting projects

By building connections, the researcher not only creates channels for his or her own use. He or she establishes connections that could potentially be used by other researchers, such as departmental colleagues, through which practice may be impacted. Just a few individuals in a department focusing on such network building could vastly increase the entire department's impact effectiveness. This will only take place, however, if the process is recognized as research and rewarded accordingly.

Motivating impactful research

Substantial effort on the part of the individual would be required to gather many of the proposed measurements for impact and its proxies. Such activities could be "encouraged" by institutional or accreditation standards that place a high priority on demonstrated impact.

The genuine risk of such encouragement is that easy-to-acquire estimates-of-fitness will be employed under the guise of objectivity. In the teaching area, I see this happening frequently as a consequence of our attempts to meet standards for assurance of learning and academic learning compacts required by accrediting agencies and our state legislature. To demonstrate our accomplishments in learning, we attempt to devise objective and replicable approaches to testing what our students are learning. Unfortunately, tests of this form are much more likely to focus on specific content—much easier to test reliably—than on skills that are less defined, such as judgment in the face of uncertainty. Regrettably, as I discuss in the next chapter, it is skills of the latter type that are critically needed to cope with a world of growing complexity.

Conclusions

On a complex landscape, the detailed and carefully made observation by the skilled reporter in the field is the most rigorous form of research. In a happy coincidence, the same process leading to such observations also tends to create research that can resonate. The research can often be presented in the form of stories [4.3]; in the process of making the observation, face-to-face channels through which it can diffuse are established. With enough of these observations, we should be able to develop a clear picture of the shape of the fitness landscape for a particular set of organizations or individuals. That will be particularly true if each of us chooses a particular landscape to investigate systematically, as part of our research agenda.

Ironically, a key technique we today employ to ensure the rigor of our research—anonymous peer review—tends to work against the publication of rigorous observational research. By demanding anonymity, we hide the experience of the observer from the reviewer thereby eliminating a potentially important source of credibility. Statistically-grounded survey work has the advantage here, since it can be rendered almost judgment-free. By emphasizing the gate keeper role in peer review, as opposed to mentorship, we greatly increase the likelihood of Type II error: excessive conservatism. Surprising observations, however, are inevitable on a rugged landscape. Rather than treat them as outliers, as we are inclined to do when we encounter them amongst a cluster of "better behaved" observations, we need to recognize that these may be the forerunners of major changes to the system that we are observing and are also likely to help us in establishing the boundaries [1.3] for any theory or conceptual scheme that we hope to develop.

If we want to motivate researchers towards engaging in more impactful research, we would do well to remember two things:

1. If you want to achieve research impact outside of academia, you should be focusing on the inter-personal networks that re-

searchers develop, rather than on the number of articles they publish.

2. Achieving a foundational impact on a few individuals is much less common, and much more valuable, than achieving a superficial impact on many people. Superficial impact will soon attenuate [3.1]. Foundational impact will last and will tend to be passed on. Researchers should be rewarded for identifying cases where their findings have demonstrated such impact and should be encouraged to identify those writings of other researchers and practitioners that have exerted a strong influence on their own thinking.

Keeping these two facts at the forefront of our thinking, we may be able to avoid developing policies that actually discourage impactful research—such as using raw citation counts—rather than motivating researchers to do more of what they are already doing.

Chapter 13 Foundational References

Colquitt, J. A., & Zapata-Phelan, C. P. (2007). Trends in theory building and theory testing: A five decade study of the Academy of Management Journal. *Academy of Management Journal, 50*(6), 1281-1303.

Gladwell, M. (2000). *The Tipping Point.* New York, NY: Back Bay Books.

Pfeffer, J. (2007). A modest proposal: How we might change the process and product of managerial research. *Academy of Management Journal, 50*(6), 1334-1345.

Rogers, E. M. (2003). *Diffusion of innovations* (5th ed.). New York, NY: Free Press.

Shanteau, J. (1992). Competence in experts: The role of task characteristics. *Organizational Behavior and Human Decision Processes, 53*, 252-266.

Chapter 13 Notes

[1] Where I specifically refer to an observation from Chapter 12, which I do quite a bit, I put the observation number in braces. [2.1] therefore refers to Observation 2.1.

[2] I have frequently heard colleagues from outside of business comment on the sheer number of publications often found on business faculty CV's, including my own. Also surprising, at least to those in the sciences, is how many of these are single-authored or have just one co-author. It is not unusual for scientific research, particularly research funded by large grants, to have a dozen or more authors.

[3] Clayton Christensen (2008) predicts that online education options will completely transform K-12 education within the next 5-10 years. I have not heard him make such a prediction for business education (perhaps because he is a professor at Harvard Business School) but I would argue that research business schools are even more vulnerable.

[4] At my university, for example, an Implementation Science task force has been created with health sciences and engineering faculty being its most active members.

[5] As an example of the diffusion of theories, my wife Clare has served as a substitute teacher in two adjacent school districts—Hillsborough County and Pasco County—and the two are premised on entirely different theories of education leading to very different classroom experiences.

[6] Naturally, I do not believe that the adoption of education theory is the sole reason that private and parochial schools generally outperform their public school counterparts. To the contrary, I believe that the nature of the students, the commitment of their parents, and the social climate of the school play a *much* greater role in the short term quality of education. I do not believe these factors are entirely divorced from the adoption of educational theory either, however. Parents who prize educational fitness will adapt by placing their students in the setting that they perceive to offer the greatest chance of success. If the best students are pulled out of public school as a consequence of a belief that private and parochial education are superior in outcome, the process can create its own reality, as only the most disadvantaged students remain in the theory-driven public educational environment. Christensen, Horn, and Johnson (2008, p. 98) predict that by 2019, 50% of high school classes will be conducted online, largely as a consequence of this disruptive student-centric technology's ability to bypass the existing public education system paradigms.

[7] *Note to myself:* I really need to meet with the chairs of these other departments and tell them about what I'm doing. It was only as I was writing this that the truly pathetic nature of what I was describing dawned on me.

[8] For example, at the *Decision Science Institute's* (DSI) annual meeting—which I have attended many times in the past—the participants typically number about 1500. There are sufficient presentations scheduled that it becomes possible for a participant to attend only those given by members of his or her own discipline. And, not surprisingly, many do. I am as guilty of this as anyone, almost exclusively attending sessions in the innovative education and classroom technology tracks. What I experience at DSI is very different from the experience at the Informing Science and IT Education (InSITE) Conference. In that conference, about 1/10th the size (150 participants), it is almost inevitable that I find myself attending presentations from disciplines whose perspective is nearly foreign to me.

[9] In my experience, considering landscape as a significant factor in recruiting is already occurring to some extent at the department level, although somewhat less so at the college level.

[10] To many of my colleagues, "strongly encouraging" junior faculty to pursue a particular research agenda might seem like an attempt to curtail academic freedom, which is premised upon being able to choose your own research topics. I would respond to that in two ways. First, if we really want to develop impactful research, we need to accept certain constraints on the research that we undertake. Second, freedom to pursue a particular research agenda does not guarantee freedom from the consequences of that choice. When a department decides to prioritize a particular journal or set of journals, for example, the researcher becomes constrained either to choose topics that the journal publishes or accept the consequences of being out of line with departmental priorities.

[11] Unfortunately, pointing out that something is a "failure of common sense" may not prevent it from happening at many research institutions. To the contrary, we, as academics, often revel in our ability to discard common sense in our pursuits—with predictable results.

¹² As Editor-in-Chief of *Informing Science: the International Journal of an Emerging Transdiscipline*, for example, I never know whether the next article I pass judgment on will come from my own area, MIS, or from education, philosophy, computer science, economics, psychology, or from some entirely different field.

¹³ Some journals choose to withhold their most recent issues from the database in order to motivate the continuance of subscriptions. Doing so, however, is likely to reduce their "impact factor", which only considers citations 2-3 years after an article is published. When libraries facing fiscal emergencies choose to abandon print copies, impact factor will surely be considered. Ultimately, that will force journals to keep database content current if they are to maintain their prestige.

¹⁴ My praise for Wikipedia will likely be treated as evidence of weakness in my scholarship by any critics who read this book. Two major criticisms are generally leveled against this tool. First, we tend to know little or nothing about the expertise of the individuals who created the articles on the site and they are not peer reviewed; its rigor can therefore not be guaranteed. My response is that the rigor of peer reviewed articles is far from assured (see Chapter 10) but that when a peer reviewed article spews self-indulgent nonsense, it lives on in the literature forever. In Wikipedia, on the other hand, it tends to get rewritten quickly.

The other common objection to the tool stems from the same dynamic aspect of its content just described: it cannot be referenced the way an article can, since the content you are referring to may have changed completely by the time a reader follows the reference. This is somewhat problematic, I admit. For this reason, I am very reluctant to reference a Wikipedia article directly. That does not, however, undermine its usefulness in rapidly confirming ideas that you are not absolutely sure about. For example, while writing Chapter 3 I looked up *superposition*, a term I learned in physics thirty five years ago but have had little reason to use since that time. Wikipedia can also serve as an excellent short cut to initial references on a new topic.

Any discomfort I have with Wikipedia stems from the fact that it serves as a constant reminder to me of my own limitations as a forecaster. Had the tool been described to me a decade ago, I would have laughed and asserted, without reservation, that such a tool could not possibly develop. The notion that collaboratively developed content, without individual credit or compensation being awarded, could lead to the most comprehensive summary of the world's knowledge ever created would have struck me as patently ridiculous. I thank my lucky stars that no one actually asked for my opinion at the time!

[15] In case the issue of anonymity in action research seems like a minor one, be assured that I do not view it as such. Last year I resigned my post as Associate Editor of the *Decision Sciences Journal of Innovative Education* in protest when I got a revise-and-resubmit of a manuscript that I submitted to a special issue on qualitative research that I happened to be in charge of. The manuscript was a case study that did a comparison of process and outcome for three classes that my co-author and I taught. Nearly all the reviewer comments were useful. The editor assigned, however, insisted on two changes: that my co-author and I make the manuscript more anonymous and that we reduce its length. When I indicated that I was enthusiastic about making all the recommended changes but those two, we were told that would *not* be sufficient. We then pulled the piece, changed it in consideration of the many other excellent reviewer suggestions, and submitted it to the *Journal of IT Education*, where it was promptly accepted (Gill & Jones, 2010).

[16] Harvard Business School, of course, ascribes to the "impact of research" philosophy and they certainly have the means to hire faculty whose research has demonstrated impact. They can also point to the case of Michael Porter, now a University Professor at Harvard, who legend has it was tenured before publishing his ground-breaking work on competitive strategy (Porter, 1980) because the dean at the time was so impressed with his ideas. That was, however, a long time ago. On the other hand, at a doctoral reunion I attended in the spring of 2009, the junior faculty I spoke to were all *very* concerned about what journals they were publishing in, so I am not sure HBS is currently as different as they make themselves out to be.

[17] To save the incredulous reader the time of doing what is a meaningless computation, the scoring scheme used by the authors of the ranking article, Im, Kim, & Kim (1998), computed rankings by taking journal pages in specific "elite" journals and multiplying them by a weighting factor, then dividing by the number of co-authors and allocating the result to the author's affiliated university. Between them, my two *MIS*

Quarterly articles were 60 pages, the weighting factor was 3.54, so I had 212.4 points. The total for FAU was 286.15, meaning I was responsible for about 75% of the points.

[18] The tenure vote was done by secret ballot but, to his credit, Ron came to my office immediately after the department meeting and explained why he had done what he did. Since it was a principled stand on his part, not a personal attack, I shrugged the whole matter off. I mention it here just to point out that the "paper count" standard *is* used by some to estimate research fitness, should there be any doubt on the matter.

[19] While researching this chapter, I discovered that *MIS Quarterly* pieces published during the mid-1990s typically garnered well over 100 citations according to Google Scholar. Only perhaps 20% of all articles published around that time were under 80 citations.

[20] The essays on how an article's research was conducted *should not* be created until the review process is complete. One can easily imagine reviewers being influenced should their own research be listed among the foundational sources.

[21] The reader may recall from Chapter 11 that undergraduate students were instrumental in helping me prepare for my expert systems research project. That made me a true believer in student involvement in research.

Chapter 14

Informing the Student Client

Roadmap & Objectives: Continuing the series of chapters devoted to recommendations, this chapter proposes that we change our curricular focus from teaching routine business processes across many disciplines to building core skills for coping with complexity and providing opportunities to practice these skills.

Throughout this book, I have emphasized the impact of system complexity on informing and decision-making. Many of the bad decisions that have recently cast such a shadow over the management profession can be described as a failure to deal with complexity and the shortened time horizons it produces. If a business school is to take an active role in addressing this problem, student and practitioner clients must be better informed regarding the perils of complex decision making.

In this chapter, we specifically consider how business schools can help students to better cope with complexity, leaving the practitioner side for Chapter 15. The chapter is organized around three issues. The first is the types of learning objectives we might expect when improved coping with complexity is our ultimate goal. What I propose is a focus on improved ability to recognize the presence of complexity, better self-understanding of how it impacts our individual decision-making, and enhancing low structure decision-making skills.

The second area examined is the nature of the content relevant to helping our students better react to complexity. Consistent with the learning objectives, the large contemporary literature on management biases and heuristics represents a good starting point. How informing impacts, and is impacted by, complexity is offered up as another. Unfortunately, there are significant limits to the degree to which "content" of any sort is likely to exert a lasting influence on students. Thus, the manner and sequence of content presentation is likely to be far more important than the actual content itself.

This leads to the third area: how content can best be conveyed in order to meet our learning objectives. In this context, alternative approaches, including lectures, case discussions, simulations, experiential learning, and other strategies are contrasted. What quickly becomes evident—and should come as no surprise—is that no single strategy is ever likely to emerge that produces optimal fit between student, instructor, and content. What I therefore propose is that an informing business school should actively seek to establish a portfolio of teaching/learning approaches and should actively manage that portfolio.

Actually Listen to Practice

I began Chapter 13 by encouraging us to "get over ourselves" when it comes to research. I begin this chapter by suggesting that we actually listen to what practitioners are telling us about what they would like from our graduates. With the exception of a small number of doctoral students, nearly all of our students are in business programs because they plan careers in business. Doesn't it make sense for our curriculum to be driven by employers?

Over the years, I have—on three different occasions—been involved in focus groups that have asked executives about what they were looking for in our undergraduate programs. Being in the MIS area, what my colleagues and I were hoping to get was specific direction—Microsoft SQL or Oracle? C++ or Java? Systems development lifecycle or agile development methods? In other words, we wanted the type of useful, constructive feedback that would allow us to fine tune our existing programs.

No matter how we phrased the question, however, the general response we got nearly always involved ensuring students had the following four categories of skills:

1. The ability to communicate effectively, both orally and in writing

2. The ability to work effectively with people (I include project management in this category).

3. Good problem solving skills

4.   The ability to learn while on the job

You could easily argue, of course, that I do not have a representative sample[1]. What I can say, however, is that I have presented this observation to many groups of academics and have published them in a number of papers (e.g., Gill, 2009a). In spite of these efforts, I have *never* had a colleague come up to me or contact me to tell me how different his or her experiences have been. I have, however, *always* seen nods of agreement in the audience when I made these observations.

That leads to two comments. The first is a trifle inconvenient. The four areas represent skills we do not directly teach[2]. Rather, we view their acquisition to be a natural (and unmeasured) side-effect of our curriculum. The second is that they encapsulate what are probably the four most valuable skills that can be acquired if one's goal is coping with complexity. This should tell us a great deal about what managers actually want. Let us now consider what a curriculum based around these skills might look like.

Complexity and the Undergraduate Curriculum

Of particular interest to this chapter is the business undergraduate curriculum. There are a number of justifications for this focus. First and foremost, undergraduate business programs dwarf graduate programs in their potential impact. According to the U.S. National Center for Educational Statistics (NCES), there were 327,531 undergraduate business degrees granted in 2006-2007 time period, compared with 150,211 masters degree granted. These numbers, however, significantly understate the importance of the business undergraduate degree since many students enrolled in masters programs have undergraduate business degrees[3].

A second reason is that master's degree programs will necessarily be much more diverse in their structure and goals than undergraduate programs. Or, at least, they should be. Whereas it is not entirely implausible to base a design on the assumption that most undergraduates have limited formal training and experience in business[4], the same cannot be said about master's candidates. Selective recruiting by graduate programs, on the other hand, allows an institution to admit students with a targeted experience levels (e.g., programs may choose to market to students right out of their undergraduate programs all the way up to seasoned executives) and set of interests (e.g., specialized master's degree programs). Each of these would have to be considered separately, as their informing needs will tend to be quite different.

Finally, there has already been quite a bit written on master's degree programs, such as Mintzberg's (2004) *Managers not MBAs* and Khurana's (2007) *From Higher Aims to Hired Hands*. These tend to ignore undergraduate business entirely[5]. I completely sympathize with their decision to focus on the students they tend to teach. But that does not change the fact that *most* business education, in the U.S. at least, is taking place at the undergraduate level and that education is also occurring at a time in life when we are more likely to be able to influence student attitudes than will be the case by the time they reach graduate school. Hence, I view undergraduate business education to be the more pressing of the two informing challenges.

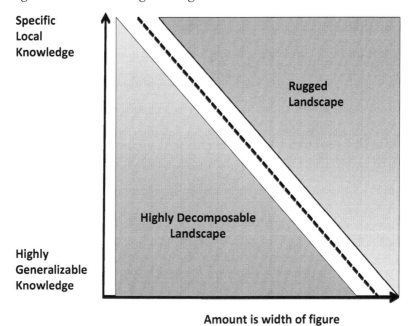

Figure 14.1: Hypothetical distribution of theory-of-fitness for a task based on the nature of the underlying landscape

Complexity and Course Content

Recognizing that a landscape is generally rugged has important implications for curriculum design. As illustrated in Figure 14.1, we would expect a decomposable environment to involve a lot of generalizable knowledge—in other words, problem spaces that broadly apply over the landscape—and relatively little activity-specific knowledge that does not generalize—problem spaces that are very task-specific. In a rugged environment, the situation is reversed; the amount of activity-specific knowledge is high, while there will be relatively little highly generalizable theory.

Today's undergraduate business curriculum

Just as I have argued that research assumptions should reflect the underlying landscape (if we care about its impact on practice), the same would make sense for our curriculum—particularly at the undergraduate level, where the assumption is that students enter with relatively minimal existing knowledge. As we just saw, tools for coping with ruggedness also happens to be the knowledge most requested by practice.

Matching curriculum content to the shape harmonious with a rugged landscape would be a major undertaking for most universities. Consider the typical undergraduate business program design, as portrayed in Figure 14.2. It begins with a disconnected series of core courses tied to the individual business functions (e.g., accounting, finance, marketing, MIS, management). These feed into a disciplinary major that begins with disconnected required courses some of which, perhaps, serve as prerequisites for some advanced courses, which may or may not be electives. Finally, many programs end with a major-specific capstone course intended to integrate the concepts; internships are also encouraged with the same integrative goal in mind. These experiences may tie to some of the courses outside of the individual's major (indicated by the light arrows from the bottom to the top); in many cases, even that is too much to hope for. If we believe the business landscape to be largely decomposable, this is not such a bad design. It encourages the perspective that effective management is a matter of breaking problems up into their functional components, then individually maximizing the fitness of each component.

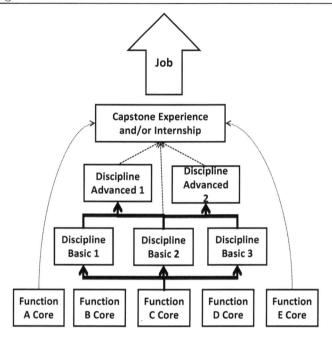

Typical Undergraduate Business Curriculum Design

Figure 14.2: Undergraduate business program typically has core courses, a couple of levels of courses in the major and some form of capstone experience

The "stacked block" approach

From a pedagogical standpoint, even if the landscape were decomposable the curriculum illustrated in Figure 14.2 leaves much to be desired. With the possible exception of one or two courses in the individual's major, there is very little opportunity to practice skills learned at the lower levels. That means that virtually every piece of knowledge acquired in the core is likely to attenuate severely [3.1]. If we really believe that the content we teach is important, then a much more sensible approach would be illustrated by the stacked block design presented in Figure 14.3. This would allow skills to be practiced, thereby allowing core skills and some intermediate skills to be retained[6].

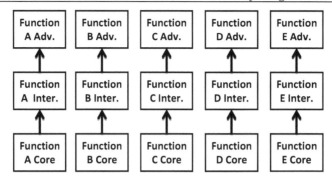

Decomposable "Stacked Block" Design

Figure 14.3: Design for decomposable disciplines, providing opportunity to practice the core skills repeated times

An inverted pyramid design for a rugged landscape

Unfortunately, the "stacked block" design is unsuited to rugged landscapes. Reinforcing the impression that functions or activities can be treated independently is the last thing we want to do when complexity is high. As suggested earlier by Figure 14.1, content relevant to most situations is rare in such a world. That argues for a much smaller core combined with numerous opportunities for practice later in the curriculum. The core would be would be much smaller—emphasizing business vocabulary and fundamental skills, such as basic accounting—and would be highly integrated across disciplines. Because our landscape is rugged, we do not want our students perceiving that the consequences of decisions in one function can be made independently of decisions in other functions. At the next level, we might have a similar intensive course in core disciplinary concepts—since businesses, like it or not, are organized around functions—but, more importantly, content focused on developing core skills applicable across all functions. Finally, to reinforce the skills taught at the lower levels, the bulk of the curriculum would consist of integrative experiences—such as internships, capstone courses, and other activities. Ideally, the individual's job activities might even begin before the program ended. This program design is illustrated, side by side with the conventional design, in Figure 14.4.

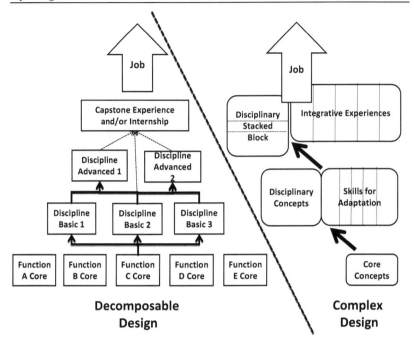

Figure 14.4 Alternative program designs appropriate for decomposable and complex fitness landscapes

Components of Proposed Design

There are many who question the wisdom of an undergraduate business major no matter how it is designed. This includes, ironically, the Carnegie and Ford foundations in the late-1950s, who led the initiative that transformed U.S. business schools[7]. It seems to me, however, that paying too much attention on *what* is being taught to undergraduates, as opposed to the *how* and *why*, is probably a mistake. I see no reason that a particular liberal arts course of study—say sociology, philosophy, Elizabethan literature, or Chinese pottery-making—is intrinsically better than business for young, impressionable undergraduate minds. If the student is interested, many important life lessons can be distilled from any subject provided we present it properly; if the student is not interested, we will likely have equal long-term success teaching a house plant.

So, if students are interested in learning about business as part of their undergraduate experience, why should we deny them that opportunity? Admittedly, there might be just a hint of self-interest here. If we stop teaching undergraduates in the U.S., we would probably need to dismiss about half of our faculty members or more. Recall from Chapter 11, I like my job.

The question then becomes: how does it make sense to teach business? To answer this question, we now consider the various layers of Figure 14.4.

Core Business Concepts

What does an undergraduate *need* to know about business? This question can be framed in terms of competing forms of complexity, as described in Chapter 3. One form of complexity, *problem space complexity*, is a function of the amount of knowledge—such as rules and concepts—that are necessary to perform the "business" task. The other is *objective complexity*—emerging from number of entities, degree of interconnection, and presence of dynamic change—that has been the central focus of this book. If you believe that the challenges businesses face are principally driven by large, stable problem spaces governing each separate function, then our goal should be to teach as many rules and concepts as the constraints of time and student cognitive capacity will allow. If rugged fitness landscapes dominate, on the other hand, there will be far too many peak-specific problem spaces to cover in any meaningful depth; we would therefore do better to focus on helping our students to develop the general skills to cope with such landscapes.

As pointed out in Chapter 1, some of the major figures in business over the past half-century did so without any formal business training. Many did not even have an undergraduate degree. This would seem to argue that there is no specific business knowledge that a student *needs to learn in school.* That does not mean that knowledge is not important in business. It just means that there are other ways of picking up whatever specific knowledge in needed, should it be that we educators happen to miss something.

A more practical way of posing the original question might be: What knowledge and skills do we want to *require* of our undergraduate students by the time they graduate? I believe the "by the time they graduate" qualification here is critical. What it implies, as a practical matter, is that the particular desired outcome must be practiced and reinforced on multiple occasions spread throughout the curriculum. Knowledge that is not practiced will attenuate [3.1]. Spreading practice over time also helps in the process (Willingham, 2008, p. 94; Rohrer & Pashler, 2007).

It is unlikely that core skills will be reinforced across a curriculum by accident. It is true that a department may be able to design a sequence of courses to ensure that its particular objectives are met. But this reinforces the very disciplinary silo mentality that we should be trying to avoid. Thus, ensuring that each skill is practiced needs to be a schoolwide priority, incorporated into the design of classes at every level.

How much time needs to be devoted to instilling the core business concepts? Not a great deal, I suspect. I base this opinion on three distinct observations, not one of which is particularly conclusive on its own:

1. *As already noted, business education does not seem to be the prerequisite to business success.* I believe this to be a function of the ruggedness of the business landscape—where relatively few universal rules apply—rather than of a systematic failure on the part of business educators. Nevertheless, it seems that much of what we teach is not necessary.

2. *My own experience distilling what I know about my own field.* Back in the mid-1990s, I was asked to write a ghost-write chapter on MIS by a finance colleague, Jeff Madura (1997), for his book *Introduction to Business*. I was surprised by how much content I could superficially cover in a single chapter and, indeed, by how much information on all fields that single book contained.

3. *The success of "business boot camp" programs.* Many top institutions, including U.C. Berkeley, Dartmouth, and NYU, run summer "business boot camp" programs, typically lasting 5-8 weeks, for liberal arts and engineering undergraduates to prepare them for a career in business.

I believe the last of these is particularly noteworthy. One of the original programs, at Dartmouth's Tuck School, was developed in close cooperation with McKinsey, the prestigious consulting firm. McKinsey viewed the program as a way to supplement MBA programs as a source of highly qualified graduates (Rafter, 2004). That a consulting firm should have been involved in the early stages of such a program is highly significant. There are few industries where the benefits of a broad knowledge of business—as opposed to disciplinary focus— match those of management consulting. Thus, their willingness to accept core business knowledge—gained in a matter of months—as a substitute for degrees lasting 2-4 years speaks volumes for the value they place upon more universal basic skills, such as those acquired in the liberal arts. Naturally, these skills include strengths in communications, problem solving, and ability to learn. Also significant is the fact that employers often recruited candidates for these programs and then paid the student's fee (e.g., $7000 for the Dartmouth program; Rafter, 2004).

Disciplinary Courses

The question of what constitutes the disciplinary core of knowledge is somewhat more variable. Accounting, in particular, might have a considerably different structure from other disciplines, assuming that a program makes preparing students for the CPA exam an objective. Otherwise, the role played by disciplinary courses would be substantially reduced in the new curriculum. This is consistent with my earlier observation that such specialization does not seem to be demanded by the managers recruiting our students.

There are, however, two advantages that are likely to accrue from having some specialization. First, it allows students to identify (and broadcast to potential employers) an area of interest in a tangible way. Since considerable functional specialization exists in practice, that will make it easier for a student to present the case that he or she is attracted by a particular job in that function. The second reason is that it is likely to be valuable for a student to have at least one mastery experience. The type of expertise that is acquired through such a sequence is qualitatively different in character from the general knowledge experience acquired in a survey course.

To incorporate specialization, the design proposed in Figure 14.4 includes one disciplinary "core concepts" course and a stacked block experience in one area of the discipline. The former meets the needs of identifying an interest area. The latter exposes the student to the process of acquiring expert knowledge. To omit that experience from an undergraduate program would place business undergraduates at a significant disadvantage to their counterparts in the sciences and engineering, all of whom will have experienced several such sequences during the course of their undergraduate years. The same applies to many of the social sciences and humanities (e.g., languages, music), where advanced knowledge cannot be acquired without prerequisite knowledge [3.2].

Skills for Adaptation

The skills for adaptation courses would be cross functional courses intended to introduce the student to tools that increase their effectiveness in the four core skills necessary for adaptation in a complex environment, namely:

- Communicating

- Working with others

- Problem solving

- Understanding how to learn

It could be argued that a generic focus on these items looks more like a liberal arts agenda than a business-focused curriculum. My response to this observation would be two-fold. First, to the extent that we do not instill these generic skills, we can expect business education to be supplanted by approaches that do; witness the success of business "boot camps", whose target student is precisely the one most likely to have acquired such skills in the course of his or her education. Second, where business programs have an advantage over liberal arts programs is in our ability to educate students in these skills without needing to be generic. The diversity of business lends itself to activities and examples involving all four core skills. As a student of literature, you can gain insights into human relations by reading the great novels of fiction. I see no reason why the same insights cannot be acquired through examining the in-depth studies of business situations. The main difference is that in the latter case, the student may also gain some specific knowledge of business practice that may prove useful in a future job. In reading Jane Austen, such incidental knowledge is more likely to consist of the importance of finding a gentleman with a suitable income should you happen to find yourself suddenly an unmarried yet attractive woman of limited financial prospects in the early 19th century[8].

A particularly problematic aspect of the suggested focus on skills for adaptation in the curriculum is that we have little experience in teaching them[9]. One solution, of course, would be to outsource. My students routinely remind me of a lesson learned in other business courses they have taken: when an activity falls outside an organization's core competencies, outsourcing is the appropriate solution[10]. Under this path, we would work closely with other areas, particularly in the liberal arts, to develop courses relating to the core skills that would then be taught by other colleges. I am certain these colleges would welcome the influx of students as a means of bolstering their enrollments. It would also afford these colleges the opportunity to disabuse our students of any notions that capitalism can be a beneficial economic system, a point I return to in Chapter 16.

My own preference would be for us to take on the task ourselves. The business context we already know (*or should* know). The concepts associated with the core skills we can—*and should*—learn. What I would also point out is that the transdisciplines proposed in Chapter 13 as plausible research areas also map quite well into the core skills. Table 14.1 is presented to capture the flavor of the mapping although there is quite a bit more overlap than the table suggests. For example, an activity involving learning could easily fall into the informing science, cognitive science, or complex adaptive systems domain of study. Thus, if we were to follow the recommendations of Chapter 13 with respect to conducting such research, we would find ourselves well prepared to design useful instruction in the core skill areas.

Table 14.1: Transdisciplines and Core Skills

Name	Core Skill	Examples
Informing science	Communications	Advertising, communications, technology diffusion
Network science	Collaboration	Leadership, project management, organizational behavior
Motivation science		
Cognitive science	Problem solving	Managerial economics, decision-making, creativity, systems analysis & design
Decision science		
Design science		
Complexity science	Learning and adaptation	Organizational dynamics, industry dynamics, innovation, design, evolutionary economics
Sustainability science		

Integrative Experiences

The typical business curriculum today ends with some sort of capstone experience, intended to integrate the lessons learned in the (largely) disconnected courses leading up to it. From the rugged landscape perspective, this could be characterized as our attempt to repair the damage we inflicted upon our students by encouraging them to think of the world as being decomposable in all of their earlier courses. My preference, however, would be to minimize the damage we inflict in the first place. Even then, we are likely to need multiple integrative experiences to repair what damage was truly unavoidable, since the same "simplicity" that facilitates informing works necessarily works against recognizing complexity.

Creating a curriculum where integrative experiences play a large role will be challenging. In the first place, I am very suspicious of integrative courses that rely heavily on lectures, or even stories. The whole purpose of integrative experiences is to force the student to confront situations of realistic complexity. Unfortunately, many of the factors that make a lecture understandable—simplifying the material and presenting it in a step-by-step manner—effectively disguise the underlying complexity of the task being described. I cannot count the number of times that I had students come up to me in my introductory programming class saying,

"I understood everything you said in class, but when I tried to do the assignment, I could not." And programming, as a task, is vastly less complex than the typical business activity[11].

The other problem associated with integrative course design comes from the fact that students are likely to be heterogeneous with respect to how they learn best. Thus, it would probably be a serious mistake to design a curriculum around a single pedagogy unless you specifically attempt to attract students most likely to thrive under that system. Harvard Business School and other case-method schools attempt to do just that in their MBA programs—emphasizing their reliance on case method teaching to potential applicants. That works to a certain extent, but is likely to fail some of the students, such as those who did not realize what they were getting into. It is also likely to be impractical for institutions that need to accept a high percentage of applicants, such as many public universities. What this means is that most schools would need to include a portfolio of teaching and learning approaches among their integrative approaches. This topic is so important that the next section specifically focuses on proposing some integrative alternatives to lectures.

Integrative Alternatives to Lectures

The lecture has been the central pedagogical pillar of business education, particularly as conducted in the U.S. at the undergraduate level. As noted in the previous section, however, if we are to provide integrative experiences that help the student practice skills for adaptation and coping with complexity, we need to employ a number of other approaches to facilitate student learning in a diverse community. In this section, some examples of these techniques are presented.

Case Method

The case method is a pedagogy that is normally conducted in a classroom and involves students discussing a situation with the goal of making a decision. The case study discussed is normally a fairly detailed document—ranging from 10-25 pages, including exhibits—that is written based upon a real world situation, usually in the form of a story [4.3] without a clear ending. The instructor, who might better be called a facilitator, calls upon students to identify relevant case facts, analyze the situation, and justify the decisions that are recommended.

The case discussion has long been the core of graduate business education at some schools (a.k.a., case method schools). Relatively few schools systematically incorporate it into the undergraduate business curriculum and many instructors are not particularly faithful to its precepts even at the graduate level. In understanding why, it is useful to begin by looking at critiques of the case method, after which we can consider its role in integrative education.

Critiques of the case method

I have been able to find relatively few systematic critiques of case method teaching. I believe this to be unfortunate, since the case method approach—or *any* pedagogical approach—is not likely to be universally useful. It is only through understanding the limits to its effectiveness that we can determine where it is best applied (and how it can be improperly applied) [3.1].

The most systematic attempt to discredit the case method that I could find was written by Steven Shugan (2006), a widely cited scholar in the marketing field, in an editorial written for *Marketing Science*. He specifically identifies seven issues that he asserts warrant abandoning case discussions in the classroom. So as to avoid introducing my own interpretations, the introductory statement for each item is quoted verbatim as follows (Shugan, 2006, pp. 113-114):

> First, the Socratic case method is extraordinarily effective for teaching many skills (e.g., applying written law); however, it is ancient and inferior to the scientific method...

> Second, the case method weakens the link between research and classroom, removing critical incentives for relevant research...

> Third, surrendering teaching to those with little knowledge of the vast marketing literature cuts the quality of marketing education...

> Fourth, the case method can teach false confidence...

> Fifth, we could lose our best students. Better students, who have already acquired analytical thinking skills and confidence, might seek more scientific content and technical training...

Sixth, some great research might never reach the classroom because translating it into the case-method format is too challenging...

Seventh, the case method rarely exposes students to the latest tools for making better decisions...

If we look at these criticisms, we can detect a number of distinct themes running throughout. First and foremost, he believes that the marketing discipline exists on a highly decomposable landscape. Thus, he equates marketing research with the hard sciences in several places (e.g., his first, fifth and seventh point). In the discussion of his fourth point, he also suggests that a tolerance for ambiguous thinking—which he concedes may be an outcome of case discussions—is probably not a good thing; I take that as meaning that he does not believe the typical real world problem has multiple viable solutions.

He also does not appear to believe that resonance is a critical component of the research process. This is suggested by the sixth and seventh points, since research that is too challenging to translate into an example problem situation is probably going to be devilishly hard to diffuse to practice[12]. Similarly, when he talks about the "latest tools", he appears to be using the academic time scale, wherein:

> many well-executed research projects, usually conducted over months (if not years) by well-trained researchers and subjected to a review process for months (if not years), produce outcomes usually vastly superior to anything even diligent students could produce in a weekend of intensive case discussion. (Shugan, 2006, p. 112)

Personal experience tells me you can go from case site identification to employing the case for classroom discussion in a few weeks (if the need is great). Which leads to the third theme: he does not believe that case development constitutes research, as noted in his second item and also as implied by the seventh, which suggests that a tool observed in practice and reported by the case-writer does not represent a valid "latest tool". In this opinion, he obviously diverges from that expressed by Jeffrey Pfeffer (2007, p. 1337) in management, who pointed out that the vast majority of tools used in practice were developed outside of academia.

At the other extreme of the case method criticism continuum, Henry Mintzberg (2004, p. 52) makes the following comments:

> Reaching a logical conclusion and knowing how to convince others of it are certainly important aspects of managing. But overemphasized, as they are in the case study classroom, they can distort the whole managerial process. Managers have to sense things; they have to weave their way through complex phenomena, they have to dig out information, they have to probe deeply, on the ground, not from the top of some mythical pyramid [the organizational hierarchy]. The "big picture" is not there for the seeing; certainly not in any twenty-page document; it has to be constructed slowly, carefully, through years of intimate experience...

In other words, he is arguing that a typical decision is far too complex to be presented accurately in a case study.

The only area where Shugan and Mintzberg appear to agree with respect to the weaknesses of the case method is their tendency to engender overconfidence to the point of arrogance. Shugan (2006, p. 113) makes this his fourth point, although he does not supply any supporting evidence for his assertion. I suspect that this is because there is none that would meet his scientific standards for rigor. My own attempts to measure this effect (described later in this section) lead to the opposite conclusion. If anything, the case discussions make my students less confident in the decisions they initially proposed upon reading the case.

Mintzberg's (2004) opinions on the subject seem to be heavily influenced by observations of Harvard Business School MBA students. It is indisputable that they are subjected to a two-year program that relies heavily on the case method. It would *mainly* be true, based on my own observations, that they graduate with an attitude sufficiently arrogant to annoy co-workers across the globe. It would, however, be *entirely untrue* to assume that they entered the program in a humble frame of mind. Thus, to assume that their arrogance was a product of the case method strikes me as an act of the most egregious sort of abduction[13].

My own view is that there is a grain of truth to both criticisms. If you truly believe the environment being studied is filled with "right answers" and universal truths that can be found through persistent research, as Shugan (2006) appears to, then the case method may not be the best tool. That he can hold such beliefs given the marketing field's appalling track record in the area of replicating its research findings (Hubbard & Armstrong, 1994, p. 233) amazes me, but that was the subject of a different chapter.

Mintzberg (2004) is certainly correct in believing that case studies in no way capture the true complexity of real world situations. On the other hand, neither do the problems that are taught in elementary physics (ignore friction—in your dreams!) or psychology or any other subject. Should we forgo reading Dickens simply because we will never be able to appreciate his descriptions of London street life the way a native of that period could? Excluding doctoral degrees, the curriculum design theme of Mintzberg's book seems to be that management training should be limited to specialized[14] master's degree programs and mid-career programs for individuals already expert in management. Is there no room for less advanced students interested in business?

Drawing upon my own experience, both as student and facilitator, I will readily concede three weaknesses inherent in the case method. The first is the dependence of discussions upon the skills of the facilitator. There are myriad ways that an instructor can mess up a case discussion—all of which I have been guilty of from time to time. He or she can over-control the discussion or under-control it. By doing the former, the case becomes transformed into a lecture or narrative; the latter tends to convey the sense that any solution proposed is workable—an entirely false notion. The instructor can choose a set of cases that leads the students to generalize ineffective rules—this is particularly true when what actually happened after the case is over-emphasized[15]. Perhaps worst of all, the instructor can ignore the inherently integrative nature of a case study and facilitate it solely from the perspective of his or her discipline. Experienced facilitators and course designers are aware of these pitfalls and can, to a certain extent, avoid them. Unfortunately, experienced instructors are increasingly difficult to come by—a fact upon which Mintzberg (2004, p. 65) and I agree.

The second weakness of the case method is that it depends heavily on the students. I can think of no pedagogical technique where participant "buy in" is more critical. No instructor can make a case discussion effective if the students arrive unprepared. A strong desire for consensus can also wreck a discussion. Cultural factors play an important role in participation that can easily be underestimated[16]. All this becomes particularly challenging when students entering the course have no prior case discussion experience. Unfortunately, at all but a few select schools, this student inexperience with the pedagogy is the rule.

Perhaps the greatest weakness of the case method is the frustrating inability to assess case method learning outcomes (fitness) in any objective way [1.1]. Where specific content or skills are being conveyed, they can be tested. Such objective testing is extremely difficult in case method courses.

I would describe the problem in the following terms. When you first pick up a new case study, you are placed in the ultimate low-structure decision-making situation. Chances are the industry is one you've never thought about, the company is one you know little about or have never heard of, the product (if applicable) is one you do not care about, and the protagonist may well be entirely different from you in personality, nationality, and gender. You are then asked to place yourself in that protagonist's shoes and make a decision. There are enough variables in this equation, however, that you will find yourself "bonding" with some cases considerably more than others[17]. The variability of such bonding is considerable, however, but plays a big role in your ability to analyze it. For example, imagine how hard it is to put yourself in the decision-making mindset of a manager whom you detest, who is working in an industry you abhor, for a company that you would gladly see go out of business. If you use case exams to assess what a student has learned, however, the error introduced by the variability in bonding is likely to be considerable. Moreover, instructors themselves tend to "bond" with different approaches to analyzing a case, so the grading variability for a given exam will also tend to be great.

Benefits of the case method

Mapped against the four core learning objectives, the case method seems to offer distinct benefits in at least two areas: communications and problem solving. Even Shugan (2006) reluctantly concedes these may be benefits[18], as does Mintzberg (2004). That these benefits should accrue makes sense given the discussion process; communications is integral and even an inexperienced instructor will call students out when the reasoning they present is faulty (which is not that uncommon, in my experience). Moreover, the story format of the typical case study should enhance the natural resonance [4.3] of the method.

The case method is frequently viewed as the epitome of the *constructivist* learning paradigm. What this means is that participants are expected to construct their own meaning out of the process, rather than have a theory or procedure presented to them by the instructor. Since this is substantially more reflective of complex "real world" situations than lectures—even accepting Mintzberg's criticisms—it can be argued that the case method serves to advance the "understanding how to learn" goal.

The goal of "collaborating with others" is the least likely to be advanced by the case method, although institutions such as Harvard now attempt to build that into the process by assigning students to study groups during their first year of the MBA program[19]. On the other hand, case discussions quickly demonstrate the diversity of perspectives encountered across a group of students. In the comments that students make to me each week, I often see specific mention of things students learned from each other. Thus, even the collaboration goal may be advanced by the case method to some extent.

The subjective assessment—on the part of the student—of case method learning is often quite high. For example, I surveyed the Harvard MBA class of 1982 for our 25th reunion. In the survey, I asked them to tell me the greatest strength of the HBS MBA Program and gave them a list of choices. The top three[20], accounting for 80% of all 143 responses, were:

1. The case method (34%)

2. The quality of my classmates and what I learned from them (while in school) (32%)

3. The networking opportunities it afforded me after I graduated (14%)

I see a similar positive reaction to the case method in the graduate courses that I have taught[21]. Obviously, assessing the fitness of the pedagogical approach therefore requires us to balance the highly positive subjective evidence of learning from students with the near-total lack of other objective evidence.

In my own classroom, I have attempted to devise techniques that make the learning that is occurring more transparent, at least to me. I begin each class with a 20 minute period during which I ask students a question that cannot easily be answered simply by referring to case facts.

For example, "If you were the manager in this case, what three actions would you take tomorrow?" Then, after each case discussion has been completed, I have students take 10-15 minutes filling out a form with two key questions:

1. What are the three most important things you learned from reading the case?

2. How did the case discussion change your understanding of the case?

From the responses I get a clear sense of the effectiveness of the discussion. What I have also found is how frequently student opinions are swayed by the discussion—often accompanied by expressions of humility. Here is an actual student response to the second question taken from a class I recently taught using the *Frontier Airlines* case:

> The discussion points definitely opened up many ideas and thoughts that I didn't really think of, allowing for me to see the case from a whole new light, ideas about niche markets and such really allowed me to think outside of the box. I did feel that I had quite a strong understanding of many of the issues that were involved in the case but my downfall was not looking at the different strategies that should be pursued, which I will be doing for the next case.

While I am not sure that this would be convincing evidence of learning to anyone but me, when I see that students are taking away from the discussion what I hoped they would, it gives me some confidence.

In total, I feel that the integrative nature of the case method combined with its self-evident contribution to three of the four core learning objectives makes it a natural component of any informing business school curriculum. Realistically, however, considerable faculty training will be required if it is to be effective. It will also not be a particularly good fit with some students. Thus, it should be viewed as part of a diverse portfolio of techniques; it should not be relied on exclusively. We return to the second element of the case method, case writing, in Chapter 15.

Experiential Learning

Experiential learning involves bringing students into the field as part of their education. There is a broad array of experiential learning opportunities. These include:

- *Internships and cooperative education programs*, where students work for local organizations that are likely to be potential employers. These positions may be paid or unpaid and may be for academic credit or non-credit.

- *Service learning*, where students perform volunteer work for non-profit organizations and small businesses to help them thrive.

- *International programs*, where students get to experience foreign cultures—particularly valuable for U.S. students, who tend to be much less well travelled than their European, Asian, or South American counterparts. Types of programs include study abroad, as well as guided and unguided travel.

The underlying idea behind experiential learning is that observation and participation in field-based activities represents an important aspect of learning that is nearly impossible to achieve in the classroom. Increasingly, U.S. universities are requiring—or strongly recommending—such activities as part of their formal curriculum. We are even seeing this movement in high schools. In Florida, for example, a student must perform at least 75 hours of volunteer (service learning activities) in order to qualify for the state's Bright Futures scholarship program[22].

In order for experiential learning to be successful, we need to ensure that what is observed is internalized by the student. Alice and David Kolb (2009) propose that such learning takes place through a cycle, such as that illustrated in Figure 14.5. The fact that this cycle involves both experimentation and reflection makes it an excellent mechanism for reinforcing the "understanding how to learn" core objective for virtually any complex (rugged landscape) domain. Additionally, experiential learning often takes place in a team or group context (collaboration) and is very likely to involve communication—including written communication if students are asked to put their reflections on paper.

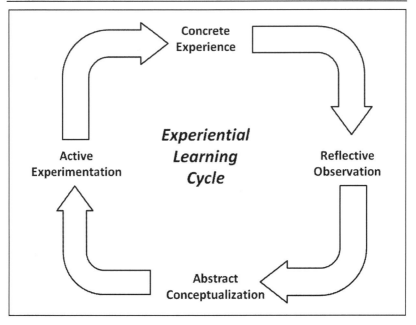

Figure 14.5: Experiential learning cycle proposed by Kolb & Kolb (2009, p. 44)

Where some care needs to be taken, in my opinion, is with respect to goals. Experiential learning, as presented in Figure 14.5, is intrinsically a problem-solving activity. Where there is inherent tension is between the goal of learning and whatever goal or goals are incorporated in the experience itself. In a service learning project, for example, should a student be expected to spend a large part of his or her time doing routine work, such as photo-copying, if the organization needs that work to be done? My own view—one that would certainly be disputed by many academics—is that an important lesson from the process is the experience of accepting the goals of the participating organization. Ensuring such lessons are internalized by the student is the role of the reflection process. Such reflection will not happen automatically, however. Assigned activities, such as keeping an online personal journal of the experience, will help to ensure that some reflection takes place. They may also help instructors identify situations where organizations are taking unfair advantage of cheap student labor.

Perhaps the greatest practical obstacle to incorporating widespread experiential learning into a curriculum is the extraordinary demands of identifying suitable sites, planning comprehensive field trips, and monitoring ongoing student progress over the duration of the experience. This set of activities requires skills that are markedly different from lecturing and even from facilitating case discussions. While some faculty members will demonstrate skills in two or even three of these areas, most are likely to gravitate towards a preferred mode of informing. Unfortunately, this is likely to be lecturing for most faculty members, the skill at which they are most practiced [2.2].

One practical suggestion for enhancing faculty skills in experiential learning would be to encourage them—through incentives—to participate in such an experience periodically, as if they were a student. A side effect of such *faculty internships* would, of course, be to build stronger person-to-person ties to the local practitioner community. While this process would be particularly beneficial to those researchers with limited prior business employment, there are few of us who would not learn a great deal through such an experience.

A variation on the general internship idea is the project-specific internship, akin to a consulting assignment. Here, a team of students is brought on by the organization to complete a project under faculty supervision. Under the direction of our department chair, Kaushal Chari, my department has recently initiated such a program for our undergraduate students. Under this program, members of the department's Executive Advisory Board (EAB) identify projects based on their needs and faculty member expertise and then, over the course of a semester, allow the student teams to complete the project. The department is paid a sum of $15,000 for each project, which goes towards compensating the participants and towards departmental needs. At our most recent board meeting, members of the board committed to supporting five projects during the pilot test, to be conducted in spring 2010. There was unanimous agreement amongst the board members that it was the faculty member involvement that made the program attractive[23].

Student Research

In many of the sciences, significant efforts are being made to bring undergraduates into the research process. The physical and life sciences already have a long history of walking students through research simulations—known as lab experiments—in addition to this more recent initiative.

Research is a very important activity in most business landscapes. It is also likely to become more important, as more frequent discontinuities in the environment, technological innovation, and globalization increase the number of opportunities that research may be able to identify and clarify. Research is, of course, the epitome of the "understanding how to learn" core objective.

The Internet has also made the process of conducting business-related research much easier. In doing so, however, it has also increased the likelihood of making Type I errors (drawing invalid conclusions) since very little quality control exists for many sources. Thus, an important skill that students should learn is how to assess the quality of their sources, and the need to verify their findings through alternative means[24].

In Chapter 15, I make the argument that field-based activities such as case writing (whether they are intended for a journal or the classroom) should be classified as research. The same standard should apply to students' activities. In fact, incorporating a case-writing component into an experiential learning activity (as previously described) would seem to offer an ideal combination of all four core skills. Moreover, faculty could then collaborate with students on further preparing the product to make it more suitable for classroom use or publication. While I have not tried this with undergraduates, I have engaged in this activity with a number of MBA and MS-MIS students and have been quite pleased with the results.

Design Projects

A design problem, particularly one involving a complex environment, can provide a unique opportunity to experience and reflect upon the multi-peaked nature of rugged landscapes. These problems generally fall into the problem solving core objective, although they are often prepared in teams (collaboration), involve presentations (communications), and require moving beyond what is already known (learning).

In the MIS discipline, it is not unusual to have semester-long project courses in which students apply the tools that they have learned in earlier course-work. It would be relatively easy to devise similar projects (e.g., creating a business plan, designing a new product) in other business disciplines. A project would seem to be a natural conclusion to a stacked block disciplinary course sequence, such as that proposed in Figure 14.4. Placing it there would reinforce skills introduced in earlier classes [3.1] and would increase the likelihood that students would be able to handle the associated complexity [3.2].

The ideal design project would have the following characteristics:

- It would be taken from a real world domain where many alternative possibilities are available; this emphasizes the design science aspect of the exercise.

- It would offer the opportunity for collaboration with other students and, perhaps, practice; projects frequently overlap with experiential learning objectives.

- It should be larger than any undertaking the typical student has undertaken (at least as part of coursework); in my experience, a truly complex task is qualitatively different from activities where the student can readily see how to proceed at the outset of the task.

- Results should be presented to both peers and, where possible, practitioners; aside from the obvious communication-skills benefit, seeing the project work of others, and having your own evaluated by an expert, helps reinforce the complex nature of the task.

An excellent example of such a project was developed by Joanne Tucker and Victor Massad (2007), of Shippensburg University in Pennsylvania. A 2006 finalist in the *Decision Sciences Institute's* Innovative Curriculum Competition, the course involved students setting up and running a business on the eBay online auction site. The process began with a $200 loan from the university's dean, after which students planned their business strategy, acquired product, developed a marketing presence on the site, conducted fulfillment and shipping operations, and finally debriefed—all over the course of one semester. Not only were student evaluations of the project high, but all five of the teams profiled made enough money to repay their loan, with an average net profit of $100.

When I have assigned such projects to my own undergraduate students, I have rarely been disappointed with the outcome. Frequently, I have found myself surprised by the highly quality of work coming from students who had not previously distinguished themselves in more routine forms of assessment (such as tests). I would also comment, however, that managing the process frequently requires considerable practical expertise. In the case of programming projects, students would occasionally come to me with errors that took me hours to diagnose. As was the case for the other non-lecture pedagogies discussed, the skills required for this type of activity are not necessarily the skills acquired by a research faculty member. This is another reason that it makes sense to involve practitioners in the assessment process.

Simulations in Virtual Worlds

Capstone courses have often employed computer-based business simulations to give students the experience of participating in a dynamic competitive environment (Gill, 2009b). The underlying concept seems sound enough, but the actual practice may be more questionable. Henry Mintzberg (2004, p. 44) responds as follows to a student's claim that participating in such games made him a better manager:

> Such claims are patent nonsense. That they are made at all suggests how distant such schools are from management practice. Making a sequence of pat decisions on fixed parameters every few minutes so that a machine can tell you instantly how well you have done is not quite like managing in that real world. Indeed, it only compounds the problem created in other courses, by giving the impression that managing is far more orderly and analytical than it really is. While managers out there work in "calculated chaos" and "controlled disorder" (Andrews, 1976), students in here write numbers down on fixed forms.

Mintzberg does go on to suggest that such games *may* have a role in a curriculum—but that role simply has nothing to do with management. Framed in the rugged landscape perspective, what simulation games emphasize is tuning behaviors that are mainly suitable for the periods of relative order that exist between discontinuities. That further implies that they emphasize activities that are likely to be very situation-specific (and that practicing managers are already good at) while making impossible—by the very constraints of the exercise—the type of low-structure innovative activities necessary to cope with discontinuities. It is very hard to "think out of the box" when you are constrained to a particular product, a particular market, a particular set of channels, and a particular set of user-controllable parameters. If practitioners were clamoring for graduates with more specific routine-management skills, I might view the value of these games quite differently. But I have not seen any evidence that they are. Nor, for that matter, have I found any compelling research demonstrating the beneficial impact of the simulation approach on practice[25].

Virtual worlds

If I had been asked five years ago about the likelihood that the nature of simulations would change, I would have expressed strong doubts. And, as so often happens when I try to predict the future, I would have been wrong. What have evolved considerably since that time are incredibly complex virtual worlds. These began with the creation of massive multi-player games (MMPGs), such as *Runescape*™ and *World-of-Warcraft*™, where a player seeks treasure and glory through performing quests in a world inhabited by avatars—controlled by other players—with whom the player can cooperate or compete, the latter often involving battles to the death. At any given time, tens of thousands of individuals are actively participating in these worlds, from all over the globe.

In parallel with these formal games, less structured virtual worlds have emerged. By far the best known of these is Linden Lab's *Second Life*™. Unlike the MMPGs, there is no specific goal established for a Second Life participant. Instead, popular PG-rated activities include socializing with other online avatars, sight-seeing, and shopping. The world is built around virtual islands that are customized by users (who rent them from Second Life) with buildings, furnishings, landscape, and activities. The world has its own currency—the Linden—that can be purchased with real world currencies at floating exchange rates. Interactions between users can be done with text chat (instant messaging) or through voice—a capability that is rapidly improving.

A particularly intriguing aspect of Second Life is the ability to build things. The environment provides a powerful scripting language and drawing tools that allow practically any virtual product to be created. It is even possible to build virtual factories that produce virtual products.

The building facility has been at the core of Second Life's success; rather than Linden Lab having to construct the entire world, the vast majority of what is present has been developed entirely by users. Buildings, cars, bicycles, all manner of clothing, and even body parts (to personalize avatars) are available for sale and, in many cases, for free.

Figure 14.6: My students starting to assemble for a case discussion in Second Life

Academics have flocked to Second Life in droves. For example, a recent issue of the *Journal of Information Systems Education* did a special feature on Web 2.0 technologies with five different articles relating to Second Life (Dreher, Reiners, Dreher, & Dreher, 2009; Robbins & Butler, 2009; Shen & Eder, 2009; Wagner & Ip, 2009; and Wang & Braman, 2009). What seems to motivate them primarily is the enhanced sense of personal presence you get when contrasted with other distance learning tools. In Figure 14.6, for example, you can see my back as my students are assembling for a case discussion that I conduct once each semester on Second Life[26].

Lest it seems as if I am waxing euphoric about Second Life, let me also add that there are currently a number of drawbacks to its educational use. In fact, I positively dread my Second Life class as it approaches each semester. To being with, the environment currently demands more computing power than some of my students have; that means I have to figure out ways of accommodating them. In addition, no matter how many practice sessions we hold, there will always be a few who lose audio or experience other problems. There is also the problem of being a relative newcomer; I would guess that it takes several days of practice to become really smooth at navigating. As for myself, I am continuously bumping into things and people. Just a week before writing this, I had to endure several students ribbing me about the fact that it had taken me over a minute to jump up on the tree stump from which I planned to facilitate the case discussion.

These inconveniences pale, however, when compared with my biggest fear. The first time I conducted the exercise, in spring 2009, after the case discussion I sent my students out into the broader Second Life world for an hour to explore. After that, they were to come back and report what they found. Nearly every female student in the class, and at least one of the males, reported that they had been propositioned by a stranger at some point during the excursion (the most common pick-up line being "do you want to cuddle?"). All it would take would be one student lacking in *either* a sense of humor or a sense of perspective—it is, after all, only a "virtual" environment—and I would probably need to curtail the exercise forever. Interestingly, since that time Linden Lab instituted some new policies intended to segregate the X-rated crowd[27] from the PG participants. When I ran the exercise in fall 2009, not one student reported being propositioned.

A business world?

It seems to be that virtual worlds—perhaps Second Life itself, perhaps a successor—offer an extraordinary opportunity to rethink the entire idea of a business simulation. Consider some of Mintzberg's (2004, p. 44) specific complaints about simulations[28]:

- "Making a sequence of pat decisions on fixed parameters": By allowing users to construct and market virtual products of almost any kind, decisions are neither pat nor are the parameters fixed.

- "every few minutes": Things on Second Life necessarily occur at their own pace, they are not synchronized by a computer that waits for moves to be entered. As a result, simulations in such worlds would need to be much longer—at least a semester long, perhaps a year. What Second Life would allow for is time compression. A facility can be designed and constructed in a few weeks, rather than years. You can teleport to China to meet a potential consumer (or producer) instantly, rather than by taking a 36 hour plane flight.

- "so that a machine can tell you instantly how well you have done": The criteria for success would necessarily be negotiated between students and instructors. Groups could, for example, get credit for service projects (e.g., building a site for a non-profit organization) and for the relationships with other groups they succeed in developing.

I am not at all convinced that such a simulation would be harmonious with the existing Second Life environment. For example, when I was first learning the environment, at one time I suddenly found myself surrounded by six giant chickens each of whom had a stick of dynamite in its respective rear end that subsequently exploded; I believe that goes beyond even Mintzberg's "calculated chaos" and "controlled disorder". Unfortunately, such experiences—along with a fairly wide range of X-rated behaviors that I simply cannot identify with—are part of the existing world's culture. Moreover, I am not sure that a highly goal-directed contingent of business students systematically seeking to use and mold the world for its own activities would be welcomed by the existing inhabitants.

Fortunately, it would also be possible to set up an entirely separate world, run on independent servers, in which global commerce was intended to be the principal activity. Students from around the world could then enter the ongoing (and evolving) environment and attempt to construct their own businesses—whose success could be judged by sales, profit, and service, much the way real businesses are. Such a world would quickly require division of labor. The skills needed to design new products (design skills), construct new the products (programming skills), sell the new products to individuals across the globe (marketing skills), develop agreements (negotiation skills), and manage the entire process to produce a profit (finance and management skills) would create a need for true collaborative efforts across an entire program. Assuming the world goes global—as is very much the case for the existing Second Life—students operating in this environment would also gain practical acquaintance with a variety of issues associated with working in the global environment, including the challenges presented by language, time zones, cultures, and diversity of goals.

Very quickly, such a world would develop its own competitive landscapes, each unique in their own ways. While it is doubtful that these would map directly to real world rugged landscapes, they would provide students with a rich experience in all four core objectives—communicating, collaborating, problem-solving, and understanding how to learn. And, because the resulting environment would necessarily be a richly connected network that is continuously evolving, we would be almost guaranteed to observe punctuated equilibrium behaviors. Because of the time compression involved, they should even occur quite frequently.

Yet again, managing the proposed activity would require instructor/facilitator skills that are far different from those of the typical faculty member. In this activity, however, the desired skills may not even exist at the present moment in time.

A Doctor of Business Education

To repeat what I have mentioned for each integrative learning example, the skills of today's typical research faculty member do not necessarily coincide with those most aligned to the pedagogical techniques just described. He or she may not be used to facilitating cases or managing the activities associated with experiential learning. The informality of the research techniques that students can most effectively apply in practice are likely to be an anathema to the serious scholar and many of us are not practiced in the skills that serious projects demand (even though we could probably identify the applicable body of published theory). As for the activities that could take place in virtual worlds, there are few of us who can face such a prospect without trembling.

Business faculty members are, as a group, among the most intelligent set of individuals that I know. As a result, it is certainly the case that many of us could muddle our way through this unfamiliar territory, perhaps even distinguishing ourselves in the process. Nevertheless, a great many of us would probably shrink at the thought of acquiring all these pedagogical skills. We might even be tempted to employ our formidable skills of logic and persuasion to write articles about the folly of being distracted from our important disciplinary research in order to acquire skills whose underlying purpose we do not grasp.

I believe that informing businesses should be treated as an inseparable element of the research process. I also believe that one of the most effective ways of accomplishing that task is through graduating students who pass their knowledge on. Thus, we need to treat our educational activities as being at least as important as our research agenda. Naturally, there are many of us who would revel in the opportunity to experiment with these new techniques. I count myself in that group. But I also see a role for faculty members who are specifically recruited and educated to be effective in these forms of instruction.

What I would therefore propose is that we need a new type of degree, one that I will call a *Doctor of Business Education (DBE)*, that specifically focuses on research and techniques related to informing business students and practice. Unfortunately, the very name of the degree would be like painting "My plan is to become a second class citizen" on your shirt at a research-intensive school; we've already seen where the AACSB places pedagogical research in the food chain. For this reason, the degree would target three distinct groups:

1. *Existing research faculty members seeking a transdisciplinary specialization.* Rename the degree a Ph.D in Informing Science and ensure that it is taught across an institution's colleges—which would make sense under any circumstances—and it could be positioned as a career enhancing degree.

2. *Faculty members at schools with a reduced research mission or at community colleges.* These faculty members often benefit from acquiring the formal degree and these institutions encourage pedagogical research.

3. *Executive-level practitioners seeking to become business faculty members.* Such a degree could benefit mid- and late-career professionals seeking to transition to faculty positions at research or other institutions. To make degrees targeting this group more palatable, it might be called a *Doctorate in Business Research and Education.*

The last of these groups may seem like a bit of an anomaly—and it is certainly an untested proposition—but there are a number of reasons to believe it might work. My colleague Uwe Hoppe and I discuss the evidence for practitioner interest in professional doctorates in some detail in a recent paper (Gill & Hoppe, 2009). Within the professional group, a substantial fraction wants the degree for career advancement (discussed more fully in Chapter 15). There is, however, another group who see a doctorate as a mechanism for transitioning to academia[29]. The particular interest here is often the desire to teach. Even where driven by the desire to research, a DBE could be quite valuable. The skills for empirical research in business and education are quite similar[30]. Thus, examples of research from both areas could be presented in such a program.

To offer some anecdotal evidence, over the years I have been approached by two MBA classmates interested in transitioning to academia[31]. I was therefore curious as to how common that interest was. So, when I customized the 25th reunion survey for my class, I gave a wide selection of career options and asked my classmates to choose which one they would like to be doing if they were to leave their present career. The winner, by far, was becoming a professor (30% of the decidedly non-scientific sample of 143 responses). By comparison, not a single one wanted to work as a lawyer—despite the fact that quite a number of them already had law degrees. What was particularly interesting was the fact that 10-15 of the respondents appeared to be seriously pursuing the academic career option. Since the survey represented only about 20% of the actual class, the actual demand for some form of convenient doctoral education could be quite large.

There would also be some logical sense to recruiting executives for such a program. Many of the pedagogies described—particularly experiential learning, student projects, and running virtual businesses— would require a set of skills that has more in common with management than with lecturing. As a result, managers who have been appropriately trained might be a better choice to run such programs than traditionally trained research faculty. Given the degree to which business schools are reducing their emphasis on the case method, noted by Mintzberg (2004), we might also more easily find individuals with case discussion experience amongst the ranks of experienced practitioners than in the class of newly minted PhDs.

For the proposed DBE degree to work for any of the three target groups, it would need to have a large distance learning component— since the majority in each group would want to continue working through much of the program. For this particular degree, however, relying heavily upon online learning would make sense under any circumstances, since the use of innovative web-based pedagogies would necessarily figure heavily in the program.

Master's Degree Programs

It is much more difficult to generalize about business master's degree programs than undergraduate programs. For undergraduate programs, we can at least be excused for making the flawed assumption that students arrive with minimal business knowledge and an unclear set of goals. For master's programs, an assumption that was merely flawed becomes ludicrous. Therefore, unless we happen to have an economist's comfort with unrealistic assumptions, it probably makes sense to abandon the pretense.

The first recommendation I would make regarding a particular master's program would be to consult employers with respect to the skills that they are looking for. If they happen to answer "a broad knowledge of business or disciplinary theory" then the problem is solved—we can and should continue doing just what we have been doing[32]. If they respond differently, however, then we would do well to heed what they say. If the survival of business schools depends upon acquiring resources from practice, then ignoring what they ask for because "we know better" would be an inopportune way to launch the relationship.

Suppose, then, practitioners were to give an answer more similar to that mentioned for undergraduates; one that emphasizes core skills. In this case, I would anticipate the essential design proposed for undergraduate education might be maintained in some form, modified in light of the program's expected market. For example, some MBA programs target students coming directly out of an undergraduate program from non-business majors. For these students, the business boot-camp and integrative learning elements of the program would remain relevant. The core skills emphasis in the middle might be reduced, however, in light of the undergraduate profile. Students coming from the liberal arts and sciences, for example, might already have communications and problem solving experience beyond what we might expect from the typical business major. (That, at least, is the assumption McKinsey employed in initiating the business boot camp program).

For students seeking a disciplinary master's degree, a program built around a series of stacked blocks might be most suitable [3.1][3.2].

Presumably, employers seeking graduates of these programs are looking for in-depth knowledge and practiced skills. That assumption needs to be tested, however.

The most difficult common case is the MBA requiring substantial work experience. This would be the typical "flagship" MBA program at top universities and Executive MBA programs at most other schools. Such a program might well choose to eliminate the entire "business boot camp" based on practical experience and instead focus more heavily on skills for adaptation and integrative experiences.

As the potential quality of the online learning experience grows—as it is now doing at a rapid rate—the opportunity for business schools to develop programs specialized to a particular type of student, business landscape, or even pedagogy will grow correspondingly. What this suggests to me is an eventual stratification of MBA programs into three categories:

1. *Prestigious full-time face-to-face experience.* Schools such as Harvard and Stanford can always be expected to have strong residential component. The bonding that occurs as a result is too valuable to the students[33] and the school to abandon.

2. *High-end global specialized programs conducted through distance learning.* With the disadvantages of distance learning becoming smaller every day, the ability to run a global program specializing in a particular function, landscape, or pedagogy will produce a new generation of programs along these lines. Relatively few first- and second-tier MBA and disciplinary master's programs will be able to compete against this onslaught. Here, I am generalizing based on the movement to distance learning that Christensen (Christensen, Horn, & Johnson, 2008) is already predicting at the primary and secondary school level in the near future. As distance learning becomes the "preferred" form of high-end education at earlier stages of education, it can hardly help but experience elevated prestige at later levels.

3. *Local part-time programs.* Most full time MBA and master's degree programs are already experiencing troubles maintaining enrollments in the U.S., part-time programs are doing better. Owing to competition from the global online category, combined with reduced state support for public institutions, we can

reasonably expect the average quality of students enrolled in these programs decline over time.

4. *Low selectivity online programs.* These programs, such as offered by the *University of Phoenix* and Walden University, are already attracting large numbers of students. Their convenience is high and the quality of many of their offerings is also high—although I frequently find this assertion disputed by colleagues whose opinions have been formed without the inconvenience of actually examining the offerings they criticize. The standards for instructor training at the University of Phoenix, for example, are much higher than what I have seen at typical research universities—where the expectation for faculty training in teaching is essentially "whatever you came in with."

This predicted pattern could, of course, prove wrong; indeed, the inability of experts to predict the future in fields such as business and education is a theme frequently repeated in this book [5.2]. What I have described is, however, completely consistent with the trends of technological innovation and globalization that are currently driving many areas of the economy. If this analysis is correct, it bodes ill for the typical, non-elite, face-to-face master's degree program. Schools that are not prepared to adapt to the changing environment can therefore expect to see losses in institutional support for business research as a result of declining enrollments.

Ethics in the Curriculum

The central theme of Chapters 1 and 2 of this book is that if students lose faith in business education, we will find ourselves stripped of the resources that support our research. I believe that there is no single factor more likely to produce such loss of faith than the widespread perception that we are ignoring ethics in our curricula or, even worse, are actively promoting theories that eventually lead to unethical behaviors on the part of managers.

There are two central questions that need to be addressed with respect to ethics. One is where they belong in the curriculum. The second is what we should actually be teaching. Since the first is considerably more straightforward, we consider it first.

Curriculum Placement

Two issues are frequently considered with respect to the placement of ethics within a business curriculum. The first is if it should be taught as a standalone course or integrated with existing courses. The second is whether it should be taught by business faculty members or by faculty from disciplines that study the topic more systematically, such as philosophy.

With respect to the choice of a standalone course or integration into other courses, it is tempting just to answer "yes". If something is important to learn, it needs to be continuously reinforced in the curriculum [3.1]. On the other hand, it is awkward trying to argue against having a course dedicated to the subject.

The concern I have with a stand-alone course on ethics is two-fold. It has been my experience that most ethical dilemmas are unrecognized as such when they first arise. They begin with an unconscious or innocuous act that later evolves into a much more severe problem. In a course devoted to ethics, students would naturally assume that every situation presented involves an ethical quandary. We need to take care that students do not leave a program assuming that every ethical problem immediately advertises itself as such. That might be worse than ignoring ethics altogether.

The second concern with a standalone course is that having such an offering may give faculty members teaching other courses the sense that they no longer need to worry about including ethics in their discussions, since ethics are "covered" elsewhere. Without an ethics-specific course, faculty will necessarily be compelled to incorporate ethical issues, if for no other reason, because accreditation requirements demand it. The view that covering a topic once is sufficient pervades today's curriculum designs (recall Figure 14.2). Once ethics occupies its own box, time will be freed up to present "other important research." I feel much the same way about leadership, globalization, and technological innovation. Each of these is too important to be pigeon-holed into a single course. Instead, we need to see these issues incorporated into *every* course.

With respect to bringing in more expert instructors to teach ethics, I cringe at the thought. To begin with, it seems likely that students will be more receptive to ethical instruction given by individuals who have a generally favorable view of business; these will be extremely hard to find in the typical liberal arts philosophy department. It also sends a very clear message; you typically do not outsource activities that you believe to be central to your mission—as mentioned earlier, this seems to be one lesson our students actually do pick up from our teaching. Finally, one of the natural side-effects of specialization is that very different and inconsistent perspectives can emerge within separate silos and flourish unchallenged [1.2]. Do we really want to give up control of what our students learn about ethics?

Weighed against these arguments is the obvious expertise differential. Wouldn't our students benefit most from access to the ethics experts? My reaction is that given the impact that substandard ethical behavior has had on the public's perception of business, we—business faculty members—would all do well to become experts. If we are unqualified to discuss ethical issues with our students, then we may well be the source of the problem in practice, as some—such as the late Sumantra Ghoshal (2005)—have suggested. In which case, we should rightly be ashamed of ourselves.

Ethics on a Rugged Landscape

A rugged landscape tends to give ethical issues a situation-specific quality that defies general rules. Consider, for example, the case of collusion between competitors. In most industries, such as retail sales, if competing firms were to get together and set prices for specific products it would be a serious ethical transgression, as well as being a criminal violation of the law. In some industries, however, the situation is quite different. The venture capital business, for example, invests money in start-up companies. The vast majority of these businesses fail. A few— the grey swans in the bunch—succeed beyond anyone's wildest dreams. The problem is that it is too expensive for each venture firm to do the type of investigating necessary to determine if a particular start up is worth investing in. So what happens is that a particular fund will investigate a start-up carefully and, if it pans out, will allow a number of other venture funds (its "competitors") to invest as well. This process of sharing investments allows the funds to diversify over a much wider range of investments; the process is critical to the industry's survival. To the start-up's founders, on the other hand, the process has serious drawbacks. It greatly reduces their ability to play one venture firm off against another to get a better offer. It also means that being turned down by one firm is tantamount to being turned down by many. This process is out in the open, however. Thus, it would be hard to describe it as unethical.

In a more general sense, ethical behavior is likely to depend on two factors: 1) the values of the individual, and 2) the conceptual scheme under which it is analyzed. Our ability to impact student and manager values appears to be somewhat limited[34]. We may have better luck in influencing students' ability to detect and analyze ethical issues.

On a rugged landscape, both the ability to distinguish between fitness and estimates-of-fitness[1.1] and the role played by informing are both critical elements of ethical analysis. Consider, for example, the following two statements:

1. The role of the CEO is to maximize shareholder wealth.

2. The role of the CEO is to maximize the organization's fitness.

The first of these describes an estimate-of-fitness that is likely be a function of share price and expected dividend payout. The second refers to a construct that is inherently unknowable; any day a black swan asteroid might wipe out the company's headquarters—meaning its actual fitness the instant before the impact was, in reality, much lower than it appeared to be.

Which of the two is a better guideline to give students? If we choose the first, we run headlong into the types of problems that Ghoshal (2005; Ghoshal, Bartlett, & Moran, 1999; Ghoshal & Moran, 1996) identified as arising from agency theory (Jensen & Meckling, 1976) and transaction cost economics (Williamson, 1975). Individuals may feel justified in taking action to impact share price—up to and including manipulating the stock—because it coincides with their goal. We have seen this problem before in this book. Almost any time an entity fixates upon a single estimate-of-fitness, long term fitness ultimately, and predictably, suffers [5.3].

Choosing the second definition creates its own set of problems. Since true fitness is likely to be unknowable and we are ruling out relying on individual estimators, how fitness is assessed is likely to require considerable justification. For example, we have seen true fitness is likely to depend upon at least three factors:

1. *Current fitness.* In the case of a company, estimators might include the income statement, balance sheet, share price, employee satisfaction surveys, customer satisfaction surveys, and so forth.

2. *Expected fitness in the future.* Fitness based upon our best existing predictions of what is likely to happen. Here we might use economic forecasts as well as some forward-looking present data (e.g., various measures of stakeholder satisfaction may prove to be good predictors of future performance).

3. *Adaptability and diversity.* As argued in Chapter 9, we can reasonably expect environmental discontinuities in the form of grey and black swans will totally transform our landscape at some unpredictable point in the future. Specific actions that we take to ensure our destruction is averted and that glorious opportunities are not missed are key contributors to true fitness [5.3].

Assigning executives the task of maximizing organizational fitness provides them with considerable flexibility in prioritizing different elements of fitness. In the U.S. automobile industry, for example, for many years car makers placed a higher priority on avoiding a strike than upon improving their long term competitiveness. The UAW was equally focused on its short term fitness. As a result, GM and Chrysler were unable to stay out of bankruptcy during the discontinuity that emanated from the housing market bubble[35].

With great flexibility comes a great responsibility to inform. As long as a company identifies as specifically as possible the means of estimating fitness that it is using, and does not make arbitrary or frequent changes to that measure, then there is no reason to assume that maximizing shareholder value is intrinsically superior as a measure—aside from the fact that it leads to more mathematically tractable theory.

As an example of this flexibility, consider the ice cream maker *Ben and Jerry's, Inc.* Despite the fact that they are a subsidiary of a multi-national public company (Unilever), social mission infuses every aspect of the company and their web site. By the shareholder wealth argument, they would need to show how each of those activities contributes to the company's bottom line or be remiss in their fiduciary duties. By the organizational fitness criterion, on the other hand, they have simply chosen to view contributions to causes to be significant in how they estimate their organization's fitness.

Another example is the *Chick-Fil-A* restaurant chain, which is privately held. They refuse to allow stores to open on Sundays, for religious reasons. If the company's executives believe that honoring the Sabbath is important to the spiritual well being of its franchisees, managers, and employees, then it would make sense to factor that into their estimate-of-fitness for the company. If they were to go public, would they need to change that policy? They probably would if they were tasked only with the duty of "maximizing shareholder wealth"—after all, their policy leaves 14% of the days of the week on the table. I would argue, from a purely ethical standpoint however, that as long as that policy was made clear in the initial public offering and they did not sell so many shares that they relinquished control of the company the Sunday-closing policy could persist.

The ethical role of informing becomes critical in both examples. If a potential buyer is aware of the manner in which a company's fitness is estimated when buying a share, then any economic consequences of that estimate should be factored into the share price. Perhaps a Ben & Jerry's share would be worth more had the founders not been activists. Perhaps it would be worth less. The point is that there are few ethical issues here provided they are consistent. Were the owners to suddenly or surreptitiously decide to start marketing their own brand of cigarettes or begin bulldozing a large area of the rainforest in order to build a coal-fired electricity generating plant, then shareholders would have a right to claim ethics had been violated. Naturally, once control has been ceded by the founders or private owners, the ability of shareholders to translate anger into action grows. But, provided management is open and consistent with respect to how it estimates the company's fitness, ethical considerations have been met (at least according to my definition). Ultimately, whether or not the estimate is a good one will be determined by the firm's survival in the marketplace.

Ghoshal (2005, p. 79) quotes economist Milton Friedman (2002, p. 133) as saying:

> Few trends could so thoroughly undermine the very foundations of our free society as the acceptance by corporate officials of a social responsibility other than to make as much money for their stockholders as possible.

While an argument can be made that forcing such a responsibility upon businesses might well undermine freedoms, allowing managers to choose to accept such a responsibility is the very essence of freedom. In doing so, however, they must provide stockholder's with a clear justification as to why they believe such responsibilities are consistent with organizational fitness. Furthermore, shareholders should have the right to take action against management should evidence suggest that management's view of fitness is changing arbitrarily or with the likely purpose of enriching themselves rather than improving organizational fitness.

In addition, management's ethical obligation in informing must be with the goal of ensuring that share price and estimated fitness reflect each other as closely as possible. Where share price is lower than estimated fitness, current shareholders are obviously being treated unfairly. Where share price is *higher* than estimated fitness, the individual buying the stock—who immediately transitions to "current shareholder"—is being treated unfairly.

Encouraging managers to focus on *fitness with transparency* as opposed to maximizing shareholder wealth would help address many of the concerns set forth by Ghoshal (2005), since it allows human concerns to be placed very high—provided that they are communicated to buyers and sellers of shares. Oftentimes a strategy will not necessarily result in the maximum share price for the assets involved, e.g., a firm that focuses on building in adaptability and diversity will likely seem less efficient in the short term. Nonetheless, provided that the fitness estimates of executives are not continuously changing, shareholders can still receive a fair deal. A thousand shares of a stock worth $5 that appreciates to $6 provide the same return as five hundred shares of a $10 stock that appreciate to $12. If the original owners of the company are willing to accept half as much for their stock when the company goes public in order to pursue their particular vision of fitness, then subsequent purchasers of the stock who have been informed of that vision have no moral right to demand that the company change its vision in order to transform the $5 stock into a $10 stock.

At the very start of this book, the importance of trust in business was emphasized. After the collapse of trust that occurred in the past year, Edelman's *Trust Barometer* mid-year survey asked 1,675 global opinion leaders what actions companies could take to rebuild trust (StrategyOne, 2009b, p. 15). The top four actions listed, followed by the percentage of respondents who listed them, were as follows:

1. Treat employees well (94%)

2. Keep producing quality products and services (93%)

3. Transparent and honest business practices (93%)

4. Communicate frequently and honestly (91%)

Contrast the last two of these—both products of informing—with "protect profit margins" (43%). If trust contributes to a company's fitness, as it surely must, then informing must be one of the most important activities of the organization.

Economists may argue, of course, that a company that does not make efficient use of its assets is unlikely to survive against competition in the long term. This would imply that managers who fail to maximize current shareholder wealth are failing in their duty regardless of their personal view of organizational fitness. I would argue, however, that the marketplace may not always value adaptability and vision appropriately, and that some of the firms that have the courage to defy short term earnings growth to pursue their own well-considered goals may, in the long run, be vindicated.

Conclusions

A rugged fitness landscape calls for a very different educational agenda than a decomposable one. Such a landscape will have a vastly reduced set of common principles of fitness. Instead, the core skills of communications, collaboration, problem solving and learning are to be particularly prized.

A curriculum based around core skills, none of which are particularly business-specific, will look very different from that of existing programs. Gone would be the isolated survey courses and highly specialized offerings taught from disciplinary silos. In their place would be far more integrative experiences, intended to provide practice in the core skills and foster a sense of interrelationship between disciplines. Technology can play a major role in these designs, since it provides a mechanism for compressing the constraints of place and time. Ultimately, we can expect technology-delivered programs to claim a substantial share of the existing face-to-face market for business education.

The type of instructor best suited to this new approach to business education is also likely to change. Facilitating courses designed around core learning objectives often demands skills much closer to that of a manager than of a research academic. Moving in that direction would make us much more like our counterparts in other professional schools such as medicine, engineering, and law, where faculty members are much more likely to act in a parallel practitioner capacity than we are. Bringing such skills into our business schools may require a new type of doctoral training; training that emphasizes the skills and technologies particularly suited to informing students and practice.

Better understanding the complex nature of the business landscape may also transform how we educate our students with respect to ethics. The mathematically tractable but narrowly focused emphasis on the ubiquitous shareholder wealth estimate-of-fitness makes less sense than the fuzzier goal of fitness with transparency when the underlying fitness landscape is rugged. Taking this broader view, it becomes possible to understand and even advocate the benefits of incorporating concerns that go well beyond current share price into the organization's objective. Organizations that do so, however, need to become far better at informing stakeholders of their perspective. Hence, the need for curricula that emphasize informing grows even more pressing.

Chapter 14 Foundational References

Christensen, C. M., Horn, M. B., & Johnson, C. W. (2008). *Disrupting class*. New York, NY: McGraw Hill.

Ghoshal, S. (2005). Bad management theories are destroying good management practices. *Academy of Management, Learning & Education, 4*(1), 75-91.

Mintzberg, H. (2004). *Managers not MBAs*. San Francisco, CA: Berrett-Koehler.

Shugan, S. M. (2006). Editorial: Save research—abandon the case method of teaching. *Marketing Science, 25*(2), 109–115.

Willingham, D. T. (2009). *Why don't students like school?* San Francisco, CA: Jossey Bass.

Chapter 14 Notes

[1] That three focus groups with executives is not a representative sample I readily concede. I would also comment, however, that a representative sample drawn from a population on a rugged fitness landscape is likely to be as useful as a representative sample of recipes drawn from a cookbook. What do you do with it?

To illustrate the problem, I refer to the most recent meeting of my department's Executive Advisory Board (EAB). One of the members, the CEO of a small business, suggested that we should be teaching more programming, since he saw considerable demand for that set of skills. Representatives from some larger organizations indicated that they did not normally hire entry level programmers—something that had become evident in previous EAB meetings where we had surveyed participants on the type of skills they were looking for in our undergraduates. The initial member persisted, however, talking about the highly creative things that someone knowledgeable in both programming and business could build. The large company representative then proposed that the type of activities just described were not really what programmers did; in his organization, the individuals performing this type of work would be called "innovators". Then he strongly agreed with the original member—even his large company hired (and prized) innovators.

What is an innovator, however? Essentially, it is someone who combines the ability to learn new things with exceptional problem solving ability. A company will always lean towards hiring someone who has mastered their specific set of tools (e.g., management tools, technical tools, research tools) in preference so someone who as not—*all other things being equal*. When all other things are *not* equal, however, core skills are usually considered the more critical. (Even the board member who was looking for more programmers agreed to this, when I spoke to him after the meeting).

Given the diversity of tools in widespread use, it makes sense for programs to pay particular attention to the timeless core skills, ensuring that these are advanced whatever specific tools happen to be taught at a particular point in time.

[2] In defense of my current department, we did add a project management course is response to a recent round of comments.

[3] NCES also reports 99,998 Associate's Degrees in business during the same period, for which much of the advice in this chapter would likely prove applicable.

[4] When I say it is not unreasonable to assume limited experience on the part of undergraduates, I am referring *only* to curriculum design purposes. Working at a metropolitan research university with a substantial commuter population, I recognize the assumption is absurd when it comes to the reality of our students—many of whom have substantial work experience and academic training in other areas. Nevertheless, they generally accept the fact that we begin with the basics and most seem to prefer it that way.

[5] Some examples of how undergraduate business education is ignored follow. In Rakesh Khurana's (2007) book, in the index the term "undergraduate" has "*See* business schools: education". Unfortunately that entry does not exist. In Ken Starkey and Nick Tiratsoo's (2007) *The Business School and the Bottom Line*, the subject of undergraduate education seems to be ignored entirely. In *Managers Not MBAs*, Henry Mintzberg (2004, pp. 384-388), to his credit, spends almost four pages on the topic. The central theme is established with his quote: "Anyone who insists on a practical undergraduate education should be sent to a trade school; he or she has no business at a university." Ironically, his overall view of undergraduate business education is perhaps the most consonant with mine of the three: at least he has a view. But I believe the notion that you cannot combine good foundational training with practical value strikes me as decidedly lacking in creativity. Just because it is not routinely accomplished is no reason to assume that it cannot be done.

[6] My wife Clare frequently marvels at how much of the knowledge I learned my undergraduate curriculum I retained. She attributed this to my good memory and, until I started working on this book, I congratulated myself by conceding that she was probably right. What I now believe is that I unintentionally designed my own "stacked" curriculum. For example, I had two years of physics in high school, took six semesters of physics and applied physics in college, then had further graduate-level training in physics while learning nuclear engineering in the Navy. The same applied to chemistry, although I only took one year while in college. I took a six semester theory sequence in economics, as

well as having had two years of it in high school. I had four semesters of advanced calculus in college (after placing out of my first year course in high school). I had two semesters of mathematical statistics, followed by another six semesters taken during graduate school.

The flip side of the coin is that I recall absolutely nothing about the remaining general education and specialty courses I took. I vaguely recollect spending a lot of time on the training of rats and pigeons in introduction to psychology (behaviorism was big at the time). All I remember about my comparative religion class is that I routinely fell asleep in the front row because of the way the professor's voice modulated and that when my brother Peter came to visit from high school, he fell asleep too. From introductory Norwegian, I can still say "Why are the white ones more expensive than the others?" and "Can you show me the way to the station?" but that is the limit of the skills that I have retained after 35 years.

[7] Mintzberg (2004, p. 387) provides quotes from Pierson (Carnegie) and Gordon & Howell (Ford) both of which question the value of having undergraduates emphasize business topics.

[8] I do not want it to appear that I am dismissing Jane Austen, whose writings I quite enjoy. Great literature holds the current advantage over business writings in that it tends to be much better written and exhibits a depth of insight into human behavior and motivation that goes far beyond "maximizing shareholder wealth" and the "art of the deal." Thus, I believe that students today would gain more benefits in many core areas from a developing a deep understanding of literature—or even the comic operettas of Gilbert and Sullivan—than from much of the business literature, particularly anything connected with Donald Trump. But I do not believe that necessarily needs to be the case in the future. The pedagogical benefits of bringing our examples closer to home is that students will not be forced to transfer their knowledge quite as far across domains, something we are not all that good at [3.3].

If we want to use business publications to as a means of providing a mirror on human behavior, we need to start elevating the quality of the works we produce in this area. One way to do so would be to classify true-to-life books and stories that depict business situations—either factual *or fictional*—as a form of research. I revisit the theme of expanding the type of activities that are viewed as research in Chapter 15.

[9] Having witnessed the manner in which many tenured faculty members react to suggested changes in policy when discussed in faculty meetings, I doubt that we, as a collective group, possess a measure of "skills for adaptation" any greater than that of the general populace.

[10] And as soon as one of these students can explain to me how the "outsource activities outside your core competencies" rule can be distinguished from short-sighted laziness, I will be inclined to pay attention. On the other hand, as findings on the high levels of business school cheating demonstrate, this is one lesson that they have clearly taken to heart.

[11] Programming does, however, provide much more immediate feedback when you do not understand what is going on than does a typical business situation. That is what my students were really complaining about.

[12] To illustrate the fact that Shugan (2006, p. 112) does not appear to worry too much about diffusion of research results, consider the following description he offers in his "research worth learning" section:

> This research combines a sliding-window logit model and a gamma diffusion pattern in an hierarchical Bayes framework. This research incorporates seasonality by using an outside good whose demand follows an autoregressive model that weights demand in the last 3 years for the same corresponding week. It is unlikely that business students could replicate this analysis.

The question then becomes, who could replicate this analysis—aside from its originator?

[13] In fairness to Mintzberg, I am not sure that he blames the case method for all the shortcomings of Harvard MBAs. As he later puts it, "The business schools of Harvard and Stanford are separated mainly by geography" (Mintzberg, 2004, p. 65). By this he means that despite employing quite different pedagogies, their underlying view of business—and the damage they do to their MBA students—is roughly equivalent.

[14] Mintzberg's (2004, p. 382) model for low level specialized master's degree programs allows for specialization either by function or by landscape.

[15] I feel that Mintzberg (2004) is quite correct in asserting that most cases do not have enough information to make anything remotely resembling an informed decision. Thus, students need to make assumptions well beyond what is presented in the case in formulating their decisions or action plan. Over-emphasis on the outcome of a case implies that the facts of the case led to the result whereas, in reality, the cause-and-effect relationship likely involved many factors that the students were unaware of.

[16] In one of my graduate courses, for example, I had three sisters from China who sat together for the entire semester and never said a word in class—despite the fact that they generally came in well prepared. I spent the whole semester wracking my brain with respect to what to do. I mentioned the situation to a colleague who had been teaching in the Far East at a conference after the course was completed. Without even an instant of hesitation, she asserted that I should have separated them after the very first class. As soon as I heard the suggestion, I judged it to be a good one. Quite honestly, however, the thought never occurred to me until my colleague offered it.

[17] Very near the beginning of my marketing course at HBS, for example, I exhibited a connection to the "Butcher Wax" case we discussed in the very first week of the course. My study group was astonished by my passion for the case. It derived from two sources. First, on several occasions I had spent more than a day applying Butcher Wax (principally used in bowling alleys) to the living room floor of my family's summer cottage in New Hampshire. Second, when I was in elementary school, our class took a tour of the Butcher Wax factory, compliments of one of the other students, the late Susan Butcher (later the four-time winner of the Iditarod dog sled race).

[18] Right after conceding that persuasion and problems solving skills may be advanced by the case method, Shugan (2006, p. 111) goes on to say: "Unfortunately, these so-called benefits are sometimes detrimental. Suppose a manager convinces everyone to take the wrong action." Apparently, there is just no satisfying some people.

¹⁹ During my time at HBS, in the early 1980s, study groups were also popular; they were not formally organized, however.

²⁰ The "quality of the faculty" in my HBS reunion survey came in a dismal fourth, at 11%.

²¹ For example, while at Florida Atlantic University, the first two case method courses that I taught were to cohorts in their new Executive MBA program. I received the "top professor" honors for both cohorts.

²² My tenth grade son currently tutors children after school at the local elementary school and is enrolled in a "Practical Arts" class where his job is to help the instructor of his high school's AP Computer Science course.

²³ Active faculty involvement in paid student projects absolutely clinched the deal. As one member pointed out, the estimated cost of a 4 person undergraduate student team would come out to $23/hour, based on the time estimates projected for the program. In the prevailing economy, the group's consensus was that experienced individuals could be acquired for a similar rate. The entire economics changed, however, if faculty members were involved; it made the wage rate seem extremely reasonable and reduced the expected supervisory burden for the company, a common complaint leveled with respect to interns.

²⁴ In their zeal to prevent students from committing Type I errors, it is equally important that academics refrain from applying their own standards of evidence to student projects. As discussed in Chapter 15, practice tends to be much more accepting of the risk of Type I error and much less accepting of the risk of making Type II errors—which can lead to opportunities lost through hesitation. We would not serve our students well if we encourage them to adopt our own standards in this area.

²⁵ It is common enough to find students recalling their participation in simulation exercises fondly. That does, in my opinion, count for something.

²⁶ In the Figure 14.6 illustration of Second Life, my back is featured because the screen capture was taken from my computer. Student names—which are their "fake" Second Life names rather than their real names—have been pixilated out.

[27] Did I mention that you can purchase naked body parts of nearly every type on Second Life?

[28] The Mintzberg (2004, p. 44) complaint that a virtual world simulation would definitely not address is, "Playing at management is not management." It seems to me, however, that this comment would be better directed at certain practicing managers—and their obsession with "winning" the salary game and with toys, such as corporate jets and shower curtains that cost as much as an Indian college professor makes in a year—rather than at students. Playing is a respected tool for learning; let us not lose sight of that.

[29] For example, after publishing my article on professional doctoral programs with Uwe Hoppe, I received an email from Dr. James Digabriele, on the faculty at Montclair State University in New Jersey. It offers some interesting insights into those who attend these professional programs, as well as the obstacles faced by such a program in today's educational climate in the U.S. He writes the following:

> I just wanted to add some information regarding the Pace University DPS program. I have a DPS degree from Pace in addition to a PhD by publication from Middlesex University in London. The DPS has been around since 1972 which makes it older than some regarded PhD programs. The truth be told Pace settled on the DPS in the same way Cleveland State did with the DBA. A few neighboring Universities in NYC balked at the idea of Pace adding a PhD. Since the New York Department of Education does not allow the title; "Doctor of Business Administration," the Doctor of Professional Studies was born! Although the web site for the DPS is full on innuendo on where the graduates intend to land upon completion of the degree, at least 90% of the entering class have intentions to transition to academia (many students already are faculty but need the doctorate for tenure). In addition, Pace really doesn't do a good job of promoting this degree because in the past they were threatened with a law suit from a graduate that did not get a faculty position at a certain University. As a result, Pace became very passive regarding the actual public description of the degree. In my opinion this has caused the DPS to become the Rodney Dangerfield of doctoral degrees! There is

an important point to note about the DPS; most DBA programs have taken the DPS model an adopted it! The most recent is Kennesaw State.

With that said, the truth is the DPS does as much as a PhD in preparing graduates for scholarly research however, from an applied point of view. It is unfortunate the widespread discrimination among academics regarding the DPS, it is a wonderful degree that truly unites the academic and practice communities. The faculty are all traditional PhD's. The combination with experienced practitioners creates very fertile ground for research.

In a later email, he points out that "the current Pace DPS student has an average of 600 on the GMAT, master's degree, and 10 years experience." The first two make their candidates comparable to what is seen in many academic doctoral programs; the last would be much less usual in top research doctoral programs today.

[30] Referring back to the continuum between science and art presented in Chapter 3, it is hard to justify placing business fitness landscapes either to the left or to the right of education fitness landscapes. Thus, it would make sense for the two fields to share similar methods when it comes to research.

[31] One of students interested in doctoral programs never followed up with me, so I do not know what the outcome of that case is. The other followed up very seriously but, sadly and unexpectedly, passed away before he could begin.

[32] The exception to the "continue what we are doing" rule would be for case method schools such as Harvard. If theory is what employers truly prize, then the case method should be abandoned and theory-based lectures substituted. Shugan (2006) would, indeed, be vindicated.

[33] As evidence in support of elite residential programs, I refer to my previously mentioned survey in which nearly half of the respondents mentioned interactions with classmates while in the program and long-term networking to be the aspects of the MBA that they liked best.

[34] There is relatively little evidence of the direct impact of faculty members on the ethical values of business students. As mentioned in Chap-

ter 1, one study, producing results largely consistent with earlier studies, found that while business students generally exhibited lower ethical values than liberal arts students, the business education itself did not appear to make their morals much worse (Milner, Mahaffey, MacCaulay, & Hynes, 1999). That certainly does not set the initial bar in business ethics education too high.

On a more positive note, the *Aspen Institute* (2008) has found the ethical awareness of business students to be slightly improving in recent years, although this trend cannot necessarily be attributed to the programs they are attending. Sadly, the study also reports that "high ethical standards" ranked ahead of only "job security" and "other" as a criterion when selecting a job among graduating MBAs (Aspen Institute, 2008, p. 13).

Somewhat related to our ability to influence values, at least in general terms, two recent studies found that faculty political values did not appear to exert a great impact on student political values (Mariani & Hewitt, 2008; Woessner & Kelly-Woessner, 2009). While both studies detected a slight leftward drift over time, it did not appear to be connected to the specific professors of the students. Peer effects therefore seemed to be a more convincing explanation.

[35] Both the GM and Chrysler organizations nonetheless survived; they did so by favoring one group of stakeholders—management and employees—over several others, most notably the former shareholders and U.S. taxpayers. The ethical question this raises is if the companies actually incorporated their too-big-to-fail status and the UAW's political clout into the estimate of fitness they were using to guide their actions *without informing the shareholders*. If so, their actions were unethical in my framework; if not, they were merely shortsighted.

Chapter 15

Informing Practice

Roadmap & Objectives: Concluding the series of chapters devoted to recommendations that began with Chapter 13, this chapter proposes that we should stop attempting to inform practitioners about the principles governing activities they already know how to perform and instead seek to work collaboratively with practice towards solving unusual or unexpected problems.

An academic discipline's long term prospects for survival are greatly enhanced if it produces a product that is either beautiful or useful. Some disciplines, such as those in the fine arts, obviously focus on beauty and our ability to appreciate it. Others, such as medicine and engineering, have demonstrated a continuing ability to create artifacts that improve our quality of life—even if the details can get a bit messy. A few, such as mathematics, are blessed with the unusual ability to produce ideas of great elegance that eventually prove to be useful, even where their utility may not be immediately obvious when the ideas are first formed.

In Chapter 4, I made the argument that the nature of business processes are sufficiently complex that ugly theory is the best we can dare to hope for. Thus, our long term access to resources is likely to depend upon our being useful. Presumably, this requires us to meet three critical prerequisites: that our research is valid (rigor), that our research results are potentially useful to our practitioner clients (relevance), and that we communicate these results effectively (resonance). Although it is tempting to look at these three prerequisites as being independent of each other, in a complex world they are not. To the contrary, I will argue that they are highly interdependent. As a result, they need to be addressed simultaneously.

The central theme of this chapter is that researchers need to spend much more time engaged in activities that create enduring relationships with practitioners and much less time worrying about communicating with other researchers. Much of the chapter is spent describing programs and activities that can promote such relationships. Towards the end of the chapter, the Harvard Business School agribusiness program is profiled as an exemplar of informing with impact. We begin the chapter, however, by considering some attitudinal changes (on the part of researchers) that are likely to be a prerequisite to a rich, two-way informing process between academics and practitioners.

We Need to Stop Treating Practitioners like Idiots

Most business professors that I have met claim to hold practitioners in reasonably high esteem. With the notable exception of economics and finance professors—who routinely assume practitioners behave like super-geniuses (*homo economicus*; Thaler, 2000)—our research often paints a very different picture. Since informing effectiveness tends to decline once you discover that the person informing you believes that you have the IQ of a lawn chair, it is worth considering some of the activities that we do that might give practitioners that impression. Not coincidentally, there is considerable overlap between these activities and the threats to rigor described in Chapter 10.

Report the Existence of Low Hanging Fruit

Imagine yourself getting behind the wheel of your car. You click your seatbelt and adjust your rear view mirror. Then you hear the passenger sitting next to you say: "To start the car, you need to insert the key into the ignition and turn it clockwise." Given that you have been driving for over 35 years, you look over at your passenger in disbelief. Is this sarcasm? Is this a joke you do not get? Is it possible that your passenger thinks this is news to you? If you conclude that it is the last of these, what are the odds that you will listen to anything else that individual suggests with respect to your driving?

Personally, I cannot see how this is so different from a practitioner discovering that MIS researchers have published hundreds of papers exploring a model whose central premise is that the usefulness of an information systems impacts our intention to use that system (see the discussion of the TAM in Chapter 10)[1].

Low hanging fruit, as defined in Chapter 10, are factors that act decomposably *and* exert a substantial effect. By their very nature, there cannot be very many of them—not every factor can have a *major* effect just as it is impossible for everyone to be above average except in Lake Wobegon—and their decomposability makes them readily detectable. As researchers, we should therefore be extremely skeptical of our ability to discover them before practitioners do. An obvious way of determining this is to *ask a group of practitioners how a particular phenomenon works before beginning to investigate it as a research project.*

Having done this myself from time-to-time, I would be willing to predict that considerable variation in opinion will result. In a decomposable world, that would mean the practitioners truly do not understand their landscape. The rugged landscape offers an alternative explanation: that the process could be quite different in the regions of the landscape where the responding managers are working. What you can be confident of, however, is that if they all agree on a particular factor, researching that factor is unlikely to do much to inform practice. Unfortunately, that same agreement may signal that the factor will be an excellent empirical research topic, since high impact decomposable factors are what our analytical tools are particularly good at capturing.

One way we might encourage our research to move in a more practitioner-useful direction would be to require researchers to submit an addendum to each theory or empirical journal submission. Not intended for publication but solely for review purposes, the supplement would contain the results of a focus group or survey performed prior to the actual research where members of the targeted practitioner audience were asked to rate the likelihood of the various hypotheses being tested in the manuscript (translated into reader friendly language) being valid. This supplement would help us identify two important characteristics of the research: 1) if the findings are "old hat" to the practitioner audience, and 2) if the hypotheses being tested in an empirical manuscript "evolved" from their initial form (as described in the focus group or survey) so as to support the actual results.

Assume Practitioners Cannot Handle Type II Error

One of the most interesting subplots of Ziliak & McCloskey's (2007) *The Cult of Statistical Significance* is the story of the relationship of William Sealy Gosset and Roland Fisher. As I mentioned earlier in a brief footnote to Chapter 10, Gosset worked for *Guinness Breweries* and was very interested in statistical process control. As part of his work on dealing with small samples, he devised a test of significance—published under the pseudonym Student, since Guinness did not want employees publishing under their own names—that became famous as Student's t-test. Ironically, he thought the test was likely to be of minimal practical use because the concept of statistical significance was far less important to him than that of economic benefit and loss. That seemed a sensible attitude given that he was trying to maximize profits.

Through much of his later life, Gosset corresponded with Roland Fisher, who came to edit the most influential journal in statistics and later became the Galton Professor of Eugenics[2] at City College in London. He took a dim view of Gosset's notions of economic value. Instead, he advocated significance testing as the basis for testing theory, devoid of economic consequences. In fact, he was largely responsible for 5% becoming the most widespread standard of significance.

In Chapter 10, the economic implications of statistical power[3] were discussed. By ignoring them, we are depriving practitioners of that which would be of greatest interest to them in our empirical research. There is, however, another aspect of focusing entirely on reducing Type I error without worrying about what Type II errors we might be introducing. Doing so carries with it the implicit assumption that managers are unable to make a judgment regarding what may or may not be useful to them. It makes sense to lock up your tools when children are around because they might hurt themselves. What does it say about our opinion of managers when we lock up those findings that do not meet our five-percent solution, regardless of what their potential economic consequences might be?

A rugged landscape greatly amplifies the inappropriateness of what we are doing. The essential character of ruggedness is that effects important in one context will be of negligible importance in another. Unrestrained creativity is a wonderful characteristic when designing an ad campaign. On the other hand, you should the head for the hills at full speed—pausing only to don your lead undergarments—when the reactor operator at your local nuclear power plant feels the same impulse to experiment on the job. As a result, every large effect associated with a particular case will tend to yield much less significant results for observations taken randomly from a rugged landscape. Managers can benefit, however, from knowing such large effects, negative or positive, have been observed in specific situations. They can then use their judgment to assess each effect's potential relevance to *their own situation*. Even more important, where judgment alone does not suffice, they can take advantage of the numerous opportunities to conduct quasi-experiments that a business setting nearly always provides. Don't know if a particular sales promotion is a good idea? Try it in a small test market and examine the results.

Call for "Evidence-based Practice"

Whenever I hear a business researcher call for *evidence-based practice*, chills run down my spine. The reason: such calls are nearly always followed by a diatribe against the observed fact that practitioners are failing to do what the academics are telling them they should be doing based upon research findings[4]. The unanswered question: why?

Does my convulsive reaction imply that I believe practitioners are never wrong? Hardly… Practitioners tend to be experts, and experts are prone to quite a variety of mistakes, not the least of which is over-confidence (as discussed in the very next section). On the other hand, it would be foolish to dismiss their expertise. There may be very good reasons a particular manager chooses to do things in a manner inconsistent with existing academic theory. After all, we are driven to explore the landscape surrounding our local fitness peak [1.2]. To suggest that such a choice is the opposite of evidence-based practice—*superstition-based practice*, possibly?—is an assertion of disrespect towards that manager's accumulated expertise and, quite possibly, wisdom. That is not a very good way to initiate a diffusion process.

If the world were as decomposable and orderly as our theories suggest it is, there might be an excuse for our arrogance. But, as noted in Chapter 10, there is ample reason to believe that our theory fragments will not generalize as well as we think they will and a lot of our statistical evidence is probably flimsier than we would wish it to be. Moreover, our studies routinely toss out observations affected by Taleb's (2007) black and grey swans as outliers. But building performance and economic models around orderly periods ignores the costs that a sensible organization will incur to ensure adaptability [5.3]. Can we be so sure that the managers that we are chiding are not wiser in this respect than we are?

If we want to be taken seriously, a little humility will go a long way.

Errors that Experts Make

Do the three examples of attitudes that might antagonize managers just presented imply that there is nothing useful that our research can tell practitioners? Not in the least. What we need to do, however, is tailor our practice-directed research to the needs of *experts*. Fortunately, for those of us hoping to make an honest living from research, experts are far from infallible. Let us therefore look at some of the types of errors that experts routinely make.

Forecasting Errors

As we saw in Chapters 10 and 13, neither expert practitioners nor expert academics are particularly good at forecasting the behavior of complex adaptive systems. Indeed, the inherent unpredictability of these systems is one of their defining characteristics [5.2].

Ironically, the most useful lessons that research may offer to practice in this area are:

1. Do not allow specific forecasts—including those made by researchers—to weigh heavily in decision-making.

2. Ensure that forecasts include allowances for the grey and black swan events that are likely to be very material to performance, yet often overlooked.

In conjunction with the first of these, we should be encouraging managers neither to overvalue performance that is linked to successful forecasting nor to be overly critical of performance that arises from missed forecasts, since both are likely to be more heavily dependent upon luck than skill. For example, in the first chapter of *The Drunkard's Walk*, Leonard Mlodinow (2008, p. 14-15) profiles the case of Sherry Lansing, an executive at Paramount, who had a string of successes with movies such as *Titanic* and *Forrest Gump*. Her ability to predict what would be popular with the public then appeared to drop after a series of expensive films bombed, at which point she was unceremoniously dumped. The year afterwards, Paramount had its best performance in a decade. The problem with Paramount's view of the story: the films that came out the following year were all ones that Lansing had placed in the pipeline. The moral: it is probably a mistake to place too great an emphasis on the ability to predict in a domain where no one can be expected to predict well. Far better to estimate fitness using measures related to those activities that the individual can control.

In the absence of feedback, experts use too much knowledge

Part of acquiring expertise is the process of developing personalized techniques for handling situations likely to be encountered. Sometimes, however, the situations being handled do not provide the expert with objective outcome feedback. In such cases, it is easy for the expert to assume his or her techniques are working; we earlier saw it as the *illusion of control*. Academics face this problem constantly in their teaching. How many of us really know how much our typical student benefits from the courses we offered once they leave school?

In *Blink*, Malcolm Gladwell (2005, p. 125-136) describes the case of a Cook County emergency room where there was a shortage of beds and yet a large number of people each day were coming in with chest pains that might—or might not—be a heart attack. The problem this created was that Type I error (assuming the patient is having a heart attack and putting him or her in the intensive care unit) was very expensive while Type II error (sending a patient home who *was* having a heart attack) could be fatal, as well as making the hospital vulnerable to lawsuits. Adding to the problem, the doctors making the diagnosis were not likely to be the ones treating the patient; as a result, they tended to get little concrete feedback on the outcomes of their decisions. This combination led to error rates averaging 11 to 25 percent.

Because the condition being diagnosed reflected a biological system, as opposed to social system, the opportunity for beneficial "evidence-based practice" was significant. In fact, a decision tree developed based on computer records proved to be accurate at the heart attack/non-heart attack classification about 95% of the time—far better than the doctors. At the same time, it required substantially less information than had been used by the typical expert. This seems to be an intrinsic aspect of expertise; as their knowledge becomes compiled, experts have the ability to process more information. Barring feedback to pare down extraneous information, they will tend to use too much.

As a sidebar, it is worth noting that Gladwell (2005, p. 138) specially mentioned how much trouble the developer of the decision tree had getting his ideas accepted[5]. This, of course, is always going to be a problem when attempting to tell experts that their expertise is sub-optimal [2.2], the *Law of Abandoned Expertise*. If researchers can identify the types of situations in which such failures routinely occur, and also emphasize to practitioners that the problem is one that *all experts* fall prey to, then there is a chance that some diffusion will take place.

Objectively analyzing low-structure situations

When an expert encounters a low-structure situation, he or she can be expected to fall prey to precisely the same types of biases and fallacies that routinely impact novices. That may be true even when the situation exists within the expert's own domain of expertise. The reader may recall, for example, how violently some statisticians and mathematicians reacted to the *Let's Make a Deal* problem (Mlodinow, 2008, pp. 42-45) presented, described in Chapter 6.

It may be for this reason that so many trade books detailing the types of fallacies that afflict us have recently been published[6]. Significantly, a great many of these findings have been known for three decades (e.g., the articles collected in Kahneman, Slovic, & Tversky, 1982). These have, however, been widely read and understood only in the parallel universe of academic research[7]. It is unfortunate when the relatively small percentage of our research that might have practical applications for managers becomes lost in the swamp of research that does not. We return to this issue later in the chapter, when discussing diffusion.

Excessive focus

The very nature of expertise will tend to lead to excessive focus during periods of relatively high landscape stability [5.3]. It feels good to exert control, and the more practice you get exerting it, the more effortless it becomes. Where the fitness landscape is very dynamic, the expert is continuously challenged, so the amount of automatized behavior is reduced. But where things seem stable, unconscious patterns of behavior can easily develop. This can happen as easily at the organizational level—for example, my study of Mrs. Fields' Cookies and Batterymarch Financial Management (Gill, 1995a)—as it does at the individual level.

The problem with developing an efficient routine tuned to a particular landscape [5.1] is that it can easily ignore the grey and black swans that will eventually, but unpredictably, perturb the landscape [5.2]. It would not be unusual for even expert managers to fail to consider the eventual possibility of the very unusual disrupting the routine; it is often much harder to identify what is missing in a system or plan than to critique what is actually present[8].

Leveraging research opportunities

The four areas just presented are intended to be examples, not an exhaustive list. Their common thread is that they represent situations commonly associated with expert fallibility. Thus, they seem to be fertile ground for finding solutions to managerial problems that are not already known.

Much managerial research today seems to be focused on achieving a generalized sense of "understanding." On a rugged landscape, such a goal is likely to experience three drawbacks: it will be local, it will be transitory, and it will nearly always annoy an expert when you imply that your "understanding" is greater than his or hers. We all have problems, however, even if we are experts. Focusing our research on problems instead of broad understanding—even if those problems are local and temporary—greatly increases the likelihood that informing will occur.

Diffusion is Part of Research!

In the very first chapter of this book, we saw the case that relatively little academic business research has made its way into practice. We therefore need to ask ourselves the question: *should we be responsible for encouraging such diffusion?*

My answer is an emphatic yes! Informing is the central theme of this book and every act of informing is an act of research—or should be. At its core, research is about finding explanations for what works and what does not; Elster (1983) and Ghosal (2005) stated this explicitly, as discussed at the end of Chapter 3. When we inform ourselves, we explore what is known (e.g., literature review), we create possible explanations (e.g., theory building), and we test existing theories (e.g., empirical research). We are completely comfortable calling each stage of this process research. Yet, somehow, we believe that designing and conducting a class is entirely different despite the fact that the process involves exploring what is known (e.g., deciding on content), creating explanations with which to present the concepts to students (e.g., design our lessons), and then searching for evidence that student mental models have been altered (e.g., examinations, student evaluation comments). That many of us do not engage in this process with the same enthusiasm for rigor that we apply to our publishable disciplinary research tells us a great deal about our own severely myopic world views and almost nothing about whether such activities are research[9].

With respect to practice, we make what is known (or what we think is known) available to practice in the form of journal articles. We anticipate that these will have a measurable impact—at least according to the implications for practice paragraph we dutifully place at the end of nearly every paper. For the most part, we voluntarily abandon the process there, however. In effect, we are making an experimental manipulation—publishing our article—but are choosing not acquire or analyze data regarding the effect of the manipulation. *The act of attempting to inform is an act of research, it is simply bad research the way we have been doing it.* The sooner we recognize this, the sooner we will begin to view diffusion as an integral part of the research process. Once we fully ascribe to that view, I have little doubt that we will begin impacting practice in a meaningful way.

The challenge presented by diffusion is that, for the most part, complex ideas will not move very well through mass media channels, such as journals [4.2]. Thus, although there would certainly be no reason to discourage researchers from publishing in practitioner journals or writing trade books, pinning all our hopes that such activities will produce a substantial improvement in our impact is quite optimistic. What really is needed is the development of personal networks that facilitate informing between academics and practitioners *in both directions*. We now consider three examples of activities that can serve such a purpose.

Case Writing in the Field

Case writing is usually viewed in terms of the output produced: the teaching or research case study. In simple terms, these types of cases can usually be distinguished on two dimensions: destination and focus. The teaching case, of course, has the classroom as its principal destination, whereas the research case targets academic journals or books. The difference in focus is considerably more subtle. The best teaching cases tend to emphasize a particular decision to be made or problem to be solved. It is much easier to conduct a discussion exploring the question of "what should this manager do?" than a discussion that is essentially a post-mortem of a decision and its consequences, i.e., "what did the manager do right?" or "what did the manager do wrong?" The research case, on the other hand, typically focuses on understanding cause and effect. Most published research cases incorporate a heavy theory component. The situation or situations described in the case are then used to support or contradict the key elements of that theory.

Case writing and informing channels

Paying too much attention to the case study as a product ignores the greatest benefit of case writing—the process itself. When we go into the field to write case studies—particularly teaching case studies—the potential for forging impactful channels *serving all our major clients* is extraordinary. With respect to practice, the intensive contact required for quality case development leads to a personal bond—a bond that, if properly maintained, can continue to serve as a two-way informing channel for decades. At Harvard Business School, this potential is fully recognized[10] and is considered central to their strategy of maintaining close relationships with business. At all but a few other research-focused schools, such as Stanford and schools affiliated with case publishers[11], developing teaching cases is, at best, considered an activity unrelated to research[12].

But informing channels to practice are not the only channels being forged or reinforced by case writing. When you write a case study on a local company, there is a very good chance that the protagonist will attend one of more class discussions of the case; many will insist upon it. When this happens, you are building channels between practitioner clients and student clients—as well as reinforcing the case-writer's ties. You are also helping to establish a bond between the practitioner and the institution—a very nice bond to have when it comes to hiring in a tough economy. This can be particularly true when students are involved in the case-writing process (e.g., McNamara, 2009), an excellent example of an integrative activity that fits well into the curriculum proposed in Chapter 14.

It is also possible to leverage the case writing process so as to expand the definition of student client to include practicing managers. At HBS, for example, their three day Agribusiness Seminar—attended by top executives from global agribusiness companies, many of whom return year after year—makes discussions of new agribusiness cases their centerpiece. A similar summer program was hosted by HBS's MIS faculty for IT professionals and academics in the 1980s, but has long since been abandoned.

Case writing benefits to research quality

The development of teaching cases, in particular, also offers another benefit in terms of diffusion. As was mentioned in the previous section, practitioners are likely to be far more suspicious of the research goal "generalized understanding" than of research that focuses on solving a specific problem. While a research case tends to focus on the former, teaching cases most definitely focus on the latter—just a few classroom experiences trying to facilitate a meaningful discussion of a "post-mortem" style case will convince the case writer that the open-ended "what should we do now?" case is far superior for classroom use. Learning to write about decisions-to-be-made[13] will nudge the researcher towards publications that are likely to be far more resonant with practice.

Teaching cases can also be beneficial in supporting the landscape focus for researchers advocated in Chapter 13. To develop a landscape focus, the researcher needs as much exposure to decision-making in the landscape as possible. Ironically, the teaching case is usually a much better source of such information than a research case. To begin with, there are practical length limits to both (imposed by journals for research cases and by student patience for teaching cases). For the research case, it is a rare article that does not use up more than half this space with its obligatory review of the literature, hypothesis presentation, hypothesis testing, and wrap-up. In the teaching case, on the other hand, nearly all that space can be employed in describing the decision maker's landscape. In addition, the researcher writing a case will normally be very oriented towards arguing that the results are generalizable—at least if the researcher wants the case to be published. Towards this end, it is in the researcher's best interest to minimize the landscape-specific aspects of the situation. A good teaching case, on the other hand, provides a rich set of details and images, a great many of which may actually be immaterial to the decision being made. These details serve an important pedagogical function, since distinguishing between what is relevant and irrelevant is a critical component of the student's case analysis.

Acquiring case writing skills

The case writer, particularly one who focuses on writing teaching cases, faces formidable obstacles in learning the craft. Many of these are the direct result of research methods training, since a number of the skills that enhance the publication potential of a research project actually work against the teaching case author. Some examples of these obstacles follow.

Focus on a pre-conceived objective.

Good business research, as it is conventionally viewed today, is driven by the hypothesis testing process. This requires the researcher to frame a situation in a particular way, usually motivated by a weakness or hole in the existing research literature. In developing a teaching case, on the other hand, the most promising decision situations to profile are the ones that the managers in the organization are currently facing. This requires considerable flexibility on the part of the case writer, since what he or she thought the case *might* be about can change quickly during the early stages of the process. I recall one experience when I went on a case site visit with a very experienced researcher (but inexperienced in the mischievous ways of teaching cases) who was determined to write about one aspect of a situation while it was immediately apparent—to me, at least—that the managers we were interviewing were much more interested in discussing another very interesting set of decisions that they needed to make. The case was written according to the researcher's plan, but the resulting case was nearly impossible to facilitate in the classroom.

Jargon- and theory-free writing.

When writing research, a very narrow audience is targeted. Knowing this, the researcher feels free to employ the jargon familiar to other researchers focusing on the same topic (who may number in the dozens). A particular culprit in this respect is the devotion to theory. In a section of an article titled "Contorted, Ponderous Prose", renowned management scholar Donald Hambrick (2007, p. 1349) describes the relationship as follows:

> Our insistence on theory in every article has led to a lot of bad writing. In every paper, we must have an obligatory section about the origins and current state of the theory we are invoking—again, no matter how strained its relevance. We must

adopt the conceptual nomenclature of the theory, instead of just referring to the phenomena or variables we are examining. And, above all, we must go to lengths to say how the paper contributes to theory. It's not enough to say how the paper contributes to our knowledge or understanding. Instead, we must do a lot of elaborate hand-waving to assert some theory or another is better off because of our paper.

Including theory in teaching cases also works against the constructivist philosophy of the case method pedagogy. In a case discussion, our hope is that students will learn to identify relevant theory *or develop their own theory* applicable to the situation. Telling them what theory to apply defeats the purpose.

Importance of skilled observation.

The current ideal of research rigor is to minimize the impact of the researcher on the findings. The underlying principle is sound—if research findings depend heavily on the observer they will be hard to replicate[14]. In writing the teaching case, on the other hand, skilled observation is a huge advantage. Unfortunately, becoming a good observer usually requires a great deal of practice [3.2]. That may explain why case writing is so often taught through an apprenticeship-style process.

Not coincidentally, the skills described above are very closely aligned with those associated with creating resonant research, described in Chapter 13. These include choosing a resonant problem (i.e., focusing on what management is interested in), creating a resonant product (i.e., a story that is well written), and becoming better observers.

Acquiring these skills will not necessarily be easy, since they work against many of the precepts of good research. Outside of institutions that value teaching case development and institutions where pedagogical activities are highly valued, it may be difficult to find individuals who can teach these skills in the business school. I would speculate, however, that the skills may exist in the institution's other schools. Creative writing, for example, incorporates many skills that could be applied to creating engaging case narratives. One rather disturbing trend I have noticed at case producing universities such as Harvard and Stanford is the increasing use of professional case writers. The rationale behind using these is to produce case studies that are well written and more accessible to students. That is precisely what disturbs me. One of the great things about writing teaching cases is that it forces you to write in a clear and compelling manner. If you do not, the consequences become obvious when your case bombs in the classroom; an example of what is sometimes referred to as "eating your own dog food." Splitting the writing and research roles may also produce cases that are somewhat schizophrenic; unable to decide if they are teaching or research cases[15].

Observational skills could be honed by training in the arts. For example, *Smithsonian* recently published an article about a program in New York where high ranking police officers attended a course titled "The Art of Perception" designed to "fine tune their attention to visual details" (Hirschfeld, 2009, p. 49). The program, which used art works to tune observation skills, was originally taught to medical students. Since that time, it has been enthusiastically received by the law enforcement community including the FBI, the U.S. Secret Service, and the U.K.'s Scotland Yard.

Identifying appropriate problems is a skill that is particularly sensitive to practice. One way to acquire that skill is through consulting—our next topic.

Consulting as Research Grants

After I had completed the first semester of my doctoral program, I started to develop a picture of the nature of academic research in business[16]; it was not a pretty picture. Being confused as to why we were conducting so much research that seemed (to me) to have no purpose, I began pestering the late Jim McKenney, the department chair, for examples where our research had made an impact on practice. Every time I did so, he began to describe his consulting activities. Each time he responded in that fashion, I explained that I was *not* asking about consulting—after all, I had been a professional consultant and was aware that impact could be exerted through that channel—I was talking about our actual research. After that exchange, a pattern of discourse we engaged in *several* times, we usually agreed to change the subject. Unfortunately, it took me decades to recognize that two quite profound points were being made in these conversations. First, that *consulting is research*. Second, that *consulting offers the researcher one of the most effective channels for achieving impact*.

There is a considerable variability in the level of institutional tolerance for consulting at business schools. At the very top tier of schools, it is encouraged, serving both a minor and a major purpose. The minor purpose is to supplement the faculty member's income so substantially that the school can justify paying a less generous salary[17] than the individual's reputation might warrant. The major reason is that consulting for the right companies creates invaluable ties for the school. Just look at the online resumes of faculty members at these institutions and see how often their consulting clients are prominently featured.

At strong research schools outside of the top tier, the situation is somewhat different. While the belief that it is acceptable to consult for up to one day a week is widely held, I have certainly seen little evidence of consulting being actively encouraged (although it may be at some schools). I can speculate as to the reasons for this. First, because it is not considered research, consulting must therefore be a distraction. To be considered a *serious* researcher, you must learn to avoid such distractions. Second, as noted in Chapters 2 and 13, business faculty members are already paid more, and in many cases *much* more, than faculty in nearly every other discipline. That we should be encouraged to further supplement our income with lucrative consulting contracts would be viewed by the rest of the institution as scandalous. Thus, consulting happens… but it happens in the shadows.

The unfortunate consequence of the informal "don't' ask, don't tell" policy towards outside consulting is that it closes out what could be one of our most effective channels for informing. Among its many benefits, consulting: a) opens a face-to-face channel, b) forces the faculty member to take a problem focus—since firms rarely pay hundreds of dollars an hour to achieve "generalized understanding," and c) it provides immediate feedback as to the impact of research. As mentioned in Chapter 13, we can hardly expect the impact of our research to be considered in our estimate-of-fitness for research if we cannot measure it.

At schools where consulting remains in the shadows, one possible remedy would be to *allow* consulting projects to be treated as research grants. Although a faculty member *could* still engage in private consulting (under the one day/week limit), *consulting-as-grant* assignments would be conducted under a very different arrangement. As would be the case with a typical research grant, the faculty member would get a limited portion of the billed amount. On the other hand, the faculty member would get all the benefits of a grant: teaching release (if desired), funds for travel and equipment, graduate student assistance and, most important, credit towards promotion, tenure, and merit. In effect, the faculty member is rewarded for bringing resources into the institution just as a scientist would be.

There would be two obvious barriers to such an arrangement. The first involves a question of trust. While it would be relatively easy for a dean or provost to offer assurance to a faculty member that consulting activities were going to be treated as the equivalent of research, doing so does not necessarily guarantee that other faculty members involved in the decision will feel the same[18]. The other barrier is opportunity; not every faculty member will immediately find his or her consulting services in demand. Fortunately, there is a relatively straightforward approach to dealing with the second issue. As faculty at HBS discovered nearly a century ago, case writing is the gateway drug that leads a firm to long term dependence on consulting.

Naturally, consulting activities do not necessarily need to be compensated; service consulting offer many of the same informing benefits as paid consulting and benefits the institution in ways beyond defraying overhead costs. My brother Geoffrey Gill, for example, received a degree in the management of technology from MIT. Since that time, he has actively participated in the school's Venture Mentoring Service (VMS). The program puts experienced entrepreneurs and, from time-to-time, MIT faculty members together with early-stage entrepreneurs. The teams meet in small groups monthly to discuss the start-up's plans and operations. Open to all members of the MIT community, the program has assisted a few hundred businesses since it began. Like many of its participants, my brother has acted in both capacities—advisee and mentor—and speaks very highly of the process and its results. It has served to maintain his close ties with MIT long after his graduation.

Professional Doctorates

If you look at the typical U.S. research doctorate in business, it is well designed to promote both learning and a certain kind of diffusion. On the learning side, beyond the obligatory course work there are numerous activities, such as acting research assistant, where students are required to apply these skills. There are opportunities to work closely with experts in developing papers. There is a highly constructivist activity, the dissertation process, where students develop their own models of research. On the diffusion side, there is an almost universal policy of institutions not hiring their own doctorates[19]. Over time, that creates a network of contacts for each faculty member that spans the country, and even the globe.

The fly in the ointment of the traditional doctorate is that the network being created is entirely focused on researchers informing each other. If we want to knowledge to diffuse to practice, we need a program with similar learning benefits (with respect to our research) that produces graduates who serve as managers. Here is the great strength—from an informing standpoint—of the professional doctorate. Unlike the trans-disciplinary doctorate of Chapter 13 and the business education-focused doctorate (DBE) of Chapter 14, the professional doctorate already exists and, in Europe[20] and Australia, is thriving. In a sense, it is the complement to the proposed DBE; although both target practicing managers, the professional doctorate is particularly designed for those individuals who intend to remain in practice.

My colleague Uwe Hoppe, a professor at the University of Osnabrueck in Germany, and I recently did a study of professional doctorates both internationally and in the U.S. (Gill & Hoppe, 2009). A particularly useful study in this area (Bourner, Bowden, & Laing, 2001) was con-ducted in England, and contrasted academic PhDs with their profes-sional counterparts. Some of the key distinctions are summarized in Table 15.1. The strong problem (vs. generalized understanding) focus of the professional programs was particularly noteworthy.

Hoppe and I concluded by arguing that having a professional doctoral student enrolled establishes a nearly ideal informing channel between practice and academia. Paradoxically, to maximize the effectiveness of the relationship, some of the most sacrosanct precepts of business doctoral education would need to be reversed. We would want to insist that the program be taken part time; as an informing channel to prac-tice, it would only be effective if our students remain in practice. We would want to emphasize distance learning as much as possible in the program; professionals move around a great deal so if we want to avoid students dropping out, we would need that flexibility. We would also benefit from students taking *as long as possible* to complete the program. As long as they remain students, they continue to serve as a channel to practice. Once they complete the program, that close tie is potentially lost. Even worse, they may want to join us in academia, thereby dis-rupting our channel to practice altogether[21].

Table 15.1: Professional vs. research doctorates (adapted from Bourner, Bowden, & Laing, 2001)

Attribute	Academic PhD	Professional Doctorate
1. Career focus	Entry into academia	Professional doctorates nearly always claim to address the career needs of aspiring professionals
2. Domain of research topic	Disciplinary theory	Professional practice
3. Research type	'original investigation undertaken to gain new knowledge and understanding but not necessarily directed towards any practical aim or application' (p. 71)	Issues of real interest to the profession
4. Research focus	A perceived gap in the literature	A problem encountered in practice
5. Starting point	Finding what is known in the literature	A problem for which the solution is unknown
6. Intended learning outcomes	Contribution to the literature	'A significant original contribution to knowledge of • professional practice through research, plus one or more of the following: • personal development (often specifying reflective practice); • professional level knowledge of the broad field of study; • understanding of professionalism in the field; • appreciation of the contribution of research to the work of senior professional practitioners.' (p.72)

A design for such a program, which I whimsically refer to as the *double decade doctorate* (DDD), might be as follows. We would recruit from the very top of our master's degree classes; we might even choose to make the degree by-invitation-only, to add to its prestige. Students would enroll in one course per year, at no cost to them beyond books for the first decade. Course work would emphasize research methods, disciplinary studies based around case work (that the students would often provide), and project development. In the latter half of the second decade, students would identify suitable research projects and would write a dissertation. During this period, they would not only pay for their courses, they would also be expected to fund some faculty research projects if they possess the requisite means to do so. (Given the selection process, a great many would have accumulated the resources to provide generous funding). Ultimately, at around the twenty year mark, they would defend their dissertation and get their doctorate. At that point, presumably, some would choose to transition to academia while others would remain in practice.

I would certainly not suggest that the DDD replace existing professional doctoral programs. For the most part, these are working quite well. For example, at Osnabrueck, the relationship between the university and doctoral students already working has been mutually beneficial in terms of research (see Gill & Hoppe, 2009). Instead, I believe it to be particularly suitable for the research university that currently engages in lots of business academic research leading to minimal impact on practice. There is no shortage of candidate institutions meeting this criterion.

A Case Study in Effective Informing: The Agribusiness Program at HBS

If I advocate forcefully for engagement with practice and students, it is mainly a result of my decade of participation in the agribusiness program at Harvard Business School. This program, under the direction of Professor Ray Goldberg, demonstrated to me the level of impact that a business school can have when it forgoes the conventional ideas of what constitutes business research. I now offer a brief description of that program.

What is Agribusiness?

Agribusiness describes the system through which agricultural products, food and fiber in particular, are produced, transformed, and distributed throughout the world economy. Rather improbably, given its geographic location, the term was coined by Harvard Business School professors John H. Davis and Ray A. Goldberg in 1957. The term was needed to capture "the closeness of interdependence and manifold interrelationships of agriculture and business" (Goldberg, 1968, p. v).

The philosophy driving agribusiness is that individual participants in the system cannot manage effectively without considering the overall behavior of the system in which they participate. As described by Dr. Ray Goldberg (1968, p. 3):

> if managers, private and public, are to develop effective strategies and policies, they must be fully aware of the total commodity system in which they participate, and they must understand the interaction of its parts.

Goldberg's assertion that agribusiness behaviors are best viewed through the lens of commodity systems quickly justifies itself when you look at the unusual nature of many agribusiness entities. For example, the farmer—the producer—often serves as a supplier of one or more inputs: selling seeds, equipment, and other production necessities on the side to neighboring farmer. Such is also true of some of the largest firms. For example, *ConAgra*—one of the world's largest food processors—owned *United Agri Products*, once the largest farm inputs supplier in the U.S. until it divested it in 2003.

The inherent price volatility and yield volatility of farm production— the latter largely attributable to weather but also a result of biological factors such as disease and pests—led to a wide range of agricultural risk management tools emerging well before their use was widespread elsewhere. For example, commodity exchanges in agribusiness could— potentially—exist without major speculator participation. The needs of farmers to reduce the price exposure of their existing crop makes it sensible for them to "go short" (i.e., sell contracts on the futures markets) in the commodities market; the need for producers to ensure they can acquire future supplies at a predictable price gives them an incentive to "go long" (i.e., buy contracts on the futures markets). In addition, even the most laissez-faire government makes exceptions in the case of its agricultural industries; price supports and centralized attempts to manage agricultural supply have long been in place. Needless to say, this process often produces unintended side effects. For example, when CocaCola was studying the possibility of building a corn wet milling plant to produce high fructose corn syrup (HFCS) plant in the 1980s, an important issue to be considered was the likelihood of further or reduced government price supports for ethanol, since that would compete for inputs and production facilities[22]. At the same time, it was trying to grapple with the expected impact of a new sweetener, aspartame, that had the potential to transform consumption (as saccharine had done previously) yet was also potentially subject to regulation—as had been the case when the U.S. banned of cyclamates in 1969.

There are few competitive landscapes where global effects are as large and as rapid as agribusiness. In the 1960s and 1970s, for example, wheat farmers in states like Kansas suddenly found themselves critically impacted by production failures in the Soviet Union. It is virtually impossible to understand commodity behaviors when considering them from a local perspective.

In the research context, the commodity system concept seems refreshingly contemporary in light of the emphasis current business research places on supply chains and value-added networks. This should not be surprising. Throughout its history, agribusiness has tended to surface important phenomena well before they are re-discovered as areas of interest in disciplinary research. Since the 1950s, for example, we have recognized that it is nearly impossible to develop a clear vision of any commodity system without considering *all* of Porter's (1980, 1985) five forces, along with the effects of government; collectively, these forces have probably been experienced in more strongly in the agribusiness sector than in any other sector of the economy.

With respect to technology, agribusiness far outdistances any other domain in terms of experienced practical impact. This may seem like an odd assertion, given that I am a researcher in information technology and the fact that technology is transforming medicine at a breathtaking pace. But consider the following. We are still trying to figure out how to measure the productivity increases brought about by the use of information technology (Brynjolfsson & Hitt, 1998). This actually represents an improvement from our earlier state of knowledge (which was wondering if such productivity increases even existed). While medicine can proudly point to ever-increasing life expectancies (in the developed world), a substantial fraction of these increases are attributable to improved nutrition (i.e., agribusiness) and better public health practices, rather than technology. Contrast these with the unequivocal record of success of agribusiness. For most of the 1800s, the farm work force consisted of 60% of the U.S. population; it is still 50% in the developing world (Federico, 2005). Almost entirely as a result of innovations in technology and practice, that labor force percentage today is closer to 2.5% of the population in the developed world—with increases, rather than declines, in actual output. The impact of technological innovation on agribusiness was not limited to the developed world, however. In a recent obituary printed in the Wall Street Journal, the late Norman Borlaug[23]—the leading pioneer of the green revolution that made much of the developing world nearly or entirely self sustaining with respect to food—was described as "arguably the greatest American of the 20th century" (Easterbook, 2009, p. A27).

Even in the area of business research, agribusiness has played an important role. For example, Everett Rogers (2003), whose *Diffusion of Innovations* is the seminal work in the field, began his career studying the introduction of crop control chemicals in Iowa. It built upon findings regarding the difficulties in getting farmers to adopt hybrid corn seed in the 1930s and 1940s. Much of the early work in applied statistics took place in agribusiness settings. William Sealy Gosset, the developer of Student's t-test who was featured earlier in this chapter, worked for Guinness Brewery, an agribusiness concern. Analysis of crop yields also proved to be a popular domain for developing new statistical techniques.

The widespread availability of higher education in the U.S. can also, to a great extent, be credited to agribusiness. Starting in the middle of the U.S. Civil War, a series of federal laws (e.g., the Morrill Acts of 1862 and 1890) established a system of "land grant" colleges specifically intended to further agricultural and mechanical education. Many of today's public universities owe their existence or size to the funding and other resources made available through these efforts. Later, government funding for agricultural experiment stations and the Cooperative Extension Service—both operating under the supervision of land grant universities—allowed farmers to observe, initiate, and participate in agricultural research projects, as well as have access to researchers. In other words, these institutions—established nearly a hundred years ago and earlier—sought to inform farmers through establishing enduring relationships with them in the field.

Professor Ray Goldberg

When I first encountered agribusiness at Harvard, the program had been active for nearly 30 years[24]. By that time, Professor Davis had retired and the program was directed by Ray Goldberg, the George M. Moffett Professor of Agriculture and Business.

Under Goldberg, the agribusiness program at HBS had evolved into a very different type of intellectual endeavor than the disciplinary research activity that is typical of today's U.S. business school. Although his education was fairly typical of HBS professors at the time (A.B. and M.B.A. from Harvard, PhD. from the University of Minnesota), he never lost sight of his roots in Fargo, North Dakota, where his family operated a milling business.

Goldberg's research record is impressive by traditional academic standards; according to his HBS biography, he authored, co-authored, or edited at least 23 books and 110 articles. What is *really* impressive, however, is the fact that he has authored or supervised the development of over 1000 HBS case studies. This accomplishment—representing about 20 case studies a year over the course of his entire academic career—is a feat that I would guess to be unparalleled in the annals of HBS.

Relationship with students

His extraordinary success in case development was inextricably linked to Goldberg's impact on students and on practice. With respect to practice, the appetite for cases was almost inexhaustible. Each year, continuing to the present day, HBS offered a three-day agribusiness seminar for executives[25] that consisted almost entirely of case discussions. Because the same people—including many, if not most, of the world's top agribusiness executives—came back year after year, the cases to be discussed needed to be renewed annually. As a result, Goldberg would usually choose one or two students from the second year MBA agribusiness elective class to act as research assistants for the following year. While some of these students went on to get doctorates, most did not. Instead, they delayed their entry into the MBA job market for a year in order to get the experience of working with Goldberg. Although he was known to be relentless task master in the area of case development, his later involvement in helping to place these students in highly desirable positions more than compensated for the hectic year they had experienced.

Based on my own observations, Goldberg's ability to recruit top students to work as case writers can only be partially explained by the rosy placement prospects that existed at the end of their term. Weighing even more heavily was the close relationship that Goldberg forged with his students while they were attending his course. Because of all the new cases being debuted in the MBA class, case protagonists attended about half of all the class discussions. Whenever this was the case, he allowed about ten students to sign up to be his lunch guests at the HBS Faculty Club so that they could talk to the executive. In doing so, he incurred the gratitude of both students and executives alike. Once a year, he also invited his entire class (close to 100 students) to attend a party at his summer home on Cape Cod.

Another facet of Goldberg's interaction with students was his willingness to sponsor elective research projects in the second semester of the second year of the MBA program. Whereas MBA independent research projects can drain a faculty member's time without necessarily offering any great rewards, Goldberg actively solicited them[26]. Indeed, he even induced the CEO of *Standard Milling*, Pat Uhlmann, to award a cash prize for the best of these projects.

Relationship with practice

When Malcolm Gladwell (2000) refers to connectors, the image of Ray Goldberg immediately pops into my head. I have never met an individual with more connections to practice than he. During his period of greatest activity, from the 1970s to the 1990s, I would feel quite safe in saying it was the rare top executive of a major agribusiness company in the world who did not know him or know of him[27].

That his relationships with practice resulted in informing is a matter to which I can personally attest. In the mid-1980s, I worked for Agribusiness Associates, Inc., a consulting firm that Goldberg had founded[28]. During the three years that I worked at the firm full time, I had many opportunities to witness the close attention paid to him as he explained his perspective on their businesses and, his favorite theme, the growing role that biotechnology would play. Frequently, my consulting colleagues and I would then spend hours with these individuals, now clients, attempting to understand and explain how his ideas could be put into action.

Evolution to the Present Day

I would characterize the late-1970s and early-1980s as the peak of the agribusiness program at HBS. Part of this can be attributed to the environment; the Russian grain deals and price spikes of commodities such as sugar in the 1970s had brought agribusiness to the forefront of the nation's consciousness. More importantly, the intellectual climate within HBS still welcomed the applied nature of the agribusiness research program.

If agribusiness had an Achilles heel at HBS, it was its lack of clear ties to a single discipline. Although technically part of the Marketing Department, the focus of agribusiness was on a competitive landscape not a discipline. An agribusiness case could just as easily focus on issues of finance, strategy, government, technology, or operations management as it did on marketing. For most of HBS's 100 year history, such a focus was not a problem. In its early days, for example, much of the school's research output consisted of industry reports. Beginning in the 1960s, however, notions of what constituted acceptable business research had started to change. The Ford Foundation's report (Gordon & Howell, 1959), had lauded HBS for its case method teaching while, at the same time, expressing a preference for a scientific research approach more closely aligned with that of Carnegie Mellon (Khurana, 2007). Since it takes a long time for focus to change in academia, it was not until the mid-1980s that real indifference to the agribusiness philosophy of research began to surface.

By the time I started my MIS doctorate at HBS, agribusiness had already been displaced from its easily accessible offices in Loeb Hall and relocated to a site within the labyrinthine recesses of the school's Baker Library[29]. More significantly, the school chose not to recruit an agribusiness research specialist as a successor to Goldberg. Instead, upon Goldberg's retirement, leadership of the agribusiness was first given to Professor Warren McFarlan, an internationally renowned MIS researcher, and subsequently to Professor David Bell[30], a faculty member with a very distinguished research record in the decision sciences[31] whose publication record, aside from case studies, is nearly devoid of agribusiness-related research. At the present time, Bell's appointment also includes serving as a Senior Associate Dean, with duties that include faculty recruiting.

To handle the day-to-day activities of the agribusiness program, a Director position was established in 2005. As of this writing, that position is occupied by Mary Shelman, who completed the HBS MBA program in the late-1980s and then served as Goldberg's research assistant for a year and established a reputation as an exceptionally talented case writer. Her key responsibility is the continued development of the case studies needed for the three day Executive Agribusiness Seminars, which still attracts 200 executives a year at a current price of $7500 per person and remains oversubscribed. A rotating international version of the seminar, recently held in Paris, Shanghai, and Mumbai, has also been instituted. Goldberg, as a professor emeritus in his early 80s, continues to participate in these seminars and also does some teaching at Harvard's Kennedy School of Government.

On the surface, then, the agribusiness program at HBS looks much as it once did. The agribusiness seminar continues to generate the type of financial contribution that would make it the crown jewel of most business schools. A dozen or so cases continue to be written each year, directed by one of the most respected case-writers in the history of the program. Its titular head is an academic of international reputation whose contributions to the decision sciences are familiar to anyone doing research in that field.

Despite these apparent signs of health, I find what I observe—entirely as an outsider—to be troubling with respect to the future of the program. While a passion for agribusiness still guides the case writing activity, evidence that other forms of academic research are being conducted by the school are not visible to the outsider. The attention of the academic researcher in charge of the program is divided among many interests, both research and administrative. There are no current agribusiness doctoral students. At an institution whose focus is increasingly being directed towards traditional research productivity measures[32], being separated from the central research mission of the school in this manner would not bode well for the status of the area within the broader institution.

If I am correct, then what I have observed is very sad. The philosophies I learned while working in agribusiness with Ray Goldberg infuse every aspect of my research (and of this book). They also infuse every aspect of agribusiness practice—the very name itself derives from the program as does the concept of commodity systems. To allow the program to become lessened in any way illustrates the harm that over-relying on a weak estimate-of-fitness, research publication productivity, can do.

Diffusion of Ethics

Of all the self-delusions in which we engage, the idea that we are impacting practitioner ethics by writing research articles on that subject may be the most fanciful. We are employing a channel to which they do not attend. We are employing language with which they are not familiar. We are preaching about pressures that, in their opinion, we do not personally experience; ask a practitioner about the logic of tenure to see what I mean. Furthermore, in the minds of a great many practitioners, we are in no position to discuss ethics. They understand that academic research is costly. They also believe its purpose should be to benefit them. Why should taxpayer and tuition dollars be expended on research whose sole purpose is to inform no one but ourselves? So believing, practitioners would have every reason to conclude that we are taking money under false pretenses.

Does this mean that business researchers cannot exert influence on practice? Not at all; what it means is that such influence is unlikely to be exerted through the channels that we currently use for our research. Channels of personal influence are another matter entirely. Over the years, I have been surprised how often my conversations with consulting clients and friends in business have turned to issues of ethics and values. This is particularly true of individuals with whom I have established long term relationships. Nearly always, these individuals are interested in doing what is right. The challenge seems to be figuring it out. The defining character of an ethical dilemma is that it is both complex and unfamiliar; were it simple or routine, it would not be a dilemma.

As alluded to in Chapter 1, improving the ethical standing of business appeared to be central motivation behind the original development of business schools. Rakesh Khurana (2007, p. 46), in *From Higher Aims to Hired Hands*, thoughtfully documents the evolution of business schools in the U.S. from the beginning of the 20th century to the present. He quotes a 1927 speech given by Wallace B. Donham, the dean of HBS who was largely responsible for the school's emphasis on the case method:

> The country has suffered less, perhaps, than England from an attitude that looks down on business as a calling, but even here young men enter business too frequently because they do not feel competent or inclined to enter any of the so-called learned

professions, rather than from a positive desire to enter upon a business career. Business has thus become in part a catch-all and a dumping ground into which in the case of many families inferior sons are advised to go.

Early business magnates, such as Amos Tuck (Dartmouth) and George F. Baker (Harvard) gave generously to establish business schools with the hope of improving this perception of business. During the 1960s through the 1990s, the efforts to revitalize business schools may have contributed to changing public attitudes towards business in a positive way. Interestingly, we have now entered an age where the reputation of business as a whole has once again become tarnished. It would probably be a mistake to blame this decline on a few isolated individuals. Where so many CEOs and top managers feel justified paying themselves hundreds of times what their lowest paid employee earns, it would be optimistic to attribute the problem to the occasional bad egg.

So how can we, as business school faculty members, help business face its ethical challenges? As a prerequisite, we need to establish personal informing channels. Then we need to offer ideas for better estimating organizational and individual fitness; rather than telling a manager what to do, we are far more likely to succeed in influencing behavior when we suggest better ways of assessing fitness [4.1]. Regrettably, the disciplines that are most likely to oversimplify the estimation of fitness— economics and finance—have gone the farthest in establishing such informing channels (e.g., by placing their doctorates in practice). As a consequence, just as Ghoshal (2005) asserts, it is easy for estimates-of-fitness that fulfill the needs of mathematical tractability and data gathering (e.g., share price and executive compensation) to become accepted as a proxy for organizational and individual fitness. If we do this long enough, we may even start to believe that these measures *are* fitness, a message that is implicit in the writings of many economists and finance researchers. It is up to other business disciplines, holding a broader view of what constitutes fitness, to exert their influence. We cannot be effective in doing so by focusing on writing about it, however [4.2].

It may well prove that through the simple act of developing close personal relationships with practitioners, we can influence how they estimate fitness. Since I have not exactly lavished praise upon business academics this book, I can perhaps be excused for mentioning one of our strengths: we rarely let the wages we earn become the preferred method for estimating our own fitness. In this respect, we are very different from many practitioners, obsessed with the compensation of colleagues and competitors. If we develop relationships characterized by mutual respect with these individuals, the very fact that we view fitness so differently[33] from the way they do may help them adopt a broader perspective—and help us to do the same in the process.

Conclusions

In their book *The Business School and the Bottom Line*, Ken Starkey and Nick Tiratsoo (2007, p. 212) suggest that a business school needs to redefine itself as an *agora*, "an ancient Greek term first used to describe a centre of political, social and philosophical activity, a place of congregation." This idea of diverse activities, of bringing parties together is central to the ideas presented in this chapter. It is a welcome contrast to the narrow and fragile estimates-of-fitness that we increasingly use to measure productivity in today's research-focused business schools.

Business researchers need to be careful, however, about viewing themselves as the "center" of anything. For far too long, we have expected practitioners to come to us, to seek out our wisdom by reading what we have written in the form that we have chosen, to accept the notion that because we are highly educated, we are also wise. For nearly five decades, we have been driven by a belief in the essential correctness of our research activities, and reassured by a faith that practice will, one day, see the light and allow themselves to be guided by our theories. In holding such beliefs—despite the flood of evidence that seems to suggest how little we know—we have done ourselves great harm in the eyes of practice. If we are to undo the damage, we cannot build a marketplace and hope that our clients will come. We must, instead, vigorously seek out practicing managers at every opportunity. We must make it clear that we see our role as first learning from them, then helping them when we can. Through that genuine spirit of service, we can forge the connections through which informing takes place in both directions. We must never forget that building an infrastructure for effective informing is as integral to the business research endeavor as creating knowledge. Once we accept these propositions and therefore appropriately reward *all* those activities that enable us to inform practice, impact will surely follow.

Chapter 15 Foundational References

Gill, T. G., & Hoppe, U. (2009). The business professional doctorate as an informing channel: A survey and analysis. *International Journal of Doctoral Studies, 4,* 27-57. Retrieved from http://ijds.org/Volume4/IJDSv4p027-057Gill267.pdf

Goldberg, R. A. (1968). *Agribusiness coordination: A systems approach to the wheat, soybean and Florida orange economies.* Boston, MA: Harvard Business School, Division of Research.

Ziliak, S. T., & McCloskey, D. N. (2008). *The cult of statistical significance.* Ann Arbor, MI: University of Michigan Press.

Chapter 15 Notes

[1] Okay, I'm not being fair here. An academic would never make a statement like: "To start the car, you need to insert the key into the ignition and turn it clockwise." It would be more along the lines of:

> Our findings support the hypothesis that the key construct interacts with the ignition slot construct when moderated by the presence of a counterclockwise rotational force at a $p<0.01$ level of significance. Since care must be taken in generalizing from a single experiment, we recognize the need for further research. Nonetheless, we believe our findings provide a valid basis for the Key-Starts-Car (KSC) model that we have proposed and, owing to the widespread use of automobiles in industry, believe that this finding should be of considerable interest to practicing managers.

[2] As I mentioned earlier, the notion of decomposability and the field of eugenics go hand-in-hand, since eugenics is based upon the premise that specific traits are beneficial to humans and should, therefore, be engineered into the population through selective breeding (not unlike what is done with dogs, where the desirable characteristics of a breed are identified and specific animals are judged according to these characteristics). For those who believe the relationship between fitness and individual traits is very complex, statistics would be of negligible value both because traits interact and because the long term survival prospects of the species will greatly benefit from diversity.

[3] Statistical power is also an idea originally developed by Gosset (Ziliak & McCloskey, 2007, p. 20).

[4] Consider, for example, the comments made by Denise Rousseau (2006, p. 258-259) in an article in the Academy of Management Review about evidence-based management:

> My great disappointment, however, has been that research findings don't appear to have transferred well to the workplace. Instead of a scientific understanding of human behavior and organizations, managers, including those with MBAs, continue to rely largely on personal experience, to the exclusion of more systematic knowledge. Alternatively, managers follow bad advice from business books or consultants based on weak evidence. Because Jack Welch or McKinsey says it, that doesn't make it true.

Were I a manager reading these words, I would just conclude that she was calling me unscientific (the opposite of scientific), unsystematic (the opposite of systematic), and gullible—since I can easily be duped by Jack Welch and McKinsey because I reflexively assume everything they say is both true and applies to my situation. I would not feel I was getting much credit for my accumulated experience, either.

Virtually every time I see the terms evidence-based practice or evidence-based management employed, I encounter the same arrogant and patronizing quality. It is detectable even in articles where academic wisdom is called into question as well (e.g., Rynes, Giluk, & Brown, 2007).

The strange thing is that I suspect the authors of these pieces do not even recognize how offensive their characterizations might be to managers. (I, on the other hand, fully recognize how offensive much of what I say in this book is likely to be to some academics. But I am a member of that community. And sometimes, as the song goes, you need to be cruel to be kind.)

As a final irony, a recent article in the *Academy of Management Perspectives* (Reay, Berta, & Kohn, 2009) examined the evidence that evidence-based management is actually effective in practice. They concluded that, up to this point, empirical support for the practical value of evidence-based management was weak and that considerably more evidence should acquired before we forcefully advocate its use by management.

[5] Aside from the Cook County emergency room—which desperately needed to free up bed space—the other highly interested party was the U.S. Navy's submarine force (Gladwell 2005, p. 138). As I can personally attest, it is a big deal to surface a submarine on patrol to evacuate a crew member, so you do not want to make that choice lightly.

[6] Just listing those published in the last two years that happened to be within three feet of me as I was writing this, I counted six books (e.g., Mlodinow, 2008; Thaler & Sunstein, 2008; Ariely, 2007; Gilbert, 2007; Gladwell, 2009; Akerlof & Shllier, 2009)

[7] Just as an example, I acquired my now weather-beaten copy of Kahneman, Slovic, and Tversky (1982) in 1986, a book that was was an assigned reading in my very first doctoral course. It would be hard to find a business academic researcher who is entirely unfamiliar with the findings.

[8] To illustrate the challenges of detecting what is missing, the first letter I received after moving into my house in Tampa was a letter from my new homeowner's association informing me that they were about to start fining me $150/day because I was missing a tree. How do you look for a tree that isn't there?

[9] Whilst I was in a somewhat whimsical mood, I wrote two conference papers that considered what might happen if our teaching was evaluated with the same sense of rigor we reply to our disciplinary research. The first, titled "The Cruelest Experiment" (Gill, 2004) considered entirely of a dream sequence in which I was forced to defend my course design to an Institutional Review Board made up of figures from the Spanish Inquisition. To my astonishment, it won the "Distinguished Paper" award for DSI's Innovative Education track (out of over 50 presented papers). The second, "The Peer Reviews and the Programming Course" (Gill, 2005) consisted of the imaginary responses I might expect to get if that same course design were submitted for anonymous peer review at a journal.

[10] It is instructive to note, for example, how many of the consulting activities (which HBS professors tend to feature prominently on their personal web pages, unlike most other schools) are with the same com-

panies that participated in case studies co-authored by the faculty member.

[11] Some of these universities maintain their own case publishing operation, such as the University of Western Ontario's Ivey School of Business. Others who host case publishers, such as Babson College in the U.S. and Cranfield University in the U.K., who both rent office space to ECCH.

[12] Just as an example, during my own promotion and tenure forays, I cannot recall the published teaching case studies that I developed or co-developed being mentioned even once, either by external reviewers or by promotion and tenure committees. I finally decided to separate the two dozen or so of these from everything else in my resume so as to ensure that my remaining publications were not "polluted" by the presence of discussion case writing activities. I mention this not so as to portray myself as a victim; it was quite clear to me that the value that I placed upon such activities was not necessarily shared by my colleagues. Rather, my hope is to make it crystal clear that I am fully aware of the fact that writing teaching case studies is not considered research at many institutions, and that I am not so naïve as to believe that it is.

[13] In general, it is better to get into the habit of referring to teaching cases as focusing on decisions-to-be-made as opposed to problems-that-need-to-be solved. The easiest way to lose a potential case site is to go in saying that you want to write about their "problems"—even when you mean it in the much more positive context of problem solving.

[14] As noted in Chapter 10, we almost never replicate our research and, in the rare cases where we do, it fails to confirm the earlier findings most of the time. Thus, the practical importance of the principle of ensuring replicability is moot, although it certainly makes us sound a great deal more scientific.

[15] I lack any hard evidence that the quality of HBS cases has declined as a consequence of the increased reliance on case writers. I will note, however, that I am not alone in questioning whether the quality of these cases has declined in recent years. At the recent doctoral reunion held by HBS in 2009, the facilitator of a case discussion on the HBS MBA program was absolutely roasted by participants—mainly from

doctoral classes that graduated in the 1960s and 1970s—on the subject of the quality of cases.

[16] The fact that it I was well into my doctoral program before I even had a clue with respect to what "real research" is can only partially be attributed to my being slow on the uptake. During my MBA, HBS took great pains to shield me from such research in anything but its most rarified forms. Thus, based upon observation, I concluded that research consisted of writing cases and occasionally—when an extremely pedantic mood struck—writing articles for the *Harvard Business Review*. As should probably be clear by now, even five years in a doctoral program and nearly twenty years employed at research universities did not entirely undo that initial damage.

[17] When I first approached HBS about my entering the doctoral program, the professor that I spoke to assured me that every year his consulting income was at least double his salary. While I was in the program during the late 1980s, typical billing rates ranged from $3000/day (untenured assistant professor) to $8000/day (widely known full professor), although I am sure that I was not made privy to the highest rates.

[18] With respect to professional credit for consulting, when I was an assistant professor at Florida Atlantic University, I developed a geographic information system under a contract with McDonald's Latin American Division, a project that brought in tens of thousands of dollars of overhead contribution to the College of Business as a result of my efforts. At the time, the dean assured me that the project would be treated as the equivalent of a top tier journal article. By the time I actually went up for promotion and tenure, however, that dean had retired and had been replaced by another dean. Suffice it to say, I'm glad that I did not have to rely on those assurances. Not once during the P&T process was serious consideration given to that particular project; I did not even bother raising the issue, since I had no reason to believe that my continued employment was in doubt. Had my "top tier" article (see Chapter 10) not been published, however, I probably would have found myself looking for a new job, since the former dean's view of the importance of the consulting project was not widely held.

[19] Harvard Business School used to be a notable exception to the principle of an institution not hiring their own doctorates. This was under-

standable, given the difficulty of finding applicants from other universities trained in its unusual pedagogy and research focus. At my recent doctoral reunion, however, we were told that this policy had changed and that HBS doctorates would normally not be hired by HBS. Instead, they would need to spend at least three years working at another university before they could be considered for an HBS position.

[20] In Germany, for example, the majority of top level executives have a doctorate (Gill & Hoppe, 2009).

[21] In *The Tipping Point*, Malcolm Gladwell (2000, p. 276-277) introduces the notion of a "maven trap." Such a "trap" is simply an opportunity or activity that will tend to be disproportionately attractive to mavens; he mentioned the help-line number on the packaging of Ivory soap as an example. I suspect that a doctoral program is precisely such a trap. Thus, the problem will not be finding enough students to fill these professional programs. Rather, it is more likely to be a challenge keeping these students out of academia long enough so that they can help to diffuse our research.

[22] I am aware of CocaCola's deliberations in the area of sweetener acquisition since I was project manager for the consulting team that conducted one of these studies.

[23] In Chapter 16 we shall point out that the "Population Bomb", defused largely by Norman Borlaug's work with dwarf wheat varieties, was projected to lead to the starvation of at least half a billion people by the year 2000.

[24] Bertrand Fox, the HBS Division of Research Director in 1967, placed the official starting date of the *Program in Agriculture and Business* at December, 1952 (Goldberg, 1968, p. v).

[25] In the 1980s, HBS would routinely run two agribusiness seminars, one in Boston and one in London.

[26] In my own case, I wrote a technical paper titled "A Note on Farm Supply Channels" that was later used in the agribusiness course for a few years and represented my first academic publication.

[27] In making the assertion about Goldberg's connectivity with business, I do so from the perspective of a consultant who worked in the field during the middle of the period described.

[28] As Goldberg explained it to me, he founded Agribusiness Associates, Inc. because he needed a firm to which he could refer the many companies that requested his services. He had little interest the day-to-day activities involved in actually running a consulting firm, however. Thus, by the time I joined the firm, he had sold controlling interest to a merchant bank operating out of London, who installed its own president.

[29] Although Goldberg never mentioned any feelings with respect to being relocated, his secretaries were not reticent about expressing their displeasure to me. This situation was made more awkward by the fact that the department that had displaced them was, in fact, the same MIS department from which I was getting my doctorate.

[30] I sourced the information about the current occupant of the Moffett chair from the HBS web site.

[31] I cite Bell's work on utility quite extensively in my own research in that area (e.g., Gill, 2008a). Unlike my own research, however, he prefers to develop mathematical models for phenomena such as regret and disappointment, as opposed to taking a psychological/connectionist approach.

[32] My assertion that HBS is increasingly driven towards traditional research productivity measures is my subjective interpretation of a number of observations I have made over the years. Most recently, at the doctoral reunion held in 2009, I heard a remark from a recently hired assistant professor about how important it had become to publish in the top tier journals of the field; during the 1980s while I was a doctoral student, such words would have never been uttered—even though they might have been thought. It was always supposed to be the quality of the idea, not the quality of the outlet that mattered. The increased importance of outlet seemed to be supported by comments made by the current director of the doctoral program, who observed that many doctoral students were delaying their completion, staying in the program 5 or even 6 years, in order to publish the requisite three articles that would ensure them placement at another top institution. While I was doing my doctorate, I was actually urged *not* to publish, lest it distract me from the more important task of getting through.

[33] In using the term "differently", I am definitely not intending to imply that the estimates-of-fitness employed by business academics are neces-

sarily better than those employed by practitioners. Not only would that be arrogant, but it would also be quite the opposite of how I feel. Given the choice between estimate the fitness of a firm using share price and estimating the quality of a business researcher using citation count, I would say the former is likely to be more accurate. Both, however, are likely to lead to aberrant behaviors, since both estimates are awful.

Chapter 16

Progress and the Future

Roadmap & Objectives: An area that has received scant attention in the book so far has been the role played by business and business schools in society as a whole. Returning to the subject of time horizons first raised in Chapter 9, this chapter proposes that the vigor and value of business schools is intimately tied to the process of progress. It therefore concludes that it would be in our best interest to take a vocal role when policy proposals are made that could undermine that process.

A recurring theme of this book is the futility of attempting to predict the long-term behavior of a complex, adaptive system. Experts tend to think they can do it but rarely achieve results much better than random guessing. Thus, it is with considerable trepidation that I conclude this book with a chapter about the future.

The chapter begins by offering some perspective on the "insoluble" problems of the past. These predicaments of progress, as they are called by my father, have been particularly commonplace since the industrial revolution, when rapid change started exerting a visible impact on every aspect of the average person's life in those nations being transformed. Common to these predicaments has been a sense of urgency, certitude that disaster was inevitable but might be somewhat ameliorated by desperate public action and, finally, outcomes that completely defied the original predictions.

We then look at three imminent crises: one environmental, one demographic, and one attitudinal. I will argue that of the three, it is the last—our loss of faith in free enterprise—that should concern us most. It is the last of these crises that is most likely to produce changes to our fitness landscape that greatly reduce our adaptability. Thus, I believe it to be the most likely to cause lasting damage. If we cannot adapt, then we are far more vulnerable to the first two crises, as well as any others that inevitably come along.

The crisis of attitude also has another aspect to it. It is the one crisis that the informing business school can play a fundamental role in addressing. If we make coping with complexity central to our mission, then we can be instrumental in preparing students and managers to deal with the landscapes they will encounter. If we help our stakeholders find the confidence that they can survive the many negative consequences of complexity and can benefit from the many opportunities it offers then they will not fear it. And—as we shall see in this chapter—the fear of complexity may be the greatest challenge that we face.

Predicaments of Progress

If you fear that your way of life is threatened in the not-too-distant future, then you are not alone. In his book, *Posterity Lost: Progress, Ideology and the Decline of the American Family*, Richard T. Gill (my father) points out that over the past 200 years, a familiar pattern has played out many times. First, some innovation or advancement occurs that, initially, appears to improve life. Next, an impending calamity triggered by that advance is identified; it seems certain to permanently damage the world, if not end it altogether. Radical public action is demanded, even though we recognize that we are probably too late[1]. Then, quite unexpectedly, technological or social transformations take place that ultimately overcome the problem. Looking back on the problem, we recognize that we had become unnecessarily alarmed—except for those of us who were most fervent in our predictions. We, the true believers, argue that we were actually right but that changes outside the system led to a completely improbable outcome or, even more often, we assert that the problem has *not* been solved, only delayed.

To illustrate just how pervasive this pattern has been, I summarize some examples from my father's book, most of which should be personally familiar to those of us who have reached middle age (particularly if we took economics in the late 1960s or early 1970s).

Starvation on a Global Scale

The first predicament of progress, and the most persistent, is that we are all destined to starve. Its origins are in the late 18th Century, when

Thomas Malthus predicted population would grow exponentially while land would grow only geometrically, owing to diminishing returns. My father (R.T. Gill, 1997, p. 124) frames the reasoning behind this predicament as follows:

> It is human nature, when the means are available, to have as many children as possible; more food makes the increased survival of children possible and also encourages earlier marriages and higher fertility. The predicament arises because the ensuing population growth quickly swallows up all gains and reduces the mass of population to subsistence again.

David Ricardo, the famous economist writing in the 19th century, framed the Malthusian predicament in economic terms. Labor, like any other economic good, is governed by the law of supply and demand. When the economy is in equilibrium, the supply of labor will match the wage rate and population will stabilize. When a change, such as the introduction of technology that improves worker output, occurs, more labor will become available (through forces such as increased reproduction). That increase in supply will, ultimately, drive the price back down to the natural (subsistence) level. To the extent that excess profits are realized, they will all accrue to the landlord.

The widespread famine predicted has not (yet) occurred for two main reasons. First, because people adapted to increased wealth by drastically reducing the number of children they have, instead of increasing that number as predicted. (Later in the chapter, I argue that this—not overpopulation—is now one of the most pressing problems facing developed nations). Second, agricultural productivity increased vastly more rapidly than Malthus or Ricardo ever anticipated[2].

In the late 1960s, computer models of world population predicted— once again, with complete certainty—that much of the world was destined to starve to death. Public health advances and incremental increases nutrition were reducing death rates, particularly in developing countries, resulting in rapid population growth. To quote a popular book at the time, *The Population Bomb*:

> The battle to feed humanity is over. In the 1970s and 1980s hundreds of millions of people will starve to death in spite of any crash programs embarked upon now. At this late date, nothing can prevent a substantial increase in the world death rate... (Ehrlich, 1978, p. xi, 24-25).

Here, the adaptation the author missed was most definitely in the area of increasing agricultural productivity (e.g., the "green revolution"), since population did continue to climb during the period. *A Blueprint for Survival* (Goldsmith & Allen, 1972) argued, however, that:

> the new genetic hybrids are not intended to solve the world food problem, but only to give us time to devise more permanent and realistic solutions. It is our view, however, that these hybrids are not the best means of doing this, since their use is likely to bring about a reduction in overall diversity, when the clear need is to develop an agriculture diverse enough to have long-term potential.

In response to these criticisms, which persist to this day, the late green revolution pioneer Norman Borlaug is quoted as saying that:

> [Most Western environmentalists] have never experienced the physical sensation of hunger. They do their lobbying from comfortable office suites in Washington or Brussels. If they lived just one month amid the misery of the developing world, as I have for 50 years, they'd be crying out for tractors and fertilizer and irrigation canals and be outraged that fashionable elitists in wealthy nations were trying to deny them these things. (Easterbook, 2009, p. A27)

There is certainly merit to seeking diversity in the crops we plant—indeed, Borlaug spent most of his life looking for new varieties with potential. The fact remains, however, that many, if not most, developed countries now have programs to encourage farmers not to grow too much and many large developing countries, such as India and China, find themselves becoming net exporters of food in some years. Thus, the threat of imminent global starvation has certainly been postponed for at least a while.

Resource Depletion

As a consequence of rapid industrialization, in the late 1960s and early 1970s, computer models predicted—as always, with complete certainty (according to their designers)—that the world would be out of many non-renewable resources by the beginning of the millennium. For example, *A Blueprint for Survival* predicted that by the year 2010, we would have exhausted the worldwide supply and projected reserves of silver, gold, copper, mercury, lead, platinum, tin, tungsten, and zinc (Goldsmith & Allen, 1972). Metals were the least of our problems, however. The real disaster that was about to happen involved oil. What their projections showed[3] was the following:

> [D]emand will exceed supply by the end of the century. What is significant, however, is not the speed at which such vast reserves can be depleted, but that as late as 1975 there will appear to be reserves fully ample enough to last for considerably longer. Such a situation can easily lull one into a false sense of security and the belief that a given growth rate can be sustained, if not indefinitely, at least for a good deal longer than is actually the case.

In the mid-1970s oil prices spiked, seeming to confirm the worst fears of the forecasters. At that point, the projections and the reality began to diverge in a big way. There seemed to be two key principles of adaptation that were in play:

1. When the price of something goes up, we buy less of it (i.e., conservation)

2. When the price of something goes up, we find clever ways to search for more of it (i.e., increasing supply).

The models being employed ignored these adaptations in their formulations. As a result, after another spike in the early 1980s, the real dollar price of many of the commodities—particularly oil—went down. Way down. In many cases, prices actually settled to their lowest levels in history.

Only recently, over the past four years, did prices start spiking again. Ironically, the major concern today is not that we will run out. The concern is almost the opposite: if we consume the supply that we have, we will irreversibly change the climate of our planet. That topic is discussed later in the chapter.

Nuclear Annihilation

Ever since World War II, when the U.S. dropped atomic bombs on Hiroshima and Nagasaki to bring the conflict to a rapid end, the threat of a nuclear conflict has loomed large in people's minds. *The Bulletin of Atomic Scientists*, for example, maintains a Doomsday Clock. Its purpose, as described on its web site[4], is as follows.

The Doomsday Clock conveys how close humanity is to catastrophic destruction—the figurative midnight—and monitors the means humankind could use to obliterate itself. First and foremost, these include nuclear weapons, but they also encompass climate-changing technologies and new developments in the life sciences that could inflict irrevocable harm.

The clock was first set at 11:53 PM (seven minutes to midnight) in 1947. Since that time, it has moved in response to world events. It reached 2 minutes to midnight after the U.S. tested its hydrogen bomb in 1953 and got as far as 17 minutes away from midnight in 1991, when the Soviet Union dissolved. Since that time it has been steadily moving back towards midnight. Its most recent move was to 11:55 PM (5 minutes to midnight). The web site explains this by asserting:

> The world stands at the brink of a second nuclear age. The United States and Russia remain ready to stage a nuclear attack within minutes, North Korea conducts a nuclear test, and many in the international community worry that Iran plans to acquire the Bomb.

Since it is not entirely clear how North Korea or Iran could start a truly global nuclear war—or why Russia and the U.S. would even consider launching an attack on each other, for that matter—the group added "climate change" as a justification for their prediction of impending doom.

In retrospect, it is certainly safe to say that there was great cause for concern in the late 1940s. The world had just experienced the most catastrophic war in its history; a war that began barely 20 years after what was supposed to be the war to end all wars. By using atomic weapons against Japan, the U.S. had supposedly removed the taboo against their use that might have otherwise existed. And, with the advent of fusion weapons such as the hydrogen bomb, the destructive power both sides possessed seemed unlimited.

Unlike the cases of starvation and resource depletion, it is harder to pinpoint any specific adaptation that prevented the beginning of nuclear war. In spite of the fact that *Mutually Assured Destruction* (MAD)—the deterrent strategy where both sides amass sufficient weaponry to wipe each other out in the event of a full-scale conflict—is ridiculed by many and parodied in films such as Dr. Strangelove, a case can be made that it contributed to our safety during the period. It is not clear that

MAD had ever previously existed between great nations; my view is therefore that we adapted to the new situation by not attacking each other directly[5]. The great fear, of course, was that with all that weaponry lying around, a sociopathic individual or a rogue nation might start a conflict that would escalate into all out global war. That was, of course, a risk. True sociopaths are rare, however. Even psychotic leaders, such as Hitler, do not generally *initiate* conflicts knowing they will lose them; it is only once they are already engaged in the war that all rationality is lost. Thus, there was always a risk to MAD—but perhaps less than supposed by some.

Of course, by the late 1980s, it was not superiority in nuclear weaponry that brought an end to the cold war. Rather, it was the fact that the Soviet economic system had been unable to grow and adapt as well as the western economies. Eventually, it became too hard for the U.S.S.R. to supply the basic needs of an increasingly restive populace and to maintain military parity. So the country broke up into separate states and the era of communist expansion ended.

Was the breakup of the Soviet Union an inevitable occurrence? Not in the minds of Soviet experts who, when asked in 1988, split almost 50-50 on whether or not the communists would still be in control by 1993 (Tetlock, 2000). Once again, we see the challenge presented by trying to predict the behavior of an adaptive system.

Failure to Adapt and "The Black Death"

The common thread in the crises described is that, through progress, we were able to adapt our way out of them. What would have happened, however, had we failed to adapt? We see such an example in the European pandemic known as *The Black Death*.

In the mid-14th century, the continent of Europe was still in a period sometimes referred to as the Middle Ages. This period, extending roughly from 1066-1485[6] was characterized by frequent European conflicts[7] and very little progress. By the end of the 13th Century, however, trade routes to the Far East began to open, starting with Marco Polo in 1295. Scarcely 50 years later, a deadly disease—now thought to be the bubonic plague—entered Europe through Italian ports and within a few years, killed somewhere around half the European population.

In Taleb's (2007) terminology, the spread of the disease and its aftermath was a black swan event. In its wake, however, the printing press and the Renaissance occurred, the precursors to the modern era of progress. Historians once argued that medieval Europe was heading towards an inevitable Malthusian population crisis that was forestalled by the outbreak. In the last few decades, however, that perception has changed dramatically. In his introduction to a book by the late historian David Herlihy, Cohn describes the change in thinking as follows:

> By the late 1980s he no longer saw medieval society headed inexorably towards a Malthusian disaster; instead, he saw it locked in a "stalemate" or "deadlock". The plague was not historically necessary, and without it Europe may well have persisted with remarkably stable institutions and systems of behavior for millennia. By his later interpretation, the Black Death had become an external factor independent of the social, political, or even the demographic environment. Once it had struck, however, it set Europe on a new path almost totally unrelated to its late medieval social past. (Cohn, 1997, p. 4)

What is significant here is that the pandemic struck a highly stable population that had very little experience at adaptation and was, therefore, particularly vulnerable. Had Europe become experienced in adapting to change, as we have necessarily become by virtue of living in the era of progress, it is doubtful that such a heavy price would have been paid. Imagine, for example, how different medicine might have been if we had not forgotten nearly as much as we had learned in the millennium following the fall of Rome. The Black Death was not unique, however. More recently, the potato famine that transformed both Ireland and the U.S. in the 19th Century[8] reminds us of the high price that can be paid for lack of diversity and failing to be adaptable.

The "Idea of Progress"

A central theme in my father's book is that of the *Idea of Progress*. Born out of the Scientific, Commercial and Industrial Revolutions, the Idea describes a faith that, in the long run, the world will become a better place. That our children and children's children will inevitably experience rising standards of living. That through our own efforts, we contribute to the process by which these positive changes occur. In the U.S., the Idea was particularly prevalent in the late 1800s and early 1900s (excluding World War I) and it experienced a rebirth in the 1950s that persisted through the early 1960s. By today's standards, however, it seems almost "quaint" (R.T. Gill, 1997, p. 2).

What is so critical about the Idea of Progress is that it helps the individual to weather the bumps that necessarily result from the *process of progress*. As I have argued throughout this book, rugged fitness landscapes are not particularly pretty. Fitness peaks can be hard to find and even harder to maintain as external and internal forces distort the landscape. The certainty that the disruptions being experienced will, in the long term, produce a better world is comforting. In practical terms, it means we have faith the validity of techniques such as dollar-cost-averaging, allowing us to smile as the stock market goes down—since we "know" that the stock we are now buying will be worth much more when it comes time to sell.

Acceptance or rejection of the idea of progress can be a powerful element of an individual's ideology. As summarized in Table 16.1, it can impact attitudes in many areas. As a matter of definition, accepters tend to feel that progress solves more problems than it creates, while rejecters feel the opposite. Similarly, accepters tend to be optimistic that solutions to progress-related problems will arrive in time. Rejecters are more likely to try to back out of that aspect of progress that caused the problem. For example, if a technology such as nuclear power exhibits an unexpected problem—as happened at Three Mile Island—accepters would assume that they could identify the source and work around it; rejecters would use the failure as an argument to abandon the technology. Accepters also view discontinuities in system behavior to be an inevitable fact of life; indeed, they can be positively viewed as the source of opportunities. Rejecters see discontinuities as evidence that the system is no longer working properly, if it ever did in the first place, and needs to be managed.

In looking at the past, accepters emphasize the positive trajectory, focusing on growth in personal income and technological accomplishment, giving progress much of the credit. Rejecters focus on mistakes of the past—wars, environmental damage, inequality, and injustice—placing much of the blame on *supposed* progress. These views carry over to the future, where accepters tend to be more optimistic about their children's future than rejecters[9]. Accepters also tend to be more confident in individual decision-making than rejecters—who are much more likely to believe that individuals need direction to compensate for flaws in the process of progress and human nature. Without such direction, they argue, selfish decisions will typically work against society's needs. Thus, accepters tend to favor leaving the landscape as is, despite its ruggedness. Rejecters seek to redesign the landscape, through policy and incentives, in order to encourage desired individual behaviors. These attitudes mirror the fact that accepters see the landscape as robust; rejecters view it as being more fragile and malleable.

Table 16.1: Ideology and Idea of Progress

Characteristic	Accept Idea of Progress	Reject Idea of Progress
Attitude towards progress	Faith in progress; solves more problems than it creates	Mistrust progress; creates more problems than it solves
Attitude towards problems	Progress will find solutions to existing problems, even those caused by progress	Where source of problems is progress, progress must be undone
The past	See progress of the past in positive light	Emphasis on the errors made in past progress
The future	On the whole, our children will be better off than we were	Our children will not necessarily be as well off as we were
Discontinuities in behavior	See discontinuities as inevitable; potential source of future opportunities	See discontinuities as evidence that progress must be contained and managed carefully
Individual decision making	Individuals generally make valid decisions on their own	Most individuals need direction in making good decisions
Landscape shape	Believe that naturally emerging rugged landscape favors long term fitness	Favor designing less rugged landscape to encourage globally sensible decisions
Nature's robustness	Believe natural landscape is generally robust	Believe natural landscape is fragile
Orientation	Individualist	Collective
Fitness	Emphasizes growth	Emphasizes equity

Accepters tend to be individualists in orientation, reflecting their view that progress is the inevitable result of individuals. Rejecters tend to have a more collective focus, reflecting beliefs that progress is acceptable only when it occurs by design, and through organized efforts. As a consequence, in the presumed trade-off between growth and equality, accepters tend to favor the growth that unconstrained progress offers, rejecters are more concerned with repairing the inevitable inequalities that such progress creates.

Naturally, the polarities listed in Table 16.1 are extremes. In fact, when respondents to the *World Values Survey* were asked to express the strength of their belief in a progress-related question using a scale of 1 to 10 to express the intensity of the individual's conviction, most responses were near the middle. Nonetheless, strong correlations between attitudes towards progress and responses to other questions do emerge[10]. For example, in the U.S. a stronger belief in individual progress was associated with individuals who:

A. Feel they have greater freedom of choice and control (V46)

B. Are more likely to believe that competition is good (V119)

C. Believe that living in a country governed democratically is important (V162)

D. Believe that people, rather than government, should take more responsibility for their own well-being (V118)

E. Believe that individual decisions, rather than fate, controls a person's destiny (V122)

F. Believe the world is better off as a result of science and technology (V123)

G. Believe that scientific advances will help us, rather than harm us, in the future (v90) and will also create more opportunities in the future (V92)

H. Describe personal ideology as being towards the right of the political spectrum (V114) and expect to vote Republican in national elections (V231)

I. Report that they feel happy (V11)

We are not necessarily fixed in our positions on the continuum between accepter and rejecter. A five year run-up in the stock market tends to breed acceptance of the Idea; an unexpected financial crisis that decimates our 401K accounts makes temporary rejecters of us all (at least for a while). I believe the Idea of Progress construct to be an important one, however. We now consider how it influences some of the greatest challenges facing in business today.

Three Challenges We Face

As stated at the very beginning of this book, recent years have been very trying for business around the globe. Businesses and business schools are still trying to decide how they should react. In many respects, however, the recent worldwide financial crisis may be the least significant of our problems. Financial crises come and go, often following the same pattern[11]. Their impact tends to be short-lived, however, at least when compared to the human life-span. Some of the greatest threats business faces remain to be addressed, however. In this section, I discuss three that concern me: the social effects of global climate change, the changing demographics of the developed world, and what my father refers to as the *Fundamental Predicament of Progress*.

Global Climate Change

There were three reasons that I felt global climate change was an appropriate subject for a book on business informing:

1. If widely accepted climate models are correct, we can expect climate change to dramatically alter the business landscape over the next 50 years.

2. A large number of business schools have, either independently or as an interdisciplinary effort, implemented programs relating to sustainability.

3. It provides an excellent case study of the uneasy mix between science and ideology that complexity can create.

Let me assert, at the outset, that I am a skeptic. Since I generally accept the Idea of Progress, it would nearly be impossible for me to be otherwise. I am also not a climatologist. To the extent I know anything at all about global warming, it is the result of an afternoon's worth of research, during which I tried to verify some basic facts and analyze some data that is widely, but not universally[12], accepted by both sides.

Let me begin by stating some beliefs I have that would certainly be consistent with those who argue that climate change is a serious problem; perhaps the most serious the world now faces. These are:

- Carbon dioxide levels have been rising over the past century.

- The global climate, being a complex system, will exhibit punctuated equilibrium and is therefore capable of very rapid transitions.

For these reasons alone, it makes sense to be concerned and—where possible—to moderate our behaviors so as not to precipitate any radical climate shifts.

It is the second of these points, that the climate is a complex system—and a complex adaptive system, if we truly believe that human beings are causing these changes—where I begin to have problems. Counter intuitively, the reported strength of the scientific consensus raises the first red flag. Naomi Orestes (2004) did a survey of 928 articles on climate change published between 1993 and 2003. According to her results, "none of the papers disagreed with the consensus position." A complex system, by its very nature, would not produce such a uniform set of results. Thus, we would either need to conclude the climate system is largely decomposable—and hold proposed models to a very high degree of accountability for the accuracy of their predictions—or conclude the scientific process itself has become derailed by ideology. As it turns out, existing climate models do not do a very good job predicting short term behaviors, as they would if the components of the climate system were decomposable and well understood. So we must consider what role ideology may have played.

Some climate trends

What about all the evidence and the scientific consensus? When you first consider the data, it appears to make a compelling case. Take, for example, the correlation between CO_2 and global temperature estimates. Over the past 50 years or so, it has been *very* impressive[13]. Indeed, there is a strong temptation to look at the plot and say "case closed." In fact, over the past 95 years, CO_2 levels predict temperature better than lots of other time series. In my tests, however, the competition for correlation was won by the unadjusted U.S. consumer price index (CPI). The fit of these series from 1958 is shown in Figure 16.1[14]. Of course, anyone familiar with time series analysis recognizes the phenomenon: whenever there is a trend, any two series that trend over the same period will be highly correlated—even if they trend in opposite directions. You need to do a lot better than that to establish causality.

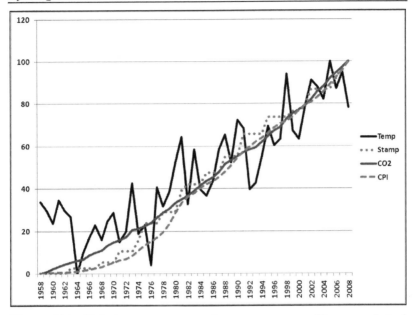

Figure 16.1: Global temperature estimates over past 50 years plotted against U.S. First Class postage stamp prices, atmospheric CO₂ levels and the U.S. Consumer Price Index. All values have been normalized so that their minimum value in the range is 0 and their maximum is 100.

Spurious correlations aside, the upward trend in Figure 16.1 is rather alarming. If we went back more than 100 years, we'd see the same trend—a total range of variation under 1.3 degrees[15]. But is this really so unusual? In Figure 16.2, I plot raw temperature estimates derived from two different Antarctic core sample studies to show our best guess is regarding the variation in past global temperatures from contemporary levels (0 on the graphs). The two series are extremely correlated, indicating high reliability. It should be noted that the present (on the right of the chart) is at or near the peak of a rapid warming trend that has occurred since the last ice age, most of which occurred well before human impact could have been material[16].

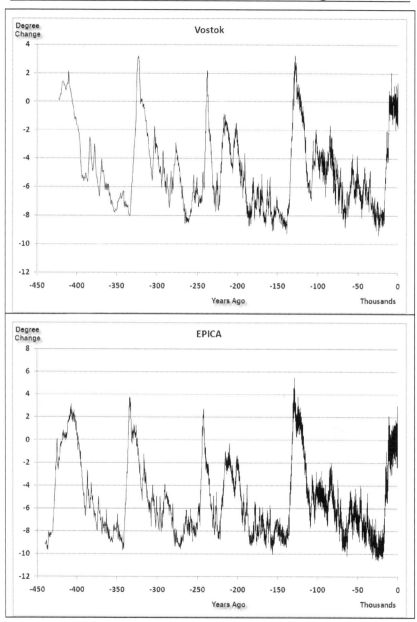

Figure 16.2: Global temperature estimates for past 400,000+ years from Vostok (Petit, et al. 1999) and EPICA (Jouzel, et al. 2007) Antarctic core estimates. Present day is on the right.

These temperature estimates are also highly correlated with CO_2 levels taken from core samples—suggesting that CO_2 levels are, in fact, a better predictor of global temperature than the CPI. The cause and effect is a bit fuzzy here, however. Anyone who has ever opened a warm soft drink knows that it is more explosive that a cold one. The oceans are among the world's greatest carbon sinks. Thus, as their temperature gets warmer, we would expect the rate of absorption of CO_2 to fall and atmospheric levels to rise. Thus, higher CO_2 is an effect of rising temperatures as well as a possible cause[17].

Climate scientists are fully aware of the problems I describe and their models are vastly more sophisticated and grounded in physical science than the simple correlations and averages I computed during my afternoon pretending to be a climatologist. My self-admitted and obvious limitations in understanding how climate works, however, do not change the fact that today's climate experts are attempting to make detailed predictions about the behavior of a complex system. As we have seen throughout this book, making such predictions is a task where experts tend to be overconfident but not very good.

Parallels to business research

As already noted, climatology is not within my sphere of expertise. I do, however, see a number of parallels to business research in terms of how it is being conducted.

Reliance on computer models

One obvious similarity between climate change science and business research—particularly as conducted in finance and economics—is heavy use of computer models. Common to both domains is a confidence in projecting long term trends in spite of an inability to accurately project the short term. To quote Andrew Dressler, a climate scientist at Texas A&M University:

> These long-term climate projections are a much easier problem than these shorter-term climate projections. It's sort of counterintuitive. (Ball, 2009, p. A21)

A statement such as Dressler's should be examined carefully. As it turns out, first noted in Chapter 3, weather models were among the first areas where the phenomenon of chaos was identified (Gleick, 1988). As a practical matter, the sensitive dependence on initial conditions exhibited by such models, sometimes called "the butterfly effect", makes it a practical impossibility to generate detailed predictions of the future. On the other hand, the tendency of such systems towards strange attractors means that patterns of behavior could be exhibited by such models over the long term, suggesting that long term predictions of general patterns of behaviors may be possible, as Dressler seems to imply. All this presumes, however, that the model being used is precisely correct—since small variations in the model could cause the long term predictions to vary wildly. As a result, it will take a really long time to determine if the model is correct[18].

To go a step further, as John D. Sterman (2002), Director of the MIT Systems Dynamics Group, pointed out when delivering the Jay Wright Forrester Prize Lecture[19], all models are necessarily wrong, although they may still be useful. Even well known climate models, such as the DICE model, chose to ignore factors—such as economic friction—that were nonetheless perceived to be important (Sterman, 2002, p. 518-519). The question then becomes, why did the developers stop at that point?

Answering that question, based on my many years experience building business computer models, involves recognizing the critical role played by the modeler's expectations. As models grow more complex, it becomes increasingly difficult to build them without knowing what effect you are trying to create. The problem is too many parameters whose values are questionable estimates and even some that are pure guesses. On the one hand, the ability to assume values for parameters gives the modeler great flexibility in demonstrating that a phenomenon *could take place* according to the model. On the other hand, our reliance on assumptions means we learn very little about whether or not a predicted phenomenon *will take place*, since demonstrating a particular set of assumptions make something possible does not make it probable. Thus, whatever confidence we have in the model must be based upon its ability to generate predictions better than any other model *and* better than the naïve type of forecasting approaches that I earlier applied.

As a practical matter, the climate models of several years back all predicted temperatures would rise. Since temperatures dropped slightly, parameters and assumptions in these models were then revisited, leading to new versions that now incorporate the drops[20]. We see the same thing constantly happening on Wall Street, where previously unpredicted changes are rapidly explained and incorporated into new models.

In neither case, however, does the confidence of the model builder appear to have been badly shaken by the lack of predictive power. That is human nature; it just does not happen to be particularly compelling science.

Powder puff tests

The switch in terminology, from "global warming" to "climate change" is a good example of movement towards powder puff testing. Global warming, at least, implies a testable hypothesis. If temperatures go down for a while, we must reject it. Climate change, on the other hand, cannot be tested. Climates always change (recall Figure 16.2), therefore support will always be available. The problem is that when the negative effects of climate change are discussed—such as rising sea levels and more violent hurricanes—they tend to be the effects of warming, not just change.

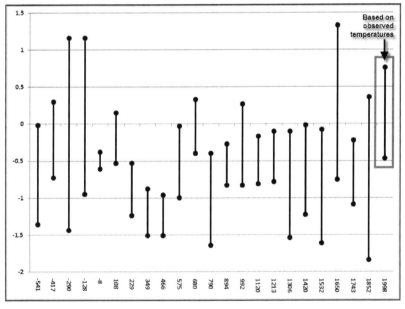

Figure 16.3: High and low temperatures for intervals of roughly 100 years based upon Vostok core sample estimates of global temperature. The final (rightmost) range is taken from actual temperature data, ending with 1998 (the hottest year on record). Earlier high temperature ranges are based on unsmoothed core sample estimates, which may (or may not) exhibit greater volatility.

Even global warming, however, is still a 50/50 powder puff test when the null hypothesis is no temperature change. A better test would be to compare the magnitude of changes experienced over the past 100 years with those typically experienced during 100 year intervals. In Figure 16.3, I take the raw Vostok core temperature estimates going back about 2500 years and break them into intervals of roughly 100 years. Viewed in High/Low/Close format[21], the case for global warming or increasing volatility does not appear as compelling.

Goal-driven research

In business research, the desire to produce theory drives a great deal of our research. In climate change research, the desire to *prove* that humans are impacting the climate seems to have become an overriding goal. The innate complexity of the global climate system facilitates that goal. As we have seen, where high levels of complexity are present, it is nearly always possible to make a cogent case for a particular point of view [1.3]. Thus, where the fitness landscape for grants and publication favors results that demonstrate the impact of human intervention, such results will be found—just as surely as there will be theory in submissions to top business journals.

It would be nearly impossible for an individual rejecting the Idea of Progress to resist the clarion call of climate change as a cause. This was verified by the *World Values Survey* results, where individuals more skeptical about progress were much less likely to be skeptical about global climate change. The reason for this relationship is that climate change has all the elements that would tend to confirm a rejecter's assumptions about the world. It is a direct consequence of uncontrolled growth; it threatens our entire species (quite a few animal and plant species, as well); it cries out for the enlightened to provide direction to the less informed masses; there is *no chance* the process of progress will help us adapt to find a solution[22]. The fact that we have encountered such predicaments in the past, and worked our way out of them, is irrelevant. In fact, in the eyes of many, *A Blueprint for Survival* actually got it right back in 1972. The catastrophe simply took a bit longer to materialize; sadly this only means that it will be worse than we ever imagined when it arrives.

Is there any other evidence that the climate change debate is more heavily colored by ideology than science? A number of aspects of the debate would suggest that it is. First, consider the assertion—frequently made by those who believe such change is imminent—that virtually all scientific evidence points to such change[23]. The only way that could be true is if our climate is not actually complex, but is instead simple. If the climate system is complex and there is such a one-sided preponderance of evidence, it can only mean that the process by which evidence is generated is extremely flawed. In fact, there is substantial anecdotal evidence suggesting that it is very difficult to get results that question the validity of climate change published or to get grants for research aimed at developing alternative explanations[24]. Under such circumstances, each new piece of supportive research tells us more about the process used to generate that research than it does about the phenomenon being investigated. We should not attach too much weight to the fact that Monty Hall shows us that there is nothing of interest behind door number 3, since we already knew that the prize behind whichever door he opened would be lame.

The role of business schools in climate change

Over the next decade or so, climate change is likely to figure very heavily into the agenda of business schools. A colleague of mine assures me that dozens of top business schools are considering sustainability programs; the Aspen Institute (2009) has started to publish rankings heavily weighted towards environmental consciousness. Issues relating to climate change, such as carbon cap-and-trade, are very much in the news and in the business consciousness.

By presenting my own skepticism regarding global climate change, it is definitely not my intent to change anyone's mind on the subject. Must I add, yet again, that I am not a climate scientist? What my goal has been is to argue that the matter is far from settled—unlike what the zealots on both sides of the debate would have us believe—and that business schools should play an active role in the discussion. What this means, in particular, is that we should be examining the economic consequences of programs and, from time-to-time, even spot checking the science. While most of us have little experience in climate modeling, we do have experience in researching complex systems.

To take an *active* role, we need to ensure that any sustainability program that we launch invites input from both sides of the ideological spectrum: those of us who believe in the Idea of Progress, and those who feel that the Idea has, perhaps, outlived its usefulness. The business school is one of the few places in the typical university where individuals ready to argue both sides of the issue can be found. Using liberal vs. conservative as a (very) weak proxy for belief in the Idea of Progress, we find vast disparities in the typical university. For example, according to recent surveys (Mariani & Hewitt, 2008, p. 775, 777):

- At U.S. Research I universities, the ratio of self-identified liberals to conservatives is 4.9:1[25].

- In the physical sciences—where climatology would normally be located—the ratio is 4.1:1.

- In history and government—where future-policy makers might reside—the ratio is 6.2:1.

- In social sciences, the ratio is 5.8:1.

Only in health sciences (1:1) and business (0.8:1) are the ratios anywhere near parity. If we are to have an honest debate—one that actually leads to informing rather than reinforcement of a shared ideology—both sides of the argument need to be seated at the table and prepared to talk. Once again, we see the value of business school faculty pursuing transdisciplinary research that engages other researchers within the university.

For my own part, while I am very suspicious of much of the current science, I believe that some of the outcomes desired by its proponents could be quite beneficial. Expanding the portfolio of energy sources we use, making more use of solar, wind, nuclear, geothermal, and other sources, makes a great deal of sense on a complex landscape; recall that diversity is one of the best ways to ensure survival. Similarly, I can think of few situations where reducing wasteful behavior is inappropriate. Conservation is typically virtuous. The danger we need to avoid is any reflexive reaction that causes us to dwell upon imperfect estimates of fitness—such as atmospheric carbon dioxide levels—as an excuse to mandate certain behaviors. Paradoxically, such a course would end up making us less adaptable (as overemphasizing *any* single estimate of fitness tends to do) in the long run. Consequently, by adopting such measures in a single-minded fashion, we may well become less able to mitigate climate effects should they arrive as some predict.

The Predicament of Aging Populations

Critics of the Idea of Progress point to the rapidly rising populations of the developing world; the fears of Malthus are still with us. Adherents of the Idea point to a very different concern: the declining birth rates of the developed world.

The predicament is well known to demographers. Once nations reach a certain level of development, birth rates start to decline—often quite sharply. In moderation, this is a very good thing; in the past, it derailed all the Malthusian predictions. Taken to excess, these declines present serious challenges for the future.

Changing age distributions

The single measure that best captures our expectations for population age distribution is fertility rate. This measure reflects the mean number of children per woman in the population. With normal mortality from other causes in a developed country, a steady state value for fertility rate is about 2.1. At that level, population will neither grow nor shrink over time and age distributions will ultimately reach a stabilize—barring major changes to life expectancy (which have been the rule rather than the exception in modern times of progress).

Table 16.2: Fertility rates and projections for selected countries (from Table A.15, *World Population Prospects, The 2006 Revision, Highlights,* U.N. Economic and Social Affairs)

	1970-1975	2000-2005	2005-2010	2020-2025	2045-2050
U.S.	2.02	2.04	2.05	1.88	1.85
Japan	2.07	1.29	1.27	1.35	1.6
Italy	2.33	1.29	1.38	1.49	1.74
U.K.	2.04	1.7	1.82	1.85	1.85
France	2.31	1.88	1.89	1.85	1.85
Germany	1.64	1.35	1.36	1.49	1.74
India	5.26	3.11	2.81	2.13	1.85
China	4.86	1.7	1.73	1.85	1.85
World	**4.47**	**2.65**	**2.55**	**2.29**	**2.02**

Fertility rates vary considerably by country, and have dropped rapidly in recent years—particularly in the developed and rapidly developing world. 1970 and present-day values, along with U.N. projections[26] for the future, are listed for selected countries in Table 16.2. What these numbers suggest is that many developing countries—such as Japan, the European countries and even China—are currently experiencing below-replacement fertility rates.

The challenge presented by rapidly changing birth rates—in either direction—is the impact on a country's dependency ratio. The ability of a population to contribute to the economy varies by age. The very young and very old tend to be net consumers of goods and services; those in the ages between therefore need to generate a surplus. Where birth rates are very high, you get a large population of individuals too young to work; this is particularly problematic as economic activity moves in the direction of knowledge work, where it takes longer to education productive workers. Where birth rates are very low, as it now true for much of the developed world, the opposite problem occurs. The number of elderly people rises.

In Figure 16.4, the 2005 values for percentage of the population between 15 and 60 (a rough proxy for the size of the working population) are presented for the same countries shown in Table 16.2. While the difference does not appear to be particularly alarming for the U.S. (which has a fertility rate close to replacement), it is still quite significant. During that 45 year period, the dependent proportion of the population grows from 37% to 44%, almost a 20% increase. Because 60-70% of U.S. federal budget outlays directly serve the dependent population[27], and because the tax burden would fall on a work force that is 10% smaller (as a percentage of the population) we could expect the U.S. federal government percentage of GDP to rise from its 2008 level of 21% to something along the lines 25-26% (making the conservative, and therefore highly unlikely, assumption that no new programs are added). Add another 20% of GDP for state and local spending[28], which is less likely to rise with dependency ratio[29], and we see government expenditures representing nearly 50% of the U.S. economy[30]. The situation is far graver for the countries in Western Europe, whose dependency ratios are changing by a much larger amount and whose governmental expenditure percentages of GDP are already 5 to 15% higher[31]. Japan, on the other hand, has government expenditures slightly below those of the U.S. but a much higher cumulative debt and by far the most severe change in projected dependency ratio.

If we continue to follow the current trend, we could easily see government spending representing 50-70% of economic activity, in the U.S.,

Japan, and Europe. At such a high level of government activity, we start to become indistinguishable from the command economies of the past. What concerns me is that we may become politically similar as well. In order to live up to past commitments, a huge transfer of wealth from the working population to the dependent population will be required. As a result, the incentive to hide economic activity from the tax collector will grow. To ensure compliance, increasingly coercive enforcement measures may be required. Such a system could easily spiral to a point where individuals participate in the system only to the extent that it keeps them from getting arrested.

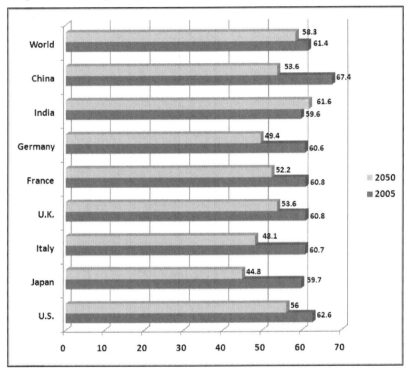

Figure 16.4: Percentage of the population in the 15-60 age range for selected countries for 2005 and estimated for 2050 (from Table A.10, *World Population Prospects, The 2006 Revision, Highlights*, U.N. Economic and Social Affairs)

Potential for progress

Fortunately, progress has the potential to alter any inevitability. In Figure 16.5, the breakdown of average expenditures for U.S. individuals over 65 is presented. If the costs associated with dependency could be reduced, the cost of government commitments would be reduced correspondingly. Looking at the figure, the obvious area where reduction needs to take place is medical expenses. Adding the cost of Medicare to out-of-pocket costs, these expenses consume about 42% of the budget of those over 65. Oddly enough, most elderly people that I know do not savor the hours they spend under medical care. If such care can be made more effective and efficient, few would object if less money was spent on it.

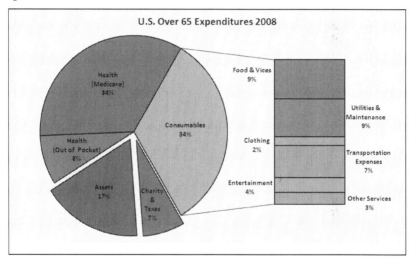

Figure 16.6: Breakdown of household expenses for U.S. individuals 65 and older, from Table 47, 2009 Consumer Expenditure Survey, U.S. Bureau of Labor Statistics. Medicare expenditures were estimated by dividing total 2008 Medicare expenses ($456 billion, as reported by the U.S. Congressional Budget Office) by the U.S. population that is over 65.

I cannot offer any concrete path to reducing medical costs. I would warn against assuming such costs are not susceptible to progress, however. Just over a hundred years ago, that same 40%+ of the individual's budget would have been devoted to food—today, it is 9%, even after including tobacco and alcohol. Manufactured goods have also declined substantially in their percentage of total spending. If individuals and companies participating on the fitness landscape believe that fitness can only be achieved by developing novel ways of reducing medical costs, then we can expect to see a steady stream of cost reducing innovations, as we saw in agriculture and the technology industries.

Unfortunately, today's system for delivering medicine has evolved into a form where actual costs are so divorced from those receiving services that cost reduction is almost entirely absent from the fitness landscape. In the U.S., for example, the vast majority of individual medical expenses are paid through health insurance or by government programs. Insurance, in turn, is largely paid for by employers; government programs through payroll and income taxes. Medical service providers, such as hospitals, bill by allocating costs—often in a manner that has little to do with actual costs. We have all heard of the $10 aspirin on a hospital bill. Doctors and other providers are generally compensated on a per-service basis, creating a strong incentive to over-provide. This incentive is exacerbated by a legal specialty built upon exacting heavy tolls for physician mistakes. Not only does this add to direct costs, it also leads to untold costs for "defensive medicine."

Under a system structured such that costs and prices are unknown—and probably unknowable—we cannot expect progress to reduce costs. We need estimates of fitness, at the consumer level, that incorporate costs if progress is to produce transformations that reduce costs. Regrettably, our current attempts to fix the system do little to make costs an important component of the fitness landscape. Indeed, the notion that insurance should cost nearly the same for everyone—despite the fact that there are huge differences in the actual services they are likely to consume—may make the problem worse. (Recall the Chapter 9 footnote, where the most expensive 50 patients collectively cost Blue Cross & Blue Shield of Ohio more than the least expensive 75,000). Indeed, I cannot recall any industries where massive government participation has actually led to a fitness function with a strong cost containment element.

The other area of large public participation in the economy is education. Here, Clayton Christensen is already predicting that distance learning technologies could have a transformative impact, reversing decades of ever-increasing costs per student (Christensen, Horn, & Johnson, 2008). Once more, existing institutions may prove to be an obstacle to progress. Regulations, established by well meaning school boards, combine with work rules and seniority-driven salary schedules negotiated by unions to protect their members, to move the fitness function away from cost recognition and containment. Progress tends to take place in the direction of what is being measured. Thus, the current emphasis on test scores has led to increases along that dimension of fitness (Christensen, Horn, & Johnson, 2008, p. 63). Until cost is similarly built into the equation, we should not expect to see much progress in that area.

Figuring out how to bring costs into the fitness function is, of course, only part of the solution to the aging population. Immigration policies—that encourage legal immigration while reducing the fitness of illegal immigration—can also serve to reduce dependency ratios. Typical retirement age will certainly increase; the system was not built for 20-25 years of retirement and 65 year olds are much younger today, in health terms, than they were when our systems were conceived. Raising birth rates could be another factor influencing the long term contributor. That the problem in the U.S. is somewhat less serious than what is being faced in Europe is a result of our higher fertility; at around 2.05, it is almost at replacement levels.

With respect to birth rates, we can also see how progress plays an important role. As nations move from developing to developed, birth rates drop sharply. Once nations reach the developed state, however, the factors impacting birth rate appear to change. In fact, as shown in Figure 16.7, when birth rates of developed countries (excluding former eastern-bloc countries) are related to their Net Happiness Index, a strong relationship (adjusted R-square of 0.56) is observed. As it turns out, happiness is one of the variables showing the strongest association with the Idea of Progress. This, of course makes sense. If you believe your children will live in a better world, you should be willing to have more of them. If, on the other hand, you are pessimistic about the future, you can easily come to view having more children as a selfish act.

The close relationship between birth rates and the Idea of Progress was, in fact, one of the central elements of the theory that my father proposed in *Posterity Lost* (R.T. Gill, 1997). In Figure 16.7 we see evidence that believing in the positive inevitability of progress may actually exert a concrete impact.

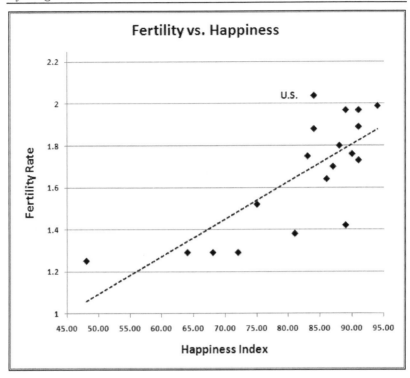

Figure 16.7: 2005 Fertility rates for Western European countries plus U.S., Canada, Japan and Australia plotted against Net Happiness Index from NationMaster.com (derived from 2005 World Values Survey)

Business schools and the aging population

Business researchers have long studied the problems of incentives. Unlike students of government and macro-economists, however, our focus has often been at the individual and organizational unit level. These are the areas where the rapid adaptation that is the driving force of the process of progress takes place. We need to sit at the table with public policy makers to ensure that the landscape structures that promote adaptation are not inadvertently dismantled through well-meaning public initiatives that too heavily rely on top-down thinking[32].

The aging population also means that business schools need to place greater emphasis on re-education and continuous education. Some elite schools, such as HBS, already do this through their executive programs.

At many universities, however, the task of providing ongoing education to adult learners is relegated to continuing education organizations, divorced from research and the academic mainstream. Ironically, a large percentage of these non-credit and certificate courses focus on business and technology. What we need to recognize is that the complexity of today's business environment will virtually mandate that many, if not most, participants in the system will find themselves changing careers later in life. If we wish to exert true impact on our local community, these individuals need to be every bit as important to us as our fresh-faced undergraduates and MBA candidates.

Serving the needs of the aging population will require greater flexibility on our part as well as the creative use of technology. We will also need to think carefully about how the needs of the experienced worker—likely to be an expert in some job area already—can be met and their skills leveraged. The changes we need to make to accommodate them will be worth the effort. If we employ pedagogies based on the assumption that students can drive their own learning process—rather than relying on our existing course designs, built around the needs of novice learners—we stand to learn as much as they do.

The Fundamental Predicament of Progress

The price we pay for each of the transformations that the process of progress brings about is relatively modest: a slight increase in the complexity of the world in which we live. These increases are cumulative, however. Eventually, complexity itself may become the problem. As we have seen, increasing system complexity tends to promote shorter time horizons. Thus, in what may be the paradox of the age, as technological changes rapidly increases our lifespan, our ability to make plans for our lives—and to plan for the needs of our children—seems to be declining at an equally rapid rate.

The nature of the Fundamental Predicament

The interaction between process and Idea leads to what my father refers to as the *Fundamental Predicament of Progress*. Up to this point in history, the process of progress has largely been sustained by the Idea of Progress. The Idea serves as our estimate-of-fitness. When the process generates some new innovation, we can rarely perceive all of its potential consequences. The Idea makes us confident that the net effect of those innovations that survive the test of the marketplace will be to improve our collective lives. Thus we are motivated to continue innovating, believing that society will develop in a positive way. The parallel to evolution is strong. In genetics, not all mutations are good—to the contrary, most are bad. Evolution works because the good ones are more likely to survive; the bad ones generally die out before they can do too much damage to the system. So it is with the Idea of Progress.

What makes the Idea sustainable is its long term perspective. We need to overcome the setbacks that the process necessarily generates. Discontinuities are inevitable in a complex system like the economy; they are also essential, as they create or unveil opportunities for innovation. The process also leads to inequalities—often huge inequalities. Try too hard to stamp these out and you also undermine the process. The good news is that the consequences of these inequalities may not be as undesirable and long lasting as they may first appear. What do John D. Rockefeller, Andrew Carnegie, Alfred P. Sloan, Henry Ford and George F. Baker have in common? They all became very rich and were vilified for it in their day. What else do they have in common? They initiated the Rockefeller Foundation, the Carnegie Foundation, the Ford Foundation and the Alfred P. Sloan Foundation; George F. Baker, who founded the precursor to Citibank, donated the entire initial funding for Harvard Business School. Who is vilified as today's biggest robber baron? Bill Gates. Who founded what is perhaps the most significant charitable foundation of all time? The same Bill Gates—with some added billions from Warren Buffet, who routinely competes with Gates for the richest person slot on the Forbes list. Does inequality guarantee generosity? Of course not... but the fact that they frequently accompany each other—in the U.S., at least—should not be ignored either.

What makes the Fundamental Predicament of Progress so fundamental is the fact that the process of progress tends to undermine time horizons. As we saw in Chapter 9, innovative technology and globalization both tend to increase the complexity of the economic system. Technology, particularly information technology, speeds up the rate at which we can gather information and react to it. Globalization increases the number of individuals in the systems whose actions can affect us. It too is a natural consequence of the process of progress—social progress, in particular. Once nations stop trying to invent reasons to fight with each other, starting to trade with each other is the next natural step.

As system complexity increases, however, it becomes increasingly difficult to make meaningful predictions about where we will be in the future. One of the first principles of finance is that we discount that about which we are uncertain. The paradoxical result: the more effective the process of progress is in producing change, the harder it is to maintain continued belief in the Idea of Progress. The growing frequency of discontinuities and the increasing tendency for inequalities to appear begin to seem like evidence that the process is no longer working. Ironically, such behaviors actually suggest that progress is still running strong. But they make it very easy to give up on the Idea.

All this does not mean that progress must be allowed to run entirely unchecked. In fact, a central premise of Kauffman's (1993) theory is that successful fitness landscapes exist on a boundary between order and chaos. The process of progress, absent constraints, could therefore drive us too far in the direction of chaos. It is very important, however, not to so heavily constrain the process that it slows to a crawl. Order may sound appealing in concept, but it will tend to freeze in place those problems created by past progress. Consider the frighteningly low birth rates, declining life expectancies, and high pollution levels left behind by the old command economies to see what "order" looks like.

Business Schools and the Fundamental Predicament

If the Idea of Progress fails, there will be no need for business schools.

This single statement is the conclusion that ties the current chapter with those that preceded it. My argument is based on the following logic:

1. In Chapters 1 and 2, I presented the case that nearly all of our research—outside of economics and finance—is largely being ignored by practice.

2. In Chapter 10, I suggested a number of reasons why current business research findings—our attempts to impose attractive, orderly theory on a rugged landscape—are not as rigorous as we presume them to be. That applies to all business disciplines.

3. In Chapter 14, supported by the analysis of informing in Chapters 4 through 7, I suggested that the design of our existing curricula was not constructed in such a manner as to produce enduring impact on our students.

4. In Chapter 14, I also pointed out that the skills that managers seem to prize—communications, collaboration, problem solving, and knowing how to learn—are at best presumed to be unmeasured side effects of the courses we currently teach.

Collectively, these support a view that business schools, operating "as usual" may not have much of a future in a resource-constrained environment.

On the other hand, I also point out that there are many areas where business schools can make a useful contribution through their informing activities. In informing our students, we can teach the skills for coping with complexity; these happen to be the very skills that managers most value. I tend to agree with Mintzberg (2004) that day-to-day management is a practice that is better learned in the field than in a classroom. Considering how we might react to the various color swans that eventually disrupt any complex environment, on the other hand, is something we need to do in the classroom; waiting around for one to happen in the field is too costly. I made a similar observation with respect to our research. Offering a manager a theory relating to the routine performance of his or her job is generally presumptuous, if not downright rude. We should anticipate they have already developed rules for behaving in such an environment. Helping them to consider how they might react to the truly unexpected or working with them to investigate new emerging peaks on the fitness landscape is another matter entirely. During disruptions, there are no established rules to follow [5.1].

Framed in the context of the current chapter, what I am suggesting is that where business schools can be most useful is in helping businesses cope with the process of progress. As long as that process continues, we will always have a useful role.

The question we need to ask then becomes: Will the process of progress continue if the Idea of Progress is lost? It is with respect to this question that I have my gravest doubts.

The Greatest Threat

At the Harvard Business School doctoral reunion that I attended in spring 2009, we discussed a case titled "Harvard Business School." At one point in the discussion, the facilitator posed the following question to the audience (all former doctoral students):

> What is the greatest competitive threat to Harvard Business School in the future?

For five minutes, the usual suspects were named: distance learning, cheaper state universities, for profit institutions, corporate training, etc. I have to admit, I was a bit disappointed by the linear thinking of my colleagues. To me, the most compelling threat was obvious: Harvard Law School.

Although I appreciated the laugh my suggestion garnered when I finally tossed it into the discussion, I did not throw it out as a joke. Rather, my purpose was to point out that losing the "best and brightest" students to other business schools is much less serious than what happens if these students abandon business altogether.

My choice of law school, in particular, was not a cynical attempt to instigate a round of lawyer-bashing (as enjoyable a pastime as that may be). Lawyers—like legislators, academics, union leadership, and, to a lesser extent, accountants—play a vital balancing role in the competitive ecology. Whereas the managers thrive through adaptation, taking full advantage of the flexibility offered by a rugged landscape and more than occasionally leaving chaos in their wake, these other professions and occupations actually acquire fitness through introducing rigidities into the landscape. Returning to the complexity definitions presented in Chapter 3, their fitness derives from *problem space complexity*, which describes the number of rules and concepts required to perform a task. Individuals in these careers benefit professionally from being purveyors of problem space complexity; their long term interest is in seeing it continually increase. The more complicated the legal system, the greater the need for lawyers[33]. The more complicated the regulatory environment, the greater the value of legislative experience and the greater the opportunity to slip in special favors to constituents. The greater the size of the body of rules, principles, and concepts that must be mastered in a discipline, the greater the need for extended academic training. Union negotiators counter the excesses of management with highly specialized inflexible work rules and detailed specific pay plans—heavily weighted towards seniority—while minimally rewarding adaptation skills. When the Sarbanes-Oxley Act of 2002 was passed, dramatically increasing reporting requirements and accountability for public companies, an accounting degree became the hottest ticket in business schools.

Without the law and appropriate regulations, the business environment might well descend into chaos. The danger we face today, however, is that in a panic we may introduce inflexibilities into the system that undermine the process of progress to a degree that will be very hard to reverse. At the present time, the forces motivating increased control of the system are great. The international economy has recently experienced great discontinuities as a result of the global credit crisis. Who could blame the people on Main Street for wanting to exert greater control over the players on Wall Street? On top of that, we have the twin long term threats discussed in this chapter. The threat of global warming is taken by many as a mandate for immediate and extensive regulation of the energy sector. The threat of an aging population has U.S. legislators approving greatly increased government involvement in the health care system.

Even assuming that we overcome the immediate threats we face, the process of progress can be seriously undermined if business loses its luster as a career. One of the greatest assets of U.S. business has been its ability to attract talented individuals[34]. If these individuals instead decide to pursue careers in fields where fitness is gained by regulating progress, the consequences for progress would not be good. A U.S. Supreme Court Justice, Antonin Scalia (2009), has already complained about the high quality of legal counsel. In an interview on CPAN he commented:

> I mean lawyers, after all, don't produce anything. They enable other people to produce and to go on with their lives efficiently and in an atmosphere of freedom. That's important, but it doesn't put food on the table and there have to be other people who are doing that. And I worry that we are devoting too many of our very best minds to this enterprise.

Sustaining the Idea of Progress

The potential usefulness of business schools is intimately tied to the process of progress. If that process ceases, then the most we can aspire to is "trade school" status: teaching the rules of routine behavior [5.1]. For much of humanity's history, slow or no progress has been the rule, rather than the exception. There are many places in the world today where progress is not applauded. Where the Idea of Progress flourishes, however, progress continues its forward, if rather bumpy, trajectory. The Idea has been the principal driver of the modern age.

What can business schools do to sustain the Idea of Progress and, thereby, justify their own continued existence? Perhaps the most important thing we can do is instill a sense of perspective in our students and in the managers we inform. The elements of that perspective can come from a number of sources. First and foremost, individuals need to become aware of how complex systems behave. When you recognize the characteristic patterns of punctuated equilibrium, it is much easier not to panic when observing the phenomenon in the real world. Progress is not always pretty in the wake of the creative destruction it leaves behind and it rarely seems to be fair when viewed in the short term. Nevertheless, it is comforting to know that these pathologies are consistent with a pattern of activity that has—for all its faults—taken humanity to a level of prosperity that is unparalleled in all its history.

An understanding of history itself can be another source of perspective. In the U.S., many of today's students have very limited knowledge of history in general, and almost no knowledge of business history. While understanding history is no substitute for actually experiencing the ups and downs of the business cycle, it is certainly better than assuming every speed bump that progress generates is unprecedented. It is difficult to develop long time horizons without a concept of the past.

Optimism is a critical component of the Idea of Progress. Lacking optimism, the disruptions created by the process are just too scary. The faculty members of a business school have a great advantage over the popular press in one important respect: they do not have to sell newspapers with anxiety-provoking headlines. To quote President Franklin D. Roosevelt's most famous line, "the only thing we have to fear is fear itself." It was spoken at his inauguration, in the midst of another dark time during which it seemed as if progress had abruptly come to an end.

Naturally, a business school is made up of a group of individuals, a substantial minority of whom may have long-since abandoned the Idea of Progress. Encouraging such dissent is healthy. Discussing differences in perspectives openly and respectfully offers its own form of comfort. It conveys the sense that our ideas are born of reason, not just ideology. It also signals our embracing of diversity—which is, after all, one of the best ways of coping with complexity.

Conclusions

In order to survive, business schools must be useful. In order to be useful, they must inform business. There are many ways we can do this. We can inform our students: the future employees and managers of industry. We can inform practice. We can inform those other disciplines that use business to translate their ideas into practical, commercial realities. And, in order to accomplish these important goals, we need to keep each other informed as well.

For too long business researchers have focused on the last of these informing activities without measuring, or even particularly caring about, the impact we exert on students, practice, and other disciplines. In an age where other social concerns seem sure to divert resources away from self-indulgent academic activities in the future, our current path is a recipe for extinction.

The focus of this chapter has been on progress. The process of progress turns out to be fundamental in terms of what can make a business school useful. For the last 50 years or so, most of our research has been directed towards building an understanding of the orderly; part of the reason that so little of what we have done has made its way into practice is that practicing managers, for the most part, are already pretty good at handling the routine. They are also good at instructing new hires in that task. To believe otherwise is little more than hubris on our part and will, with considerable justification, be viewed as arrogance by those we intend to inform. Progress, on the other hand, continually presents managers with the unexpected, the unexplored, and the uncomfortable. By emphasizing, in our research and teaching, what can be done to prepare for and cope with discontinuities, we enter an area of the fitness landscape where *everyone* can benefit from an outside opinion. Because globalization and information technology tend to accelerate the process of progress, the value of help in dealing with its vagaries is ever growing.

Sustained progress is not inevitable, however. To the contrary, periods such as the last three centuries have been relatively rare in human history. For progress to flourish, it must be nurtured by a complementary ideology, known as the Idea of Progress. This ideology, based on a foundation of optimism and a faith that the world will ultimately be a better place as a result of progress, allows us to weather the turbulence of the process without abandoning the system. Lose faith in the Idea, and the process will soon be undermined by our attempts to "fix it".

Today, much of the Western world is at an ideological crossroads. While rapidly developing nations, such as China, India, and Brazil, retain a strong faith in progress, many in Europe and the U.S. seem to be losing confidence. Truly, the challenges we face are great. We may be doing serious damage to our planet's climate. We certainly are facing an aging population that will strain our future resources to a degree unparalleled in human history. Inequalities between rich and poor have never seemed so stark. Many argue that progress is to blame; they are, of course, right. The question is, will further progress clean up the problems it created—as it has done so often in the past—or is what we face today truly different from anything that has come before?

It is impossible to answer questions such as the last with complete confidence. That is why ideology is at least as important as science in this particular debate. If research business schools want to flourish, however, we would do well to subscribe to the Idea of Progress a little while longer, and to ensure the rest of society is aware of our view. Progress provides the most compelling justification for our existence. I, for one, will do my best to continue to nurture it.

Chapter 16 Foundational References

Gill, R. T. (1997). *Posterity lost: Progress, ideology, and the decline of the American family*. Lanham, MD: Rowan & Littlefield.

Chapter 16 Notes

[1] Consider, for example, the series of quotes taken from the introductory paragraphs of *A Blueprint for Survival* (Goldsmith & Allen, 1972), a special issue of *The Ecologist* later reprinted as a book:

> 110. The principal defect of the industrial way of life with its ethos of expansion is that it is not sustainable. Its termination within the lifetime of someone born today is inevitable-unless it continues to be sustained for a while longer by an en-

trenched minority at the cost of imposing great suffering on the rest of mankind. We can be certain, however, that sooner or later it will end (only the precise time and circumstances are in doubt), and that it will do so in one of two ways: either against our will, in a succession of famines, epidemics, social crises and wars; or because we want it to-because we wish to create a society which will not impose hardship and cruelty upon our children-in a succession of thoughtful, humane and measured changes...

111. Radical change is both necessary and inevitable because the present increases in human numbers and per capita consumption, by disrupting ecosystems and depleting resources, are undermining the very foundations of survival...

130. Increases in food production in the undeveloped world have barely kept abreast of population growth. Such increases as there have been are due not to higher productivity but to the opening up of new land for cultivation. Unfortunately this will not be possible for much longer: all the good land in the world is now being farmed and according to the FAO[2] at present rates of expansion none of the marginal land that is left will be unfarmed by 1985 - indeed some of the land now under cultivation has been so exhausted that it will have to be returned to permanent pasture...

132. Whatever their virtues and faults, the new genetic hybrids are not intended to solve the world food problem, but only to give us time to devise more permanent and realistic solutions. It is our view, however, that these hybrids are not the best means of doing this, since their use is likely to bring about a reduction in overall diversity, when the clear need is to develop an agriculture diverse enough to have long-term potential. We must beware of those 'experts' who appear to advocate the transformation of the ecosphere into nothing more than a food-factory for man. The concept of a world consisting solely of man and a few favoured food plants is so ludicrously impracticable as to be seriously contemplated only by those who find solace in their own wilful ignorance of the real world of biological diversity...

150. The developed nations consume such disproportionate amounts of protein, raw materials and fuels that unless they considerably reduce their consumption there is no hope of the undeveloped nations markedly improving their standards of living…

[2] Recall from Chapter 15 how the percentage of the U.S. population actively engaged in farming dropped from about 60% to 2.5% in a period of just over 100 years.

[3] *A Blueprint for Survival*'s projections for oil consumption and supply were illustrated with two curves that ominously intersected around 1999, presumably the year that we would run out of oil. I recall those curves from my 1973 introductory economics course at Harvard. At the time, I thought to myself: "this can't be good".

[4] Accessed from the Bulletin of Atomic Scientists web site on 10/27/09 at http://www.thebulletin.org/content/doomsday-clock/overview

[5] Certainly, there was no shortage of conflicts during the Cold War in which the superpowers engaged each other by proxy, either overtly or surreptitiously; Korea, Vietnam, and Afghanistan are all examples of these. Thus, no one can argue that there was little hostility during the period from 1947-1991. Nevertheless, the U.S. and U.S.S.R. both avoided direct aggressions.

[6] Since the precise dates are not very important, I used the timeline from http://www.middle-ages.org.uk/middle-ages-timeline.htm

[7] The Middle Ages began with the Battle of Hastings in 1066, included four Crusades, and concluded with the 100 Years War followed by the War of the Roses.

[8] By the mid-1800s, the majority of Irish farmers had become completely dependent upon one crop—the potato—for sustenance. When blight destroyed most of the crop, mass starvation and immigration to the U.S. occurred.

[9] My father's thesis is that the strength of the traditional family and the Idea of Progress are very intimately related. Thus, when one breaks down, so will the other.

[10] To assess if personal values clustered, I tested U.S. results from the *World Values Survey 2005-2008* (http://www.worldvaluessurvey.org/), which included over 1200 responses. As an anchor, I performed cross tabulations with the question (V121) that best seemed to capture the *Idea of Progress*, the continuum between:

> 1. People can only get rich at the expense of others

> 10. Wealth can grow so there's enough for everyone

Roughly 2/3 of U.S. respondents replied with values of 5 through 8. To look at the relationship between other variables and progress, I performed a cross-tabulation with each variable and the progress variable (V121), seeing how the mean value for the progress variable differed based upon responses to the compared variable. Because of the large sample size, statistical significance for any observed differences was nearly guaranteed. I therefore assumed the weighted average of positive vs. negative responses of the compared variables needed to be at least a 0.5 difference in the average "progress" values for the same individuals.

[11] In just the last one hundred years, there have been at least ten according to Carmen Reinhart and Kenneth Rogoff (2009, p. 254) in their recent book *This Time Is Different: Eight Centuries of Financial Folly*, which details the history of such crises. The authors argue that many of these crises exhibit a remarkable similarity of structure, suggesting that their impact does not exert a lasting impression on the affected communities.

[12]The data I use would be more likely to be rejected by climate change skeptics, some of whom accuse certain scientists of manipulating the data to favor their own position. In general, believers in global warming tend to use the same series that I acquired.

[13] When I ran the numbers, using data from NASA and scientific journals, I found an R-square of nearly 0.90, quite high enough to publish, had such analyses not already been published many times.

[14] I start the Figure 16.1 series in 1958, which is when the temperature station in Hawaii began recording temperatures (prior to that, ice core temperature estimates were used—which were adjusted to make them consistent with the Hawaii values). The series in the figure are all normalized over the period, so their lowest value is 0, their highest is 100.

If the actual regression fit results were plotted, the curves would be slightly displaced in the graph to obtain the best possible fit.

An anonymous source on the Internet suggested that U.S. stamp price mapped well to global temperature and, sure enough, it does.

[15] The 1.23 degree difference between maximum and minimum global temperatures over the period from 1897 to 2006 does not appear to be particularly unusual. Using the Vostok core sample temperatures, for example, and intervals of roughly a century each (the core samples were not taken at precisely even intervals), the range of variation within each interval *averaged* about 1.14 degrees over the previous 2500 years, with 8 of 22 periods having higher variations.

[16] If temperature stops rising where it is now, we would have experienced one of the *lower* major peaks of the past 450,000 years. In fact, the range of variation *in this period* was about 12-15 degrees. From this, it is reasonable to conclude that "expected natural variations" should be advanced as a viable alternative hypothesis to explain recent global temperature increases.

[17] If CO_2 levels were to be the major cause of global warming, then the result would be a positive feedback loop, where rising CO_2 raises temperature leading to reduced CO_2 absorption by ocean surface layers (Sterman, 2002, p. 517), leading to further temperature rise, leading to further release, and so forth. There need to be other effects—such as increased cloud cover—that work in the opposite direction otherwise the climate would be so unstable that most forms of life could not survive.

[18] If a climate model is not governed by sensitive dependence on initial conditions, Dressler's claim would seem to be much weaker. For non-chaotic models, which tend to produce trends and/or repetitive cycles, we would expect the uncertainty associated with predictions to grow over time. Thus, if the model proves to be wrong in the short run—as was the case for nearly all the climate models after 2005, when actual temperatures dropped slightly instead of rising as predicted—then we would hardly expect the model to grow more accurate in its future predictions.

[19] Jay Forrester is generally acknowledged to be the father of systems dynamics, and his influence was strongly felt in many of the global

models that produced doomsday forecasts, as well as in much of the business modeling done today.

[20] For example, a recent *Wall Street Journal* article (Ball, 2009, A21) identifies two studies, one British and one German, that now assert that the recent cooling trend was to be expected as a consequence of climate change. The article concludes by saying:

> But they disagree among themselves on how long the cooling will last. The British paper says warming will resume as early as this year. The German paper says warming won't resume for perhaps a decade.
>
> Such disagreements aren't unusual in a nascent science. "I don't think anybody is surprised that we're going to get one model that suggests it's going to cool and another that suggests it's going to warm," says Vicky Pope, a scientist at the Hadley Center, the U.K. institute where the research for the British paper was done. "That's consistent with where we are with the science."

[21] There are all sorts of potential problems with the way the raw data is presented—the largest of which is that core sample data is not necessarily a valid proxy for global temperature and there were not measurements for very recent years, so the final range was taken using actual global temperature estimates (the same series used in Figure 16.1). What is significant, on the other hand, is the high level of volatility experienced in past century long periods.

[22] When I left the Navy in 1980, I taught a high school project course in nuclear power. Since I had just spent three years serving on submarines, principally as a reactor control officer, this was a domain that I happened to know quite a bit about. While preparing for that course—a central theme of which was to understand both the pro- and anti-nuclear positions—I got my first real taste of opposition to the Idea of Progress. Of particular note was the fact that, at the time, radioactive waste was considered to be the principle "unsolvable" barrier to greater use of the technology. The problem was, every time a proposal was made to create a facility to solve the problem, the opponents of the technology voted it down. That same opposition exists today. As Lawrence Summers and Richard Zeckhauser (2008) note, planners for such a facility are now being asked to predict what will happen *one million*

years into the future, up from 10,000 years. Given that our historical record only goes back about 6,000 years, it is hard to view this as anything other than a roadblock. Counter-intuitively, nuclear power has virtually no carbon footprint and produces a power output per unit area of disrupted environment that is unsurpassed by any other technology of which I am aware. It is, however, precisely the type of technology that those who favor the Idea of Progress are comfortable with, and that opponents hate.

Even technologies that might address global warming directly are being discounted. In *Super Freakonomics*, Levitt and Dubner (2009, p. 192-196) describe a number of proposed technologies, including an improbable 100 mile long garden-hose sized device to pump sulfur dioxide into the stratosphere to reflect incoming sunlight. The estimated cost of the 10-15 hoses necessary to halt global warming would be around $150 million, plus $100 million per year operating costs. According to the authors, when former U.S. Vice President and Nobel Laureate Al Gore was presented with this and other geo-engineering options, he responded: "In a word, I think it's nuts" (Levitt & Dubner, 2009, p. 200).

The irony here is that I am suspicious of the simple solutions proposed in the book precisely because their feasibility is predicated on the very same models that predict global warming. Those who believe these models, however, are suspicious of such solutions because their success would support the abhorrent Idea of Progress—which predicts innovative technology and adaptation will find a way around such problems when they arise.

[23] The level of certainty among those who are convinced that climate change is occurring is quite impressive. Consider the following remarks from Alex Beam (2006), a columnist for The Boston Globe (not normally considered a conservative news outlet):

> Speech codes are rare in the industrialized, Western democracies. In Germany and Austria, for instance, it is forbidden to proselytize Nazi ideology or trivialize the Holocaust. Given those countries' recent histories, that is a restraint on free expression we can live with.
>
> More curious are our own taboos on the subject of global warming. I sat in a roomful of journalists 10 years ago while

Stanford climatologist Stephen Schneider lectured us on a big problem in our profession: soliciting opposing points of view. In the debate over climate change, Schneider said, there simply was no legitimate opposing view to the scientific consensus that man-made carbon emissions drive global warming. To suggest or report otherwise, he said, was irresponsible.

I am quite certain that I could find right wing blogs, and perhaps even some scientists, expressing the same sentiments regarding the opposite point of view.

[24] A good place to become aware of the problem is in a heavily footnoted work of fiction, Michael Crichton's (2004) *State of Fear.* As it happens, I have a friend who expressed skepticism in the past and was soundly criticized for her science. As an exercise, the reader is encouraged to look up MIT's Richard Lindzen, verify that his credentials are impeccable, then look at the vitriolic comments that have been made against him, both by bloggers and other scientists. His typical "offense" is attempting to use actual data to determine whether certain climatic components (e.g., clouds, gasses) trap or reflect heat; obviously, the answer to such questions would have a huge impact on climate models.

Most recently, there has been the widely reported "Climategate" scandal (Henninger, 2009), originating in the U.K.'s University of East Anglia. Hackers retrieved several thousand emails from the servers of the well respected East Anglia Climate Unit that detailed a wide range of efforts to discredit climate researchers who did not share the prevailing set of beliefs, deny those individuals access to data, castigate peer-reviewed journals that published articles questioning the consensus, and prevent the discussion of information from such research in major climate policy documents.

[25] There is actually a reasonably consistent relationship between the higher levels of institutional research intensity and liberal-to-conservative ratio, 4.9:1 for Research I, 2.7:1 for Research II, 2.0:1 for Doctoral I (Mariani & Hewitt, 2008, p. 775). It also seems to be supported by the *World Values Survey* where, in the U.S., the lowest score on the confidence in individual progress question was from respondents with a doctoral degree, while the highest was from respondents with a professional master's degree (5.5 vs. 6.9).

I have heard those in the liberal camp justify the preponderance of the left among the highly educated as evidence that "intelligent people are liberal;" individuals in the conservative camp are slightly less enthusiastic about such an interpretation of the findings. Although not in the liberal camp myself, I believe there may be a grain of truth to their explanation. What got me thinking about it was something that Taleb (2007) mentioned about beginner's luck. He argued that most gamblers believe in it precisely because if you do not have luck when you start gambling, you stop. Therefore, it follows that most people who continue to gamble a lot must have experienced such luck when they started.

The parallel to this in the academic world is that people who are very good at academic scholarship are attracted to academia. They also develop a high level of confidence in their own differential ability to figure out how things work; they are used to doing better than their peers at such tasks. Thus, the notion that certain individuals—specifically more intelligent individuals with the proper socially conscious motivation—could manage things better than the entirely unmanaged process of progress would be very consistent with their experience.

Weighing against this would be their field of research. In some fields, such as the physical sciences (4.1:1; Mariani & Hewitt, 2008, p. 777) and mathematics (1.9:1), the notion that the world can be represented using orderly models is continuously reinforced. In other fields, such as the humanities (5.4:1), fine arts (4.3:1) and social sciences (5.8:1), there is very little unambiguous feedback; it is therefore very hard to prove a particular theory or position is wrong. Working in fields of either type would tend to reinforce the belief that individuals can successfully understand and control systems. At the other extreme, there are a number of applied fields where the researcher is continually confronted with complexity and then receives rapid and unambiguous feedback when things do not go as planned. These fields should tend to attract and foster individuals skeptical that complex systems can be completely controlled. These fields would include business (try to outguess the market; 0.8:1), engineering (bridges collapse if they are not properly designed; 1.5:1), health sciences (patients die despite doing all the right things; 1.0:1), and agriculture (crops sometimes fail; 0.0:1).

[26] As we might expect, projections for future fertility rates and population are just as prone to inaccuracy as every other type of projection of complex system behavior. The U.N.'s range for 2050 world population is 8 to 12 billion. Even that, however, does not include any grey swans. The baby boom after World War II, for example, involved U.S. fertility rates jumping from as low as 2.2 in 1940 to 3.8 in 1957 (Gill, Glazer, & Thernstrom, 1992, p. 42). Its occurrence was entirely unpredicted.

[27] According to the U.S. Congressional Budget Office, in 2008 about 60% of all outlays were programmatic (Social Security, Medicare, Medicaid, unemployment, and other retirement programs making up the vast majority) and likely to be proportional to the dependent population percent. In fact, since many are dependent upon the elderly percentage (e.g., the 80 years and older percentage of the population is expected to more than double from 2005 to 2050), we can expect the numbers to grow by more than 20%.

[28] In 2007, U.S. Federal expenditures were approximately $2.7 trillion, and 20% of GDP. According to the U.S. Census, total state and local outlays that year were $2.66 trillion. Thus, they account for roughly 20% of GDP as well.

[29] With respect to education expenditures, while the percentage of students in the population should fall owing to reduced birth rates, the cost of preparing a student to be a knowledge worker is likely to rise. Thus, the total percentage of GDP devoted to education could remain relatively constant, although it has risen much faster historically.

[30] Using 2050 for population age projections is convenient, since the U.N. publishes projections for that date. In the intermediate term, however, the problem is likely to be worse. Because the baby boom (individuals born in the period 1946-1964) is disproportionately large, 20 years from now—when the vast majority will have retired—could well be the worst point in time. According to the U.S. Census, for example, the over-65 percentage of the U.S. population will have increased by 59% between 2004 and 2030 (Table 3 on http://www.census.gov/population/www/projections/projectionsages ex.html)

[31] According to the *2009 OECD in Figures*, which uses slightly different numbers from the CBO and the U.S. Census, in 2008 government

expenditures as a percentage of GDP for selected countries were as follows:

- U.S. – 37.3%

- U.K. – 47.7%

- France – 52.7%

- Germany – 43.9%

- Japan – 36%

[32] As an example of the problems of top-down thinking in the U.S., one only needs to look as far as physician reimbursement. Because Medicare, a U.S. government program, plays a large role in U.S. medicine, it has considerable power to set reimbursement rates. One obvious way to reduce costs is to lower these rates or to lock them in place. Congress chose to do so a number of years ago. Subsequently, each year it has to override its previously established rates, the "doc-fix" bill, since these rates would be disastrous to the medical community. Today, in fact, the more serious threat is that artificially low rates are driving doctors out of the areas where they are most needed as the population ages, such as primary care (Pardes, 2009).

[33] Recall the old adage: In a community with one lawyer, the lawyer starves; in a community with two lawyers, they both get rich.

[34] In fact, the draw of the U.S. business environment is truly global; about a quarter of high tech startups are founded by individuals who came to this country to study (Schramm, Litan. & Stangler, 2009).

Chapter 17

Reflections

Roadmap & Objectives: To reflect upon what I have learned in writing this book and summarize the key recommendations.

In the Preface to this book, I identified three priorities for research and informing that every business school needs to consider. These were:

1. Is our emphasis on understanding the general principles of business behavior or on building a tool bag of techniques for dealing with individual problems?

2. Are we utilizing one way channels to communicate our knowledge or are we interactively constructing knowledge with our practitioner and student clients?

3. Is our focus on exploring the routine activities of business or on creatively responding to the unexpected?

In this brief chapter that reflects on the book, we first review the overall picture of the business environment that has been presented then summarize the key recommendations.

The Complex Environment

The conceptual scheme used throughout the book involves treating the environment as a fitness landscape. One such a landscape, the various choices that we make, combined with those aspects of our situation that we cannot change, determine how well we succeed or, alternatively, the likelihood that we will not survive. Where such landscapes are decomposable, we can make decisions incrementally, with predictable outcomes. As they grow more complex, many combinations of attributes make sense—a fact further complicated a dynamically changing relationship between our choices and fitness.

Looking at the world as broadly as possible, over the past decades two major trends—1) innovation in information and communications technologies, and 2) globalization—have been particularly influential in reshaping the business environment. As illustrated in Figure 17.1, these forces tend to increase the fundamental sources of complexity: the number of entities in the system, the degree of interrelationship between entities and the extent to which fitness relationships are dynamically changing. Increases in underlying system complexity, in turn, lead to a more turbulent, rugged landscape. Dealing with that landscape requires us to rethink how we inform business.

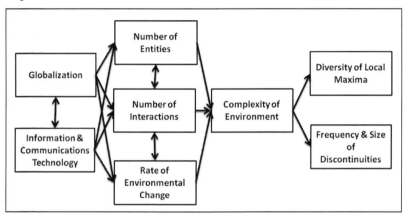

Figure 17.1: How globalization and technology are impacting the typical fitness landscape upon which a business operates

Increased diversity means that the range of combinations that can lead to success grows, making it harder to be an expert across the entire environment. The increased rate and potential size of discontinuities means that system-altering changes play an ever-greater role in shaping the landscape. Both of these serve to reduce the certainty of our knowledge. Paradoxically, they also increase the need for whatever knowledge can be acquired, drawing a more diverse set of students into the educational system and producing a greater variety of practitioners seeking expert help. Thus, at the same time we are becoming less confident of our own knowledge, we are confronted by clients whose pre-existing knowledge is less well understood by us. Together, these forces lead us away from routine informing and towards non-routine and low structure informing, as illustrated in Figure 17.2. The arrow pointing down highlights the growing fragility of our general knowledge about the landscape. The arrow pointing to the left signifies the growing diversity of the student and practitioner clients we inform.

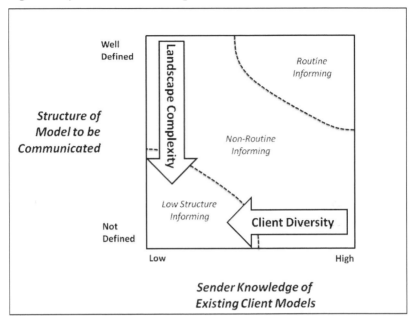

Figure 17.2: Continuum of informing settings, based upon the dimensions of model structure and knowledge of client models

In view of these forces, our three Preface priorities need to shift as follows:

1. Towards increased focus on specific problems, and seeking to understand the boundaries of fitness relationships, rather than seeking out general principles governing behaviors.

2. Towards greater reliance on interactive informing—where informer and client each share their models and mutual understanding grows through enduring relationships—in preference to one-way channels from informer to client.

3. Towards learning how to adapt to changing conditions as opposed to developing rules for routine behavior.

Based on these conclusions, there are a number of concrete recommendations that could be implemented. Those presented in previous chapters are now summarized.

Recommendations

Many recommendations for coping with a rugged business landscape have been sprinkled throughout this book. Some of the most significant of these are now summarized, organized according to the priority they most directly impact. Within the presentation that follows, the division of these recommendations is somewhat arbitrary. There are few, if any, that apply to only a single priority.

Priority 1: Focus on Problem Solving

Research findings accumulate with time. In an increasingly complex environment, this process will lead to an expanding base of knowledge, as the discovery of new relationships will not necessarily invalidate old relationships. As a consequence, the natural tendency will be for the amount of "content", in the form of theory fragments, to grow.

From a pedagogical standpoint, increases in content tend to lead to declines in retention. As discussed in Chapter 6, we quickly forget that which we do not practice. As a consequence, adding more content to a curriculum to account for new research findings is likely to be counterproductive in terms of learning. This further underscores the wisdom of moving away from curricula based upon systematic surveys of the "general principles" that apply to business and more narrowly focusing on core skills that facilitate problem solving in a complex environment.

As it turns out, the set of core skills that are most valued by practice are also those particularly useful coping with a complex environment: the ability to communicate effectively, the ability to work with others, problem solving ability and the ability to learn. As discussed in Chapter 14, it therefore makes sense to build our curricula around instilling these skills. As discussed in Chapter 13, it also makes sense to us to focus our research on solving specific problems, rather than upon developing general theories that help us to understand the behavior of routine business processes.

Where we feel the need to develop general understanding, the greatest value we can offer will be in helping describe the structure of a specific landscape (such as a particular industry). Where complexity is present, there is greater value to specifying the boundaries of observed relationships than to noting that the relationships exist. A problem solving focus to research also involves the collaboration of disciplinary researchers. It is the very rare business problem that can be described in terms of a single business function. Some of the key recommendations presented in Chapters 13 through 16 that relate to this priority are summarized in Table 17.1.

Table 17.1: Recommendations relating to problem solving

Area	Recommendation (Chapter)	Explanation
Education	Inverted pyramid curriculum (Chapter 14)	Vastly reduce the amount of survey course content and instead focus on providing numerous capstone opportunities to practice core skills.
	Emphasize experiential learning (Chapter 14)	Internships, coops, and service learning activities all tend to focus students on handling the specific challenges facing the organization.
	Develop student research opportunities (Chapter 14)	Research projects that emphasize acquiring knowledge related to specific research questions
	Expand role of project courses (Chapter 14)	Projects involve problem solving and teamwork; subsequent presentations hone communications skills
Research	Encourage action research (Chapter 13)	Action research involves the researcher playing an active role in area of investigation; nearly always requires a problem-centered focus
	Reward transdisciplinary research (Chapter 13)	Transdisciplinary research typically involves researchers from disparate disciplines cooperating to work on a common problem
	Develop detailed maps of specific landscapes (Chapter 15)	Focus research on establishing the boundaries of behavior within a specific landscape, rather than on characterizing the behaviors themselves
	Triangulate evidence of research impact on practice (Chapter 13)	Rather than over-relying on fragile measures of research productivity (e.g., article placement, citation counts), broader measures of impact on business decision making and problem solving should be incorporated into assessments of research quality.

Table 17.2: Recommendations relating to interactive informing

Area	Recommendation (Chapter)	Explanation
Education	Emphasize peer-driven educational techniques (Chapter 14)	Techniques such as the case method and projects demand that student learn from each other; in complex settings, this is likely to be the most effective informing approach.
	Emphasize informing aspects of ethics in the curriculum (Chapter 14)	With growing complexity, general rules of ethical behavior that apply to every situation will be hard to formulate. As a consequence, the relative importance of transparent informing in ethical situations will expand. If these principles are to be learned, they must be reinforced throughout the curriculum through frequent discussion.
	Active teaching case development programs (Chapter 15)	Developing local teaching cases encourages faculty to build relationships with practice and brings practitioners into the classroom.
	Develop distance learning, part time programs for professionals (Chapter 14)	Programs that target mid- and late-career professionals build potential pathways through which knowledge can diffuse to practice.
Research	Treat consulting projects as research grants (Chapter 15)	Ongoing consulting encourages engagement with practice; successful ongoing consulting relationships build the school's network.
	Reward development of networks (Chapter 13)	Diffusion needs to be considered an integral part of research; activities that build networks should be viewed as important as knowledge creation.
	Doctorate in transdisciplinary studies (Chapter 13)	A late career second doctorate intended to build relationships with researchers in domains outside of business.
	Professional doctorates (Chapter 15)	Degrees intended to build long term relationships with professionals who remain in business. By extending the duration of these doctorates and encouraging distance learning, candidates can act as a beachhead in diffusing research to practice.

Priority 2: Emphasize Interactive Informing

Very little informing is likely to be accomplished by broadcasting complex content to a highly diverse clientele. As discussed in Chapter 8, complex informing, whether it involves student clients, practitioner clients, or clients in other disciplines, requires a great deal of interaction. It also tends to rely heavily on peer-to-peer informing within the client community.

These conclusions lead to two general recommendations. The first is that we need to place far greater emphasis on developing relationships as part of our informing activities, both in research and teaching. Building an informing network is as important to informing success as the content we create or convey. The second, is that we should foster peer-to-peer informing within our informing designs.

Some of the key recommendations presented in Chapters 13 through 16 that relate to this priority are summarized in Table 17.2.

Priority 3: Learn to Deal with the Novel

As a general rule, businesses are well prepared to train employees to deal with routine situations. The greatest value we can therefore offer in our informing efforts involves those situations where the routine is disrupted. As it turns out, in such situations experts often make bad decisions in a reasonably predictable way. Chapters 5, 6, 7 and 9 offer a catalog of examples that describe our foibles in making decisions in unfamiliar settings.

More broadly, learning to deal with the novel, as opposed to the routine, involves developing a philosophy that embraces the growing diversity of students and practitioners participating in the system as a consequence of innovations in technology, increasing inclusiveness of our educational systems and globalization. These forces virtually guarantee that we—as faculty members—will face a growing need to address the unfamiliar in our teaching and research.

Some of the key recommendations presented in Chapters 13 through 16 that relate to this priority are summarized in Table 17.3.

Table 17.3: Recommendations relating to non-routine behavior

Area	Recommendation (Chapter)	Explanation
Education	Draw upon pedagogical methods employed in the arts (Chapter 14)	The arts exist on landscapes that can reasonably be characterized as more complex than business environments; we can learn much from them in areas such as theater (improvisation) and observation.
	Develop real world simulations around evolving landscapes (Chapter 14)	Where a simulation is driven by computer rules, it is unlikely to exhibit the spontaneous chaos of the real world. Massive multi-player environments, such as Second Life, offer the potential of realistic discontinuities emerging spontaneously.
	Encourage design projects (Chapter 14)	Whereas traditional projects often constrain students and limit spontaneity, design projects—e.g., creating a new type of software application, business planning for a novel product—force exploration of fitness landscape.
	Emphasize heuristics and biases in core curriculum (Chapter 14)	Heuristics and biases exert their greatest effect in novel situations. Students can be taught to recognize these predispositions and, if practiced extensively in subsequent courses, better avoid them on the job.
	Doctorate in Business Education (Chapter 14)	A doctorate to develop business educators who can address the needs of a diverse body of students using techniques built around encouraging non-routine thought.
Research	Focus research on those areas where expertise predictably fails (Chapter 13)	Experts are unlikely to feel they need our help with routine activities, therefore our striving to develop a better understanding of them is largely self indulgent. Helping experts understand where their expertise fails offers a better value proposition.
	Promote a better understanding of the process of progress (Chapter 16)	Ultimately, the survival of business schools as anything more than trade schools depends upon continued progress; our research needs to explore the adaptability-efficiency tradeoffs and help business better understand and address turbulent environments without unnecessary anxiety.

Conclusions

In a world of increasing complexity, the conventional U.S. business school design becomes ever-more inadequate. We provide more and more content to our students, thereby ensuring any important lessons we offer stand little chance of being retained. We engage in research that is more and more specialized in our attempts to describe a world whose behavior grows continually more dependent upon acknowledging the importance of broad interactions. Our focus moves towards informing our colleagues in spite of the fact that the only conceivable purpose that this activity serves is to ensure that those colleagues can better inform a subsequent generation of colleagues.

There is a delicious irony to this process. We who study the rough and tumble world of business nevertheless believe that we can continue to thrive without producing a product that meets the needs of our ultimate client—the businesses that employ our students and, at least in theory, seek our advice. From an evolutionary standpoint, the conventional U.S. business school is rapidly approaching a dead end. The signs of this decay are easily observed to anyone who cares to look for them, as detailed in Chapters 1 and 2 of this book.

Despite this rather gloomy prognosis, I remain optimistic with respect to the future of business research and education. My reason is simple. While the growing complexity of the world renders most of what we now do irrelevant, it also increases the *potential* value that we could add if we direct the considerable pool of talent that exists in today's business faculty towards the problem of designing approaches to informing business that make sense based on nature of the environment we face. While complexity makes complete understanding much more difficult to attain, it also provides opportunities that simply are not available in a simpler world. In the simple world, small incremental changes necessarily produce only small incremental improvements. In a complex world, the small adjustment can, under some circumstances, lead to dramatic benefits. Such effects are intrinsic to complex landscapes. If we can help our students and practitioners develop techniques that help them identify these opportunities, we will add far more value than ever would have been possible in the world of simple, attractive theories. The complex world particularly rewards the sensitive, creative and flexible individual, not just the driven workaholic. For my own part, I'd rather do research that is most likely to benefit the former...

In this book, I have outlined how complex environments differ from simple environments in their structure and behavior. I have pointed out the dangers of confusing what we are broadcasting to students and practitioners with what they are actually learning from us. I have identified areas where research and education could be particularly valuable *assuming* that the environments we face are complex. Finally, I have presented a series of design principles, summarized in this chapter, which could be employed if we chose to build an institution, from the ground up, whose overriding goal was to inform business. Not surprisingly, the result would look very different from any of today's business schools.

Despite the radical nature of much of what I have proposed, I suspect that there is not a single recommendation contained in this book that has not been implemented somewhere. What I therefore hope to see, within my lifetime, is an institution that incorporates a collection of these ideas (as well as many more ideas that I have failed to consider) into a design based around the mission of informing business. I am confident that just one such institution would be enough. I am sure it would be quickly copied by others seeking to have the same impact. My fondest wish is that this book might, in some small way, help to encourage some institution somewhere in the globe to take the leadership role in initiating this noble endeavor.

T. Grandon Gill
Informing Business
Santa Rosa, California: Informing Science Press.

References

AACSB. (2008). Final report of the AACSB International impact of research task force. *AACSB International*, Retrieved from http://www.aacsb.edu/resource_centers/research/Final/Impact of_Research_Report-FINAL.PDF

Adval, R. (2001). Sometimes it just feels right: The differential weighting of affect-consistent and affect- inconsistent product information. *Journal of Consumer Research, 28*(1), 1-17.

Ainslie, G. (2001). *Breakdown of will*. Cambridge, UK: Cambridge University Press.

Akerlof, G. A., & Shiller, R.J. (2009). *Animal spirits: How human psychology drives the economy and why it matters for global capitalism.* Princeton, NJ: Princeton University Press.

Alba, J. W., & Marmorstein, H. (1987). The effects of frequency knowledge on consumer decision making. *Journal of Consumer Research, 14*, 14-26.

Allison, K. R., & Rootman, I. (1996). Scientific rigor and community participation in health promotion research: are they compatible? *Health Promotion International, 11*(4), 333-340.

Alonzo, M., & Aiken, M. (2004). Flaming in electronic communication. *Decision Support Systems. 36*, 205-213.

Amabile, T.M. (1997). Motivating creativity in organizations: On doing what you love and loving what you do. *California Management Review, 40*(1), 39-58.

Ambady, N., & Rosenthal, R. (1993). Half a minute: Predicting teacher evaluations from thin slices of nonverbal behavior and physical attractiveness. *Journal of Personality and Social Psychology, 64*(3), 431-441.

Ambrose, S. H. (1998). Late Pleistocene human population bottlenecks, volcanic winter, and differentiation of modern humans. *Journal of Human Evolution, 34*(6), 623–651.

Anderson, L. R., & Holt, C. A. (1997). Information cascades in the laboratory. *American Economic Review, 87*(5), 609-615.

Andrews, F. (1976, October 29). Management: How a boss works in calculated chaos. *New York Times*, p. 79 (Business and Finance section).

Applegate, L., Austin, R., & Collins, E. (2005). *IBM's decade of transformation (A): The turnaround.* Harvard Business School Publishing, Case 9-805-130.

Ariely, D. (2008). *Predictably irrational.* New York: Harper Collins.

Ariely, D. (2009). The end of rational economics. *Harvard Business Review,* July-August, 1-7 (HBS reprint page numbers).

Armstrong, J. S., & Hubbard, R. (1997). Publication bias against null results. *Psychological Reports, 80,* 337-338. Retrieved from http://ssrn.com/abstract=665387

Arthur, W. B. (1988). Self-reinforcing mechanisms in economics. In P. W. Anderson, K. J. Arrow, & D. Pines (Eds.). *The economy as an evolving complex system* (pp. 9-32). Reading, MA: Addison Wesley.

Arthur, W. B. (1989). The economy and complexity. In D. L. Stein (Ed.), *Lectures in the sciences of complexity* (pp. 713-774). Reading, MA: Addison Wesley.

Aspen Institute. (2008). *Where will they lead?* The Aspen Institute Center for Business Education. Retrieved from http://www.aspeninstitute.org/publications/where-will-they-lead-2008-executive-summary-pdf

Aspen Institute. (2009). *Aspen's Global 100: Beyond grey pinstripes, 2009-2010,* The Aspen Institute Center for Business Education Retrieved from http://www.beyondgreypinstripes.org/pdf/2009-2010BGP_Brochure.pdf

Arya, A., Glover, J., & Mittendorf, B. (2006). Hierarchical reporting, aggregation, and information cascades. *Managerial and Decision Economics, 27,* 355–362.

Axelrod, R. (1984). *The evolution of cooperation.* New York, NY: Basic Books.

Bain, K. (2004). *What the best college teachers do.* Cambridge, MA: Harvard University Press.

Bak, P. (1996). *How nature works: The science of self-organized criticality.* New York: Copernicus.

Baldridge, D. C., Floyd, S. W., & Markoczy, L. (2004). Are managers from Mars and academics from Venus? Toward an understanding of the relationship between academic quality and practical relevance. *Strategic Management Journal, 25*(11), 1063-1074.

Ball, J. (2009, October 30). The earth cools, and fight over warming heats up. *The Wall Street Journal,* p. A21.

Banerjee, A. V. (1992). A simple model of herd behavior. *Quarterly Journal of Economics, 107*(3), 797-817.

Barabasi, A. L. (2002). *Linked.* New York, NY: Plume.

Barings debacle. (2008). Retrieved on 4/22/2008 from
http://www.riskglossary.com/link/barings_debacle.htm

Barman, S., Buckley, M. R., & DeVaughn, W. L. A. (1997). Pedagogical
concerns in business education: The case of management science.
S.A.M. Advanced Management Journal, 62(1), 28-34.

Barley, S. R., Meyer, G. W., & Gash, D. C. (1988). Cultures of culture:
academics, practitioners and the pragmatics of normative control.
Administrative Science Quarterly, 33(1), 24-60.

Baskerville, R., & Meyers, M. (2002). Information systems as a
reference discipline. *MIS Quarterly, 26*(1), 1-14.

Beam, A. (2006, August 30). MIT's inconvenient scientist. *Boston Globe.*
Retrieved from
http://www.boston.com/news/science/articles/2006/08/30/mits
_inconvenient_scientist/

Becker, G. S., Grossman, M., & Murphy, K. M. (1992). Rational
addiction and the effect of price on consumption. In G.
Loewenstein & J. Elster, *Choice over time* (pp. 361-382). New York,
NY: Russell Sage Foundation.

Benbasat, I., & Zmud, R. (1999). Empirical research in information
systems: The practice of relevance. *MIS Quarterly, 23*(1), 3-16.

Bennis, W. G., & O'Toole, J. (2005). How business schools lost their
way. *Harvard Business Review*, May, Reprint R0505F, 1-10.

Berkowitz, P. (2010, 13 March). Climategate was an academic disaster
waiting to happen, *The Wall Street Journal*, p. A13.

Bikhchandani, S., Hirshleifer, D., & Welch, I. (1992). A theory of fads,
fashion, custom, and cultural change as informational cascades. *The
Journal of Political Economy, 100*(5), 992-1026.

Bloom, B. S. (Ed.), Engelhart, M. D., Furst, E. J., Hill, W. H., &
Krathwohl, D. R. (1956). *Taxonomy of educational objectives: The
classification of educational goals. Handbook 1: Cognitive domain.* New
York, NY: David McKay.

Bombardieri, M. (2005, December 18). In computer science, a growing
gender gap: Women shunning a field once seen as welcoming.
Boston Globe. Retrieved from
http://www.boston.com/news/local/articles/2005/12/18/in_co
mputer_science_a_growing_gender_gap/

Bowden, M., & McDonald, S. (2008). The impact of interaction and
social learning on aggregate expectations. *Computational Economics,
31*, 289–306.

Bourgeois, L. J. & Eisenhardt, K. M (1988). Strategic decision processes in high velocity environments: Four cases in the microcomputer industry. *Management Science,* 34(7), 816-835.

Bourner, T., Bowden, R., & Laing, S. (2001), Professional doctorates in England. *Studies in Higher Education, 26*(1), 65-83.

Brier, D. J. (2005). Marking the future: A review of time horizons. *Futures, 37,* 833-848.

Brynjolfsson, E., & Hitt, L. M. (1998). Beyond the productivity paradox. *Communications of the ACM, 41*(8), 49-55.

Burry, J. Jr. (1992). The 10 percent solution. *Chief Executive.Net.* Retrieved from http://www.chiefexecutive.net/ME2/Sites/dirmod.asp?sid=&nm =&type=Publishing&mod=Publications%3A%3AArticle&mid=8F 3A7027421841978F18BE895F87F791&tier=4&id=B5AD73ED1F A047BF80BE9BDFD9AC1198&SiteId=6817839757EF444181872 6B97A2175A5

Camerer, C. F., & Johnson, E. J. (1991). The process-performance paradox in expert judgment: How can experts know so much and predict so badly? In K. A. Ericsson & J. Smith (Eds.), *Towards a general theory of expertise: Prospects and limits* (pp. 195-217). Cambridge, U.K.: Cambridge University Press.

Card, S. K., Moran, T. P., & Newell, A. (1983). *The psychology of human-computer interaction.* Hillsdale NJ: Earlbaum.

Ceci, S. J., & Peters, D. (1984). How blind is blind review? *American Psychologist,* 39(12), 1491-1494.

Chapman, G. B. (2004). The psychology of medical decision making. In D. J. Koehler & N. Harvey (Eds.), *Blackwell handbook of judgment and decision making* (pp. 585-603). Malden, MA: Blackwell Publishing.

Charness, N. (1991). Knowledge and search in chess. In K. A. Ericsson & J. Smith (Eds.), *Towards a general theory of expertise: Prospects and limits* (pp. 39-63). Cambridge, U.K.: Cambridge University Press.

Cheit, E. F. (1985). Business schools and their critics. *California Management Review, 27*(3), 43-62.

Chevalier, J., & Ellison, G. (1999). Are some mutual fund managers better than others? Cross-sectional patterns in behavior and performance. *Journal of Finance, 54*(3), 875-899.

Christensen, C. M., Horn, M. B., & Johnson, C. W. (2008). *Disrupting class.* New York, NY: McGraw Hill.

Cialdini, R. B. (2005). Don't throw in the towel: Use social influence research. *Observer, 18*(4). Retrieved from http://www.psychologicalscience.org/observer/getArticle.cfm?id=1762

Clark, A. E., Frijters, P., & Shields, M. A. (2008). Relative income, happiness and utility: An explanation for the Easterlin Paradox and other puzzles. *Journal of Economic Literature, 46*(1), 95-144.

Cohen, E. (1999). Reconceptualizing information systems as a field of the transdiscipline informing science: From ugly duckling to swan. *Journal of Computing and Information Technology, 7*(3), 213-219.

Cohn, S. K. (1997). Introduction. In D. Herlihy & S. K. Cohn (Eds.), *The black death and the transformation of the west* (pp. 1-15). Cambridge, MA: Harvard University Press.

Coleman, S. (1996). The Minnesota income tax compliance experiment: State tax results. *Minnesota Department of Revenue*, Retrieved from: http://www.taxes.state.mn.us/legal_policy/research_reports/content/complnce.pdf

Colquitt, J. A., & Zapata-Phelan, C. P. (2007). Trends in theory building and theory testing: A five decade study of the Academy of Management Journal. *Academy of Management Journal, 50*(6), 1281-1303.

Commission on Presidential Debates. (2004). *The Bentsen-Quayle Vice Presidential Debate*, Retrieved from http://www.debates.org/pages/trans88c.html

Companario, J. M. (1993). Consolation for the scientist: Sometimes it is hard to publish papers that are later highly-cited. *Social Studies of Science, 23*(2), 342-362.

Conniff, R. (2009). Mad about shells, *Smithsonian, 40*(5), 44-51.

Crichton, M. (1992). *Rising sun.* New York, NY: Ballantine Books.

Crichton, M. (2004). *State of fear.* New York, NY: Harper Collins.

Cummings, J. J., & Elkins, J. (1999). Lack of automaticity in the basic addition facts as a characteristic of arithmetic learning problems and instructional needs. *Mathematical Cognition, 5*(2), 149–180.

Daft, R. L., Lengel, R. H., & Trevino, L. K. (1987). Message equivocality, media selection, and manager performance: Implications for information systems. *MIS Quarterly, 11*(3), 355-366.

Dahringer, L. (2003). A dean on deaning. *Decision Line, September/October*, 19-21.

Datar, S. M., Garvin, D. A., & Knoop, C. (2008a). Harvard Business School. *Harvard Business School Publishing, 9-308-012.*

Datar, S. M., Garvin, D. A., & Knoop, C. (2008b). Stanford Graduate School of Business. *Harvard Business School Publishing, 9-308-010.*

Datar, S. M., Garvin, D. A., & Weber, J. (2008a). University of Chicago Graduate School of Business. *Harvard Business School Publishing, 9-308-014.*

Datar, S. M., Garvin, D. A., & Weber, J. (2008b). Yale School of Management. *Harvard Business School Publishing, 9-308-011.*

Davenport, T., & Markus, M. L. (1999). Rigor vs. relevance revisited: Response to Benbasat and Zmud. *MIS Quarterly, 23*(1), 19-23.

Davenport, T. H., Prusak, L., & Wilson, H. J. (2003). *What's the big idea? Creating and capitalizing on the best management thinking.* Boston, MA: Harvard Business School Press.

Davis, F. D., Bagozzi, R. P. & Warshaw, P. R. (1989). User acceptance of computer technology: A comparison of two theoretical models, *Management Science, 35*(8), 982-1003.

Davis, M. (1971). That's interesting!: Towards a phenomenology of sociology and a sociology of phenomenology. *Philosophy of the Social Sciences, 1*, 309-344.

Deary I. J., Irwing, P., Der, G., & Bates, T. C. (2007). Brother–sister differences in the g factor in intelligence: Analysis of full, opposite-sex siblings from the NLSY1979. *Intelligence, 35*, 451–456.

De Bondt, W. F. M. (1991). What do economists know about the stock market? *Journal of Portfolio Management, 17*, 84-91.

De Vany, A., & Lee, C. (2001). Quality signals in information cascades and the dynamics of the distribution of motion picture box office revenues. *Journal of Economic Dynamics & Control, 25*, 593-614.

Dertouzos, M. L., Lester, R. K., & Solow, R. M. 1989. *Made in America: Regaining the productive edge.* Cambridge, MA: MIT Press.

Dewhurst, S. A. & Marlborough, M. A. (2003). Memory bias in the recall of pre-exam anxiety: The influence of self-enhancement. *Applied Cognitive Psychology, 17*, 695–702.

Dijksterhuis, A., & van Knippenberg, A. (1998). The relation between perception and behavior or how to win a game of trivial pursuit. *Journal of Personality and Social Psychology, 71*(2), 865-877.

Dreher, C., Reiners, T., Dreher, N., & Dreher, H. (2009). Virtual worlds as a context suited for information systems education: Discussion of pedagogical experience and curriculum design with reference to Second Life. *Journal of Information Systems Education, 20*(2), 211-214.

Drucker, P. (1989). *The new realities.* New York: Harper & Row.

Dunn, D. S., & Wilson, T. D. (1991). When the stakes are high: A limit to the illusion of control effect. *Social Cognition, 8,* 305-328.

Easterbrook, G. (2009, September 15). The man who defused the 'Population Bomb'. *The Wall Street Journal,* p. A27.

Edwards, J. P., & Harris, D. J. (1977). Planning in a state of turbulence. *Long Range Planning, 10,* 43-49.

Ehrlich, P. R. (1978). *The Population Bomb* (2nd ed.). New York: Ballantine Books.

Einhorn, H. J., & Hogarth, R. M. (1975). Unit weighting schemes for decision making. *Organizational Behavior and Human Performance, 13,* 171-192.

Elster, J. (1983). *Explaining technical change.* Cambridge, U.K.: Cambridge University Press.

Evanschitzky, H., Baumgarth, C., Hubbard, R., & Armstrong, J. S. (2007). Replication research's disturbing trend. *Journal of Business Research, 60*(4), 411–415.

Federico, G. (2005). *Feeding the world.* Princeton, NJ: Princeton University Press.

Feeley, T. H. (2002). Evidence of halo effects in student evaluations of communication instruction. *Communication Education, 51*(3), 225-236.

Frank, R. H. (1992). The role of moral sentiments in the theory of intertemporal choice. In G. Loewenstein & J. Elster, *Choice over time* (pp. 265-284). New York, NY: Russell Sage Foundation.

Frederick, S., & Loewenstein, G. (2008). Conflicting motives in evaluations of sequences. *Journal of Risk and Uncertainty, 37,* 221–235.

Friedman, M. (2002). Capitalism and freedom (40th anniversary edition), Chicago, IL: University of Chicago Press.

French bank blames trader for $7 billion fraud. (2007). *Associated Press.* Retrieved on 4/22/2008 from http://www.msnbc.msn.com/id/22818054

Frensch, P. A. (1994). Composition during serial learning: A serial position effect. *Journal of Experimental Psychology: Learning, Memory, and Cognition, 20*(2), 423-443.

Frey, B. S. (2003). Publishing as prostitution? Choosing between one's own ideas and academic success. *Public Choice, 116*(1/2), 205-223.

Gandolfi, A. E., Gandolfi, A. S., & Barash, D. (2002). *Economics as an evolutionary science: From utility to fitness.* New Brunswick, NJ: Transaction Publishers.

Gardner, M. (1970). The fantastic combinations of John Conway's new solitaire game "life". *Scientific American, 223*(4), 120-123.

Garvey, M. J. (2004, November 1). Is an MBA worth it? *Information Week*. Retrieved from http://www.informationweek.com/news/global-cio/compensation/showArticle.jhtml?articleID=51201467

Gersick, C. J. G. (1991). voluationary change theories: A multilevel exploration of the punctuated equilibrium paradigm. *Academy of Management Review, 16*(1), 10-36.

Ghoshal, S. (2005). Bad management theories are destroying good management practices. *Academy of Management Learning & Education, 4*(1), 75-91.

Ghoshal, S., Bartlett, C. A., & Moran, P. (1999). A new manifesto for management. *Sloan Management Review, 40*(3), 9-20.

Ghoshal, S., & Moran, P. (1996). Bad for practice: A critique of transaction cost theory. *Academy of Management Review, 21*(1), 13-47.

Giacalone, R. A. (2004). A transcendent business education for the 21st century. *Academy of Management Learning & Education, 3*(4), 415–420.

Gigerenzer, G. (2004). Fast and frugal heuristics: The tools of bounded rationality. In D. J. Koehler & N. Harvey (Eds.), *Blackwell handbook of judgment and decision making* (pp. 62-88). Malden, MA: Blackwell Publishing.

Gilbert, D. (2007). *Stumbling on happiness.* New York: Knopf.

Gill, C. (2006). Confessions of a neophyte distance learner and full-time procrastinator. *eLearn Magazine, 38*(1). Retrieved from http://www.elearnmag.org/subpage.cfm?section=case_studies&article=38-1

Gill, R. T. (1997). *Posterity lost: Progress, ideology, and the decline of the American family.* Lanham, MD: Rowan & Littlefield.

Gill, R. T., Glazer, N., & Thernstrom, S.A. (1992). *Our changing population.* Englewood Cliffs, NJ: Prentice Hall.

Gill, T. G. (1991). *Expert systems: A mapping between symbol susceptible tasks and software tools.* Un-published doctoral dissertation. Boston, MA: Harvard Business School.

Gill, T. G. (1995a). High tech hidebound: Case studies of information technologies that inhibited organizational learning. *Accounting, Management, & Information Technologies, 5*(1), 41-60.

Gill, T. G. (1995b). Early expert systems: Where are they now? *MIS Quarterly, 19*(1), 51-81.

Gill, T. G. (1996). Expert systems usage: Task change and intrinsic motivation. *MIS Quarterly, 20*(3), 301-329.

Gill, T. G. (2001). What's an MIS paper worth? (An exploratory analysis). *Database for Advances in Information Systems, 32*(2), 14-33.

Gill, T. G. (2004). The cruelest experiment. *Proceeding of the Decision Sciences Institute, Boston, MA*, 4141-4147.

Gill, T. G. (2005). The peer reviews and the programming course. *Issues in Informing Science and Information Technology, 2*, 205-217. Retrieved from http://2005papers.iisit.org/I17f83Gill.pdf

Gill, T. G. (2008a). A psychologically plausible goal-based utility function. *Informing Science: The International Journal of an Emerging Transdiscipline, 11*, 227-252. Retrieved from http://inform.nu/Articles/Vol11/ISJv11p227-252Gill220.pdf

Gill, T. G. (2008b). Reflections on researching the rugged fitness landscape. *Informing Science: The International Journal of an Emerging Transdiscipline, 11*, 165-196. Retrieved from http://inform.nu/Articles/Vol11/ISJv11p165-196Gill219.pdf

Gill, T. G. (2008c). Resonance within the client-to-client system: Criticality, cascades, and tipping points. *Informing Science: The International Journal of an Emerging Transdiscipline, 11*, 311-348. Retrieved from http://inform.nu/Articles/Vol11/ISJv11p311-348Gill221.pdf

Gill, T. G. (2008d). Structural complexity and effective informing. *Informing Science: The International Journal of an Emerging Transdiscipline, 11*, 253-279. Retrieved from http://inform.nu/Articles/Vol11/ISJv11p253-279Gill223.pdf

Gill, T. G. (2009a). Coping with complexity. *Decision Sciences Journal of Innovative Education*, 339-340.

Gill, T. G. (2009b). Technology in the classroom. In S. J. Armstrong & C. V. Fukami (Eds.), *Sage handbook of management learning, education and development* (pp. 213-230). Los Angeles, CA: Sage.

Gill, T. G., & Bhattacherjee, A. (2007). The informing sciences at a crossroads: The role of the client, *Informing Science: The International Journal of an Emerging Transdiscipline, 10*, 17-39. Retrieved from http://inform.nu/Articles/Vol10/ISJv10p017-039Gill317.pdf

Gill, T. G., & Bhattacherjee, A. (2009). Whom are we informing? Issues and recommendations for MIS research from an informing sciences perspective. *MIS Quarterly, 3*(2), 217-235.

Gill, T. G., & Hicks, R. (2006). Task complexity and informing science: a synthesis. *Informing Science: The International Journal of an Emerging*

Transdiscipline, 9, 1-30. Retrieved from http://inform.nu/Articles/Vol9/v9p001-030Gill46.pdf

Gill, T. G., & Hoppe, U. (2009). The business professional doctorate as an informing channel: A survey and analysis. *International Journal of Doctoral Studies, 4,* 27-57. Retrieved from http://ijds.org/Volume4/IJDSv4p027-057Gill267.pdf

Gill, T. G., & Jones, J. (2010). A tale of three classes: Case studies in course complexity. *Journal of Information Technology Education, 9,* 1-29. Retrieved from http://www.jite.org/documents/Vol9/JITEv9p001-029Gill717.pdf .

Gill, T. G., & Saunders, C. S. (1997). Intrinsic motivation and IT adoption. *Journal of Management Systems, 9,* 1-4.

Gill, T. G., & Sincich, A. (2008). Illusions of significance in a rugged landscape. *Informing Science : The International Journal of an Emerging Transdiscipline, 11,* 197-226. Retrieved from http://inform.nu/Articles/Vol11/ISJv11p197-226GillIllusions.pdf

Gladwell, M. (2000). *The Tipping Point.* New York, NY: Back Bay Books.

Gladwell, M. (2005). *Blink.* New York, NY: Back Bay Books.

Gladwell, M. (2008). *Outliers.* New York, NY: Little, Brown & Co.

Glaser, M., Noth, M., & Weber, M. (2004). Behavior finance. In D. J. Koehler & N. Harvey (Eds.), *Blackwell handbook of judgment and decision making* (pp. 527-546). Malden, MA: Blackwell Publishing.

Gleick, J. (1988). *Chaos.* New York, NY: Penguin Books USA.

Glick, W. H., Miller, C. C., & Cardinal, L. B. (2007). Making a life in the field of organization science. *Journal of Organizational Behavior, 28,* 817–835.

Glick, W. H., Miller, C. C., & Cardinal, L. B. (2008). Reality check on career success and weak paradigms: Chance still favors the hearty soul. *Journal of Organizational Behavior, 29,* 715–723.

Goeree, J. K., Palfrey, T. R., Rogers, B. W., & McKelvey, R. D. (2007). Self-correcting information cascades. *Review of Economic Studies, 74,* 733–762.

Goldberg, R. A. (1968). *Agribusiness coordination: A systems approach to the wheat, soybean and Florida orange economies,* Boston, MA: Harvard Business School, Division of Research.

Goldsmith, E., & Allen, R. (1972). A blueprint for survival. *The Ecologist, 2*(1). Retrieved from http://www.theecologist.info/page33.html

Gordon, R. A., & Howell, J. E. (1959). *Higher education for business*. New York, NY: Columbia University Press.

Gottesman, A. A., & Morey, M. R. (2006a). Manager education and mutual fund performance. *Journal of Empirical Finance, 13*(2), 145-182.

Gottesman, A. A. & Morey, M. R. (2006b). Does a better education make for better managers? An empirical examination of CEO educational quality and firm performance. *SSRN, April 21*. Retrieved from http://ssrn.com/abstract=564443

Gottfredson, S. D. (1978). Evaluating psychological research reports: Dimensions, reliability, and correlates of quality judgments. *American Psychologist, 33*(10), 920–934.

Grebe, T., Schmid, J., & Stiehler, A. (2008). Do individuals recognize cascade behavior of others? – An experimental study. *Journal of Economic Psychology, 29*, 197–209.

Guber, P. (2007). The four truths of the storyteller. *Harvard Business Review, December*, 52-59.

Gupta, H. M., Campanha, J. R., & Pesce, R. A. G. (2005). Power-law distributions for the citation index of scientific publications and scientists. *Brazilian Journal of Physics, 35*(4A), 981-986.

Hackman, J. R., & Oldham, G. R. (1980). *Work redesign*. Reading, MA: Addison Wesley.

Halhoun, I. A., & Hestenes, D. (1985). The initial knowledge state of college physics. *American Journal of Physics, 53*, 1043-1055.

Hambrick, D. C. (2007). The field of management's devotion to theory: Too much of a good thing? *Academy of Management Journal, 50*(6), 1346-1352.

Handy, C. (1990). *The age of unreason*. Boston, MA: Harvard Business School Press.

Harmon, P., Maus, R., & Morrissey, W. (1988). *Expert systems: Tools and applications*. New York, NY: Wiley.

Hawk, T. F., & Shah, A. J. (2007). Using learning style instruments to enhance student learning. *Decision Sciences Journal of Innovative Education*, 1–19.

Hayden, T. (2009). What Darwin didn't know. *Smithsonian, 39*(11), 41-48.

Hayes, R. H., & Abernathy, W. J. (1980). Managing our way to economic decline. *Harvard Business Review, July-August*, 67-77.

HBS. (2008). *2008 Global Summit on Business Education in the 21st Century*, Retrieved from http://www.hbs.edu/centennial/businesssummit/business-society/business-education-in-the-21st-century.pdf

Heath, C., & Heath, D. (2007). *Made to stick*. New York, NY: Random House.

Henninger, D. (2009, December 4). Climategate: Science is dying. *The Wall Street Journal*, p. A21.

Hevner, A. R., March, S. T., Park, J., & Ram, S. (2004). Design science in information systems research. *MIS Quarterly, 28*(1), 75-106.

Hillinger, C. (1986, August 11). Long Island duck farms fly the coop - Traditional industry fades as producers sell to developers. *Los Angeles Times*. Retrieved from http://articles.latimes.com/1986-08-11/business/fi-2568_1_long-island-duck

Hirschfeld, N. (2009). Teaching cops to see. *Smithsonian, 40*(7), 49-54.

Hofstede, G. (2001). *Culture's consequences: Comparing values, behaviors, institutions, and organizations across nations* (2nd ed.). Thousand Oaks, CA: SAGE Publications.

Holland, J. H. (1992). *Adaptation in natural and artificial systems*. Cambridge, MA: MIT Press.

Hotz, R. L. (2009, October 9). A neuron's obsession hints at biology of thought, *The Wall Street Journal*, p. A14.

Hubbard, R., & Armstrong, J. S. (1992). Are null results becoming an endangered species in marketing? *Marketing Letters, 3*(2), 127-136.

Hubbard, R., & Armstrong, J. S. (1994). Replications and extensions in marketing: Rarely published but quite contrary. *International Journal of Research in Marketing, 11*(3), 233-248.

Hubbard, R., & Vetter, D. E. (1991). Replication in the finance literature: An empirical study. *Quarterly Journal of Business and Economics, 30*, 70-81.

Hubbard, R., & Vetter, D.E. (1996). An empirical comparison of published replication research in accounting, economics, finance, management, and marketing. *Journal of Business Research, 35*, 153-164.

Im, K. S., Kim, K. Y., & Kim, J. S. (1998). An assessment of individual and institutional research productivity in MIS. *Decision Line, December/January*, 8-12.

INSAG-7. (1992). *The Chernobyl accident: Updating of INSAG-1 -- A report by the International Nuclear Safety Advisory Group*. Vienna, Austria: International Atomic Energy Agency.

Jamieson, K., & Hyland, P. (2006). Good intuition or fear and uncertainty: The effects of bias on information systems selection decisions. *Informing Science: The International Journal of an Emerging*

Transdiscipline, 9, 49-69. Retrieved from
http://inform.nu/Articles/Vol9/v9p049-069Jamieson60.pdf

Janssen, O., & Van Yperen, N. (2004). Employees' goal orientations,
the quality of leader-member exchange, and the outcomes of job
performance and job satisfaction. *Academy of Management Journal,
47*(3), 368–384.

Jacobs, M. T. (1991). *Short-term America: The causes and cures of our business
myopia.* Boston: Harvard Business School Press.

Jensen, M. C., & Meckling, W. H. (1976). Theory of the firm:
Managerial behavior, agency costs and ownership structure. *Journal
of Financial Economics, 3,* 305-360.

Johnson-Laird, T. (1985). Deductive reasoning ability. In R. J.
Sternberg (Ed.), *Human abilities: An information processing approach* (pp.
173-194). New York, NY: W.H. Freeman.

Jouzel, J., Masson-Delmotte, V. , Cattani, O., Dreyfus, G., Falourd, S.,
Hoffmann, G., Minster, B., Nouet, J., Barnola, J. M., Chappellaz, J.,
Fischer, H., Gallet, J. C., Johnsen, S., Leuenberger, M., Loulergue,
L., Luethi, D., Oerter, H., Parrenin, F., Raisbeck, G., Raynaud, D.,
Schilt, A., Schwander, J., Selmo, E., Souchez, R., Spahni, R.,
Stauffer, B., Steffensen, J. P., Stenni, B., Stocker, T. F., Tison, J. L.,
Werner, M., & Wolff, E. W. (2007). Orbital and millennial
Antarctic climate variability over the past 800,000 years. *Science,
317*(5839*)*, 793-797.

Judge, T. A., Cable, D. M., Colbert, A. E., & Rynes, S. L. (2007). What
causes a management article to be cited--article, author, or journal?
Academy of Management Journal, 50(3), 491-506.

Kacmar, K. M., & Whitfield, J. M. (2000). An additional rating method
for journal articles in the field of management. *Organizational
Research Methods, 3,* 392-406.

Kahneman, D., Slovic, P., & Tversky, A. (Eds.). (1982). *Judgement under
uncertainty: Heuristics and biases.* Cambridge, UK: Cambridge
University Press.

Kahneman, D., & Tversky, A. (1979). Prospect theory: An analysis of
decision under risk. *Econometrica, 47*(2), 263-292.

Kahneman, D., & Tversky, A. (1982). On the study of statistical
intuitions. In D. Kahneman, P. Slovic, & A. Tversky (Eds.),
Judgement under uncertainty: Heuristics and biases (pp. 493-508).
Cambridge, UK: Cambridge University Press.

Kauffman, S. A. (1993). *The origins of order.* Oxford, UK: Oxford
University Press.

Keen, P. G. W.. and Scott Morton, M. S. (1978). *Decision support systems: An organizational perspective.* Reading, MA: Addison Wesley.

Khurana, R. (2007). *From higher aims to hired hands.* Princeton, NJ: Princeton University Press.

Kirchheimer, S. (2004). Coffee: The new health food? *WebMD.* Accessed on 9/8/2008 from http://men.webmd.com/features/coffee-new-health-food.

Klein, H., Wesson, M., Hollenbeck, J., & Alge, B. (1999). Goal commitment and the goal setting process: Conceptual clarification and empirical synthesis. *Journal of Applied Psychology, 84*(4), 885-895.

Kolb, A. Y., & Kolb, D. A. (2009). Experiential learning theory: A dynamic, holistic approach to management learning, education and development. In S. J. Armstrong & C. V. Fukami (Eds.), *The Sage handbook of management learning, education and development* (pp. 42-68). Los Angeles, CA: Sage.

Krathwohl, D. R. (2002). A revision of Bloom's taxonomy: An overview. *Theory Into Practice, 41*(4), 212-218.

Ku, G., Malhotra, D., & Murnighan, J. K. (2005). Towards a competitive arousal model of decision-making: A study of auction fever in live and Internet auctions. *Organizational Behavior and Human Decision Processes, 96*, 89–103.

Kubler, D., & Weizsacker, G. (2003). Information cascades in the labor market. *Journal of Economics, 80*(3), 211–229.

Kubler, D., & Weizsacker, G. (2004). Limited depth of reasoning and failure of cascade formation in the laboratory. *Review of Economic Studies, 71*(247), 425-441.

Kuhn, T. S. (1970). *The structure of scientific revolutions* (2nd ed., enlarged). Chicago, IL: University of Chicago Press.

Lahart, J. (2009, September 22). New light on the plight of winter babies. *The Wall Street Journal,* p. A14.

Langer, E. J. (1975). The illusion of control. *Journal of Personality and Social Psychology, 32*, 311-328.

Langer, E. J., & Rodin, J. (1976). The effects of choice and enhanced personal responsibility for the aged: A field experiment in an institutional setting. *Journal of Personality and Social Psychology, 34*(2), 191-198.

Larkin, J. H. (1981). Enriching formal knowledge: A model for learning to solve textbook physics problems. In J. R. Anderson (Ed.), *Cognitive skills and their acquisition* (pp. 311-334). Hillsdale, NJ: Lawrence Earlbaum.

Latham, G., & Locke, E. (2006). Enhancing the benefits and overcoming the pitfalls of goal setting. *Organizational Dynamics, 35*(4), 332–340.

Latham, G., & Locke, E. (2009). Science and ethics: What should count as evidence against the use of goal setting? *Academy of Management Perspectives, 23*(3), 88-91.

Latham, G., & Steele, T. (1983). The motivational effects of participation versus goal setting on performance. *Academy of Management Journal, 26,* 406-417.

Lawrence, P. R., & Nohria, N. (2002). *Driven: How human nature shapes our choices.* San Francisco, CA: Josie-Bass.

Lee, A. (1999). Rigor and relevance in MIS research: Beyond the approach of positivism alone. *MIS Quarterly, 23*(1), 31-33.

Lee, H. L., Padmanabhan, V., & Whang, S. (1997). The bullwhip effect in supply chains. *Sloan Management Review, 38*(3), 93-102.

Leonard-Barton, D., & DeLacey, B. (1987). *Skunkworks at Digital Equipment Corporation: The tale of XCON, Case 9-687-051.* Boston, MA: Harvard Business School Publishing.

Levitt, S. D., & Dubner, S. J. (2009). *Super freakonomics: Global cooling, patriotic prostitutes and why suicide bombers should buy life insurance.* New York, NY: William Morrow.

Levitt, S. D., & List, J. A. (2007). What do laboratory experiments measuring social preferences reveal about the real world? *Journal of Economic Perspectives, 21*(2), 153–174.

List, J. A. (2007). On the interpretation of giving in dictator games. *Journal of Political Economy, 115*(3), 482-493.

Lo, A. W. (2005). *Reconciling efficient markets with behavioral finance: The adaptive markets hypothesis.* Retrieved from SSRN: http://ssrn.com/abstract=728864

Locke, E. (2004). Goal-setting theory and its applications to the world of business. *Academy of Management Executive, 18*(4), 124-125.

Locke, E., & Latham, G. (2009). Has goal setting gone wild, or have its attackers abandoned good scholarship? *Academy of Management Perspectives, 23*(1), 17-23.

Loewenstein, G. (1994). The psychology of curiosity: A review and reinterpretation. *Psychological Bulletin, 116*(1), 75-98.

Loewenstein, G. (1992). Fall and rise of psychological explanations in the economics of temporal choice. In G. Loewenstein & J. Elster, *Choice over time* (pp. 3-34). New York, NY: Russell Sage Foundation.

Loewenstein, G., & Prelec, D. (1992). Anomalies in intertemporal choice: Evidence and an interpretation. In G. Loewenstein & J. Elster, *Choice over time* (pp. 119-146). New York, NY: Russell Sage Foundation.

Loewenstein, G., & Sicherman, N. (1991). Do workers prefer increasing wage profiles? *Journal of Labor Economics, 9*(1), 67–84.

Lord, K. R., & Burnkrant, R. E. (1993). Attention versus distraction: The interactive effect of program involvement and attentional devices on commercial programming. *Journal of Advertising, 22*(1), 47-60.

Luce, M. F., Payne, J. W., & Bettman, J. R. 1999). Emotional trade-off difficulty and choice. *Journal of Marketing Research, 36*(2), 143-159.

Lyytinen, K. (1999). Empirical research in information systems: On the relevance of practice in thinking of IS research. *MIS Quarterly, 23*(1), 25-28.

Madura, J. (1997). *Introduction to business*. Mason, OH: South-Western Publishing.

Maher, M. W. (1995). The evolution of management accounting research. *Management Accounting, 76*(11), 72.

Majaran, V., Muller, E., & Bass, F. M. (1991). New product diffusion models in marketing: A review and directions for research. In N. Nakicenovic & A. Grubler (Eds.), *Diffusion of technologies and social behavior* (pp. 125-177). New York, NY: Springer.

Mandelbrot, B. (1963). The variation of certain speculative prices. *The Journal of Business, 36*(4), 394-419.

Malhotra, Y. (2001). *Knowledge management and business model innovation*. Hershey, PA: Idea Group.

Mariani, M. D., & Hewitt, G. J. (2008). Indoctrination U.? Faculty ideology and changes in student political orientation. *PS: Political Science & Politics, 41*(4), 773-783.

Mauboussin, M. J. (2008). *More than you know: Finding financial wisdom in unconventional places*. New York, NY: Columbia.

McCabe, D. L., Butterfield, K. D., & Trevino, L. K. (2006). Academic dishonesty in graduate business programs: Prevalence, causes, and proposed action. *Academy of Management Learning & Education, 5*(3), 294–305.

McCabe, D. L., & Trevino, L. K. (1995). Cheating among business students: A challenge for business leaders and educators. *Journal of Management Education, 19*(2), 205–218.

McClelland, J. L., & Rumelhart, D. E. (1981). An interactive activation model of context effects in letter perception: Part 1. An account of basic findings. *Psychological Review, 88*(5), 375-407.

McFarlan, F. W. (Ed.) (1985). *The information systems research challenge: Proceedings.* Boston: HBS Press.

McGurn, W. (2009, September 15). Let's grade Wall Street like colleges. *The Wall Street Journal,* p. A19.

McNamara, P. (2009). Benefits of writing teaching case studies with students for credit. *MED Newsletter,* 11-12. Retrieved from http://division.aomonline.org/med/images/newsletter-fall-2009.pdf

Merton, R. K. (1968). The Matthew effect in science. *Science, 159*(3810), 56-63.

Meyer, A. D. (1982). Adapting to environmental jolts. *Administrative Science Quarterly, 27,* 515-537.

Milgram, S. (1967). The small world problem. *Psychology Today, 1*(1), 60-67.

Miller, C. C. (2006). Peer review in the organizational and management sciences: Prevalence and effects of reviewer hostility, bias, and dissensus. *Academy of Management Journal, 49*(3), 425–431.

Miller, G. A. (1967). *The psychology of communication.* New York, NY: Basic Books.

Milner, D., Mahaffey, T., MacCaulay, K., & Hynes, T. (1999). The effect of business education on the ethics of students: An empirical assessment controlling for maturation. *Teaching Business Ethics, 3*(3), 255-267.

Minsky, M. L., &Papert, S. A. (1969). *Perceptrons.* Cambridge, MA: MIT Press.

Mintzberg, H. (2004). *Managers not MBAs.* San Francisco, CA: Berrett-Koehler.

Mirels, H. L. (1980). The avowal of responsibility for good and bad outcomes. *Personality and Social Psychology Bulletin, 6*(2), 299-306.

Mitchell, T. R., Thompson, L., Peterson, E., & Cronk, R. (1997). Temporal adjustments in the evaluation of events: The "rosy view". *Journal of Experimental Social Psychology, 33*(4), 421-448.

Mlodinow, L. (2009). *The drunkard's walk.* New York: Vintage Books.

Mol, M. J., & Birkinshaw, J. (2008). *Giant steps in management.* Harlow, U.K.: Prentice Hall-Financial Times.

Morison, E. (1966). *Man, machines and modern times.* Cambridge, MA: MIT Press.

Morris, J. A., & Feldman, D. C. (1996). The dimensions, antecedents, and consequences of emotional labor. *Academy of Management Review, 21*(4), 986-1010.

Moss Kanter, R., Schlesinger, L., & Richardson, L. (1989). Mastering the art of change: Managing convergence and upheaval. *Harvard Business School Press*, Teaching Note: 9-389-168.

Mussweiler, T., Englich, B., & Strack, F. (2004). Anchoring effect. In R. F. Pohl (Ed.), *Cognitive illusions* (pp. 183-200). Hove, UK: Psychology Press.

Naik, G. (2009, September 8). Deep inside bacteria, a germ of human personality. *The Wall Street Journal*, p. A18.

Navarro, P. (2008). The MBA core curricula of top-ranked U.S. business schools: A study in failure? *Academy of Management Learning & Education, 7*(1), 108-123.

Nelson, A. (2008). Is an MBA worth it? *CNBC, 17 November*. Retrieved from http://www.cnbc.com/id/27767506

Newell, A. (1990). *Unified theories of cognition*. Cambridge, MA: Harvard University Press.

Newell, A., & Rosenbloom, P. S. (1981). Mechanisms of skill acquisition and the law of practice. In J. R. Anderson (Ed.), *Cognitive skills and their acquisition* (pp. 1-55). Hillsdale, NJ: Lawrence Earlbaum.

Newell, A., & Simon, H. A. (1972). *Human problem solving*. Englewood Cliffs, NJ: Prentice-Hall.

Newcombe, N. S., & Bouton, M. E. (2009). Masked reviews are not fairer reviews. *Perspectives on Psychological Science, 4*(1), 62-64.

Newton, B. D. (2003, September 26). All-you-can-eat was too much. *St. Petersburg Times*. Accessed on 8/8/2009 from http://www.sptimes.com/2003/09/26/news_pf/State/All_you_c an_eat_was_t.shtml

Nunes, J., & Drèze, X. (2006). The endowed progress effect: How artificial advancement increases effort. *Journal of Consumer Research, 32*(4), 504-512.

Oreskes, N. (2004). Beyond the ivory tower: The scientific consensus on climate change. *Science, 306*(5702), 1686.

Ordonez, L. D., Schweitzer, M. E., Galinsky, A. D., & Bazerman, M. H. (2009a). Goals gone wild: The systematic side effects of overprescribing goal setting. *Academy of Management Perspectives, 23*(1), 6-16.

Ordonez, L. D., Schweitzer, M. E., Galinsky, A. D. & Bazerman, M. H. (2009b). On good scholarship, goal setting, and scholars gone wild. *Academy of Management Perspectives, 23*(3), 82-87.

Oswald, M. E., & Grosjean, S. (2004). Confirmation bias. In R. F. Pohl (Ed.), *Cognitive illusions* (pp. 79-96). Hove, U.K.: Psychology Press.

Pardes, H. (2009, November 5). The coming shortage of doctors. *The Wall Street Journal*, p. A19.

Payne, J. W. (1976). Task complexity and contingent processing in decision making. *Organizational Behavior and Human Performance, 16*, 366-387.

Payne, J. W., Bettman, J. R., & Johnson, E. J. (1993). *The adaptive decision maker*. Cambridge, UK: Cambridge University Press.

Peters, D. P., & Ceci, S. J. (1982). Peer-review practices of psychological journals: The fate of published articles, submitted again. *Behavioral and Brain Sciences, 5*(2), 187-255.

Petit, J. R., Jouzel, J., Raynaud, D., Barkov, N. I., Barnola, J. M., Basile, I., Bender, M., Chappellaz, J., Davis, J., Delaygue, G., Delmotte, M., Kotlyakov, V. M., Legrand, M., Lipenkov, V., Lorius, C., Pépin, L., Ritz, C., Saltzman, E., & Stievenard, M. (1999). Climate and atmospheric history of the past 420,000 years from the Vostok ice core, Antarctica. *Nature, 399*, 429-436.

Pfeffer, J. (2007). A modest proposal: How we might change the process and product of managerial research. *Academy of Management Journal, 50*(6), 1334-1345.

Pfeffer, J. & Fong, C. (2002). The end of business schools? Less success than meets the eye, *Academy of Management Learning & Education*, 1(1), 78–95.

Pierson, F. C. (1959). *The education of American businessmen: A study of university-college programs in business administration*. New York, NY: McGraw-Hill.

Politser, P. (2008). *Neuroeconomcs*. Oxford, UK: Oxford University Press.

Porter, L. W., & McKibbin, L. E. (1988). *Management education and development: Drift or thrust into the 21st century*. New York, NY: McGraw-Hill.

Porter, M. E. (1980). *Competitive strategy*. New York, NY: Free Press.

Porter, M. E. (1985). *Competitive advantage*. New York, NY: Free Press.

Prelec, D., & Simester, D. (2001). Always leave home without it: A further investigation of the credit-card effect on willingness to pay. *Marketing Letters, 12*(1), 5-12.

Rachlinski, J. L. (2004). Heuristics, biases and governance. In D. J. Koehler & N. Harvey (Eds.), *Blackwell handbook of judgment and decision making* (pp. 567-584). Malden, MA: Blackwell Publishing.

Rafter, M. V. (2004). Looking for business-ready candidates, companies turn to finishing schools of commerce. *Workforce Management*, Online, August. Retrieved from http://www.workforce.com/archive/feature/23/79/86/index.php

Read, D., & Loewenstein, G. (1995). Diversification bias: Explaining the discrepancy in variety seeking between combined and separated choices. *Journal of Experimental Psychology: Applied, 1*(1), 34-49.

Reay, T., Berta, W., & Kohn, M. K. (2009). What's the evidence on evidence-based management? *Academy of Management Perspectives, 23*(4), 5-18.

Reber, R. (2004). Availability. In R. F. Pohl (Ed.), *Cognitive illusions* (pp. 147-164). Hove, U.K.: Psychology Press.

Reinhart, C. M., & Rogoff, K. S. (2009). *This time is different: Eight centuries of financial folly*. Princeton, NJ: Princeton University Press.

Robbins, R. W., & Butler, B. S. (2009). Selecting a virtual world platform for learning. *Journal of Information Systems Education, 20*(2), 199-210.

Roberts, R. (2010, February 27). Is the dismal science really a science? *The Wall Street Journal*, A13.

Rodin, J., & Langer, E. J. (1977). Long-term effects of a control-relevant intervention with the institutionalized aged. *Journal of Personality and Social Psychology, 35*(12), 897-902.

Roediger III, H. L., & Gallo, D. A. (2004). Associative memory illusions. In R. F. Pohl (Ed.), *Cognitive illusions* (pp. 309-326). Hove, U.K.: Psychology Press.

Roethlisberger, F. (1977). *The elusive phenomena*. Boston, MA: HBS Press.

Rogers, E. M. (2003). *Diffusion of innovations* (5th ed.). New York, NY: Free Press.

Rohrer, D., & Pashler, H. (2007). Increasing retention without increasing study time. *Current Directions in Psychological Science, 16*(4), 183-186.

Rottenstreich, Y., & Shu, S. (2004). The connections between affect and decision making: Nine resulting phenomena. In D. J. Koehler & N. Harvey (Eds.), *Blackwell handbook of judgment and decision making* (pp. 444-463). Malden, MA: Blackwell.

Rumelhart, D. E., & McClelland, J. L. (1982). An interactive activation model of context effects in letter perception: Part 2. The contextual enhancement effect and some tests and extensions of the model. *Psychological Review, 89*(1), 60-94.

Rumelhart, D. E. & Norman, D. A. (1981). Analogical processes in learning. In J. R. Anderson (Ed.), *Cognitive skills and their acquisition* (pp. 335-359). Hillsdale, NJ: Lawrence Earlbaum.

Russo, J. E., & Dosher, B. A. (1983). Strategies for multiattribute binary choice. *Journal of Experimental Psychology: Learning, Memory and Cognition, 9*, 676-696.

Russo, J. ,& Shoemaker, P. (1989). *Decision traps: Ten barriers to brilliant decision making and how to overcome them.* New York, NY: Simon & Schuster.

Ruth, A. (2007). Hard things about using the internet in HE. Retrieved from: http://apps01.domino.griffith.edu.au/apps/blogs/ed-tech.nsf/dx/hard-things-about-using-the-internet-in-he

Rynes, S. L., Giluk, T. L., & Brown, K. G. (2007). The very separate worlds of academic and practitioner publications in human resources management: Implications for evidence-based management. *Academy of Management Journal, 50*(5), 987-1008.

Salvia, J., Algozzine, R., & Scheare, J.B. (1977). Attractiveness and school achievement. *Journal of School Psychology, 15*(1), 60-67.

Samuelson, P. (1937). A note on measurement of utility. *Review of Economic Studies, 4*, 155-161.

Scalia, A. (2009, October 9). Notable and quotable. *The Wall Street Journal*, p. A17.

Schank, R. C. (1986). *Explanation patterns: Understanding mechanically and creatively.* Hillsdale, NJ: Lawrence Earlbaum.

Schein, E. H. (1999). Kurt Lewin's change theory in the field and in the classroom: Notes toward a model of managed learning. *Reflections, 1*(1), 59-74.

Schmidt, F. L., & Hunter, J. E. (1998). The validity and utility of selection methods in personnel psychology: Practical and theoretical implications of 85 years of research findings. *Psychological Bulletin, 124*(2), 262-274.

Schramm, C., Litan, R., & Stangler, D. (2009, November 6). New business, not small business, is what creates jobs, *The Wall Street Journal*, p. A25.

Selfridge, O. G. (1958). Pandemonium: A paradigm for learning. In J. A. Anderson & E. Rosefield. (1988). *Neurocomputing: Foundations of research* (pp. 117-122). Cambridge, MA: MIT Press.

Shen, J., & Eder, L. B. (2009). Intentions to use virtual worlds for education. *Journal of Information Systems Education, 20*(2), 225-233.

Shannon, C. E., & Weaver, W. (1949). *The mathematical theory of communications.* Urbana: University of Illinois Press.

Shanteau, J. (1992). Competence in experts: The role of task characteristics. *Organizational Behavior and Human Decision Processes, 53,* 252-266.

Shiller, R. J. (1995). Conversation, information, and herd behavior. *American Economic Review, 85*(2), 181-185.

Shiffrin, R. M., & Dumais, S. T. (1981). The development of automatism. In J. R. Anderson (Ed.), *Cognitive skills and their acquisition* (pp. 111-140). Hillsdale, NJ: Lawrence Earlbaum.

Shirky, C. (2003). Power laws, weblogs, and inequality. Retrieved from http://www.shirky.com/writings/powerlaw_weblog.html

Shugan, S. M. (2006). Editorial: Save research—abandon the case method of teaching. *Marketing Science, 25*(2), 109–115.

Siegel, J. J. (2009, October 29). Efficient market theory and the crisis, *The Wall Street Journal,* p. A23.

Sierra, J. J., & Hyman, M. R. (2006). A dual-process model of cheating intentions. *Journal of Marketing Education, 28*(3), 193-204.

Simon, H. A. (1955). A behavioral model of rational choice. *Quarterly Journal of Economics, 69,* 129-138.

Simon, H. A. (1981). *The sciences of the artificial* (2nd ed.). Cambridge: MIT Press.

Simon, H. A., & Hayes, J. R. (1976). The understanding process: Problem isomorphs. In H. A. Simon, (1979). *Models of thought* (pp. 477-512). New Haven, CT: Yale University Press.

Soman, D., & Cheema, A. (2002). The effect of credit on spending decisions: The role of the credit limit and credibility. *Marketing Science, 21*(1), 32-53.

Starbuck, W. H. (2003). Turning lemons into lemonade: Where is the value in peer reviews? *Journal of Management Inquiry, 12*(4), 344-351.

Starbuck, W. H. (2005). How much better are the most-prestigious journals? The statistics of academic publication. *Organization Science, 16*(2), 180-200.

Starkey, K., & Tiratsoo, N. (2007). *The business school and the bottom line.* Cambridge, UK: Cambridge University Press.

Stix, G. (2009). The science of bubbles and busts. *Scientific American, 301*(1), 78-85.

Sterman, J. D. (2002). All models are wrong: Reflections on becoming a systems scientist. *System Dynamics Review, 18*(4), 501–531.

StrategyOne. (2009a). 2009 Edelman trust barometer. *Edelman.* Retrieved from http://www.edelman.com/trust/2009/

StrategyOne. (2009b). Edelman trust barometer: 2009 special midyear trust survey. *Edelman.* 9 August, Retrieved from http://www.edelman.com/trust/midyear/docs/Mid-Year2009TrustBarometer_ClientDeck.pdf

Stroop, J. R. (1935). Studies of interference in serial verbal reactions. *Journal of Experimental Psychology, 18,* 643-662. Retrieved from http://psychclassics.yorku.ca/Stroop/

Summers, L., & Zeckhauser, R. J. (2008). Policymaking for posterity. *Journal of Risk and Uncertainty, 37,* 115–140.

Taleb, N. N. (2007). *The Black Swan.* New York, NY: Random House.

Tapp, A. (2004). A call to arms for applied marketing academics. *Marketing Intelligence & Planning, 22*(5), 579-590.

Teigen, K. H. (2004). Judgment by representativeness. In R. F. Pohl (Ed.), *Cognitive illusions* (pp. 165-182). Hove, U.K.: Psychology Press.

Tetlock, P. E. (1999). Theory driven reasoning about plausible pasts and probable futures in world politics: Are we prisoners of our preconceptions? *American Journal of Political Science, 43*(2), 335-366.

Thaler, R. H. (2000). From homo economicus to homo sapiens. *Economic Perspectives, 14*(1), 133-141.

Thaler, R. H., & Sunstein, C. R. (2008). *Nudge.* New York, NY: Penguin Group USA

Thompson, S. C. (2004). Illisions of control. In R. F. Pohl (Ed.), *Cognitive illusions* (pp. 115-126). Hove, U.K.: Psychology Press.

Travers, J., & Milgram, S. (1969). An experimental study of the small world problem. *Sociometry, 32*(4), 425-443.

Trieschmann, J., Dennis, A., Northcraft, G., & Niemi Jr., A. (2000). Serving multiple constituencies in business schools: M.B.A. program versus research performance. *Academy of Management Journal, 43*(6), 1130-1141.

Tucker, J. M., & Massad, V. (2007). Student-managed eBay business: A tool for applying business learning. *Decision Sciences Journal of Innovative Education, 5*(2), 383-389.

Tversky, A. (1969). Intransitivity of preferences. *Psychological Review, 76,* 31-48.

Tversky, A. (1972). Elimination by aspects: A theory of choice. *Psychological Review, 79,* 281-299.

Tversky, A., & Kahneman, D. (1982a). Availability: A heuristic for judging frequency and probability. In D. Kahneman, P. Slovic, & A. Tversky (Eds.), *Judgement under uncertainty: Heuristics and biases* (pp. 163-178). Cambridge, UK: Cambridge University Press.

Tversky, A., & Kahneman, D. (1982b). Introduction. In D. Kahneman, P. Slovic, & A. Tversky (Eds.), *Judgment under uncertainty: Heuristics and biases.* (pp. 1-20). Cambridge, UK: Cambridge University Press.

Tversky, A., & Kahneman, D. (1982c). Judgments of and by representativeness. In D. Kahneman, P. Slovic, & A. Tversky (Eds.), *Judgement under uncertainty: Heuristics and biases* (pp. 84-98). Cambridge, UK: Cambridge University Press.

Usher, M., & McClelland, J. L. (2001). The time course of perceptual choice: The leaky, competing accumulator model. *Psychological Review, 108*(3), 550-592.

Usher, M., & McClelland, J. L. (2004). Loss aversion and inhibition in dynamical models of multialternative choice. *Psychological Review, 111*(3), 757-769.

Van Der Werf, M. (2009, June 3). Researcher offers unusually candid description of university's effort to rise in rankings. *Chronicle of Higher Education.* Retrieved from http://chronicle.com/daily/2009/06/19270n.htm

Virany, B., Tushman, M. L., & Romanelli, E. (1982). Executive succession and organization outcomes in turbulent environments: An organizational learning approach. *Organization Science, 3*(1), 72 91.

Vittor, E. M. (2004, June 8). New title to honor Tribe, Whitesides. *The Harvard Crimson.* Retrieved from http://www.thecrimson.com/article.aspx?ref=502753

Wade, M., Biehl, M., & Kim, H. (2006). Information systems is not a reference discipline (and what we can do about it). *Journal of the Association for Information Systems, 7*(5), 247-269.

Watts, D. J. (2003). *Six degrees: The science of a connected age.* New York, NY: Norton.

Wagner, C., & Ip, R. K. F. (2009). Action learning with Second Life - A pilot study. *Journal of Information Systems Education, 20*(2), 249-258.

Wang, Y., & Braman, J. (2009). Extending the classroom through Second Life. *Journal of Information Systems Education, 20*(2), 235-247.

Weinstein, N. D. (1980). Unrealistic optimism about future life events. *Journal of Personality and Social Psychology, 39*(5), 806-820.

Williamson, O. E. (1975). *Markets and hierarchies: Analysis and anti-trust implications.* New York, NY: Free Press.

Willingham, D. T. (2009). *Why don't students like school?* San Francisco, CA: Jossey Bass.

Woessner, M., & Kelly-Woessner, A. (2009). I think my professor is a democrat: Considering whether students recognize and react to faculty politics. *PS: Political Science & Politics, 42*(2), 343-352.

Wolfram, S. (1994). *Cellular automata and complexity.* Reading, MA: Addison-Wesley.

Wood, R. (1986). Task complexity: Definition of the construct. *Organizational Behavior and Human Decision Processes, 37,* 60-82.

Zand, D.E. & Sorensen, R.E. (1975). Theory of change and the effective use of management science, *Administrative Science Quarterly,* 20(4), 532-545.

Zeckhauser, R. J., & Viscusi, W. K. (2008). Discounting dilemmas: Editors' introduction. *Journal of Risk and Uncertainty, 37,* 95-106.

Ziliak, S. T., & McCloskey, D. N. (2008). *The cult of statistical significance.* Ann Arbor, MI: University of Michigan Press.

About the Author

T. Grandon Gill is a professor in the Information Systems & Decision Sciences department of the College of Business at the University of South Florida. He holds a doctorate in Management Information Systems from Harvard Business School, where he also received his M.B.A. His principal research areas are the impacts of complexity on decision-making and IS education, and he has published many articles describing how technologies and innovative pedagogies can be combined to increase the effectiveness of teaching across a broad range of IS topics. Currently, he is an Editor of the *Journal of IT Education* and an Editor-in-Chief of *Informing Science: the International Journal of an Emerging Transdiscipline*.

Email: grandon@usf.edu

Index

10,000 Hour Rule, 161
2008 Global Summit on Business Education in the 21ˢᵗ Century, 7
21, the movie, 289
A Blueprint for Survival, 545, 547
AACSB International, 8, 14, 15, 16, 19, 37, 43, 45, 79, 106, 376, 377, 380, 400, 401, 405, 448
research impact report, 14
abduction, 132, 133, 166, 205, 328, 432
Abernathy, W. J., 10, 11, 21, 25, 271, 281, 282
abstract concepts, 173, 372
academic experts, 168
academic freedom, 410
academic informing systems, 27, 31
Academy of Management Journal, 100, 296
Academy of Management Review, 296, 328, 502
Accounting, Management. & Information Technologies, 399
accretion, 186
Administrative Science Quarterly, 316
Adval, R., 216
affect, 211
agency theory, 15, 16, 18, 43, 294, 455
agora, 500
agribusiness, 228, 280, 338, 339, 385, 472, 481, 490, 493, 495, 497, 506

Agribusiness Seminar, 481, 497
Aiken, M., 214
Ainslie, G., 259
airline crashes, 61
airline industry, 98
AIS. See Association for Information Systems
Akerlof, G.A., 219, 225, 503
Alba, J. W., 135
Alge, B., 210
Algozzine, R., 212
Allen, P., 7
Allen, R., 512, 513, 545
Allison, K.R., 284
all-you-can-eat, 99
Alonzo, M., 214
altruism, 214, 291
Amabile, T.M., 192
Ambady, N., 212
Ambrose, S.H., 274
American Express, 104, 280, 342
anchoring, 140, 205, 206, 214, 216
attraction, 141
compromise, 141
similarity, 141
Anderson, L.R., 236
Andrews, F., 442
anger, 213
anticipated emotions, 212, 217
antikythera, 70, 84
Applegate, L., 104
applied research, 5, 32, 89
Arco College Guide, 65

Ariely, D., 100, 107, 138, 141, 142, 144, 145, 146, 147, 148, 166, 178, 179, 213, 215, 292, 328, 331, 503

Armstrong, J.S., 314, 324, 333, 433

arousal, 172, 199, 201, 202, 203, 212, 213, 215, 218, 279, 343, 351

arousal interest, 172

Arthur, W.B., 82

Arya, A., 237

Ask Marilyn, 179, 331

Aspen Institute, 468, 528

assessing landscape complexity, 59

Association for Information Systems, 39, 40

associative storage, 119

assurance of learning, 8, 406

asteroid collision, 274, 281

attention filter, 83, 199, 200, 201, 212, 221

attractive students and instructors, 212

attractive theory, 22, 70, 72, 74, 78, 81, 87, 105, 108, 115, 287, 346

attributes, 70

auction exercise, 128

Austen, J., 426, 463

Austin, R., 104

Authorizer's Assistant, 280, 342

automatization, 161

automatize, 162, 163, 167, 175, 180, 206, 301, 365, 478

availability, 130

Axelrod, R., 127

axons, 136

baby and the bath water paradox, 98

Bagozzi, R.P., 300, 332

Bain, K., 182

Bak, P., 58, 83, 246, 247, 264, 327

Baldridge, D.C., 15

Ball, J., 524, 550

Ballmer, S., 7

Banerjee, A. V., 236

Barabasi, A. L., 242, 247

Barash, D., 51

Barings debacle, 101

Barley, S.R., 15

Barman, S., 26

Bartlett, C.A., 455

Baskerville, R., 40, 332

Bass, F.M., 15, 231, 400

Bates, T.C., 330

Batterymarch Financial Management, 104, 271, 478

Baumgarth, C., 324

Bazerman, M.H., 210, 224

Beam, A., 551

Beaver, W., 15

Becker, G.S., 258

behaviorist theory, 187

Benbasat, I., 37, 38

Bennis, W.G., 13, 21

Berkowitz, P., 315

Berlin Philharmonic, 312

Berlin, I., 18

Berta, W., 502

Betamax, 55, 82, 105

Bettman, J.R., 82, 134, 216

Bhattacherjee, A., 25, 36, 39, 332

bias filter model, 198

Biehl, M., 41

Bikhchandani, S., 235

Birkinshaw, J., 14, 319
Black Death, 266, 515
Black Swan, The, 18, 132, 224, 277
black swans, 18, 19, 109, 132, 274, 279, 292, 311, 360, 368, 369, 454, 456, 476, 478, 515
Blink, 86, 223, 312, 477
Bloom, B.S., 160, 183, 184
Bloom's Taxonomy, 160, 183
Bloomberg, M., 7
Blue Cross & Blue Shield of Ohio, 246, 281, 534
Blue's Clues, 220
Blueprint for Survival, 512, 527
Bombardieri, M., 46
boot camp, 7, 424
boredom, 201
Borlaug, N., 493, 506, 512
Boston Consulting Group, 8
Boston, Massachusetts, 84, 243
Bourgeois, L.J., 105
Bourner, T., 488, 489
Bouton, M.E., 320
Bowden, M., 236, 488, 489
Bowden, R., 236, 488, 489
Braman, J., 444
Brazil, 4, 61, 545
bread makers, 141
Breakdown of Will, 259
Brier, D.J., 250, 270
Bright Futures, 437
Brin, S., 7
Brinker, S., 190
Brown, K.G., 100, 219, 502
Brynjolfsson, E., 492
Buckley, M.R., 26
Buffet, W., 7, 538
Bulletin of Atomic Scientists, 513, 547

bullwhip effect, 267, 280
Burnkrant, R.E., 203
Burry, J. Jr., 246, 281
Bush, G.W., 257
business degrees conferred in U.S., 6
business plan, 124, 441
Business School and the Bottom Line, 462, 500
business schools, 42
Business Week, 9, 36
Butcher Wax, 465
Butler, B.S., 444
Butterfield, K.D., 4
butterfly effect, 85, 525
Cable, D.M., 318, 332, 402
Camerer, C.F., 190, 329
Campanha, J.R., 296
Canary Islands, 282
capital asset pricing model, 19, 292
capitalism, 1, 427
Card, S. K., 119
Cardano, G., 252
Cardinal, L.B., 325, 336
Carnegie Foundation, 3, 10, 538
Carnegie Mellon, 496
case method, 429
cash, 145
Ceci, S.J., 313, 315, 317, 319
cellular automata, 58, 83
channel capabilities, 200
chaos, 58, 78, 85, 276, 442, 446, 524, 539, 541, 542
chaotic landscape, 53, 55, 73, 335
Chapman, G.B., 144
Chari, K., 439
Charness, N., 121, 122, 154

cheating, 217
Cheema, A., 215
Cheit, E.F., 6, 10
Chernobyl, 101
chess, 121, 154, 162, 170, 266
chest pains, 477
Chevalier, J., 8
China, 4, 195, 395, 446, 465, 512, 530, 531, 545
Chinese Tea Ceremony, 180, 366
choice strategies
  elimination by aspects, 135
  equal weight heuristic, 134
  frequency of good and bad features, 135
  lexicographic heuristic, 135
  majority of confirming dimensions, 135
  satisficing, 135
Christensen, C.M., 62, 88, 92, 104, 409, 451, 534
chunk, 161, 167, 175, 180, 365
chunking, 161, 162, 175
citation analysis, 40
Clark, A. E., 115, 127
Clemson University, 64
client filters, 199, 201, 220
client-to-client informing, 227, 231
CocaCola, 491, 506
cockroaches, 196
co-evolution, 55, 57, 59
co-evolving systems, 272
coffee, 69, 78, 86, 251
cognitive functions, 212
cognitive load, 120, 134
Cohen, E., 28, 30, 31, 45, 82, 316
Cohn, S.K., 516

Colbert, A.E., 318, 332, 402
Coleman, S., 144
College Expert, 64, 65, 66
college rankings, 64
Collins, E., 104
Colquitt, J.A., 297, 298, 332, 381, 408, 571
Commission on Presidential Debates, 216
commodity systems, 280, 491, 497
Companario, J.M., 318, 404
competing senders, 29
compiled knowledge, 167, 185, 206, 365
complex adaptive systems, 58, 263, 281, 283, 372, 386, 427, 476
complexity, 47
  and individual resonance, 193
complexity indicators, 97
compromise effect, 141, 205, 291
ConAgra, 491
concept acquisition, 160, 165, 186, 187
conceptual scheme, 18, 74, 118, 129, 136, 146, 157, 160, 165, 168, 176, 183, 184, 194, 198, 221, 223, 272, 317, 327, 339, 359, 370, 454
Conchylomania, 236
confirmation bias, 130, 209, 228
confirmation heuristic, 209
conjunction effect, 112, 130, 176
conjunctive fallacy, 176
connectionism, 136, 138, 386

connectionist model, 138, 161
connectors, 234, 243, 244
Conniff, R., 236
constructivist, 435, 484, 487
consulting-as-grant, 486
continuous aiming, 195
control processes, 161
Cook County emergency room, 477
cooperative education, 437
Cooperative Extension Service, 493
Copernicus, 70
coping with complexity, 415, 417, 429, 510, 540, 544
core skills, 365, 420, 421, 424, 426, 427, 440, 450, 459, 461
cow paths, 84
crab legs, 99
Crichton, M., 276, 552
critical mass, 231
critical thinking, 183
Cronk, R., 257
Cult of Statistical Significance, 95, 298, 473
cultural dimensions, 60
Cummings, J.J., 180
curiosity, 129, 172, 201, 219, 284
curriculum undergraduate, 417
d'Alembert, J.L.R., 277
Daft, R. L., 200, 216
Dahringer, L., 362
Darwin, C., 286, 329, 383
Datar, S.M., 24
Davenport, T., 13, 37, 367
Davis, F.D., 300
Davis, J.H., 490, 493

Davis, M., 129, 173, 181, 201, 202, 221
Dawes, W., 243
De Bondt, W.F.M., 293
De Vany, A., 245
Deary I.J., 330
Decision Line, 398
Decision Sciences Institute, 441
decision support systems, 299
decomposability, 53, 54, 65, 67, 75, 76, 77, 88, 90, 91, 93, 97, 110, 111, 112, 168, 285, 301, 350, 360, 473, 501
decomposable fitness landscape, 55
deep knowledge, 174
DeLacey, B., 350
delivery system, 28
Dell, M., 7
dendrites, 136
Dennis, A., 33, 36
Der, G., 330
Dertouzos, M. L., 276
DeVaughn, W.L.A., 26
Dewhurst, S.A., 257, 278
Dictator, 290
difficulty, 210
diffusion, 15, 366, 479, 498
diffusion models, 15, 231, 232
Diffusion of Innovations, 218, 231, 493
Digital Equipment Corporation, 349
Dijksterhuis, A., 142
dinosaurs, 274, 281, 369
directing processing, 165, 176
disciplinary informing systems, 27, 31
disciplinary silos, 285, 294, 325, 383, 384

discontinuous change, 59, 103, 104, 105, 263, 271
discussion group trolling, 214
disinforming, 154
disruptive innovation, 104
distortion, 198
distractibility, 202
divergent change, 105
diversity, 57, 68, 98, 118, 150, 235, 246, 287, 317, 369, 376, 391, 426, 435, 447, 456, 458, 461, 501, 512, 529, 544, 546
Doctor of Business Education, 447, 448
doctoral programs, 38, 390, 467, 468, 490
dominant estimate-of-fitness, 361
Donham, W.B., 498
Doomsday Clock, 513
Dosher, B.A., 135
double decade doctorate, 489
Dreher, C., Dreher, N. & Dreher, H., 444
Drèze, X., 210
drive
  control, 129
  curiosity, 129
  feedback, 129
  for fairness, 127
  to acquire, 126
  to bond, 126
  to defend, 126
  to learn, 126
  to win, 126
drives, 212
Drucker, P., 29
Drunkard's Walk, 154, 178, 277, 476
Dubner, S.J., 290, 291, 551

Dumais, S.T., 161
Dunlap, Al, 18
Dunn, D. S., 254
DVD, 56
early adopters, 232, 268
Easterbook, G., 493, 512
economic schools, 295
economic theory, 17, 98, 106, 107, 148, 290, 292, 328
Edelman trust barometer, 3, 458
  StrategyOne, 3, 4, 458
Eder, L.B., 444
Edwards, J.P., 105
efficiency vs. adaptability, 126, 369
efficient market hypothesis, 69, 295
Ehrlich, P.R., 511
Einhorn, H. J., 134
Eisenhardt, K.M, 105
Elkins, J., 180
Ellison, G., 7, 8
Ellison, L., 7
Elster, J., 79, 80, 479
emotional anchoring, 216
emotional framing, 215
emotional impact on choice strategies, 216
emotional labor, 218
emotions, 211
emotions and information processing, 213
endowment effect, 144
Englich, B., 140
enhanced memory of emotionally significant events, 213
Enron, 3
Epcot Center, 180

epidural anesthesia, 259
ERP, 266
estimate-of-fitness, 69, 71, 73,
    85, 101, 108, 110, 115, 121,
    135, 147, 148, 211, 237, 245,
    296, 324, 360, 361, 363, 364,
    366, 367, 371, 372, 374, 377,
    394, 397, 399, 402, 406, 455,
    460, 486, 497, 499, 500, 507,
    537
ethics, 4, 11, 21, 41, 225, 314,
    452, 457, 460, 468, 498
eugenics, 112, 501
Evanschitzky, H., 324
evidence-based management,
    100
evolutionarily stable strategy,
    126
exaggerated anticipation, 257,
    261
Executive Advisory Board,
    439, 460
experiential learning, 111, 416,
    437, 438, 440, 441, 447, 449
expert system, 155, 180, 334,
    337, 340, 341, 342, 347, 348,
    349, 351
expertise, 159
    acquisition of, 160
Explanation Patterns, 225
explanation-based taxonomy of
    disciplines, 79
external clients, 32, 35, 37, 45,
    159
exuberance, 237
faculty internships, 439
Federico, G., 492
Feeley, T. H., 212
feelings, 211
Feldman, D.C., 218

Fisher, R., 112, 299, 334, 473
fitness function, 51, 53, 54, 55,
    57, 59, 64, 65, 79, 97, 112,
    317, 382, 534, 535
    of a recipe, 51
fitness landscape, 47, 51, 56,
    60, 69, 70, 71, 76, 98, 103,
    106, 108, 109, 111, 125, 135,
    149, 152, 185, 305, 308, 310,
    311, 317, 362, 367, 381, 384,
    407, 460, 478, 509, 527, 534,
    540, 544
fitness of a company, 108
fitness peak, 52, 55, 57, 63, 105,
    351, 369, 372, 382, 475
    formula, 57
fitness with transparency, 458,
    460
Florida Atlantic University,
    114, 190, 337, 340, 341, 354,
    398, 413, 465, 505
Floyd, S.W., 15
Fong, C., 7, 14
forces of cohesion, 238, 242
forces of entropy, 238, 242
Ford Foundation, 3, 10, 89,
    283, 375, 496, 538
Forrest Gump, 476
Forrester, J.W., 525, 549
Foundational References, xviii
framing, 140, 205, 206, 214,
    256, 257, 331, 361
Frank, R.H., 258
Franklin, B., 383
Frederick, S., 258
free, effect of, 146
Frensch, P. A., 130
Frey, B.S., 321
Friedman, M., 329, 457
Friedman, T., 282

Frijters, P., 115, 127
From Higher Aims to Hired Hands, 418, 498
fundamental drives, 126, 145
Fundamental Predicament of Progress, 520, 537, 538
future preference, 255
Gackowski, Z., 84, 153
gain-loss discounting asymmetry, 256
Galacticomm, 190
Galinsky, A.D., 210, 224
Gallo, D.A., 175
gambler's fallacy, 131, 253, 261
Gandolfi, A. E. & Gandolfi, A. S., 51
Garvey, M.J., 25
Garvin, D.A., 8, 24
Gash, D.C., 15
Gates, W., 7, 102, 103, 114, 311, 538
GCA, 280
Georgia State University, 68
Germany, 112, 281, 488, 506, 530, 551, 555
Gersick, C.J.G., 105
Gerstner, L., 104
Ghoshal, S., 16, 17, 19, 21, 79, 80, 290, 454, 455, 457, 458, 499
Giacalone, R.A., 11
Gigerenzer, G., 130, 131, 148
Gilbert, D., 113, 129, 143, 217, 254, 255, 257, 259, 262, 356, 503
Gilbert, W., 463
Gill, C., 217
Gill, C.B., 180, 393, 409, 462
Gill, G.K., 280, 487
Gill, P.S., 463

Gill, R.T., 187, 189, 509, 510, 511, 516, 517, 520, 535, 537, 554
Giluk, T.L., 100, 219, 502
Gladwell, M., 60, 61, 86, 103, 114, 142, 150, 158, 161, 189, 220, 223, 234, 243, 312, 331, 404, 477, 495, 503, 506
Glaser, M., 176
Glazer, N., 554
Gleick, J., 85, 524
Glick, W.H., 325, 336
global climate change, 520, 527, 528
Glover, J., 237
goal setting, 209, 210, 211, 224, 294, 362
goal setting literature, 209
goal setting theory, 50
goal space, 119, 121, 122, 124, 129, 135, 145, 161, 167, 184
Goeree, J. K., 245
Goldberg, R.A., 280, 338, 339, 490, 491, 493, 495, 496, 497, 506, 507
Goldsmith, E., 512, 513, 545
Google, 7, 326, 328, 392, 397, 399, 413
Google Scholar, 393, 402, 403
Gordon, R.A., 3, 89, 283, 375, 463, 496
Gore, A., 257, 551
Gosset, W.S., 305, 334, 473, 493, 502
Gottesman, A.A., 8
Gottfredson, S. D., 336
Grebe, T., 236
Green and Rao, 15
grey swans, 273, 311, 368, 475, 554

Griffith, M., 344
Grosjean, S., 130
Grossman, M., 258
grounded theory, 290, 298
Guam, 61
Guber, P., 219
Guinness Book of World Records, 331
Guinness Brewery, 474, 493
Gunfire at Sea, 194
Gupta, H.M., 296
Gupta, Y., 66, 83
Gutenberg-Richter law, 239
Hackman, J.R., 129, 201, 279, 342, 343, 346, 348, 351
Halhoun, I. A., 182
Hambrick, D.C., 90, 285, 298, 328, 483
Handy, C., 105, 279
Harmon, P., 344
Harris, D.J., 105
Harvard Business Review, 10, 25, 219, 292, 339, 505
Harvard Business School, 3, 7, 9, 11, 12, 24, 73, 113, 128, 155, 253, 277, 334, 338, 339, 341, 355, 356, 385, 409, 412, 429, 432, 435, 465, 472, 481, 487, 490, 494, 495, 496, 497, 498, 503, 504, 505, 506, 507, 538, 540
Harvard Law School, 541
Hawk, T.F., 61
Hawthorne experiments, 73
Hayden, T., 286
Hayes, R. H., 10, 11, 21, 25, 177, 180, 271, 281, 282
heart attack, 255, 477
Heath, C. & Heath, D., 154, 189, 194, 219, 220, 234

Henninger, D., 552
Herlihy, D., 516
Hershey's Kiss, 147
Hestenes, D., 182
heuristics, 117, 129, 131, 132, 134, 148, 149, 150, 151, 174, 185, 201, 205, 206, 208, 216, 223, 251, 252, 255, 415
for low structure tasks, 125
goal space, 135
money and price, 145
operator space, 131
state space, 129
Hewitt, G.J., 469, 529, 552, 553
Hicks, R., 48, 82
high velocity, 105
Hillinger, C., 245
Hirschfeld, N., 485
Hirshleifer, D., 235
History Channel, 282
Hitt, L.M., 492
Hofstede, G., 14, 15, 60
Hogarth, R. M., 134
Holland, J. H., 236, 383
Hollenbeck, J., 210
Holt, C.A., 236
homo economicus, 132, 134, 292, 472
homogeneous clients, 29
Hoppe, U., 448, 467, 488, 490, 506
Horn, M.B., 62, 89, 104, 409, 451, 534
Hotz, R.L., 156
How Nature Works, 247
Howell, J.E., 3, 89, 283, 375, 463, 496
Hubbard, R., 323, 324, 333, 433

human cognitive system, 120, 126, 213
Human Problem Solving, 118
Hunter, J.E., 100, 101
Hyland, P., 177, 198, 210
Hyman, M.R., 217
Hynes, T., 5, 468
hyperbolic discounting, 207, 258, 262
IAT. *See* implicit associations test
IBM, 14, 102, 104, 114, 349
Idea of Progress, 516, 518, 519, 520, 527, 528, 530, 535, 537, 539, 540, 542, 543, 544, 545, 547, 548, 550, 551
IDEO Product Development, 378
illusions of control, 133, 254, 477
Im, K.S., 398, 412
immediacy effect, 258
Implementation Science, 378
implicit associations test, 204
India, 395, 512, 530, 545
indicators of ruggedness, 62
individual resonance, 193
individualism vs. collectivism, 60
induction, 132, 155, 166, 205, 206
information cascades, 59, 103, 144, 147, 215, 228, 235, 236, 237, 239, 244, 245, 264, 296, 362, 394
information overload, 201, 202
information processing, 48, 50, 117, 118, 121, 151, 165, 169, 182, 201, 206
and emotions, 213

informational cascades. *See* information cascades
informing environment, 28, 29, 272
informing instance, 28, 30
informing science, xii, 28, 30, 31, 45, 191, 194, 396, 427
foundations of, 45, 82
Ph.D in, 448
Informing Science Conference, 410
Informing Science Institute, 316, 385
Informing Science journal, 296, 336, 411
informing science research, 31
informing system, 28, 31, 40, 217, 221, 264, 270
informing system design, 31
innovators, 232
INSAG-7., 101
instance creation, 31
institutional client constituencies, 33
institutional informing systems, 27, 32
interdependence, 55
interference, 203, 213
internal clients, 32, 35
Internet bubble, 20, 25, 36
internships, 437
interrelatedness, 31
intrinsic motivation, 50, 129, 197, 198, 208, 210, 211, 212, 342, 343, 350
intrinsic motivators
achievement, 208
arousal, 208
control, 208
Introduction to Business, 424

invisible hand, 98, 292, 328
Ip, R.K.F., 444
Irwing, P., 330
isomorphic problems, 177
Jacobs, M.T., 276
James Bond, 289
Jamieson, K., 177, 198, 210
Janssen, O., 210
Japan, 276, 281, 514, 530, 531, 532, 536, 555
Jensen, M.C., 16, 294, 455
Johns Hopkins University, 83
Johnson, C.W., 62, 89, 104, 409, 451, 534
Johnson, E.F., 190
Johnson, E.J., 134
Johnson-Laird, T., 177, 178
jolts, 105
Jones, J., 82, 412
Journal of IS Education, 40
Jouzel, J., 523
Judge, T.A., 318, 319, 332, 402
Kacmar, K.M., 328
Kahneman, D., 21, 100, 130, 131, 140, 176, 252, 294, 331, 478, 503
Kauffman, S.A., 54, 56, 57, 58, 83, 149, 334, 335, 383, 539
Kauffman's NK Model, 54
Keen, P.G.W., 299
Keil, M., 342
Keller, 15
key informants, 232
Khurana, R., 2, 5, 379, 418, 462, 496, 498
Kim, H., 41
Kim, K.Y. & Kim, J.S., 398, 412
Kindle DX, 393
Kirchheimer, S., 79

Klein, H., 210
Knoop, C., 24
knowledge
  levels of structure, 165
knowledge compilation, 162
knowledge conflicts, 181
knowledge work, 531
knowledge workers, 29
Kohn, M.K., 502
Kolb, A.Y & Kolb, D.A., 111, 437, 438
Korean Air, 61
Koslowski, D., 18
Krathwohl, D.R., 184, 192
Ku, G., 215
Kubler, D., 235, 245
Kuhn, T. S., 76, 134, 182, 362
lab experiments, 211, 290, 440
laggards, 232
Lahart, J., 158
Laing, S., 488, 489
land grant, 493
landscape specialization, 384, 385, 388
landscapes, 51
Langer, E.J., 254, 263
Lansing, S., 476
Larkin, J.H., 188
Latham, G., 210, 224, 225
Law of Abandoned Expertise, 134, 181, 209, 218, 225, 228, 317, 364, 478
Law of Limited Visibility, 69, 211, 361
law of practice, 162
law of small numbers, 131
Law of the Few, 234
Lawrence, P. R., 10, 126, 127, 172, 329, 550
Leamer, E., 107

learning, 159
learning by analogy, 177
learning curve, 162, 163, 247
learning styles, 61
Lee, A., 37
Lee, C., 245
Lee, H.L., 267
Lengel, R. H., 200
Leonard-Barton, D., 350
Lester, R. K., 276
Let's Make a Deal, 178, 478
levels of abstraction, 30
Levitt, S.D., 290, 291, 328, 551
Linden Lab, 443, 445
Lindy truffle, 147
Lindzen, R., 552
List, J.A., 291, 328
Litan, R., 555
Lo, A.W., 148, 254, 277
Locke, E., 209, 210, 224, 225
Loewenstein, G., 129, 212, 213,
    214, 256, 258, 259, 260
Long Island Duck Farmer's
    Cooperative, 228
long tail, 311
Long Term Capital Management,
    19
long term memory, 119, 120,
    163, 165, 169, 170, 171, 189,
    199, 200, 208
long term self interest, 213
Longfellow, H.W., 243
longitudinal investigation, 382
Lord, K.R, 203
low hanging fruit, 300, 301,
    302, 332, 350, 361, 473
low structure informing, 230
low structure problem, 123,
    125, 129, 131, 135, 148, 151,
160, 174, 176, 177, 185, 207,
    230, 243, 264, 271, 366
subtask, 125
low structure problems, 136
LTCM. See Long Term Capital
    Management
Luce and Tukey, 15
Luce, M.F., 216
ludic fallacy, 18, 19
Lyytinen, K., 37
MacCaulay, K., 5, 468
Made to Stick, 154, 189
Madoff, 4
Madura, J., 424
magnitude effects in
    discounting, 260
Mahaffey, T., 5, 468
Mahajan, V., 231
Maher, M.W., 25
main effect, 93, 264, 308, 361
Malhotra, D., 215
Malhotra, Y., 15, 398, 400, 401
Malthus, T., 511, 530
Man, Machines and Modern Times,
    194
management information
    systems. *See* MIS
Managers Not MBAs, 11, 462
Managing Our Way to
    Economic Decline, 10
Mandelbrot, B., 246, 292
Mariani, M.D., 469, 529, 552,
    553
market value, 108, 111, 125
Marketing Science, 430
Markoczy, L., 15
Markowitz, 26
Markus, M. L., 37
Marlborough, M.A., 257, 278
Marmorstein, H., 135

masculinity vs. femininity, 60
mass media, 221, 231, 243, 379, 480
Massad, V., 441
master's degree programs, 450
mathematical/deductive operators, 131
Matthew Effect, 285, 295, 296, 301, 331, 333
Mauboussin, M.J., 247, 263
Maus, R., 344
mavens, 234, 243, 244, 506
MBA, 7, 8, 9, 11, 12, 25, 36, 44, 190, 254, 277, 278, 280, 338, 424, 429, 432, 435, 440, 449, 450, 451, 464, 465, 468, 495, 496, 504, 505, 537
payback period, 9
McCabe, D.L., 4, 24
McClelland, J.L., 141, 155
McCloskey, D.N., 84, 95, 112, 298, 299, 301, 302, 303, 305, 326, 333, 334, 350, 473, 502
McDonald, S., 236
McDonald's, 505
McFarlan, F.W., 35
McGurn, W., 64
McKelvey, R.D., 245
McKibbin, L.E., 10
McKinsey, 7, 8, 44, 424, 450, 502
McNamara, P., 481
Meckling, W.H., 16, 294, 455
media richness, 200, 214
medical diagnosis, 122
Mega Disasters, 282
mental model, 117, 118, 186, 206, 210, 211, 214, 244, 278
Merck, 302
Merton, R. Jr., 19, 26, 109

Merton, R.K., 296, 333
meta-cognitive knowledge, 184
meta-knowledge, 165
Meyers, M., 40, 332
Microsoft, 7, 102, 416
Milgram, S., 232, 245
Miller, C.C., 316, 325, 394
Miller, G.A., 161
Milner, D., 5, 468
Minnesota tax compliance, 144
Minsky, M.L, 137
Mintzberg, H., 8, 10, 11, 12, 21, 23, 24, 25, 90, 418, 432, 433, 434, 442, 445, 446, 449, 462, 463, 464, 466, 540
Mirels, H.L., 261, 279
MIS, 15, 21, 25, 27, 28, 35, 36, 40, 45, 86, 106, 109, 113, 294, 296, 299, 300, 325, 385, 398, 399, 400, 401, 411, 416, 419, 424, 440, 472, 482, 496, 507
disciplinary informing system, 35
practitioner clients, 37
research, 37, 41, 43, 300
rise and fall, 36
student clients, 38
MISQ, 35, 37, 41, 296, 332, 336, 352, 353, 354, 398, 399, 402, 413
MIT, 339, 340, 355, 487, 525, 552
Mitchell, T.R., 82, 257
Mittendorf, B., 237
Mlodinow, L., 71, 114, 131, 149, 154, 178, 179, 277, 331, 476, 478, 503
Mol, M.J., 14, 319
Mona Lisa, 63, 76, 201

Montclair State University, 467
Monty Hall, 178, 191, 301, 528
moods, 212
Moran, P., 17, 455
Moran, T.P., 119
Morey, M.R., 8
Morison, E., 194, 195, 196, 197
Morrill Acts of 1862 and 1890, 493
Morris, J.A., 218
Morrissey, W., 344
Moss Kanter, R., 105
motivational conflicts, 197
Mrs. Fields' Cookies, 271, 478
Muller, E., 231
multiple clients, 30, 32, 231, 232
multiple communications pathways, 29
multiple informing systems, 29
multiple regression analysis, 65, 112, 308
Murnighan, J.K., 215
Murphy, K.M., 258
Mussweiler, T., 140
Mutually Assured Destruction, 514
Mythbusters, 83
Naik, G., 264
narrative fallacy, 20, 307, 328, 334
National Science Foundation, 40, 46
naval gunnery, 194
Navarro, P., 294
Nelson, A., 9
network effects, 55
neural networks. *See* connectionism
neurons, 136, 137, 156

Newcombe, N.S., 320
Newell, A., 118, 119, 162, 184, 202
Newton, I., 286, 327
Niemi, Jr. A., 33
NK, 54, 56, 59, 73, 308, 327, 335, 383
NK landscapes, 73, 383
Nobel Laureates, 26, 76, 126, 296, 551
Nohria, N., 172
non-pecuniary benefits, 17
non-routine informing, 193, 227, 230, 243
normal science, 76
Norman, D.A., 177, 186
Northcraft, G., 33
Norway, 240, 246, 265
Noth, M., 176
nuclear conflict, 513
Nuclear Regulatory Commission, 259
Nunes, J., 210
objective complexity, 49, 50, 56, 73, 105, 165, 264, 423
observation skills, 485
Occam's Razor, 70, 84
Oceans 11 & 13, 289
offshored, 281
Oldham, G.R., 129, 201, 279, 342, 343, 346, 348, 351
operator space, 119, 121, 122, 124, 129, 167
opinion leaders, 232, 236, 458
opportunism, 17
optimism, 89, 208, 254, 278, 543, 545
Ordonez, L.D., 210, 211, 224
Oswald, M.E., 130
Outliers, 60, 103, 150, 161, 331

overconfidence, 208, 254, 261, 432
overlap of teaching and research interests, 39
overlapping systems, 272
Pace University, 467
Padmanabhan, V., 267
pain, 212
Palfrey, T. R., 245
Pandemonium, 137
Papert, S.A., 137
Parade Magazine, 179
paradigm shift, 76
paradox of expertise, 167
Paramount, 476
Pardes, H., 555
Pareto distributions, 239
Pareto, A., 239, 246
Pashler, H., 164, 424
Paul Revere, 243
payday loans, 260
Payne, J.W., 82, 134, 216
Pearson, E., 112, 305
pecuniary benefits, 17
peer review, 312, 313, 320, 322, 353, 394, 395, 396, 407, 503
perceptron, 137, 156
persuaders, 234
Pesce, R.A.G., 296
Peters, D., 313, 315, 319
Peterson, E., 257
Petit, J.R., 523
Pfeffer, J., 7, 14, 25, 90, 318, 319, 321, 322, 378, 379, 380, 395, 397, 431
Pierson, F.C., 3, 463
poetry, 171
Politser, P., 255
Ponzi scheme, 1, 4, 249
Population Bomb, The, 511

Porter, L., 10
Porter, M.E., 99, 412, 492
portfolio theory, 18, 19, 20, 26, 292
Posterity Lost, 510, 535
powder puff tests, 300, 301, 332, 350, 526, 527
power distance, 60, 61
power law, 162, 228, 238, 239, 240, 242, 244, 246, 263, 265, 266, 268, 269, 273, 282, 292, 293, 296, 311, 329, 330, 331, 368
  examples, 239
Power of Context, 234
power test, 303, 304
practitioner clients, 37
practitioner experts, 168
predicaments of progress, 509
Predictably Irrational, 178, 179
predictive accuracy, 11
preference for escalating gains, 258
preferences, 36, 65, 87, 100, 113, 124, 136, 138, 141, 143, 144, 147, 148, 152, 184, 206, 207, 208, 215, 216, 250, 256, 258, 260, 262, 279, 294, 331
Prelec, D., 145, 256, 260
presentism, 207, 259, 262
prices, effect of, 146
priming, 142, 205
prior client knowledge, 206
prior mental models, 197
Prisoner's Dilemma, 127
private information, 235, 245
probability theory, 252, 277
problem solving, 120, 125, 154, 160, 165, 180, 183, 184, 204,

205, 210, 362, 365, 416, 425,
434, 440, 450, 459, 504, 540
problem space, 49, 118, 120,
121, 122, 123, 129, 160, 166,
167, 176, 178, 179, 180, 183,
198, 200, 205, 220
choosing, 177
definition, 119
updating or replacing, 181
problem space complexity, 423,
541
process of progress, 517, 527,
536, 537, 539, 540, 542, 544,
553
procrastination, 217
profession
criteria for, 5
professional doctorate, 488
projection heuristic, 144
prospection, 262
Prusak, L., 13, 367
pseudo-random, 251
pseudo-randomness, 348
public information, 166, 236
punctuated equilibrium, 58, 63,
105, 110, 250, 263, 268, 270,
274, 367, 372, 447, 521, 543
pure research, 5, 32
quality control of research, 312
Rachlinski, J.L., 176
Rafter, M.V., 425
range brackets, 253
ranking organizations, 33, 35
Read, D., 259
reasoning by analogy, 206
Reay, T., 502
Reber, R., 130
recency effect, 130
recipe fitness, 51
recognition heuristic, 130

recommendations, summary
of, 560
recreating knowledge, 174
recycle towels, 143
Red Lobster, 99
refusal to be informed, 217
Reiners, T., 444
Reinhart, C.M., 548
relevance filters, 209
replication research, 63, 323
representativeness, 130
research impact, 14, 43, 45,
400, 401, 402, 403, 407
research rankings by business
discipline, 36
resistance, 197
resonance, 194, 197, 198, 199,
200, 221, 285, 316, 325, 332,
360, 367, 373, 381, 431, 471
cognitive filters, 199, 204,
221
information filters, 199, 204,
206
motivation filters, 199, 208
risk & time preference
filters, 199, 207, 221
visceral filters, 199, 211, 221
restaurant dinners preference,
258
restructuring, 186
retrieving knowledge, 165, 174
Ricardo, D., 511
rich get richer, 237, 238, 242,
263, 269, 330
Richardson, L., 105
rigor
definition, 284
rigor versus relevance, 196,
198, 381
rigor-relevance filters, 208, 209

Rising Sun, 276
risk, 251
risk & time preference filters, 206
Robbins, R.W., 444
Roberts, R., 106
Rodin, J., 263
Rodriguez, A., 344
Roethlisberger, F., 73, 74
Rogers, B.W., 245
Rogers, E.M., 218, 231, 232, 243, 367, 493
Rogoff, K.S., 548
Rohrer, D., 164, 424
Romanelli, E., 105
Romer, P., 282
Roosevelt, T., 198
Rootman, I., 284
Rosenbloom, P.S., 162
Rosenthal, R., 212
Rottenstreich, Y., 216
router, 243, 247
rugged fitness landscape, 53, 167, 168, 283, 287, 298, 305, 336, 354, 360, 362, 371, 373, 376, 459, 460, 517
components, 56
ruggedness, 91
Rumelhart, D.E., 155, 177, 186
Russo, J. E., 135, 254
Ruth, A., 403
Rynes, S.L., 100, 219, 318, 332, 402, 502
Salvia, J., 212
Samuelson, P., 256
Santa Fe Institute, 385, 387
satisficing, 135, 269
Saunders, C.S., 46, 218, 341
scale free networks, 241
Scalia, A., 542

Schank, R.C., 225
Scheare, J.B., 212
Schein, E.H. & Lewin, K., 362, 374
schema creation, 186
schema evolution, 186
schemata, 130, 131, 161, 166, 186
Schlesinger, L., 105
Schmid, J., 236
Schmidt, F.L., 100, 101
Schneider, S., 552
scholarship of teaching, 32
scholarship of teaching research, 40
Scholes, M., 19, 26, 109
Schramm, C., 555
Schweitzer, M.E., 210, 224
science vs. art continuum, 75
Scott Morton, M.S., 299
Scott, P. (Admiral), 195
sea shells, 236
Second Life, 443, 445, 466
Selfridge, O.G., 137, 155
self-serving bias, 261
service learning, 437
Sesame Street, 220
sexual arousal, 213
Shah, A.J., 61
Shannon, C.E., 28
Shanteau, J., 375, 378
Sharpe, 26
Shelman, M., 496
Shen, J., 444
Shields, M.A., 115, 127
Shiffrin, R.M., 161
Shiller, R.J., 219, 225, 245
Shirky, C., 247
Shoemaker, P., 254
Shu, S., 216

Shugan, S.M., 430, 431, 432, 434, 464, 465, 468
Sicherman, N., 258
Siegel, J.J., 69, 166
Siegfried and Roy, 289
Sierra, J.J., 217
SIM. See Society for Information Management
Simester, D., 145
Simon, H.A., 31, 76, 118, 135, 177, 180, 181, 184
Sims, W.S., 195, 196, 197, 198
Sincich, A., 308, 310, 335, 348
Single Client Resonance Model, 198, 200, 221
Six Degrees, 245
six degrees of separation, 232
skunkworks, 350
Slovic, P., 478, 503
small world model, 232, 243
Smithsonian, 485
social influence, 143, 212, 218, 228, 244, 245, 363, 372
Societe Generale, 101
Society for Information Management, 35, 38
Solow, R. M., 276
Soman, D., 215
Sorensen, R.E., 363
SOT. See Scholarship of Teaching
South Korea, 61
spacing vs. massing, 164
stagflation, 281
Standard Milling, 495
Stanford University, 14, 378
Stangler, D., 555
Starbuck, W.H., 316, 317, 320, 321, 325
Starkey, K., 500

state space, 119, 121, 122, 124, 125, 129, 131, 161, 166
statistical significance, 61, 79, 84, 90, 95, 110, 112, 298, 301, 302, 303, 304, 306, 309, 334, 346, 351, 355, 474, 548
Steele, T., 210
stereopsis, 170
Sterman, J.D., 525, 549
stickiness, 103, 220, 234
stickiness of entities, 63
sticky communications, 194
Stiehler, A., 236
Stix, G., 237
stock price, 69, 83, 108, 459
stories, 171, 381
    resonance of, 219
storing knowledge, 165, 169
Strack, F., 140
Stroop Effect, 203
Stroop, J.R., 203
structural complexity, 165
student clients, 38
Student's t-test, 474
Stumbling on Happiness, 356
sub-system/super-systems, 272
SUCCESs model, 194, 220, 221
Sullivan, A., 463
Summers, L., 259, 329, 550
Sunstein, C.R., 100, 144, 153, 223, 254, 503
Super Freakonomics, 290, 551
superposition, 75, 77, 92, 411
survey courses, 38, 459
survivability, 51
Sviokla, J., 339, 349
swimming class, 188
symbolic processing, 136
Taffinder, C., 344

Taleb, N.N., 18, 19, 20, 21, 26, 105, 109, 132, 149, 224, 247, 253, 264, 273, 277, 288, 292, 293, 307, 311, 326, 328, 329, 368, 369, 475, 515, 553
TAM. *See* technology acceptance model
Tapp, A., 25
task completion environment, 28
task complexity, 48, 49, 82
  experienced, 48
  information processing, 48
  objective, 48
  problem space, 48
  structural, 48
task complexity classes, 48
taxonomies, 132
teaching versus research interests in MIS, 39
technology acceptance model, 300, 301, 332, 472
technology-induced changes, 31
Teigen, K H., 130, 176
Tetlock, P.E., 209, 224, 293, 515
Thaler, R.H., 100, 132, 144, 153, 223, 254, 292, 472, 503
theory boundaries, 288
theory fragment, 291, 306, 317, 348, 350
theory of evolution, 70, 93, 111, 286, 329
theory of reasoned action, 332
theory-of-fitness, 70, 72, 78, 79, 81, 90, 91, 93, 100, 105, 108, 110, 111, 125, 284, 285, 286, 287, 289, 308, 324, 336, 418

theory-of-process, 71, 93, 104, 108, 383
Thernstrom, S.A., 554
thinking, 183
Thompson, L., 257
Thompson, S.C., 133
time horizons, 25, 60, 162, 206, 249, 250, 263, 270, 271, 274, 275, 276, 400, 415, 537, 538, 543
Tipping Point, The, 103, 189, 220, 234, 245, 506
tipping points, 234
Tiratsoo, N., 500
Titanic, 476
Tower of Hanoi, 177, 180, 181, 365
trained incapacity, 301, 333
transaction cost economics, 16, 17, 18, 43, 455
transaction processing system, 31
transdisciplinary specialization, 385, 386, 448
transdiscipline, 28, 385, 386, 387, 391, 396
Travers, J., 232
Trevino, L.K., 4, 24, 200
Trieschmann, J., 33
trombone auditions, 312
Trump, D., 463
Tuck School, 3, 7, 424
Tucker, J.M., 441
tulip bubble, 236
tuning, 186
turbulence, 105, 545
turbulent dynamics, 63
Tushman, M.L., 105
TV remote control, 169

Tversky, A., 100, 130, 131, 135, 140, 176, 252, 478, 503
Type I error, 25, 284, 288, 302, 305, 316, 347, 440, 466, 474, 477
Type II error, 25, 284, 288, 302, 303, 305, 316, 407, 466, 474, 477
U.S. News & World Report, 35
ugly theory, 72, 74, 81, 96, 288, 381, 471
Uhlmann, P., 495
Ultimatum, 290
uncertainty, 251
uncertainty avoidance, 60
uncertainty versus risk, 18
unexpected, 201
United Agri Products, 491
University of California at Berkeley, 7
University of Central Florida, 41, 46
University of Osnabrueck, 488
University of Phoenix, 375, 451
University of South Florida, xix, 35, 593
user resistance, 302
Usher, M., 141, 155
utility, 17, 51, 56, 80, 100, 115, 124, 125, 126, 129, 136, 138, 148, 154, 177, 199, 208, 209, 256, 259, 290, 291, 294, 331, 360, 471, 507
utility preferences, 51
Van Der Werf, M., 64
van Knippenberg, A., 142
Van Yperen, N., 210
VCR standards, 55
Venture Mentoring Service, 487

Vetter, D.E., 324
VHS, 55, 82, 105
vice presidential debate, 216
Vioxx, 302, 303
Virany, B., 105
visceral factors, 133, 200, 201, 211, 212, 213, 215, 217
Viscusi, W.K., 277
Vittor, E.M., 389
volcanic eruption, 274
vos Savant, M., 331
Wade, M., 41
Wagner, C., 444
Wall Street, 16, 114, 150, 493, 525, 542
Wall Street Journal, 550
Walmart, 7, 55, 268, 271
Walt Disney World, 180
Wang, Y., 444
Warshaw, P.R., 300, 332
Watts and Zimmerman, 15
Watts, D.J., 15, 232, 239, 243, 245, 246
Weaver, W., 28
Weber, J., 24
Weber, M., 176
Web-of-Science, 399, 402
Weinstein, N.D., 254, 255, 278
Weizsacker, G., 235, 245
Welch, I., 235, 502
Wesson, M., 210
Western Electric, 73
Western Washington University, 68
Whang, S., 267
white swans, 273
Whitfield, J.M., 328
Wikipedia, 24, 84, 154, 327, 394, 411
Williamson, O.E., 17, 455

Williams-Sonoma, 141
Willingham, D.T., 61, 120, 129,
  164, 171, 173, 178, 183, 187,
  188, 189, 219, 223, 225, 331,
  424
Wilson, H.J., 13, 367
Wilson, T.D., 254
Woessner, M. & Kelly-
  Woessner, A., 469
Wolfram, S., 281
Wood, R., 48, 50
word of mouth, 30, 244
working memory, 119, 123,
  151, 161, 165, 169, 170, 171,
  180, 181, 183, 185, 189, 199,
  200, 208, 330, 365

World Values Survey, 519, 527,
  536, 548, 552
World Wide Web, 242
XCON, 349, 350
Yellowstone National Park,
  282
Zand, D.E., 363
Zapata-Phelan, C. P., 297, 381
Zeckhauser, R.J., 259, 277, 550
Ziliak, S.T., 84, 95, 112, 298,
  299, 301, 302, 303, 305, 326,
  333, 334, 350, 473, 502
Zipf's Law, 239, 247
Zmud, R., 37, 38

Made in the USA
Charleston, SC
29 August 2012